PRACTICAL GUIDE TO
S CORPORATIONS

SIXTH EDITION

MICHAEL SCHLESINGER

Wolters Kluwer
CCH

Editorial Staff

Production .... Jennifer Schencker

This publication is designed to provide accurate and authoritative information in regard to the subject matter covered. It is sold with the understanding that the publisher is not engaged in rendering legal, accounting, or other professional service and that the author is not offering such advice in this publication. If legal advice or other expert assistance is required, the services of a competent professional person should be sought.

In the course of preparing this publication, the author has randomly selected names for use in providing examples and describing situations. Any similarity to persons living or dead, fictional or nonfictional is purely coincidental and the author and publisher disclaim any responsibility of liability therefor.

ISBN 978-0-8080-3294-6

©2013 CCH Incorporated. All Rights Reserved.

4025 W. Peterson Ave.
Chicago, IL 60646-6085
800 248 3248
CCHGroup.com

Printed in the United States of America

SFI Certified Chain of Custody
Product Line Contains At Least
20% Certified Forest Content
www.sfiprogram.org
SFI-00756

This book is dedicated to my grandchildren, Eli and Morgan, who were born after my wife died and the publication of the fifth edition of this book. They, who represent the sixth generation of my family in America, have given me great comfort and inspiration to continue writing this book.

Preface

S corporations, at present, are the largest tax filer in the United States of America. This book provides, in a single volume, a complete guide and reference tool for the tax practitioner to solve the many problems arising in regard to S corporate taxation. While this book does not cover every single case, ruling, or procedure on a particular point, the reader is provided with the main case or point in a particular area, so that this situation can be understood quickly. Further, the Appendices provide practical information for the tax practitioner to utilize in his or her practice. To assist the reader, tax planning situations are presented throughout the book.

This book is organized into sixteen chapters. Chapter 1 discusses the tax considerations in electing S corporate status, as well as the advantages and disadvantages of S corporate taxation. Chapters 2-10 detail operations of an S corporation, discussing the statutory requirements to be an S corporation, the types of taxpayer who can qualify as shareholders, considerations that one must make before converting a C corporation to S status, etc. Chapter 11 sets forth income and estate planning situations for S corporations. Chapter 12 covers changes which could occur in the life of an S corporation, namely, termination and revocation of the S corporate status, sale of S corporate stock, reorganization of the corporation, etc.

Chapter 13 provides the reader with a comparison of S corporations to other business entities, such as one-person limited liability companies, partnerships, and C corporations. Chapter 14 discusses S corporation subsidiaries, Chapter 15, employee stock ownership plans ("ESOPs") for S corporations, and Chapter 16, a detailed discussion of the proposed regulations under Code Sec. 1411.

This book is not intended to apply to all circumstances, and the Forms contained herein may not be applicable in every situation. Further, the law is constantly changing in the field of S corporations. Accordingly, it is strongly urged that the current status of all statutes, case law, rulings, regulations, revenue procedures, announcements, notices, Forms and/or applications thereof be confirmed before relying on the information set forth in this book.

It should be noted that in writing this book, the author has attempted to make the table of contents read like an index. The reader has three easy means to solve a problem or locate a topic: the Contents, Contents in Detail on page xiii and the Index. In addition, the author has provided a table of cases, statutes, treasury regulations, rulings, and procedures so that the reader will have an easy-to-use method to solve a specific problem. To assist the reader in practice, the Appendices supply sample language for various situations regarding S corporations.

This book is intended to remove some of the mystery surrounding S corporations and their complexities. Because of its thoroughness, multitudinous examples, and tax pointers, this book should provide the reader with a unique resource tool to be utilized as a major addition to a tax library.

Michael Schlesinger

August 2013

About the Author

Michael Schlesinger is a partner in the New York and New Jersey law firm Schlesinger & Sussman. He has over 40 years of experience in business, tax, income, and estate planning for corporations, limited liability companies, partnerships, and small, closely held family businesses. Mr. Schlesinger taught these subjects for 12 years as an adjunct professor at Pace University School of Law in White Plains, New York. He is the author of several books and numerous articles on the taxation of business entities. Mr. Schlesinger has dabbled in the entertainment field writing a column in *Variety* about tax problems of entertainment personalities, sports stars, etc. He has been quoted in the *New York Times*, *Smart Money*, *Federal Tax Weekly* and *Fortune Small Business*. He has represented famous authors, playwrights, professional athletes, public officials including a member of a United States President's cabinet, judges, and Fortune 50 CEOs. Mr. Schlesinger is a member of the New York bar and has an LL.M. in taxation from the New York University School of Law.

Acknowledgments

Writing a book of this magnitude requires an allotment of tremendous time and effort and cannot be done without the support of various individuals, namely my editor Jennifer Schencker, and my companion Carol Schwebel. Carol is the one who provided support during the writing process as I tried to balance the needs of writing this book, my practice of law, and life. Jennifer is the one who took my raw manuscript and made it into this book. Last year, I co-authored the CCH Expert Treatise Library: Federal Taxation of Subchapter S Corporations with Robert W. Jamison. Some of the cases, rulings, etc. in this 6th edition of my book have been previously summarized or discussed in the Treatise I co-wrote with Robert W. Jamison.

Contents

Contents in Detail

Chapter 13—Comparisons to Other Business Entities

Paragraph

Chapter 16—The Effect That Code Sec. 1411 Has on S Corporate Shareholders

Chapter 1

Tax Considerations in Electing S Corporation Status

¶ 101 Introduction

The S corporation entity form has changed significantly since its creation by Congress in 1958. Even its name has changed from the legalese "Subchapter S corporation" to the current "S corporation" after passage of the Subchapter S Revision Act of 1982. It is favored by many because it offers many of the benefits of partnership taxation while giving shareholders limited liability from creditors, bankruptcy, and the like. Law changes continue to fine-tune the S corporation form making it a valuable vehicle for conducting business both in the United States and abroad.

Today, the S corporation, a federal tax hybrid entity, must also be compared with the limited liability company (LLC), a state tax hybrid entity. An S corporation resembles an LLC in operation and concept; however, there are distinct differences. LLCs composed of two or more members work strictly on partnership taxation principles.[1] In many ways, the taxation of an S corporation resembles a partnership; however, partnership tax law does not always apply (e.g., an S corporation cannot allocate income the way a partnership can; distributions of appreciated property are generally taxable[2]).

It may be asked why taxpayers would want to use an S corporation rather than an LLC in view of the similarity of tax principles. Under current tax law, the unique partnership tax principles are only available in an LLC if there are two or more taxpayers. In contrast, S corporations require only one taxpayer to operate.[3] Also, S corporations offer unique planning possibilities not available in LLCs (e.g., the creation of capital gains).

---

[1] Although an LLC can elect to be treated as a corporation for federal income tax purposes (and could therefore elect to be treated as an S corporation), the vast majority will elect to be treated as partnerships because of the favorable tax treatment provided by partnership taxation.

[2] Compare Code Secs. 704(b) (allocation of partnership income among partners) and 1377(a) (determination of S corporation shareholders' pro rata share). See also ¶ 1304.03 for more discussion.

[3] In almost all states, a person can form a one-member LLC. The taxation of the one-member LLC will depend on the type of entity that forms it. See ¶ 1307 to compare one-member LLCs to S corporations.

An S corporation's ordinary income and loss is not taxed at the corporate level; rather, it is passed through to the shareholders as in a partnership.[4] Likewise, an S corporation's foreign income and loss, tax-exempt interest, charitable contributions, and passive income are also passed through to the shareholders.[5] Because of this one level of taxation, many individuals elect S corporation status to operate their corporations. In doing so, they avoid the tax technicalities of "regular Form 1120 corporations," commonly known as C corporations (e.g., tax on accumulated surplus, disguised dividends, personal holding company taxation).

The text that follows discusses the primary advantages of using the S corporation form. Additionally, tax pointers offer methods to take advantage of the quirks in the law as well as ways to avoid the pitfalls. To determine which business entity to use for federal tax purposes, Chapter 13 compares the S corporation to C corporations (personal service and regular Form 1120), partnerships (general and limited), and LLCs (one-member and two-or-more-members).

¶ 102 Advantages of Having an S Corporation

Below are 17 income tax reasons why taxpayers elect S corporation status.

.01 Tax-Free Contribution to the S Corporation

When certain requirements are met, taxpayers can contribute assets to an S corporation tax free.

> **Tax Pointer:** Sales tax could arise on a transfer however, if the transfer is not done properly. In *Weichbrodt*,[6] sales tax was imposed when a shareholder contributed additional property to his S corporation. For a discussion of the imposition of sales tax on a transfer of property and the means to avoid it, see ¶ 103.

Contributions of property when debt exceeds basis. When an S corporation shareholder contributes appreciated property encumbered by debt in excess of basis, gain must be recognized.[7] The character of this gain (capital or ordinary) will depend upon the nature of the contributed property.

> **Example 1-1:** Marlene Smith contributes real estate to a newly formed corporation in exchange for 30% of its stock. Her tax basis in the real estate is $150,000; its fair market value is $250,000. The property is encumbered by a $200,000 mortgage. Because the mortgage on the real estate exceeds Smith's basis in the property, she will be required to recognize a $50,000 gain upon transfer of this property to the corporation.[8] The character of this gain will depend upon the nature of the property in Smith's hands prior to the transfer. If it was a capital asset to her, the gain will be capital.

---

[4] Code Sec. 1366(b).

[5] Code Sec. 1366(b). See Chapters 6 and 7 for a detailed explanation of the tax treatment of S corporation ordinary income, deductions, capital gains, and the like.

[6] NEW YORK TAX REPORTER ¶ 404-103, New York Division of Tax Appeals, ALJ (2002).

[7] Code Sec. 357(c). See ¶ 1117 for further discussion.

[8] If Code Sec. 351 does not apply to the transfer, her gain will be even greater.

.02 Protection from Creditors

An S corporation, because it is a corporation, provides its shareholders with protection from corporate debts and against the corporation's creditors throughout the world. The only statutory requirement that the S corporation has to meet for this worldwide creditor protection is to be a domestic corporation.[9] Like any other corporation, certain formalities must be observed, such as an annual meeting of shareholders.[10]

In contrast, LLCs are a relatively new concept in the United States, having started in 1977. While LLCs do have their counterparts in other areas of the world, such as the Satre in France and the GmbH in Germany, there is not a body of law established (as with the S corporation) to detail protection to the owners. Thus, particularly for international operations, until there is an adequate body of law established for LLCs, the better business vehicle is often an S corporation. While an S corporation by definition provides liability protection, shareholders may want additional protection from creditors by creating a chain of entities to own the stock such as having a grantor trust own a single member limited liability company which in turn owns the S corporate stock. Such an ownership situation was approved in IRS Letter Ruling 200339026 (June 23, 2003).

.03 Avoidance of Double Taxation

For individuals starting a business, the S corporation is an ideal business vehicle because unlike a C corporation it avoids double federal taxation, having only one level of taxation at the shareholder level.[11] The S corporation's income is taxed to the shareholders. In contrast, a C corporation's income is taxed twice: first at the corporate level and again when the income is distributed to the shareholders.

> **Tax Pointer 1:** A C corporation can convert to an S corporation to avoid double taxation; however, the S corporation may be subject to a built-in gains tax, a passive investment income tax, a LIFO recapture tax, and general business credit recapture.[12]

> **Tax Pointer 2:** Conversion from a C corporation to an S provides interesting tax planning possibilities when the C corporation has suspended passive losses. For a discussion of this planning possibility, see ¶ 404.08.

.04 No Recharacterization of Pass-Through Items

S corporations pass through certain items of income, expense, and the like to the shareholder without recharacterization.[13] Consequently, S corporation charitable contributions are not subject to the 10 percent limitation imposed on C

[9] See Chapter 2 for a discussion of other requirements to become an S corporation.

[10] If a corporation does not observe the formalities of a corporation, creditors can "pierce the corporate veil" and hold the shareholders liable for corporate debt. In some circumstances, shareholders can remain liable for corporate debts even if the formalities are observed. See, for instance, the Business Corporation Law of the State of New York, Code Sec. 630, where the ten largest shareholders are liable for employee wages.

[11] There are exceptions to the one level of S corporation taxation, namely Code Sec. 1374 transactions (discussed at ¶ 802) and Code Secs. 1375 and 1362(d) transactions (discussed at ¶ 804). However, with careful planning, the statutory provisions of Code Secs. 1374, 1375, and 1362(d) can usually be overcome.

[12] Code Secs. 1374, 1375, and 1362(d). See Chapter 8 and ¶ 1204 for a discussion of these Code Secs.

[13] Code Sec. 1366(a)(1)(A).

corporations.[14] However, S corporations cannot take advantage of two charitable contribution techniques available to C corporations: contributions of inventory[15] and scientific equipment.[16]

.05 Immediate Deduction for Losses

If heavy start-up losses are expected or an operating C corporation anticipates a period of heavy losses, an S election should be considered since S corporation losses are deductible in the year incurred to the extent of a shareholder's basis in S corporation stock and loans to the corporation.

> **Tax Pointer 1:** If the shareholder has more losses than basis in stock and loans, the unusable losses generally may be carried forward indefinitely and taken when the shareholder's basis increases.[17]

> **Tax Pointer 2:** If the loss from an S corporation is passive, the passive loss is only deductible to the extent of passive income.[18]

.06 No Alternative Minimum Tax

S corporations do not pay the alternative minimum tax on preference items that C corporations pay.[19] Instead, the S corporation shareholders include in their alternative minimum tax calculation the pass-through of preference items to determine if they are liable for any alternative minimum tax.

.07 No Personal Holding Company Tax or Accumulated Earnings Tax

An S corporation, unless it has C corporation earnings and profits,[20] can engage in 100 percent passive investment activities[21] without adverse tax consequences or additional tax liability. In contrast, a C corporation can have a tax imposed on it for its passive investment activities,[22] depending upon the number of its shareholders and the dollar amount of its passive investment income.

Also, a C corporation is subject to penalty taxes if it accumulates its earnings and profits excessively instead of distributing them as dividends to its shareholders.[23] In contrast, an S corporation can accumulate its earnings and profits with impunity, as can an LLC and a partnership. However, the following nontax risk should be noted—creditors have a source of funds for satisfying their claims.

> **Example 1-2:** Bill Ortiz, a pediatrician, incorporates himself as a professional corporation, electing S status on formation. Rather than distributing the earnings and profits of the corporation as they are earned, Ortiz leaves the funds in the corporation for its future growth. The corporation purchases a building, and one day, a brick of the building drops on a patient, Andrea Cruz,

---

[14] Code Sec. 170(b)(2). For further discussion about charitable deductions and S corporations, see ¶ 703.

[15] Code Sec. 170(e)(3)(A).

[16] Code Sec. 170(e)(4)(D).

[17] See ¶ 903.08 and ¶ 904.06 for more discussion.

[18] Code Sec. 469. See ¶ 911 et seq. for more discussion.

[19] Code Secs. 55 et seq. and 1363(a).

[20] For a definition of C corporation earnings and profits, see ¶ 1204.01.

[21] Code Sec. 1362(d)(3)(C)(i) defines "passive investment income" generally as gross receipts derived from royalties, rents, dividends, interest, annuities, and sales or exchanges of stock or securities (gross receipts from such sales or exchanges being taken into account only to the extent of gains therefrom). See ¶ 804 for further discussion of this area.

[22] Code Sec. 541 et seq.

[23] Code Sec. 531.

¶102.05

and seriously injures her. Cruz sues the corporation, but discovers that the corporation accidentally let the insurance on the building lapse. In the course of the lawsuit, the corporation's profits of $1 million are discovered. Because Cruz learns of the accumulated profits, settlement becomes difficult. If Ortiz had distributed the earnings and profits by salary or as a distribution,[24] only the assets remaining in the corporation would be available to the injured party.

.08 One Level of Taxation in the Sale of a Business

When an S corporation sells its business assets, the shareholders pay tax at one level—the shareholder's level.[25] In contrast, a C corporation will generally pay tax at two levels—once at the corporate level when the assets are sold and again at the shareholder level when the net proceeds are distributed.

> **Example 1-3:** Omega Inc., a calendar-year C corporation, has one share-holder, Bud Taylor, who started the corporation on January 1, 1995. On that date, Taylor contributed $5,000 for 100 shares of stock. On January 2, 1995, Omega Inc. bought vacant land, Glenwood, for $5,000 and held the land, its sole asset, until December 31, 2012. Omega Inc. had no other transactions since inception, and on December 31, 2012, Omega Inc. sold Glenwood for $55,000 to an unrelated third party, Sam Peterson, realizing a gain of $50,000 ($55,000 – $5,000 of basis in the land). Assume that Omega Inc. is in its lowest income tax bracket of 15%, and that it distributed the net proceeds from the sale of Glenwood to Taylor. This would mean Taylor will receive a dividend of $42,500 ($50,000 – (.15 × $50,000)). Assume that Taylor's tax rate is 35%. The net proceeds to Taylor on the transaction are $27,625 computed as follows: (corporate net income of $50,000 – (.15 × $50,000) = $42,500) and ($42,500 – (.35 × $42,500) = $27,625). In contrast, if Omega Inc. was an S corporation from inception and the capital gains rate was 15%, Taylor would have paid tax of only $10,000 (.15 × $50,000) leaving him a net of $42,500 on the sale ($50,000 – $7,500).

Clearly, operation of an S corporation in situations such as Example 1-3 produces significant tax savings; in Example 1-3, the tax savings were $14,330 ($42,500 – $27,625).[26]

.09 Distribute Earnings Free of FICA, FUTA, and Employment Taxes

Under *Radtke*,[27] S corporations are required to pay reasonable salaries to S corporation shareholders.[28] However, the *Radtke* court and other courts since that decision have not defined exactly what is a reasonable salary. To the uninitiated, the definition of "reasonable salary" may seem inconsequential and like splitting hairs since the salary is taxed to the shareholder at ordinary income rates, just like distribution of income. However, distributions from an S corporation are free from

---

[24] See ¶ 1204.02 for further discussion.

[25] If Code Sec. 1374 is applicable, see ¶ 802 for a discussion of the built-in gains tax.

[26] Note that if the corporate tax rate in Example 1-3 was higher than 15 percent, then the results would be skewed even more in favor of an S corporation format

depending on the corporate activities and tax bracket of the shareholder.

[27] *J. Radtke*, CA-7, 90-1 USTC ¶ 50,113, 895 F2d 1196.

[28] Note, however, *C. Davis*, DC Colo., 95-2 USTC ¶ 50,374, 887 FSupp 1387, refused to recharacterize distributions as salary where the two shareholders were husband and wife.

¶102.09

Federal Insurance Contributions Act (FICA), Federal Unemployment Tax Act (FUTA), and other employment taxes such as State Unemployment Insurance (SUI). Since the FICA tax rate is currently over 15 percent, the potential savings can be substantial if a shareholder receives distributions from an S corporation rather than salary. Because there is no "bright line" as to what is a reasonable salary, shareholders have become aggressive in pursuit of such distributions.[29]

Example 1-4: Alice Jenson is the sole shareholder of AJ Inc., a qualified S corporation. This year, Jenson received a salary from the corporation of $75,000 on which she paid FICA taxes of $5,737.50 (7.65%). The corporation paid the employer's share of FICA taxes in a like amount for a total cost of $11,475. If Jenson reduced her salary to $50,000 and took an additional $25,000 as a distribution of profits, she and the corporation would save $3,825 in FICA taxes ($25,000 × .153) because S corporation distributions are not treated as earned income for federal tax purposes.

In contrast, by definition, two-or-more-member LLCs and limited partnerships do provide in certain circumstances that distributions from them can be free of FICA, FUTA, and employment taxes. Specifically, all distributions to limited partners are free of FICA, FUTA, and employment taxes. An individual is treated as a limited partner unless the individual (1) has personal liability for the debts of or claims against the partnership by reason of being a partner, (2) has authority to contract on behalf of the partnership, or (3) participates in the partnership for more than 500 hours during the partnership's tax year.[30] S corporations, however, put no such restrictions on their shareholders; thus, S corporations provide their shareholders with the ability to manage the business and at the same time exempt some of their earnings from FICA, FUTA, and employment taxes. The only requirement is that shareholders who operate the business must take a reasonable salary.

Tax Pointer 1: The Department of the Treasury has recommended new legislation. Deputy Inspector General for audit, Pamela J. Gardner, reported on May 20, 2005 that 36,000 one-owner S corporations with profits of $100,000 or more paid no payroll taxes on profits; 40,000 S corporations with profits in the $50,000–$100,000 range paid no payroll taxes on the profits because no salary was taken. Accordingly, the Department of the Treasury has recommended that Congress close this loophole by subjecting to employment taxes all operating gains of S corporations that accrue to more than fifty-percent owners and their relatives.

Tax Pointer 2: Depending on the activity of the shareholder and the S corporation, the distribution of S corporate earnings could be classified as net investment income under Code Sec. 1411. For a discussion of Code Sec. 1411, see Chapter 16.

---

[29] Code Sec. 3101(b)(2)(A) prescribes that for tax years beginning after 2012, the employee's portion of the Medicare component of FICA taxes is increased by an additional 0.9 percent to a total of 2.35% for wages in excess of $200,000 ($250,000 in the case of a joint return, $125,000 in the case of a married taxpayer filing separately). See ¶ 616 for a discussion of Code Sec. 3101(b)(2)(A).

[30] Reg. §301.7701-3(b)(2)(ii) and Prop. Reg. §1.1402(a)-2(h)(2); For additional discussion of self-employment tax issues involving partners, see ¶ 716.03.

.10 Create Capital Gains for a Shareholder by Borrowing Money

Frequently, to offset capital losses, it is necessary to create capital gains, especially at the end of a tax year, so that a taxpayer will not be forced to carry forward capital losses subject to limited deductibility (i.e., $3,000 per year). S corporations offer a unique vehicle to create capital gains in that, by definition, any distribution in excess of a shareholder's basis will produce capital gains (with long-term or short-term capital gains treatment, depending on how long the shareholder owned the stock in the S corporation). However, an S corporation might be cash-tight so the distribution cannot be made. In that case, an S corporation can borrow money to create the distributions. Example 1-5 illustrates this concept in a simplified sense.

> **Example 1-5:** Alvin Garber is the sole shareholder of Alsa Inc., a calendar-year S corporation. On June 30, 2008, Garber incurs $100,000 in capital losses in the stock market. Under Code Sec. 1211, if Garber has no capital gains in 2008 to offset the capital losses, he will only be able to deduct $3,000 of the losses. Assume that Garber's basis in his Alsa Inc. stock is zero. Alsa Inc. owns a building without a mortgage that is worth $150,000 on December 15, 2008. On December 15, 2008, Alsa Inc. borrows $100,000 from a bank, securing the loan with a mortgage on its building, and distributes the $100,000 to Garber. Alsa Inc. breaks even for 2008. Garber will report the distribution as a capital gain because the distribution was $100,000 in excess of basis. On his Schedule D on Form 1040, Garber will offset the entire $100,000 capital loss with the $100,000 of capital gain created from the stock distribution.

In Example 1-5, Garber could not do the same thing in a partnership tax framework, either through an LLC or partnership, because when a partnership or LLC borrows money, the debt increases the basis of the partner or member, as the case may be.[31]

.11 Create Gains for a Shareholder by Distribution of Appreciated Property

When an S corporation distributes appreciated property (other than an obligation of the corporation or its stock) to a shareholder at fair market value, a gain will result, equaling the difference between the S corporation's basis and the fair market value of the property.[32] The resulting gain will be passed through to the shareholders in proportion to their stock ownership, increasing the basis of their stock.[33] The character of the gain will depend upon the nature of the property distributed by the corporation.

> **Example 1-6:** Alpha Inc., a calendar-year S corporation, is owned by three individual shareholders: Jill Allen, Jane Mays, and Joan Gibson. Alpha Inc. owns Wildwood, a piece of land that cost $100,000. On December 31, 2008, when the land was worth $160,000, it was distributed to Jill Allen. Jill's basis for her Alpha Inc. stock is $200,000. Jill's father, Sam, was an Alpha Inc. shareholder, and on his death on January 1, 2008, Jill acquired her S corporation

[31] Code Sec. 752.
[32] Code Sec. 311(b).
[33] Code Sec. 1367(a)(1).

stock from Sam.[34] The value of Alpha Inc. stock on Sam's estate tax return was $200,000. Alpha Inc. broke even for 2008 and had no other transactions other than the distribution of Wildwood to Jill on December 31, 2008. The tax consequence of the distribution of Wildwood to Jill is as follows: the three shareholders will each report capital gains of $20,000 (($160,000 – $100,000) ÷ 3). Jill's basis in her stock in Alpha Inc. will decline to $60,000, computed as follows: $200,000 less the $160,000 fair market value of Wildwood plus $20,000 of capital gains. Jill also has a basis in Wildwood of $160,000.

In contrast to Example 1-6, if property other than cash and marketable securities is distributed to partners in a partnership, no capital gain will be generated by the distribution; rather, the partners as a general rule take the lesser of the partnership's basis or the partner's individual basis in the partnership. The same is true for LLCs and LLC members electing to be treated as partnerships for federal tax purposes.

> **Example 1-7:** Assume the same facts as in Example 1-6, except that Alpha is an LLC. No capital gain will be generated on the distribution of Wildwood, and Jill's basis in Alpha LLC on December 31, 2008, will be $100,000 ($200,000 – Alpha LLC's $100,000 in basis in Wildwood).

If a C corporation distributes appreciated property to a shareholder, gain is recognized by the corporation at the corporate level.

> **Example 1-8:** Assume the same facts as in Example 1-6, except that Alpha Inc. is a C corporation. The tax consequences are as follows: Alpha Inc. would report a capital gain of $60,000 ($160,000 – $100,000) on its Schedule D on Form 1120. There is no change in the basis of Jill's stock, and she reports $160,000 as a dividend, the fair market value of Wildwood.[35]

Distribution of previously depreciated property. Gain recognized on the distribution of depreciable (or depletable) property will be recaptured as ordinary income to the extent of excess depreciation (or depletion) previously claimed.[36] In addition, *all gain* recognized by the corporation on the distribution of depreciable property to a 50-percent-or-more shareholder will be classified as ordinary income.[37]

.12 Shareholders Allowed to Redeem Stock at Death with Impunity

There are two basic ways to buy out a shareholder at death: either the shareholder's stock is redeemed at death[38] or the other shareholders buy out the stock at death (the shareholders' purchase of the stock at death is called a "cross-purchase buyout").[39] There are no adverse tax consequences with an S corporation in either type of buyout. With a C corporation, however, there could be a problem if the redemption is funded by life insurance on the deceased shareholder's life. Code Sec. 56 provides that the death benefit under a life insurance contract is included in

---

[34] For a discussion of basis, see ¶ 903 and ¶ 1124.

[35] Note that there may be a problem under state law if the corporation was insolvent at the time of the distribution, or if only one shareholder received a dividend, but it is beyond the scope of this book to discuss such issues.

[36] Excess depreciation is defined in Code Secs. 1245 and 1250. Excess depletion is defined in Code Sec. 1254.

[37] Code Sec. 1239.

[38] A redemption under Code Secs. 302 or 303. See ¶ 1209 for a discussion of this topic.

[39] A cross-purchase agreement is discussed at ¶ 1106.11.

a corporation's alternative minimum taxable income. For a C corporation with little or no earnings in the year of death, the C corporation could be caused to pay a tremendous amount of alternative minimum tax solely as a result of the shareholder's death.

> **Example 1-9:** ACC Inc., a calendar-year C corporation, is composed of three equal shareholders: Catherine Akers, Jim Becker, and Jane Grant. The C corporation was established to buy Prairie Grove. The shareholders have a redemption agreement under which the corporation will be required to redeem a deceased shareholder's stock, with the buyout price being funded by life insurance on each of the shareholders' lives. Prairie Grove is worth $1.5 million when Becker dies, and the corporation receives $500,000 of life insurance on Becker's death. The corporation pays Becker's estate $500,000, the fair market value of Becker's one-third interest in the $1.5 million corporation. Since inception, ACC Inc. has broken even; tax-wise, it has no earnings and profits, and no assets other than its interest in Prairie Grove. Becker's death will cause ACC Inc. to pay alternative minimum tax on roughly $500,000 under Code Sec. 56, or approximately $135,500 ((26% × $175,000) + (28% + $325,000)). If ACC Inc. had been an S corporation, no such alternative minimum tax could have been generated since an S corporation is not subject to the alternative minimum tax.

.13 One Level of Taxation on Disallowed Travel and Entertainment Expenses

One of the IRS's favorite audit areas is to review travel and entertainment expenses of closely held corporations because shareholder-employees frequently have the corporation pay for items that are clearly personal in nature, such as vacations that are billed as business trips for the corporation and meals for friends that are billed as business meals. If these items are disallowed in a C corporation, there is a double tax effect: one at the corporate level on the income "created" by the disallowed expenses, plus one at the shareholder-employee level on the constructive dividend associated with disallowed expenses. In contrast, a disallowance in an S corporation has only one level of income tax generated—at the shareholder-employee level.

> **Example 1-10:** Sam Larsen is the sole shareholder of Sam Inc., a calendar-year S corporation. Sam Inc. is profitable, and Larsen runs all sorts of personal expenses through Sam Inc. that are deducted on the corporation's tax return. In 2006, Sam Inc. deducted $5,000 for Larsen's vacation to Florida that Larsen claimed was a business trip, and $10,000 for meals for friends and family that Larsen claimed were business meals. For 2006, Sam Inc. broke even tax-wise after deducting these expenses. On an IRS audit for the year 2006, the IRS disallowed all $15,000 of deductions claimed by the S corporation. Larsen was then required to report an additional $15,000 of income on his 2006 Form 1040.

In contrast to Example 1-10, if Sam Inc. had been a C corporation, the results would have been as follows: Sam Inc. would have reported an additional $15,000 of income, paying an additional $2,250 in tax ($15,000 × .15). Sam would also be

¶102.13

required to report $15,000 as a dividend on his own tax return, thereby incurring double tax.

   Tax Pointer: C corporations, in an attempt to minimize disallowance situations with shareholder-employees, frequently adopt "payback" resolution procedures in their corporate minutes, employment agreements, etc.;[40] however, these payback arrangements do not work in all circumstances.

.14 Sale of a Residence

If an individual sells his or her principal residence, regardless of the taxpayer's age, up to $500,000 ($250,000 if the individual is not married) of the gain can be excluded if certain conditions are met.[41] While it is beyond the scope of this text to provide a detailed description of the sale of a residence, under prior law, a homeowner could sell his or her residence to his or her wholly-owned S corporation and defer the gain.[42] It remains to be seen whether the homeowner could still do this under current law, but arguably, the same concept would apply.

The sale of the primary residence of a taxpayer could involve a Code Sec. 1031 transaction. For a discussion of the relationship of Code Sec. 1031 to Code Sec. 121, see: Michael Schlesinger, "Combined Tax-Free Exchange with Home-Sale Exclusion", *Practical Tax Strategies*, Vol. 74, No. 6 at 343 (June 2005).

.15 Income and Estate Tax Planning

An S corporation provides a means for income and estate tax planning for a shareholder and his or her family, though limited in comparison to the planning opportunities offered by a family partnership or an LLC. In contrast to a one-member LLC, estate-planning opportunities for a one-member S corporation are easier to implement because the taxation of the entity does not change upon the death of the shareholder. In contrast, a one-member LLC, if the owner were to leave it to more than one individual, would change from a Schedule E or C taxpayer (depending on the type of business in which the one-member LLC was engaged) to a partnership for tax purposes.

.16 ESOP Planning

Code Sec. 1042(b)(4) prescribes that for a shareholder to receive favorable tax results in selling stock to a C corporation ESOP, the shareholder must hold the stock for three years. IRS Letter Ruling 200003014 (October 20, 1999) prescribes that the taxpayer's holding period will include the time during which the corporation's subchapter S election was in effect.

Thus, an individual shareholder could start an S corporation utilizing its pass-through abilities to grow, take losses, etc. Once the S corporation is successful, then the shareholders can terminate the S election, form the C corporation ESOP to utilize the tax benefits of Code Sec. 1042, and use IRS Letter Ruling 200003014 to utilize the holding period of S corporation stock for purposes of the three-year test under Code Sec. 1042(b)(4). For a further discussion of ESOPs, see Chapter 15, particularly ¶ 1501–¶ 1506.

---

[40] See, e.g., *V.E. Oswald*, 49 TC 645, Dec. 28,879 (Acq.).

[41] Code Sec. 121.

[42] IRS Letter Ruling 8646036 (August 19, 1986).

.17 Code Sec. 199 Deduction

As discussed at ¶ 722, Code Sec. 199 provides a deduction for domestic production activities. However, to obtain the deduction, wages have to be paid. By definition, sole proprietorships, whether they operate as unincorporated Schedule C filers, or as a one-member LLC, do not generate any wages, since all their income is self-employment; likewise, partners do not generate any salaries for their activities; guaranteed payments are not classified as W-2 wages for Code Sec. 199 purposes. However, if a business person forms a one-person S corporation to conduct activities, then the S corporation can pay the business person a salary, thereby satisfying Code Sec. 199's wage requirement.

¶ 103 State Issues

.01 State Tax Issues

Normally, when one does tax planning with S corporations, the focus is mainly federal tax issues. However, states, in an effort to balance their budgets, have been focusing more on business entities to raise funds from taxation. Accordingly, tax practitioners, once they solve their federal tax planning problems, must now concentrate on state tax laws to determine if the federal tax planning would not be unduly burdensome from a state tax perspective. Cases in point: mergers and Code Sec. 1031 exchanges. For a discussion of planning under Code Sec. 1031 to avoid transfer taxes, see IRS Letter Ruling 200118023, discussed at ¶ 1307.16. For cases involving mergers, see IRS Letter Ruling 20010718 discussed at ¶ 1307.17.

New York State Department of Taxation and Finance, TSB-A-08(1)M[43] offers an interesting situation where utilization of a Florida S corporation which is owned by a non-resident individual escaped estate taxation when the corporation owned real estate in New York. In contrast, this same pronouncement held that a single member LLC organized in Florida which owned real estate in New York was liable for estate taxation. The only requirement for the S corporation to escape taxation was that there had to be a "business purpose" for its existence.

The case of *Weichbrodt d/b/a McDonalds*[44] also illustrates another problem which has to be considered—namely, sales tax. In *Weichbrodt*, the taxpayer owned eight McDonald's restaurants—four directly as sole proprietorships, and four through his wholly-owned S corporation, where the taxpayer owned 100 common shares out of a total of 200 common shares which could be issued. The taxpayer was the sole shareholder, president and CEO of the S corporations. All eight of the restaurants were commonly managed and supervised. On June 30, 1996, the taxpayer decided to transfer the assets of the sole proprietorships to his wholly-owned S corporation for ten shares of common stock, with the corporation filing a Notification of Sale Transfer or Assignment in Bulk with the New York Sales Tax Department, listing the value of all the assets being transferred as "zero." The Division of Tax Appeals held that, pursuant to New York State Tax Law § 1101(b)(4), the transfer of assets to a corporation can be a sale. The Division,

---

[43] NEW YORK TAX REPORTER ¶ 406-279, New York Commissioner of Taxation and Finance, October 24, 2008.

[44] NEW YORK TAX REPORTER ¶ 404-103, New York Division of Tax Appeals, ALJ (2002).

citing *Sunny Vending Co. v. State Tax Commission,*[45] held that "the broad and inclusive language of the taxing statute 'clearly expresses an intent to encompass most transactions involving the transfer or use of commodities in the business world.'"

In terms of assessing the sales tax, the taxpayer argued that none could be imposed, because there was no material consideration for the sale, and he owned 100% of the assets before and after the transaction. Alternatively, the taxpayer argued that if a taxable sale occurred, the tax should be imposed on the increase in the shareholder's equity in the S corporation, to wit $115,604, thus yielding a sales tax of $8,092. However, the Division sustained the Administrative Law Judge's determination by holding that the fair market value of the assets transferred should be used. In reaching its decision, the Division noted that the S corporation assumed the shareholder's debts in connection with the § 351 transaction (as to the shareholder guaranteeing these debts to the lender, the Division gave no cognizance).

> **Tax Pointer:** 20 NYCRR 526.6(d)(1)(iv) prescribes that the transfer of property to a corporation upon its *organization* in consideration of issuance of its stock is not deemed a retail sale; thus, it is not subject to sales tax (emphasis added). 20 NYCRR 526.6(d)(1)(i) prescribes that the "transfer of property to a corporation solely in consideration for the issuance of its stock pursuant to a merger or consolidation effected under the laws of New York or any other jurisdiction, is not a retail sale." Thus, to avoid sales tax, the taxpayer in *Weichbrodt* should have incorporated the sole proprietorship as a separate corporation, and then merged it into his existing corporation. However, from a liability standpoint, it may be wise to have separately incorporated each property, rather than placing all the properties in one corporation.

.02 Operating a Business for State Tax Purposes as a Partnership, but for Federal Tax Purposes as an S Corporation

As detailed at ¶ 206, in certain states, there may be a tax advantage to operate a business as an S corporation for federal tax purposes, but as a partnership for state tax purposes.

.03 Location of the Domicile of the S Corporation and Its Shareholders

The case of *Est. of Bernard Shapiro,*[46] illustrates the fact that care must be practiced in terms of location of the S corporation and its shareholders. In *Shapiro,* Mr. Shapiro was living with a woman named Cora Jane Chenchark in the state of Nevada. They were not married and after a lengthy relationship, Cora sued Mr. Shapiro for palimony. Mr. Shapiro's estate settled Ms. Chenchark's claim for $1,000,000 and deducted the claim as a debt of the estate. The court sustained the claim on the grounds that palimony existed in Nevada. If Mr. Shapiro and Ms. Chenchark had lived in California instead of Nevada, such a claim could not have arisen. Thus, domicile and residence of the S corporation and shareholders should be a key consideration for operation of the S corporation.

---

[45] New York Tax Reporter ¶ 251-027, 475 N.Y.S.2d 896 (3d Dept. 1984).

[46] 2011-1, USTC ¶ 60,614 (9th Cir. 2011).

¶ 103.02

Chapter 2

Requirements to Be an S Corporation

¶ 201 Basic Requirements

Because an S corporation is a creature of statute, Congress has prescribed that all of the following requirements be met for a corporation to achieve S corporation status:[1]

- Have no more than 100 shareholders
- Have only eligible shareholders (e.g., individuals, decedents' estates, certain prescribed trusts, but not nonresident aliens)
- Be a domestic corporation
- Have only one class of stock

> *Tax Pointer 1:* Even if a corporation meets all of the above requirements, it may not want S status because of the shareholder limitations. When parents who are eligible shareholders undertake estate planning, the S corporation limitations on trusts may make them opt for another business structure such as a limited liability company classified as a partnership for tax purposes.

> *Tax Pointer 2:* In terms of the definition of "domestic corporation," it may be advantageous for a business to operate as a partnership for state tax purposes, but as an S corporation for federal tax purposes. For a discussion of this area, see ¶ 206.

---

[1] Code Sec. 1361(b)(1).

¶ 202 Counting the Shareholders

.01 Meeting the 100-Shareholder Limit

An S corporation may not have more than 100 shareholders at any time during the tax year or it will lose its S status. Cumulatively, an S corporation may show more than 100 shareholders during a tax year due to transfers of stock, but the total shareholders at any one time cannot exceed 100.[2]

In the case of S corporations which will exceed one hundred shareholders, shareholders may consider doing an "end run" around Code Sec. 1361(b)(1)(A)'s one hundred shareholder limit by forming a partnership of S corporations. Rev. Rul. 94-43[3] approved such a procedure. In Rev. Rul. 94-43, the IRS sustained a partnership of three S corporations where each S corporation had the maximum number of shareholders permitted. So if three hundred shareholders wanted to operate as a single business, they could form three S corporations comprised of one hundred shareholders each, and have these three S corporations enter into a partnership to do business.

Today, however, the partnership anti-abuse regulations, Reg. § 1.701-2, support deliberate attempts to subvert Code Sec. 1361(b)'s requirements. Example 2-1 illustrates this administrative approval:[4]

> **Example 2-1:** Marcata Inc. and Juan Gomez form partnership Salina to conduct a bona fide business. Marcata Inc. is a corporation that has elected to be treated as an S corporation under subchapter S. Gomez is a nonresident alien. Salina is properly classified as a partnership under the check-the-box regulations. Because Code Sec. 1361(b) prohibits Gomez from being a shareholder in Marcata Inc., Marcata Inc. and Gomez chose partnership form (rather than admit Gomez as a shareholder in Marcata Inc.) as a means to retain the benefits of subchapter S treatment for Marcata Inc. and its shareholders.
>
> Subchapter K is intended to permit taxpayers to conduct joint business activity through a flexible economic arrangement without incurring an entity-level tax. The decision to organize and conduct business through partnership Salina is consistent with this intent. In addition, on these facts, the requirements of Reg. § 1.701-2(a) have been satisfied. Although it may be argued that the form of the partnership transaction should not be respected because it does not reflect its substance (inasmuch as application of the substance-over-form doctrine arguably could result in Gomez being treated as a shareholder of Marcata Inc., thereby invalidating Marcata Inc.'s subchapter S election), the facts indicate otherwise. The shareholders of Marcata Inc. are subject to tax on their pro rata shares of Marcata Inc.'s income (see Code Sec. 1361 et seq.), and Gomez is subject to tax on Gomez's distributive share of partnership income (see Code Secs. 871 and 8100). Thus, the form in which this arrangement is

---

[2] Code Sec. 1361(b)(1)(A) and Rev. Rul. 78-390, 1978-2 CB 220. The 10-shareholder limit under prior law was not violated when a corporation had a cumulative total of 15 shareholders during a tax year, but no more than 10 shareholders at any one time.

[3] IRB 1994-27, 8 (6/17/94).

[4] Reg. § 1.701-2(d).

cast accurately reflects its substance as a separate partnership and S corporation. The Commissioner therefore cannot recast the transaction by claiming the partnership is inconsistent with the intent of subchapter K.

.02 Stock Held by a Husband and Wife

When stock is held jointly by a husband and wife, either as joint tenants or as tenants in common, the husband and wife are treated as one shareholder,[5] although both spouses must personally consent to the S corporation election.[6] If a husband and wife each own stock separately as well as jointly, they are still treated as one shareholder.[7]

Community property states. In a community property state, the husband and wife are treated as one shareholder if they each own stock, regardless of whether or not they each own stock as common property.

Death of a spouse. If a spouse dies, stock owned by the surviving spouse and the estate of the deceased spouse will be treated as one shareholder. Likewise, if both spouses die, the two estates will be treated as one shareholder.[8]

.03 Stock Held with Children, Grandchildren, or Parents

An individual who owns stock with his or her children, grandchildren, or parents is counted separately along with the shareholder children, grandchildren, or parents (e.g., if a father and his two children are shareholders of an S corporation, they count as three shareholders, not one, for the 100-shareholder numerical limit).[9] Constructive ownership rules do not apply in determining the 100-shareholder numerical limit.

> **Tax Pointer:** See discussion at ¶ 202.08 where the family can file an election to be treated as one shareholder.

.04 Stock Held by a Nominee or Agent

If stock is held by a nominee, only the beneficial owner will be treated as a shareholder for the 100-shareholder numerical limit. Likewise, stock held by an agent is deemed to be stock owned only by the principal.[10]

> **Example 2-2:** ADF Inc., an S corporation, issued 15 stock certificates: 13 to individuals; one to Commerce Bank, who is the agent for Don Adams; and one to Bob Jones, who is holding the stock as a nominee for his three sisters, Doris, Martha, and Sally Jones. ADF Inc. has the following 17 shareholders, although only 15 certificates were issued: the 13 individuals, Adams, and the three Jones sisters.

---

[5] Code Sec. 1361(c)(1).

[6] Reg. § 1.1362-2(b)(2).

[7] Reg. § 1.1361-1(e)(2).

[8] Reg. § 1.1361-1(e)(2).

[9] Code Sec. 1361(b).

[10] Reg. § 1.1361-1(e)(1) states that "[t]he person for whom stock of a corporation is held by a nominee, guardian, custodian, or an agent is considered to be the shareholder."

.05 Stock Held by a Custodian

When stock is held by a custodian under the Uniform Transfer to Minors Act (UTMA), the minor is deemed the owner, not the custodian.[11] Thus, if one person acts as a custodian for four different minors, there are four shareholders.

.06 Stock Held by Unmarried Joint Tenants and Tenants in Common

If two or more unmarried persons own S corporation stock as joint tenants, tenants in common, and so on, each person counts as a shareholder.[12]

.07 Beneficial Ownership

Occasionally, stock is not issued to a shareholder; yet, the parties and the S corporation treat the taxpayer as a shareholder. Such a situation arose in the case of *Feraco*.[13] In *Feraco*, a father and son owned the stock of the corporation. A third taxpayer, Bob Butler ("Butler") was given an option to purchase stock in the S corporation; however, no stock was issued to him. Nevertheless, the S corporation issued a Form 1120S, Schedule K-1 to Butler each year that he was involved in the corporation. The Court held that Butler was a shareholder of the S corporation, even though he lacked legal title to the shares. In reaching its decision, the Court noted that besides Butler being listed as a shareholder on the S corporation's tax return, Butler held executive positions typical of an owner of a corporation.

If an S corporation has beneficial owners before it issues stock, Reg. § 1.1377-1(a)(2)(i) treats the taxpayer as a shareholder for any day on which the corporation has not issued any stock.

.08 Family Members Treated as One Shareholder

Effective for tax years beginning after December 31, 2004, Code Sec. 1361(c)(1) has been amended to provide that, for purposes of counting the number of shareholders of an S corporation, "members of the family" can elect to be treated as one shareholder. Code Sec. 1361(c)(1)(B)(i) defines the term "members of the family" as the common ancestor, the lineal descendants of the common ancestor, and the spouses (or former spouses) of the lineal descendants or common ancestor. However, Code Sec. 1361(c)(1)(B)(ii) prescribes that the common ancestor cannot be more than six generations removed from the youngest generation of shareholders at the time the S election is made, or the effective date for tax years beginning after December 31, 2004. A spouse (or former spouse) will be treated as being of the same generation as the individual to which he or she is (or was) married.

Code Sec. 1361(c)(2)(B) prescribes that the members of a family may be treated as one shareholder, for the purposes of determining the number of shareholders, whether a family member holds stock directly or is treated as a shareholder by reason of being a beneficiary of an electing small business trust or qualified subchapter S trust. A legally adopted child, a child who is lawfully placed

---

[11] Rev. Rul. 66-226, 1966-2 CB 239.

[12] Reg. § 1.1361-1(e)(1).

[13] *F.J. Feraco*, 80 TCM 463, Dec. 54,072(M), TC Memo. 2000-312; *accord, S.D. Pahl*, 71 TCM 2744, Dec. 51,287(M), TC Memo. 1996-176, aff'd CA-9, 98-2 USTC ¶ 50,602, 150 F3d 1124 (court provides excellent discussion of the federal and state law issues involving beneficial ownership of stock).

with a household for legal adoption, and a foster child are considered a member of the family.

The Internal Revenue Service in Notice 2005-51[14] prescribed certain rules of operation and definitions for the family provisions for ownership of S corporate stock, namely:

> [any] member of the family who is (or is treated under Section 1361 and the regulations thereunder as) a shareholder of the S corporation may make the election. The election is made by notifying the corporation to which the election applies. The notification shall identify by name the member of the family making the election, the "common ancestor" of the family to which the election applies, and the first taxable year of the corporation for which the election is to be effective. For purposes of making the election the common ancestor does not have to be alive at the time the election is made.

For purposes of the election, the estate of a deceased member of the family will be considered to be a member of the family during the period in which the estate, or a trust described in Section 1361 (c) (2) (A) (iii), holds stock in the S corporation. The members of the family will include:

(1) Each potential current beneficiary of an electing small business trust (ESBT) who is a member of the family,

(2) The income beneficiary of a qualified subchapter S trust (QSST) who makes the QSST election, if that income beneficiary is a member of the family,

(3) Each beneficiary of a trust who is a member of the family, if the trust was created primarily to exercise the voting power of stock transferred to it,

(4) The member of the family for whose benefit a trust described in Section 1361 (c) (2) (A) (vi) was created,

(5) The deemed owner of a trust treated as wholly owned under subpart E of Part I of subchapter J of Chapter 1 of Subtitle A of the Internal Revenue Code, if that deemed owner is a member of the family, and

(6) The owner of an entity disregarded as an entity separate from its owner under § 301.7701-3 of the Procedure and Administration Regulations, if that owner is a member of the family.

If a corporation has two or more elections in effect and the members of one family for which the election has been made (the inclusive family) include all the members of another family for which the election was also made (the subsumed family), then the members of the inclusive family will be counted as one shareholder for purposes of Section 1361 (b) (1) (A) as long as the inclusive family's election is in effect, and the members of the subsumed family will not be counted as a separate and additional shareholder.

The election will be effective as of the first day of the corporation's taxable year designated by the shareholder making the election. Any election will remain in effect until terminated as provided in regulations.

---

[14] 2005-51 IRB.

¶202.08

If taxpayers have already taken certain actions in order to make this election by various forms of notification to the corporation or to the IRS, in order for the election to be effective for taxable years beginning after December 31, 2004, taxpayers will need to provide the information described in Notice 2005-91 to the corporation (to the extent not already provided to the corporation).

The corporation is required to keep records in accordance with Section 6001 and the regulations thereunder.

Tax Pointer 1: To protect family members and the S corporation from one family member electing termination, provisions should be inserted in the S corporate shareholders agreement mandating that all family members vote to maintain the election, with the proviso that if a family member wants to break the election, leave the corporation, etc., the corporation and/or the remaining shareholders must purchase this shareholder's interest.

Tax Pointer 2: Code Sec. 1361(c)(1) does not detail what happens if a member of this six-generation family S corporate group conveys stock to a member outside the family group. Presumably, this will not cause the destruction of the six-generation family group, with the recipient of the stock being counted as an additional shareholder.

One of the primary benefits in having various generations of a family treated as one shareholder is that it makes it easier to make other individuals, such as employees, shareholders.

¶ 203 Eligible Shareholder Entities

Limitations are imposed on what types of entities can be shareholders of an S corporation.[15] Discussed briefly below are five types of entities that can and should be considered for shareholders of an S corporation because of their tax-planning opportunities.[16]

.01 Estates

Because of the transitory nature of estates, in that they act as conduits for disposing of a decedent's net assets, estates are not often thought of as a tax-planning device. However, they can, in certain circumstances, provide assistance and prevent adverse tax consequences from arising.

In the case of an S corporation, if an S corporation shareholder left his or her estate by will to a nonresident alien (who cannot be an S corporation shareholder[17]), the corporation's S status would terminate when the nonresident received the S corporation shares. However, if the shareholder's estate was kept alive and delayed making the bequest, the S corporation status could be maintained until the crisis generated by the decedent's bequest to the nonresident alien was resolved. Steps the S corporation could take would be to redeem the shares bequeathed to

---

[15] Code Sec. 1361(b)(1).
[16] Other entities such as the employee stock ownership plans (ESOPs) can be S corporation shareholders, but Congress has placed restrictions on them that make

it difficult from a tax-planning perspective to use them in operating S corporations. For a discussion of ESOPs and their limitations, see Chapter 15.
[17] Code Sec. 1361(b)(1)(C).

the nonresident alien, or have the nonresident alien become a resident alien. Alternatively, the stock could be sold by the estate to a permitted shareholder.

From a tax-planning perspective, it may be desirable for an estate of a deceased C corporation shareholder (where the decedent owned 100 percent of the corporation's stock) to elect S status for the corporation to take advantage of the S status's single level of taxation.[18]

.02 Six Types of Trusts

Only certain trusts can be shareholders of an S corporation. If an ineligible trust is admitted as a shareholder (e.g., a foreign trust[19] or trust for an individual retirement account (IRA)), the S corporation election will be terminated when the nonpermitted trust becomes a shareholder. As discussed in Chapter 3, only the following six types of trusts are permitted to be S corporation shareholders:[20]

(1) Grantor trusts

(2) Code Sec. 678 trusts

(3) Testamentary trusts

(4) Voting trusts

(5) Electing small business trusts (ESBTs)

(6) Qualified subchapter S trusts (QSSTs)

.03 Bankrupt Shareholders and Bankruptcy Estates

A shareholder who has filed under any provision of the bankruptcy code can be an S corporation shareholder.[21] A bankruptcy estate can also be a shareholder in an S corporation.[22] In the case of a husband and wife where just one of the spouses goes bankrupt, presumably, on the bankruptcy of one of the spouses, two shareholders will be created: one, the bankrupt spouse's estate, and the other, the nonbankrupt spouse.[23]

An S corporation can revoke its status whereupon it becomes a C corporation. If an S corporation revokes its status in a bankruptcy, this revocation can have enormous tax consequences. For instance, in *The Majestic Star Casino, LLC v. Barden Development, Inc.*,[24] a case involving a QSUB, the court held that S corporation status is not a property right; thus, creditors cannot object if the S corporation shareholders revoke S status. The result was that approximately 2.26 million dollars of estimated income tax was not paid to the Indiana Department of Revenue for 2010 by the shareholders on revocation. The court in reaching its decision acknowledged *In re Trans-Line West, Inc.*[25] and its ilk, but stated that it "decline[d] to follow the rationale of Trans-Line West and its progeny, and we conclude that S-corp status is not 'property' within the meaning of the Code."

---

[18] For a discussion of these estate-planning situations, see ¶ 1109.05 et seq.

[19] For a definition of "foreign trusts" see Code Sec. 7701(a)(31) and Reg. § 1.1361-1(h)(2).

[20] Code Sec. 1361(c)(2) and (d).

[21] Code Sec. 1361(c)(3).

[22] Reg. § 1.1361-1(b)(2).

[23] Code Sec. 1361(c)(1) would normally treat them as just one shareholder.

[24] 2013-1 USTC ¶ 50,338 (3rd Cir. 2013).

[25] 203 B.R. 653, 97-1 USTC ¶ 50,252 (Bankr. ED Tenn. 1996) S status a property right.

.04 Charitable Organizations

A charitable organization can be a shareholder in an S corporation provided that the charitable organization is exempt from taxation and, therefore, classified as a "qualified tax-exempt shareholder."[26] Thus, an individual shareholder can donate S corporation stock to a charitable organization (e.g., church, synagogue, private foundation, Red Cross, community chest) and receive a charitable contribution for it. The charitable organization will be counted as one shareholder for establishing the 100-shareholder limit, according to the Small Business Job Protection Act (SBJPA) Committee Reports.[27]

Income or stock from the S corporation. The SBJPA Committee Reports also prescribe that items of income or loss of an S corporation will flow through to the charitable organization (qualified tax-exempt shareholder) as unrelated business taxable income (UBTI) regardless of the source or nature of such income (e.g., passive income of an S corporation will flow through to the qualified tax-exempt shareholder as UBTI). If a qualified tax-exempt shareholder has gain on the sale of the stock in a C corporation that once was an S corporation while held by the shareholder, the tax-exempt shareholder will treat as UBTI the amount of gain that the shareholder would have recognized had it sold the stock for its fair market value as of the last day of the corporation's last tax year as an S corporation.

Example 2-3: GoodHomes, a qualified tax-exempt organization, acquired stock in a for-profit S corporation several years ago. Two years ago, when GoodHomes' tax basis in its stock in the S corporation was $70,000, the shareholders voted to revoke its S election. The revocation was effective as of January 1 of that year. GoodHomes estimated that its stock in the company was worth approximately $200,000 at the date of revocation of the election. This year, it sold its stock in the company for $320,000, realizing a $250,000 gain. $130,000 of this gain must be treated as UBTI (the difference between the $200,000 value of the stock at the date of revocation and GoodHomes' $70,000 tax basis). The remainder of GoodHomes' gain will presumably be treated as investment income.

Income or stock from C corporation earnings and profits. If a charitable organization (qualified tax-exempt shareholder) purchased stock in an S corporation[28] and subsequently received a dividend distribution on that stock that reflected subchapter C earnings and profits accumulated in prior years, the organization must reduce its basis in the stock by the amount of the dividend. The SBJPA Committee Reports prescribe that regulations may provide that the basis reduction only would apply to the extent the dividend is deemed to be allocable to subchapter C earnings and profits that accrued on or before the date of acquisition.

Example 2-4: UWC is a qualified charitable organization that purchased stock in an S corporation three years ago for $50,000. This year, when UWC's basis in the stock was still $50,000, it received a distribution from the S

---

[26] Code Sec. 1361(b)(1)(B) and (c)(6) and Code Sec. 501(a).

[27] Small Business Job Protection Act of 1996 (P.L. 104-188).

[28] Stock could have been acquired when the corporation was a C or an S corporation.

¶203.04

corporation of $43,000, all of which was deemed to be attributable to earnings and profits accumulated in prior years when it was a C corporation. UWC must reduce its basis in the S corporation stock by the $43,000 dividend distribution, thus increasing the amount of any future gain realized on sale of that stock that will be classified as UBTI. Note that non-charitable shareholders do not adjust the basis of their S corporation stock on receipt of distributions classified as dividends for federal income tax purposes.

.05 Employee Benefit Trusts

Employee benefit trusts can be shareholders in an S corporation provided they are exempt from taxation.[29] Trusts specifically mentioned in the SBJPA Committee Reports are employee stock ownership plans (ESOPs).[30] As is the case with charitable organizations, employee benefit trusts are classified as one shareholder for the 100-shareholder limit regardless of the number of employees covered by the plan.

.06 Disregarded Entities—Limited Liability Companies

While the law is not dispositive, it appears based on IRS Letter Ruling 9745017 (August 8, 1997) that a one-taxpayer LLC that is classified as a disregarded entity can be a shareholder in an S corporation providing that the underlying member can qualify as a permissible S corporation shareholder, and no election has been made to tax the limited liability company as an association.[31]

Besides IRS Letter Ruling 9739014, there have been two private letter rulings sustaining LLC ownership—IRS Letter Ruling 9745017 (August 8, 1997) sustained the transfer of shares held by a QSST [32] to an LLC owned exclusively by the QSST, and IRS Letter Ruling 20008015 (February 28, 2000) held that the transfer of shares by individual shareholders to disregarded entities would be sustained where a partnership was involved as one of the disregarded entities. The facts in IRS Letter Ruling 20008015 are as follows: X is an S corporation which has two equal individual shareholders, A and B. Pursuant to an overall business plan, A plans to form a one-person LLC, "LLCA," and a limited partnership, "LPA." A plans to exchange N% of A's ownership in the S corporation for 100% ownership in the one-person LLC. Subsequently, A plans to transfer A's remaining interest in the S corporation ("M%") to the limited partnership, taking back a limited partnership interest. Simultaneously, the one-person LLC will transfer its interest in the S corporation to the limited partnership, with the final result being that A will own 100% of the limited partnership, with the LLC being a general partner. Similarly, B plans to do the same with respect to B's ownership in the S corporation. Neither LLCA, LPA, nor the business entities owned by B (LLCB and LPB) will elect to be treated as an association taxable as a corporation for federal income tax purposes. Instead, each of the entities would exist according to their default classification obtained under Reg. § 301.7701-3(b), and S corporation status would remain intact.

---

[29] They must be exempt from taxation under Code Sec. 501(a). Code Sec. 1361(c)(6) and Code Sec. 401(a).

[30] For a discussion of ESOPs, see Chapter 15.

[31] Cf. IRS Letter Ruling 9739014 (June 26, 1997).

[32] For a definition of "QSST," see ¶ 307.

IRS Letter Ruling 199949019 (September 10, 1999), however, has ruled that the transfer of stock to a multiple member LLC terminated the S election.

From a planning perspective based on the letter rulings, IRS Letter Rulings 20008015 and 9739014 offer tremendous planning possibilities due to the tax treatment afforded one-member LLCs.[33]

To illustrate, an individual, Sam, could start out as a one-person LLC, because he wants a home-office deduction for his fledgling business as well as a medical reimbursement plan for his family, providing Sam hires his spouse.[34]

After Sam becomes successful, he could convert the one-person LLC to a one-person S corporation. Sam may want to do this conversion to an S corporation for several reasons: (a) avoidance of Code Sec. 1402's self-employment tax on every dollar earned (in an S corporation as detailed at ¶ 716.03, Sam only has to take a reasonable salary and can distribute the rest of the earnings to himself, self-employment tax-free); (b) estate planning. As detailed at ¶ 1307.08, a one-member LLC does not offer any estate tax planning possibilities. In contrast, with an S corporation, Sam could establish trusts for his family with the S corporation stock and make gifts to his family of S corporation stock utilizing minority discounts (for a discussion of minority discounts, see ¶ 1110.07); and (c) operate in areas where a one-person LLC is not recognized (for a discussion of this point, see ¶ 1307.04).

Sam may also want to own his own S corporation stock through a one-member LLC for additional liability protection from creditors. While an S corporation (as detailed in ¶ 102.02) protects a shareholder from corporate creditors, there is always the risk that creditors of the S corporation could pierce the corporate veil and seek payment from the individual shareholders (for a discussion of the protection that an S corporation offers shareholders, see ¶ 102.02). If a shareholder were to own stock in the S corporation through a one-member LLC, then the creditor would have to work twice as hard, in that the creditor would have to pierce two veils of protection—the S corporation and the LLC.

.07 IRAs Can Be Bank Shareholders

Code Sec. 1361(c)(2)(A) and Code Sec. 4975(d) have been amended to provide that IRA and Roth IRA ownership of S corporate bank stock is allowed to the extent that such stock is held by the IRA or Roth IRA on October 22, 2004.

¶ 204 Ineligible Shareholder Entities

.01 Nonresident Aliens

A nonresident alien is defined as an individual who is neither a citizen of the United States nor a resident in the United States for at least one-half of a year.[35] Nonresident aliens cannot be shareholders of S corporations.[36]

---

[33] For a discussion of one-member LLCs, see ¶ 1307.

[34] For a more detailed discussion of this point, see ¶ 1307.09.

[35] Code Sec. 7701(b)(1)(B).

[36] Code Sec. 1361(b)(1)(C). *But see,* ¶ 202.01 which discusses an indirect means to involve a non-resident alien in an S corporation.

Dual-status individuals. Under current laws, it is possible for an individual to be both a resident of the United States and of a foreign country, and to claim benefits as a nonresident of the United States under tax treaties. To ensure that at least one level of taxes are paid on an S corporation's earnings, a dual-resident taxpayer who claims any treaty benefits as a nonresident, so as to reduce his or her U.S. income tax liability, will be treated as a nonresident alien for S corporation eligibility rules.[37] Accordingly, if the dual-resident taxpayer is a shareholder in an S corporation for any portion of the year while claiming a treaty benefit, then the S corporation will lose its S status effective the first day of the tax year in which the dual resident became an S corporation shareholder and claimed the treaty benefit as a nonresident.[38] If the dual resident does not claim treaty benefits to reduce U.S. tax liability, then he or she can be an S corporation shareholder.[39]

Nonresident alien spouse. If a U.S. shareholder's spouse is a nonresident alien who has a current ownership interest (as opposed to a survivorship interest) in the stock of an S corporation (by reason of any applicable law, such as a state community property law or a foreign country's law), the corporation does not qualify as an S corporation from the time the nonresident alien spouse acquires the interest in the stock.[40] If a corporation's S election is inadvertently terminated as a result of a nonresident alien spouse being considered a shareholder, the corporation may request relief.[41]

Example 2-5: In 2005, Karen Walters, a U.S. citizen, married David Cohen, a citizen of a foreign country. At all times, David meets the definition of a nonresident alien.[42] Under the foreign country's law, all property acquired by a husband and wife during the existence of the marriage is community property and owned jointly by the husband and wife. In 2005, while residing in the foreign country, Karen formed Epicure, a U.S. corporation, and Epicure simultaneously filed an election to be an S corporation. Epicure issued all of its outstanding stock in Karen's name. Under the foreign country's law, Epicure's stock became the community property of and jointly owned by Karen and David. Thus, Epicure does not meet the definition of a small business corporation and, therefore, cannot file a valid S election because David, a nonresident alien, has a current interest in the stock.

Example 2-6: Assume the same facts as Example 2-5, except that in 2006, Karen and David file a Code Sec. 6013(g) election allowing them to file a joint U.S. tax return and causing David to be treated as a U.S. resident for chapters 1, 5, and 24 of the Internal Revenue Code. The Code Sec. 6013(g) election applies to the tax year for which made and to all subsequent tax years until terminated. Because David is treated as a U.S. resident under Code Sec.

---

[37] Eligibility rules under Code Sec. 1361. Proposed Reg. §301.7701(b)-7(a)(4)(iii) and (iv).

[38] Code Sec. 1362(d)(2).

[39] An exception will be provided by Proposed Reg. §301.7701(b)-7(a)(4)(iv), which allows a dual-resident taxpayer to be treated as a U.S. resident even if he or she claims a treaty benefit. This exception will apply if the

dual-resident alien and the S corporation enter into an agreement to be subject to tax and withholding as if the dual resident were a nonresident alien partner in a partnership.

[40] Reg. §1.1361-1(g)(i).

[41] Code Sec. 1362(f). See ¶1205 for further discussion.

[42] Code Sec. 7701(b)(1)(B).

6013(g), Epicure now meets the requirements to be an S corporation. Thus, the election filed by Epicure to be an S corporation is valid.

.02 Nonqualifying Trusts

The following trusts cannot be S corporation shareholders. However, with proper planning, these "prohibited" trusts can indirectly participate in S corporations. For a discussion of this point see ¶ 202.01.

Foreign trusts. A foreign trust cannot be an S corporation shareholder.[43] Although a foreign trust is recognized under a foreign law, it does not satisfy Code Sec. 1361's rules mainly because of its nonresident alien shareholders.

Charitable remainder trusts. A charitable remainder trust cannot be an S corporation shareholder.[44] While tax-exempt organizations can be S corporation shareholders,[45] the charitable remainder trust will not qualify, because, as a rule, charitable trusts do not distribute all of their income to the beneficiaries; rather, they distribute a fixed amount of income in the case of a charitable remainder trust, or a percentage of income in the case of a charitable unitrust. Thus, because all of the trust's income is not distributed, it cannot satisfy Code Sec. 1361's strict rule of complete income distribution. Further, Code Sec. 1361(e)(1)(B)(ii) and (iii) prescribe that (1) a trust exempt from federal income tax and (2) a charitable remainder annuity trust or charitable remainder unitrust cannot be an electing small business trust.

Charitable lead trusts. A charitable lead trust cannot be an S corporation shareholder since it, like a charitable remainder trust, distributes a fixed or percentage unit of income to its charitable beneficiaries. Thus, because all the trust's income is not distributed, it cannot satisfy Code Sec. 1361's strict rule of complete income distribution.[46]

.03 Partnerships and Limited Liability Companies (LLCs)

A partnership (and, by definition, an LLC) cannot be an S corporation shareholder.[47] However, under "old" law pertaining to pre-1982 "subchapter S" corporations, a partnership or LLC could apparently act as a nominee or trustee of an allowable trust without destroying the S corporation election.[48] Presumably, this position has not changed. The IRS has also struck down attempts to subvert this prohibition on partners owning stock in an S corporation. But the anti-abuse regulations[49] published for partnerships and limited liability companies sustain use of a partnership and/or LLC to avoid Code Sec. 1361(b)(1)(B)'s strictness.

---

[43] Code Sec. 1361(c)(2)(A).

[44] Code Sec. 1361(e)(1)(B).

[45] Code Sec. 501(a) pursuant to Code Sec. 1361(b)(1)(B), based on a strict reading of Code Sec. 1361(c)(2)(A)(i)-(iv)'s trust rules.

[46] However, see IRS Letter Ruling 199936031 (June 10, 1999) for a means to allow a charitable lead annuity trust to operate with S corporation stock.

[47] Code Sec. 1361(b)(1)(B). See also *F.J. Kling*, 41 TCM 1133, Dec. 37,770(M), TC Memo. 1981-133 (partnership owned all of the stock of an S corporation; partners were denied a distributive-share deduction of corporate losses).

[48] Reg. § 1.1361-1(e)(1); see also *R. Guzowski*, 26 TCM 666, Dec. 28,535(M), TC Memo. 1967-145.

[49] Reg. § 1.701-2(b).

Tax Pointer: While a partnership and/or an LLC cannot be an S corporation shareholder, the S corporation can be a partner in a partnership or a member in an LLC.[50]

.04 C Corporations

A C corporation, whether foreign or domestic, cannot own stock in an S corporation.[51] Under old law, however, a C corporation could apparently hold title to the stock as a nominee or trustee of an allowable trust.[52] Again, this position is presumably still valid. Notwithstanding the general restriction on a C corporation owning S corporation stock, there is this exception: Code Sec. 1361(c)(6) permits nonprofit or charitable corporations to be shareholders.[53]

.05 Individual Retirement Accounts (IRAs)

Except for an IRA which held bank stock on October 22, 2004, an IRA cannot be an S corporation shareholder.[54] If a shareholder innocently transfers stock in an S corporation to an IRA, the IRS will in many cases agree to waive the effect of the terminating event if the stock is timely removed from the IRA.[55]

While an IRA cannot be an S corporation shareholder, it is possible in connection with an ESOP (see discussion at Chapter 15) that the ESOP could provide that every participant who receives a distribution of stock can direct that the distribution be rolled over to an IRA. IRS Letter Ruling 200122034 (February 28, 2000) prescribes that the S corporation's status will not be terminated if the S corporation redeems the stock immediately on the rollover designation before the IRA custodian receives the stock. Roth IRAs cannot be shareholders of an S corporation.[56]

.06 Overcoming Ineligibility

While the above shareholder entities (¶ 204.01–¶ 204.05) are ineligible to hold shares in S corporations based on Code Sec. 1361(b)'s requirements, Reg. § 1.701-2(d) does offer a way to overcome their ineligibility by forming a partnership or limited liability company with the S corporation.[57]

¶ 205 Owning C Corporations and Being a Member of a Controlled Group

.01 Owning C Corporations

An S corporation may own all or part of a C corporation by vote or value.[58] For tax purposes, the S corporation shall report its ownership in the C corporation as if it were an individual.[59] Thus, the S corporation will report dividends received as income without a dividends-received deduction.[60]

---

[50] See discussion at ¶ 1108.

[51] Code Sec. 1361(b)(1)(B).

[52] Reg. § 1.1361-1(e)(1).

[53] See discussion at ¶ 203.04.

[54] For a discussion of this limited exception for an IRA holding bank stock, see ¶ 203.07.

[55] IRS Letter Ruling 8915067 (January 23, 1989).

[56] *Taproot Administrative Services,* 2012-1 USTC ¶ 50,256 (9th Cir. 2012).

[57] For an example, see Example 2-1 at ¶ 202.01.

[58] Code Sec. 1361(b)(2).

[59] Code Sec. 1363(b). See also ¶ 1402.02.

[60] Code Sec. 243.

Tax Pointer: An S corporation with earnings and profits should proceed with care in acquiring any C corporation stock because of the effects of the passive investment income tax and the loss of S election.[61]

While an S corporation can own more than 80 percent of a C corporation, the S corporation may not join in the filing of a consolidated return with any of its affiliated C corporation subsidiaries unless the C corporation is a qualified subchapter S subsidiary as discussed in Chapter 14.[62] A C corporation subsidiary of an S corporation, however, can file consolidated returns with an affiliated C corporation.[63]

.02 Transactions with a C Corporation Subsidiary

Depending upon the amount of ownership the S corporation has in its C corporation subsidiaries, the related-party rule could recharacterize transactions, classifying gains as ordinary or disallowing losses.[64] If there is an installment sale between the S corporation and its controlled C corporation (i.e., the S corporation owns more than 50 percent of the C corporation's stock) and the disposition of the property takes place within two years before the installment sale payments are completed, then the gain is recognized in full.[65]

.03 Tax Consequences of Being a Member of a Controlled Group

There is nothing in the law to prevent an S corporation from being a member of a controlled group (i.e., brother-sister corporations[66] connected through common ownership by individuals, estates, or trusts). Controlled group ownership could arise in various situations, for example, when the same shareholder owns a C and an S corporation or two or more S corporations that are brother-sister corporations. Certain tax situations become affected when an S corporation is a member of a controlled group, for example, membership in retirement plans,[67] the work opportunity credit,[68] and the research credit.[69]

Example 2-7: Hank Young, a taxpayer, owns all the stock in Youngans Inc., an S corporation, and BarBQ Inc., a C corporation. Young establishes a profit sharing plan in BarBQ Inc., where there are many employees but very little profits, and a pension plan in Youngans Inc., where Young is the sole employee. Because Youngans Inc. and BarBQ Inc. are members of a controlled group, the employees of Youngans Inc. and BarBQ Inc. have to be combined to see if the top-heavy rules have been abridged, if the proper amount of contributions are being made, and so on.[70]

---

[61] Tax provisions under Code Sec. 1375; loss of S election procedure under Code Sec. 1362(d)(3). For more discussion, see ¶ 804 and ¶ 1204.

[62] Code Sec. 1504(b)(8).

[63] The C corporation must meet the definitions of Code Secs. 1361(b)(3) and 1504. For a further discussion of C corporation subsidiaries, see ¶ 1409 and Michael Schlesinger, "S Corporations Can Now Have Subsidiaries, but Proceed With Caution," *Taxation for Accountants,* at 132 (September 1998).

[64] Code Sec. 1239 (see also ¶ 607) and Code Sec. 267 (see also ¶ 712).

[65] Code Sec. 453(c).

[66] As defined by Code Sec. 1563(a).

[67] Code Sec. 410.

[68] Code Sec. 52(a).

[69] Code Sec. 41(f).

[70] Code Sec. 410 et seq. and Code Sec. 401 et seq. (For a discussion of retirement plans, see ¶ 707.)

.04 Tax Rates as a Member of a Controlled Group

An S corporation, by being a member of a controlled group, does not affect the tax rates of C corporations that are members of the controlled group, accumulated earnings credit of the corporations, and so on.[71]

> **Example 2-8:** Leo Harms forms Haven Inc., a C corporation, to engage in a venture. It is profitable, and Harms is contemplating another venture. In 2006, Harms forms Salvi Inc. to engage in this new enterprise, which elects S corporation status on formation. Salvi Inc. and Haven Inc. earn $100,000 each in 2006. Haven Inc.'s corporate income tax for 2006 will be computed by using the tax rates under Code Sec. 11 without allocation as would be required for brother-sister C corporations under Code Sec. 1561 et seq., and Harms, as sole shareholder of Salvi Inc., will report $100,000 of income on his Form 1040.

> **Tax Pointer:** Although a C and an S corporation will not have to share the corporate tax rate schedule when they are members of a controlled group, Code Sec. 482 can apply to reallocate income between the two entities.[72]

.05 Intercompany Loans from a C Corporation to an S Corporation to Create Basis for a Shareholder to Recognize Losses from Operations

During the course of operating an S corporation, a shareholder may realize that he, she or it may not have sufficient basis to take a loss from S corporation operations. To remedy this situation, the shareholder may lend money to the S corporation.[73] However, rather than utilizing a shareholder's own funds directly, a shareholder may want to utilize a brother-sister entity to advance the funds. Such was the situation in the recently-decided case of *Culnen*.[74]

In *Culnen*, from 1987 to 1990, taxpayer was a shareholder in Wedgewood Associates, Inc., an S corporation engaged in the restaurant business. During this period of time, taxpayer increased his shareholder ownership from 39% to 73%. During the same period of time, taxpayer was the sole shareholder of Culnen & Hamilton, Inc., an insurance producer in the State of New Jersey, which was an S corporation from February 1, 1986 through May 31, 1987; thereafter, Culnen & Hamilton was a C corporation. Culnen & Hamilton made advances to Wedgewood, allowing the shareholder to deduct the losses arising from Wedgewood's operation, which totaled approximately $2,500,000. The Court felt that Culnen & Hamilton was an "incorporated pocketbook" of the shareholder; thus, the payments made by Culnen & Hamilton to the S corporation, which were posted as loans, were such, and thus the shareholder could deduct the losses.[75] It is to be noted, however, that as a rule, a situation like *Culnen* is not a wise course because of challenge from the

---

[71] Code Sec. 1561(a).

[72] See, e.g., *W.H. Bell III,* 45 TCM 97, Dec. 39,495(M), TC Memo. 1982-660 (income paid to S corporation by a related corporation should be adjusted downward by Code Sec. 482), but see *Bank of Winnfield & Trust Co.,* DC, 82-1 USTC ¶ 9292, 540 FSupp 219 (no allocation of insurance premiums from an S corporation to a bank controlled by the stockholders of S corporation).

[73] For a discussion of utilizing debt to create basis for deducting S corporation losses, see ¶ 904.

[74] *D.J. Culnen,* 79 TCM 1933, Dec. 53,856(M), TC Memo. 2000-139, rev'd and rem'd on other grounds CA-3, 2002-1 USTC ¶ 50,200.

[75] In *F.H. Hitchens,* 103 TC 711, Dec. 50,309 (1994), the Court held that an indebtedness to a pass-through entity that had advanced the funds to an S corporation and is closely related to the taxpayer did not satisfy the basis rules of Code Sec. 1366. However, the Court felt the facts in the instant case were different than *Hitchens,* allowing the Court to find debt basis for the shareholder.

IRS. For discussion of this point, see ¶ 904.10. A simple means to avoid IRS challenge is to use wire transfers to create basis for taking losses. Wire transfers usually occur the same day; thus, the funds are on deposit in the S corporate checking account rather than being there on a bookkeeping entry.

¶ 206 Eligible Corporations

Only domestic corporations can be S corporations.[76] A "domestic corporation" is defined as one organized or created in the United States.[77] A foreign corporation could qualify as a domestic corporation if it files a certificate of domestication and a certificate of incorporation with a state within the United States.[78] Code Sec. 1361(b)(2)(A) prescribes that a bank which does not use the reserve method of accounting for bad debts can be an eligible corporation for S corporate purposes.

.01 A Business Operating as a Partnership for State Tax Purposes, but as an S Corporation for Federal Tax Purposes, Qualifies as a Domestic Corporation under Code Sec. 1361(b)(1)

The IRS has issued a number of private rulings allowing a business to operate in partnership format for state law purposes, but qualifying as a domestic corporation for S corporate purposes. See, for example, IRS Letter Ruling 200201005 (limited partnership for state tax purposes); IRS Letter Ruling 200215006 (limited liability partnership). A business would be desirous of becoming a partnership for state tax purposes if it would yield significant savings. A reading of the private letter rulings indicates that for a partnership to be sustained as a domestic corporation for S corporation purposes, the partnership agreement has to provide for equal distribution of assets, income, losses, etc. among the partners; thus, the partnership will not violate Code Sec. 1361's rules regarding one class of stock. However, for the partnership to utilize this partnership concept, it must file Form 8832, checking the box to be classified as a corporation. For a discussion of Form 8832, see ¶ 401.08.

In terms of converting an existing S corporation to a partnership for state tax purposes, but retaining the S corporation's identity as an S corporation for federal tax purposes, see the discussion at ¶ 1211.08.

¶ 207 Ineligible Corporations

Even when all of the other requirements of S corporation status have been satisfied (e.g., the corporation only has 100 individual shareholders, the shareholders are not nonresident aliens), to remain eligible, the corporation to elect S status must also *not* be any of the following:[79]

- Financial institution that is a bank which uses a reserve method of accounting for accounting for bad debts.[80]

- Insurance company subject to tax.[81]

- Corporation electing the Puerto Rico or possession tax credit.[82]

- Domestic international sales corporation (DISC), or former DISC.

---

[76] Code Sec. 1361(b)(1).

[77] Reg. § 1.1361-1(c) as defined in Reg. § 301.7701-5.

[78] For a discussion of this point, see IRS Letter Ruling 9512001 (September 30, 1994).

[79] Code Sec. 1361(b)(2).

[80] As defined in Code Sec. 585(a)(2) or to which Code Sec. 593 applies.

[81] Subchapter L of the Code.

[82] Code Sec. 936.

¶ 208 One-Class-of-Stock Requirement

For a corporation to qualify as an S corporation, it can only have one class of stock.[83] The following situations will not create a second class of stock leading to the revocation of the S election: voting and nonvoting stock, stock that can vote on certain issues, and one class of stock that can elect certain members of the board of directors. However, the one-class-of-stock requirement severely limits estate and income tax planning possibilities since S corporations are prohibited from adopting recapitalizations, creating preferred stock, and so on.[84] The following planning possibilities are available to S corporations.

.01 Voting and Nonvoting Common Stock

An S corporation is permitted to have voting and nonvoting common stock, provided that all shares have the same economic rights to corporate income and assets.[85] This statutory exception to having only one class of stock gives S corporations the following tax and business planning flexibility.

Shifting income among family members. One tax-planning device is to shift income by having various family members (i.e., children over the age of 14) own stock in the S corporation together with their parents. Estate tax savings are reaped as well for the controlling shareholder by using minority and lack of marketability discounts (see discussion at ¶ 1110.07). To prevent loss of voting control over corporate affairs, the S corporation can issue nonvoting common stock to the children over the age of 14 and voting common stock to the parents.[86]

> **Example 2-9:** Abby and Ben Schwartz, husband and wife, have three minor children, Adam, Chad, and Nathan. They plan to start Abby Inc., an S corporation. To keep control over the corporation, Abby and Ben will have Abby Inc. issue all voting common stock to themselves and nonvoting common stock to their three children.

> **Information Pointer:** Family members who have voting stock must be careful not breach their fiduciary duty to the corporation (e.g., the minority shareholders); otherwise they may be sued by the non-voting shareholders in a civil derivative shareholder suit. An example of such a situation could arise if the nonvoting shareholders felt that the voting shareholders took excessive salaries.

Some parents want sole ownership and control of their S corporation during their lives, and, at their deaths, they want to pass the ownership and control of the S corporation to their children and trusted employees. In this situation, a parent may

---

[83] Code Sec. 1361(b)(1)(D).

[84] See ¶ 1109.02 for discussion.

[85] Code Sec. 1361(c)(4). Operationally, all shares must provide proportional interests to their holders in corporate distributions and liquidation proceeds.

[86] Care must be taken not to run afoul of the reallocation rules of Code Sec. 1366(e). (See discussion at ¶ 1119.01–¶ 1119.04.) Care must also be taken in family estate-planning situations not to run afoul of Code Secs. 2701–2704 (discussed at ¶ 1120).

¶208.01

pass stock in the S corporation to children and trusted employees by means of his or her last will and testament without creating a second class of stock.[87]

> **Tax Pointer 1:** Care must be practiced with respect to involving family members in an S corporation; in particular, the grasp of Code Sec. 2036. For a discussion of Code Sec. 2036 and how it applies to S corporations, see ¶ 1109.03.

Raising business capital with nonvoting common stock. While an S corporation cannot issue preferred stock, nonvoting common stock can serve some of the same purposes.[88]

> **Example 2-10:** Vetta Bhella owns all the voting common stock in Pharmox Inc., an S corporation. Pharmox Inc. needs to raise additional capital, so it issues nonvoting common stock to a new stockholder, Terry Holt. Holt is willing to make the investment, giving all of the control in Pharmox Inc. to Bhella while enjoying the economic rights to dividends and liquidation proceeds from the stock. If Holt is issued a tremendous amount of shares (instead of a minimal amount), Holt will receive a tremendous amount of income because S corporation income is distributed on a per-share, per-day basis.

> **Tax Pointer 2:** Private letter rulings have indicated that corporations can have a great deal of flexibility in raising business capital (see, e.g., IRS Letter Ruling 8247017 [August 13, 1982] where an agreement gave minority shareholders the option of having their stock redeemed under certain conditions but did not create a second class of stock).

Attracting key personnel with equity in nonvoting common stock. Frequently, key personnel who are running a business want equity participation in the business to compensate them for their efforts. In addition to establishing an employee stock ownership plan (ESOP),[89] an S corporation can establish nonvoting common stock to give key personnel an equity interest in the corporation. Alternatively, the S corporation can issue voting stock but restrict its rights by a shareholders' agreement. The corporation can have restrictions on transferability or require repurchase by the corporation upon the occurrence of certain events.[90]

IRS Letter Ruling 200029050 (April 26, 2000) sustains an employment stock situation used frequently with key executives: the executive receives nonvoting stock in the S corporation as part of his employment package. When certain events occur (i.e., death, disability, divorce, termination of employment with or without cause), the S corporation is required to buy back the stock for a premium price. The IRS sustained a stock-employment agreement with these types of provisions, holding that this agreement does not create a second class of stock, because the agreement did not alter the stock's distribution, dividend, or liquidation rights.

Stock appreciation rights (SARs). Private letter rulings periodically detail planning possibilities permitted with stock of an S corporation. In IRS Letter Ruling 8828029 (April 14, 1988), stock appreciation rights (SARs) were not deemed a

---

[87] For more detail of such a situation, see discussion at ¶ 1119.
[88] Code Sec. 1361(b)(1)(D).
[89] See Chapter 15 for a discussion of ESOPs.
[90] IRS Letter Rulings 9043013 (July 26, 1990), 9049049 (September 30, 1990), and 9101019 (October 5, 1990).

¶208.01

second class of stock. The facts of IRS Letter Ruling 8828029 were that X, an S corporation, had one class of stock and allowed selected employees to participate in its SAR program. Using the plan provisions, each SAR was assigned a value according to a formula, roughly equal to the value of one share of X's stock. The SAR, however, did not entitle the employee to vote as a shareholder or share in the assets of the corporation on liquidation. Participants in the plan were allowed to redeem the SARs at certain times during the term of their employment, but when they terminated their employment, they were required to redeem their entire SAR interest. When the employee redeemed an SAR, the employee received an amount equal to the increase of the SAR's value from issue date to termination date.

Stock option plans. In IRS Letter Ruling 8819041 (November 21, 1989), a stock option plan was deemed not to create a second class of stock. The pertinent facts of the Ruling were that the S corporation's board of directors would authorize stock options that would be nontransferable and nonexercisable in five years. For the options to be exercisable, the S corporation had to achieve a certain specified minimum rate of return on its assets, and on exercise, the optionee would have to make a Code Sec. 83(b) election, recognizing the value of the stock acquired as income in the year.

Tax Pointer 3: Code Sec. 409A discussed at ¶ 723 provides various restrictions on employment agreements, stock option plans, etc. It remains to be seen how Code Sec. 409A will apply to S corporate shareholder agreements.

.02 What Is and Is Not a Second Class of Stock

Equity interests. For stock to be classified as a second class of stock,[91] there must be two "equity" interests created. In IRS Letter Ruling 9112017 (December 21, 1990), the IRS provided clarification regarding the definition of equity. In this ruling, the Class A shareholders did not receive any cash or property distributions, had no right to assets from the corporation's liquidation, and the shares could not be transferred. However, they could elect a majority of the board of directors. These shares were created solely to provide a particular shareholder with additional voting rights. The Class B shareholders were entitled to cash and property dividends, liquidation proceeds, and could vote on mergers and dissolutions. IRS Letter Ruling 9112017 concluded that the Class A common stock did not represent an equity interest and was not considered a "class of stock" for purposes of Code Sec. 1361(b)(1)(D).

Voting rights, buy-sell agreements, commercial contractual arrangements, and redemption agreements. Differences in voting rights among shares of stock of the S corporation are disregarded in determining whether a corporation has more than one class of stock. Likewise, buy-sell agreements among shareholders and restrictions on the transferability of stock are disregarded unless a principal purpose of the agreement is to circumvent the one-class-of-stock requirement.[92] Additionally, commercial contractual arrangements such as leases, employment agreements, or loan agreements are disregarded unless a principal purpose of the

---

[91] Code Sec. 1361 contains the proscription against two classes of stock.

[92] Code Sec. 1361(b)(1)(D).

agreement is to circumvent the one-class-of-stock requirement. Redemption agreements are similarly disregarded to determine whether an S corporation has more than one class of stock unless the agreement restricts the rights of the holders of the stock to share in liquidation proceeds or provides for distributions that would be treated as nonconforming distributions.

In IRS Letter Ruling 200329011 (March 26, 2003), a second class of stock was not found under Reg. § 1.1361-1(l)(2)(iii)(A) in a personal injury law firm, where two different arrangements were established to redeem stock of shareholders. One arrangement provided an incentive shareholders agreement which was tailored for younger firm members that required each contracting shareholder to sell his or her shares on death, disability, retirement or termination of employment at a price determined through a complex formula, engineered to reward long-term employment. The other agreement (the "old redemption agreement") which applied to two senior firm members required them to redeem their shares at book value on a terminating event, with the two agreements creating different redemption rights on the occurrence of a terminating event.[93]

State income taxes paid or withheld. State laws that require a corporation to pay or withhold state income taxes on behalf of some or all of the corporation's shareholders are disregarded to determine whether all outstanding shares of stock of the corporation confer identical rights to distribution and liquidation proceeds. A difference in timing between the constructive distributions and the actual distributions to the other shareholders generally does not cause the corporation to be treated as having more than one class of stock.

Redemption agreements. Redemption agreements for stock will be considered as establishing a second class of stock if, at the time the agreement is entered into, the contractual redemption price "is significantly in excess of or below the fair market value of the stock." Reg. § 1.1361-1(l)(2)(iii)(A) also prescribes that "[a]greements that provide for the purchase or redemption of stock at book value or at a price between fair market value and book value" will not establish a second class of stock. In order for a price to be accepted by the regulations, there must be a "good faith determination of fair market value." However, Reg. § 1.1361-1(l)(2)(iii)(B) prescribes that bona fide agreements to redeem or purchase stock at the time of death, divorce, disability, or termination of employment are disregarded in determining whether a corporation's shares of stock confer identical rights.

> **Tax Pointer:** For redemption agreements involving members of a shareholder's family, the special valuation rules in Codes Secs. 2701-2704 should be consulted to ensure that all transactions are done at "fair market value," not "book value" where a gift would be deemed to occur.[94]

---

[93] See also IRS Letter Ruling 200429012 (anti-dilution clause in a shareholders agreement applicable to two out of the four shareholders will not terminate the S status); IRS Letter Ruling 8506114 (November 19, 1984) (no second class of stock when S corporation permitted to impose stock restrictions on stock issued to employees but not required to place same restrictions on principal shareholder); IRS Letter Ruling 9011055 (December 14, 1989) (founding shareholder of S corporation exempted from S corporate employment agreement which affected shareholder-employee rights).

[94] See further discussion at ¶ 1120.

Determining book value of stock. Reg. § 1.1361-1(l)(2)(iii)(C) prescribes that "determination of book value will be respected if—(1) The book value is determined in accordance with Generally Accepted Accounting Principles (including permitted optional adjustments); or (2) The book value is used for any substantial nontax purpose."

Change of stock ownership distributions. An agreement will not create a second class of stock where "as a result of change in stock ownership, distributions in a tax year are made on the basis of shareholders' varying interest in the S corporation's income in the current or immediately preceding tax year." Reg. § 1.1361-1(l)(2)(iv) also prescribes that "[i]f distributions pursuant to the provisions are not made within a reasonable time after the close of the tax year in which the varying interests occur, the distributions may be recharacterized depending on the facts and circumstances, but will not result in a second class of stock."

Distributions that differ in timing and amount. The thrust of Reg. § 1.1361-1(l)(2) is such that a facts and circumstances test will be used to determine if a second class of stock is created for "any distributions (including actual, constructive, or deemed distributions) that differ in timing or amount."

Reg. § 1.1361-1(l)(2) examples. Reg. § 1.1361-1(l)(2) offers the following nine examples of how to determine what is and is not a second class of stock.

> *Example 1: Determination of whether stock confers identical rights to distribution and liquidation proceeds.* (i) The law of State A requires that permission be obtained from the State Commissioner of Corporations before stock may be issued by a corporation. The Commissioner grants permission to S, a corporation, to issue its stock subject to the restriction that any person who is issued stock in exchange for property, and not cash, must waive all right to receive distributions until the shareholders who contributed cash for stock have received distributions in the amount of their cash contributions.

If stock is issued that does not confer identical rights to distributions and liquidation proceeds, then a second class of stock will exist.[95] The rights to distribution and liquidation proceeds can be found in the corporate charter, bylaws, administrative law operation, state law, or agreement. The conditions imposed by the State Commissioner of Corporations in Example 1 above causes the S corporation to have more than one class of stock.

> *Example 2: Distributions that differ in timing.* (i) S, a corporation, has two equal shareholders, A and B. Under S's bylaws, A and B are entitled to equal distributions. S distributed $50,000 to A in the current year, but does not distribute $50,000 to B until one year later. The circumstances indicate that the difference in timing did not occur by reason of a binding agreement relating to distribution or liquidation proceeds.

The difference in timing of the distributions to A and B in Example 2 above does not create a second class of stock; however, Code Sec. 7872 or other recharacterization principles may apply to determine the appropriate tax consequences.

---

[95] Reg. § 1.1361-1(l).

Example 3: Treatment of excessive compensation. (i) S, a corporation, has two equal shareholders, C and D, who are each employed by S and have binding employment agreements with S. The compensation paid by S to C under C's employment agreement is reasonable. The compensation paid by S to D under D's employment agreement, however, is found to be excessive. The facts and circumstances do not reflect that a principal purpose of D's employment agreement is to circumvent the one class of stock requirement of section 1361(b)(1)(D) and this paragraph (l).

In Example 3 above, Reg. § 1.1361-1(l)(2) states that "S is not treated as having more than one class of stock by reason of the employment agreements, even though S is not allowed a deduction for the excessive compensation paid to D."

Example 4: Agreement to pay fringe benefits. (i) S, a corporation, is required under binding agreements to pay accident and health insurance premiums on behalf of certain of its employees who are also shareholders. Different premium amounts are paid by S for each employee-shareholder. The facts and circumstances do not reflect that a principal purpose of the agreements is to circumvent the one class of stock requirement of section 1361(b)(1)(D) and this paragraph (l).

In Example 4 above, Reg. § 1.1361-1(l)(2) states that "S is not treated as having more than one class of stock by reason of the agreements. In addition, S is not treated as having more than one class of stock by reason of the payment of fringe benefits."

Example 5: Below-market corporation shareholder loan. (i) E is a shareholder of S, a corporation. S makes a below-market loan to E that is a corporation-shareholder loan to which section 7872 applies. Under section 7872, E is deemed to receive a distribution for S stock by reason of the loan. The facts and circumstances do not reflect that a principal purpose of the loan is to circumvent the one class of stock requirement of section 1361(b)(1)(D) and this paragraph (l).

In Example 5 above, Reg. § 1.1361-1(l)(2) states that "S is not treated as having more than one class of stock by reason of the below-market loan to E."

Example 6: Agreement to adjust distributions for state tax burdens. (i) S, a corporation, executes a binding agreement with its shareholders to modify its normal distribution policy by making upward adjustments of its distributions to those shareholders who bear heavier state tax burdens. The adjustments are based on a formula that will give the shareholders equal after-tax distributions.

Because the binding agreement in Example 6 above relates to distribution of liquidation proceeds, and the rights are altered, Reg. § 1.1361-1(l)(2) states that "S is treated as having more than one class of stock."

Example 7: State law requirements for payment and withholding of income tax. (i) The law of State X requires corporations to pay state income taxes on behalf of nonresident shareholders. The law of State X does not require corporations to pay state income taxes on behalf of resident shareholders. S is incorporated in State X. S's resident shareholders have the right (for example, under the law of State X or pursuant to S's bylaws or a binding agreement) to distributions that take into account the payments S makes on behalf of its nonresident shareholders.

In Example 7 above, the payment by S of state income taxes on behalf of its nonresident shareholders results in constructive distributions to these shareholders. However, Reg. § 1.1361-1(l)(2) states that "the state law requiring S to pay state income taxes on behalf of its nonresident shareholders is disregarded in determining whether S has more than one class of stock."

> *Example 8: Redemption agreements.* (i) F, G, and H are shareholders of S, a corporation. F is also an employee of S. By agreement, S is to redeem F's shares on the termination of F's employment.

In Example 8 above, Reg. § 1.1361-1 (l) (2) states that the redemption agreement "is disregarded in determining whether all outstanding shares of S's stock confer identical rights to distribution and liquidation proceeds."

> *Example 9: Analysis of redemption agreements.* (i) J, K, and L are shareholders of S, a corporation. L is also an employee of S. L's shares were not issued to L in connection with the performance of services. By agreement, S is to redeem L's shares for an amount significantly below their fair market value on the termination of L's employment or if S's sales fall below certain levels.

The portion of the agreement in Example 9 above providing for redemption of L's stock on termination of employment is disregarded. Furthermore, Reg. § 1.1361-1 (l) (2) (iii) (A) prescribes that "the portion of the agreement providing for redemption of L's stock if S's sales fall below certain levels is disregarded unless a principal purpose of that portion of the agreement is to circumvent the one class of stock requirement of section 1361 (b) (1) (D) and this paragraph (l)."

.03 Other Issued Instruments, Obligations, or Arrangements

To determine whether other instruments, obligations, or arrangements will be treated as a second class of stock, Reg. § 1.1361-1 (l) (4) (ii) (A) prescribes that

> any instrument, obligation or arrangement issued by a corporation . . . regardless of whether designated as debt, is treated as a second class of stock of the corporation—
>
> > (1) If the instrument, obligation or arrangement constitutes equity or otherwise results in the holder being treated as the owner of stock under the general principles of Federal tax law; and
> >
> > (2) A principal purpose of issuing or entering into the instrument, obligation, or arrangement is to circumvent the rights to distribution or liquidation proceeds conferred by the outstanding shares of stock or to circumvent the limitation on eligible shareholders contained in paragraph (b) (1) of this section.

Short-term unwritten advances. Reg. § 1.1361-1 (l) (4) (ii) (B) prescribes, however, a safe harbor for certain short-term unwritten advances and proportionately held obligations. It also states that for short-term unwritten advances

> from a shareholder that do not exceed $10,000 in the aggregate at any time during the taxable year of the corporation, are treated as debt by the parties, and are expected to be repaid within a reasonable time are not treated as a second class of stock for that taxable year, even·if the advances are considered equity under general principles of Federal tax law.

Proportionately held obligations. As to proportionately held obligations, Reg. § 1.1361-1 (l) (4) (ii) (B) *(2)* prescribes that

> Obligations of the same class that are considered equity under general principles of federal tax law, but are owned solely by owners of, and in the same proportion as, the outstanding stock of the corporation, are not treated as a second class of stock. Furthermore, an obligation or obligations owned by the

sole shareholder of a corporation are always held proportionately to the corporation's outstanding stock.

.04 Call Options

A call option (or similar instrument) according to Reg. § 1.1361-1 (l) (4) (iii) (A) is not treated as a second class of stock unless, taking into account all the facts and circumstances,

> the call option is substantially certain to be exercised . . . and has a strike price substantially below the fair market value of the underlying stock on the date that the call option is issued, transferred by a person who is an eligible shareholder . . . to a person who is not an eligible shareholder . . . , or materially modified. For purposes of [this rule], if an option is issued in connection with a loan and the time period in which the option can be exercised is extended in connection with (and consistent with) a modification of the terms of the loan, the extension of the time period in which the option may be exercised is not considered a material modification.

The determination of whether an option is substantially certain to be exercised takes into account not only the likelihood that the holder may exercise the option, but also the likelihood that a subsequent transferee may exercise the option. Reg. § 1.1361-1 (l) (4) (iii) (A) goes on to say:

> A call option does not have a strike price substantially below fair market value if the price at the time of exercise cannot, pursuant to the terms of the instrument, be substantially below the fair market value of the underlying stock at the time of exercise.

Exceptions for certain call options. Reg. § 1.1361-1 (l) (4) (iii) (B) provides two exceptions for call options. First, a call option is not treated as a second class of stock if it is issued to a person who is actively and regularly engaged in the business of lending and if it is issued with a loan to a corporation that is commercially reasonable. Second, a call option that is issued to an individual who is either an employee or an independent contractor who performs services for the corporation (and the call option is not excessive according to the services performed) is not treated as a second class of stock if the call option is nontransferable within the meaning of Reg. § 1.83-3 (d) and the call option does not have a readily ascertainable fair market value as defined in Reg. § 1.83-7 (b) at the time the option is issued. If the call option becomes transferable, however, the exception ceases to apply.

Safe harbor for call options. Reg. § 1.1361-1 (l) (4) (iii) (C) provides a safe harbor for certain call options issued by a corporation. A call option is not treated as a second class of stock if, on the date the call option is issued, it has not been transferred to a person who is not an eligible shareholder or materially modified, and the strike price of the call option is at least 90 percent of the fair market value of the underlying stock on that date. Under this safe harbor, a good faith determination of fair market value by the corporation will ordinarily be respected, unless it can be shown that the value was substantially in error and the determination of the value was not performed with reasonable diligence to obtain a fair value. Example 2-11 illustrates the rules regarding options.

Example 2-11: Stanwich, a corporation, has 100 shareholders. Stanwich issued call options to April Good, Brett Holt, and Cindi Lewis, who are not shareholders, employees, or independent contractors of Stanwich. The options have a strike price of $40 and are issued on a date when the fair market value of Stanwich stock is also $40. A year later, Pronto, a partnership, purchases April Good's option. On the date the call option is purchased, the fair market value of Stanwich stock is $80.

On the date the call option is issued, its strike price is not substantially below the fair market value of Stanwich stock. Under Reg. § 1.1361-1(l)(4)(iii)(A), however, whether the call option is a second class of stock must be redetermined if the call option is transferred to a person who is not an eligible shareholder of Stanwich. Pronto is not an eligible shareholder of Stanwich because Stanwich already has 100 shareholders and Pronto is a partnership.

Because on the date the call option is transferred to Pronto its strike price is 50% of the fair market value, the strike price is substantially below the fair market value of Stanwich stock. Accordingly, the call option is treated as a second class of stock as of the date it is transferred to Pronto if, at that time, it is determined that the option is substantially certain to be exercised based on all the facts and circumstances.

Reg. § 1.1361-1(l)(4)(iii)(C) offers the following example for applying the regulations.

> *Example 2: Call option issued in connection with the performance of services.* (i) E is a bona fide employee of S, a corporation. S issues to E a call option in connection with E's performance of services. At the time the call option is issued, it is not transferable and does not have a readily ascertainable fair market value. However, the call option becomes transferable before it is exercised by E.
>
> (ii) While the option is not transferable, . . . it is not treated as a second class of stock, regardless of its strike price. When the option becomes transferable, . . . if the option is materially modified or is transferred to a person who is not an eligible shareholder . . . , and on the date of such modification or transfer, the option is substantially certain to be exercised and has a strike price substantially below the fair market value of the underlying stock, the option is treated as a second class of stock.

.05 Debt

Straight debt safe harbor. Straight debt is not treated as a second class of stock even if it would otherwise be treated as equity under general principles of federal tax law. Reg. § 1.1361-1(l)(5) follows the definition of straight debt provided by Code Sec. 1361(c)(5) (i.e., the debt is in writing, payment of the interest is not contingent on profits, etc.).

"Straight debt" of a C corporation converting to S status may be considered equity under general principles of federal tax law, but the obligation is not treated as a second class of stock if the C corporation converts to S status.[96] In addition, the conversion from C corporation status to S corporation status is not treated as an exchange of debt for stock on such an instrument. Also, the fact that an obligation

---

[96] Reg. § 1.1361-1(l)(5)(v).

is subordinated to other debt of the corporation does not prevent the obligation from qualifying as straight debt.[97]

The safe harbor for debt was created in 1982 in Code Sec 1361(c)(5) by a Congress sympathetic to the reclassification problem of debt as a second class of stock. For S shareholder loans, straight debt will not be considered a second class of stock if the loans[98]

- are in writing;

- constitute an unconditional promise to pay in money a sum certain on a specified date or on demand;

- provide for an interest rate and interest payment dates that are not contingent on the S corporation's profits, borrower's discretion, or similar factors;

- are not convertible directly or indirectly into S corporation stock; and

- are owed to a creditor that would be a permitted S shareholder, or a person who is actively and regularly engaged in the business of lending money.

Debts that meet all of the above criteria will not be vulnerable to the charge that they are merely a disguised form of equity and therefore constitute a second class of stock.

Tax Pointer 1: The interest rate should be able to be computed by outside factors such as the prime rate.[99]

Tax Pointer 2: If the debt falls outside of the safe harbor test in Code Sec. 1361(c)(5) (e.g., it is not in writing), it still will not be classified as a second class of stock if the debt is incurred proportionally to stock ownership.[100]

Debt as a second class of stock. There is no restriction against S corporations incurring debt; however, there is a potential problem if debt is not issued pro rata to shareholders in that it could be classified as a second class of stock and thus destroy the S corporation election.[101] Fortunately, the safe harbor rules[102] are sufficiently broad that most S corporations, with a little care, should be able to avoid this problem.[103]

Situations not treated as a second class of stock are detailed in the following cases:

- *S. Novell.*[104] Disproportionate advances were deemed "loans and not advances of equity capital."

[97] Reg. § 1.1361-1(l)(5)(ii).

[98] Reg. § 1.1361-1(l)(5)(i).

[99] See H.R. Rep. No. 826, 97th Cong. 2d Sess. 8, and S. Rep. No. 640, 97th Cong. 2d Sess. 8.

[100] See, e.g., *W.C. Gamman,* 46 TC 1, Dec. 27,900 (1966) (debt issued in proportion to stock ownership is not second class of stock). See also ¶ 904.08 for the tax-planning possibilities with S corporation debt.

[101] Code Sec. 1361(b)(1).

[102] Code Sec. 1361(c).

[103] See also the discussion in *J.L. Stinnett, Jr.,* 54 TC 221, Dec. 29,955 (1970) and *W.M. Allison Est.,* 57 TC 174, Dec. 31,053 (1971).

[104] *S. Novell,* 28 TCM 1307, Dec. 29,854(M), TC Memo. 1969-255.

- *A.F. Nielsen Co.*[105] Debt was not in proportion to stock ownership, but the debt did not affect the stockholder's corporate control and thus was not classified as stock.

- *J.L. Stinnett, Jr.*[106] Non-interest bearing notes did not carry with them the right to vote, participate in earnings growth or decision making, and so on; thus the debt was not classified as a second class of stock.

Debt preferred to acquiring more stock. Due to the Code's onerous rules for withdrawing capital contributions,[107] it is easier for a shareholder to remove funds lent to a corporation rather than contributed, proceeding carefully not to create a taxable situation.[108] However, other creditors (e.g., a bank making a loan to the corporation) may restrict the repayment of loans by requiring that unrelated creditors be paid first before the shareholder-creditor, or they may impose restrictions preventing the corporation from incurring junior debt, distributing earnings, etc.[109]

.06 Inadvertently Losing S Status

A corporation that has elected S status and subsequently is treated as having more than one class of stock loses its S corporation status. In such a case, the corporation's S election terminates on the date the corporation is first treated as having more than one class of stock. Inadvertent termination relief under Code Sec. 1362(f) will be available in appropriate cases. In general, a corporation that qualifies under Code Sec. 1362(f) will have its S status restored retroactive to the date the S election was terminated. The S corporation can use an agreement to prevent termination by having the corporation and shareholders take all steps to eliminate the terminating act and then apply to have its S status restored retroactively. The requirements for notifying the IRS if the S corporation loses its status are discussed at ¶ 1205.01.

.07 Correcting Violations to Not Lose S Status

Because an S corporation could lose its status if it violates Code Sec. 1361's strictures about one class of stock, the S corporation should adopt measures to ensure that it does not violate any of the regulations in the future. One possible scenario could be to adopt corporate provisions similar to C corporation provisions involving unreasonable compensation (e.g., *Oswald*[110] and *Van Cleave*[111] permitted shareholder-employees who had unreasonable compensation to repay the excess compensation back to the C corporation rather than have it treated as a dividend). In the case of S corporations, the corporate provision would provide that if the S corporation is found to have violated Code Sec. 1361's one-class-of-stock requirement, the shareholders would be permitted to correct the violations, thereby not

---

[105] *A.F. Nielsen Co., Inc.,* 27 TCM 44, Dec. 28,817(M), TC Memo. 1968-11.

[106] *J.L. Stinnett, Jr.,* 54 TC 221, Dec. 29,955 (1970).

[107] See Code Sec. 1368 and ¶ 903 and ¶ 904, and Code Sec. 302 and ¶ 1209.

[108] See ¶ 904.08.

[109] There are also tax-planning possibilities with debt; see ¶ 904.08.

[110] *V.E. Oswald,* 49 TC 645, Dec. 28,879. Acq., 1968-2 CB 2.

[111] *E. Van Cleave,* CA-6, 83-2 USTC ¶ 9620, 718 F2d 193.

causing the S election to be terminated. It remains to be seen if this type of provision will be effective.

Tax Pointer 1: In determining whether there is more than one class of stock, Reg. § 1.1361-1(l)(3) prescribes that all outstanding shares of stock are considered. The fact that the articles of incorporation provide for other classes of stock that have not been issued, and thus are not outstanding, will not disqualify the S corporation election.[112]

Tax Pointer 2: Care must be taken in issuing stock since state law may create a difference in shareholder rights to receive dividends or liquidation proceeds.

Tax Pointer 3: If nonvoting stock and/or voting stock is issued to key personnel to give them equity participation, the key personnel could be taxed for the value of the stock furnished and/or a gift tax situation could occur, depending upon how the key personnel were issued the stock.

.08 Changing from S Status

If Code Sec. 1361's strictures prove to be onerous, corporations may consider liquidating and becoming a partnership or a limited liability company (LLC). Taxpayers may decide to operate under another business form such as an LLC when the 100-shareholder limit is exceeded or a nonpermitted shareholder wishes to become an "equity" owner.[113]

Tax Pointer: As an alternative to liquidation, an S corporation may decide to enter into a partnership with an LLC as the nonpermitted shareholder.[114]

.09 Restricted Stock

S corporations, like C corporations, can issue restricted stock to its employees to motivate performance or achievement of certain goals. To ensure achievement of performance or goals, the stock is not vested until performance of certain events, such as completion by the employee of 5 years of service. Because the employee cannot freely transfer the stock, it is labeled "restricted stock." Reg. § 1.1361-1(b)(3) provides that stock that is issued in connection with the performance of services (within the meaning of Reg. § 1.83-3(f)) and that is substantially nonvested (within the meaning of Reg. § 1.83-3(b)) is not treated as outstanding stock of the corporation, and the holder of that stock is not treated as a shareholder solely by reason of holding the stock, unless the holder makes an election with respect to the stock under Code Sec. 83(b) or the risk of forfeiture ceases. Until the risk of forfeiture ceases or the shareholder makes an election under Code Sec. 83(b), there can be no distributions regarding the restricted stock; rather, any payments on the restricted stock are treated as compensation to the restricted stockholder.

---

[112] See also Reg. § 1.1371-1(g), adopted under former Code Sec. 1371.

[113] For discussion of liquidation of an S corporation, see ¶ 1209 and ¶ 1210. For a discussion of partnerships, see ¶ 1305 and ¶ 1306; for LLCs, see ¶ 1304 and ¶ 1307.

[114] See discussion of Reg. § 1.701-2 discussed at ¶ 202.01, Example 2-1.

.10 Contingent Sales of Stock; Earn Outs

At times, companies are sold with "earn outs;" that is, the purchase price is adjusted based on corporate operations after the sale of the company. In IRS Letter Ruling 9821006 (February 5, 2008) the shareholders sold their stock subject to an "earn out" based on corporate performance after the date of sale. Under the contingent sale terms, some shareholders were paid additional cash; others were paid additional consideration. The Internal Revenue Service held that no second class of stock was created immediately before the sale. In a subsequent letter ruling, IRS Letter Ruling 201241001 (July 10, 2012) the Internal Revenue Service allowed an S corporation where there was an "earn out" payout to use an alternative basis recovery method rather than the installment method to report income.

¶ 209 Compliance with State Laws Regarding S Corporations

In many states, S corporations have to follow various formalities to either come into existence for state purposes, or, if in existence, to do annual filing, such as file a franchise tax return. If the S corporation does not comply with the various state requirements, this could have a disastrous consequence to the shareholders of the corporation. This was recently illustrated in *David Dung Le, M.D., Inc.*[115]

On April 1, 1991, the State of California suspended the corporation's powers, rights and privileges for failure to pay state income tax. The IRS issued a notice of deficiency to the corporation on July 1, 1999, with the corporation filing a timely petition for redetermination of the tax deficiency on August 12, 1999. On February 22, 2000, taxpayer learned of its lack of status from the IRS's District Counsel. Taxpayer then promptly made payment of the arrearage in franchise taxes which totaled approximately $6,000. Notwithstanding, the Court refused to allow tax-payer's proceeding to continue in Tax Court because of lack of status. As to the taxpayer's claim under U.S. Tax Court Rule 60(a), which provides that a petition filed timely by an improper party can be continued in the name of the proper party is not applicable, because taxpayer never had the requisite capacity to bring the action in Tax Court initially.

Accordingly, if an S corporation is under audit and it is projected that the corporation will have to resort to Tax Court for resolution of the controversy, the corporation should ensure that its charter is not revoked for nonpayment of franchise tax payments prior to entering into Tax Court.

¶ 210 S Corporate Shareholders Owe a Fiduciary Duty to the Corporation and Each Other

Chesterton, Inc. v. Chesterton[116] held that shareholders owe a fiduciary duty to each other and the company not to terminate an S election. In *Chesterton*, a closely held family S corporation formed under Massachusetts law adopted a shareholders agreement which gave the corporation a right of first refusal. Arthur W. Chesterton, grandson of the founder and owner of the largest minority interest, was dissatisfied with the operations of the corporation. He tried to offer his stock for sale, but found

---

[115] *David Dung Le, M.D., Inc.*, 114 TC 268, Dec. 53,859, aff'd CA-9, 2002-1 USTC ¶ 50,112.   [116] 97-2 USTC ¶ 50,809 (1st Cir. 1997).

no buyers. So, he decided to establish two shell corporations owned by him to purchase his shares, which would have destroyed the S corporation status. The S corporation refused to make the purchase and sued Arthur for various actions including an injunction against him to prevent him breaching his fiduciary duty to the corporation under Massachusetts law. The court enjoined Arthur holding under Massachusetts law that a shareholder owes the company and its other owners an elevated fiduciary duty of utmost good faith and loyalty. The court noted that Arthur's proposed transfer was motivated by self-interest and would have resulted in the company and other owners losing substantial financial benefits; thus, he would breach his fiduciary duty. Even if Arthur had a valid reason for wanting to transfer his stock, there was no legitimate business purpose for the company. The company would have suffered irreparable harm from the loss of its S status since the amount of its increased tax liability was contingent on its future earnings and distributions and, therefore, was immeasurable. Also, the damage to the company if the transfer was permitted would outweigh any injury to the shareholder if the transfer was enjoined.

Chapter 3

Trusts That Qualify as S Corporation Shareholders

¶ 301 Six Types of Eligible Trusts

Only the following six types of trusts are permitted to be S corporation shareholders.[1] A discussion of each of the trusts and their unique qualifications follows in the paragraph number shown.

- Grantor trusts (¶ 302)
- Trusts owned by a beneficiary (Code Sec. 678 trusts) (¶ 303)
- Testamentary trusts (¶ 304)
- Voting trusts (¶ 305)
- Electing small business trusts (ESBTs) (¶ 306)
- Qualified subchapter S trusts (QSSTs) (¶ 307)

.01 Code Sec. 1411's Effect on Trust Operations

Code Sec. 1411 could impose taxation on a trust's income. For a discussion of this topic, the reader should consult Chapter 16.

.02 Material Participation of a Trustee for Purposes of Satisfying Code Secs. 469 and 56(b)

Code Sec. 469 prescribes for purposes of making an activity "active" rather than "passive" for purposes of deducting losses there has to be material participation. In the case of a trust, *Mattie K. Carter Trust v. U.S.*,[2] "material" participation by a trustee of a testamentary trust engaged in a ranching business was determined by addressing the activities of the trust through its fiduciaries, employees, and agents,

---

[1] Code Sec. 1361(c)(2) and (d).

[2] 2003-1 USTC ¶ 50,418, (Apr. 11, 2003).

and could not be decided by evaluating only the activities of the trustee. However, IRS Letter Ruling 201029014 (Jul. 24, 2010) held that a trust may only have "active" participation in a business for Code Sec. 469 purposes if only the trustee materially participates.[3]

In the case of an S corporation trust, Technical Advice Memorandum 201317010 (4/26/13), a trustee of a complex trust was deemed not to actively participate in the management of an S corporation where the grantor of the trust actively ran the business. Thus, under Code Sec. 56(b)(2) the trust could not deduct research and experimental expenses in the year incurred for alternative minimum tax; rather they had to be amortized over 10 years.

¶ 302 Grantor Trusts

.01 Qualifications of Grantor Trusts

A grantor trust is allowed to be a shareholder of an S corporation, provided that the grantor is

- an individual,
- not a nonresident alien, and
- treated as owning all of the trust.[4]

In addition, the grantor must also consent to the S election.[5] A grantor trust does not have to qualify as an S corporation shareholder for its entire life—only for the period that it is to be a shareholder of an S corporation.[6] Thus, a trust could be a qualifying S corporation grantor trust for the first 20 years of its life, then terminate (e.g., when the beneficiary turns 20), and then prescribe different provisions that would prevent the trust from qualifying as an S corporation shareholder (e.g., becoming a trust for a nonresident alien).

.02 Characteristics of a Grantor and Trust

A grantor of a grantor trust qualifying as an S corporation shareholder can

- retain the right to revoke the trust;[7]
- retain a reversionary power in the trust;[8]
- retain certain administrative rights normally designated to the trustee, such as the right to decide to distribute income or accumulate it for the grantor, the grantor's spouse, or both;[9] and/or
- control beneficial enjoyment of the corpus or income.[10]

The fact that income and principal of the trust can be distributed to individuals other than the grantor (e.g., the grantor's children and grandchildren) does not

---

[3] *Accord*, Technical Advise Memorandum 200733023 (Aug. 17, 2007).

[4] Code Sec. 1361(c)(2)(A)(i) and Code Secs. 671-677.

[5] Reg. § 1.1362-6(b)(2). See also ¶ 403.08.

[6] Reg. § 1.1361-1(h)(1)(i).

[7] Code Sec. 676(a).

[8] Code Sec. 673(a). An example of this type of trust is a grantor retained annuity trust (GRAT). See IRS Letter Rulings 9625001 (February 26, 1996), 9525032 (March 22, 1995), and 9448018 (August 30, 1994) for examples that sustain GRATs.

[9] Code Sec. 677(a).

[10] Code Sec. 674(a).

prevent the trust from qualifying as an S corporation shareholder.[11] Also, the trust may continue as a shareholder for up to two years after the grantor's death.[12]

> *Tax Pointer:* If the S corporation's shareholders' agreement does not provide for a distribution of funds to pay income taxes, the grantor may want to consider funding the trust with additional income-producing assets to pay taxes.[13]

.03 Example of Grantor Trusts

Living trusts. A common example of a grantor trust is the revocable *inter vivos* trust or living trust, which is often used as an estate-planning device to minimize estate probate of assets.

¶ 303 Trusts Owned by a Beneficiary (Code Sec. 678 Trusts)

.01 Qualifications of Trusts Owned by a Beneficiary

A trust owned by a beneficiary (a person other than the grantor) is allowed to be a shareholder of an S corporation, provided that the beneficiary is

- an individual and
- not a nonresident alien.[14]

.02 Characteristics of a Beneficiary and Trust

A beneficiary of a trust who holds a *Crummey* [15] power to withdraw the trust corpus is deemed the owner of the trust even if the beneficiary never exercises the withdrawal power.[16] Generally, the beneficial owner of the trust becomes the shareholder for receiving the taxable income of the S corporation; however, the trust is the legal owner of the stock and, therefore, receives the distributions from the S corporation.[17]

At the death of the beneficiary/owner, the trust may continue as an S corporation shareholder for two years after the time the beneficiary's gross estate includes the entire corpus of the trust.[18]

.03 Reasons for Code Sec. 678 Trusts

A Code Sec. 678 trust allows a donor gift-giving flexibility in that the donee (i.e., the beneficial owner) can elect or not elect to be an S corporation shareholder. Practically, this means that the donor is not "ruling from the grave." To illustrate, assume a parent establishes a Code Sec. 678 trust for a child and places C corporation stock in it. Under this scenario, the child can decide to elect S status.

> *Tax Pointer:* A simple reading of Code Sec. 1361(c)(2)(A) indicates that a foreign trust cannot be a shareholder in an S corporation even if it is described in Code Sec. 678.

---

[11] See, e.g., IRS Letter Ruling 9037011 (June 14, 1990).

[12] Code Sec. 1361(c)(2)(A)(ii).

[13] For further discussion, see ¶ 1106.06.

[14] Code Sec. 1361(c)(2)(A)(i), in conjunction with Code Sec. 678.

[15] *D.C. Crummey,* CA-9, 68-2 USTC ¶ 12,541, 397 F2d 82.

[16] See IRS Letter Rulings 9506011 (November 3, 1994), 9625031 (March 21, 1996), 9311021 (December 18, 1992), and 9009010 (November 29, 1989).

[17] Code Secs. 1361(c)(2)(B)(ii) and 1366(a)(1).

[18] Code Sec. 1361(c)(2)(A)(ii).

¶ 304 Testamentary Trusts

.01 Reasons for Testamentary Trusts

Frequently, an individual is very concerned that after his or her death the beneficiaries named in his or her will may not be able to handle their own affairs. Consequently, trusts called "testamentary trusts" are provided in the individual's will for such a situation. One primary reason for establishing a testamentary trust is to prevent a beneficiary from owning S corporation stock until such time as the decedent dictates in his or her will. This added control could be beneficial when a parent fears that a child receiving S corporation stock at the parent's death would not act responsibly (e.g., the child has a drug habit). Consequently, the parent may establish a testamentary trust for the S corporation stock so that the child will not receive the stock until he or she reaches an age which the grantor of the trust feels the child will have the maturity, wellness or ability to handle his or her own affairs.

Testamentary trusts are also used in second marriage situations through qualified terminal interest property (QTIP) trusts. Example 3-1 will illustrate.

> **Example 3-1:** Gary Nemeth, a 100% owner of S corporation stock, divorced Helena, his wife of many years. In the divorce settlement, Gary was allowed to keep all the S corporation stock. Shortly after his divorce from Helena, Gary met Donna Dodds and married her. Gary was so much in love with Donna that he ignored his lawyer's advice and did not enter into a prenuptial agreement with Donna. At the time of Gary's marriage to Donna, Gary had only one asset in his estate, the S corporation stock. Shortly after his marriage to Donna, Gary came to his senses and realized that Donna could become a shareholder in the S corporation by electing against Gary's will if he did not make adequate provision for her in his will. To protect his children by his first marriage, Gary, in his will, establishes a QTIP trust for the S corporation stock that provides Donna the use of the stock's income during her life (from the principal), and at her death, the QTIP trust will terminate and all the S corporation stock will be given to Gary's children from his first marriage. Thus, Gary's children from his first marriage can operate the S corporation free of management control by Donna while Donna is living, and they will keep the stock ownership intact by receiving the stock at Donna's death.

In some states, Donna (in Example 3-1), notwithstanding the QTIP provisions, trust, etc., can still fight against Gary's will demanding one-third of the S corporation stock outright. Thus, Gary, at the time he drafts his will and until his death must keep a careful eye on state law to ensure that his plans for giving his entire stock to his children are not sabotaged. Donna, assuming she does not elect against the QTIP trust, could sue the QTIP trustee for corporate waste if she can establish that corporate excesses are occurring (e.g., the S corporation employs Gary's minor children and pays them exorbitant salaries).

.02 Characteristics of Testamentary Trusts

A trust that receives S corporation stock under a will can remain as an S corporation shareholder for up to two years, beginning on the day that the stock was transferred to it.[19] Thereafter, unless the testamentary trust qualifies as a type of permitted S corporation trust (e.g., a qualified terminal interest property trust (QTIP Trust)), the S election will be lost. This time restriction on testamentary trusts severely limits estate planning, forcing a testamentary trustee to either sell and/or redeem the stock in a limited period of time or make a distribution to the beneficiaries of the stock, assuming they are all eligible shareholders.

> *Tax Pointer:* When faced with a testamentary trust that will cause the S corporation to lose its S election, the corporation could redeem the trust's stock, converting the "tainted" stock in the trust to cash and/or notes. This would preserve the S corporation's status.

.03 Advantages of Testamentary Trusts

One advantage of transferring stock to a testamentary trust is that a sale can frequently be made from a trust without court approval, whereas sale of stock by an estate could require court approval.

¶ 305 Voting Trusts

.01 Qualifications of Voting Trusts

The requirements a trust must meet to qualify as a voting trust are not clearly defined in Code Sec. 1361(c)(2)(A)(iv). However, below are a number of requirements provided in Reg. § 1.1361-1(h)(1)(v):

- The trust must be in writing.
- The trust must give right-to-vote stock to one or more trustees.
- All distributions must be for the benefit of the beneficial owners.
- The title and possession of the S corporation stock must vest in the beneficiaries at the end of the trust.
- The trust must terminate on or before a specific time period or event under its terms, or by state law.

.02 Characteristics of Voting Trusts

Voting trusts are defined by state law. Normally, their existence is only for 10 years, subject to renewal. By definition, voting trusts can have multiple owners. Code Sec. 1361(c)(2)(B)(iv) prescribes that each beneficiary of a voting trust is a shareholder. Accordingly, each beneficiary should sign the Form 2553 consent form for an S election, and it would be advisable to have the trustee of the trust sign the form as well.

.03 Advantages of Voting Trusts

A voting trust allows a parent to transfer S corporation voting shares to children but keep the right to vote. However, the parent as trustee also has a fiduciary duty to the beneficiary; thus, the parent could be sued if he or she permits corporate waste to occur (e.g., draws too much salary from the S corporation). Further, there are other means than a voting trust for a parent to control the S

---

[19] Code Sec. 1361(b)(1)(B) and (c)(2)(A)(iii).

corporation. One means is to have all the children sign a shareholders' agreement where they all agree to vote to have the parent as a director, president, CEO, etc. Another means to obtain voting control is for the S corporation to issue nonvoting stock to the children, but voting control to the parent.

> **Tax Pointer:** Whatever agreement is developed, the parent who is controlling the S corporation always faces a challenge from his or her children for corporate waste.

¶ 306 Electing Small Business Trusts (ESBTs)

.01 History of ESBTs

Congress created the electing small business trusts (ESBTs) in an effort to level the playing field for estate and income tax planning between S corporations and other business entities (mainly partnerships and limited liability companies).[20] The simple tax advantage of an ESBT over a qualified subchapter S trust (QSST) is that the trustee can sprinkle income among the beneficiaries of the trust as well as accumulate income rather than be mandated to distribute all income to a beneficiary as is required in a QSST.

Regulations have been issued in an attempt to provide guidance in the area. Set forth below is a brief discussion of the regulations and how they interplay with the law for ESBTs. It is beyond the scope of this book to provide a detailed description of the regulations; accordingly, the reader should consult the regulations for further guidance.

.02 Qualifications of ESBTs

All beneficiaries of ESBTs must be

- individuals,
- estates, or
- charitable organizations that are eligible to be shareholders in an S corporation.[21]

Nonresident alien beneficiaries will not disqualify an ESBT trust. Only "potential current beneficiaries" of an ESBT are treated as shareholders of the S corporation.[22] Thus, a trust can qualify as an ESBT if an ineligible shareholder is a contingent beneficiary (i.e., one who is not vested). However, if the contingent beneficiary becomes vested and no longer contingent because the conditions preventing the contingent beneficiary from vesting are removed, then the trust would be disqualified at the time the contingency lapses.[23] For trusts established for C corporations, LLCs, and partnerships, there are no similar restrictions regarding who can or cannot be a beneficiary, because anyone can be a beneficiary of these entities: a nonresident alien, a C corporation, a personal service corporation, an S corporation, etc.

---

[20] Small Business Job Protection Act of 1996 (P.L. 104-188).

[21] Code Sec. 1361(e)(1)(A)(i) prescribes that, prior to 1998, charitable organizations may hold only contingent remainder interests in an ESBT.

[22] Code Sec. 1361(c)(2)(B)(v).

[23] Code Sec. 1361(e)(2) provides for conditions that will prevent disqualification of the ESBT when a contingent beneficiary becomes a shareholder. See also discussion at ¶ 306.03 about the termination of an ESBT.

Certain trusts cannot be ESBTs. Code Sec. 1361(e)(1)(B) lists certain trusts that cannot be ESBTs: QSSTs, charitable remainder trusts, and any trust exempt from income tax.

Code Sec. 678 and grantor trusts can be ESBTs. As stated at ¶ 302 and ¶ 303, a grantor trust and a Code Sec. 678 trust can be an S corporation shareholder. However, Code Sec. 1371 is silent as to whether or not these two types of trusts can be ESBTs. The reason why a grantor may want the conversion of a grantor trust to an ESBT is because he or she does not want to pay income tax on income that the grantor does not receive, as can happen with a QSST. Reg. § 1.1361-1(m)(4)(ii) provides that a grantor trust can become an ESBT to the extent all or a portion of the trust is treated as owned by a person under the grantor trust rules. Thus, a trust which contains a Crummey Power to withdraw the Code Sec. 2503(b)'s annual exclusion will cause the donee beneficiary to be treated as a deemed owner for a portion of the trust which is allocable to the lapsed withdrawal right. With respect to the value of the S corporation shares in excess of the annual donee exclusion, this would be included in the non-grantor trust portion. By definition, this means that if there are multiple beneficiaries in a Crummey trust, a greater portion of the corpus of the trust will qualify as an ESBT.

Trusts can be beneficiaries of an ESBT. Reg. § 1.1361-1(m)(4)(iv)(C) prescribes generally that trusts which receive ESBT distributions in the future, like contingent beneficiaries, are disregarded as beneficiaries until they become actual beneficiaries. But when the trust becomes a beneficiary, the trust has to be a qualified trust to hold stock.

Election required for ESBT status. For a trust to qualify as an ESBT and become a shareholder in an S corporation, the trustee has to make an election.[24] The trustee makes the election, providing information needed on the election form, and the election must be filed within two months and 16 days of the date that the stock is transferred to the ESBT.[25] If an election is made late, relief may be available under Rev. Proc. 2007-62 discussed at ¶ 401.04.[26]

.03 Characteristics of ESBTs

Income taxes. An ESBT is simple in concept. Unfortunately, in practice, it is a complex undertaking, not simplified by the regulations. While per Reg. § 1.1361-1(m)(3)(ii), an ESBT is a single trust for tax reporting purposes, with one employer identification number, Reg. § 1.641(c)-1 indicates that items are required to be reported differently. An ESBT is divided into two separate trusts for income tax purposes: one portion for S corporation income[27] and the other for non-S corporation transactions.[28] In contrast to the rules for QSSTs, ESBTs are taxed on S corporation income, and there is no credit for pass-through of income. An ESBT must pay income tax on the trust income at the highest rate for trusts and estates, without benefit of the personal exemption or standard deduction.[29] The highest rate

---

24 Code Sec. 1361(e)(1)(A)(iii).

[25] Reg. § 1.1361-1(j)(6).

[26] Rev. Proc. 2007-62, 2007-41 IRB 786.

[27] Code Sec. 641(c)(1)(A).

[28] Code Sec. 641(c)(1)(B).

[29] Code Sec. 641(c)(2)(A) and (B). The joint explanatory statement of the Committee of Conference (HR 3448 Statement of Managers) prescribed that the income tax

for trusts and estates in 2005 was 35 percent on ordinary income and 15 percent on net capital gains.

Code Sec. 641(c)(2)(A) and (B) prescribes that there is no exemption amount for alternative minimum tax purposes. Reg. § 1.641(c)(1)(a) prescribes that an ESBT which contains S corporate stock and C corporate stock, for purposes of Subchapter J, the portion of the trust which holds the S corporate stock is treated as a separate trust. Further, a grantor or other person could be treated as the owner of a portion of the assets held in trust; so there may also be a "deemed owner" portion of the trust.

In terms of deductions, Reg. § 1.641-1(c) takes a narrow view. For instance, Reg. § 1.641-1(c)(4)(i) provides that state and local income taxes and administration expenses must be directly related to the S corporate portion to be deductible. For taxable years beginning after December 31, 2006, Code Sec. 641 provides that a deduction for interest paid or accrued on indebtedness to acquire stock in an S corporation may be taken into account in computing the taxable income of the S portion of an ESBT. Reg. § 1.641-1(d)(4)(ii), only applicable for taxable years prior to December 31, 2006, details that interest paid by an ESBT to purchase stock in an S corporation is allocated to the S portion of the ESBT and is not a deductible administrative expense for purposes of determining the taxable income of the S portion.

For purposes of charitable contributions, there are a number of unique rules. While Code Sec. 642(c)(1) prescribes that a trust is entitled to deduct contributions to the extent of the amount paid from gross income, Code Sec. 642 provides that the charitable contribution must be authorized by the trust instrument. Thus, if the S corporation makes a charitable contribution, the ESBT can only deduct the contribution if the trust instrument specifically permits charitable contributions. Accordingly, care must be exercised in drafting any ESBT to ensure that the matter of charitable contributions is covered, assuming that the settlor of the trust desires such a situation.

While these rates may be onerous, Code Sec. 641(c) makes it worse by prescribing that the trust is denied any deduction for distribution of S corporation income to the beneficiaries in computing its income tax. Accordingly, the ESBT cannot shift income tax to the beneficiary(ies) who may be in a lower tax bracket. In contrast, trusts established for C corporations, LLCs, and partnerships have no such restrictions, nor are they taxed initially at such a high rate of income tax.

> **Tax Pointer:** Accordingly, the only taxpayers who can effectively use ESBTs for tax-planning purposes are those taxpayers who are in the highest income tax bracket (i.e., 35 percent for 2005) and will consistently stay in the highest bracket. Since very few taxpayers meet this qualification, ESBTs have very little utility.

(Footnote Continued)

rate is to be the highest individual tax rate for an individual.

Code Sec. 1361(e)(2) provides that for purposes of the term "potential current income beneficiary," a power of appointment to the extent it is not exercised is disregarded in determining the potential current beneficiaries of an ESBT. Examples illustrating this rule are found under the subparagraph "Termination of an ESBT."

For income passed through from an S corporation, Code Sec. 641(c) provides some further restrictions. For instance, capital losses (to the extent they exceed capital gains) are not allowed.[30] Also, in determining the trust taxable income, the only items of income, loss, deduction, or credit to be considered in the computation are as follows:[31]

- Items required to be taken into account under Code Sec. 1366
- Gain or loss from distributions on S corporation stock
- State or local income taxation or administration expenses to the extent allocable to S corporation income items already included

Reg. § 1.641(c)-1(C) and (3) prescribes that if an item of income, expense, etc. is S or non-S corporation related, if these items are attributable to a grantor, then these items will be included in the grantor's income. Reg. § 1.641(c)-1(f)(2) prescribes that dividends attributable to C corporation earnings are "includible in the gross income of the non-S [corporation] portion" of the trust. Interest on funds borrowed to purchase S corporation shares per Reg. § 1.641(c)-1 is allocated to the S corporation portion; however, interest "is not a deductible expense for purposes of determining taxable income of the S [corporation] portion."

Reg. § 1.641(c)-1(f)(4) limits the ESBT's charitable contribution in a controversial position, holding that the contributions can only come from the non-S corporation portion. If an ESBT owns stock in more than one S corporation, Reg. § 1.641(c)-1(d)(2)(iii) prescribes that "all the S corporations are aggregated for purposes of determining the S [corporation] portion's taxable income."

S corporation stock purchase not allowed. If an S corporation stock interest is acquired by purchase in an ESBT, the trust will not qualify as an ESBT.[32] A "purchase" is "any acquisition if the basis of the property acquired" is determined by Code Sec. 1012.[33] Thus, a beneficiary can only acquire an interest in an ESBT by gift or bequest.

Each beneficiary counted as one shareholder. Every "potential current beneficiary" is counted as a shareholder to determine the 100-shareholder limit prescribed by Code Sec. 1361(b)(1)(A).[34] A "potential current beneficiary" is "any person who at any time . . . is entitled to, or at the discretion of any person may receive, a distribution from the principal or income of the trust."[35]

To prevent violating the S corporation 100-shareholder limitation, it may be advisable to draft in the ESBT a limitation as to the number of beneficiaries permitted. Sample language might be: "For purposes of the number of beneficiaries

---

[30] Code Sec. 641(c)(2)(D).
[31] Code Sec. 641(c)(2)(C).
[32] Code Sec. 1361(e)(1)(A)(ii).

[33] Code Sec. 1361(e)(1)(C).
[34] Code Sec. 1361(c)(2)(B)(v).
[35] Code Sec. 1361(e)(2).

in this trust, no beneficial interest shall be created that would cause the corporation to lose its S corporation status established under Code Sec. 1361," or words to that effect.[36]

Termination of an ESBT. A one year transition period is required for a trust to qualify as an ESBT.[37] As discussed previously, Code Sec. 1361(e)(1) prescribes that only permitted shareholders who can be shareholders of an S corporation can be current beneficiaries of an ESBT. However, Code Sec. 1361(e)(2) permits nonpermitted taxpayers to be contingent shareholders (e.g., an LLC). In the event that the contingency preventing the nonpermitted taxpayer to become a beneficiary is removed or ceases to exist (e.g., a vested beneficiary dies), Code Sec. 1361(e)(2) prescribes the following:

> If a trust disposes of all of the stock which it holds in an S corporation, then, with respect to such corporation, the term "potential current beneficiary" does not include any person who first met the requirements of [qualifying as a potential current beneficiary] during the one year period ending on the date of such disposition.

Thus, if the ESBT sells or disposes of the S corporation stock within one year of the date when the nonpermitted shareholder becomes a beneficiary of the trust, the S corporation status will not be jeopardized. If the trust does not sell or dispose of the stock within the one year period, it will cease to qualify as an ESBT, with the S corporation status terminating.

Reg. §1.641(c)-1(i) prescribes that if an ESBT terminates because the S election is terminated, an allocation is made on the trust's tax return between the S portion of the year and the C portion, pursuant to Code Sec. 1362(e)(1)(A),[38] with any S corporation items not reflected in the S corporation portion to be included in the non-S corporation portion. If the entire trust is terminated, then items are allocated to the beneficiaries. Examples illustrating Code Sec. 1361(e)(2) which encompass the material discussed above under the subparagraph "Each beneficiary counted as one shareholder"" are set forth below:

Example 3-2: L, the sole shareholder of XYZ, Inc., an S corporation, creates on January 1, 2004 a trust for the benefit of B. B also has a current exercisable power of appointment to appoint income or principal to B's six children. The potential current beneficiaries of the trust, pursuant to Reg. §1.1361-1(m)(4)(vi) will be B and his six children. At the time the trust is created, XYZ, Inc. had 71 shareholders. Because all of these children are counted as shareholders, Code Sec. 1361(b)(1)(A)'s 100-shareholder limit will be exceeded, and the corporation's S election will terminate, unless the trust disposes of all the stock within sixty days of creation.

Example 3-3: Assume the same facts as in Example 3-2, except L creates the trust on January 1, 2005, and XYZ, Inc. has 98 shareholders. B's unexercised power of appointment, pursuant to Code Sec. 1361(e)(2) will not cause

---

[36] Local law should be consulted to determine if this provision is valid and enforceable.

[37] Code Sec. 1361(e)(2).

[38] For a discussion of Code Sec. 1362(e)(1)(A), see ¶1207.01.

¶306.03

XYZ, Inc.'s S corporate election to terminate, since it will now have 99 shareholders (the 98 shareholders plus B).

Example 3-4: Assume the same facts as in Example 3-3, except that B appoints the income and principal to his six children. The S election will terminate unless the trust disposes of all its stock within one year of creation.

.04 Disadvantages of ESBTs

As discussed above, income and estate tax planning with ESBTs is very limited because ESBTs have to pay tax at the highest rate for trusts and estates without the beneficiaries receiving any credit. Accordingly, if the beneficiaries are in brackets equivalent to the highest rates for trusts and estates, then an ESBT becomes viable without adverse tax results. However, the chances of this occurring consistently during the entire life of the trust are very, very rare. Thus, as a general rule, LLC and partnership trusts, which have none of the above S corporation restrictions of ESBT and QSST trusts, become the vehicle of choice for estate and income tax planning. Further, because of the unique properties that Code Secs. 704, 752, and 754 have in the area of partnerships, it is rare today to use S corporations for estate and income tax planning (see Chapter 11 for discussion).

As the brief discussion of the regulations indicate, the rules regarding ESBTs are complex; thus, it is very difficult to do complete tax planning, at least until the regulations become finalized.

.05 Conversion of an ESBT to a QSST

If there is a single beneficiary of an ESBT, conversion of an ESBT to a QSST may be desirable if the beneficiary receives all the trust distributions, mainly because a QSST is not subject to income tax and the highest income tax bracket, as is the case with an ESBT.

.06 Deductibility of Interest Expense on Indebtedness Incurred by an Electing Small Business Trust to Acquire S Corporation Stock

For taxable years beginning after December 31, 2006, Code Sec. 641 provides that a deduction for interest paid or accrued on indebtedness to acquire stock in an S corporation may be taken into account in computing the taxable income of the S portion of an ESBT. Reg. § 1.641(c)-1(d)(4)(ii), which detailed that interest paid by an ESBT to purchase stock in an S corporation was allocated to the S portion of the ESBT but was not classified as a deductible administrative expense for purposes of determining the taxable income of the S portion, is now reversed.

.07 The Effect That Code Sec. 1411 Has on Electing Small Business Trust Operations

Chapter 16 details the effect that Code Sec. 1411 has on S corporate operations. For specific details for ESBTs, see ¶ 1603.03 and Example 16.4 which sets forth an example showing the computation of taxation under Code Sec. 1411.

¶ 307 Qualified Subchapter S Trusts (QSSTs)

.01 History of QSSTs

In 1981, Congress established the concept of a qualified subchapter S trust (QSST) to own stock in an S corporation. Since then, the definition of a QSST (an estate and income planning trust) has been revised by regulations,[39] rulings, and case law to its current status.

.02 Qualifications of QSSTs

Basically, a QSST is a "simple trust"[40] that can be established during life (*inter vivos*) or at death in a will (testamentary). Examples of trusts that can qualify as QSSTs are

- qualified terminable interest property (QTIP) trusts,
- trusts for minor children,[41]
- trusts that pay income for life to a beneficiary,[42]
- trusts that will terminate when a beneficiary attains a certain age, and
- other trusts given as examples in IRS Letter Rulings 8514018 and 8435153.[43]

A QSST must also be a trust that is not a foreign trust described in Code Sec. 7701(a)(31).

While, by definition, a simple trust qualifies as a QSST, a complex trust could qualify if mandatory distribution of income is required. Likewise, a minor's trust (Code Sec. 2503(c)) where the trustee accumulates income can qualify as a QSST, providing distribution of all the income of the trust is made annually.[44]

.03 Characteristics of QSSTs

Legal support obligations. If a QSST distributes income to an income beneficiary to satisfy the grantor of the trust's legal support obligation under local law, the trust will cease to qualify as a QSST as of the date of the distribution. The following example from Reg. § 1.1361-1(j)(2)(ii)(C) illustrates this point:

> *Example:* F creates a trust for the benefit of F's minor child, G. Under the terms of the trust, all income is payable to G until the trust terminates on the earlier of G's attaining age 35 or G's death. Upon the termination of the trust, all corpus must be distributed to G or G's estate. The trust includes all of the provisions prescribed by section 1361(d)(3)(A) and [Reg. § 1.1361-1(j)(1)(ii)], but does not preclude the trustee from making income distributions to G that will be in satisfaction of F's legal obligation to support G. Under the applicable local law, distributions of trust income to G will satisfy F's legal obligation to support G. If the trustee distributes income to G in satisfaction of F's legal obligation to support G, the trust will not qualify as a QSST because F will be treated as the

---

[39] Namely Reg. § 1.1361-1(j).

[40] Code Sec. 651(a) defines a simple trust as one that provides that "all of its income is required to be distributed currently" and that does not make any distributions in a given year other than its current income.

[41] Reg. § 1.1361-1(j).

[42] IRS Letter Ruling 8336069 (June 9, 1983) where a testamentary trust that paid income to a widow for her life was a qualified subchapter S trust.

[43] IRS Letter Rulings 8514018 (June 2, 1985) and 8435153 (June 1, 1984). For an example of a qualified subchapter S trust that did not qualify, see IRS Letter Ruling 8434091 (May 24, 1984) where a trust that could pay income and corpus to either a woman or her son was found not to be a qualified subchapter S trust.

[44] IRS Letter Ruling 8717024 (January 17, 1987).

owner of the ordinary income portion of the trust. Further, the trust will not be a qualified subpart E trust because the trust will be subject to tax on the income allocable to corpus.

Power to appoint income or corpus. If, under the terms of a QSST, a person (including the income beneficiary) has a special power to appoint, during the life of the income beneficiary, trust income or corpus to any person other than the current income beneficiary, the trust will not qualify as a QSST.[45] However, if the power of appointment results in the grantor being treated as the owner of the entire trust under the rules of subpart E, the trust may be a permitted shareholder.[46]

The QSST election. A QSST will not qualify as an S corporation shareholder unless the beneficiary irrevocably elects to have the trust qualify for the special QSST tax treatment. The IRS, in Reg. § 1.1361-1(j), has prescribed the manner in which the beneficiary must elect QSST status. Care must be exercised in a QSST election since Code Sec. 1361(d)(2)(D) prescribes that the beneficiary must make the election within two months and 16 days after the trust acquires the S corporation stock. If the election is premature or late, it could cause the S corporation to lose its status because there is not a qualified shareholder. When making a QSST election, Reg. § 1.1361-1(j)(6) contains the following requirements:

(i) *In general.* . . . This election must be made separately with respect to each corporation whose stock is held by the trust. The QSST election does not itself constitute an election as to the status of the corporation; the corporation must make the election provided by section 1362(a) to be an S corporation. Until the effective date of a corporation's S election, the beneficiary is not treated as the owner of the stock of the corporation for purposes of section 678.

(ii) *Filing the QSST election.* The current income beneficiary of the trust must make the election by signing and filing with the service center with which the corporation files its income tax return the applicable form or a statement that—

(A) Contains the name, address, and taxpayer identification number of the current income beneficiary, the trust, and the corporation;

(B) Identifies the election as an election made under section 1361(d)(2);

(C) Specifies the date on which the election is to become effective (not earlier than 15 days and two months before the date on which the election is filed);

(D) Specifies the date (or dates) on which the stock of the corporation was transferred to the trust; and

(E) Provides all information and representations necessary to show that:

(1) Under the terms of the trust and applicable local law—

(i) During the life of the current income beneficiary, there will be only one income beneficiary of the

---

[45] Reg. § 1.1361-1(j)(2)(iii).

[46] Code Sec. 1361(c)(2)(A)(i) and Reg. § 1.1361-1(h)(1)(i).

> trust (if husband and wife are beneficiaries, that they will file joint returns and that both are U.S. residents or citizens);

> (ii) Any corpus distributed during the life of the current income beneficiary may be distributed only to that beneficiary;

> (iii) The current beneficiary's income interest in the trust will terminate on the earlier of the beneficiary's death or upon termination of the trust; and

> (iv) Upon the termination of the trust during the life of such income beneficiary, the trust will distribute all its assets to such beneficiary.

(2) The trust is required to distribute all of its income currently, or that the trustee will distribute all of its income currently if not so required by the terms of the trust.

(3) No distribution of income or corpus by the trust will be in satisfaction of the grantor's legal obligation to support or maintain the income beneficiary.

(iii) *When to file the QSST election.*

(A) If S corporation stock is transferred to a trust, the QSST election must be made within the 16-day-and-2-month period beginning on the day that the stock is transferred to the trust. If a C corporation has made an election under section 1362(a) to be an S corporation (S election) and, before that corporation's S election is in effect, stock of that corporation is transferred to a trust, the QSST election must be made within the 16-day-and-2-month period beginning on the day that the stock is transferred to the trust.

(B) If a trust holds C corporation stock and that C corporation makes an S election effective for the first day of the taxable year in which the S election is made, the QSST election must be made within the 16-day-and-2-month period beginning on the day that the S election is effective. If a trust holds C corporation stock and that C corporation makes an S election effective for the first day of the taxable year following the taxable year in which the S election is made, the QSST election must be made within the 16-day-and-2-month period beginning on the day that the S election is made. If a trust holds C corporation stock and that corporation makes an S election intending the S election to be effective for the first day of the taxable year in which the S election is made but, under § 1.1362-6(a)(2), such S election is subsequently treated as effective for the first day of the taxable year following the taxable year in which the S election is made, the fact that the QSST election states that the effective date of the QSST election is the first day of the taxable year in which the S election is made will not cause the QSST election to be ineffective for the first year in which the corporation's S election is effective.

(C) If a trust ceases to be a qualified subpart E trust but also satisfies the requirements of a QSST, the QSST election must be filed within the 16-day-and-2-month period beginning on the date on which the trust ceases to be a qualified subpart E trust. If the estate of the deemed owner of the trust is treated as the shareholder under paragraph (h)(3)(ii) of this section, the QSST election may be filed at any time but no later than the end of the 16-day-and-2-month period beginning on the date on which the estate of the deemed owner ceases to be treated as a shareholder.

(D) If a corporation's S election terminates because of a late QSST election, the corporation may request inadvertent termination relief under section 1362(f). See § 1.1362-4 for rules concerning inadvertent terminations.

If an election is made late, relief may be available under Rev. Proc. 2007-62.[47]

Tax Pointer 1: By law, an S corporation would lose its status if the QSST does not file a valid QSST beneficiary election on time,[48] but in practice, strict adherence of the rule is not required as is the case with a Form 2553, "Election by a Small Business Corporation." Technical Advice Memorandum 8035012 (April 29, 1980) prescribes that if the beneficiaries of a QSST fail to sign the QSST consent form, it is not considered a substantive omission for S election purposes.

Successive income beneficiary. A successive income beneficiary is considered to have consented to the original QSST election and does not have to file a subsequent election with the IRS.[49] However, if the successive income beneficiary does not wish to continue the QSST, and, by extension, the S election (assuming there is no procedure for preserving the S election, such as requiring a beneficiary to serve notice on the trustee of the desire to terminate the QSST and allowing the trustee to redeem the S corporation stock), Reg. § 1.1361-1(j)(10) imposes an affirmative duty on this successive income beneficiary to make an affirmative refusal to consent by signing and filing with the service center (where the corporation files its income tax return) a statement that has all of the following:

(1) Contains the name, address, and taxpayer identification number of the successive income beneficiary, the trust, and the corporation for which the election was made;

(2) Identifies the refusal as an affirmative refusal to consent under Code Sec. 1361(d)(2); and

---

[47] Rev. Proc. 2007-62, 2007-41 IRB 786. See IRS Letter Ruling 201144018 (11/4/11) for a situation where the QSST trustees made mistakes 3 times in filing the election; yet the IRS allowed the election.

[48] Code Sec. 1361(d)(1).

[49] Reg. § 1.1361-1(j).

(3) Gives the date on which the successive income beneficiary became the income beneficiary.

The filing date and effectiveness of a QSST termination requires that the affirmative refusal to consent be filed within two months and 16 days after the date on which the successive income beneficiary becomes the income beneficiary. The affirmative refusal to consent will be effective as of the date on which the successive income beneficiary becomes the current income beneficiary.

The following examples from Reg. § 1.1361-1(j)(9)(ii) deal with the successive income beneficiary.

> *Example 1:* Shares of stock in Corporation X, an S corporation, are held by Trust A, a QSST for which a QSST election was made. B is the sole income beneficiary of Trust A. On B's death, under the terms of Trust A, J and K become the current income beneficiaries of Trust A. J and K each hold a separate and independent share of Trust A within the meaning of section 663(c). J and K are successive income beneficiaries of Trust A, and they are treated as consenting to B's QSST election.

> *Example 2:* Assume the same facts as in *Example 1,* except that on B's death, under the terms of Trust A and local law, Trust A terminates and the principal is to be divided equally and held in newly created Trust B and Trust C. The sole income beneficiaries of Trust B and Trust C are J and K, respectively. Because Trust A terminated, J and K are not successive income beneficiaries of Trust A. J and K must make QSST elections for their respective trusts to qualify as QSSTs, if they qualify. The result is the same whether or not the trustee of Trusts B and C is the same as the trustee of trust A.

Revocation of the QSST election. A beneficiary may desire to terminate a QSST election, and thus an S election, unless steps are undertaken to preserve the S election (e.g., redeeming the QSST corporation stock). Reg. § 1.1361-1(j)(11), below, prescribes the procedure for revocation:

> *Revocation of QSST election.* A QSST election may be revoked only with the consent of the Commissioner. The Commissioner will not grant a revocation when one of its purposes is the avoidance of federal income taxes or when the taxable year is closed. The application for consent to revoke the election must be submitted to the Internal Revenue Service in the form of a letter ruling request under the appropriate revenue procedure. The application must be signed by the current income beneficiary and must—

>> (i) Contain the name, address, and taxpayer identification number of the current income beneficiary, the trust, and the corporation with respect to which the QSST election was made;

>> (ii) Identify the election being revoked as an election made under section 1361(d)(2); and

>> (iii) Explain why the current income beneficiary seeks to revoke the QSST election and indicate that the beneficiary understands the consequences of the revocation.

Tax Pointer 2: A QSST is not limited to owning stock only in an S corporation—it can own other property in other situations (e.g., stock in a C corporation). Thus, the revocation of the QSST election would apply to the S corporation stock owned by the trust.

The following example from Reg. § 1.1361-1(k)(1) illustrates the QSST rules:

¶307.03

Example 1: (i) *Terms of the trust.* In 1996, A and A's spouse, B, created an inter vivos trust and each funded the trust with separately owned stock of an S corporation. Under the terms of the trust, A and B designated themselves as the income beneficiaries and each, individually, retained the power to amend or revoke the trust with respect to the trust assets attributable to their respective trust contributions. Upon A's death, the trust is to be divided into two separate parts; one part attributable to the assets A contributed to the trust and one part attributable to B's contributions. Before the trust is divided, and during the administration of A's estate, all trust income is payable to B. The part of the trust attributable to B's contributions is to continue in trust under the terms of which B is designated as the sole income beneficiary and retains the power to amend or revoke the trust. The part attributable to A's contributions is to be divided into two separate trusts both of which have B as the sole income beneficiary for life. One trust, the *Credit Shelter Trust,* is to be funded with an amount that can pass free of estate tax by reason of A's available estate tax unified credit. The terms of the Credit Shelter Trust meet the requirements of section 1361(d)(3) as a QSST. The balance of the property passes to a Marital Trust, the terms of which satisfy the requirements of section 1361(d)(3) as a QSST and section 2056(b)(7) as QTIP. The appropriate fiduciary under § 20.2056(b)-7(b)(3) is directed to make an election under section 2056(b)(7).

(ii) *Results after deemed owner's death.* On February 3, 1997, A dies and the portion of the trust assets attributable to A's contributions including the S stock contributed by A, is includible in A's gross estate under sections 2036 and 2038. During the administration of A's estate, the trust holds the S corporation stock. Under section 1361(c)(2)(B)(ii), A's estate is treated as the shareholder of the S corporation stock that was included in A's gross estate for purposes of section 1361(b)(1); however, for purposes of sections 1366, 1367, and 1368, the trust is treated as the shareholder. B's part of the trust continues to be a qualified subpart E trust of which B is the owner under sections 676 and 677. B, therefore, continues to be treated as the shareholder of the S corporation stock in that portion of the trust. On May 13, 1997, during the continuing administration of A's estate, the trust is divided into separate trusts in accordance with the terms of the trust instrument. The S corporation stock that was included in A's gross estate is distributed to the Marital Trust and to the Credit Shelter Trust. A's estate will cease to be treated as the shareholder of the S corporation under section 1361(c)(2)(B)(ii) on May 13, 1997 (the date on which the S corporation stock was transferred to the trusts). B, as the income beneficiary of the Marital Trust and the Credit Shelter Trust, must make the QSST election for each trust by July 28, 1997 (the end of the 16-day-and-2-month period beginning on the date the estate ceases to be treated as a shareholder) to have the trusts become permitted shareholders of the S corporation.

Tax Pointer 3: Using multiple trusts can produce estate tax savings. In *Mellinger,*[50] a minority interest in a corporation held by the decedent's own trust and her late husband's QTIP trust cannot be merged for purposes of valuation; accordingly, a minority interest valuation discount can be taken, even though the two interests would equal a majority ownership if they were combined.

For other examples concerning the application of the QSST rules, see Reg. § 1.1361-1(k).

---

[50] *H.R. Mellinger Est.,* 112 TC 26, Dec. 53,218.

Liquidation of the corporation. In IRS Letter Ruling 9721020 (February 20, 1997), the IRS ruled that upon complete liquidation of the company, any gain or loss recognized on the liquidation under both Code Secs. 331 and 336 will belong to the trust, not the income beneficiaries.

Use of passive activity losses and at-risk amounts by QSST income beneficiaries. Reg. § 1.1361-1(j)(8) prescribes that, for purposes of a QSST, the QSST beneficiary is taxed on all income, loss, deductions and credits attributable to ownership of S corporate stock by the QSST, but the trust, not the beneficiary, is treated as the owner of the S corporate stock for purposes of determining tax consequences on the disposition by the trust of the S corporate stock. Code Sec. 1361(d)(1) was amended, effective for taxable years beginning after December 31, 2004, to prescribe that for purposes of Code Sec. 469 and Code Sec. 465, the QSST beneficiary is allowed to deduct suspended losses under Code Sec. 465's at-risk rules, and Code Sec. 469's passive activity loss rules when the trust disposes of its S corporate stock.

.04 Disadvantages of QSSTs

Estate-planning limitations of a QSST. With a QSST, the trustee does not have any discretion in the distribution of income and in spreading income among beneficiaries. For S corporations, the general principles of trusts collide with the following congressional directions for QSSTs, thereby making estate and income tax planning with QSSTs difficult.[51] A QSST must[52]

- distribute all of its income to a citizen or resident of the U.S.;
- have only one income beneficiary;[53]
- distribute trust corpus to only the current income beneficiary during the beneficiary's lifetime, including the time when the trust terminates; and
- the income interest (i.e., the life estate) ceases on the earlier of the beneficiary's death, or the termination of the trust.

The limitations in estate planning with QSSTs are exemplified by the following two examples: the first with international families and the second with "problem" children.

Example 3-5: A grandfather, Miles LeBlanc, wants to establish a QSST for his grandchild, Ann Rue, a Canadian citizen residing in Canada (i.e., a nonresident alien). The QSST would be a shareholder in his S corporation. LeBlanc cannot establish the QSST for his grandchild unless the U.S.-Canadian treaty allows it.

Example 3-6: A mother, Katherine Ryan, wants to establish a trust where the trustee will have the right to control the distribution of income and/or principal in the event her son, Art Ryan, becomes drug crazed and debt ridden. Katherine cannot do this in an S corporation framework with a QSST, because

---

[51] Code Sec. 1361(d)(3).

[52] Reg. § 1.1361-1(j)(1).

[53] While a simple reading of the regulation makes it appear that there cannot be multiple beneficiaries of a

QSST, in reality, there can be if the trust is drafted properly. See IRS Letter Rulings 8721045 (February 19, 1987), 9506011 (November 3, 1994), 9119070 (November 19, 1990), and 9115020 (January 1, 1991).

a QSST has the requirement that the income be distributed annually to the beneficiary.[54]

Tax Pointer 1: Care should be taken in selecting the trustee of a QSST, especially when a minor child is the beneficiary and the child's parent is the trustee. If any of the trust's income is used for the minor child's support, the trust may lose its QSST qualification because all of the S corporation income is not passing through to the beneficiary, and thus the corporation's S status will be destroyed.

Tax Pointer 2: Since Code Sec. 1361(d) allows state law and the trust instrument to define what is trust income and corpus, there is room for tax planning because, depending on where the parties want to be, certain items could be classified as corpus rather than income and thereby save income taxes.

Tax Pointer 3: In Rev. Rul. 89-45,[55] a QSST was not approved because it was to be used to fund a new trust for after-born grandchildren.

Trusts in general. Trusts, whether they are established during life (*inter vivos*) or at death in a will (testamentary), are invaluable for estate and income tax planning purposes. Their primary use is "control," and because of this "control" aspect, they have become known as "rulers from the grave," particularly the testamentary trusts established in wills.

A trust allows an individual to make a gift to the trust for gift tax purposes, thereby omitting future appreciation on the gift property for his or her estate and, at the same time, dictating when and how the beneficiary will receive the income and principal. Parents like trusts because they can give gifts to their children while at the same time protect their children against themselves. For example, parents can instruct that should a child be on drugs, the trustee can withhold distribution of the income and/or principal until the child straightens out to the trustee's satisfaction; parents can also insert spendthrift provisions so that if a child incurs gambling debts, the bookie will not be able to reach trust assets to collect his or her mark, etc.

LLC and partnership trusts do not have QSST limitations. The QSST is not a favorable tax-planning device for an international family or a family where problems could develop with a family member. In contrast, LLC and partnership trusts, whether limited or general, have none of the QSST restrictions detailed above. Thus, in Example 3-5, the grandfather could use a LLC instead of an S corporation and establish a trust for his grandchild, whether the trust was in Canada or the United States, because nonresident aliens can be members of LLCs. The grandfather could provide that the trustee have discretion in distributions of

[54] There is an end-run solution to the mother's problem if her son becomes drug addicted and debt ridden. If the mother serves as an officer of the S corporation, has a controlling interest, and has control of the board of directors, then when it comes time to distribute profits, the board of directors can declare a bonus to her of the entire net income of the S corporation, thereby precluding any net income to be distributed to the shareholders (i.e., the son as beneficiary of the QSST). However, the difficulty with this approach is that the son could demand that the trustee of the QSST sue the corporation for "waste" because the officers (i.e., the mother) are being overpaid and the shareholders are not receiving a fair return on their investment.

[55] Rev. Rul. 89-45, 1989-1 CB 267.

income and/or principal so that if the grandchild should go on drugs, incur gambling debts, etc., the trustee would have the power to withhold income and/or principal until the child straightens out.

QSSTs compared to ESBTs. Congress created the electing small business trusts (ESBTs) in an effort to provide alternatives to the limitations of QSSTs. An ESBT in comparison to an QSST can withhold income and principal for a beneficiary if the beneficiary is on drugs, has gambling debts, etc. Further, an ESBT can have multiple beneficiaries, and the trustees can pick and choose which beneficiaries receive principal and/or income, when the distribution(s) of principal and/or income will occur, and how much.[56] However, there is a price to be paid for such freedom in comparison to QSSTs. For a discussion of ESBT limitations, see ¶ 306.04.

Converting a QSST to an ESBT. Because of the advantages for ESBTs discussed at ¶ 306.01, it may be desirable to convert a QSST to an ESBT. Reg. § 1.1361-1 (j) (12) details the steps for conversion.[57]

> *Tax Pointer 4:* If a QSST contains other assets besides S corporation stock, the other assets are reported for tax purposes as if no QSST rules applied. Therefore, the income and expense of the non-S corporation assets are reported per Code Sec. 1361(d)(1)(B) according to Subparts A through D of the Code, with the QSST trust segment reported according to Subpart E of the Code.

---

[56] Code Secs. 1361(e) and 641(c).

[57] See IRS Letter Ruling 200227027, which sets forth circumstances allowing the revocation of the ESBT election and conversion of the trust to a QSST.

Chapter 4

Filing of an S Corporation Election and Tax Return

¶ 401 Filing Form 2553

.01 Tax Years Covered

Although a corporation may satisfy all the requirements to be an S corporation, it does not become one automatically—first it must elect S status by filing Form 2553, "Election by a Small Business Corporation."[1] Once Form 2553 is filed and accepted by the IRS, the election becomes effective for the corporation's tax year granted and for all succeeding tax years until the election is terminated.[2]

.02 Notification of S Status

Once the IRS has accepted or rejected an S election, it will notify the corporation of its decision. The corporation should follow-up with its IRS service center if does not receive the IRS's determination in the time frame given below (quoted from the Instructions for Form 2553, December 2007):

> The service center will notify the corporation if its election is accepted and when it will take effect. The corporation will also be notified if its election is not accepted. The corporation should generally receive a determination on its election within 60 days after it has filed Form 2553. If box Q1 in Part II is checked on page 2,[3] the corporation will receive a ruling letter from the IRS, that either approves or denies the selected tax year. When box Q1 is checked, it will generally take an additional 90 days for the Form 2553 to be accepted.
>
> Care should be exercised to ensure that the IRS receives the election. If the corporation is not notified of acceptance or nonacceptance of its election within 2

---

[1] See Form 2553 at Appendix 1.

[2] Code Sec. 1362(c) and (d).

[3] This indicates that a corporation is requesting a tax year other than the one ending December 31, except for an automatic 52-53-week tax year ending in the month of December. (For a discussion of calendar- or fiscal-year reporting, see ¶ 502.)

¶401.02

months of the date of filing (date faxed or mailed), or within 5 months if box Q1 is checked, take follow-up action by calling 1-800-829-4933.

If the IRS questions whether Form 2553 was filed, an acceptable proof of filing is (a) certified or registered mail receipt (timely postmarked) from the U.S. Postal Service, or its equivalent from a designated private delivery service (see Notice 2004-83, 2004-52 IRB 1030 (or its successor)); (b) Form 2553 with an accepted stamp; (c) Form 2553 with stamped IRS received date; or (d) IRS letter stating that Form 2553 has been accepted.

.03 When to File Form 2553

A corporation can only file for S status once it is incorporated.[4] It may then file for S status at any time during the tax year; however, for the S status to be effective for the current tax year, it must be filed on or before the 15th day of the tax year's third month.[5]

Example 4-1: Klein Inc. is a calendar-year corporation. On January 1, 2009, the shareholders of Klein Inc. decide they want to elect S corporation status for the tax year 2009. They have until March 15, 2009, to file the election. If the shareholders don't file the election until July 1, 2009, the election will not be effective until January 1, 2010.

Short tax years. When corporations have a short tax year of 2½months or less, the election must be filed within 2 months and 15 days *after the start* of the tax year, regardless of when the tax year ends.[6]

Example 4-2: Adam Hamilton, Brian King, and Claire Roper form ADJ Inc. on December 1, 2009, and desire S corporation status. The three shareholders must file Form 2553 on or before February 15, 2010, for the short calendar-tax-year from December 1 to December 31, 2009.

.04 Errors in Filing Form 2553

The IRS can reject a Form 2553 for not being properly filed (e.g., the corporation did not obtain the consent of all shareholders). If such a rejection occurs, the shareholders are forced to operate as a C corporation for the current tax year, or liquidate the corporation—either situation creates adverse tax consequences until S status can be adopted the next year. Because of the serious tax consequences, a corporation may correct an error on Form 2553 if it was inadvertent (by following Rev. Proc. 2007-62 discussed below under "Filing late") and if the corporation takes steps to correct the error within a reasonable period of time.[7]

Incorrect or missing dates. The following minor filing errors by a corporation and its shareholder(s) have been excused, allowing the corporation to operate under the S status in the current year:

- Failing to furnish the date on Form 2553 was deemed a minor error, allowing Form 2553 to be accepted when it was filed.[8]

---

[4] IRS Letter Ruling 8530100 (May 1, 1985).
[5] Code Sec. 1362(b)(1)(B).
[6] Code Sec. 1362(b)(4).

[7] Code Sec. 1362(f) and (b)(5).
[8] IRS Letter Ruling 8835011 (June 2, 1988).

- Failing to provide the correct date of incorporation of the S corporation was deemed not fatal to the election.[9]

Filing late. If a corporation fails to file the S corporation election on time and good cause is shown, the IRS may retroactively provide relief to the corporation and shareholders, if the following requirements are met:[10]

(1) The entity is an eligible entity as defined in Reg. § 301.7701-3(a);

(2) The entity intended to be classified as a corporation as of the intended effective date of the S corporation status;

(3) The entity fails to qualify as a corporation solely because Form 8832 was not timely filed under Reg. § 301.7701-3(c)(1)(i), or Form 8832 was not deemed to have been filed under Reg. § 301.7701-3(c)(1)(v)(C);

(4) The entity fails to qualify as an S corporation on the intended effective date of the S corporation status solely because the S corporation election was not timely filed pursuant to Code Sec. 1362(b);

(5) The entity has reasonable cause for its failure to file a timely Form 2553 and a timely Form 8832;

(6) The entity seeking to make the S corporation election has not filed a tax return for the first taxable year in which the election was intended; and

(7) No taxpayer whose tax liability or tax return would be affected by the S corporation election (including all shareholders of the S corporation) has reported inconsistently with the S corporation election, on any affected return for the year the S corporation election was intended.

An entity may request relief for a late S corporation election by (1) filing with the applicable IRS campus a properly completed Form 2553 with a Form 1120S for the first taxable year the entity intended to be an S corporation and (2) the forms must be filed together no later than 6 months after the due date of the tax return (excluding extensions) of the entity for the first taxable year in which the S corporation election was intended. A properly completed Form 2553 includes a statement establishing reasonable cause for the failure to file the S corporation election timely. The Form 2553 will be modified to allow for the inclusion of such statement.[11]

Relief is also available for late elections for electing small business trusts (ESBTs) (see ¶ 306), qualified subchapter S trusts (QSSTs) (see ¶ 307), and 100 percent subsidiaries (see Chapter 14).[12]

Requesting a private letter ruling for relief of filing errors. A corporation that does not qualify for any of the relief described above may still request relief by private letter ruling for an inadvertent termination, inadvertent invalid election, or a late election. Errors that have been provided relief include the following:

---

[9] IRS Letter Ruling 9424022 (March 15, 1994).

[10] Rev. Proc. 2007-62, Par. 5.01 (as provided under Code Sec. 1362(b)(5)).

[11] Rev. Proc. 2007-62, 2007-41 IRB 786. The instructions for Form 2553, December 2007 also provide guidance for filing a late election.

[12] Rev. Proc. 2007-62, 2007-41 IRB 786. Note that Rev. Proc. 2007-62 is an alternative to letter ruling relief ordinarily used to obtain relief for late S elections and related election under Code Sec. 1362(b)(5), Code Sec. 1362(f), or Reg. § 301.9100-1 through Reg. § 301.9100-3.

- Taxpayers who have not used certified mail to file Form 2553 have prevailed to show timely filing.[13]

- When Form 2553 is postmarked on the last day of the election period, the election will be good although the IRS may receive the Form 2553 several days later.[14]

- An S corporation can issue a different number of shares from the number detailed on Form 2553 and not lose its election.[15]

- If the corporation fails to specify the precise number of shareholders or the acquisition date of the shares, it is not fatal to the S election.[16]

- Taxpayers who have used the wrong year in the effective date have had the obvious error disregarded so that their S election began when intended.[17]

Relief not always given. Some cases do not get relief when filing late. In *Leather*,[18] the corporation's attorney prepared a Form 2553 and placed it in an envelope addressed to the IRS in Ogden, Utah. By habit, the attorney ran the envelope through her postage meter in the law office in July 1986, following the usual procedure for outgoing mail. Because the service center did not receive the Form 2553 on time and because the taxpayer could not show its actual date of deposit in the U.S. mail, no S election was permitted for the year in question. The Tax Court stated that an actual deposit or proof of mailing must be evidenced by certified mail with a return receipt requested.

.05 S Status Requirements Must Be Met During Entire Tax Year

A corporation, if it wants to elect S corporation status, must satisfy all S corporation requirements on every day during the tax year before the election is made.[19] If the corporation cannot meet this requirement, then the election will be effective for the following tax year. Examples 4-3 through 4-10 illustrate S status requirements (Examples 4-3 through 4-7 are adapted from Reg. § 1.1362-6):

> **Example 4-3:** *Effective election; no prior taxable year.* A calendar-year small business corporation begins its first tax year on January 7, 2010. To be an S corporation beginning with its first tax year, the corporation must make its election during the period that begins January 7, 2010, and ends before March 22, 2010. An election made earlier than January 7, 2010, will not be valid.

> **Example 4-4:** *Effective election; taxable year less than 2½ months.* A calendar-year small business corporation begins its first tax year on November 8, 2009. To be an S corporation beginning with its first tax year, the corporation

---

[13] See, e.g., *Mitchell Offset Plate Serv., Inc.*, 53 TC 235, Dec. 29,829. Acq., 1970-1, CB XVI (1970); IRS Letter Ruling 9716024 (January 21, 1997) where a corporation was treated as an S corporation even though Form 2553 was never filed; *accord*, IRS Letter Rulings 9735008 (May 23, 1997), 9735019 (May 30, 1997), and 9719009 (January 29, 1997).

[14] Code Sec. 7502.

[15] Rev. Rul. 74-150, 1974-1 CB 241 (facts contained in Form 2553 that are not relevant to the corporation's

qualification as an S corporation will not invalidate an otherwise valid election).

[16] IRS Letter Ruling 9424022 (March 15, 1994).

[17] See IRS Letter Ruling 8835011 (June 2, 1988) where an election was filed on December 23, 1986, that detailed an effective date of January 1, 1987; the election was held valid for tax years beginning December 1, 1986.

[18] *H.S. Leather*, 62 TCM 1087, Dec. 47,708(M), TC Memo. 1991-534.

[19] Code Sec. 1362(b)(2)(B)(i).

must make its election during the period that begins November 8, 2009, and ends before January 23, 2010.

Example 4-5: *Election effective for the following taxable year; ineligible shareholder.* On January 1, 2009, two individuals and a partnership own all of the stock of a calendar-year C corporation. On January 31, 2009, the partnership dissolved and distributed its shares in the corporation to its five partners, all individuals. On February 28, 2009, the seven shareholders of the corporation consented to the corporation's election of subchapter S status. The corporation files a properly completed Form 2553 on March 2, 2009. The corporation is not eligible to be a subchapter S corporation for the 2009 tax year because during the period of the tax year prior to the election it had an ineligible shareholder. However, under Reg. § 1.1362-6(a)(2)(ii)(B), the election is treated as made for the corporation's 2010 tax year.

Example 4-6: *Effective election; shareholder consents.* On January 1, 2009, the first day of its tax year, a subchapter C corporation had 15 shareholders. On January 30, 2009, two of the C corporation's shareholders, Michael Arndt and George Breen, both individuals, sold their shares in the corporation to three individuals. On March 1, 2009, the corporation filed its election to be an S corporation for the 2009 tax year. The election will be effective (assuming the other requirements of Code Sec. 1361(b) are met) provided that all of the shareholders as of March 1, 2009, as well as former shareholders Arndt and Breen, consent to the election.

Example 4-7: *Consent of new shareholder unnecessary.* On January 1, 2009, three individuals own all of the stock of a calendar-year subchapter C corporation. On April 15, 2009, the corporation, in accordance with Reg. § 1.1362-6(a)(2), files a properly completed Form 2553. The corporation anticipates that the election will be effective beginning January 1, 2010, the first day of the succeeding tax year. On October 1, 2009, the three shareholders collectively sell 75% of their shares in the corporation to another individual. On January 1, 2010, the corporation's shareholders are the three original individuals and the new shareholder. Because the election was valid and binding when made, it is not necessary for the new shareholder to consent to the election. The corporation's subchapter S status election is effective on January 1, 2010 (assuming the other requirements of Code Sec. 1361(b) are met).

Example 4-8: Aback Inc. is a calendar-year corporation. Aback Inc. has two shareholders: Roxy Partnership and James Jones, an individual. On January 10, 2009, Jones buys out Roxy Partnership's stock interest and then elects S status. Aback Inc. cannot be an S corporation for 2009 because it failed to meet all the requirements of S status on every day of the tax year (i.e., it had an improper shareholder for 10 days). Consequently, Aback Inc. will have S status starting January 1, 2010.

Example 4-9: On January 1, 2009, the first day of its tax year, Cable Corp., a C corporation, had three individuals as shareholders. On April 15, 2009, the corporation, in accordance with Reg. § 1.1362-6(b), filed a properly completed Form 2553. The corporation anticipated that the election would

¶401.05

become effective January 1, 2010, the first day of the succeeding tax year. On October 1, 2009, one of the shareholders sold 40% of his shares in the corporation to a partnership. On January 1, 2009, the corporation had as its shareholders the original three individuals as well as the partnership. The corporation fails to meet the definition of a small business corporation on January 1, 2010, and its election will be treated as having terminated on that date.

Example 4-10: On July 15, 2009, Mortor Corp., a C corporation that uses a June 30 tax year, files a properly completed Form 2553 to be an S corporation for its tax year beginning on July 1, 2010. On Form 2553, Mortor Corp. states that it will use a calendar year as its tax year. On June 15, 2010, one of the shareholders of Mortor Corp. sells his entire interest in the corporation to a partnership. Mortor Corp. fails to meet the definition of a small business corporation on July 1, 2010, and its election will be treated as having terminated on that date.

.06 Reelecting S Status After Prior Termination

If a corporation's S status has been terminated after 1982, then the corporation and any successor corporation is not eligible to make an election to acquire S status until the fifth year after the termination of the election, unless the IRS consents to an earlier election.[20]

Tax Pointer 1: Although Code Sec. 1362(g) requires that an S corporation wait five years after terminating its S status before it can reelect, this waiting period will not be enforced when the termination was inadvertent. Under Code Sec. 1362(f), an S corporation whose S status is inadvertently terminated can apply to have its status reinstated if it acts promptly to correct the terminating event. See ¶ 1205 and ¶ 1206 for a discussion of the waiting period for reelection and the waiver of that waiting period.

Substantial change in ownership. The IRS has usually permitted S status reelection when there was a substantial change of ownership in the corporation (i.e., more than 50 percent after the year of termination).[21] In the absence of a substantial change of ownership, an S corporation can reelect S status if it can show that (1) termination was reasonably beyond the control of the corporation and its substantial shareholders and (2) the substantial shareholders did not participate in the plan to terminate the election.[22] The IRS has issued a large number of private letter rulings on allowing and rejecting requests for reelection of the S status; the particular facts of the letter rulings are likely to reflect many current situations.[23]

Tax Pointer 2: A request to reelect S status does not affect the time to timely file an S election. Thus, a corporation may consider filing a timely election while its request for reelection is pending.[24]

---

[20] Code Sec. 1362(g).

[21] Reg. § 1.1362-5(a) prescribes that if there was a change in ownership of more than 50 percent after the year of termination, it will tend to establish that consent should be granted.

[22] Reg. § 1.1362-5(a).

[23] See also discussion at ¶ 1206.

[24] See, e.g., IRS Letter Ruling 8203017 (October 20, 1981).

¶401.06

.07 Existing S Corporations

If a corporation has already elected S status and a new shareholder joins the corporation, the election continues without any additional action by the new or existing S shareholders.[25] If any shareholder does not want to continue operating the corporation as an S corporation, however, the shareholder can take one of two steps:

(1) File a consent to revocation, provided more than 50 percent of the shares of stock of the corporation are in agreement,[26] or

(2) Do a terminating event (e.g., transfer stock to a nonpermitted shareholder or a partnership) provided the corporation's shareholders' agreement does not prevent this.[27]

Tax Pointer: If new shareholders do not want S status in the future (see ¶ 1115 and ¶ 1301 for reasons they may not want S status), they should conduct a careful investigation before becoming a shareholder in an existing S corporation. Otherwise, they could find themselves in a very difficult situation with no legal way of extrication.

.08 Entity Classification—the "Check-the-Box" Regulations, Form 8832

Reg. § 301.7701-1 prescribes a check-the-box procedure (hereinafter the "Check-the-Box Regulations") for an entity to classify itself for tax purposes. Code Sec. 1361(b), as discussed at ¶ 206, provides that only domestic corporations can be S corporations. The Check-the-Box Regulations prescribe that certain entities will qualify as domestic corporations without further action by the corporation. For instance, a business entity organized under a federal or state statute, or under a statute of a federally recognized Indian tribe if the statute describes or refers to the entity as incorporated, or as a corporation, body corporate, or body politic, is classified as a corporation for tax purposes. Foreign entities can qualify as well. IRS Letter Ruling 9512001 discussed at ¶ 206 details the procedures for a foreign business to qualify as an S corporation.

However, business entities that are not automatically classified as corporations (i.e., partnerships) can elect to be classified as a corporation for federal tax purposes. An example would be a partnership which, for federal tax purposes, wants to be classified as an S corporation, but for state tax purposes wants to be classified as a partnership, because under state tax law where this partnership operates, the tax rate is lower for partnerships than for S corporations.

Eligible entities which want to be classified as an S corporation have to make two timely elections—one on Form 8832, Entity Classification Election, and the other on Form 2553. Temp. Reg. § 301.7701-3T(c)(v)(C) prescribes that after July 20, 2004, if an eligible entity makes a timely and valid election to be an S corporation, the Service will treat the entity as having made a proper election to be classified as an association taxable as a corporation. Temp. Reg.

---

[25] Code Sec. 1362(d).

[26] See also ¶ 1202.

[27] See also ¶ 1203.

§ 301.7701-3T(h)(3) provides that the eligible entity which files a timely S election before July 20, 2004 can also rely on this Temporary Regulation.

¶ 402 Shareholders Must Consent to an S Election

.01 All Shareholders Must Consent

To make the S corporation election on Form 2553, all shareholders on the day an election is made must consent to the election.[28] If the election is filed after the first day of a corporation's tax year, the consent is required of any person who held stock during the tax year and before the election.[29] If a shareholder does not consent, the election will not take effect until the next tax year.

> **Example 4-11:** Keifer Inc. is a C corporation whose stock is owned entirely by Andra Orzo. Keifer Inc. reports on the calendar year, and on February 1, 2009, Jack Fiala buys all of Orzo's stock, with the intention of having Keifer Inc. become an S corporation as of January 1, 2009. If Fiala does not obtain Orzo's consent on Form 2553, the election will not be effective until January 1, 2010.

.02 Signing the Shareholders' Consent Statement

Shareholders make the consent by signing Column K of Form 2553 (see Form 2553 at Appendix 1). To overcome last-minute situations, it is possible for shareholders to sign a copy of Form 2553 and then attach the copy of Form 2553 to the actual Form 2553, or they can sign a substitute form that covers all the elements of Form 2553 (see an example of such a form at Appendix 2, Consent to Election to Be Treated as an S Corporation). By using this approach, the corporation is saved the task of sending one Form 2553 all over the country to obtain necessary signatures. Once a shareholder has consented to a valid S election by the corporation, the shareholder cannot later withdraw the consent.[30]

> **Tax Pointer:** Failing to state the number of shares owned by each shareholder in Column L of Form 2553 can cause the S corporation election to be invalid.[31] However, the IRS has ruled that a minor error in completing Form 2553 (failing to furnish the date the election was to take effect) did not prevent the corporation from making an S election.[32]

.03 Consent Extensions

In the event a shareholder's consent is missing as described in Example 4-11, the corporation can file an extension to obtain the missing consent.[33] In order for the extension to be granted, the corporation must show to the satisfaction of the IRS's district director or the director of the service center where the corporation files its income tax return that there was "reasonable cause for the failure to file such consent and that the interest of the government will not be jeopardized by treating such election as valid." The shareholder(s) who did not consent to the

---

[28] Code Sec. 1362(a)(2). See Form 2553 at Appendix 1.
[29] Code Sec. 1362(b)(2)(B)(ii).
[30] Reg. § 1.1362-6(b)(3)(i).

[31] *R.E. Brutsche*, CA-10, 78-2 USTC ¶ 9745, 585 F2d 436.
[32] IRS Letter Ruling 8835011 (June 2, 1988).
[33] Reg. § 1.1362-6(b)(3)(iii).

corporation's S election in the original filing of Form 2553 must file a consent to the election within the extension time period granted by the IRS.[34]

¶ 403 Who Must Sign a Shareholders' Consent Statement

The shareholders' consent portion of Form 2553 (Column K) must be signed by the various S corporation shareholders as detailed below.

.01 Stock Held by a Nominee

The actual beneficial owner must sign the consent on Form 2553.[35]

.02 Minor's Stock Held by a Custodian

Form 2553 must be signed by the minor or the minor's legal representative for any minor's stock held by a custodian under the Uniform Transfers to Minors Act (UTMA). If the minor has no legal representative, then the minor's natural or adoptive parent can sign the consent form.[36] A custodian under the UTMA does not have the capacity to sign the consent for a minor.[37] If the custodian happens to be the minor's legal representative or parent, and if no legal representative has been appointed, the custodian may then consent in the capacity as legal representative or parent.[38]

> **Tax Pointer 1:** The term "minor" is not defined by the Code or regulations with respect to S corporation situations. Presumably, the state law where the S corporation is formed will define the term "minor."[39]

> **Tax Pointer 2:** Under the UTMA, care must be taken to ensure that the *inter vivos* donor of stock to the minor is also not the custodian since the donor custodian will have the stock included in his or her estate if the donor custodian should predecease the minor.[40]

.03 Joint Tenants

Each tenant in common, joint tenant, and so on is treated as a separate shareholder who must consent to the S corporation election.[41]

.04 Spouses

Even though Code Sec. 1361(c)(1) provides that a husband and wife are treated as one shareholder for purposes of the 100-shareholder limit, they both must sign the consent.[42]

---

[34] Reg. § 1.1362-6(b)(3)(iii).

[35] *H.C. Kean*, CA-9, 72-2 USTC ¶ 9764, 469 F2d 1183. Aff'g in part 51 TC 337.

[36] Reg. § 1.1362-6(b)(2)(ii).

[37] Rev. Rul. 66-116, 1966-1 CB 198, amplified by Rev. Rul. 68-227, 1968-1 CB 381.

[38] Rev. Rul. 68-227, 1968-1 CB 381.

[39] See Rev. Rul. 71-287, 1971-2 CB 317 (the terms "minor" and "majority" were determined by the California Uniform Gifts to Minor Act).

[40] *L. Lober*, 53-2 USTC ¶ 10,922, 346 US 335, 74 SCt 98.

[41] Reg. § 1.1362-6(b)(2)(i); IRS Letter Ruling 9803008 (October 14, 1997) (ownership of S corporate shares as tenants in common does not rise to the level of a partnership; thus tenants in common are permitted S corporate shareholders).

[42] Reg. § 1.1362-6(b)(2)(i). *Accord, H.W. Forrester*, 49 TC 499, Dec. 28,852.

.05 Community Property

If stock is community property, each person having a community property interest is treated as a shareholder and must sign the consent.[43]

.06 Estates

An executor, fiduciary, or an administrator of an estate will sign the consent on behalf of the estate. In the event that there are multiple executors or administrators, only one executor or administrator has to consent.[44]

.07 Voting Trusts

Each beneficiary of a voting trust is a shareholder. Accordingly, each beneficiary should sign the consent form, and it would be advisable to have the trustee of the trust sign the consent as well.[45]

.08 Grantor Trusts

Under a grantor trust, the grantor is treated as a shareholder and therefore must sign the consent.[46] If there are multiple grantors, then each must sign the consent. If an individual created three separate grantor trusts, each owning stock in the S corporation, the three trusts are treated as one shareholder, not three.[47]

.09 Testamentary Trusts

Since the estate is treated as a shareholder rather than the trust, the executor of the estate makes the consent, not the trustee.[48]

.10 Trusts Owned by the Beneficiary (Code Sec. 678 Trusts)

Each deemed beneficial owner of the trust should consent to the election.[49]

.11 Qualified Subchapter S Trusts (QSSTs)

The income beneficiary who is the deemed owner of the stock should sign the consent form.[50] Because the law is not clear on this point, most likely the trustee should sign the consent form as well.

Electing the QSST. The current income beneficiary of the QSST must sign a special election form.[51] A person holding a power of attorney for the QSST beneficiary may also sign the election.[52] The determination of whether the trust qualifies as a QSST depends upon the terms of the trust instrument as interpreted under local law. Some grantor trusts could qualify as QSSTs by permitting the trust to file a protective election.[53] A trust may want to file this special election to ensure that the trust will qualify as an S corporation shareholder.

---

[43] Reg. § 1.1362-6(b)(2)(i).

[44] Reg. § 1.1362-6(b)(2)(iii).

[45] Code Sec. 1361(c)(2)(B)(iv).

[46] Code Sec. 1361(c)(2)(B)(i).

[47] IRS Letter Ruling 9526021 (April 3, 1995).

[48] Code Sec. 1361(c)(2)(B)(iii).

[49] Reg. § 1.1362-6(b)(2)(ii); IRS Letter Ruling 9803008 (October 14, 1997) (ownership of S corporate shares as tenants in common does not rise to the level of a partnership; thus tenants in common are permitted S corporate shareholders).

[50] Code Sec. 1361(d)(2)(A) and (B).

[51] Code Sec. 1361(b)(2)(B) and (d)(1). For the requirements of the QSST election, see ¶ 307.

[52] IRS Letter Ruling 9314022 (January 7, 1993).

[53] Reg. § 1.1361-1(j)(6)(iv).

The IRS over the years has shown some liberality toward the QSST election. When a beneficiary of a QSST failed to consent to the QSST election, but did consent individually to the S corporation election, the IRS sustained the QSST as a shareholder.[54]

.12 Bankrupt Shareholders

If an individual shareholder is in bankruptcy under Title 11, the bankruptcy estate consents to the election presumably by the estate's administrator signing Form 2553.[55] For a discussion of how a bankrupt estate reports income, loss, etc., see ¶ 612.

.13 Gifts of S Corporation Stock

If a gift of stock is incomplete, the donor should sign the consent.[56] If a gift is complete, then the donee will sign as the stockholder.

.14 Conditional Sales of Stock

If a conditional sale of stock occurs, the buyer can only sign the form when the buyer becomes the beneficial owner of the stock.[57]

.15 Incompetent Individuals

If a conservatorship has been established for an incompetent person, the conservator is the individual who signs the form.[58]

.16 Employee Stock Ownership Plans (ESOPs)

The trustee of an ESOP will sign the consent for the S corporation status.

.17 Charitable Organizations

Most likely, the individual who is in charge of a charitable organization (i.e., the president of a charitable organization meeting Code Sec. 501(c)(3)'s requirements) will sign the consent for the S corporation status.

.18 Qualified Subchapter S Subsidiaries (QSubs)

An S corporation may elect to treat an eligible subsidiary as a QSub by filing a completed form to be prescribed by the IRS[59] (unless the corporation is under the five-year prohibition for reelecting S status).[60] The election form must be signed by a person authorized to sign the S corporation's tax return[61] and must be submitted

---

[54] IRS Letter Ruling 9316015 (January 21, 1993); IRS Letter Ruling 9626035 (April 2, 1996) (taxpayers who were both individual shareholders and beneficiaries of QSSTs signed the S corporate election only as individual shareholders; Internal Revenue Service sustained the S election even though the shareholders did not sign the QSST election form on the grounds of "substantial compliance" with the Internal Revenue Code and its regulations); IRS Letter Ruling 201144018 (July 13, 2011) (inadvertent errors in connection with an S corporate election waived to allow S status).

[55] Code Sec. 1361(c)(3). While Reg. §1.1362-6(b)(2) does not have a specific reference to bankruptcy, it does discuss estates in general. Presumably, its language applies to bankruptcy situations.

[56] See, e.g., *F.G. Auld,* 37 TCM 1851-86, Dec. 35,598(M), TC Memo 1978-508 (stock was still deemed to be held by the father since beneficial ownership of stock was not transferred to the son; the son's letter to the IRS advised that he had not consented to the S corporation election and was treated as having no legal validity).

[57] See, e.g., *Pacific Coast Music Jobbers, Inc.,* CA-5, 72-1 USTC ¶ 9317, 457 F2d 1165. Aff'g 55 TC 866, Dec. 30,667.

[58] Cf. IRS Letter Ruling 9314022 (January 7, 1993).

[59] Reg. §1.1361-3(a)(2). See also Chapter 14.

[60] Code Sec. 1361(b)(3)(D).

[61] The tax return required to be filed under Code Sec. 6037.

¶403.18

to the service center where the subsidiary filed its most recent tax return (if applicable).

.19 Corporate Officers

Form 2553 can be signed by any person who is authorized to sign the corporation's Form 1120S.[62] Individuals who can sign Form 1120S are the president, vice president, treasurer, assistant treasurer, chief accounting officer, or any officer duly authorized.[63] (The corporation secretary is not one of the listed signatories.)

.20 Family Member Shareholder Ownership

Code Sec. 1361(c)(1)(D) prescribes that the member of the family making the election signs.

Tax Pointer: As discussed at ¶ 202.08, the family should adopt a shareholders agreement so that no unwarranted tax results will occur, such as one family member conveying stock to a member outside of the family; doing something which would affect the S corporation maintaining its election, etc.

.21 IRA Bank Shareholders

Congress did not detail the means the IRA bank shareholder utilizes to make the S election. Presumably, until defined by regulation, the trustee of the IRA, similar to the trustee of an ESOP, will make the election.

¶ 404 Considerations Before Converting a C Corporation to an S Corporation

Before a C corporation becomes an S corporation, certain points should be considered to prevent unwarranted tax consequences from arising. Some of the factors to consider are detailed below in ¶ 404.01–¶ 404.12.

.01 Shareholder Loans from Retirement Plans

Under prior law, shareholder-employees borrowing from the C corporation retirement plan had to repay the debt on conversion on the corporation from C to S status. For taxable years beginning after December 31, 2001, Code Sec. 4975 was amended to eliminate this restriction.[64]

.02 Accounting Method

An S corporation cannot adopt a method of accounting that is different from the method it used as a C corporation without obtaining the IRS's consent, according to at least two court cases.[65]

Recovery of a deduction taken in a C corporation year. When an S corporation recovers an expense that was previously deducted in a C corporation year, the recovery must be passed through as income to the S corporation share-

---

[62] Reg. § 1.1362-6(a).

[63] Code Sec. 6062.

[64] See ¶ 1302.06 for a detailed discussion of shareholder loans from a retirement plan.

[65] *C.C. Weiss,* CA-10, 68-1 USTC ¶ 9380, 395 F2d 500. Aff'g, 26 TCM 564, Dec. 28,489(M), TC Memo. 1967-125. *W.H. Leonhart,* 27 TCM 443, Dec. 28,975(M), TC Memo. 1968-98.

holders to the extent that the prior C corporation benefited from the initial deduction.[66]

Tax shelters. If a C corporation is classified as a tax shelter under Code Secs. 448(a)(3) and 461(i), it must use a modified accrual method to report its income.

.03 General Business Credit

An S corporation election will not trigger the recapture of any general business credit, assuming that the C corporation assets are still subject to the general business credit recapture.[67] Instead, the S corporation is liable for any recapture of general business credit claimed during a prior non-S corporation year if the S corporation disposes of the asset prior to the expiration of its useful life.[68]

.04 Permitted Tax Year

An S corporation can only have a fiscal year under limited circumstances with an interest-free deposit being made to the IRS.[69] Consequently, when a fiscal-year C corporation converts to S, it should give serious consideration to reporting its income using calendar-year status to avoid the complications of the interest-free deposit required by Code Secs. 444 and 7519.

> **Example 4-12:** Abba Inc., a fiscal-year C corporation engaged in manufacturing, has a fiscal year ending July 31, 2010. It has three shareholders—Murray Lee, Taylor McGinnis, and Al Jones, all individuals. On August 1, 2010, it adopts S status. Rather than make the required payment as prescribed by Code Secs. 444 and 7519, Abba Inc. adopts calendar-year status pursuant to Code Sec. 1378. Consequently, Abba Inc. will file two tax returns for 2010—Form 1120 for the fiscal period ending July 31, 2010, and Form 1120S for the period August 1–December 31, 2010.

.05 Tax on Passive Investment Income and Loss of S Status

If a C corporation on conversion to an S corporation has one dollar or more of earnings and profits, the earnings and profits could cause the S corporation to lose its status,[70] if for each of three consecutive years, the S corporation has gross receipts in excess of 25 percent from passive investment income. Further, the S corporation will, if it fails the passive investment income test in a year when it has earnings and profits, pay an income tax on the lower of the excess net passive income or its taxable income.[71]

Consequently, to avoid this problem, the C corporation may consider, before electing S status, eliminating all earnings and profits by declaring a dividend or opting to have a special distribution made under Code Sec. 1368(e)(3).[72]

---

[66] *T.A. Fredrick,* 101 TC 35, Dec. 49,165.

[67] Code Sec. 1371(d)(1). See also ¶ 803 and Code Sec. 38.

[68] Code Sec. 1372(d)(2). See also Code Sec. 38.

[69] See ¶ 502.01 for further discussion.

[70] Code Sec. 1362(d)(3). See ¶ 1204 for further discussion.

[71] For further discussion, see ¶ 804.

[72] For further discussion, see ¶ 804.12 and ¶ 1004.03.

.06 Loss of Fringe Benefits

Certain tax-free fringe benefits are denied to more-than-2-percent shareholder-employees of S corporations.[73] An example of where fringe benefits are denied to a more than 2 percent shareholder would be group life insurance. Consequently, prior to converting from C to S status, the shareholders of the C corporation should determine any adverse tax consequences that might result from the loss of tax-free fringe benefits.

If an S corporation pays for the fringe benefits of a more-than-2-percent shareholder-employee, the payments are treated as wages for withholding tax purposes, Social Security, and Medicare.[74] The more-than-2-percent shareholder-employee may also take a deduction on his or her personal Form 1040 for health insurance premiums (for 2005 and thereafter, 100 percent of the premiums included in income is deductible).[75]

Some states do not allow a corporation to purchase a group health insurance plan with one participant. Thus, the S corporate shareholder would be required to purchase the health insurance in his or her own name. However, in the IRS publication "Headliner"[76] the IRS stated that an S corporation's sole shareholder-employee cannot purchase health insurance in his or her own name and be eligible for Code Sec. 162(l)'s above-the-line deduction for medical insurance. Thus, the shareholder can only deduct the health insurance as an itemized deduction subject to the 7.5% floor.

.07 Tax on Built-In Gains

A tax on built-in gains is imposed when a C corporation elects S status after December 31, 1986.[77] The tax is triggered if the S corporation sells or distributes to its shareholders any assets that had appreciated in value prior to the corporation's conversion to S status. The tax applies to sales or distributions occurring within 10 years of the effective date of the S election.

.08 No Carryforward or Carryback of Losses and Credits

No carryforwards and no carrybacks arising from transactions while the S corporation was in C status can be carried to a tax year for which it is an S corporation.[78] Examples would be net operating loss (NOL) carryforwards under Code Sec. 172, general business credit carryforwards under Code Secs. 38, 39, and so on.

Net operating losses (NOLs). Although NOLs that arise when the S corporation was a C cannot be carried forward to S years, Code Sec. 1371(b)(3) provides that when determining the number of years the NOL can be carried forward, the years that the corporation is an S are counted. This counting procedure prescribed

---

[73] Code Sec. 1372.

[74] Announcement 92-16, IRB 1992-5, 53.

[75] Code Sec. 162(l)(5).

[76] *Headliner* Volume 163 (May 15, 2006).

[77] Code Sec. 1374(a). The tax is subject to certain restrictions that the S corporation inherits. See ¶ 802 for further discussion of the built-in gains tax.

[78] Code Sec. 1371(b)(1) and *A. Rosenberg,* 96 TC 451, Dec. 47,219 (a corporation which had a net operating loss (NOL) of $353,733 as a C corporation could not use the NOL carryover to offset income earned after electing S status under Code Sec. 111; Code Sec. 1371(b)(1), which specifically forbids the carryover of an NOL from a C corporation year to an S corporation year, prevails).

by Code Sec. 1371(b)(3) becomes of importance to a C corporation that converts to an S that has an NOL—the NOL could be lost forever if the S never terminates its election or terminates it beyond the period of carryforward provided in Code Sec. 172.

> **Tax Pointer 1:** If an S corporation loses or terminates its S election while the NOL carryforward is still open, the corporation, which would then be a C, can use the NOL carryforward in computing its corporate income tax.

> **Tax Pointer 2:** C corporation NOLs may be used, however, to offset corporate-level taxes paid by the S corporation after conversion. For example, LIFO recapture income triggered under Code Sec. 1363(d)[79] and built-in gains recognized (and taxed) under Code Sec. 1374[80] may be offset by NOL carryforwards from periods preceding the S election.

Passive activity losses (PALs). In *St. Charles Investment Co.*,[81] S corporation shareholders could deduct suspended Code Sec. 469 passive activity losses arising from C corporation years in the year that the S corporation disposed of the activity that gave rise to the losses. The facts which gave rise to this decision are as follows: On January 1, 1991, a closely held C corporation that was engaged in a real estate rental business elected S status. At the time of its election, the corporation had suspended passive losses arising from its rental activities. In 1991, during its first year as an S corporation, the corporation disposed of the passive activities, with the S corporation deducting on its tax return the suspended passive activity losses. The Court held that Code Sec. 469(b) overrides Code Sec. 1371(b)(1) (the prohibition on an S corporation from carrying forward any C activities to the S corporation). In reaching its decision, the Court noted that the shareholders of the corporation were receiving a windfall, in that the shareholders were able to offset income with losses arising from a different taxpayer (i.e., the former C corporation).[82]

.09 C Corporation Debt

When a C corporation with debt converts to S status, the conversion will not be treated as an exchange of debt for stock. Furthermore, if the C corporation's debt satisfies the straight debt standard, the debt will be treated as straight debt, even though it may be considered equity under the general principles of federal tax law.[83]

.10 Investment Interest Expense

If a C corporation shareholder borrows money to purchase stock in the corporation, basically, the interest expense on the debt is classified as investment interest expense. However, if an S corporation shareholder borrows money to purchase stock,[84] the tax treatment of the interest expense depends on the assets and activities of the corporation. For instance, the interest expense to incur the debt

[79] See ¶ 806 for a discussion of LIFO recapture.
[80] See ¶ 802 for a discussion of built-in gains tax.
[81] *St. Charles Investment Co.*, CA-10, 2000-2 USTC ¶ 50,840, 232 F3d 773.
[82] But see Technical Advice Memorandum 9628002 (October 10, 1995) which stated that suspended passive activity losses of a C corporation that converted to an S could not be recognized subsequently by the S corporation.
[83] Reg. § 1.1361-1(l)(5)(v). See also ¶ 208.05.
[84] See discussion at ¶ 702.

may not be deductible as incurred if the S corporation is engaged in 100 percent passive activities and losses, and the S corporation shareholder who borrowed the funds is "passive."[85] Consequently, to prevent unwarranted tax results, an analysis should be undertaken before incurring debt as to the deductibility of the interest expense on money borrowed to purchase S corporation stock.

The case of *Russon*[86] illustrates the effect that conversion from C status to S status can have. In *Russon*, a case of first impression, the Tax Court has held that interest paid by an individual on a loan to acquire a business organized as a C corporation by buying its stock is deemed investment interest, and subject to the rules regarding investment interest deductions. The facts were as follows:

> Three brothers owned stock in Russon Brothers Mortuary, a C corporation, and decided to step aside to allow the younger generation to acquire the stock interest. The brothers sold their stock interest to the children in exchange for 10 percent down and the balance payable with interest over 15 years. The C corporation never paid dividends during its existence, and the stock purchase agreement specified that the buyers could not declare or pay any dividends until the purchase price was paid in full. The Court held that Code Sec. 163(d)(3)(A) prescribes that interest paid on property held for investment is treated as investment interest, and under Code Sec. 163(d)(5)(A)(i), property held for investment includes any property that produces income, such as interest, dividends, annuities or royalties not derived in the ordinary course of business. In construing the situation, the Court, citing Rev. Rul. 93-68, held that Congress clearly intended to cover property that normally produces dividends, whether or not dividends actually are produced, and thus the interest was deemed investment interest. However, the Tax Court pointed out that, had the Russon Brothers been an S corporation (or a partnership), the children would have been able, as active managers of the business, to deduct the interest expense without limitation, as direct owners of the business.

.11 Alternative Minimum Tax

An alternative minimum tax is imposed on all C corporations.[87] However, when a C corporation converts to an S corporation, it is not liable for alternative minimum tax.[88] In that regard, if an S corporation has to pay the built-in gains tax according to Code Sec. 1374 (see ¶ 802), it does not have to pay alternative minimum tax on the transaction even though the Code Sec. 1374 tax is generated by activities clearly related to the prior C corporation. Note, however, shareholders can be liable for the alternative minimum tax individually as a result of items passed through from the S corporation.

.12 Tax Year

As a general rule, a C corporation (except for personal service corporations) can adopt any fiscal year (regardless of business purpose) or calendar year for reporting its income, expenses, etc.[89] In contrast, an S corporation, unless it can establish a business purpose for reporting on a fiscal-year basis, must use a calendar year, or a fiscal year as prescribed by Code Sec. 444. When a C corporation goes to S status, it must change its tax year to a calendar year, or another

---

[85] Code Sec. 469.
[86] *S.C. Russon,* 107 TC 263, Dec. 51,639.
[87] Code Sec. 55.

[88] Code Sec. 1363(a).
[89] For further discussion, see ¶ 502.

¶404.11

reporting period permitted by Code Sec. 444. The C corporation, however, cannot shorten its last corporate tax year to make the election.[90]

In other words, assume that a C corporation is reporting its income, loss, etc. on a fiscal year July 1-June 30, and on December 31, 2009, it decides that it wants to elect S status. The C corporation cannot file as a C corporation for the period July 1-December 31, 2009, cutting its year short, and then as an S corporation for the period January 1-December 31, 2010. Instead, the C corporation must file as a C corporation for the period July 1-June 30, 2010, and then as an S corporation for July 1-December 31, 2010, unless on conversion, the S corporation can establish a business purpose for reporting its income, loss, etc. or a fiscal year under Code Sec. 444.[91]

.13 Conversion to an S Corporation Will Allow Shareholders to Recognize C Corporation Passive Losses on Disposition of Passive Activity

St. Charles Investment Co.[92] held that when a closely held C corporation which was engaged in real estate business converted to S status, and then began to dispose of its real estate holdings, the S corporation could deduct these passive activity losses on its tax return. While the Court felt that the S corporation shareholders were receiving a windfall in that the shareholders were able to offset income with losses arising from a different taxpayer (i.e., the former C corporation), the Court felt that Code Sec. 469(b) overrides Code Sec. 1371(b)(1). It remains to be seen what planning opportunities will arise from this case.

> **Tax Pointer:** Based on the holding of *St. Charles Investment Co.*, it remains to be seen whether suspended Code Sec. 465 at-risk losses can be utilized to offset S corporation income on the conversion.

.14 Code Sec. 172(b)(1)(H)'s Special Carry Back Provision

Congress, for any tax year which ends after December 31, 2007 and begins before January 1, 2010, added Code Sec. 172(b)(1)(H) to allow an "eligible small business to elect to carry back NOLs for up to 5 years." ¶ 614 sets forth a discussion of Code Sec. 172(b)(1)(H).

¶ 405 Filing an S Corporate Return

.01 Filing the Form 1120S

Code Sec. 6037 requires that an S corporation file an information return on Form 1120S for each year there is a valid S corporation election. The S corporation reports its operations and activities on Form 1120S. The return is due by the 15th day of the third month following the close of the corporation's tax year unless timely extended. Form 1120S, Schedule K summarizes all shareholders' shares of corporate income, deductions, credits, etc. for the taxable year. The Form 1120S, Schedule K-1 is prepared to reflect each shareholder's portion of every item reflected on the Form 1120S, Schedule K with one copy to be delivered on or before the filing due date of the return to each shareholder and attached to the corporate

---

[90] IRS Letter Ruling 8938079 (June 30, 1989).
[91] For further discussion, see ¶ 502.

[92] *St. Charles Investment Co.*, CA-10, 2000-2 USTC ¶ 50,840, 232 F3d 773.

return. The instructions to the Form 1120S prescribe that: (1) a corporation which has been dissolved must generally file its final return by the 15th day of the 3rd month after the date it is dissolved and (2) if the S election is terminated (see Chapter 12 for a discussion of termination of the S election and the consequences which flow from it) during the taxable year and the corporation reverts to a C corporation, the Form 1120S is to be filed for the S corporation's short year by the due date, including extensions, of the C corporation's short year.

.02 *Signature on the Return*

The instructions to the Form 1120S prescribe that the Form 1120S must be signed and dated by the president, vice president, treasurer, assistant treasurer, chief accounting officer, or any other corporate officer (such as tax officer) author-ized to sign.

If a return is filed on behalf of a corporation by a receiver, trustee, or assignee, the fiduciary must sign the return, instead of the corporate officer. Returns and forms signed by a receiver or trustee in bankruptcy on behalf of a corporation must be accompanied by a copy of the order or instructions of the court authorizing signing of the return or form.

If an employee of the corporation completes Form 1120S, the paid preparer's space should remain blank. Anyone who prepares Form 1120S but does not charge the corporation a fee for preparation should not complete that section. Generally, anyone who is paid to prepare the return must sign it and fill in the "Paid Preparer's Use Only" area.

Paid preparers. The paid preparer must complete the required preparer information, sign the return in the space provided for the preparer's signature and give a copy of the return to the taxpayer. A paid preparer may sign original or amended returns by rubber stamp, mechanical device, or computer software program.

Paid preparer authorization. If the corporation wants to allow the IRS to discuss its tax return with the paid preparer who signed it, the corporation can authorize this. This authorization applies only to the individual whose signature appears in the "Paid Preparer's Use Only" section of the return. It does not apply to the firm, if any, shown in that section.

.03 *Electronic Filing of Form 1120S*

Reg. § 1.6037-2 requires that beginning in 2006, S corporations which have assets of fifty million dollars or more are required to file Form 1120S electronically providing the corporation files at least 250 returns a year. For years ending after 2006, the filing requirement drops to assets of ten million dollars or more. There are exceptions however:

(1) The S corporation was not required to file Form 1120S for the prior taxable year or the corporation has not been in existence for a least one calendar year prior to the due date of the return excluding extensions of the Form 1120S, or

(2) It would be an undue hardship for the S corporation to file electronically.

.04 Tax Shelter Reporting

Reg. § 53.6011-4(a) and Reg. § 1.6037-1(c) prescribe that an S corporation which participates, directly or indirectly, in a tax shelter is required to file a disclosure of such participation with its tax return by attaching a statement to Form 1120S. Additionally, the shareholders are required to disclose their participation by attaching a statement to their individual Form 1040.

.05 Penalties for Failing to File an S Corporate Return

If an S corporation fails to file the information return required by Code Sec. 6037, Code Sec. 6699 imposes an entity level penalty on the S corporation with the penalty being assessed each month (or portion thereof) that the failure continues, for a maximum of 12 months. Per Code Sec. 6699(a), an S corporation can abate the penalty if it can show reasonable cause for failing to meet the filing obligation. Code Sec. 6699(b) details that the imposition of the penalty depends on the taxable year where the return was not filed timely. For returns required to be filed after December 31, 2009, the monthly penalty amount is increased from $89 to $195 per month per shareholder for each month or fraction of a month during which the failure continues, up to a maximum of 12 months.

If an S corporation fails to furnish Schedules K-1s to its shareholders or delivers to them an incomplete form, Code Sec. 6722 prescribes that for each such failure to furnish Schedule K-1 to a shareholder when due and/or to include on the Schedule K-1 all the information required to be shown, the IRS can impose a $100 penalty in regard to each Schedule K-1 for which a failure occurs. Further, if the requirement to report correct information is intentionally disregarded, each penalty is increased to $250 or, if greater, 10 percent of the aggregate amount of items required to be reported.

Chapter 5

Accounting Methods and Tax Years of S Corporations

¶ 501   Accounting Method Choices
¶ 502   Calendar- or Fiscal-Year Reporting

¶ 501 Accounting Method Choices

S corporations can adopt any permissible method of accounting (i.e., cash, accrual, or any other method prescribed by the Code).[1] If an S corporation is engaged in more than one trade or business, it can use a different method of accounting for each trade or business.[2] If the S corporation is deemed a tax shelter, however, the accrual method must be used.[3] Unlike a partnership, the S corporation is not bound by the accounting method of its shareholders.

.01 Deductibility of Expenses and Interest

Even if the S corporation elects the accrual method to report income and expense, it must still use the cash method for deducting business expenses and interest owed to certain related-party, cash-method taxpayers.[4] The certain related-party, cash-method taxpayers are[5]

- any shareholder who owns stock in the corporation and
- any person related to a shareholder as defined in Code Sec. 267(b) or Code Sec. 707(b)(1).[6]

As a result, the S corporation will receive the deduction for the expense items when the payment is includible in the recipient's income.

> **Tax Pointer:** There is no time limit when these accrued items must be paid.[7] Prior law required payment within 2½ months from the end of the tax year; otherwise, the deduction was lost.

---

[1] Code Sec. 446(a).

[2] Code Sec. 446(d).

[3] Code Sec. 448(a)(3).

[4] Code Sec. 267(a)(2). S. Rep. No. 640, 97th Cong. 2d. Sess. 24, reprinted in 1982-2 CB 718, 729 states: "The bill places a Subchapter S corporation on the cash method of accounting for purposes of deducting business expenses and interest owed to a related party cash basis taxpayer . . ." *See also* H.R. Rep. No. 826, 97th Cong., 2d. Sess. 23, reprinted in 1982 CB 730, 740. For a further discussion of Code Sec. 267, see ¶ 712.

[5] Code Sec. 267(e).

[6] Note, also, if a shareholder owns more than a 50-percent-profits interest in a partnership, the partnership and the S corporation are related for this purpose (Code Sec. 707(b)(1)(A)). Additionally, the restriction on the deduction by the S corporation in a particular year only applies if the corporation and shareholder to whom the expense or interest is being paid are related on the last day of the corporation's year in which the amount would normally be deductible.

[7] Code Sec. 267.

Example 5-1: Alpha Corporation, an S corporation, is owned by two unrelated individuals, Ann West and Betty Meade, who report their income on the cash basis. Meade owns one share, and West owns 99 shares of Alpha Corporation. Alpha Corporation adopts the accrual method of accounting and the calendar year for reporting income. Alpha Corporation, on January 1, 2003, signs a lease with West. As of December 31, 2003, Alpha Corporation has accrued rent of $6,000 owed to West. Because West has not received the $6,000 rent by December 31, 2003, Alpha Corporation cannot deduct the $6,000 for rent in 2003 on its Form 1120S.

Example 5-2: Assume the same facts as in Example 5-1, except that on January 1 of the next year (2004), Alpha Corporation delivers a $6,000 check to West who deposits the check and reports it as income. Alpha Corporation will be able to deduct the $6,000 for rent in 2004 on its Form 1120S.

Example 5-3: Assume the same facts as in Example 5-1, except that Alpha Corporation delivers a $6,000 rent check to West on December 31, 2003, and West deposits the check that day. Alpha Corporation will be able to deduct the $6,000 for rent in 2003 on its Form 1120S.

.02 Change of Accounting Method When Converting to S Corporation

An S corporation may not adopt a method of accounting that is different from the method it used as a C corporation without obtaining the IRS's consent, according to at least two court cases.[8] An S corporation, however, can elect a different accounting method than a predecessor partnership.[9]

.03 Cash Method of Accounting

As a rule, the IRS is hostile to the cash method of accounting because of the manipulation that can occur with the receipt of income. By definition, the cash method prescribes that income is not earned by an S corporation until received. Consequently, if a cash-basis corporation wants to reduce its income, it can enter into an agreement prior to performing a contract that the corporation is not to be paid until the following year. In the case of *Austin,*[10] the IRS attacked the cash-basis method of a service business. In losing the attack, the IRS had to pay more than $15,000 in legal fees to the taxpayer. The facts were as follows:

> Associated Services of Accountable Professionals Ltd. (ASAP) was incorporated in 1986 and elected to be an S corporation in 1989. ASAP was in the business of providing nurses to hospitals and other health-care facilities at an agreed hourly rate. ASAP paid the nurses and billed the clients at their contracted rates. ASAP had no inventory, had never had gross receipts that exceeded $5 million, and had always used the cash method of accounting. The IRS audited ASAP, and prior to trial, the Commissioner conceded the method of accounting issue

---

[8] *C.C. Weiss,* CA-10, 68-1 ustc ¶ 9380, 395 F2d 500. Aff'g, 26 TCM 564, Dec. 28,489(M), TC Memo. 1967-125. *W.H. Leonhart,* CA-4, 69-2 ustc ¶ 9597, 414 F2d 749. Aff'g 27 TCM 443, Dec. 28,975(M), TC Memo. 1968-98.

[9] Because Code Sec. 381(a) does not apply to the incorporation of a partnership, Code Sec. 381(c)(4), set forth below, cannot apply: "The acquiring corporation shall use the method of accounting used by the distributor or transferor corporation on the date of distribution or trans-

fer unless different methods were used by several distributor or transferor corporations or by a distributor or transferor corporation and the acquiring corporation. If different methods were used, the acquiring corporation shall use the method or combination of methods of computing taxable income adopted pursuant to regulations prescribed by the Secretary."

[10] *L.E. Austin,* 73 TCM 2470, Dec. 51,969(M), TC Memo. 1997-157.

¶501.02

stipulating that the only deficiency would be $4,898 for travel and entertainment expenses. Because the Court felt that the IRS was not substantially justified in its attack of the taxpayer's method of accounting, legal fees were awarded to the taxpayer.

A number of cases have arisen concerning the use of the cash method. *RACMP Enterprises*[11] held that contractors could use the cash method of accounting if the material that was utilized in providing services are deemed "not merchandise held for sale." As to another taxpayer victory, *Osteopathic Medical Oncology and Hematology, P.C.*[12] held that drugs used as part of chemotherapy treatment were not considered merchandise, because their use was an indispensable and inescapable part of the rendering of services. However, in *Von Euw & L.J. Nunes Trucking*,[13] the Court distinguished *RACMP Enterprises*, holding that a company that acquires and transports sand and gravel for its customers is required to maintain inventories, even though the company usually has no goods on hand at the end of the day.

> **Tax Pointer:** For purposes of utilizing Code Sec. 199's domestic production deduction discussed at ¶ 722, the taxpayer may want to be classified as a contractor rather than be engaged in a service business.

In an effort to clarify some of the uncertainty in the area caused by *RACMP Enterprises* and the cases spawned by it, the IRS issued Field Service Advice 200125001 (January 18, 2001), which stated that the IRS would not pursue further litigation against taxpayers that had similar situations as *RACMP Enterprises*. On January 8, 2001, the IRS issued Rev. Proc. 2001-10,[14] modifying Rev. Proc. 2000-22,[15] stating that any qualifying S corporation (e.g., one that is not a tax shelter) that has annual average gross receipts of $1,000,000 or less for three consecutive years does not have to use the accrual method of reporting income if it has inventories.

Then, the IRS issued Rev. Proc. 2002-28,[16] which prescribes that the IRS will allow qualifying small business taxpayers with gross receipts of $10,000,000 or less to use the cash method of accounting for tax years ending after December 31, 2001; however, Rev. Proc. 2002-28, Section 9 prescribes that the IRS will not challenge a taxpayer's use of the cash method for earlier years if the taxpayer, for a year in question, was eligible to use the cash method as detailed in Rev. Proc. 2002-28.

Rev. Proc. 2002-28, Section 5.01 defines a "qualifying small business taxpayer" (QSBT) as any taxpayer (i.e., an S corporation) with average annual gross receipts of more than $1,000,000 but less than or equal to $10,000,000. Rev. Proc. 2002-28, Section 5.02 prescribes that a taxpayer has average annual gross receipts of $10,000,000 or less if, for each prior taxable year ending on or after December 31, 2000, the taxpayer's average annual gross receipts for the three-taxable-year period ending with the applicable prior taxable year does not exceed $10,000,000. Rev.

---

[11] *RACMP Enterprises*, 114 TC 211, Dec. 53,825.

[12] *Osteopathic Medical Oncology and Hematology, P.C.*, 113 TC 376, Dec. 53,629.

[13] *Von Euw & L.J. Nunes Trucking*, 79 TCM 1793, Dec. 53,830(M), TC Memo. 2000-114.

[14] Rev. Proc. 2001-10, 2001-1 CB 272.

[15] Rev. Proc. 2000-22, 2000-1 CB 1008.

[16] Rev. Proc. 2002-28, IRB 2002-18, 815; modified and amplified in Rev. Proc. 2008-52, 2008-36 IRB 587.

Proc. 2002-28, Section 5.04(2) covers the situation where a taxpayer has not been in existence for three years with Rev. Proc. 2002-28, Section 3.02(1), detailing that this special cash method situation will not apply to the farming business.

Rev. Proc. 2002-28 also discusses situations where it will apply. For instance, Rev. Proc. 2002-28, Section 4.01(5) prescribes that a QSBT is eligible to use the cash method if the taxpayer's principal business activity is the provision of services, including the provision of property incident to the service.

> *Tax Pointer:* While Rev. Proc. 2002-28 generally applies to a qualifying business under $10,000,000 of average annual gross receipts, it does not apply to C corporations (or partnerships with a C corporation partner) with average gross receipts over $5,000,000 that are barred from using the cash method by Code Sec. 448.[17]

¶ 502 Calendar- or Fiscal-Year Reporting

.01 Selection Considerations

An S corporation can use a calendar year or a fiscal year to report its income, whether it is a new or existing corporation. With fiscal-year reporting, unless a business purpose can be established (e.g., a cherry orchard harvests its crop in April each year), there is a price to be paid for this special treatment: an interest-free deposit to the IRS that is adjusted each year to reflect changes in S corporation income (i.e., if the S corporation income goes up, the deposit has to go up; if the income decreases, then a refund has to be made[18]). Further, the S corporation can only choose a fiscal year ending September 30, October 31, or November 30.

From a tax perspective, there is really no long-term benefit to fiscal-year reporting due to deposit requirements. However, from a bookkeeping perspective, fiscal-year reporting eases an accountant's work load since some S corporation tax returns will be due on dates other than March 15.

In the course of operations, an S corporation may desire to change its taxable year. However, Reg. § 1.442-1 prescribes that once a taxpayer adopts a taxable year, it can only be changed by permission of the Internal Revenue Service. To obtain the year change, the taxpayer has to file a Form 1128 and pay a user fee. The Service issued three lengthy Revenue Procedures to prescribe guidelines in terms of adopting fiscal years, which are detailed below.

- Rev. Proc. 2006-45[19] which applies to C corporations and S corporations electing S status. The Revenue Procedure sets forth procedural rules when the IRS will automatically approve retention of a corporation's taxable year when it adopts S status or changes the corporation's taxable year.

---

[17] Code Sec. 448 generally prohibits the use of the cash method by a C corporation (other than a farming business and a qualified personal service corporation) and a partnership with a C corporation partner (other than a farming business and a qualified personal service corporation), unless the C corporation or partnership with a C corporation partner meets a $5,000,000 gross receipts test. Code Sec. 448 also prohibits tax shelters from using the cash method.

[18] Code Sec. 7519.

[19] 2006-2 CB 581.

- Rev. Proc. 2006-46[20] provides for situations where the Service will automatically grant approval for an S corporation to use fiscal years.

- Rev. Proc. 2002-39[21] provides for situations where the Service will not grant automatic approval.

Tax Pointer: If corporation is under audit, the automatic change rules of Rev. Procs. 2006-45 and 2006-46 do not apply.

.02 Calendar-Year Reporting

Newly formed S corporations. Newly formed S corporations (i.e., those starting *de novo* as an S corporation and never having existed as a C corporation) must use a calendar year for reporting income, loss, gain, etc. unless they can justify a fiscal-year status. Thus, there is no opportunity for deferral, assuming that all the shareholders are calendar-year taxpayers. Although calendar-year reporting is required unless the S corporation can justify a business purpose,[22] the S corporation must still take steps to acquire a calendar year. On Form 2553, "Election by a Small Business Corporation," the S corporation must designate a calendar year at Item 1. Additionally, Item O has to be checked to denote whether it is a new corporation, or an existing corporation retaining or changing its tax year. The consent of the IRS is not required for S corporations to use calendar-year reporting.

C corporations. For C corporations converting to S status, the process for establishing a calendar year is slightly more complex.

Calendar-year C corporation converting to S status. If a calendar-year C corporation is electing S status, it can retain calendar-year status without IRS consent by filing Form 2553, filling in Item I, and checking Item O, Box 2.

Fiscal-year C corporation converting to calendar-year S status. A fiscal-year C corporation can change to calendar-year S status on conversion without consent of the IRS by filing Form 2553, filling in Item I, and checking Item O, Box 3.[23]

.03 Fiscal Year Reporting

If an S corporation wishes to establish a natural business year, the S corporation has to qualify under one of the following three tests:

- Natural business-year test
- Ownership tax-year test
- Relevant facts and circumstance test

Natural business year. Rev. Proc. 2002-38 provides that the Internal Revenue Service will automatically approve a natural business year for operation of the S corporation. In order to qualify for this fiscal year reporting, Rev. Proc. 2006-46, Sec. 5.07 prescribes that the S corporation must satisfy a mechanical gross receipts test, namely that 25 percent of the S corporation's gross receipts are consistently recorded in the final two months of the selected year. In order to obtain this type of

---

[20] 2006-2 CB 859.

[21] 2002-22 IRB 1046, modified and clarified by Notice 2002-72, 2002-2 CB 843, and modified by Rev. Proc. 2003-34, 2003-18 IRB 856, and Rev. Proc. 2003-79, 2003-45 IRB 1036.

[22] Code Sec. 1378.

[23] Rev. Proc. 2006-46, Sec. 4.01(1), 2006-2 CB 859. If a corporation is under examination, then consent must be obtained from the IRS, or if there is an income tax issue being tried, then the court must grant permission.

fiscal year reporting, the S corporation first computes its gross receipts from sales and services during the most recent 12-month period selected as the desired tax year. Gross receipts for the last two months of this 12-month period are also computed. This yearly figure is divided into the two-month figure, and must equal at least 25 percent. The same calculations are made for two 12-month periods preceding the 12-month period used for the initial calculations. Gross receipts for the last two months of the two preceding 12-month periods must also equal or exceed 25 percent of the total.

Procedure. Rev. Proc. 2006-46, Sec. 7, details the procedural requirements for obtaining natural business year. Part II of Form 2553 must be completed as well, with the S corporation checking the appropriate box in Item O, and completing Box P1.

S Corporation no longer qualifies under the natural business year test. Rev. Proc. 2006-46, Sec. 6.05, prescribes that if the S corporation no longer qualifies for a natural business year, the S corporation must change to another permitted taxable year; otherwise, the S corporation will forfeit its S corporate status.

Ownership taxable year. Rev. Proc. 2006-46 prescribes that an S corporation can obtain a fiscal year based on the fiscal year of the shareholders owning a majority of the stock. Rev. Proc. 2006-46, Sec. 5.08, prescribes that an S corporation satisfies the ownership taxable year test if the shareholder(s) owning more than one-half of the stock as of the first day of the desired fiscal year, maintains or concurrently changes to the same fiscal year. If a Code Sec. 501 tax-exempt charity is a shareholder, its taxable year is generally disregarded. However, if the S corporation is wholly owned by tax-exempt entity(ies), then the taxable year for the majority shareholder is utilized.

Procedure. Rev. Proc. 2006-46, Sec. 7.03 prescribes that if the S corporation can qualify for the ownership taxable year test, the corporation checks the second box under Item P, as well as fills in the appropriate box under Item O of Part II of Form 2553. At the top of the first page of Form 2553 or 1128 (if applicable), state that "Form is filed under Rev. Proc. 2006-46". If the S corporation is under audit, then it must comply with Rev. Proc. 2006-46, Sec. 7.03.

Facts and circumstances text. Rev. Proc. 2002-39 and Rev. Rul. 87-57[24] prescribes that for a corporation to obtain a fiscal year reporting, non-tax considerations must be compelling. Rev. Rul. 87-57 sets forth various examples where a fiscal year would be appropriate (for example, weather conditions requiring a business to be operated only during certain months).[25] Examples where a corporation would not be granted a fiscal year under the facts and circumstances test would be to permit the corporation to obtain a reduced rate for an accountant's services.[26] Another example where a fiscal year would be denied is where the corporation seeks to change its reporting so that shareholders can receive their tax information on a timely basis.[27]

---

[24] 1987-2 CB 117.
[25] Rev. Rul. 87-57, Situation 7.
[26] *Id.*, Sec. 2.
[27] *Id.*, Sec. 4.

¶502.03

Procedure. To obtain fiscal year reporting under the facts and circumstances test, the S corporation checks Form 2553, Part II, Item Q, checking the appropriate box, as well as completing the appropriate box for Item O of Part II of Form 2553.

Back-up Code Sec. 444 election to obtain limited fiscal year reporting. When an S corporation is electing a fiscal year other than Code Sec. 444's limited fiscal year reporting, it can make a "back-up election" at the same time for a fiscal year of September 30, October 31, or November 30.[28] If the IRS denies a natural business-year status, then the S corporation can use the back-up election for reporting purposes in its first tax year. By making the back-up election, the S corporation will not be forced to use a calendar year for its first year of operation if it does not obtain a natural business-year status.

.04 Code Sec. 444 Fiscal Years of September 30, October 31, or November 30

S corporations can use a fiscal year of September 30, October 31, or November 30 for tax-reporting purposes by filing Form 8716, "Election To Have a Tax Year Other Than a Required Tax Year," even though the S corporation cannot establish a business purpose for any of these fiscal years.[29] However, for this limited fiscal-year reporting status, Code Sec. 7519 requires that a deposit be made on Form 8752, "Required Payment or Refund Under Section 7519," and be filed each year that the Code Sec. 444 election is effective, even if no payment is due for a particular year. It also should be noted that an S corporation cannot make a Code Sec. 444 election if a prior Code Sec. 444 election was effective at any time.[30] Thus, if an S corporation made a Code Sec. 444 election and lost it due to failure to make a required payment (a "lapsed" corporation), the S corporation cannot file a new Code Sec. 444 election and must revert to a calendar year. Also, end runs are precluded around Code Sec. 444 by denying Code Sec. 444 treatment to a "lapsed" S corporation that merges into a newly formed S corporation.[31]

Fiscal years prohibited for members of a tiered structure. Since S corporations can be members of LLCs, partnerships, etc., an abuse could occur in reporting (i.e., a September 30 fiscal-year S corporation is a member of a October 31 LLC). Accordingly, an S corporation cannot make a Code Sec. 444 election if it is a member of a tiered structure (i.e., when an S corporation owns an interest in a tiered entity such as a partnership or LLC).[32] If an S corporation is a member of a deferral entity, then all members of the deferral entity have to have the same tax reporting year.[33]

C corporations electing S status. Code Sec. 444(b) prescribes that an existing C corporation can elect on conversion to S status to keep its fiscal year of September 30, October 31, or November 30 providing its "deferral period" is three months or less. The "deferral period" is generally defined as the number of months that elapse before the beginning of the desired tax year and December 31.[34] A

---

[28] Temp. Reg. § 1.444-3T(b)(4)(i).
[29] Code Sec. 444.
[30] Temp. Reg. § 1.444-1T(a)(5)(i)(C).
[31] Temp. Reg. § 1.444-1T(b)(5)(iii)(B).
[32] Code Sec. 444(d)(3).
[33] *Ibid.*
[34] Temp. Reg. § 1.444-1T(b)(2)(iii).

corporation can elect a September 30, October 31, or November 30 fiscal year if the desired fiscal year does not exceed the shorter of (1) three months or (2) the deferral period of the tax year being changed. The reason for the imposition of a deferral period is to prevent a prolonged deferral of taxation of S corporation income due to electing a fiscal-year status, notwithstanding the depository rules of Code Sec. 7519.

Example 5-4: Wells, a June 30 fiscal-year C corporation, elects S status and a fiscal year ending September 30 under Code Sec. 444. Because the deferral period of the desired fiscal year of three months (October 1-December 31) is shorter than the six-month period of its original tax year (July 1-December 31), the September 30 fiscal year is permissible.

Example 5-5: Assume the same facts as in Example 5-4, except that Wells, the C corporation, had an October 31 fiscal year, wanting to change to a September 30 fiscal year. Here, the three-month deferral for a September 30 fiscal year exceeds the two-month deferral period of its original tax year (November 1-December 31) and the Code Sec. 444 election cannot be made. The choice for the C corporation under Code Sec. 444 is to keep its existing fiscal year of October 31, or change its tax year to one ending November 30 (or December 31).

Example 5-6: SavAlot is a C corporation having a September 30 fiscal year when it elects S status. It files under Code Sec. 444 to keep its existing fiscal year of September 30. There is no problem with any deferral period, so the election is allowed.

Tax Pointer: If a fiscal year C corporation converting to S status will be facing a "Built In Gains" tax under Code Sec. 1374, it may be advantageous to shorten Code Sec. 1374's recognition period by adopting under Code Sec. 444, a fiscal year of 9/30, 10/31 or 11/30. See the illustration below which assumes that the C corporation is on a 6/30 fiscal year. For a discussion of Code Sec. 1374 see ¶ 802.

A June 30th fiscal year C corporation converts to an S corporation and adopts under Code Sec. 444 a 10/31 fiscal year for its year of operation, and then after the first full fiscal year of operation terminates its October 31st fiscal year to operate under a calendar year; the S corporation will be able to shorten the 5 year recognition period to 4 calendar years as illustrated below.

7/01/y1–10/31/y1	1st year of recognition
11/1/y1-10/31/y2	2nd year of recognition
11/1/y2-12/31/y2	3rd year of recognition
1/1/y3-12/31/y3	4th year of recognition
1/1/y4-12/31/y4	5th year of recognition

S corporations making a Code Sec. 444 election. A Code Sec. 444 election for fiscal-year reporting of September 30, October 31, or November 30 is made on

¶502.04

Form 8716.[35] Form 8716 may be executed on behalf of the S corporation by any of the corporation's officers or chief accounting officer.[36]

> *Due date of Form 8716.* For the Form 8716 fiscal election to be effective for the first tax year, it must be filed by the earlier of (1) the 15th day of the fifth month following the month that includes the first day of the fiscal year for which the election will be effective or (2) the due date (determined without regard for extensions) for the S corporation income tax return for the short tax year resulting from the Code Sec. 444 election.[37]

> ***Example 5-7:*** NexStar, an S corporation, begins operations on September 10, 2006, and elects a September 30 fiscal year. NexStar must file Form 8716 by December 15, 2006. This is the earlier of the 15th day of the fifth month following the month that includes the first day of the fiscal year for which the election will be effective (February 15, 2007) or the due date for the S corporation income tax return (December 15, 2006).

> ***Example 5-8:*** Assume the same facts as in Example 5-7, except that the S corporation NexStar commences operations on October 20, 2006. NexStar must file Form 8716 by March 15, 2007, which is the 15th day of the fifth month following the month that includes the first day of the tax year for which the election will first become effective.

> Form 8716 is filed with the IRS service center where the S corporation will file its income tax return. Moreover, in addition to filing the Form 8716 with the IRS by the due date described above, the S corporation must also attach a copy of Form 8716 with its first return for the first tax year for which the Code Sec. 444 election is effective.[38]

> *Termination of the Code Sec. 444 election.* An S corporation's Code Sec. 444 election will terminate when the S corporation does any of the following:[39]

- Changes its required tax year (i.e., December 31)
- Liquidates
- Willfully fails to comply with the required payments mandated by Code Secs. 7519 or 280H
- Becomes a member of a tiered structure that does not have the same tax year
- Affirmatively terminates its election

Code Sec. 7519 required payments. As a general rule, an S corporation must make payments on Form 8752 for each tax year that a Code Sec. 444 election is effective. Form 8752, "Required Payment or Refund Under Section 7519," must be filed even if no required payment is due for any particular tax year.[40]

> *Penalties for failure to make Code Sec. 7519 payments.* An S corporation that willfully fails to make a required payment may have its Code Sec. 444 election terminated.[41] Further, if an S corporation fails to make a required payment, a penalty equal to 10 percent of the difference between the amount, if any, of the required payments already made and the amount of required payments that

---

[35] Temp. Reg. § 1.444-3T(b)(1).

[36] Reg. § 1.444-3T(b)(1) and Code Sec. 6062.

[37] Temp. Reg. § 1.444-3T(b)(1).

[38] *Ibid.*

[39] Temp. Reg. § 1.444-1T(a)(5)(i)(A)-(E).

[40] Temp. Reg. § 1.7519-2T(a)(2).

[41] Temp. Reg. § 1.7519-2T(c).

must be made will be imposed.[42] Additionally, in some circumstances, the S corporation could be liable for negligence and fraud penalties.[43]

Exceptions for Code Sec. 7519 payments. No payment is required on Form 8752 in the following two circumstances:[44]

1. **Exception for first-year situations.** An existing corporation making a Code Sec. 444 election need not make a Code Sec. 7519 required payment for its first tax year if such first tax year ends prior to December 31.[45]

Example 5-9: Somu, a September 30 fiscal-year C corporation, converts to S status, and, upon conversion, makes a Code Sec. 444 election to retain its tax year ending September 30. For Somu's first applicable election year, Somu's required payment is $700,[46] but Somu does not have to make a required payment for that year. However, Somu is required to file the return.[47]

2. **Liability not exceeding $500.** An S corporation does not need to make a required payment if, for a particular tax year, the amount of the required payment is not more than $500 and the S corporation was not required to make a required payment for a prior year.[48]

Example 5-10: Assume the same facts as in Example 5-9, and, in addition to those facts, for Somu's second applicable election year, the payment amount is $800.[49] Because Somu did not actually make a required payment for Somu's first applicable election year, Somu's required payment is $800 for its second applicable election year. Since the required payment is greater than $500, Somu must make a required payment for its second applicable election year. Furthermore, Somu must file the required return.[50]

Example 5-11: Assume the same facts as in Example 5-10, and, in addition to those facts, for Somu's third applicable election year, the payment amount is $1,200, but Somu's required payment is $400 ($1,200 – $800).[51] Although Somu's required payment for its third applicable election year is not more than $500, Somu must make its required payment for such year because the required payment for a preceding applicable election year exceeded $500. Somu must also file the required return for its third applicable election year.[52]

---

[42] Code Sec. 7519(f)(4).

[43] Temp. Reg. § 1.7519-2T(d).

[44] Temp. Reg. § 1.7519-1T(a)(2) and (b)(4).

[45] Temp. Reg. § 1.7519-1T(b)(4).

[46] Temp. Reg. § 1.7519-1T(a)(3).

[47] Temp. Reg. § 1.7519-1T(a)(2).

[48] *Ibid.*

[49] Temp. Reg. § 1.7519-1T(a)(3)(i).

[50] Temp. Reg. § 1.7519-2T(a)(2).

[51] Temp. Reg. § 1.7519-1T(a)(3)(i) and (ii).

[52] Temp. Reg. § 1.7519-2T(a)(2).

¶502.04

Chapter 6

Income and Loss

¶ 601 Income Taxation of an S Corporation

A prime reason for establishing an S corporation is the single level of tax.[1] However, preparing the income tax return for an S corporation on Form 1120S can be quite confusing. S corporation income, expense, loss, and so on need to be pigeonholed in the right areas. For instance, charitable contributions that are treated as an expense for a C corporation (to arrive at taxable income) are reported as itemized deductions by individual S corporation shareholders.

On Form 1120S, there are two types of income and loss:

(1) "separately stated items" that are passed directly to shareholders on Schedule K (and K-1) and

(2) "nonseparately stated items" that are aggregated on Form 1120S, lines 6 and 20, with the total income or loss reflected on line 21 and then passed through to shareholders on Schedule K (and K-1), line 1.

---

[1] Code Sec. 1363(a) and (b).

If the net result of the separately stated items and the nonseparately traded items passed through to a shareholder is a loss, the shareholder can use the loss on his, her, or its return only to the extent of the shareholder's basis in stock and debt. The loss reduces the shareholder's basis in stock first and then debt. Gains, whether taxable or nontaxable, increase the shareholder's basis in stock. If debt basis has previously been reduced by losses, it must first be restored before adjusting the shareholder's stock basis.

> **Example 6-1:** Ernie Richards is a 25 percent shareholder in JD Inc., a qualified S corporation. His basis in his JD stock at the beginning of the year was $12,000. In addition, he made a loan to JD Inc. in which his basis was $50,000. This year, his share of separately and nonseparately stated items from JD Inc. was a net loss of $18,000. He can deduct the entire $18,000 (assuming no other limitations), reducing his stock basis to zero and his debt basis to $44,000 ($12,000 stock basis *less* $12,000 of loss; $50,000 of debt basis *less* $6,000 of loss remaining). If next year, his share of S corporation items results in net income of $8,000, his debt basis will be restored to $50,000 and his stock basis will be increased to $2,000.

An S corporation provides liability protection to the corporate shareholder for corporate debts while establishing one level of taxation at the shareholder level. Thus, S corporation shareholders can have their cake and eat it too—they are themselves protected from certain corporate debts while reporting S corporation activities on their individual tax return (individual shareholders use Form 1040; estates and trusts use Form 1041; etc.).

An S corporation generally computes its taxable income in the same manner as an individual, subject to certain modifications.[2] For instance, an S corporation is not entitled to a dividends-received deduction.[3]

Shareholders include their shares of separately and nonseparately stated items on their returns for the tax year with which or within which the S corporation's tax year ends.[4] When a shareholder dies, or in the case of a trust or estate that terminates before the end of the S corporation's tax year, the S corporation's books are closed with respect to that shareholder as of the date of death or termination; the shareholders' share of income or loss to that point is then included on the shareholder's final return.

> **Example 6-2:** Jean Jones is a shareholder in Jones Inc., a qualified S corporation. Jean is a calendar-year taxpayer. Jones Inc. uses a fiscal year ending on October 31 for tax purposes. On her current year's return, Jean will report her share of S corporation income or loss for the period ending October 31. S corporation income for the months of November and December will be included on Jean's next year's tax return.

---

[2] Code Sec. 1363.
[3] Code Sec. 243.

[4] Code Sec. 1366(a)(1).

.01 Preparation of the Form 1120S

Question 9 of Schedule B, Form 1120S, advises that if the S corporation's total receipts for the taxable year and its total assets at the end of the year are less than $250,000, then the corporation does not have to complete Schedules L and M-1 of Form 1120S.

¶ 602 Separately Stated Items

Some items are passed through to S shareholders as separately stated items while other items (nonseparately stated items) are aggregated and reported as net income or loss to the corporation. The basic rule of pass-through is that an item of income, expense, and so on remains separate and may be subject to special treatment on the tax return of any shareholder, while the remainder of the items are combined to form either ordinary income or ordinary loss for the corporation.[5] Unfortunately, the Code does not specify all of the items that require separate treatment, and future Code changes may change the items currently specified for separate treatment.

The following items commonly pass through separately to S shareholders to be reported on their individual tax return (Form 1040 or Form 1041), lumped with the shareholder's other income, expenses, capital gains and losses, and so on:

Income
- Net short-term capital gain and loss
- Net long-term capital gain and loss
- Net gain and loss from involuntary conversions due to casualty or theft
- Net Code Sec. 1231 gain or loss
- Foreign income and loss
- Portfolio income and loss (i.e., interest, dividends, royalties, net short-term capital gain and loss, net long-term capital gain and loss, other portfolio income and loss)
- Tax-exempt income
- Passive income and loss (real estate and all others)

Tax Pointer: Tax-exempt bonds should generally not be held by S corporations.[6]

Deductions
- Charitable contributions
- Code Sec. 179 expense deductions
- Certain foreign taxes
- Investment interest expenses
- Oil and gas productions for purposes of depletion
- Certain itemized deductions

[5] *Ibid.*

[6] See discussions at ¶ 1006 and ¶ 1118.

Other Items

- Items used in determining certain credits
- Corporation's adjustments in computing alternative minimum tax under Code Secs. 56 and 58
- Items of tax preference under Code Sec. 57

.01 Alternative Minimum Tax

Code Sec. 1363(a) provides that an S corporation is not subject to alternative minimum tax (AMT) except for transactions involving assets from a predecessor C corporation. However, the S corporation could be involved with tax preference items which would affect a shareholder's alternative minimum tax calculation. Consequently, the AMT items have to be separately stated. Some of the items are:

- Income from the completed contract method of accounting,
- Depletion on minerals (other than oil and gas) propert, and
- Accelerated depreciation on all property placed in service after 1986.

.02 Passive Loss Rules

Code Sec. 469's passive loss rules apply at two levels—corporate and shareholder. As to the corporation, the S corporation will detail to its shareholder(s) its involvement with passive activity, such as rental income and/or loss. As to shareholders, the S corporation may or may not know if its shareholders are active or passive for Code Sec. 469 purposes. Thus, if a shareholder is passive, the burden falls on the shareholder to make the determination as to how to report income, loss, etc. arising from the S corporate activities. For a fuller discussion of Code Sec. 469, see ¶ 911.

¶ 603 Nonseparately Stated Items

.01 Corporation Gross Income

The Code does not define the gross income of an S corporation; however, Code Sec. 1363(b) states that taxable income of an S corporation "shall be computed in the same manner as in the case of an individual." Thus, for the most part, the S corporation computes its gross income and deductions as would an individual.[7] Accordingly, an S corporation recognizes income in the following situations (among others):

- The reallocation of income rules prescribed by Code Sec. 482[8]
- Transfer of installment debt under Code Sec. 453[9]

---

[7] An S corporation would not be taxed as an individual when it deals with its own stock. Code Sec. 1032 exempts an S corporation from taxation when it issues stock in exchange for property. See also IRS Letter Ruling 8417042 (January 24, 1984) where an S corporation recognized no gain under Code Sec. 1032 when it issued its stock in a merger. Further, in some instances, the non-recognition of income rules apply in certain instances, namely, Code Sec. 354 (exchanges of stock as security in a reorganization) or Code Sec. 311(a)(1) (distributions of a corporation's own stock or rights to acquire its stock).

[8] See *R.A. Hennessey,* 36 TCM 536, Dec. 34,378(M), TC Memo. 1997-122 (interest income allocated to S corporations under Code Sec. 482 because of interest-free loan to related corporations). Also see, *Bank of Winnfield & Trust Co.,* DC La., 82-1 USTC ¶ 9292, 540 FSupp 219 (court refused to sustain Code Sec. 482 allocation).

[9] *R. Dessauer,* CA-8, 71-2 USTC ¶ 9675, 449 F2d 562. Rev'g and rem'g 54 TC 327, Dec. 29,974.

- Assignment of income principles[10]
- Cancellation of debt rules[11]

The S corporation does not recognize income from items that are excluded from gross income under Code Secs. 101-132.[12]

.02 Special Situations

Some of the situations that could arise in the computation of S corporation income that would not arise for an individual include

- Distribution of appreciated property,
- Issuance of stock for property, and
- Liquidating dispositions of installment obligations.

Issuance of S corporation stock for property. An S corporation can issue its own stock in exchange for property without recognition of taxable income.[13]

Disposition of an installment obligation. Since an S corporation may use the installment method,[14] the income may be reported as received under the installment sales contract (i.e., the installment note or obligation).[15] If the corporation disposes of the installment sale obligation other than by liquidation (e.g., distributes the note to one of the S corporation shareholders), the S corporation must recognize income equal to the remaining deferred gain inherent in the note.[16]

Example 6-3: Folk Inc., composed of Phyllis and Sue Folk who each own 50 percent of the S corporation, sold land that it owned, which had a basis of $200,000, for $500,000 to a publicly listed company, Blair Inc. The sale was structured as an installment contract starting January 1, 2009, for $200,000 down and the balance ($300,000) payable on January 1, 2010, with interest. The installment obligation was evidenced by a note and mortgage. Folk Inc., after entry into the contract, decided on January 1, 2009, to distribute Blair Inc.'s note and mortgage to Phyllis, one of the shareholders of Folk Inc. On January 1, 2009, Folk Inc. had income of $300,000 reportable by the shareholders ($150,000 by each shareholder, Phyllis and Sue) because Blair Inc.'s note was distributed before it matured.

Example 6-4: Assume the same facts as in Example 6-3, except Folk Inc. sells the land to Sue Folk. The same result occurs as in Example 6-3 (i.e., Folk Inc. has $300,000 income which is reportable by the shareholders ($150,000 by each shareholder, Phyllis and Sue)).

When the installment method cannot be used. If an S corporation sells depreciable property to a related party, the installment method cannot be used to report the sale.[17] Also, the installment method cannot be used to report the sale of stock or securities traded on an established security market (e.g., the New York

---

[10] *S. Johnston,* 35 TCM 642, Dec. 33,808(M), TC Memo. 1976-142.

[11] *R.L. Brutsche,* CA-10, 78-2 USTC ¶ 9745, 585 F2d 436. Rem'g 65 TC 1034, Dec. 33,685. For a discussion of Code Sec. 108's rules, see ¶ 905.02, item (viii) and ¶ 610.

[12] See discussion at ¶ 905.02, item (viii).

[13] Code Sec. 1032 and IRS Letter Ruling 8417042 (January 24, 1984).

[14] Code Sec. 453.

[15] Code Secs. 453 and 1363.

[16] Code Sec. 453(b).

[17] Code Sec. 453(g).

Stock Exchange); rather, all the payments to be received must be treated as received in the year of sale of the stock and/or securities.[18]

Original issue discount. Taxpayers (including S corporations) must include in gross income the original issue discount (OID) inherent in certain debt obligations.[19] There are some exceptions to the rule, such as for short-term obligations;[20] however, the exceptions do not apply to S corporations.[21]

Future contracts. Taxpayers (including S corporations) must include the unrealized appreciation inherent in future contracts in income as they pertain to hedging transactions.[22]

When a shareholder's income cannot be assigned. A shareholder may attempt to have the S corporation realize income that is really his or hers. Several recent cases illustrate that the courts will not sustain such attempts. In *Isom*,[23] the court found that an insurance agent, not his S corporation, was the true earner of an insurance commission that an agent had under an employment agreement with an insurance company. In *Martin Ice Cream Co.*,[24] the court refused to sustain the sale of assets by an S corporation owned by a father and son of a customer list that the father had developed by himself and committed to memory; rather, the court treated the asset (the customer list) as property of the father alone.

¶ 604 Elections Regarding Gross Income

.01 Elections Made at the Corporate Level

Most elections regarding methods of accounting, inclusion or exclusion of income, etc. must be made at the S corporation level rather than by the shareholders individually.[25] Thus, for example, if S corporation property is "sold" in an involuntary conversion, one shareholder cannot opt to recognize gain (e.g., from insurance proceeds), while another opts to defer gain under Code Sec. 1033 by reinvesting the proceeds. Examples of elections that must be made by the S corporation rather than the shareholders are:

- The election to defer recognition of gain under Code Sec. 1033,
- The election to deduct intangible drilling costs under Code Sec. 263,
- The election not to use the installment method under Code Sec. 453 to report income realized on an installment sale, and
- The election to deduct research and development costs under Code Sec. 174.

Tax Pointer: To ensure that elections that have to be made at the corporate level will occur and that there will not be deadlocks on these issues, the shareholders, by their shareholders' agreement, may want to prescribe that if one shareholder wants a corporate election made, all the shareholders will consent. Of course, this is binding the shareholders in advance to a

---

[18] Code Sec. 453(k)(2)(A).
[19] Code Secs. 1272-1281.
[20] Code Sec. 1272(a)(2)(C).
[21] Code Sec. 1281(b)(2)(A).

[22] Code Sec. 1256(a)(1).
[23] *B.M. Isom,* 70 TCM 376, Dec. 50,826(M), TC Memo. 1995-383.
[24] *Martin Ice Cream Co.,* 110 TC 189, Dec. 52,624.
[25] Code Sec. 1363(c)(1).

position, but it is best to flesh out matters like this in advance, rather than when it is too late.

.02 Elections Made at the Shareholder Level

Although most elections must be made at the S corporation level, a few must be made by the shareholders.[26] The following elections must be made by the shareholders:

- The election to exclude foreign earned income under Code Sec. 901
- The election to claim a deduction or credit for foreign income taxes paid
- The election under Code Sec. 617 to deduct mining and exploration expenditures

¶ 605 Capital Gains and Losses

.01 Reported on Schedule D

Capital gains and losses are reported by the S corporation on Schedule D, just like an individual reports gains and losses from capital transactions. If capital losses exceed capital gains in any year, those losses are passed through to the shareholders without reduction. The holding period rules that apply to individuals to determine long-term and short-term gain and loss also apply to S corporations.

> **Tax Pointer:** S corporations that have converted from C corporations can pay a tax on net capital gains. (For instances when this might occur, see discussions at ¶ 802 and ¶ 804.)

The *Arrowsmith*[27] and *Corn Products*[28] doctrines do apply to S corporations to recharacterize capital gain and loss transactions.[29]

.02 Code Sec. 1231 Transactions

An S corporation's Code Sec. 1231 gain and loss on property are passed through separately to be aggregated with the shareholders' other Code Sec. 1231 gains and losses; there is no netting at the corporation level.[30] The determination of whether an asset qualifies as a business-use asset under Code Sec. 1231 is done, however, at the corporate level. The S corporation does not recharacterize Code Sec. 1231 gains based on previous Code Sec. 1231 losses; any recharacterization takes place at the shareholder level.

> **Example 6-5:** Moon Inc., an S corporation, in the year 2009 sold equipment at a loss producing a $2,000 net Code Sec. 1231 loss. The next year, 2010, Moon Inc. sold land it held for two years for a $5,000 gain. Moon Inc. in 2010 will report a $5,000 Code Sec. 1231 gain on Form 1120S, Schedules K and K-1.

---

[26] Code Sec. 1363(c)(2).

[27] *F.D. Arrowsmith,* SCt, 52-2 USTC ¶ 9527, 344 US 6, 73 SCt 71.

[28] *Corn Products Ref. Co.,* SCt, 55-2 USTC ¶ 9746, 350 US 46, 76 SCt 20.

[29] An example where the *Arrowsmith* doctrine was applied is *D. Bresler,* 65 TC 182, Dec. 33,478. Acq., 1976-2 CB 1 (most of payment received by S corporation in antitrust suit settlement characterized as ordinary income because prior loss in the sale of corporation's business reflected as ordinary loss). In *J.F. Shea Est.,* 57 TC 15, Dec. 31,020. Acq., 1973-2 CB 3, the IRS asserted the *Corn Products* doctrine, but the court rejected its application be83 cause of the facts involved. (It is beyond the scope of this book to discuss or define the *Arrowsmith* and the *Corn Products* doctrines; however, discussion of these topics can be found in any general textual discussion about capital gains.)

[30] Code Sec. 1366.

.03 Tax-Exempt Income

Tax-exempt income is income that is *permanently* excludible from gross income in all circumstances.[31] For example, death benefits payable under a life insurance policy[32] and interest on state and local bonds[33] are tax-exempt because they are permanently excludible from gross income. In contrast, income from improvements made by a lessee on a lessor's property is not tax-exempt income because the lessor would recognize the value of the improvements as income when the property is sold.[34] Similarly, income from the discharge of indebtedness does not constitute tax-exempt income because the attribute reduction provisions[35] have the effect of deferring the recognition of such income in some circumstances while permanently excluding it, in whole or in part, in other circumstances.[36]

¶ 606 Dealer Transactions

In determining whether an S corporation has realized a capital gain or loss rather than ordinary income or loss, the IRS normally will not look at the activities of the shareholders; rather it looks at the corporation's activities. However, if the S corporation is availed of by any shareholder or group of shareholders owning a substantial portion of the stock of such corporation for the purpose of selling property which in the hands of such shareholder or shareholders would not be a capital asset,[37] then profit on the sale will be ordinary income to the corporation, even if the property was a capital asset in its hands. Further, in determining the character of the asset in the hands of the stockholder, the activities of other S corporations in which the individual is a stockholder will be taken into account.

In other words, if an S corporation holds a property interest as a capital asset and has a substantial stockholder who is a dealer in such property, the corporation's capital gain on the sale of the property could be converted into ordinary income.

> **Example 6-6:** Doug Brown, who owns 55 percent of Sail Inc., an S corporation, is a dealer in real estate. The other stock of Sail Inc. is owned by Brown's children. Sail Inc. has as its only asset a piece of real estate that it is selling for a gain of $100,000. The $100,000 gain on the sale may be classified as an ordinary income transaction rather than a capital gain because of Brown's controlling interest and dealer status.

How much control a dealer must have to taint the character of a capital gain is not clear. However, a technical advice memorandum (TAM) shed some light on the IRS's position with respect to dealer status. In TAM 8537007 (June 10, 1985), an S corporation owned mineral property with the following shareholders: a father owned 55 percent of the stock and was assumed to be a dealer in mining properties, and his children owned the rest. A Code Sec. 1231 gain resulted from a corporate

---

[31] Reg. § 1.1366-1(a)(2)(viii).
[32] Code Sec. 101.
[33] Code Sec. 103.
[34] Code Sec. 109.
[35] For a discussion of discharge of indebtedness income, see ¶ 610.

[36] For a further discussion on why income from the discharge of indebtedness is not tax-exempt income, see the Preamble to the Proposed Regulations, Reg. 209446-82, 63 Fed. Reg. 44181 (8/18/98).
[37] Reg. § 1.1366-1(b)(3).

transaction that was treated as a capital gain and was not recharacterized as ordinary income under Reg. § 1.1375-1(d). No recharacterization was made because the corporation offered the property for sale only after failing to raise funds for the mineral property's development.

The IRS has not always been successful in converting capital gain to ordinary income. For instance, in *Buono,*[38] the Court did not believe that the corporation's three largest shareholders were dealers, and land was treated as a capital asset even though it was purchased for resale and the corporation received subdivision approval prior to sale as a single parcel. Other cases where the IRS lost its recharacterization argument are *Ofria*[39] in which the S corporation qualified for capital gain on sale of an unpatented invention and *Dean*[40] in which the land that was held for development and sale to customers in the ordinary course of business was treated as held for investment when its sale produced capital gains.

¶ 607 Related-Person Transactions

Capital gains may be recharacterized as ordinary income when they are realized on the sale or exchange of depreciable property between certain "related persons."[41] "Related persons" as they pertain to S corporations are defined as:[42]

- A person and an S corporation when such person owns directly or indirectly 50 percent or more of the value of the outstanding stock, and

- An employer- and employee-controlled welfare benefit fund or such fund controlled by a party related to the employees per the rules of Code Sec. 1239.

The 50-percent-or-more ownership test is determined taking into account Code Sec. 267(c)'s attribution rules with certain modifications. Example 6-7 illustrates the application of the rules as they apply to S corporations.

> ***Example 6-7:*** Henri Swift, an individual, owns 49 percent of the stock (by value) of Maple Corporation, an S corporation, and a trust for Swift's children owns the remaining 51 percent of the stock. Swift's children are deemed to own the stock (owned for their benefit by the trust) in proportion to their actuarial interests in the trust.[43] Swift, in turn, constructively owns the stock so deemed to be owned by his children.[44] Thus, Swift is treated as owning all the stock of Maple Corporation, and any gain Swift recognizes from the sale of depreciable property to Maple Corporation is treated under Code Sec. 1239 as ordinary income.

¶ 608 Property Distributions to Shareholders

.01 Distributing Appreciated Property

In general, when an S corporation distributes appreciated property (other than an obligation of the corporation) in a nonliquidating distribution, the distribution is

[38] *G. Buono,* 74 TC 187, Dec. 36,925. Acq., 1981-2 CB 1.
[39] *C. Ofria,* 77 TC 524, Dec. 38,198. Nonacq., 1983-2 CB 1.
[40] *W.K. Dean Est.,* 34 TCM 631, Dec. 33,192(M), TC Memo. 1975-137.
[41] Code Sec. 1239.
[42] Code Sec. 1239(c) and (d).
[43] Code Sec. 267(c)(1).
[44] Code Sec. 267(c)(5).

treated as if the property had been sold to the shareholder at fair market value.[45] This gain, in turn, will pass through to shareholders,[46] and its character will likewise pass. Thus, if the S corporation distributes appreciated Code Sec. 1231 property to a shareholder, the shareholders will, in turn, recognize Code Sec. 1231 gain at the shareholder level. The shareholder's basis in the property is equal to its fair market value.

> *Example 6-8:* Wood Inc., an S corporation owned entirely by Theresa Tanner, distributes to Tanner, in a non-Code Sec. 1374 transaction,[47] capital stock of a company traded on the New York Stock Exchange. Wood Inc.'s basis is $10,000, and on the date of the transfer, the stock's value was $17,000. Wood Inc. purchased the stock several years ago. Tanner's basis in the stock is $17,000, and Tanner realizes as the sole shareholder of Wood Inc. a $7,000 long-term gain.

> *Tax Pointer 1:* The distribution of appreciated property could trigger the built-in gains tax and the passive investment income tax on the S corporation under Code Secs. 1374 and 1375.[48]

Exceptions to distributing appreciated property. Code Sec. 311(b)'s recognition rule regarding gain does not apply to reorganization(s) and division(s) involving the S corporation under Code Secs. 354, 355, or 356.

> *Tax Pointer 2:* Depending on the type of asset, ordinary income under the depreciable property provisions of Code Secs. 1239, 1245, and 1250 could be triggered by the distribution.

.02 Distributing Depreciated Property

There is generally no loss recognition by a corporation on a nonliquidating distribution of depreciated property to a shareholder.[49] Thus, rather than create a nondeductible loss situation, the S corporation should sell the depreciated asset at a loss and pass the loss through to the shareholder.[50]

¶ 609 Earnings and Profits

.01 When an S Corporation Can Have Earnings and Profits

Under the law prior to 1983, an S corporation could have earnings and profits[51] (e.g., from being the beneficiary of a life insurance contract). Under current law, an S corporation by definition cannot have any earnings and profits from its operations unless it does one of the following:[52]

- Operates as a C corporation with earnings and profits and subsequently converts to S status,

---

[45] Code Sec. 311(b). If a loss is generated in the nonliquidating distribution, Code Sec. 311 precludes the S corporation from recognizing the loss.

[46] Code Sec. 1366.

[47] For a definition and discussion of Code Sec. 1374, see ¶ 802.

[48] See more detailed discussion at ¶ 802 and ¶ 804.

[49] Code Sec. 311(a).

[50] Code Sec. 267(a)(1) will generally preclude the loss if the depreciated asset is sold to a more-than-50-percent-in-value shareholder; thus, the asset has to be sold to unrelated third parties.

[51] For a definition of earnings and profit, see Code Secs. 312 and 316.

[52] Code Sec. 1371(c)(1).

- Acquires the earnings and profits of a C corporation in a merger or similar arrangement pursuant to Code Secs. 368, 381(c)(2), and 1371(c)(2), or

- Operates as a corporation that is the product of a tax-free division under Code Sec. 355.

.02 Earnings and Profits Can Penalize an S Corporation

An S corporation can be severely penalized for having one dollar or more of earnings and profits.[53] An S corporation with earnings and profits has to pay at the highest income tax rate specified in Code Sec. 11(b) on its excess passive investment income.[54] Further, the dollar or more of earnings and profit could cause the corporation to lose its S election if it has too much passive income for three consecutive years.

.03 Methods to Eliminate Earnings and Profits

One obvious way to eliminate earnings and profits is to declare a dividend. However, due to the complexities of S corporation taxation, an S corporation, unless all the shareholders receiving distributions elect otherwise, has to go through detailed steps to make the dividend distribution.[55]

.04 Methods to Reduce Earnings and Profits

Dividends. If dividends aren't used to eliminate earnings and profits, they may be used to reduce them.[56]

> **Tax Pointer 1:** Investment interest expense can only be deducted by shareholders to the extent they have investment interest income.[57] One source of investment interest income is dividends. Thus, by declaring a dividend from earnings and profits, the S corporation creates investment interest income for the shareholder.

> **Tax Pointer 2:** Code Sec. 1(h)(11) provides that dividends received by an S corporation shareholder after 2002 and before 2013 are eligible for a special tax rate of 5 percent for individuals in the 10 percent-15 percent bracket, and then a maximum of 15 percent thereafter. Thus, because of the favorable tax rates, shareholders have an incentive to declare dividends out of S corporation earnings and profits, thereby eliminating the problem under Code Sec. 1375 and Code Sec. 1362(d)(3). Dividends can likewise be used to offset interest expense. For a discussion of the rules, see ¶ 702.

Subchapter C transactions. Earnings and profits may also be reduced by Subchapter C transactions such as redemptions, reorganizations, divisions, and so on.[58]

---

[53] Code Secs. 1375 and 1362(d)(3), and as discussed at ¶ 804 and ¶ 1204.

[54] Code Sec. 1375.

[55] Code Sec. 1368(e)(3). See also discussion at ¶ 1004 et seq. for the rules regarding distributions as they apply to earnings and profits. For a discussion of the mechanics of Code Sec. 1368(e)(3), see ¶ 804.17 and ¶ 1004.03.

[56] See ¶ 1004.02 for using dividends to reduce earnings and profits.

[57] Code Sec. 163.

[58] Code Sec. 1371(c)(2). See discussion at ¶ 1003.

.05 Elimination of All Earnings and Profits Attributable to Pre-1983 Years for Certain Corporations

The Small Business Jobs Protection Act of 1996 provided that if a corporation was an S corporation for its first taxable year beginning after December 31, 1996, the accumulated earnings and profits of the corporation as of the beginning of that year were reduced by the accumulated earnings and profits (if any) accumulated in a taxable year beginning before January 1, 1983, for which the corporation was an electing small business corporation under Subchapter S.

Congress now provides for taxable years beginning after May 25, 2007 in the case of any corporation which was not an S corporation for its first taxable year beginning after December 31, 1996, the accumulated earnings and profits of the corporation as of the beginning of the first taxable year beginning after May 25, 2007 is reduced by the accumulated earnings and profits (if any) accumulated in a taxable year beginning before January 1, 1983, for which the corporation was an electing small business corporation under Subchapter S.

¶ 610 Cancellation of Indebtedness

.01 Income Reporting of a Debt Discharge

When a solvent debtor is discharged of a debt, the debtor usually realizes income from the discharge of debt.[59]

> **Example 6-9:** Alpha Inc. is an S corporation purchasing R Ranch on January 1, 2010, for $1,000,000, borrowing the entire $1,000,000 from its bank, State National, on a nonrecourse basis (i.e., State National only looks to the corporation to pay the debt). State National did not ask for the shareholders of Alpha Inc. to guarantee the debt, but it did request that a mortgage be placed on the property. Alpha Inc., a short time after it purchased R Ranch, experienced financial difficulties, causing it to have difficulties making the payments on the mortgage, and eventually stopping all payments when the principal on the debt was $950,000. In addition, Alpha Inc. discovered that R Ranch had environmental problems that, while solvable, were very expensive. When Alpha Inc., which is solvent, owed $950,000 on its note, State National negotiated with Alpha Inc. a complete payoff of the debt for $850,000 rather than foreclosing on the property. Alpha Inc. has forgiveness of debt income of $100,000 ($950,000 – $850,000) reportable by the shareholders as income.

However, in the above Example 6-9, if: (a) Alpha Inc. was insolvent at the time of the forgiveness of debt; (b) the debt was discharged in a bankruptcy; (c) the debt was qualified farm indebtedness as defined in Code Sec. 108(a)(1)(C); or (d) the debt was qualified real property business indebtedness as defined in Code Sec. 108(a)(1)(D), then Code Sec. 108(a)(1) prescribes that the income realized from the discharged debt is excluded from income. See ¶ 610.07 for a discussion of qualified real property business indebtedness.

---

[59] Code Sec. 61(a)(12).

.02 Reduction of Taxpayer Attributes Due to Cancellation of Indebtedness

Code Sec. 108(b)(1) prescribes that when discharge of indebtedness is excluded from gross income because the discharge from debt occurred pursuant to one of the grounds under Code Sec. 108(a)(1), then the taxpayer (e.g., the S corporation in Example 6-9) must generally make corresponding reductions to the taxpayer's attributes in the following order as detailed in Code Sec. 108(b)(1) and (2):[60]

(1) Net operating losses and carryovers of net operating losses

(2) Carryovers to and from the tax year of discharge for purposes of determining the general business credit

(3) Minimum tax credits (after 1993)

(4) Net capital losses and carryovers

(5) Bases of depreciable and nondepreciable assets

(6) Passive activity loss or credit carryovers (after 1993)

(7) Foreign tax credit carryovers

An S corporation by definition does not have net operating losses, capital loss carryover, or credits carryover. Code Sec. 108(d)(7)(A) prescribes that, with respect to an S corporation, debt discharge and attribute reductions are made at the corporate level, not the shareholder level. Accordingly, Code Sec. 108(d)(7)(B) prescribes that debt discharge income is applied to reduce pass-through losses and deductions (including capital losses) for the year of debt discharge that would have been allocated to the shareholders of the S corporation but for the fact that their basis (basis is discussed at Chapter 9) was less than the losses. Any remaining discharged debt is to be used to reduce the basis of the assets of the S corporation. In the case of the basis of depreciable assets, the S corporation, pursuant to the rules of Code Sec. 108, can elect to reduce the basis of depreciable assets first.

Generally, under Code Sec. 108(d)(7)(A), reductions in these tax attributes are made at the S corporation level rather than at the shareholder level, but with respect to application of Code Sec. 108's rules, Code Sec. 108(d)(7)(A) was amended for discharge of debt after October 11, 2001, to prescribe that while forgiveness of debt income is excluded from income taxation, the amount of the exclusion will not increase the shareholder's basis.[61]

> **Example 6-10:** Bret is the sole shareholder of Widget, Inc., a calendar-year S corporation, contributing $100 to start the corporation on January 1, 2010. During the first corporate year, Widget borrowed money from banks, but due to poor economic conditions at the end of the year, Widget was insolvent, having an operating loss of $250, and forgiveness of debt income on renegotiation of the bank loan of $300. Under Code Sec. 108(d)(7)(A), Bret will be allowed to deduct only $100 of loss equal to his stock basis; he will not be able

---

[60] Code Sec. 108(d)(7)(A) also makes it clear that on the S corporation's insolvency or bankruptcy, the adjustment prescribed by Code Sec. 108(b)(1) and (b)(2) is generally made at the corporate level; the status of a shareholder is irrelevant.

[61] Code Sec. 108(d)(7)(A) was amended on October 11, 2001, to overturn *D.A. Gitlitz*, SCt, 2001-1 USTC ¶ 50,147, 531 US 206, 121 SCt 701.

to utilize the $300 of forgiveness of debt income to step up his basis to be able to deduct the remaining portion of the operating loss of $150 ($250 – $100 of basis for the capital stock contributed).

In terms of application of Code Sec. 108(b)(1) and (b)(2)'s pecking order rules as they apply to an S corporation for reducing corporate attributes, the following should be noted:

Code Sec. 108(d)(7)(B). Code Sec. 108(d)(7)(B) prescribes that since, as a rule, an S corporation does not have any operating losses or net operating loss carryovers unless they arise from C corporation years, a special rule is prescribed to handle losses which can arise with S corporations as reflected in a shareholder's basis. Specifically, Code Sec. 108(d)(7)(B) states that any loss which is disallowed for the taxable year for the cancellation of the debt is treated as a "net operating loss." To illustrate, assume a shareholder has a zero basis for stock and debt in the year of discharge of a debt owed to a third party. Any deduction of loss under Code Sec. 1366(d)(1) has to be reduced per Code Sec. 108(d)(7)(B).

> ***Example 6-11:*** Rella is the sole shareholder of Iron, Ltd., a calendar-year S corporation. After several years of operation, Rella's stock basis is zero. However, due to corporate losses, over the years she has $1,000 of suspended losses. In 2010, Iron, Ltd. became insolvent, and one of its creditors, a bank, forgave $200 of the debt to help Iron, Ltd. rebound. Iron, Ltd. reports a loss of $50 from operations in 2010. The $50 loss is reduced to zero because of the $200 of cancellation of indebtedness income, leaving $150 ($200 – $50) to be utilized under Code Sec. 108(b)(2)(B) et seq.

> ***Tax Pointer:*** Code Sec. 108(d)(7)(B) prescribes that if losses are suspended under Code Sec. 465, Code Sec. 469, or investment interest limitation, there is to be no reduction of suspended losses under Code Sec. 108(d)(7)(A).

Code Sec. 108(e)(6) and Code Sec. 108(d)(7)(C). Code Sec. 108(e)(6) prescribes that if there is a discharge of S corporation debt owed to an S corporation shareholder, gross income results to the S corporation equal to the extent that the face amount of the debt exceeds the shareholder's adjusted basis in the debt. Code Sec. 108(d)(7)(C) prescribes that, for purposes of application of Code Sec. 108(e)(6)'s rule, the S corporation ignores the reduction in the basis of a debt attributable to the pass-through of S corporation losses.

.03 Definition of Insolvency for Cancellation of Indebtedness Income Purposes

Code Sec. 108(d)(3) defines "insolvency" as "the excess of liabilities over the fair market value of the assets," with the amount by which an S corporation is insolvent to be determined "on the basis of taxpayer's assets and liabilities immediately before discharge." Neither the Internal Revenue Code nor the regulations define "insolvency" other than in general terms. However, there have been several rulings issued to define "insolvency." IRS Letter Ruling 9125010 prescribes that the value of assets exempt from creditors is not included as assets in the computation of insolvency. Rev. Rul. 92-53[62] prescribes that the amount of nonrecourse debt over the fair market value of the property securing the debt (i.e., excess nonrecourse debt) is deemed a liability to the extent it is discharged, but excess nonrecourse debt that is not discharged is not considered a liability for insolvency purposes. Code Sec. 108(a)(3) prescribes that the amount of cancellation of indebtedness income that can be excluded is limited to the excess of liabilities over the fair market value of assets. In bankruptcy, there is no such similar limitation on the amount excludable.

   Example 6-12: Strokes, Inc., a calendar-year S corporation, purchased a building utilizing a nonrecourse mortgage. As of January 1, 2010, the building is worth $8,000, but the unpaid principal balance is $10,000. The lender agrees to reduce the debt to $8,350. Strokes, Inc. has cash at the time of the debt reduction equal to $1,000, and owes $500 to trade creditors which is not being reduced. Strokes, Inc. has excludable cancellation of indebtedness income equal to $1,150, and taxable income of $500 computed as detailed below:

Assets

Cash	$ 1,000
Building	8,000
Total Assets	9,000

Liabilities

Trade creditors	500
Nonrecourse mortgage equal to the fair market value of the building	8,000
Excess debt discharged	1,650
Total Liabilities	10,150

   For Code Sec. 108 purposes, Strokes, Inc. is insolvent to the extent of $1,150 ($10,150 − $9,000). However, the corporation has forgiveness of debt income of $1,650 ($10,000 − $8,350 [the amount to which the lender is willing to reduce the debt] = $1,650). Accordingly, Strokes, Inc. excludes $150 of cancellation of indebtedness income, reporting $500 ($1,650 − $1,150) of cancellation of debt income.

.04 Reduction of Tax Attributes and Basis

   As discussed at ¶ 610.01, Code Sec. 108(b)(2)(E) (the fifth attribute) requires that the basis of depreciable and nondepreciable property has to be reduced. Code Sec. 1017 prescribes that the basis reduction rules apply to property held by a

[62] Rev. Rul. 92-53, 1992-2 CB 48.

taxpayer at the beginning of the taxable year following the tax year in which the discharge of indebtedness occurs. Because Code Sec. 1017 prescribes that the basis reduction does not occur until the tax year following the year of discharge of debt, this means that the assets disposed of during the year of discharge are not subject to basis reduction. For examples of how the basis reduction rules work, see Reg. § 1.108-7(e), Examples 5-7.

> *Example 6-13:* Sinclair, Inc., a calendar-year S corporation, has debts of $200 and property with a basis and fair market value of $75. Sinclair is discharged of $135 of debt on December 1, 2010. If Sinclair retains the property, by Code Sec. 1017 its basis is reduced to zero on January 1, 2011; however, if Sinclair sold the property for $75, its fair market value on December 31, Sinclair will not recognize any gain under Code Sec. 1017, nor will it have taxable income from the sale in 2010, because its basis of $75 equals its fair market value.

.05 General Rules Regarding Discharge of Indebtedness

Code Sec. 108(e) prescribes some ground rules regarding discharge of debt. Two rules are noteworthy:

Code Sec. 108(e)(2)—Loss deductions. Code Sec. 108(e)(2) deals with a situation that frequently arises in insolvency and bankruptcy situations—an individual forgives payment which would give rise to a deduction. For instance, the taxpayer's lawyer forgives part of his, her or its fee for legal services; the taxpayer (assuming taxpayer is on a cash basis) does not have cancellation of debt income, because such services would have been deductible as a business expense.

Purchase money debt reduction. Code Sec. 108(e)(5) prescribes that if a taxpayer purchases property using seller financing, and the seller reduces the amount which the taxpayer owes, generally, the debt reduction is treated as an adjustment to the purchase price, with a corresponding reduction in taxpayer's basis in the property.

.06 Contribution of Debt to an S Corporation—Code Sec. 108(d)(7)(C)

When a shareholder contributes debt to an S corporation as a contribution to capital, corporate income does not result to the extent that the basis of the old debt had previously been reduced by the pass-through of losses from the corporation.

> *Example 6-14:* At the beginning of 19X4, A, Inc., a calendar year S corporation, which has one shareholder, B, has on its balance sheet, corporate stock, $200, and loan from B, $100. At the end of 19X4, A, Inc., has a loss of $250, which pursuant to Chapter 9, reduces B's stock basis to zero and the debt to $50. In 19X5, B contributes the note to A, Inc. The consequence is that both B and A, Inc., have no income from the cancellation of the indebtedness; A, Inc.'s assets are not changed, and B's stock basis is raised to $50.

.07 Qualified Real Property Business Indebtedness

Code Sec. 108(c) prescribes that a taxpayer, other than a C corporation, may elect to exclude from gross income cancellation of qualified real property business indebtedness (QRPBI). Code Sec. 108(c)(3) defines QRPBI as debt incurred or assumed on real property which is used in a trade or business and is secured by this real property. Per Code Sec. 108(c)(4), an S corporation can exclude up to the outstanding principal amount of the debt minus the fair market value of the property securing it. The excluded amount of debt reduces the basis of depreciable real property. Reg. § 1.1017-1(c) states that the maximum exclusion from gross income is any excess immediately before the discharge of the debt principal over the "net fair market value" of the qualifying property with "net fair market value" being fair market value less the outstanding principal of qualified real property business debt except the discharged debt secured by the property immediately before and after the discharge.

Code Sec. 108(d)(7)(A) prescribes that the QRPBI rules are applied at the S corporate level with the S corporation making the election. The discharge of debt that is excluded from an S corporation's income is not passed through to shareholders; consequently there is no adjustment to a shareholder's basis.

.08 Discharge of Indebtedness Arising from Purchase or Exchange of an S Corporation of Its Own Debt Obligations at a Discount—Code Sec. 108(i)

Reg. § 1.61-12(c)(2) prescribes that an S corporation will realize Code Sec. 61 cancellation of indebtedness income when it purchases its own debt obligation for less than the adjusted issue price of the debt with the income arising at the time of repurchase or cancellation of the obligation. Reg. § 1.61-12(c)(2)(i) prescribes that discharge of indebtedness income can arise when a debt instrument is retired, converted into the issuer's stock or is acquired in exchange for newly issued debt instruments of the issuer. Reg. § 1.61-12(c)(2)(ii) details that the amount of income recognized is generally the excess of the adjusted issue price over the repurchase price. For the period of December 31, 2008 through January 10, 2011, Code Sec. 108(i) prescribes that at the election of the S corporation, a shareholder can elect to defer any cancellation of indebtedness over a 5-year period reporting the income ratably over this period. However, for reacquisitions occurring in 2009, the 5-year period commences with the 5th taxable year following the taxable year when acquisition occurs. For 2010 reacquisitions, the 5-year inclusion period commences with the 4th taxable year following the taxable year in which the acquisition occurs. To assist S corporations and their shareholders in applying the special Code Sec. 108(i) rules, Rev. Proc. 2009-37[63] should be consulted.

.09 Discharge of a Shareholder's Debt to the Corporation

If an S corporation cancels the debt a shareholder owes to the corporation, the cancellation is treated as a property distribution subject to Code Secs. 301(c) and 1368. If the S corporation has accumulated earnings and profits then it is dividend to the extent of the corporation's earnings and profits. If the S corporation has no accumulated earnings and profits, the distribution is nontaxable to the extent of the shareholder's adjusted basis in the stock per Code Sec. 1368(b)(1). Distributions in excess of adjusted basis are treated as gains from the sale or exchange of property under Code Sec. 1368(b)(2).[64]

---

[63] 2009-36 IRB 309.　　　　　　　　　[64] *Toberman v. Commissioner*, TC Memo 2000-221.

¶ 611 Recharacterization of Capital Transactions

When stock in an S corporation held for more than one year is sold or exchanged, the transferor may recognize ordinary income on the transaction under Code Secs. 304, 306, and 1254. Further, under Code Sec. 1(h), an allocation is to be made for the sale or exchange of a collectible in connection with the sale of S corporation stock. A "collectible" is defined by Code Sec. 408(m) without regard to Code Sec. 408(m)(3) if the collectible is held for more than one year. The above recharacterization rules for Code Secs. 304, 306, 1254, and 1(h) are in addition to the dealer transactions discussed at ¶ 606 and the related-person transactions discussed at ¶ 607. Example 6-15 illustrates the application of Code Sec. 1(h) to a sale of S corporation stock.

> ***Example 6-15:*** Corporation Alpha has always been an S corporation and is owned by individuals Phil Jones, Charles Smith, and Laurie Cohen. In 2010, Alpha invested in antiques. Subsequent to their purchase, the antiques appreciated by $300. Laurie Cohen owns one-third of the shares of Alpha's stock and has held that stock for more than one year. Laurie's adjusted basis in the Alpha stock is $100. If Laurie were to sell all of the Alpha stock to her sister Irene for $150, Laurie would realize $50 of long-term capital gain before applying Code Sec. 1(h).
>
> If Alpha were to sell its antiques in a fully taxable transaction immediately before the stock transfer to Irene, Laurie would be allocated $100 of collectibles gain from the sale. Therefore, Laurie will recognize $100 of collectibles gain from the collectibles held by Alpha.

The difference between a transferor's long-term capital gain or loss, before applying the look-through capital gain determined under Code Sec. 1(h), is the transferor's residual long-term capital gain or loss on the sale of S corporation stock. In Example 6-15, Laurie will recognize $100 of collectibles gain under Code Sec. 1(h) and a $50 residual long-term capital loss on account of the sale of her stock interest in Alpha.

¶ 612 Effect That Bankruptcy or Insolvency Can Have on an S Corporation

When an S corporation faces financial difficulty, and debt restructuring is contemplated due to insolvency,[65] a number of scenarios could occur, such as a termination of the corporation's S status, because the lender (i.e., a C corporation) became a shareholder.[66] Alternatively, the shareholder of the S corporation, realizing that bankruptcy is imminent, may want to revoke S status, so that any gain realized on the sale of the assets on bankruptcy will not be taxed to the shareholder individually, but to the C corporation.[67]

If the S corporation's status remains, it is probable that the creditors of the S corporation will impose restrictions on the distribution of corporate funds. Thus, the shareholders will find themselves being forced to report the S corporation

---

[65] See ¶ 610.03 for a definition of "insolvency."
[66] For the effect of termination of S status, see ¶ 1207.
[67] For a discussion of this point, see ¶ 203.03 and ¶ 1202.04.

income, but having no corporate funds to use to pay the tax on the income. If cancellation of indebtedness income arises, complex tax issues can occur, as discussed at ¶ 610.

If an S corporation goes bankrupt during its taxable year, *Williams v. Comm.*[68] holds that the S corporate shareholders are not entitled to report losses generated by the corporation before the bankruptcy using Code Sec. 1377 to allocate them; rather, the losses are reported for the entire year by the bankruptcy estate. The S corporation shareholder can claim the unused losses after the bankruptcy is over, but the loss must be reduced by the amount of taxable income the shareholder obtained when the debts are excused.

.01 Bankruptcy Abuse Prevention and Consumer Protection Act of 2005—Super Discharge Eliminated

On April 20, 2005, President Bush signed into law the Bankruptcy Abuse Prevention and Consumer Protection Act of 2005 (BPACP). While it is beyond the scope of this book to provide a detailed description of the BPACP, several points should be noted. The law, which does not go into effect until October 17, 2005, contains many complex provisions, some of which are draconian in approach. For instance, Congress eliminated the super-discharge procedures in Chapter 13. Under the prior provisions, some courts allowed debtors who have not filed tax returns to discharge their taxes under a Chapter 13 plan. Additionally, some courts have allowed debtors to discharge taxes due within three years of the date of the bankruptcy petition, or assessed within 240 days under a Chapter 13 plan. Chapter 7 does not provide such an option, because failure to file a return or untimely filing of a return generally makes a tax liability non-dischargeable under Chapter 7. Some bankruptcy courts have held that this non-dischargeability under Chapter 7 regarding failure to file a tax return or untimely filing of a tax return does not apply in Chapter 13 filings. As to tax debts arising from fraudulent returns, Chapter 7 prescribes that they are not dischargeable; however, some courts have allowed them to be discharged under a Chapter 13 plan.

The BPACP was enacted to curb bankruptcy abuses, but it also expands bankruptcy protections previously available for a debtor's retirement funds. Bankruptcy Code § 522(b) provides a new federal exemption for retirement funds held in several types of tax-favored plans which applies to cases begun after October 17, 2005 (See ¶ 1103.15 for a discussion of this topic).

¶ 613 Code Sec. 199—Domestic Manufacturing Deduction

¶ 722 details the deduction for domestic production provided by Code Sec. 199. Code Sec. 199(d)(1)(A) and (B) prescribe that the Code Sec. 199 deduction is generally applied at the S corporation shareholder level. Accordingly, the S corporation must aggregate and assemble its Code Sec. 199 items of income loss, expense, etc. so that the shareholder(s) of the S corporation can utilize this deduction.

---

[68] 123 TC No. 8.

¶ 614 Code Sec. 172(b)(1)(H)—Carryback for Net Operating Losses

Code Sec. 172(b)(1) states that a taxpayer can carry back net operating losses (NOL) two years and forward 20 years. Code Sec. 172(b)(3) states that an NOL is automatically carried back unless the taxpayer waives the carry back and elects to carry the loss forward. Congress, for any tax year which ends after December 31, 2007 and begins before January 1, 2010, added Code Sec. 172(b)(1)(H) to allow an "eligible small business" (an ESB) to elect to carry back NOLs for up to 5 years. Code Sec. 172(b)(1)(H)(v)(II) defines an "eligible small business" as one which meets a fifteen million dollar (or less) gross receipts test for the tax year in which the loss arose applying the gross receipts test set forth in Code Sec. 448(c).

Rev. Proc. 2009-26[69] sets forth two examples illustrating the application of the rules. The examples have been modified to include an S corporation. They are set forth as Examples 6-16 and 6-17 below:

Example 6-16: Tom Jones owns a 40% interest in Partnerships AX and BY, plus a 40% shareholder interest in an S corporation CX, Inc. AX, BY and CX, Inc. have average annual gross receipts of $10 million, $12 million, and $14 million, respectively. Neither the partnerships nor the S corporation is required to be aggregated with any other entity for purposes of the aggregation rules of Code Sec. 448(c)(2). Tom Jones may apply its election under Code Sec. 172(b)(1)(H) to the portion of its applicable NOL attributable to its distributive share of the income, gain, loss, and deduction of each of Partnerships AX and BY and to S corporation CX, Inc. Rev. Proc. 2009-26 § 4.03(5) prescribes that the amount of the taxpayer's loss is limited to the lesser of (a) The taxpayer's items of income, gain, loss or deduction that are allowed in calculating the taxpayer's applicable NOL and are from one or more partnerships, S corporations or sole proprietorships that qualify as ESBs, or (b) The taxpayer's applicable NOL.

Example 6-17: The facts are the same as in Example 6-16, except that Partnerships AX and BY are under common control within the meaning of Code Sec. 52(b)(1). Accordingly, Partnerships AX and BY are treated as one person under the aggregation rules of Code Sec. 448(c)(2). Because the aggregated average annual gross receipts of Partnerships A and B exceed $15 million, Partnerships AX and BY do not qualify as ESBs. Tom Jones may not apply its election under Code Sec. 172(b)(1)(H) to the portion of its applicable NOL attributable to its distributive share of the income, gain, loss, and deduction of Partnerships AX and BY. However, subject to the limitations in Rev. Proc. 2009-26 § 4.03(5), Tom Jones may apply its election under Code Sec. 172(b)(1)(H) to the portion of its applicable NOL attributable to its distributive share of income, gain, loss, and deduction of S corporation CX, Inc.

For purposes of S corporations, the S corporate shareholders make the election. Congress prescribed two types of NOL carry backs, one for the year 2008 and

---

[69] 2009-19 IRB 935.

the other for 2009. If an eligible small business did not make a timely election for a 2008 NOL, then it can only make an election under the amended carry back provision for a 2008 or a 2009 NOL. In such case, a 50-percent of taxable income limitation will apply to the NOL carried back to the fifth tax year preceding the loss year.

Code Sec. 172(b)(1)(H)(iv) prescribes that if a S corporate taxpayer elects to use a five-year carry back period, the NOL amount that can be carried back to the fifth tax year cannot exceed 50% of the S corporation's taxable income for such preceding tax year (computed without regard to the NOL for the loss year or any tax year thereafter). In determining the amount of carry backs and carry overs to other tax years, adjustments have to be made to account for this 50% limitation. Further, the limitation does not apply if an S corporation made a five-year carry back election under the Code Sec. 172(b)(1)(H) as originally enacted in 2008.

To assist taxpayers regarding Code Sec. 172(b)(1)(H)'s carry backs, see Notice 2010-58.[70] Code Sec. 172(b)(1)(H)(v) prescribes that S corporate shareholders who made the election to carry back a 2008 NOL for three, four or five years under Code Sec. 172(b)(1)(H) as originally enacted in 2008 can also make an election for a 2009 NOL; thus, the Code Sec. 172(b)(1)(H) election can be made for 2008 and 2009.

> *Tax Pointer:* Congress has not changed Code Sec. 172's 20-year carryforward provision; so if a taxpayer wishes to carryforward the losses instead of going back there is no precedent.

¶ 615 Patient Protection and Affordable Care Act of 2010

While it is beyond the scope of this book to provide a detailed discussion of the Patient Protection and Affordable Care Act of 2010, there are certain aspects of the legislation which affect S corporations.

.01 Health Insurance Informational Reporting

Optional in 2011 but mandatory thereafter, employers are required to disclose the aggregate cost of applicable employer-sponsored coverage provided to employees annually on the employee's Form W-2. This reporting requirement has to be made regardless of whether the employer or the employee pays for the coverage with pre- or post-tax contributions.[71] Reg. §54.4980B-8 specifies that the aggregate cost of the coverage reported is determined under rules similar to those used in determining applicable premiums for purposes of the COBRA continuation coverage requirements of group health plans. In any event, Notice 2012-9, Q & A, A-15[72] states that the amount reportable on the Form W-2 has to include the cost of the employee coverage as well as any person covered by the plan due to relationship (the employee's spouse, dependents or a child under the age of 27). For 2% or more S corporate shareholder-employees, Notice 2012-9, Q & A, A-23[73] the cost of coverage excludes the amount the shareholder would report in income.

---

[70] 2010-37 IRB.
[71] Notice 2012-9, Q & A, A-14, 2012-4 IRB 315.

[72] 2012-4 IRB 315.
[73] *Id.*

Code Sec. 6051(a)(14) states that the applicable employer-sponsored coverage for reporting purposes does not include any salary reduction contributions to a flexible spending arrangement under a cafeteria plan, contributions to an Archer medical savings account or health savings account of the employee or the employee's spouse.

Notice 2012-9, Q & A, A-2[74] states that the disclosure requirement is informational only for the employee. Failure to comply does not affect whether any particular coverage is excludable from gross income, and compliance does not affect the amount includable in income or the amount reported in any other box on Form W-2.

Each employer providing employer-sponsored coverage must report the aggregate reportable cost of coverage it provides. Code Sec. 3121(s) details that if the employers are related employers and one such employer is a common paymaster for wages paid to the employee, the common paymaster must include the aggregate reportable cost of the coverage provided to that employee by all the employers for whom it serves as the common paymaster on the Form W-2 issued by the common paymaster. If the employers are related employers but do not compensate an employee with a common paymaster, then pursuant to Notice 2012-9, Q & A, A-7[75] with respect to that employee, the related employers may either report the entire aggregate reportable cost on one of the Forms W-2 provided to the employee, or allocate the aggregate reportable cost among the employers that concurrently employ the employee using any reasonable method of allocation. If an individual transfers to a new employer that qualifies as a successor employer, per Code Sec. 3121(a)(1) both the predecessor and successor employers report the aggregate reportable cost each provided, unless the successor employer follows an optional procedure and issues one Form W-2 reflecting wages paid to the employee during the calendar year by both the predecessor employer and the successor employer.[76]

.02 Additional 0.9% Medicare Tax

Code Sec. 3101(b)(2)(A) prescribes that for tax years beginning after 2012, the employee's portion of the Medicare component of FICA taxes is increased by an additional 0.9 percent to a total of 2.35 percent for wages in excess of $200,000 ($250,000 in the case of a joint return, $125,000 in the case of a married taxpayer filing separately). For couples who file a joint return, the additional tax is imposed on the couple's combined wages. Although the employer is generally required to withhold the employee's portion from the employee's wages, the employer is not obligated to withhold the additional tax unless (and until) the employee receives wages from the employer in excess of $200,000. For this purpose, the employer is permitted to disregard the amount of wages received by the taxpayer's spouse. Accordingly, because an employee may receive wages from more than one employer, or because the employee's spouse may receive wages, an employee may be subject to the additional tax without the tax being withheld from the employee's

[74] *Id.*
[75] *Id.*
[76] Notice 2012-9, Q & A, A-8, 2012-4 IRB 315.

wages. The employee is responsible for any portion of the additional 0.9 percent tax that is not withheld, and calculates and reports the tax on his or her Form 1040 for the year. Code Sec. 3102(f) states that if an employer fails to withhold the additional tax and the employee pays that amount, the employer is not obligated to pay the additional tax but may be subject to penalties and additions to tax for failing to withhold. In the event that the tax is over-withheld, the employee may claim a credit against income tax. For the self-employed, Code Sec. 1401(b)(2) imposes a similar additional 0.9 percent Medicare tax.

> *Tax Pointer:* Under present law, shareholder-employees of an S corporation are only required to take a reasonable salary from which FICA is taken; they can take the rest of the earnings from their S corporation as a distribution of earnings, FICA free. Earnings from an S corporation engaged in a trade or business which is not passive or trading in financial instruments or commodities is not subject to Code Sec. 1411's 3.8 percent surtax. Thus, S corporations offer a means to minimize the effect of Code Secs. 3102 and 1411.

On May 8, 2013, the Internal Revenue Service published "Questions and Answers for the Additional Medicare Tax." Set forth below are some pertinent points. Question & Answer 17 states that: "the value of taxable wages not paid in cash, such as noncash fringe benefits, are subject to Additional Medicare Tax, if, in combination with other wages, they exceed the individual's applicable threshold. Noncash wages are subject to Additional Medicare Tax withholding, if, in combination with other wages paid by the employer, they exceed the $200,000 withholding threshold."

Question and Answer 19 deals with the situation where an individual has both wages subject to FICA and Self-Employment income subject to SECA. They have to calculate their additional Medicare tax as follows:

Individuals with wages subject to FICA tax and self-employment income subject to SECA tax calculate their liabilities for Additional Medicare Tax in three steps:

> **Step 1:** Calculate Additional Medicare Tax on any wages in excess of the applicable threshold for the filing status, without regard to whether any tax was withheld.

> **Step 2:** Reduce the applicable threshold for the filing status by the total amount of Medicare wages received—but not below zero.

> **Step 3:** Calculate Additional Medicare Tax on any self-employment income in excess of the reduced threshold.

The following examples are set forth to illustrate the computation of the tax:

> *Example 6-18:* C, a single filer, has $130,000 in wages and $145,000 in self-employment income.

>> (1) C's wages are not in excess of the $200,000 threshold for single filers, so C is not liable for Additional Medicare Tax on these wages.

>> (2) Before calculating the Additional Medicare Tax on self-employment income, the $200,000 threshold for single filers is reduced by C's

¶615.02

$130,000 in wages, resulting in a reduced self-employment income threshold of $70,000.

(3) C is liable to pay Additional Medicare Tax on $75,000 of self-employment income ($145,000 in self-employment income minus the reduced threshold of $70,000).

Example 6-19: D and E are married and file jointly. D has $150,000 in wages and E has $175,000 in self-employment income.

(1) D's wages are not in excess of the $250,000 threshold for joint filers, so D and E are not liable for Additional Medicare Tax on D's wages.

(2) Before calculating the Additional Medicare Tax on E's self-employment income, the $250,000 threshold for joint filers is reduced by D's $150,000 in wages resulting in a reduced self-employment income threshold of $100,000.

(3) D and E are liable to pay Additional Medicare Tax on $75,000 of self-employment income ($175,000 in self-employment income minus the reduced threshold of $100,000).

Example 6-20: F, who is married and files separately, has $175,000 in wages and $50,000 in self-employment income.

(1) F is liable to pay Additional Medicare Tax on $50,000 of his wages ($175,000 minus the $125,000 threshold for married persons who file separately).

(2) Before calculating the Additional Medicare Tax on self-employment income, the $125,000 threshold for married persons who file separately is reduced by F's $175,000 in wages to $0 (reduced, but not below zero).

(3) F is liable to pay Additional Medicare Tax on $50,000 of self-employment income ($50,000 in self-employment income minus the reduced threshold of $0).

(4) In total, F is liable to pay Additional Medicare Tax on $100,000 ($50,000 of his wages and $50,000 of his self-employment income).

Example 6-21: G, a head of household filer, has $225,000 in wages and $50,000 in self-employment income. G's employer withheld Additional Medicare Tax on $25,000 ($225,000 minus the $200,000 withholding threshold).

(1) G is liable to pay Additional Medicare Tax on $25,000 of her wages ($225,000 minus the $200,000 threshold for head of household filers).

(2) Before calculating the Additional Medicare Tax on self-employment income, the $200,000 threshold for head of household filers is reduced by G's $225,000 in wages to $0 (reduced, but not below zero).

(3) G is liable to pay Additional Medicare Tax on $50,000 of self-employment income ($50,000 in self-employment income minus the reduced threshold of $0).

¶615.02

(4) In total, G is liable to pay Additional Medicare Tax on $75,000 ($25,000 of her wages and $50,000 of her self-employment income).

(5) The Additional Medicare Tax withheld by G's employer will be applied against all taxes shown on her individual income tax return, including any Additional Medicare Tax liability.

Chapter 7

Deductible Expenses

¶ 701 Types of Deductible Expenses

An S corporation computes its deductions in almost the same manner as an individual, except that certain deductions pass through as separate items and others are aggregated.[1] Deductible expenses that are passed through as separate items on Schedules K and K-1 end up on each shareholder's individual tax return; these separately stated items are discussed in ¶ 702–¶ 704. Deductible expenses that are nonseparately stated items are aggregated on Form 1120S, line 20, then

---

[1] See also discussion at ¶ 601.

subtracted from the total income or loss on line 6, and the balance is entered on line 21. This final figure is then passed through to shareholders on Schedules K and K-1, line 1; nonseparately stated items are discussed in ¶ 705–¶ 719.

.01 Reimbursable Expenses

Code Sec. 274 details standards for reimbursing S corporate shareholder-employees for their expenses on company business. If an S corporate shareholder-employee is entitled to reimbursement, but opts not to do it, the expenses become non-deductible.[2]

.02 Capitalization of Expenses

In a trade or business, a taxpayer, when making an expense, has to make a determination regarding tax treatment—expense or capitalize it. Code Sec. 179 as discussed at ¶ 709 helps make the decision easier because of expensing of the property in the year of purchase or upon completion subject to certain limits. However, the S corporation may not be able to avail itself of Code Sec. 179 due to the limitations imposed by this Code section (e.g., the S corporation has a loss; thus there is no benefit under Code Sec. 179 since Code Sec. 179's deduction is geared to income for expensing). The United States Supreme Court recognized the problem of capitalization versus expensing in *Welch v. Helvering*,[3] by stating "One struggles in vain for any verbal formula that will supply a ready touchstone," as to what should be capitalized and what should be expensed. The case of *Lychuk v. Commissioner*[4] illustrates this dilemma. In *Lychuk*, it was held that an S corporation which was engaged in making long-term installment loans on automobile purchases was required to capitalize the salaries of the employees involved in these transactions. It is beyond the scope of this book to discuss capitalization versus expensing.

¶ 702 Interest Expense Paid on Investment Debts

The amount of interest expense that a person can deduct on debt incurred to purchase or carry investments is limited to the amount of net investment income.[5] Examples of income classified as investment income include portfolio income under the passive loss rules,[6] gain from the disposition of investment property,[7] and income from a trade or business when the taxpayer does not materially participate, provided that the activity is not a passive activity under the passive loss rules.[8]

An S corporation's investment interest expense (*and* investment income and expense) passes through to shareholders as a separate item.[9] The consequence of this pass-through is that if the shareholder's share of investment interest of the S corporation together with his or her personal investment interest from other

---

[2] *Horwath v. Commissioner*, TC Memo 1999-141.

[3] 3 USTC ¶ 1164, 290 US 111 (1933).

[4] 116 TC 374.

[5] Code Sec. 163(d)(1). Code Sec. 163(d)(4)(A) defines "net investment income" generally as the excess of (i) investment income *over* (ii) investment expenses. "Investment income" is defined in Code Sec. 163(d)(4)(B) as gross income from property held for investment, including any net gain attributable to the disposition of the

property held for investment, but only to the extent that it is not derived from the conduct of a trade or business.

[6] See ¶ 911.06 for more discussion.

[7] Code Sec. 163(d)(5)(A).

[8] Code Sec. 163(d)(5)(A)(ii). A common example of a trade or business in which a taxpayer does not materially participate is a working interest in oil or gas property. (See Code Sec. 469(c)(2) for a definition of a working interest in oil or gas property.)

[9] Code Sec. 1366(a)(1)(A).

sources exceeds net investment income, the shareholder may not deduct any of the excess investment interest. The classification of interest as investment interest is generally made by reference to the use of the proceeds from the loan (e.g., a loan to purchase portfolio income property).[10]

Example 7-1: Adam Dowd is a shareholder in an S corporation, Hydraulics Inc., that is engaged in the automobile business. Hydraulics Inc. is very profitable, distributing most of its income to its shareholders. Dowd has large investment interest deductions that were incurred borrowing money to engage in various investment activities other than real estate. If the Hydraulics Inc. income taxable to Dowd could be construed entirely as dividend income (i.e., investment income) rather than as automobile business income, Dowd could deduct more of his investment interest expense. However, because Hydraulics Inc. is an S corporation rather than a regular corporation, the pass-through income from its business operations will not be treated as investment income, but as active business income. Dowd's share of income from Hydraulics Inc. will be investment income only to the extent that the S corporation had income from investments (e.g., dividends, interest, capital gains).[11]

When a shareholder borrows money to purchase stock in an S corporation, there is a dichotomy in the handling of investment interest expense.[12] First, the shareholder is allowed to deduct the interest incurred to finance the acquisition of stock (assuming that there is investment income (i.e., dividends)), thereby treating the stock as an investment. Second, the tax treatment of the interest incurred depends on the assets and the activities of the corporation.[13] If the shareholder materially participates in S corporation activities, the interest can be deducted by the shareholder as business interest against both passive and nonpassive income.[14]

For taxpayers who have investment interest expense (e.g., they have margin accounts for stock investments), Code Sec. 1(h)(11)(D)(i) prescribes that the taxpayers have a right to make an election with respect to dividend income received in such situations. The taxpayers can elect to offset the dividend income against investment interest expense, and if there is any excess dividend income, they can use the new 5/15 percent rates to report the income. If there is excess investment interest expense (i.e., the taxpayer paid more margin interest than dividend interest received), the taxpayer can carry forward the investment interest expense to future years. If the taxpayer in the future year has capital gains, the taxpayer can exclude from taxation the carry-over investment interest expense, with any excess capital gains being subject to the new 5/15 percent rates.

¶ 703 Charitable Contributions

An S corporation does not claim charitable deductions; rather, charitable deductions are passed through as separate items to the shareholders and reported on Form 1120S, Schedules K and K-1. The shareholder deducts the contributions

---

[10] Temp. Reg. § 1.163-8T(n)(3).
[11] Code Sec. 163(d).
[12] Code Secs. 163(d)(5) and 469(e)(1).

[13] Temp. Reg. § 1.163-8T(a)(4).
[14] Code Sec. 469 and Temp. Reg. § 1.163-8T(a)(4)(i). For further discussion of the reporting of interest expense, see ¶ 911.06.

on his, her, or its tax return subject to the charitable contribution limits prescribed by Code Sec. 170.

If an S corporation makes a noncash contribution (e.g., contributes a car to charity), the S corporation must complete and attach Form 8283, "Noncash Charitable Contributions," if the contributions total more than $500 in a tax year. Further, if the value of a contributed item or group of similar items is more than $5,000, the corporation must give a copy of its Form 8283 to each shareholder, even though the amount allocated to each shareholder is $5,000 or less. Effective for contributions made after June 3, 2004, Congress amended Code Sec. 170, by prescribing at Code Sec. 170(f)(11)(F) and (G) that:

- For purposes of determining threshold values of contributions, all similar items of non-cash property donated to one or more donees shall be aggregated and treated as single property.

- Contribution reporting requirements are applied at the corporate level; however, if the S corporation fails to meet the requirements for reporting the denial for the deduction will be made at the shareholder level.

Tax Pointer 1: S corporations may make charitable contributions without regard to the 10 percent limit imposed on contributions for C corporations.[15] Since the charitable contributions are passed through to the shareholders, the adjusted gross income limitations are applied at the shareholder level.

Tax Pointer 2: S corporations are deprived of the tax benefits associated with the following two charitable contributions available to C corporations: contributions of inventory[16] and contributions of scientific equipment.[17]

Tax Pointer 3: Since charitable organizations can be S corporation shareholders,[18] S corporation shareholders can claim a charitable deduction for any S corporation stock they give to a charitable organization.

Tax Pointer 4: Since charitable contributions can be made in connection with employee stock ownership plans (ESOPs),[19] contributions to ESOPs should be considered in tax planning.[20]

Tax Pointer 5: An S corporation may make deductible charitable contributions to foreign charities.[21] The limitation of Code Sec. 170(c)(2) (providing that a contribution by a corporation to a charitable organization is qualified only if the organization exists to serve domestic interests) does not apply to S corporations.

.01 Special Rule for Contribution of S Corporate Property

Effective for contributions made in taxable years beginning after December 31, 2005, and taxable years beginning before January 1, 2014, Code Sec. 1367(a)(2) is amended to provide a tax break for S corporations contributing appreciated capital

[15] Code Sec. 170(b)(2).
[16] Code Sec. 170(e)(3)(A).
[17] Code Sec. 170(e)(4)(D).
[18] See further discussion at ¶ 203.04.
[19] See discussion at ¶ 1507.05.

[20] See example in IRS Letter Ruling 9732023 (May 12, 1997) where a contribution of qualified replacement property to a charitable remainder unitrust did not cause a recapture of the gain deferral under Code Sec. 1042(a) with respect to an ESOP.
[21] IRS Letter Ruling 9703028 (October 22, 1996).

gain property by providing that the amount of a shareholder's basis reduction in the stock of an S corporation by reason of a charitable contribution made by the corporation will be equal to the shareholder's pro rata share of the adjusted basis of the contributed property, not the fair market value. An example to illustrate the operation of the new law is set forth below:

Example 7-2: Assume an S corporation, XYZ Inc. has one individual shareholder, James Jones. XYZ has on its balance sheet appreciated AT&T stock held by the S corporation (basis $200, fair market value $500) which it donates to a charity on December 31, 2012. The XYZ gets a charitable contribution of $500 which is reflected on Jones' Form 1120S, Form K-1 at $500, but the shareholder's basis in the S corporation is reduced only $200.

Tax Pointer 1: Code Sec. 1367(a)(2)'s change is favorable in that stock basis is reduced only by basis of the contributed property, not fair market value, thus leaving a larger portion of a shareholder's remaining basis for tax free distributions, computation of gain or loss, etc.

Tax Pointer 2: Unknown is what the tax result will be if a shareholder does not have at least as much basis (stock and debt) as the shareholder's share of the charitable contribution deduction. Assume that in the above example, Jones only had $200 of basis. Under Code Sec. 1366(d) Jones would take $200 of a deduction carrying forward $300 until he has sufficient basis to take the loss.

In *Stamoulis*,[22] an overly optimistic valuation of clothing donation done by the taxpayer did not result in imposition of any penalties on disallowance. The facts of the case were rather straight forward. The taxpayer was an investment banker with Goldman Sachs in New York and her adjusted gross income for 2002 was less than $115,000. She claimed a $55,764 charitable contribution deduction on her 2002 Federal income tax return filing Forms 8283, Noncash Charitable Contributions (this amount consisted of $5,917 in cash contributions, $48,954 in property contributions, and an $893 carryover from a prior taxable year). The IRS disallowed, for lack of substantiation and other reasons, the entire charitable contribution deduction (i.e., $55,764) claimed on taxpayer's 2002 return and imposed a $2,930 accuracy-related penalty.

Taxpayer, in court, described herself as an "impulsive buyer" whose annual expenditures for clothing and shoes might be deemed by some to be rather extravagant. Furthermore, it appears that her wardrobe was constantly changing. According to the taxpayer, she routinely purchased designer clothing and shoes, wore the items once or twice, and then donated them to an upscale thrift shop in New York, New York. Despite the fact that her 2002 income was substantially less than usual, taxpayer claimed she did not to have to modify this routine during that year.

On the several Forms 8283 which the taxpayer submitted with her return, taxpayer stated that the value was "actual value." The court slashed her charitable

---

[22] TC Summ. Op. 2007-38.

deduction to $8,949.15 and imposed no penalties against her on the donation of clothing even though she attempted to rip off the government by almost $47,000. The reason why the court did not feel that a penalty should be imposed against the taxpayer was that "the determination of the fair market values of personal items is less than an exact science. In light of the circumstances presented in this case, we are not persuaded that Taxpayer's overly optimistic valuation estimates of many items of donated property constitutes 'negligence' sufficient to warrant a penalty." The court also stated that "[i]f the donation is a small amount, any written or other evidence from the donee charitable organization acknowledging receipt is generally sufficient. See Reg. § 1.170A-13(a)(2)(i)(C)..."

.02 Recapture of Tax Benefit on Donated Property Not Used for Exempt Purposes

In an effort to prevent abuse with respect to contributions of property to a charity, Code Sec. 170(e)(7) has been added to the Code for capital gain property ("appreciated property") effective for contributions made and returns filed after September 1, 2006, and with respect to the penalty, for identifications made after August 17, 2006, to provide that there is a recovery of the tax benefit for charitable contributions of tangible personal property with respect to which a fair market value deduction is claimed and which is not used for exempt purposes. Code Sec. 170(e)(7) applies to appreciated tangible personal property that is identified by the donee organization, for example on the Form 8283, as for a use related to the purpose or function constituting the donee's basis for tax exemption, and for which a deduction of more than $5,000 is claimed ("applicable property").

Code Sec. 170(e)(7) provides that if a donee organization disposes of applicable property within three years of the contribution of the property, the donor is subject to an adjustment of the tax benefit. If the disposition occurs in the tax year of the donor in which the contribution is made, the donor's deduction generally is basis and not fair market value. If the disposition occurs in a subsequent year, the donor must include as ordinary income for its taxable year in which the disposition occurs an amount equal to the excess (if any) of (i) the amount of the deduction previously claimed by the donor as a charitable contribution with respect to such property, over (ii) the donor's basis in such property at the time of the contribution.

There is no adjustment of the tax benefit if the donee organization makes a certification to the Secretary, by written statement signed under penalties of perjury by an officer of the organization. The statement must either (1) certify that the use of the property by the donee was related to the purpose or function constituting the basis for the donee's exemption, and describe how the property was used and how such use furthered such purpose or function; or (2) state the intended use of the property by the donee at the time of the contribution and certify that such use became impossible or infeasible to implement. The organization must furnish a copy of the certification to the donor (for example, as part of the Form 8282, a copy of which is supplied to the donor).

A penalty of $10,000 applies to a person that identifies applicable property as having a use that is related to a purpose or function constituting the basis for the

¶703.02

donee's exemption knowing that it is not intended for such a use. The Pension Protection Act of 2006 (PPA) Committee Reports state that other present-law penalties also may apply, such as the penalty for aiding and abetting the understatement of tax liability under Code Sec. 6701.

> **Tax Pointer 1:** To minimize the impact of Code Sec. 170(e)(7) the S corporation could impose restrictions on the donation, such as the charity cannot dispose of the property for 3 years; or if it does, that it will make the S corporation and its shareholders "whole" for any expense it incurs including additional tax if the charity disposes of the property within 3 years of the gift.

Reporting of exempt use property contributions. Code Sec. 170(e)(7) modifies the present-law information return requirements that apply upon the disposition of contributed property by a charitable organization (Form 8282, Code Sec. 6050L). The return requirement is extended to dispositions made within three years after receipt (formerly two years). The donee organization also must provide, in addition to the information already required to be provided on the return, a description of the donee's use of the property, a statement of whether use of the property was related to the purpose or function constituting the basis for the donee's exemption, and, if applicable, a certification of any such use (described above).

.03 Qualified Appraiser Defined for Charitable Purposes

Accuracy related penalties. Generally for income tax returns filed after August 17, 2006, Congress lowered Code Sec. 6662's thresholds for imposing accuracy-related penalties on a taxpayer. Under Code Sec. 6662 a substantial valuation misstatement exists when the claimed value of any property is 150 percent or more of the amount determined to be the correct value. A gross valuation misstatement occurs when the claimed value of any property is 200 percent or more of the amount determined to be the correct value.

Code Sec. 6662(g) and (h) was amended to tighten the thresholds for imposing accuracy-related penalties with respect to the estate or gift tax. Under Code Sec. 6662(g) and (h), a substantial estate or gift tax valuation misstatement exists when the claimed value of any property is 65 percent or less of the amount determined to be the correct value. A gross estate or gift tax valuation misstatement exists when the claimed value of any property is 40 percent or less of the amount determined to be the correct value. However, there is no penalty for estate and gift tax misstatements that total $5,000 or less. Further, the Joint Committee on Taxation prescribed that Code Sec. 6664(c)(2) provides that the reasonable cause exception to the accuracy-related penalty does not apply in the case of gross valuation misstatements with respect to charitable donation property.

Appraiser penalties. Congress added Code Sec. 6695A to establish a civil penalty on any person who prepares an appraisal that is to be used to support a tax position if such appraisal results in a substantial or gross valuation misstatement. The penalty is equal to the greater of $1,000 or 10 percent of the understatement of tax resulting from a substantial or gross valuation misstatement, up to a maximum of 125 percent of the gross income derived from the appraisal. Under Code Sec.

¶703.03

6695A, the penalty does not apply if the appraiser establishes that it was "more likely than not" that the appraisal was correct. Note, this new penalty is in addition to other penalties which could be imposed.

Disciplinary proceeding. Code Sec. 6695A eliminates the requirement that the Secretary assess against an appraiser the civil penalty for aiding and abetting the understatement of tax before such appraiser may be subject to disciplinary action. Thus, the Secretary is authorized to discipline appraisers after notice and hearing. Disciplinary action may include, but is not limited to, suspending or barring an appraiser from: preparing or presenting appraisals on the value of property or other assets to the IRS; appearing before the IRS for the purpose of offering opinion evidence on the value of property or other assets; and that the appraisals of an appraiser who has been disciplined have no probative effect in any administrative proceeding before the IRS.

Qualified appraisers. Code Sec. 170(f)(11)(E)(ii) defines a qualified appraiser as an individual who (1) has earned an appraisal designation from a recognized professional appraiser organization or has otherwise met minimum education and experience requirements to be determined by the IRS in regulations; (2) regularly performs appraisals for which he or she receives compensation; (3) can demonstrate verifiable education and experience in valuing the type of property for which the appraisal is being performed; (4) has not been prohibited from practicing before the IRS by the Secretary at any time during the three years preceding the conduct of the appraisal; and (5) is not excluded from being a qualified appraiser under applicable Treasury regulations.

Qualified appraisals. Code Sec. 170(f)(11)(E)(i) defines a qualified appraisal as an appraisal of property prepared by a qualified appraiser (as defined by the provision) in accordance with generally accepted appraisal standards and any regulations or other guidance prescribed by the Secretary.

Tax Pointer 2: Notice 2006-96[23] prescribes that until regulations are effective, an appraisal that meets the requirements of Notice 2006-96 will be treated as a qualified appraisal. Thus, Notice 2006-96 applies to contributions of property (other than readily valued property) by individuals, partnerships, or corporations for which a deduction of more than $5,000 is claimed on returns filed after August 17, 2006, and before the effective date of regulations to be issued. Whether an appraiser is qualified under Notice 2006-96 is based on the appraiser's qualifications as of the date the appraisal is made. Notice 2006-96 basically tracks the Pension Protection Act of 2006 (PPA) Committee Reports, however, the Notice does provide additional detail as set forth below:

Qualified appraisal defined. The Notice provides that an appraisal will be treated as a qualified appraisal if it complies with all of the requirements of Reg. § 1.170A-13(c)—the preexisting regulations—(except to the extent the regulations are inconsistent with Code Sec. 170(f)(11)), and is conducted by a qualified appraiser in accordance with generally accepted appraisal standards. For example, the appraisal is consistent with the substance and principles of the Uniform

---

[23] 2006-46 IRB.

Standards of Professional Appraisal Practice (USPAP), as developed by the Appraisal Standards Board of the Appraisal Foundation.

The Notice provides that an appraiser is treated as having earned an appraisal designation from a recognized professional appraiser organization if such a designation is awarded on the basis of demonstrated competency in valuing the type of property for which the appraisal is performed.

An appraiser is treated as having demonstrated verifiable education and experience in valuing the type of property subject to the appraisal if he makes a declaration in the appraisal that, because of his background, experience, education, and membership in professional associations, he is qualified to make appraisals of the type of property being valued.

The Notice details that an appraiser is treated as having met these minimum requirements for real property if:

- For returns filed on or before October 19, 2006, a person will be qualified as a "qualified appraiser" if the person meets the requirements under Reg. § 1.170A-13(c)(5).
- For returns filed after October 19, 2006, the person is licensed or certified for the type of property being appraised in the state in which the appraised real property is located.

Education and experience. An appraiser is treated as having met minimum education and experience requirements for property other than real property if:

- For returns filed on or before February 16, 2007 the person meets the requirements under Reg. § 1.170A-13(c)(5).
- For returns filed after February 16, 2007, the person has (i) successfully completed college or professional-level coursework that is relevant to the property being valued, (ii) obtained at least two years of experience in the trade or business of buying, selling, or valuing the type of property being valued, and (iii) fully described in the appraisal his education and experience that qualify him to value the type of property being valued.

Appraiser declaration. For returns filed after February 16, 2007, the declaration required in Reg. § 1.170A-13(c)(5)(i) must include a statement that the appraiser understands that a substantial or gross valuation misstatement resulting from an appraisal of the value of property that he or she knows, or reasonably should have known, would be used in connection with a return or claim for refund, may subject him or her to a civil penalty under Code Sec. 6695A.

.04 Contributions of Real Property Made for Conservation Purposes

To encourage contributions of appreciated real property, Code Sec. 170(b) was modified in taxable years beginning after December 31, 2005 to provide benefits to individuals and corporations. For individuals the 30-percent contribution base limitation on contributions of capital gain property does not apply to qualified conservation contributions (as defined under present law). Instead, individuals may deduct the fair market value of any qualified conservation contribution to an organization described in Code Sec. 170(b)(1)(A) to the extent of the excess of 50 percent of the contribution base over the amount of all other allowable charitable contributions. Examples of situations where conservation easements might apply would be vacation homes, business property, etc. These contributions are not taken into account in determining the amount of other allowable charitable contributions. Individuals are allowed to carryover any qualified conservation contributions that exceed the 50-percent limitation for up to 15 years. To illustrate the new rules, an example is set forth.

> *Example 7-3:* Assume Mitan Michael, an individual with a contribution base in real property of $100, makes a qualified conservation contribution of property with a fair market value of $80 and makes other charitable contributions subject to the 50-percent limitation of $60. The individual is allowed a deduction of $50 in the current taxable year for the non-conservation contributions (50 percent of the $100 contribution base) and is allowed to carryover the excess $10 for up to 5 years. No current deduction is allowed for the qualified conservation contribution, but the entire $80 qualified conservation contribution may be carried forward for up to 15 years.

Farmers and ranchers.

Individuals. Code Sec. 170(b)(iv) provides in the case of an individual who is a qualified farmer or rancher for the taxable year in which the contribution is made, a qualified conservation contribution allowable up to 100 percent of the excess of the taxpayer's contribution base over the amount of all other allowable charitable contributions. To illustrate:

> *Example 7-4:* Assume in Example 7-3 Mitan is a qualified farmer or rancher. In addition to the $50 deduction for non-conservation contributions, an additional $50 for the qualified conservation contribution is allowed and $30 may be carried forward for up to 15 years as a contribution subject to the 100-percent limitation.

Contributions by S corporations. Code Sec. 170(b)(1)(E)(iv)(I) indicates that a qualified farmer or rancher must be an individual. Notice 2007-50[24] prescribes at Q&A 5 that if a qualified conservation contribution is made by an S corporation or other pass-through entity, the determination is made at the shareholder level (or partner level as the case may be) to determine whether the shareholder (or partner) is a qualified farmer or rancher for the taxable year of the contribution.

Corporations. In the case of a corporation (other than a publicly traded corporation) that is a qualified farmer or rancher for the taxable year in which the contribution is made, Code Sec. 170(b)(2)(A) provides that any qualified conservation contribution is allowable up to 100 percent of the excess of the corporation's taxable income (as computed under Code Sec. 170(b)(2)) over the amount of all other allowable charitable contributions. Any excess may be carried forward for up to 15 years as a contribution subject to the 100-percent limitation.

Requirement that land be available for agriculture or livestock production. As an additional condition of eligibility for the 100 percent limitation, Code Sec. 170(b)(2)

---

[24] 2007-25 IRB.

¶703.04

provides that with respect to any contribution of property in agriculture or livestock production, or that is available for such production, by a qualified farmer or rancher, the qualified real property interest must include a restriction that the property remain generally available for such production. (There is no requirement as to any specific use in agriculture or farming, or necessarily that the property be used for such purposes, merely that the property remain available for such purposes.) Such additional condition does not apply to contributions made after December 31, 2005, and on or before August 17, 2006.

Definition of a qualified farmer or rancher. Code Sec. 170(b)(1)(E)(v) defines a qualified farmer or rancher as a taxpayer whose gross income from the trade of business of farming (within the meaning of Code Sec. 2032A(e)(5)) is greater than 50 percent of the taxpayer's gross income for the taxable year. Code Sec. 61(a) and Reg §1.61-3 define gross income to include all income from whatever source derived, except as otherwise provided. Gross income from the trade or business of farming is the gross income from activities described in Section 2032A(e)(5). Such activities include cultivating the soil; raising or harvesting any agricultural or horticultural commodity; raising, shearing, feeding, caring for, training, and management of animals; handling, drying, packing, grading, or storing on a farm any agricultural or horticultural commodity in its unmanufactured state but only if the owner, operator, or tenant of the farm regularly produces more than one-half of the commodity; and the planting, cultivating, caring for, or cutting of trees, or the preparation (other than milling) of trees for market.[25]

Tax Pointer 3: In *Knapp v. Comm.*,[26] a taxpayer who donated undivided interests in marshland property to a conservation group was required to adjust the charitable donation to reflect the fact that minority undivided interests in real property might sell at discounts.

.05 Fractional Interests

In general, under present law (See, e.g., *Winokur v. Commissioner*[27] a donor may take a deduction for a charitable contribution of a fractional interest in tangible personal property (such as an artwork), provided the donor satisfies the requirements for deductibility (including the requirements concerning contributions of partial interests and future interests in property), and in subsequent years make additional charitable contributions of interests in the same property. Code Sec. 408(p) applicable for contributions, bequests, and gifts made after August 17, 2006 provides that the value of a donor's charitable deduction for the initial contribution of a fractional interest in an item of tangible personal property (or collection of such items) shall be determined based upon the fair market value of the artwork at the time of the contribution of the fractional interest and considering whether the use of the artwork will be related to the donee's exempt purposes. For purposes of determining the deductible amount of each additional contribution of an interest (whether or not a fractional interest) in the same item of property prescribes that the fair market value of the item is the lesser of: (1) the value used for purposes of

---

[25] Notice 2007-50, 2007-25 IRB Q&A 4.
[26] TC Memo 1977-389.
[27] 90 TC 733 (1988).

determining the charitable deduction for the initial fractional contribution; or (2) the fair market value of the item at the time of the subsequent contribution. Code Sec. 170(o)(2) applies for income, gift, and estate tax purposes. For purposes of valuation of "fractional interests" for gift and estate tax purposes, *Elkins, Jr., Est.*[28] holds that the waiver of the right to partition is disregarded under Code Sec. 2703(a).

The following examples illustrates the basic operation of Code Sec. 170(o):

Example 7-5: Tracey, Inc., an S corporation owned by Charles Philip in year 1 makes a donation of 25% of a Modigliani painting to MOMA. The S corporation displays the painting for 9 months in its corporate offices and MOMA for 3 months. Tracey, Inc. can deduct 25% of the Modigliani's fair market value in year 1 which Charles Philip reports on his personal tax return. In year 9, when the Modigliani has tripled in value, Tracey, Inc. conveys to MOMA the remaining 75%, however Tracey, Inc.'s contribution is geared to the Year 1 value and albeit, Charles Philip's as well.

Code Sec. 170(o)(3)(A) provides for recapture of the income tax charitable deduction and gift tax charitable deduction under certain circumstances. First, if a donor makes an initial fractional contribution, then fails to contribute all of the donor's remaining interest in such property to the same donee before the earlier of 10 years from the initial fractional contribution or the donor's death, then the donee's charitable income and gift tax deductions for all previous contributions of interests in the item shall be recaptured (plus interest). If the donee of the initial contribution is no longer in existence as of such time, the donor's remaining interest may be contributed to another organization described in Code Sec. 170(c) (which describes organizations to which contributions that are deductible for income tax purposes may be made). Second, if the donee of a fractional interest in an item of tangible personal property fails to take substantial physical possession of the item during the period described above (the possession requirement) or fails to use the property for an exempt use during the period described above (the related-use requirement), then the donor's charitable income and gift tax deductions for all previous contributions of interests in the item shall be recaptured (plus interest). If, for example, an art museum described in Code Sec. 501(c)(3) that is the donee of a fractional interest in a painting includes the painting in an art exhibit sponsored by the museum, such use generally will be treated as satisfying the related-use requirement of the provision.

In any case in which there is a recapture of a deduction under Code Sec. 170(o)(3)(A), Code Sec. 170(o)(3)(B) imposes an additional tax in an amount equal to 10 percent of the amount recaptured.

Code Sec. 170(o)(1)(A) provides that no income or gift tax charitable deduction is allowed for a contribution of a fractional interest in an item of tangible personal property unless immediately before such contribution all interests in the item are owned (1) by the donor or (2) by the donor and the donee organization. The Secretary is authorized to make exceptions to this rule in cases where all

---

[28] 140 TC No. 5.

¶703.05

persons who hold an interest in the item make proportional contributions of undivided interests in their respective shares of such item to the donee organization. For example, if A owns an undivided 40 percent interest in a painting and B owns an undivided 60 percent interest in the same painting, the Secretary may provide that A may take a deduction for a charitable contribution of less than the entire interest held by A, provided that both A and B make proportional contributions of undivided fractional interests in their respective shares of the painting to the same donee organization (e.g., A contributes 50 percent of A's interest and B contributes 50 percent of B's interest).

It is intended that a contribution occurring before August 17, 2006 not be treated as an initial fractional contribution for purposes of the provision. Instead, the first fractional contribution by a taxpayer after August 17, 2006 would be considered the initial fractional contribution under the provision, regardless of whether the taxpayer had made a contribution of a fractional interest in the same item of tangible personal property prior to August 17, 2006.

> **Tax Pointer:** It is unclear if a donor who makes a fractional interest donation has to take a minority discount in terms of valuing the gift. Hopefully, Congress or the IRS will provide guidance. Note, In *Knapp v. Comm.*,[29] a taxpayer who donated undivided interests in marshland property to a conservation group was required to adjust the charitable donation to reflect the fact that minority undivided interests in real property might sell at discounts.

.06 Contributions of S Corporate Stock

If a shareholder makes a contribution during a shareholder's life of S corporate stock that has appreciated to a charity, the contribution of partnership interest rules apply; thus, an allocation is made for income tax purposes and the contribution is reduced by the percentage of the gain which would be realized as ordinary income if the assets of the S corporation had been sold. However, if the shareholder prescribes at death a charitable contribution of S corporate stock by will, then no allocation is made and the full value of the S corporate stock is treated as charitable contribution by the estate.

> **Example 7-6:** Carol Rosa owns 10% of the stock of Saradavid, Inc., an S corporation. Carol's basis in the stock is $10,000 and it is worth $100,000. Carol wants to contribute 10% of her stock, or $10,000 worth. Part of the appreciation in Carol's stock is due to appreciated inventory which has a fair market value of $350,000 and a cost basis of $250,000. Carol must reduce her charitable contribution by $1,000 (10% of $350,000 – $250,000 = $10,000 [Carol's portion of the appreciation in the stock]; 10% × $10,000 = $1,000 [charitable portion of the appreciation]; Carol must reduce her charitable contribution from $10,000 to $9,000 ($10,000 – $1,000 = $9,000). If Carol had bequeathed 10% of her stock to a charity through her will, the estate would have taken a contribution deduction for $10,000; no reduction would have been required.

---

[29] TC Memo 1977-389.

¶ 704 Taxes

.01 Foreign Taxes

An S corporation does not deduct the foreign taxes it pays; rather, foreign taxes are passed through to the shareholders[30] on Form 1120S, Schedules K and K-1. Shareholders have the choice of either deducting the foreign taxes as an itemized deduction on their Form 1040, Schedule A, or claiming a foreign tax credit on Form 1116, "Foreign Tax Credit."[31] Even though an S corporation can have worldwide activities, it cannot have a nonresident alien as a shareholder.[32]

.02 State Income Taxes

In a number of states, an S corporation may be liable for state and local taxes. The deduction for the taxes paid passes through to the shareholders and is reported on Form 1120S, Schedules K and K-1.[33]

> ***Tax Pointer:*** If an S corporation is liable for state and local franchise taxes (i.e., for state purposes, the S corporation files as if it were a C corporation), care must be exercised as to how corporate income is paid to any shareholder-employee (i.e., salary or distribution of stock). If a distribution is made in stock, it probably will be construed as a dividend for state corporate tax purposes, while if a salary is paid, there is the risk that it could be deemed unreasonable.[34]

¶ 705 Trade or Business Expenses

An S corporation can deduct trade or business expenses paid or incurred while carrying on its trade or business.[35] The expenses are deducted on page 1 of Form 1120S. Code Secs. 1363(b)(2) and 703(a)(2)(E) provide that deductions under Code Sec. 212, expenses for the production of income, cannot be taken by an S corporation.

> ***Tax Pointer 1:*** One prime reason that a shareholder-employee forms an S corporation is that should a deduction for any trade or business expense be disallowed (e.g., salary, travel expense, rental), the disallowed expense would come under only one level of taxation (i.e., at the shareholder level) rather than the two levels of taxation in a C corporation.

> ***Tax Pointer 2:*** Even when an S corporation is not engaged in a trade or business, it may be able to deduct certain expenses such as interest,[36] taxes,[37] and hobby losses up to the amount of income.[38]

---

[30] Code Sec. 1366(a)(1)(A).

[31] Foreign tax credits are subject to the rules of Code Secs. 164 and 901.

[32] Code Sec. 1361.

[33] Code Sec. 1366.

[34] For a discussion of these points, see ¶ 1301.03 and ¶ 716.01 and ¶ 716.02.

[35] Code Sec. 162.

[36] Code Sec. 163.

[37] Code Sec. 164.

[38] Code Sec. 183.

¶ 706 Fringe Benefits

.01 Partnership Benefit Rules

Partnership benefit rules apply to the deductions S corporations may claim for fringe benefits.[39] Under prior law, one key reason for electing S status was the tax-free benefits available to shareholder-employees such as medical reimbursement plans, $50,000 group term life insurance, and so on. However, when Congress adopted the Subchapter S Revision Act of 1982, it eliminated the prior fringe benefit rules and substituted the partnership benefit rules. Today, more-than-2-percent S corporation shareholders (by value or vote) in corporations must live with the fringe benefits provisions applicable to partnerships.[40]

Tax Pointer 1: If an S corporation pays any benefits for its 2 percent shareholder-employees that are not covered under the partnership rules, the S corporation will not be able to deduct them.[41] Instead, each nondeductible benefit is passed through to the shareholder-employee as "wages" for withholding tax purposes.[42] If the benefit is a medical one, the 2 percent shareholder-employee will be allowed the medical expense to the extent he or she can deduct it as an itemized deduction.[43] The S corporation shareholder can also deduct a portion of accident and health insurance premiums directly[44] without the stricter requirements for deducting medical expenses.[45]

Tax Pointer 2: An S corporation can deduct all fringe benefits for all 2-percent-or-less shareholders and all rank and file employees subject to the standards of the Employee Retirement Income Security Act of 1974 (ERISA).

Tax Pointer 3: For a more detailed discussion of fringe benefits available to shareholder-employees of S corporations, see ¶ 1103.

.02 Definition of 2 Percent Shareholders

A 2 percent shareholder is "any person who owns (or is considered as owning within the meaning of Code Sec. 318) on any day during the tax year of the S corporation more than 2 percent of the outstanding stock of such corporation or stock possessing more than 2 percent of the total combined voting power of all stock of such corporation."[46]

.03 Travel and Entertainment Expenses

Code Sec. 274 disallows deductions attributable to certain types of travel, entertainment expense, and gifts. While Code Sec. 274 and its regulations do not discuss S corporations directly, there have been a number of cases applying the statute to S corporations. In *Sutherland Lumber Southwest, Inc.*,[47] a corporation was allowed to deduct its entire costs in supplying a jet for vacation travel for employ-

---

[39] Code Sec. 1372.

[40] Code Sec. 1372(a)(1) and (2).

[41] Code Secs. 1363(b)(2) and 703(a)(2)(E).

[42] Announcement 92-16, IRB 1992-5, 53. Clarifying Rev. Rul. 91-26, 1991-1 CB 184.

[43] Code Sec. 213.

[44] Code Sec. 162(l)(5), see also discussion at ¶ 404.06.

[45] Code Sec. 213.

[46] Code Sec. 1372(b).

[47] *Sutherland Lumber Southwest, Inc.*, 114 TC 197, Dec. 53,817, aff'd per curiam CA-8, 2001-2 USTC ¶ 50,503, 255 F3d 495, acq. IRB 2002-6.

ees, with the employer not limited to the amount that an employee would recognize as fringe benefit income. Congress overruled *Sutherland Lumber Southwest, Inc.* by enacting Code Sec. 274(e)(2). For a discussion of Code Sec. 274(e)(2), see ¶ 1103.14.

.04 Contributions to an Educational IRA

Code Sec. 530(c)(1) prescribes that a corporation can make contributions to educational IRAs for a beneficiary regardless of the income of the corporation during the year of the contribution. For a discussion of this point, see ¶ 1128.

¶ 707 Retirement Plans

.01 5-Percent-or-More Shareholder-Employee-Participants

Over the years Congress has done much to establish parity in retirement plans for various entities. The Tax Equity and Fiscal Responsibility Act of 1982 (TEFRA), did much to eliminate the disparity in retirement plans for various entities, some differences remain. Code Sec. 4975 now allows S corporate shareholder-employee-participants to borrow from their retirement plans.

> **Tax Pointer:** Since the deduction of interest on loans from pension plans is limited,[48] the tax benefit of being able to borrow from retirement plans for shareholder-employee-participants may not be very great.

.02 Unreasonable Contributions

Contributions to a qualified retirement plan are deductible to the extent that the contributions together with other compensation are reasonable in amount.[49] In the case of *LaMastro*,[50] contributions to a retirement plan were disallowed when an S corporation was formed 14 days before the end of the S corporation's tax year. The sole shareholder-employee took a salary, and the S corporation established a defined benefit plan for the sole shareholder-employee that created a loss for the tax year. The Tax Court ruled the contribution to the plan was unreasonable.

.03 Tax Planning with Retirement Plan Assets

As with retirement plans for C corporations, partnerships, and so on, there are tax-planning possibilities for S corporation retirement plans. Because retirement plans have the potential for accumulating vast assets, they should be considered in any tax planning. Due to the depth of the law concerning retirement plans, it is beyond the scope of this book to offer a detailed discussion of retirement plans. Accordingly, the reader is directed to consult Code Sec. 401 et. seq. and its regulations. However, a brief discussion of some points in the law is set forth.

One area to explore is prohibited transaction exemptions (PTEs). In PTE 85-68, a corporation was able to factor its secured accounts receivables with its retirement plan, and in PTE 79-10, a corporation that owned land and a building, instead of making only a regular cash contribution, was able to contribute the land

[48] Code Sec. 163(h)(1).
[49] Reg. § 1.404(a)-1(b).

[50] *A. LaMastro,* 72 TC 377, Dec. 36,093. See also *A.J. Bianchi,* 66 TC 324, Dec. 33,833. Aff'd CA-2, 77-1 USTC ¶ 9270, 553 F2d 93.

and building, leasing the building back. By doing this, the corporation accomplished the following:

- Any future appreciation arising from the land and building passed to the retirement plan.

- If the building was fully depreciated, the corporation now had a rental deduction that was to be paid to a related entity.

- On the negative side, the retirement plan assets are tied somewhat to the employer's financial condition (i.e., if the employer cannot pay the rent, the plan will have to evict the employer and obtain a new tenant). Also, real estate, by definition, is illiquid (i.e., if the land and building depreciate in value rather than appreciate, the retirement plan made a bad investment, etc.).

Tax Pointer 1: For retirement plans to exist and grow, they need contributions based on salary. If shareholder-employees take the bulk of their earnings by distribution rather than salary to save on employment taxes, then the contributions to their retirement plan will be limited. Retirement contributions are limited to a proportion of an employee's salary. Salary also is a factor in the Code Sec. 199 deduction. For a discussion of Code Sec. 199, see ¶ 722.

Tax Pointer 2: If a participant in an S corporation retirement plan has tax problems with the IRS, the IRS can levy against the retirement plan to collect the unpaid taxes.[51] Care should be exercised in retirement plans if a participant has tax problems or foresees them in the future.

Tax Pointer 3: In *Watson v. Proctor,*[52] creditors were allowed to attack a retirement plan established by a taxpayer because it had no common-law employees, and thus was not protected by ERISA. The Bankruptcy Abuse Prevention and Consumer Protection Act of 2005 (BPACP), effective October 17, 2005, will now protect this type of plan from attack by creditors. For a fuller discussion of this topic, see ¶ 1103.15.

.04 Individual Retirement Accounts (IRAs)

An individual who receives a salary can use the salary to establish an IRA.[53] Because distributions and pass-through items from an S corporation are not self-employment income,[54] a shareholder-employee cannot use his or her distributive share of S corporation income to establish the amount he or she is allowed to contribute to an IRA. However, if the S corporation shareholder is a participant in a retirement plan, the shareholder's share of income from an S corporation is included in the computation of adjusted gross income to establish the limitations for contributions.[55] Likewise, the share of income from an S corporation is counted to determine the $100,000 income limitation for Roth IRAs.

---

[51] Reg. § 1.401(a)-13.

[52] 161 F.3d 593 (9th Cir. 1998).

[53] Code Sec. 219 (assuming that the individual is not disqualified from establishing an IRA under Code Secs. 401 and 219).

[54] *P.B. Ding,* 74 TCM 708, Dec. 52,269(M), TC Memo. 1997-435. Aff'd, CA-9, 2000-1 USTC ¶ 50,137, 200 F3d 587 (S corporation pass-through of income deemed not self-employment income).

[55] Code Sec. 219.

Tax Pointer: Care must be exercised with respect to the establishment of IRAs since IRA assets, other than "rollovers," are not exempt from attack by creditors in a bankruptcy. For a discussion of the bankruptcy provisions, see ¶ 1103.15.

.05 Employee Stock Ownership Plans (ESOPs)

Since ESOPs are permitted to be shareholders in an S corporation, they offer valuable planning opportunities.[56] IRS Private Letter Rulings illustrating the planning opportunities are: IRS Letter Ruling 9846005 (August 6, 1998) where an ESOP assisted a taxpayer in achieving a tax-free diversification of assets for a family with a limited partnership; and IRS Letter Rulings 9801053-055 (October 8, 1997) where stock of a newly formed corporation acquired a building partly leased to an ESOP sponsor, and the building was deemed qualified replacement property for stock the ESOP sponsor sold to the ESOP.

.06 Code Sec. 401(k) Plans

An S corporation can establish a Code Sec. 401(k) plan for their employees. In a Code Sec. 401(k) plan, a deferral arrangement is established whereby the participating employee has the option of receiving a portion of their compensation in cash or making a pre-tax contribution to the plan. It is beyond the scope of this book to discuss in detail Code Sec 401(k) plans or retirement plans in general, except to note the following: An example of a Code Sec. 401(k) plan would be a Savings Incentive Match Plan for Employees (a SIMPLE) plan established under Code Sec. 401(k)(11). In Code Sec. 401(k) plans there are a number of basic requirements. For instance, the plan must: not require that an employee complete more than one (1) year of service to participate. Another is that an employee is fully vested at all times in their elective contributions. Code Sec. 402A(c)(4)(B) provides that a Code Sec 401(k) plan can include a Roth 401(k) plan. Code Sec. 414(x) provides that effective for plan years beginning after Januay 1, 2010 small employers (i.e., those with 500 employees or less) can establish a combined defined benefit plan and a Code Sec. 401(k) plan.

In an effort to encourage individuals to provide for their retirement, Congress has provided that Code Sec. 401(k) plans can provide that elective contributions will be made for a participant unless he or she affirmatively elects otherwise. Plans with these features are often referred to as "automatic enrollment" or "negative election" plans. Before Congress changed the law, there were no safe-harbor rules that enabled specially defined automatic enrollment plans to meet the actual contribution percentage (ACP) nondiscrimination test for matching contributions or the actual deferral percentage (ADP) nondiscrimination test for elective contributions.

ADP and ACP Requirements. Code Sec. 401(k)(13)(A) now provides that an automatic deferral arrangement satisfies the ADP and ACP requirements if there is an automatic deferral where the employees that are eligible to participate in the enrollment arrangement are treated as having elected to have the employer make

---

[56] See Chapter 15 detailing how ESOPs work and the planning opportunities presented with them.

elective contributions equal to a qualified percentage of compensation. Code Sec. 401(k)(13)(B) and (C) prescribe that the qualified percentage must be at least three percent of compensation, with the minimum rising by one percent for each successive year the deemed election applies to the participant, up to six percent. However, the percentage cannot exceed 10 percent.

In the case of matching contributions under the Code Sec. 401(k) plan, Code Sec. 401(k)(13)(D)(i) prescribes that the requirement is satisfied if the employer makes matching contributions on behalf of each employee who is not a highly compensated employee of 100 percent of elective deferrals up to one percent of compensation, plus 50 percent of elective deferral between one percent and up to six percent of compensation An alternative is allowed if the employer is required to make contributions to a defined contribution plan of at least three percent of compensation of behalf of each non-highly compensated employee.

Code Sec. 416(g)(4)(H) provides an exception to the top-heavy rules for these new automatic arrangements. In addition, under a vesting requirement, participants who have completed at least two years of service must be 100 percent vested with respect to matching or other employer contributions to their accounts under these arrangements.

.07 Diversification Requirements for Defined Contribution Plans

Effective generally for plan years beginning after December 31, 2006, Code Sec. 401(a)(35) was added to provide that in order to satisfy the plan qualification requirements and the vesting requirements of ERISA, certain defined contribution plans are required to provide diversification rights with respect to amounts invested in employer securities. Such a plan is required to permit applicable individuals to direct that the portion of the individual's account held in employer securities be invested in alternative investments. An applicable individual includes: (1) any plan participant; and (2) any beneficiary who has an account under the plan with respect to which the beneficiary is entitled to exercise the rights of a participant. The time when the diversification requirements apply depends on the type of contributions invested in employer securities.

Plans subject to requirements. The diversification requirements generally apply to an "applicable defined contribution plan," (i.e., "applicable individual account plan") which means a defined contribution plan holding publicly-traded employer securities (i.e., securities issued by the employer or a member of the employer's controlled group of corporations (For this purpose, "controlled group of corporations" has the same meaning as under Code Sec. 1563(a), except that, in application, 50 percent is substituted for 80 percent.) that are readily tradable on an established securities market).

.08 Rollovers of Retirement Accounts by Non-Spouse Beneficiaries

Code Sec. 402(c)(11) prescribes that effective for distributions after December 31, 2006, benefits of a beneficiary other than a surviving spouse may be transferred directly to an IRA by means of a trustee-to-trustee transfer. The IRA is treated as an inherited IRA of the nonspouse beneficiary thereby allowing the beneficiary to use his or her life expectancy for distributions from the IRA with payments to start the

¶707.08

year after the decedent's death. The provision applies to amounts payable to a beneficiary under a qualified retirement plan, Code Sec. 401(k), governmental Code Sec. 457 plan, or a tax-sheltered annuity. To the extent provided by the Secretary, the provision applies to benefits payable to a trust maintained for a designated beneficiary to the same extent it applies to the beneficiary.

Tax Pointer 1: Code Sec. 402(c)(11) will no longer require life partners, children, etc. to take lump sum payments or over a 5 year period on the death of the decedent.

Tax Pointer 2: Code Sec. 402(c)(11) applies only to employer-provided securities, not to existing IRAs.

Notice 2007-7[57] has provided some clarification with respect to the operation of this Code provision, to wit:

Nonspousal rollovers optional. A qualified plan does not have to provide nonspousal rollovers; they are optional. (Q&A 14 & 15). Accordingly, the distribution is not subject to the direct rollover requirements of Code Sec. 401(a)(31), the notice requirements of Code Sec. 402(f), or the mandatory withholding requirements of Code Sec. 3405(c). Q&A 14 prescribes that if the plan offers direct rollovers to nonspouse beneficiaries of some, but not all, participants, the rollovers must be offered on a nondiscriminatory basis because pursuant to the nondiscrimination rules of Code Sec. 401(a)(4), the opportunity to make a direct rollover is a benefit, right, or feature that is subject.

Direct rollovers of the IRA. Q&A 13 states that the IRA must be established in a manner that identifies it as an IRA with respect to a deceased individual and also identifies the deceased individual and the beneficiary, for example, "Tom Smith as beneficiary of John Smith."

Qualified plan Required Mandatory Distributions (RMD) is not eligible for rollover. Q&A 17 and 18 prescribe that an RMD which the decedent should have taken from the qualified plan under Code Sec. 401(a)(9) but did not, is not eligible for a rollover. The determination of what that qualified plan RMD is depends on whether the plan account owner died before, or on or after, his required beginning date (RBD). Note, Q&A 1 states that the RBD for a participant who isn't a 5% company owner is April first of the calendar year following the later of the year in which he or she attains age 70½ or the year in which he or she retires. A 5% company owner's RBD is April first of the year following the year in which he or she attains age 70½. IRS in its Special Edition Newsletter dated February 13, 2007 qualified the operation of this special rule by stating that the general rule of Q&A 19 (discussed below) is not intended to override this special rule.

Q&A 17(c)(2) describes a special rule that is an exception to the general rule in Q&A 19 (discussed below). If, under a plan, the 5-year rule applies for determining required minimum distributions, a nonspouse designated beneficiary may,

---

[57] 2007-5 IRB as amplified by Notice 2009-82, 2009-41 IRB 491.

¶707.08

nevertheless, treat the plan as using the life expectancy rule provided the rollover into the IRA is made prior to the end of the year following the year of the participant's death. Thus, despite a plan provision for the 5-year rule, the nonspouse designated beneficiary is permitted to treat the plan as using the life expectancy rule both for determining the amount eligible for rollover and for determining the required minimum distributions under the IRA, but only if the rollover is made prior to the end of the year following the year of the participant's death. For example, if a participant in a Code Sec. 401(k) plan dies in 2007 before his required beginning date and under the plan the 5-year rule applies for determining required minimum distributions, the participant's nonspouse designated beneficiary is permitted to roll over the deceased participant's entire account balance into an IRA in 2007 and take required minimum distributions from the IRA under the life expectancy rule. If the account balance is rolled over in 2008, the amount eligible for rollover must be reduced by the amount of the required minimum distribution for 2008, determined using the life expectancy rule. After 2008, the nonspouse designated beneficiary may still roll over funds from the Code Sec. 401(k) plan, but would have to take required minimum distributions from the IRA under the 5-year rule. No amount can be rolled over after 2011.

Post rollover RMDs from recipient IRA. Q&A 19 describes the general rule for determining required minimum distributions in the case of a nonspouse beneficiary rollover. It provides that the rules for determining required minimum distributions under a plan with respect to a nonspouse designated beneficiary also apply to an IRA. If a participant dies before his or her required beginning date, the required minimum distributions for purposes of determining the amount eligible for rollover with respect to a nonspouse designated beneficiary are determined under either the 5-year rule described in Code Sec. 401(a)(9)(B)(ii) or the life expectancy rule described in Code Sec. 401(a)(9)(B)(iii).

.09 Direct Rollovers from Eligible Retirement Plans to Roth IRAs

Code Sec. 408A(e) has been amended effective for distributions made after December 31, 2007 to allow distributions from tax-qualified retirement plans, tax-sheltered annuities, and governmental 457 plans to be rolled over directly trustee to trustee from such plan into a Roth IRA, subject to the present law rules that apply to rollovers from a traditional IRA into a Roth IRA. For example, a rollover from a tax-qualified retirement plan into a Roth IRA is includible in gross income (except to the extent it represents a return of after-tax contributions), and the 10-percent early distribution tax does not apply. Similarly, an individual with AGI of $100,000 or more could not roll over amounts from a tax-qualified retirement plan directly into a Roth IRA.

¶ 708 Organizational Expenses and Start-up Expenses

After October 22, 2004, start-up and organizational expenses amortized under Code Sec. 248 will be deductible by an S corporation in the taxable year when it begins business. Start-up and organizational expenses that are incurred on or before October 22, 2004 will continue to be eligible to be amortized pursuant to Code Sec. 248 over a period not exceeding sixty months. The S corporation will be able to deduct the lesser of the organizational expenses (of the business) or $5,000, reduced (but not below zero) by the amount of the organizational expenses that exceed $50,000. The remaining organizational expenses can be amortized ratably over 180 months, beginning with the month that the business begins.

.01 Organizational Expenses

Organizational expenses include fees for legal services such as organizing the corporation, drafting the bylaws, and the like, plus the state filing fees for forming the corporation. Additionally, fees for accounting services relative to the organization can be amortized.[58] However, commissions and other expenses incurred in selling and issuing the capital stock of a corporation cannot be deducted by the corporation—they merely reduce the amount of capital raised through the sale of stock.[59] A name change by a corporation was also classified as a non-deductible capital expenditure.[60]

.02 Start-up Expenditures

Code Sec. 195 prescribes that taxpayers for tax years beginning in 2010, the S corporation can elect to deduct, if it is engaged in a trade or business, up to $10,000 of start up expenses in the year the trade or business begins. If the start up expenditures are in excess of $10,000, then the $10,000 amount is reduced by the amount that the start up expenses exceed $60,000 but not below zero (for years beginning before January 1, 2010 and after December 31, 2010, the amount of start-up expenses of a trade or business that may be deducted by a taxpayer is increased from $5,000 with the threshold amount for reducing the deduction being $50,000). The remainder of any start-up expenditures must be amortized ratably over the 180-month period beginning with the month in which the active trade or business begins.

Code Sec. 195(c) defines start-up expenses as those amounts paid or incurred for: (1) investigating the creation or acquisition of an active trade or business, (2) creating an active trade or business, or (3) activities engaged in for profit and for the production of income before the day on which the active trade or business begins, in anticipation of the activities becoming an active trade or business. The expenditure must be one which would have been allowable as a deduction in the tax year paid or incurred if it were paid or incurred in connection with the operation of an existing active trade or business in the same field.

Field Service Advice 789 sets forth common types of expenses which would qualify as start-up expenses, namely: advertising costs; salaries and wages paid to employees and their instructors for training; travel and related expenses incurred in the course of finding potential distributors, suppliers and customers; and salaries and fees paid to executives and consultants, as well as for professional services. Code Sec. 195(c) details that expenditures attributable to an investment, but not to an anticipated trade or business, are not amortizable. Care must be practiced in utilizing Code Sec. 195's expensing provision. For instance, in IRS Letter Ruling

---

[58] Code Sec. 248.
[59] Reg. § 1.248-1(b)(3)(i).

[60] *U.S. General Banc Shares Corp.*, 388 F2d 184 (8th Cir. 1968).

¶708.01

9331001 (April 23, 1993), it was ruled that the company's first boutique was a new business, not the expansion of an existing one. Accordingly, Code Sec. 195 applied. When it added additional boutiques, they were classified as the expansion of an existing business, not a new one.

¶ 709 Election to Expense Recovery Property (Code Sec. 179)

Shareholders of an S corporation may expense a portion of tangible personal property each year. The same is true for partnerships. The Code Sec. 179(d)(8) dollar limitation for 2012 and 2013 is $500,000 plus inflation adjustment, and it applies at both the shareholder and corporation level. For 2012 and later years, the maximum deduction is $125,000 with no inflation adjustment. Because Code Sec. 179 is used to stimulate the economy (i.e., the amount goes up or down, depending on Congress's whim), shareholders should follow Congress closely to determine when investments should be made.

Code Sec. 179(f)(3) for the years 2012 and 2013 expands the definition of property qualifying for expensing to include certain real property—specifically, qualified leasehold improvement property, qualified restaurant property, and qualified retail improvement property. The maximum amount with respect to real property that may be expensed is $250,000.[61] The example set forth below illustrates the operation of this provision.

> *Example 7-7:* Assume that during 2012, a company's only asset purchases are Code Sec. 179-eligible equipment costing $100,000 and qualifying leasehold improvements costing $350,000. Assuming the company has no other asset purchases during 2012, and is not subject to the taxable income limitation, the maximum Code Sec. 179 deduction the company can claim for 2012 is $350,000 ($100,000 with respect to the equipment and $250,000 with respect to the qualifying leasehold improvements).

An S corporation makes an election to expense an asset under Code Sec. 179.[62] When the S corporation elects to expense the asset under Code Sec. 179, the corporation must reduce the basis of the property by the amount expensed.[63] Further, for 2012 through 2013, if more than $2,000,000 plus inflation adjustment of qualifying property is placed in service during the tax year, Code Sec. 179(b)(2) prescribes that the expense deduction is reduced dollar for dollar. Code Sec. 179(b)(3) provides that the expensed amount may not exceed the taxable income from the S corporation's (or the shareholder's) active trade or business. Further, Code Sec. 179(b)(3) provides that the expensed amount may not exceed the taxable income from the taxpayer's trade or business. Any amount disallowed as a result of the taxable income limitations is carried forward. The regulations under

---

[61] For purposes of the provision, qualified leasehold improvement property has the meaning given such term under Code Sec. 168(e)(6), qualified restaurant property has the meaning given such term under Code Sec. 168(e)(7) (and includes a building described in Code Sec. 168(e)(7)(A)(i) that is placed in service after December 31, 2009 and before January 1, 2012), and qualified retail improvement property has the meaning given such term under Code Sec. 168(e)(8) (without regard to Code Sec. 168(e)(8)(E)).

[62] Code Sec. 1363(c)(1), Code Sec. 179, and Proposed Reg. § 1.179-1(h).

[63] Reg. § 1.179-1(f)(2). Note, however, that because a trust or estate shareholder cannot deduct the expense per Reg. § 1.179-1(f)(3), the S corporation does not reduce the basis for the expense allocated to the trust or estate.

Code Sec. 179 indicate that this taxable income limitation is applied at *both* the S corporation and the shareholder level.[64] Thus, the S corporation may pass through to the shareholders as a deduction only that much of the amount elected to be expensed as does not exceed its trade or business income. Moreover, each shareholder may claim as a deduction on his or her tax return only so much of the amount(s) expensed under Code Sec. 179 as does not exceed his or her income from the active conduct of one or more trades or businesses (including salaries earned as an employee). Any amounts expensed under Code Sec. 179 that are not currently deductible due to the income limitations may be carried forward indefinitely.[65] However, deductibility of the expenses carried forward depends on the whims of Congress in terms of what amounts can be expensed. Thus, Congress in future years could prescribe that the Code Sec. 179 deduction is limited to $25,000 per year.

> *Example 7-8:* Swift Inc., an S corporation, purchased $21,000 of new 10-year MACRS recovery property in 2012. Swift Inc. has one shareholder, Ross Unger. Swift has $25,000 of taxable income from its trade or business. Swift elects to expense $19,000 of the assets under Code Sec. 179. Unger will have a $19,000 expense deduction on his tax return.

> *Example 7-9:* Assume the same facts as in Example 7-8, except that Swift Inc. only had $6,000 of income. Unger would only be able to take a $6,000 Code Sec. 179 deduction on his tax return.

> *Example 7-10:* Wyman Inc., an S corporation, is composed of two equal shareholders, Beth Carter and Austin Hart. Carter and Hart are both married and file joint returns with their respective spouses. Wyman Inc., in 2012, elects to expense under Code Sec. 179 the $19,000 cost of new 10-year MACRS recovery property it purchased. Carter and Hart, in addition to being shareholders of Wyman Inc., are each engaged as sole proprietors in separate businesses. Carter, in her proprietorship, acquires a qualifying asset for $25,000, and Hart acquires a qualifying asset in his proprietorship for $30,000. Accordingly, Carter on her tax return will report $24,000 of Code Sec. 179 expense deductions ($9,500 [½ × $19,000] from the S corporation and $25,000 from the proprietorship). Likewise, Hart will have a $24,000 expense deduction ($9,500 [½ × $19,000] from the S corporation and $30,000 from his proprietorship).

When the S corporation makes the election under Code Sec. 179, it must reduce the basis of the expensed property to "reflect the amount of section 179 expense elected by the [S corporation]. This reduction must be made for the tax year for which the election is made even if the section 179 expense amount, or a portion thereof, must be carried forward by the [S corporation]."[66]

> *Example 7-11:* Bluebaker Inc., a calendar-year S corporation, owns and operates a restaurant business. During 2012, Bluebaker purchased and placed in service two items of Code Sec. 179 property—a cash register costing $4,000

---

[64] Reg. § 1.179-2(c)(3).
[65] Code Sec. 179(b)(3)(B).
[66] Reg. § 1.179-3(g)(2).

¶709

and office furniture costing $6,000. Bluebaker elects to expense under Code Sec. 179(c) the full cost of the cash register and office furniture. For 2012, Bluebaker has $6,000 of taxable income derived from the active conduct of its restaurant business. Therefore, Bluebaker may deduct only $6,000 of Code Sec. 179 expenses at the S corporation level.

Reg. § 1.179-2(c)(6)(iv) prescribes that wages, salaries, tips and other compensation earned by employees are counted to determine Code Sec. 179's income limit for deductibility. An example will illustrate:

> *Example 7-12:* Barbara is a shareholder employee in an S corporation which broke even in 2012, but paid her a salary of $50,000 for the year. Barbara also operates a kitchen design business as a single person LLC and has purchased some design equipment costing $2,500. However, Barbara's LLC only generated $1,000 of income for the year 2012. Barbara can fully expense the design equipment utilizing Code Sec. 179 as follows: $1,000 from her LLC and $1,500 of her wages.

If an S corporation has an estate and/or a trust for a shareholder, Reg. § 1.179-1(f)(3) provides that the trust or estate may not deduct its allocable share of the Code Sec. 179 expense elected by the S corporation and the S corporation's basis in Code Sec. 179 property shall not be reduced to reflect any portion of the Code Sec. 179 expense that is allocable to the trust or estate. However, the S corporation may claim a depreciation deduction under Code Sec. 168 or a Code Sec. 38 credit (if available) with respect to any depreciable basis resulting from the trust or estate's inability to claim its allocable portion of the Code Sec. 179 expense. Thus, if an S corporation has an estate or trust as shareholder, careful planning must be done to determine if Code Sec. 179's election should be made when the S corporation acquires Code Sec. 179 assets.

.01 Grantor Trusts

While there is no statutory authority, Internal Revenue Service pronouncement, regulation, case, etc., Rev. Rul. 85-13[67] states that if a grantor is treated as the owner of the entire trust, the grantor is the owner of trust's assets for tax purposes. Applying this holding to Code Sec. 179, logic would dictate that the grantor in a grantor trust is a "shareholder;" thus, the grantor should be entitled to the trust's proportionate share of any Code Sec. 179 expensing deduction.

> *Tax Pointer 1:* If an S corporate shareholder plans to dispose of his or her stock where gain or loss is not recognized in whole or in part (including transfers of an S corporate interest at death) and the shareholder has not been able to fully utilize his or her Code Sec. 179 deduction due to Code Sec. 179's income limitation, Reg. § 1.179-3(h)(2) states that immediately before the transfer of the shareholder's stock in the S corporation, the shareholder's basis is increased by the amount of the shareholder's outstanding carryover of disallowed deduction with respect to his or her S corporate interest.

---

[67] 1985-1 CB 184.

Tax Pointer 2: Reg. § 1.179-2(b)(4) states that Code Sec. 179's dollar limitation (Code Sec. 179(b)(1)'s current limit is $500,000) applies to the S corporation as well as to each S corporate shareholder. In applying the dollar limitation to a taxpayer that is a S corporate shareholder in one or more S corporations, the S corporate shareholder's share of Code Sec. 179 expenses allocated to the S corporate shareholder from each S corporation is aggregated with any non-S corporation Code Sec. 179 expenses of the taxpayer for the taxable year. So, assume that a calendar year S corporation owned equally by two individual shareholders, Mike and Laurie, purchases $800,000 of Code Sec. 179 property on January 1, 2012 and elects to expense all of it. On December 31, 2012, Mike individually for his sole proprietorship purchases $200,000 of Code Sec. 179 property. Mike cannot take a Code Sec. 179 deduction of $600,000 ($400,000 from the passthrough of 50% of the S corporation's Code Sec. 179 deduction and $200,000 from his proprietorship) on his 2012 Form 1040; rather, he can only take under Code Sec. 179(b)(1) a maximum of $500,000. Accordingly, $100,000 of a Code Sec. 179 deduction is wasted due to bad timing of purchases (½ × $800,000 + $200,000 = $600,000; $600,000 – $500,000 [Code Sec. 179's limitation of $500,000] = $100,000 to be carried over).

Tax Pointer 3: Code Sec. 179(d)(6) prescribes that members of a controlled group cannot expense totally more than $500,000 in a taxable year. Code Sec. 179(d)(7) states that for purposes of determining a control group for Code Sec. 179 purposes, the group is determined using a "more than 50%" ownership test rather than "at least an 80%" one. So, if an S corporation owns more than 50% of the stock of another corporation, then care must be practiced so as not to run afoul of Code Sec. 179(b)(1)'s dollar limitation.

¶ 710 At-Risk Loss Limitations

In an effort to curb the use of nonrecourse debt to finance tax-motivated transactions (i.e., where a creditor of an S corporation does not look to hold the shareholder(s) liable for the debt on default), Congress limited the deductibility of losses generated by the following activities:[68]

(A) holding, producing, or distributing motion picture films or videotapes;

(B) farming (as defined in Code Sec. 464(e));

(C) leasing any Code Sec. 1245 property (as defined in Code Sec. 1245(a)(3));

(D) exploring for, or exploiting, oil and gas resources; or

(E) exploring for, or exploiting, geothermal deposits (as defined in Code Sec. 613 (e)(2)) as a trade or business or for the production of income.

Tax Pointer 1: The at-risk loss limitations do not apply to C corporations.[69] Consequently, Code Sec. 465 should be consulted before deciding between an S corporation and a C corporation.

---

[68] Code Sec. 465(c)(1).   [69] Code Sec. 465(c)(7).

A shareholder can only deduct losses from the above activities to the extent of the amount that they have "at risk" as defined by Code Sec. 465(b)[70] with a carryover permitted for later tax years for the portion of the deduction that exceeds the amount at risk.

Code Sec. 465's "at-risk" rules are similar in operation to Code Sec. 469's passive loss rules, in that they restrict an S corporation shareholder in deduction of losses after the fact. In other words, Code Sec. 465 imposes a two-step process for a shareholder to determine the deductibility of a loss passed through from an S corporation. First, losses, regardless of origin, are charged against a shareholder's basis in S corporation stock and debt; second, Code Sec. 465 limits the losses passing through the first step to the shareholder's "amount at risk" with regard to the investment in the S corporation.

> **Example 7-13:** Diane Mott is the sole shareholder of Semco Inc., an S corporation. On January 1, 2010, Mott acquired her stock in Semco Inc. for $100 cash and $1,000 from a nonpermitted Code Sec. 465 lender. In its first tax year, Semco Inc.'s operations resulted in a $1,000 net loss, all of which passes through to Mott. Mott's basis in her Semco Inc. stock is reduced from $1,100 to $100; however, on her personal tax return, she can deduct only $100 of the loss, the amount she personally stands to lose if her investment in Semco Inc. becomes worthless.[71]

Van Wyk[72] offers a variation of Example 7-13. In *Van Wyk*, the taxpayer and his brother-in-law each owned 50 percent of the stock of an S corporation engaged in farming. In 1991, the taxpayer and his wife borrowed $700,000 from his brother-in-law and his wife in exchange for a promissory note bearing 10.5 percent annual interest, with the note being unsecured. The taxpayer used the majority of the funds for a loan to the corporation. The Court held, pursuant to Code Sec. 465(b)(3), that the taxpayer was not at risk with respect to this loan for purposes of deducting losses from the S corporation because the Code provision provides: "Amounts borrowed shall not be considered to be at risk with respect to an activity if such amounts are borrowed from any person who has an interest in such activity, or from a related person to a person (other than the taxpayer) having such an interest." Notwithstanding, the Court refused to impose a penalty under Code Sec. 6662, citing Code Sec. 6664(c)(1), which excuses imposition of a penalty where a taxpayer acted in good faith. The Court, in not sustaining the penalty, held that the complexity of Code Sec. 465 and the lack of express guidance in the regulations led the taxpayers to what the Court called "an honest mistake of law for which it is improper to penalize them."

> **Tax Pointer 2:** Van Wyk could have avoided this Code Sec. 465 disallow-ance by borrowing the $700,000 from a bank directly and having his brother-in-law guarantee the loan.

---

[70] Code Sec. 465(a)(1).

[71] For a discussion of the computation of basis, see ¶ 902.

[72] *L.W. Van Wyk*, 113 TC 441, Dec. 53,664.

.01 Deduction of Suspended Code Sec. 465 Losses on Conversion of a C Corporation to an S Corporation

If a C corporation has suspended Code Sec. 465 losses on conversion to S status, they can be lost forever. If there is a recognition event in the S corporation operations which would allow the recognition of suspended losses, they might be deductible utilizing the reasoning of *St. Charles Investment Co.*[73] discussed at ¶ 404.13.

¶ 711 Hobby Losses

If an S corporation is found not to be engaged in a profit-making activity, it will be permitted only limited deductions for the activity's expenses.[74] In the *Bingo* case,[75] an S corporation shareholder could not deduct hobby losses from horse-racing activities because there was no profit motive.

>   *Tax Pointer 1:* Hobby loss disallowance is not a problem for an S corporation during the first two years of its life since an activity will not be considered a hobby loss if the activity has produced a profit in three out of five consecutive years (horse activities must produce a profit in two out of seven years).[76]

In *Payne,*[77] an individual taxpayer was denied deductions related to a tax consultation service operated by the taxpayer when activity generally decreased and the taxpayer did not try to replace or obtain new clients. Foreseeably, this case would apply to S corporations involving professionals (lawyers, architects, etc.).

>   *Tax Pointer 2:* In *Osteen,*[78] the court held that the substantial understatement penalty (20 percent of the tax due) cannot be imposed automatically in the case of hobby losses; rather, a hearing must be conducted to determine if the taxpayer legitimately thought the business was a real one, not a hobby, notwithstanding how the court construes the situation.

>   *Tax Pointer 3:* C corporations are not subject to the hobby loss rules.[79] So an S corporation, which could be classified as a hobby loss situation under Code Sec. 183, could incur losses for its first two years of life and then convert to C status, thereby maximizing the situation.

¶ 712 Losses and Expenses Incurred in Transactions with Shareholders

The deduction of certain losses may be disallowed or suspended,[80] and the deduction of certain expenses may be suspended.[81] Initially the loss and/or ex-

---

[73] *St. Charles Investment Co.*, CA-10, 2000-2 USTC ¶ 50,840, 232 F3d 773.

[74] Code Sec. 183.

[75] *W. Bingo,* 61 TCM 2782, Dec. 47,384(M), TC Memo. 1991-248. Aff'd, CA-11 (unpublished opinion 2/25/93).

[76] Code Sec. 183(d).

[77] *A.H. Payne,* 51 TCM 579, Dec. 42,914(M), TC Memo. 1986-93. But see, *Rabinowitz*, TC Memo 2005-188, where an S corporation which operated at a loss for 12

consecutive years was classified as an "active business" and not a "hobby" thereby allowing the shareholders to deduct the losses in full subject to their basis limitations.

[78] *H.E. Osteen,* 66 TCM 1237, Dec. 49,388(M), TC Memo. 1993-519. Aff'd and rev'd, CA-11, 95-2 USTC ¶ 50,465, 62 F3d 356.

[79] Code Sec. 183(a).

[80] Code Sec. 267(a)(1) and (f)(2).

[81] Code Sec. 267(a)(2).

pense is charged to a shareholder's basis on the S corporation books, then after the fact, the shareholder determines if it can be deducted on his or her return.

The Internal Revenue Service has various provisions under the Internal Revenue Code to strike down transactions between an S corporation and its shareholders. For instance, in *Wysong v. Commissioner*,[82] the court struck down under Code Sec. 162 a situation where taxpayers were trying to shift income from an S corporation to a sister C corporation by means of unreasonably high rents. As discussed at ¶ 911.05, Code Sec. 469 prevents passive income to be generated with related party rentals. Code Sec. 482 deals with transactions among related parties involving other situations where income, expenses, etc. are trying to be shifted from one taxpayer to another. Code Sec. 704(e) discussed at ¶ 1119.03 et seq. details the family S corporation rules to prevent S corporation shareholders from performing services or furnishing capital without receiving reasonable compensation. The safest bet for transactions between related parties is to do them at fair market value or pursuant to the reasonable party standard. Further, there must be a business purpose for the transaction between the S corporation and its shareholders. The business purpose concept was clearly illustrated in *Chin v. Commissioner*.[83] In *Chin*, a surgeon's S corporation engaged in a medical practice, paid rent to the shareholder's mother for use of her home. However, the surgeon failed to acquire business permits or licenses, did not maintain any type of local telephone listing, did not have any local hospital privileges, and was not a member of the local medical society. Moreover, the taxpayer failed to explain how he could have conducted his medical practice at the property while failing to generate any revenue. The court disallowed the deduction under Code Sec. 162.

.01 Losses

Disallowance of losses. An otherwise deductible loss on a sale or exchange of property is nondeductible if the transaction is between certain related parties as detailed below.[84] It makes no difference whether the transaction is bona fide and/or arises in the ordinary course of business.

Definition of related person. Related person(s) as they pertain to S corporations are:[85]

(1) A shareholder owning more than 50 percent of the stock of the corporation (by value).[86]

(2) An S corporation and a C corporation if the same persons own more than 50 percent in value of each corporation's stock.[87]

(3) Two S corporations if the same persons own more than 50 percent in value of each corporation's stock.[88]

(4) Two corporations that are members of the same controlled group.[89]

[82] TC Memo 1998-128.
[83] TC Memo 2003-30.
[84] Code Sec. 267(a)(1).
[85] Code Sec. 267(b).
[86] Code Sec. 267(b)(2).
[87] Code Sec. 267(b)(12).
[88] Code Sec. 267(b)(11).
[89] Code Sec. 267(b)(3) and (f)(1).

(5) A corporation and a partnership if the same persons own more than 50 percent in value of the corporation's stock and more than 50 percent of the partnership's capital or profits interest.[90]

(6) A trust fiduciary and a corporation if the trust or grantor of the trust owns more than 50 percent in value of the outstanding stock of the corporation.[91]

(7) The grantor and a fiduciary of any trust.[92]

(8) A fiduciary of a trust and a beneficiary of such trust.[93]

Constructive ownership of stock. Code Sec. 267(c) requires that stock owned both directly and indirectly (i.e., "constructively") be considered in determining whether a person or entity is a related party. In this regard, "stock owned, directly or indirectly, by or for a corporation, partnership, estate, or trust" is considered to be owned proportionately by or for its shareholders, partners, or beneficiaries.[94] In addition, individuals are deemed to be constructive owners of stock owned, directly or indirectly, by members of their family[95] (spouse, siblings, half-siblings, ancestors, or lineal descendants only)[96] and by their partners, though in the latter case, constructive ownership is imposed from a partner only if the individual also owns stock directly in the S corporation.[97]

> **Example 7-14:** Watson Inc. is a qualified S corporation owned by three shareholders. Tim Watson owns 40% of the outstanding shares and his two children each own 30%. Tim is also a 50% partner in an accounting partnership, the other partner of which owns no stock in Watson Inc. Under the constructive ownership rules, Tim is deemed to own 100% of the stock of Watson Inc. Accordingly, any loss realized by the corporation on the sale of property to Tim will not be deductible under Code Sec. 267. Note, however, that the corporation could deduct losses realized on the sale of property to Tim's partner in the accounting firm. Since the partner owns no stock in Watson Inc. directly, Tim's stock in Watson Inc. will not be attributed to the partner.

Effect of disallowed loss on basis and later transactions. Although the seller may not deduct losses realized on the sale of property to a related buyer, the buyer still takes a cost basis in the property acquired (rather than a carryover basis from the seller).[98] However, when the buyer disposes of the property at a later date, his or her gain will be recognized only to the extent that it exceeds the loss previously disallowed under Code Sec. 267.[99]

> **Example 7-15:** Jack Fox and Deann Sun are related parties. Fox sells property to Sun that has an adjusted basis of $25,000 for $21,000, generating a loss of $4,000. Under Code Sec. 267(a)(1) the $4,000 loss is disallowed. Sun's basis is $21,000, and when she has depreciated the asset to $19,000, she sells it

---

[90] Code Sec. 267(b)(10).

[91] Code Sec. 267(b)(8).

[92] Code Sec. 267(b)(9).

[93] Code Sec. 267(b)(6).

[94] Code Sec. 267(c)(1).

[95] Code Sec. 267(c)(2).

[96] Code Sec. 267(c)(4).

[97] Code Sec. 267(c)(5).

[98] Code Sec. 267.

[99] Code Sec. 267(d) and Reg. § 1.267(d)-1.

to an unrelated third party for $24,000. Sun's recognized gain is $1,000 ($5,000 – $4,000).

Example 7-16: Assume the same facts as in Example 7-15 except that Sun sold the property to an unrelated third party for $15,000. Sun's recognized loss is $4,000 ($19,000 – $15,000).

Tax Pointer 1: Losses can arise indirectly. For example, a loss was disallowed to a taxpayer on the sale of corporation stock to a related party who was the sole bidder at an IRS forced tax sale.[100]

Tax Pointer 2: If several items or classes of items are sold or exchanged where the loss is disallowed, an allocation based on fair market value is required.[101]

Tax Pointer 3: The holding period for the property acquired in the hands of the transferee is dependent on whether the transferee had a gain or loss. If there is a gain, the holding periods of the transferor and the transferee are added together. If the asset is sold at a loss, the holding period includes only the time the asset was held by the transferee.[102]

.02 Suspension of Expenses and Interest

Payments made by an accrual S corporation to its cash-basis shareholder(s) cannot be accrued and deducted by the corporation in one year and paid in the next.[103] An accrual-basis corporation may, however, be converted to a cash-basis one to deduct interest and expense (such as salary) paid to cash-basis shareholders.[104] Thus, the S corporation will deduct the expense and/or interest in the year the shareholder reports the payment and income. The following should also be noted:

(1) The rule for disallowance applies based on the payee; thus, if the shareholder is on an accrual basis and makes a payment to a cash-basis S corporation, the deductibility by the shareholder of the payment will depend when the S corporation recognizes income.

(2) Rule (1) above covers the corporation and payor who are "related" on the last day of the corporation's year in which the payment would be deductible.[105] Thus, a recharacterization will apply even if the relationship between the parties terminates before the expense or interest are includible in gross income by the recipient (i.e., if a calendar-year S corporation in 2000 accrues an item of expense to an S shareholder, David Young, and Young redeems his stock interest in 2000 with payment being made of the accrued expense by the S corporation to Young in 2001, the S corporation deducts the expense in 2001). The "related" shareholder is *any* shareholder, regardless of his or her ownership interest, and any person related to the shareholder within the meaning of Code Secs.

---

[100] *J.H. Merritt, Sr.,* 47 TC 519, Dec. 28,350. Aff'd on another issue, CA-5, 68-2 USTC ¶ 9539, 400 F2d 417.

[101] Reg. § 1.267(d)-1(b).

[102] Reg. § 1.267(d)-1(c)(3).

[103] Code Sec. 267(a)(2), 267(b), and 267(e).

[104] Code Sec. 267(a).

[105] Code Sec. 267(a)(2).

267(b) or 707(b)(1).[106] An example that applies the rules for related parties is an S corporation and a partnership where the shareholder in the S corporation owns directly or indirectly more than 50 percent of the capital and/or profit interest in the partnership.[107]

¶ 713 Vacation Homes, Personal Residences, Boats, and Recreational Vehicles

In an attempt to limit liability from negligence action, breach of contract suits, and so on, an individual may decide to place his or her vacation home or residence in an S corporation. In such cases, the deduction for expenses related to the vacation home or residence is limited.[108] The following points should be noted:

(1) The limitations on the amount and type of deduction for personal residences and vacation homes are described in Code Sec. 280A(c)(5).

(2) The personal use of a vacation home or personal residence owned by an S corporation is determined by the total amount of personal use by all of the S corporation shareholders (as well by members of their family).[109] If two or more S shareholders use the home on the same day, it only counts as one personal-use day.

Under proposed regulations issued in 1975, the IRS has indicated that a personal-use day is any day in which the residence is used by a shareholder, a family member, or *any person* other than certain employees unless such person pays rent at fair rental value.[110]

Examples 7-17 and 7-18 illustrate how Code Sec. 280A applies to S corporations.

Example 7-17: Cindy Lee, Dawn Dickson, and Effie Eastman form an S corporation, Pet Inc., in which each holds a one-third interest. Pet Inc. acquires a dwelling unit that Eastman rents from Pet Inc. at fair rental for use as Eastman's principal residence. All items of income, gain, loss, deduction, or credit of Pet Inc. that are related to the unit are allocated one-third to each shareholder. Under these circumstances, the personal use of the unit by Eastman is not treated as personal use by Pet Inc. (because Eastman pays market rent for her use of the dwelling). Consequently, the use of the unit by Eastman does not subject Lee and Dickson to the limitations of Code Sec. 280A(c)(5) on their shares of the items related to the unit. Eastman, however, is subject to the limitations of Code Sec. 280A(c)(5) on her share of those items.

Example 7-18: Zenda Inc., an S corporation in which Guy Spear and Nancy White are shareholders, is the owner of a fully equipped recreational vehicle. During the month of July, the vehicle is used by three individuals. Spear uses the vehicle on a 7-day camping trip. Allison, who is White's daughter, rents the vehicle from Zenda Inc. at fair rental for 10 days. Walter

---

[106] Code Sec. 267(e)(1)(B)(ii).
[107] Code Sec. 267(b)(10).
[108] Code Sec. 280A.

[109] Code Sec. 280A(f)(2) and Prop. Reg. §1.280A-1(e)(5).
[110] Prop. Reg. §1.280A-1(e)(1).

Nelson rents the vehicle at fair rental for 12 days under an arrangement whereby White is entitled to use an apartment owned by Richard Grant, a friend of Nelson, for 9 days. Zenda Inc. is deemed to have used the dwelling unit for personal purposes on any day on which any of its shareholders would have so used the unit. Therefore, Zenda Inc. is deemed to have used the recreational vehicle for personal purposes on 29 days.

Tax Pointer 1: Code Sec. 280A only applies to individuals, partnerships, trusts, estates, and S corporations; it does not apply to C corporations.

Tax Pointer 2: Because of the complexities of S corporation taxation, an individual desiring liability protection for a boat, vacation home, etc. may consider the use of a one-person LLC to own the vacation home, boat, etc. Under the "check-the-box" regulations, the individual would report all the vacation home's activities directly on the individual's personal tax returns without the intervening S corporation reporting.[111]

¶ 714 Corporate Interest

.01 Proper Reporting

The tax treatment of interest paid or incurred by an S corporation is quite complex. The complexity is due to various Code provisions, such as Code Sec. 469's passive loss rules, Code Sec. 263A's capitalization of interest during construction rules, Code Sec. 163's investment interest and personal interest expense rules, and Code Sec. 265(a)'s rule excluding deduction of interest to acquire tax-exempt obligations. Because of the treatment required by the various Code provisions regarding interest, tracing is required in many instances to ensure proper reporting. Temp. Reg. § 1.163-8T(a)(3) provides general guidance in how to report interest, requiring that the debt be allocated by tracing the disbursement of the debt proceeds. Because of the nature of business, tracing the disbursement of funds may prove difficult.

Example 7-19: Seltor, a calendar-year S corporation, borrows $100,000 from a bank on January 1, 2010, and immediately uses the funds to open a non-interest-bearing checking account. No other amounts are deposited in the account during the year, and no portion of the principal amount of the debt is repaid during the year. On April 1, 2010, Seltor uses $20,000 of the debt proceeds held in the account for a passive activity expenditure. On September 1, 2010, Seltor uses an additional $40,000 of the debt proceeds held in the account for a personal expenditure for Seltor's shareholder, Megan Ryan. Under Temp. Reg. § 1.163-8T(c)(4)(i), from January 1 through March 31 the entire $100,000 debt is allocated to an investment expenditure for the account. From April 1 through August 31, $20,000 of the debt is allocated to the passive activity expenditure, and $80,000 of the debt is allocated to the investment expenditure for the account. From September 1 through December 31, $40,000 of the debt is allocated to the personal expenditure, $20,000 is allocated to the passive activity expenditure, and $40,000 is allocated to an investment expendi-

[111] See ¶ 1307.06 for a discussion of one-person LLCs.

ture for the account. If the assets to which the debt is allocated were sold, or the asset's use changed during the tax year, then the tracing rules become even more elaborate.[112]

.02 Shareholder Acquisition of Stock Using Debt to Finance the Acquisition

When a shareholder acquires stock in an S corporation, either by purchase of the stock or by making a capital contribution to the S corporation, and uses borrowed funds in whole or in part to make the acquisition, the shareholder is required to allocate the interest expense incurred in making the acquisition using a reasonable allocation method.[113] Notice 89-35[114] suggests a number of methods for allocating the interest expense based on fair market value, book value, adjusted basis, or the S corporation's actual use of the proceeds from the stock acquisition.

> **Example 7-20:** Andy Brady, an individual, forms Monster Inc. and elects S status for the corporation on the day of incorporation. Brady makes a capital contribution of $1,000, funding the entire purchase price by borrowing the money from a bank. Monster Inc. engages in two activities during its first tax year, generating the following results at the end of its tax year. Monster Inc. did not use any borrowed funds to engage in the two activities:

	Fair Market Value	Adjusted Basis	Book Value
Activity 1	$1,500	$ 500	$1,000
Activity 2	500	1,000	1,000

> Using the fair market valuation method, Brady could allocate 75 percent of the initial expense to activity 1, and 25 percent to activity 2; if the adjusted basis method were used, then the allocation would be 33 percent to activity 1 and 66 percent to activity 2; and if the book valuation method were used, the allocation would be 50 percent to activity 1 and 50 percent to activity 2.

> **Example 7-21:** Assume the same facts as in Example 7-20, except Andy Brady and Lisa Flynn form Monster Inc., with Brady and Flynn being equal shareholders. Flynn likewise contributed $1,000 for her capital contribution. Monster Inc. took Brady's $1,000 capital contribution to purchase assets used in a third activity. Rather than using one of the above allocation methods, Brady can allocate the debt entirely to activity 3, reflecting the corporation's actual use of the contributed funds.

> **Tax Pointer:** Allocation of interest can be a multilayered process. In Examples 7-20 and 7-21 where the allocation of interest is detailed with borrowed funds, a determination has to be made on whether the interest expense is passive or active,[115] investment debt interest,[116] etc.

---

[112] For an example of the complexity regarding tracing, see Temp. Reg. § 1.163-8T(j).

[113] Notice 89-35, 1989-1 CB 675.

[114] *Ibid.*

[115] For further discussion, see ¶ 911.06.

[116] For further discussion, see ¶ 702.

¶714.02

.03 Passive Loss Rules

Interest paid or incurred in a passive activity must be determined at the shareholder level.[117]

.04 Tax-Exempt Obligations

Interest on debt incurred to purchase or carry tax-exempt obligations is nondeductible[118] whether the debt is incurred directly to purchase a tax-exempt bond (e.g., the corporation purchases a tax-exempt bond on margin), or indirectly, providing there is a direct relationship between the debt and the acquisition of the tax-exempt obligation.[119] Because of the probable disallowance of interest expense, an S corporation should proceed cautiously in the acquisition of tax-exempt obligations. Any tax-exempt interest can also affect distributions from an S corporation.[120]

.05 Personal Interest

Personal or consumer interest is not deductible (e.g., interest that an individual incurs to purchase a personal automobile).[121] However, corporate interest is still deductible. Consequently, S corporation shareholders may attempt to cast consumer interest situations as business interest situations. Preparers of Form 1120S should exercise care to prevent tax abuse.

.06 Interest Paid or Incurred During Construction

Interest paid or incurred during construction of certain property must be capitalized as part of the basis of the property.[122] The capitalization rules are first applied at the S corporation level and then at the shareholder level.[123] Special provisions for dealing with flow-through entities, such as S corporations, and how to report the transaction are illustrated in Example 7-19.[124]

> **Example 7-22:** Corporation Hilltop, a calendar-year S corporation, is producing qualified property (to which the interest capitalization rules apply under Code Sec. 263A) and does not elect to use the substitute cost method. The production period of the qualified property being produced by Hilltop lasts throughout the entire tax year. The monthly average balance of accumulated production expenditures for the entire year is equal to $1,000,000, and the monthly average balance of Hilltop's traced and avoided cost debt for the entire year is equal to $400,000. Hilltop is owned by two calendar-year, accrual-method shareholders, April Frink and Mark Peterson, whose interests in Hilltop are identical. Frink has eligible debt of $600,000 with an annual interest rate of 10 percent. Peterson has eligible debt of $100,000 with an annual interest rate of 12 percent. In addition, the eligible debt of Frink and Peterson is outstanding during the entire production period of the property. Frink and Peterson are therefore required to capitalize interest on their proportionate share of Hilltop's remaining production expenditures (equal to $300,000 each),

---

[117] Code Sec. 469. For discussion of the passive loss rules, see ¶ 911.

[118] Code Sec. 265(a).

[119] Cf. *Anclote Psychiatric Center, Inc.*, 76 TCM 175, Dec. 52,809(M), TC Memo. 1998-273.

[120] For further discussion, see ¶ 1006.

[121] Code Sec. 163(h)(1) (Tax Reform Act of 1986).

[122] Code Sec. 263A(f)(1).

[123] Code Sec. 263A(f)(2)(C).

[124] Notice 88-99, 1988-2 CB 422.

in the same manner as if they were producing the property themselves. Thus, Frink is required to capitalize interest equal to $30,000 (i.e., interest for one year on $300,000 of debt with an annual interest rate of 10 percent). Peterson is required to capitalize interest equal to $12,000 (i.e., interest for one year on $100,000 of debt with an annual interest rate of 12 percent).

.07 Interest Expense Allocated to Debt-Financed Distributions

If an S corporation distributed borrowed funds to a shareholder, the corporation should separately state the interest expense on these funds and list as "interest expense allocated to debt-financed distributions" under other deductions on the shareholder's Schedule K-1. Whether the shareholder can deduct this interest on his or her tax return depends on how the shareholder uses the funds.

¶ 715 Legal Expenses and Accounting Fees

Miscellaneous itemized deductions claimed by an individual taxpayer, such as tax preparation fees, legal fees for tax matters, financial planning, and subscriptions to financial publications, must exceed 2 percent of adjusted gross income to qualify as an itemized deduction.[125] Each shareholder of an S corporation must take into account his or her share of miscellaneous itemized deductions of the S corporation (e.g., a shareholder's personal legal expenses).[126]

Occasionally, shareholders pay expenses on behalf of the corporation. In *D'Angelo v. Commissioner,*[127] a Subchapter S shareholder was allowed under Code Sec. 162 legal fees incurred in connection with lawsuits involving his dealings with partnerships and S corporations where he owned an interest. A similar result occurred in *Craft v. Commissioner,*[128] however, the taxpayer, a 50% S corporate shareholder and officer of the corporation, was able to deduct business expenses incurred in his roles as an officer and employee of the corporation but they were treated as unreimbursed employee business expenses on his Form 1040, Schedule A. The reason why the taxpayer was able to deduct the business expenses of the S corporation was due to the fact that the corporation adopted a resolution requiring the officers to incur expenses as necessary or required.

¶ 716 Reasonable Compensation

.01 Salaries or Distributions on Stock

In the case of shareholder-employees, the question often arises as to how they should be compensated—by salary or distributions of cash on stock.[129]

> **Example 7-23:** Reeves Inc. is an S corporation with no earnings and profits. Reeves Inc. has one shareholder, John Rosen, who is also the only employee of the corporation. In 2010, Reeves Inc. has $100 of taxable income. If Reeves Inc. distributes the $100 of income to Rosen as a distribution with respect to stock, Rosen will report $100 of income free of self-employment

---

[125] Code Sec. 67.
[126] Temp. Reg. § 1.67-2T(b)(1).
[127] TC Memo 2003-295.

[128] TC Memo 2005-197.
[129] Code Sec. 1368. For a detailed discussion of Code Sec. 1368, see Chapter 10.

tax.[130] Alternatively, if Reeves Inc. pays Rosen $100 of salary, Rosen will still report $100 of income. However, the income will now be subject to payroll taxes.

While the net effect of corporate payments to a shareholder-employee is basically the same whether the payment is made by salary or an actual distribution free of self-employment tax, the method of payment could impact other areas. Salary payments form the basis for corporate contributions to qualified retirement plans, are treated as active income for the passive loss rules,[131] and are subject to employment taxes and social security taxes. In contrast, cash distributions on stock do not generate additional tax consequences to the shareholder-employee. However, if the distributions are in excess of the shareholder-employee's basis in stock (or the accumulated adjustments account if the S corporation still has earnings and profits),[132] the distribution would generate taxable income to the shareholder-employee.

> **Example 7-24:** Mineco Inc., a calendar-year S corporation, has one shareholder, Dennis White. White, as of January 1, 2010, has no basis in his stock or debt; thus, any loss for Mineco Inc. will be suspended for White.[133] In 2010, Mineco Inc. pays White a salary of $200 and reports a $200 loss. The tax consequences to White are that he will report $200 of salary as ordinary income, but since he has no basis in stock or debt, he will have to defer the $200 loss until he obtains basis.

In addition, some states do not recognize S corporations for tax purposes. In those states, corporate earnings distributed in the form of distributions instead of salaries could be treated as dividends, thereby creating a double tax situation.

Code Sec. 409A's deferred compensation rules. As the discussion at ¶ 723 details, shareholders in employment agreements are subject to Code Sec. 409A. At this stage, it is difficult to project what effect Code Sec. 409A will have on compensation agreements; however, it is probable that certain language will be deemed to apply. It is foreseeable that the IRS and the courts will incorporate Code Sec. 409A's distribution provisions in employment agreements, shareholders agreements, etc. to detail when an individual will be disabled; when there is a change of corporate control allowing an employee to terminate employment; obtain a severance payment, etc. Accordingly, the reader should consult ¶ 723 as well as follow the developments under Code Sec. 409A.

.02 Reasonable Salaries

Whether to compensate by salary or distribution was solved in part by *Radtke*,[134] which prescribes that a shareholder-employee cannot just receive distributed earnings from their S corporation, but must also take a reasonable salary. However, how much salary is reasonable was not defined in the case.

---

[130] See discussion at ¶ 716.03.
[131] Code Sec. 469. See further discussion at ¶ 911.04.
[132] For further discussion of distributions, see ¶ 1004.02.

[133] Code Sec. 1367(a)(2).
[134] *J. Radtke,* CA-7, 89-2 USTC ¶ 9466, 712 FSupp 143. Aff'g per curiam CA-7, 90-1 USTC ¶ 50,113, 895 F2d 1196.

But in *Barron*,[135] some guidance was established in that statistical data gathered for an industry can help the court determine reasonable compensation. In *Barron*, the taxpayer, a CPA, was the sole shareholder of an S corporation, Wiley L. Barron, CPA, Ltd. In 1994, the taxpayer's S corporation paid the taxpayer a salary of $2,000 for the year; the taxpayer did not receive a salary for 1995 and 1996. However, for the years 1994 through 1996, the taxpayer's corporation made distributions of over $50,000 to the shareholder; in 1996, the distribution was $83,341. The Court sustained the IRS's estimates of reasonable compensation for the taxpayer, based on statistical data, at $45,000, $47,500, and $49,000 for the years under review, together with penalties under Code Sec. 6656 for failure to make deposit of taxes. The taxpayer's claim for relief under Code Sec. 530 of the Revenue Act of 1978 was denied because the taxpayer was treated as an employee by his corporation for one year (for Code Sec. 530 to apply, one threshold to be satisfied is that the corporation never treated the taxpayer as an employee).

> **Tax Pointer:** The Department of the Treasury has recommended new legislation. Deputy Inspector General for audit, Pamela J. Gardner, reported on May 20, 2005 that 36,000 one-owner S corporations with profits of $100,000 or more paid no payroll taxes on profits; 40,000 S corporations with profits in the $50,000–$100,000 range paid no payroll taxes on the profits because no salary was taken. Accordingly, the Department of the Treasury has recommended that Congress close this loophole by subjecting to employment taxes all operating gains of S corporations that accrue to more than fifty-percent owners and their relatives.

.03 Tax Advantages Over Partnerships and LLCs

In *Radtke*,[136] shareholder-employees are required to take a reasonable salary from an S corporation, allowing the balance to be distributed as distributions free of Social Security, Medicare, and self-employment taxes.[137] In contrast, partnership and LLCs generally require (unless there is a statutory exception) all distributions to general partners to be subject to self-employment tax. Example 7-18 illustrates the significance of this disparity.

> **Example 7-25:** Lawyer Alex Dunn is considering opening his practice as either an S corporation or an LLC. He contemplates that he will earn $400,000 in his first year. If Dunn establishes himself as a one-person LLC, all $400,000 in earnings will be subject to self-employment tax. In contrast, if he establishes himself as a one-person S corporation, he could take a reasonable salary of $100,000, and also take a distribution of earnings of $300,000 that would be free of self-employment and Medicare taxes. Dunn would save $8,700 in self-employment taxes ($300,000 × .029) by using an S corporation rather than an LLC.

> **Tax Pointer 1:** Reg. § 1.1402(a)-2(h) prescribes that "a proprietor of an unincorporated business enterprise with respect to which an election has been

---

[135] TC Summary Opn. 2001-10.

[136] *J. Radtke*, CA-7, 89-2 USTC ¶ 9466, 712 FSupp 143. Aff'g per curiam CA-7, 90-1 USTC ¶ 50,113, 895 F2d 1196.

[137] *P.B. Ding*, 74 TCM 708, Dec. 52,269(M), TC Memo. 1997-435. Aff'd, CA-9, 2000-1 USTC ¶ 50,137, 200-F3d 587 (S corporation pass-through of income deemed not self-employment income).

made pursuant to Code Sec. 1361 . . . to be taxed as a domestic corporation shall compute his (or her) earnings from self-employment without regard to the fact that such election has been made." Presumably, this regulation applies to partnerships as well. Reg. § 1.1402(a)-2(h) was promulgated in 1974. Hopefully, due to the changes made under Code Sec. 7701, the IRS will clarify this situation with respect to entities classified as an S corporation for federal tax purposes but something different for state purposes (i.e., a partnership). In terms of partners, the Taxpayer Relief Act of 1997, P.L. 105-34 Act Sec. 935, prescribes that for purposes of imposing self-employment tax on a limited partner, no temporary or final regulations can be issued or made effective before July 1, 1998. While July 1, 1998 is long past, the IRS has not issued regulations or guidance for this area. For a discussion of the Taxpayer Relief Act of 1997, see the discussion below.

Tax Pointer 2: As discussed at ¶ 1305.10, Code Sec. 761 was amended to provide Code Sec. 761(f) effective for taxable years beginning after December 31, 2006 that if a "qualified joint venture" is conducted by a husband and wife who file a joint return, they can elect to have this venture not treated as a partnership for Federal tax purposes. All items of income, gain, loss, deduction and credit are divided between the spouses in accordance with their respective interests in the venture. Each spouse takes into account his or her respective share of these items as a sole proprietor. Thus, it is anticipated that each spouse would account for his or her respective share on the appropriate form, such as Schedule C. The provision is not intended to change the determination under present law of whether an entity is a partnership for Federal tax purposes (without regard to the election provided by the provision).

For purposes of determining net earnings from self-employment, each spouse's share of income or loss from a qualified joint venture is taken into account just as it is for Federal income tax purposes under the provision (i.e., in accordance with their respective interests in the venture). Congress provided a corresponding change to the definition of net earnings from self-employment under the Social Security Act. The Small Business and Work Opportunity Tax Act of 2007 Committee Reports detail that the change to Code Sec. 761 is not intended to prevent allocations or reallocations, to the extent permitted under present law, by courts or by the Social Security Administration of net earnings from self-employment for purposes of determining Social Security benefits of an individual.

Qualified joint venture. Code Sec. 761(f)(2) states that a qualified joint venture is one where (1) the only members of the joint venture are a husband and wife, (2) both spouses materially participate in the trade or business, and (3) both spouses elect to have the provision apply.

Self-employment tax regarding limited partnerships and LLCs. Code Sec. 1402(a)(13) and Prop. Reg. § 1.1402(a)-2(g) prescribe generally that (a) a limited partner's distributed share of partnership income is not subject to self-employment tax; however, (b) guaranteed payments made to a limited partner for services actually rendered to or on behalf of a partnership, are included. The House

¶716.03

Committee Report to P.L. 95-216 (1977)[138] prescribed that an individual who is both a general and limited partner in the same partnership is subject to self-employment tax on any distributed share of partnership income received as a general partner, but not as a limited partner.

Prop. Reg. §301.7701-3(b)(2)(ii) discussed at ¶ 102.09 prescribes situations under Prop. Reg. §1.1402(a)-2(b) and (h) when a partner will be found liable for self-employment tax. These same standards apply to LLCs classified as partnerships for tax purposes. Thus, if a member of an LLC would be classified as a limited partner because the member flunks the test under Reg. §301.7701-3(b)(2)(ii) and Prop. Reg. §1.1402(a)-2(h)(2), the member will not be liable for Code Sec. 1402's self-employment tax. Further, Prop. Reg. §1.1402(a)-2(h)(5) and (6)(iii) provides that if substantially all the activities of an LLC can be classified as a partnership for tax purposes involved the performance of services in the fields of health, law, engineering, architecture, accounting, actuarial science or consulting, the LLC members will be taxed on their distributive share of partnership income.

The Taxpayer Relief Act of 1997 (P.L. 105-34) at Act. Sec.135 prescribes that no temporary or final regulations on the definition of a limited partner for purposes of self-employment tax may be issued or made effective before July 1, 1998. Because Congress and the IRS have done nothing since July 1, 1998 to clarify this issue, the law is in a state of flux, with practitioners basically treating non-manager LLC members in a managed LLC, where the LLC has been classified as a partnership, as limited partners, thereby creating substantial tax benefits for businesses able to operate in a limited partnership format (In a managed LLC, a manager(s) runs the LLC day-to-day operations subject to being overruled by a majority vote of the members).

.04 Compensation-Related Deductions

An S corporation could decide to pay a shareholder with corporate property. If the property used for compensation purposes is appreciated, then the S corporation is required to recognize the gain or loss, as the case may be[139] on the disposition.[140] If a loss is generated with respect to the property, the corporation may be precluded from recognizing the loss under Code Sec. 267;[141] however, the shareholder-employee will still be required to report the property received as compensation at the fair market value of the property. If there is a gain on the property and the property is used to pay the compensation, the gain may be allocated to the shareholder as ordinary income instead of capital gain.[142]

The corporation, whether the property is appreciated or depreciated, obtains a deduction for salary for the fair market value as of the date of the transfer.

---

[138] H.R. Rep. 95-70.

[139] Cf. *T.C. Davis,* SCt, 62-2 USTC ¶ 9509, 370 US 65, 82 SCt 1190.

[140] If S corporation stock is used for compensation, it is exempt pursuant to Reg. §1.83-6(d).

[141] Code Sec. 267. See also ¶ 712.01.

[142] Code Sec. 1239. See also discussion at ¶ 607.

¶716.04

.05 S Corporation's Income from a Personal Service Partnership Is Not Subject to Self-employment Tax under Code Sec. 1402

In *Grigoraci v. Commissioner*,[143] an accountant formed an S corporation named Grigoraci S Corporation to protect himself from liability upon joining an accounting partnership. The accountant's S corporation received a distribution from the partnership of $124,470 which the accountant's S corporation reported. From this $124,470 of income, the S corporation paid the accountant a salary of $32,000 and distributed the balance of the income, to wit $92,470, to the accountant as the S corporation's sole shareholder. The IRS sought to reclassify the $92,470 as personal service income subject to self-employment tax. Likewise, the IRS tried to do the same with the accountant's $32,000 salary. The court refused to reclassify the S corporation's income.

.06 Payment Formulas Regarding Compensation

In *DeLorean v. Commissioner*,[144] the court sustained a corporation imposed requirement that a shareholder-employee who was the sole shareholder had to repay compensation in any year when the corporation sustained a loss. In reaching this decision the court stated that repayment of salary in accordance with Code Sec. 162 was not a contribution to capital. The shareholder claimed that this repayment approach was to motivate him to effectively manage the corporation; not do so for tax purposes. This type of agreement might prove helpful to motivate shareholder employees.

¶ 717 Meal and Entertainment Expenses

Only 50 percent of meal and entertainment expenses are allowed as a deduction to the S corporation.[145] Each shareholder shall take into account separately his or her pro rata share of meal, travel, and entertainment expenses paid or incurred.[146] In addition, each shareholder shall take into account separately his or her pro rata share of any skybox rentals paid or incurred by an S corporation.[147]

¶ 718 Nonbusiness Bad Debts

An S corporation can have a nonbusiness bad debt (i.e., a debt arising other than in a trade or business context). An example would be lending money to an employee who subsequently files for bankruptcy and defaults on the loan. An S corporation that has a nonbusiness bad debt must separately state the debt as a short-term capital loss in the year it becomes totally worthless.[148]

Determination of whether a debt is a business bad debt or non-business bad debt is a fact question and the write-off is subject to the same rules as individuals. Many times the write off involves form versus substance as was indicated in *Rogers v. U.S.*[149] which involved the owners of the Kansas City Royals Major League Baseball team and the propriety of a $34 million bad debt deduction taken by the Royals on a purported loan to one of the part owners. The end result was that the

---

[143] TC Memo 2002-202.

[144] TC Memo 1995-287.

[145] Code Sec. 274(n).

[146] Reg. § 1.1366-2.

[147] Code Sec. 274(l)(2).

[148] Code Sec. 166(d).

[149] 2000-1 USTC ¶ 50,237, 58 FSupp2d 1235 (USDCD Kan.1999).

team could not deduct its payments to its former owner as an ordinary and necessary business expense.

¶ 719 Oil and Gas Depletion

An S corporation cannot take a deduction for oil and gas depletion; rather, the depletion allowance is computed at the shareholder level.[150]

¶ 720 Golden Parachute Payments

.01 Background

Key personnel of a corporation, as part of their compensation package, enter into "golden parachute" arrangements whereby the corporation agrees to pay them large compensation packages in the event the corporation control changes. Code Sec. 4999 bars the corporation from deducting the payment if (a) it is made to a "disqualified individual," and (b) the payments are in excess of the employee's base amount of salary. Code Sec. 280G(c) defines a "disqualified individual" as an employee or independent contractor who performs services for the corporation, and is an officer, personal service corporation, shareholder or highly compensated individual. Code Sec. 280G(b) defines the "base amount of salary" which serves as the measuring point the individual's annualized includable compensation for a period consisting of the most recent five tax years beginning before the date on which the ownership or control of the corporation changed, or the portion of this period during which the individual was an employee of the corporation.

For a golden parachute payment to exist, besides being dependent on a change of effective control of the corporation, or a substantial portion of the corporation's assets, the aggregate payment's value must equal or exceed three times the disqualified individual's base amount of salary.

.02 S Corporations Not Subject to Golden Parachute Payments

Code Sec. 280G(b)(5)(A)(i) and Reg. § 1.280G-1, Q&A 6(a)(1) state that the "golden parachute rules" do not apply to S corporations.

¶ 721 Health Savings Accounts (HSAs)

Code Sec. 223 established HSAs for taxable years for 2004 and later. HSAs provide tax-favored treatment for amounts contributed and used to pay the account beneficiary's "qualified medical expenses." HSAs are trusts which basically are Archer Medical Savings Accounts (MSAs), with the eligibility restrictions removed. Money invested in HSAs grows tax-free. Distributions from HSAs, when they are used for "qualified medical expense" as that term is defined below, are tax-free, and they are penalty-free if withdrawal occurs after retirement age. Employers can offer HSAs either as a stand-alone benefit, or as part of a cafeteria plan. HSAs are portable, and move with employees when they change jobs. They do not contain a "use-it-or-lose-it" feature, like other savings accounts. It is beyond the scope of this book to provide a detailed discussion of Archer MSAs and HSAs; however, the following is noted:

---

[150] Code Sec. 1363(b)(2).

Tax Pointer 1: State law will determine if HSAs are exempt from creditor attack.

Tax Pointer 2: Employers do not like HSAs since once an employer makes a contribution to an HSA it is the employee's money and the employer has no control over the funds.

Tax Pointer 3: DOL Field Assistance Bulletin 2004-1 prescribes that HSAs are not subject to ERISA rules.

.01 Definition of HSA

Sec. 223(d)(1)(A) prescribes that, except for rollover contributions from an Archer MSA or HSA, no contributions can be accepted unless the following conditions are met:

(1) The contribution is in cash, or to the extent such contribution, when added to previous contributions to the trust for the calendar year, exceeds the sum of the dollar limits prescribed by Code Sec. 223(b)(2) and (3) (see discussion below).

(2) The trustee must be a bank, insurance company, or any recognized person pursuant to Code Sec. 223(d)(1)(B).

(3) No part of the trust assets can be invested in life insurance contracts.

(4) There is no commingling of the trust assets with any other property unless it is a common trust or investment fund.

(5) The individual's interest in the account is non-forfeitable.

.02 Qualification for an HSA

Code Sec. 223(c) prescribes that to be a participant in an HSA, certain requirements must be satisfied:

(1) The participant is covered by a high deductible health insurance plan (HDHP).

(2) The participant has no other health coverage except what is permitted under any other health plan.

(3) The participant is not enrolled in Medicare.

(4) The participant cannot be claimed as a dependent in someone else's plan.

.03 High Deductible Health Insurance Plan (HDHP)

Code Sec. 223(c)(2)(A) prescribes that an HDHP is a typical health insurance plan, with a high annual deductible. The HDHP must have a maximum limit on the amount of the annual deductible and out-of-pocket medical expense for covered expenses which the participant must pay. Out-of-pocket expenses include co-payments and other amounts, but not insurance premiums. The HDHP may provide preventive care benefits without a deductible, or with a deductible below the minimum amount deductible. Examples of preventive care would be screening tests, routine pre-natal, and well-child care, etc. Rev. Proc. 2004-71, Code Sec.

¶721.03

3.22(2)[151] prescribes that HDHP annual deductibles for a participant are as follows: If the plan is a self-coverage one, the HDHP annual deductible has to be at least $1,000, and limits the annual expenses (the sum of the annual deductible and other annual out-of-pocket expenses) required to be paid under the plan (other than premiums) to $5,100. For family coverage, the plan has an annual deductible that is at least $2,000, and limits the annual expenses (the sum of the annual deductible and other annual out-of-pocket expenses) to $10,200.

A self-only HDHP covers only the participants. A family HDHP covers the participant and any other individual (whether or not that individual is an eligible individual).

.04 Amount of Contribution

Code Sec. 223(b)(2) prescribes the amount of a contribution which can be made to an HSA. The amount of the contribution depends on the type of HDHP which the taxpayer has; for 2004, if the taxpayer has a self-covering plan, the contribution is the lesser of the amount of the taxpayer's annual HDHP deductible, but not more than $2,600; if the taxpayer has family coverage, the taxpayer can contribute the lesser of the taxpayer's annual HDHP deductible, but not more than $5,150. Code Sec. 223(b)(3) provides that if a taxpayer is over 55, an additional contribution can be made to the plan. In 2005, it is $600.

IRS Publication 969 provides guidance as to how HSAs operate for families and married individuals.

Married people. If either spouse has family coverage, both spouses are treated as having family coverage. If each spouse has family coverage under a separate plan, both are treated as having family coverage under the plan with the lower annual deductible. If taxpayers have family HDHP coverage, they are generally permitted to divide the HSA annual contribution limit for family coverage between themselves as they wish, but if they each have self-only HDHP coverage, they are subject to separate annual contribution limits.

If both spouses are 55 or older and not enrolled in Medicare, each spouse's contribution limit is increased by the additional contribution. If both spouses meet the age requirement, the total contributions under family coverage cannot be more than $6,150.

An example illustrating the married couple contribution rules is set forth below:

> **Example 7-26:** For 2010, Mr. Auburn and his wife both have family coverage under separate HDHPs. Mr. Auburn is 58 years old and Mrs. Auburn is 53. Mr. Auburn has a $3,000 deductible under his HDHP and Mrs. Auburn has a $2,000 deductible under her HDHP. Mr. and Mrs. Auburn are both treated as being covered under the HDHP with the $2,000 deductible. Mr. Auburn can contribute $1,500 to an HSA (one-half the $2,000 deductible + $500 additional contribution) and Mrs. Auburn can contribute $1,000 to an HSA (unless Mr. and Mrs. Auburn agree to a different division for the year).

[151] 2004-50 IRB 970.

¶721.04

Family coverage with embedded deductible. An HDHP with family coverage may have deductibles for both the family as a whole (the umbrella deductible) and for individual family members (the embedded deductible). In this situation the limit on contributions is the least of the following amounts:

(1) The maximum annual contribution limit for family coverage ($5,150 for 2004).

(2) The umbrella deductible.

(3) The embedded deductible multiplied by the number of family members covered by the plan.

Examples illustrating the family coverage with embedded deductibles are set forth below:

Example 7-27: For 2010, taxpayer has an HDHP with family coverage for taxpayer, taxpayer's spouse, and two dependent children. The HDHP will pay benefits for any family members whose covered expenses exceed $2,000 (the embedded deductible) and will pay benefits for all family members after the family's covered expenses exceed $5,000 (the umbrella deductible). The maximum annual contribution limit is $5,000 (the least of $5,150, $5,000, or $8,000 ($2,000 x 4)).

Example 7-28: Use the same facts as in Example 7-27, except the HDHP provides coverage only for taxpayer and taxpayer's spouse. The maximum annual contribution limit is $4,000 (the least of $5,150, $5,000, or $4,000 ($2,000 x 2)).

Tax Pointer: A plan will not qualify as an HDHP if either the umbrella deductible or the embedded deductible is less than the minimum annual deductible ($2,000) for family coverage. If there is no umbrella deductible, the deductible for each family member multiplied by the number of family members cannot exceed the maximum annual deductible and other out-of-pocket expenses ($10,000) for family coverage.

Reduction of contribution limit. Taxpayers must reduce the amount they, or any other person, can contribute to the taxpayer's HSA by the amount of any contributions made by the taxpayer's employer that are excludable from the taxpayer's income.

Rollovers. Taxpayers can roll over amounts from Archer MSAs and other HSAs into an HSA. Rollover contributions do not need to be in cash. Rollovers are not subject to the annual contribution limits.

.05 Qualified Medical Expenses

Code Sec. 223(d)(2)(A) prescribes that only qualified medical expenses as defined in Code Sec. 213(d) can be paid to an HSA beneficiary "to the extent that such amounts are not compensated by insurance or otherwise." Code Sec. 223(d)(2)(B) prescribes that health insurance cannot be purchased for an HSA, but Code Sec. 223(d)(2)(C) exempts certain insurance, such as qualified long-term care insurance. Congress has prescribed that with respect to over the counter drugs, for

¶721.05

taxable years beginning after December 31, 2010, this type of medication is not deductible through an HSA unless it is obtained by means of a prescription.

.06 Employer Contributions

An employer can fund an HSA; however, the employer must make comparable contributions to all comparable participants of the employer's HSA. IRS Publication 969 prescribes that contributions are comparable if they are either the same amount or the same percentage of the annual deductible limit under the HDHP covering the employees.

Comparable participating employees are covered by the HDHP and are eligible to establish an HSA, have the same category of coverage (either self-only or family coverage), and have the same category of employment (either part-time or full-time).

The comparability rules do not apply to contributions made through a cafeteria plan.

.07 S Corporation Contributions to HSAs

S corporations can make contributions to HSAs for the two-percent or more shareholder-employees,[152] with the result being, pursuant to Notice 2005-8,[153] that S corporations can deduct the contributions. Specifically, Notice 2005-8 prescribes that under Code Sec. 1372, for purposes of applying the provisions that relate to fringe benefits, an S corporation is treated as a partnership, and any 2-percent shareholder of the S corporation is treated as a partner of such partnership. Therefore, contributions by an S corporation to an HSA of a 2-percent shareholder-employee in consideration for services rendered are treated as guaranteed payments under Code Sec. 707(c). Accordingly, the contributions are deductible by the S corporation under Code Sec. 162 (if the requirements of that section are satisfied (taking into account the rules of Code Sec. 263)) and are includible in the 2-percent shareholder-employee's gross income. In addition, the 2-percent shareholder-employee is not entitled to exclude the contribution from gross income under Code Sec. 106(d). See Rev. Rul. 91-26.[154]

For employment tax purposes, when contributions are made by an S corporation to an HSA of a 2-percent shareholder-employee, the 2-percent shareholder-employee is treated as an employee subject to Federal Insurance Contributions Act (FICA) tax and not as an individual subject to Self-Employment Contributions Act (SECA) tax. (See Announcement 92-16, 1992-5 IRB 53, clarifying the FICA (Social Security and Medicare) tax treatment of accident and health premiums paid by an S corporation on behalf of a 2-percent shareholder-employee.) However, if the requirements for the exclusion under Code Sec. 3121(a)(2)(B) are satisfied, the S corporation's contributions to an HSA of a 2-percent shareholder-employee are not wages subject to FICA tax, even though the amounts must be included in wages for income tax withholding purposes on the 2-percent shareholder-employee's Form W-2, Wage and Tax Statement. The 2-percent shareholder-employee, if an eligible

[152] A two-percent or more shareholder is defined at ¶ 706.02.

[153] IRB 2005-4.

[154] 1991-1 CB 184.

individual as defined in Code Sec. 223(c)(1), is entitled under Code Sec. 223(a) and Code Sec. 62(a)(19) to deduct the amount of the contributions made to the 2-percent shareholder-employee's HSA during the taxable year as an adjustment to gross income on his or her federal income tax return. See Notice 2004-2, Q&A 19, 2004-2 IRB 269, for employment tax rules for employer contributions to HSAs of employees other than 2-percent shareholder-employees.

.08 Trustee Rollover of IRAs to HSAs Permitted

Code Sec. 408(d)(9) provides that for tax years beginning after December 31, 2006, a taxpayer can make a one time only tax free rollover using a trustee-to-trustee-transfer, from an IRA (but not a simplified employee pension or SIMPLE plan) to an HSA. There are tax consequences if a taxpayer does not remain an eligible individual (except because of death or disability) under the HSA for one year during the testing period (which starts with the month of the contribution and ends on the last day of the 12th month following that month), namely, the amount of the IRA distribution that would otherwise have been includible is taxed to the taxpayer and is subject to a 10% penalty tax.

¶ 722 Code Sec. 199—Deduction Relating to U.S. Production Activities

In response to the World Trade Organization's (WTO) findings regarding United States export subsidy provisions, Congress enacted Code Sec. 199 to assist domestic producers of products from a tax perspective. Code Sec. 199 is far-reaching, and affects a number of taxpayers, such as manufacturers, farmers, architects, engineers, artists, writers, etc. Code Sec. 199 provides the tax relief to the "domestic producers" by means of a deduction.

.01 Amount of Deduction

Effective for taxable years beginning after December 31, 2004, Code Sec. 199(a)(1) creates a deduction equal to an amount of 9 percent of the lesser of:

(A) the qualified production activities income of the taxpayer for the taxable year, or

(B) taxable income (determined without regard to this section) for the taxable year.

Code Sec. 199(a)(2) phases in the deduction as follows:

For taxable years beginning in:	The transition percentage is:
2005 or 2006	3
2007, 2008, or 2009	6

Tax Pointer: Reg. § 1.199-4(c)(2) states that deduction under Code Sec. 172 for a net operating loss is not allocated or apportioned to Domestic Production Gross Receipts (DPGR) or gross income attributable to DPGR.

.02 W-2 Wage Limitation

Code Sec. 199(b) provides a ceiling on the deduction, namely that the Code Sec. 199 deduction cannot exceed 50 percent of the W-2 wages of the employees for the taxable year. Reg. § 1.199-2(e) defines "W-2 Wages" as the amount paid "to any person for any taxable year of such person, the sum of the amounts described in Code Sec. 6051(a)(3) and (8) paid by such person with respect to employment of employees by such person during the calendar year ending during such taxable year. Thus, the term W-2 wages includes the total amount of wages as defined in Code Sec. 3401(a); the total amount of elective deferrals (within the meaning of Code Sec. 402(g)(3)); the compensation deferred under Code Sec. 457; and for taxable years beginning after December 31, 2005, the amount of designated Roth contributions (as defined in Code Sec. 402A)."

The IRS was concerned that the Code Sec. 199 deduction would result in tax disparities such as allowing taxpayers to use a maid to reach Code Sec. 199's 50% W-2 wage limitation; thus, it enacted Reg. § 1.199-2 to cover various situations:

Wages paid by another taxpayer. Reg § 1.199-2(a)(2) and Rev. Proc. 2006-47,[155] detail that a taxpayer may take into account any wages paid by another entity and reported by the other entity on Forms W-2 with the other entity as the employer, provided that the employee is listed in Box c of the Forms W-2. The Preamble to the regulations (TD 9263, 5/24/2006) prescribes that whether amounts paid to workers who receive Forms W-2 from professional employer organizations (PEOs) or employee leasing firms may be included in the W-2 wages of the clients of the PEOs or employee leasing firms depends on an application of the common law rules in determining whether the PEO, the employee leasing firm, or the client is the employer of the worker.

Treatment of W-2 wages paid by spouses to determine domestic production activities deduction. Reg § 1.199-2(a)(4) prescribes that an individual and his or her spouse are considered one taxpayer for purposes of determining the amount of W-2 wages for a tax year, provided that they file a joint return for the tax year. Thus, an individual filing as part of a joint return may include the wages of employees of his or her spouse in determining W-2 wages, provided the employees are employed in a trade or business of the spouse and the other relevant requirements are met. However, a married taxpayer filing a separate return from his or her spouse for the tax year may not include the wages of employees of the taxpayer's spouse in determining the taxpayer's W-2 wages for the tax year. To illustrate the application of this rule, an example is set forth below:

> *Example 7-29:* John and Jane Smith, husband and wife, file a joint return reporting two schedule C activities, one for John who is engaged exclusively in a Code Sec. 199 activity operating without any employees and one for Jane, who operates a beauty parlor and has employees. For purposes of Code Sec. 199, the couple can utilize Jane's employees from the beauty parlor for purposes of calculating the W-2 wage limitation. If the couple filed a separate return, John could not utilize his wife's employees for such a determination.

---

[155] 2006-45 IRB, Sec. 3.02.

Short taxable year. Reg. § 1.199-2(b) prescribes that if a taxpayer has a short taxable year, the taxpayer only includes W-2 wages paid during the short taxable year.

Acquisition or disposition of a trade or business (or major portion). Reg. § 1.199-2(c) prescribes that if a taxpayer (a successor) acquires a trade or business, the major portion of a trade or business, or the major portion of a separate unit of a trade or business from another taxpayer (a predecessor), then, for purposes of computing the respective Code Sec. 199 deduction of the successor and of the predecessor, the W-2 wages paid for that calendar year shall be allocated between the successor and the predecessor based on whether the wages are for employment by the successor or for employment by the predecessor. Thus, in this situation, the W-2 wages are allocated based on whether the wages are for employment for a period during which the employee was employed by the predecessor or for employment for a period during which the employee was employed by the successor, regardless of which permissible method for Form W-2 reporting is used.

W-2 wages have to be allocable to domestic production receipts. Reg. § 1.199-2T(e)(2)(i) prescribes that for purposes of W-2 Wages, they must be allocable to domestic production gross receipts (see the definition of this term below) with these wages demarcated as "threshold W-2 wages." Reg. § 1.199-2T(e)(2)(ii) details that there are 2 safe harbors to compute threshold W-2 wages, "the 861 method" utilizing Code Sec. 861 and "the simplified deduction method" with the regulations providing six examples illustrating the concept. Two of the examples are set forth below to illustrate the safe harbors:

> *Example 7-30: Code Sec. 861 method and no expanded affiliated group (EAG).* X, a United States corporation that is not a member of an EAG (as defined in Reg. § 1.199-7) or an affiliated group as defined in the regulations under Code Sec. 861, engages in activities that generate both domestic production gross receipts (DPGR) and non-DPGR. X's taxable year ends on April 30, 2011. For X's taxable year ending April 30, 2011, X has $3,000 of wages reported on 2010 Forms W-2. All of X's production activities that generate DPGR are within Standard Industrial Classification (SIC) Industry Group AAA (SIC AAA). All of X's production activities that generate non-DPGR are within SIC Industry Group BBB (SIC BBB). X is able to specifically identify cost of goods sold (CGS) allocable to DPGR and to non-DPGR. X incurs $900 of research and experimentation expenses (R&E) that are deductible under Code Sec. 174, $300 of which are performed with respect to SIC AAA and $600 of which are performed with respect to SIC BBB. None of the R&E is legally mandated R&E as described in Reg. § 1.861-17(a)(4) and none of the R&E is included in CGS. X incurs Code Sec. 162 selling expenses that are not includible in CGS and are definitely related to all of X's gross income. For X's taxable year ending April 30, 2011, the adjusted basis of X's assets is $50,000, $40,000 of which generate gross income attributable to DPGR and $10,000 of which generate gross income attributable to non-DPGR. For X's taxable year ending April 30, 2011, the total square footage of X's headquarters is 8,000 square feet, of which 2,000 square feet is set aside for domestic production

activities. For its taxable year ending April 30, 2011, X's taxable income is $1,380 based on the following Federal income tax items:

DPGR (all from sales of products within SIC AAA)	$ 3,000
Non-DPGR (all from sales of products within SIC BBB)	3,000
CGS allocable to DPGR (includes $200 of wage expense) . . .	(600)
CGS allocable to non-DPGR (includes $600 of wage expense)	(1,800)
Code Sec. 162 selling expenses (includes $600 of wage expense)	(840)
Code Sec. 174 R&E-SIC AAA (includes $100 of wage expense)	(300)
Code Sec. 174 R&E-SIC BBB (includes $200 of wage expense)	(600)
Interest expense (not included in CGS)	(300)
Headquarters overhead expense (includes $100 of wage expense)	(180)
X's taxable income	1,380

X's Qualified Production Activities Income "QPAI". X allocates and apportions its deductions to gross income attributable to DPGR under the Code Sec. 861 method in Reg. § 1.199-4(d). In this case, the Code Sec.162 selling expenses and overhead expense are definitely related to all of X's gross income. Based on the facts and circumstances of this specific case, apportionment of the Code Sec. 162 selling expenses between DPGR and non-DPGR on the basis of X's gross receipts is appropriate. In addition, based on the facts and circumstances of this specific case, apportionment of the headquarters overhead expense between DPGR and non-DPGR on the basis of the square footage of X's headquarters is appropriate. For purposes of apportioning R&E, X elects to use the sales method as described in Reg. § 1.861-17(c). X elects to apportion interest expense under the tax book value method of Reg. § 1.861-9T(g). X has $2,400 of gross income attributable to DPGR (DPGR of $3,000—CGS of $600 allocated based on X's books and records). X's QPAI for its taxable year ending April 30, 2011 is $1,395, as shown in the following table:

DPGR (all from sales of products within SIC AAA)	$ 3,000
CGS allocable to DPGR	(600)
Code Sec. 162 selling expenses ($840 × ($3,000 DPGR/$6,000 total gross receipts))	(420)
Code Sec. 174 R&E-SIC AAA	(300)
Interest expense (not included in CGS) ($300 × ($40,000 (X's DPGR assets)/$50,000 (X's total assets)))	(240)
Headquarters overhead expense ($180 × (2,000 square feet attributable to DPGR activity/total 8,000 square feet))	(45)
X's QPAI	1,395

W-2 wages. X chooses to use the Reg § 1.199-2T(e)(2)(ii) wage safe harbor to determine its W-2 wages, as shown in the following steps:

(A) Step one. X determines that $625 of wage expense were taken into account in determining its QPAI as shown in the following table:

CGS wage expense	$200
Code Sec. 162 selling expenses wage expense ($600 × ($3,000 DPGR/$6,000 total gross receipts))	300
Code Sec. 174 R&E-SIC AAA wage expense	100
Headquarters overhead wage expense ($100 × (2,000 square feet attributable to DPGR activity/8,000 total square feet))	25
Total wage expense taken into account	625

(B) Step two. X determines that $1,042 of the $3,000 in paragraph (e)(1) wages are properly allocable to DPGR, and are therefore W-2 wages, as shown in the following calculation:

$$\frac{\text{Step one wage expense}}{\begin{array}{c}\text{X's total wage expense for}\\ \text{taxable year ending}\\ \text{April 30, 2011}\end{array}} \times \text{X's paragraph (e)(1) wages}$$

$$\frac{\$625}{\$1,800} \times \$3,000 = \$1,042$$

Code Sec. 199 deduction determination. X's tentative deduction under Reg. § 1.199-1(a) (Code Sec. 199 deduction) is $124 (.09 × (lesser of QPAI of $1,395 or taxable income of $1,380)) subject to the wage limitation under Code Sec. 199(b)(1) (W-2 wage limitation) of $521 (50% × $1,042). Accordingly, X's Code Sec. 199 deduction for its taxable year ending April 30, 2011 is $124.

Example 7-31: *Simplified deduction method.* Z, a corporation that is not a member of an Expanded Affiliated Group (EAG), engages in activities that generate both DPGR and non-DPGR. Z is able to specifically identify CGS allocable to DPGR and to non-DPGR. Z's taxable year ends on April 30, 2011. For Z's taxable year ending April 30, 2011, Z has $3,000 wages reported on 2010 Forms W-2, and Z's taxable income is $1,380 based on the following Federal income tax items:

DPGR...	$ 3,000
Non-DPGR....................................	3,000
CGS allocable to DPGR (includes $200 of wage expense) ...	(600)
CGS allocable to non-DPGR (includes $600 of wage expense)	(1,800)
Expenses, losses, or deductions (deductions) (includes $1,000 of wage expense)	(2,220)
Z's taxable income	1,380

Z's QPAI. Z uses the simplified deduction method to apportion deductions between DPGR and non-DPGR. Z's QPAI for its taxable year ending April 30, 2011 is $1,290, as shown in the following table:

DPGR...	$ 3,000
CGS allocable to DPGR	(600)
Deductions apportioned to DPGR ($2,220 × ($3,000 DPGR/$6,000 total gross receipts))	(1,110)
Z's QPAI...	1,290

W-2 wages. Z chooses to use the wage expense safe harbor under Reg § 1.199-2T (e)(2)(ii) to determine its W-2 wages, as shown in the following steps:

(A) Step one. Z determines that $700 of wage expense were taken into account in determining its QPAI, as shown in the following table:

Wage expense included in CGS allocable to DPGR	$200
Wage expense included in deductions ($1,000 in wage expense x ($3,000 DPGR/$6,000 total gross receipts))	500
Wage expense allocable to DPGR	700

(B) Step two. Z determines that $1,167 of the $3,000 paragraph (e)(1) wages are properly allocable to DPGR, and are therefore W-2 wages, as shown in the following calculation:

$$\frac{\text{Step one wage expense}}{\substack{\text{Z's total wage expense for} \\ \text{taxable year ending} \\ \text{April 30, 2011}}} \times \text{Z's paragraph (e)(1) wages}$$

$$\frac{\$700}{\$1,800} \times \$3,000 = \$1,167$$

Code Sec. 199 deduction determination. Z's tentative Code Sec. 199 deduction is $116 (.09 × (lesser of QPAI of $1,290 or taxable income of $1,380)) subject to the W-2 wage limitation of $584 (50% × $1,167). Accordingly, Z's Code Sec. 199 deduction for its taxable year ending April 30, 2011 is $116.

Tax Pointer 1: Calculation of W-2 Wages has various effective dates. For taxable years prior to May 18, 2006, there was no requirement that W-2 wages be allocated to domestic production gross receipts. Thus, if a taxpayer was engaged in various activities, (i.e., a service business and manufacturing), the taxpayer could allocate all the W-2 wages (manufacturing and service) for purposes of determining the W-2 wage limitation.

¶722.02

Tax Pointer 2: The Preamble to the Proposed Regulations dated October 21, 2005 state that guaranteed payments to partners are not W-2 wage.

Tax Pointer 3: Because partners in a partnership cannot be employees for purposes of Code Sec. 199, the partnership (or an LLC classified as a partnership for tax purposes) if it has no employees will have to convert to an S corporation in order to take advantage of the Code Sec. 199 deduction.

.03 Definition of "Qualified Production Activities Income" (QPAI)

To obtain a Code Sec. 199 deduction, a taxpayer must have Qualified Production Activities Income (QPAI). Code Sec. 199(c)(1) defines "QPAI" to mean, for any taxable year, an amount equal to the excess (if any) of:

(a) the taxpayer's domestic production gross receipts (DPGR) for such taxable year, over

(b) the sum of:

　(i) the cost of goods sold that are allocable to such receipts,

　(ii) other deductions, expenses, or losses directly allocable to such receipts, and

　(iii) a ratable portion of other deductions, expenses, and losses that are not directly allocable to such receipts or another class of income.

Tax Pointer: Code Sec. 199's deduction is geared to the taxpayer's "domestic production gross receipts," with the location of the production activity, rather than the source of the income, determining whether the deduction is available. Thus, in some cases, QPAI could be foreign-source income.

Code Sec. 199(c)(2) prescribes that the Secretary shall prescribe rules for the proper allocation of items of income, deduction, expense, and loss for purposes of determining income attributable to domestic production activities.

.04 Cost of Goods Sold (CGS) Allocable to DPGR

Reg. § 1.199-4(b) prescribes detailed rules for calculation of CGS. Pertinent provisions are detailed below. Reg. § 1.199-4(b)(1) generally prescribes that when determining its QPAI, a taxpayer must subtract from DPGR the CGS allocable to DPGR. In the case of a sale, exchange, or other disposition of inventory, CGS is equal to beginning inventory plus purchases and production costs incurred during the taxable year and included in inventory costs, less ending inventory. CGS is determined under the methods of accounting that the taxpayer uses to compute taxable income. In computing CGS, the taxpayer should incorporate Code Secs. 263A, 471, and 472.

Special rules for imported items or services. Reg. § 1.199-4(b)(3) provides that the cost of any item or service brought into the United States without an arm's length transfer price may not be treated as less than its value immediately after it entered the United States for purposes of determining the CGS to be used in the computation of QPAI. Similarly, the adjusted basis of leased or rented property that gives rise to DPGR that has been brought into the United States without an arm's length transfer price may not be treated as less than its value immediately after it entered the United States. When an item or service is imported into the United States that had been exported by the taxpayer for further manufacture, the increase in cost may not exceed the difference between the value of the property when exported and the value of the property when imported back into the United States after further manufacture. For this purpose, the value of property is its customs value as defined in Code Sec. 1059A(b)(1).

Rules for inventories valued at market or bona fide selling prices. Reg. § 1.199-4(b)(4) prescribes that if part of CGS is attributable to inventory valuation adjustments, then CGS allocable to DPGR includes inventory adjustments to Qualified Production Property (QPP) that is MPGE in whole or in significant part within the United States. Accordingly, taxpayers that value inventory under Reg. § 1.471-4 (inventories at cost or market, whichever is lower) or Reg. § 1.471-2(c) (subnormal goods at bona fide selling prices) must allocate a proper share of such adjustments (for example, writedowns) to DPGR based on a reasonable method that is satisfactory to the Secretary based on all of the facts and circumstances.

Rules applicable to inventories accounted for under the last-in, first-out (LIFO) inventory method and taxpayers using the simplified production method or simplified resale method for additional Code Sec. 263A costs. Reg. § 1.199-4(b)(5) and (6) provide rules for computation of the inventory under these methods.

Examples illustrating some of the provisions of Reg. § 1.199-4(b) are set forth below:

> **Example 7-32:** *Advance payments.* T, a calendar year taxpayer, is a manufacturer of furniture in the United States. Under its method of accounting, T includes advance payments and other gross receipts derived from the sale of furniture in gross income when the payments are received. In December 2007, T receives an advance payment of $5,000 from X with respect to an order of furniture to be manufactured for a total price of $20,000. In 2008, T produces and sells the furniture to X. In 2008, T incurs $14,000 of Code Sec. 471 expense and additional Code Sec. 263A costs to produce the furniture ordered by X. T receives the remaining $15,000 of the contract price from X in 2008. Assuming that in 2007 the advance payment qualifies as DPGR in 2007 and 2008, the remaining $15,000 of the contract price must be included in income and DPGR when received by T in 2008. T must include the $14,000 it incurred to produce the furniture in CGS and CGS allocable to DPGR in 2008.

> **Example 7-33:** *Use of standard cost method.* X, a calendar year taxpayer, manufactures item A in a factory located in the United States and item B in a factory located in Country Y. Item A is produced by X within the United States and the sale of A generates DPGR. X uses the FIFO inventory method to account for its inventory and determines the cost of item A using a standard cost method. At the beginning of its 2007 taxable year, X's inventory contains 2,000 units of item A at a standard cost of $5 per unit. X did not incur

significant cost variances in previous taxable years. During the 2007 taxable year, X produces 8,000 units of item A at a standard cost of $6 per unit. X determines that with regard to its production of item A it has incurred a significant cost variance. When X reallocates the cost variance to the units of item A that it has produced, the production cost of item A is $7 per unit. X sells 7,000 units of item A during the taxable year. X can identify from its books and records that CGS related to the sales of item A during the taxable year are $45,000 ((2,000 x $5) + (5,000 x $7)). Accordingly, X has CGS allocable to DPGR of $45,000.

.05 Allocation of Gross Receipts between DPGR and non-DPGR

Reg. § 1.199-1(d)(1) provides that a taxpayer must determine the portion of its gross receipts for the taxable year that is DPGR and the portion of its gross receipts that is non-DPGR. Applicable Federal income tax principles apply to determine whether a transaction is, in substance, a lease, rental, license, sale, exchange, or other disposition the gross receipts of which may constitute DPGR, whether it is a service the gross receipts of which may constitute non-DPGR, or some combination thereof. For example, if a taxpayer leases QPP and in connection with that lease also provides services, the taxpayer must allocate its gross receipts from the transaction using any reasonable method based on all of the facts and circumstances and that accurately identifies the gross receipts that constitute DPGR and non-DPGR.

De minimis rules. Reg. § 1.199-1(d)(3)(i) provides that if less than 5% of the taxpayer's gross receipts are from non-DPGR, then all the taxpayer's gross receipts can be treated as DPGR. However, if the non-DPGR exceed 5%, then an allocation is required.

S corporations and other pass-through entities method of allocation. Reg. § 1.199-1(d)(3)(ii) states that in the case of an S corporation, partnership, trust or estate, or other pass-through entity, the determination of whether less than 5 percent of the pass-through entity's total gross receipts are non-DPGR is made at the pass-through entity level. In the case of an owner of a pass-through entity, the determination of whether less than 5 percent of the owner's total gross receipts are non-DPGR is made at the owner level, taking into account all gross receipts of the owner from its other trade or business activities and the owner's share of the gross receipts of the pass-through entity.

An example will illustrate the allocation procedure between DPGR and non-DPGR:

Example 7-34: X derives its gross receipts from the sale of gasoline refined by X within the United States and the sale of refined gasoline that X acquired by purchase from an unrelated person. If at least 5% of X's gross receipts are derived from gasoline refined by X within the United States that qualify as DPGR and at least 5% of X's gross receipts are derived from the resale of the acquired gasoline (that do not qualify as DPGR), then X does not qualify for the de minimis rules and X must allocate its gross receipts between the gross receipts derived from the sale of gasoline refined by X within the

United States and the gross receipts derived from the resale of the acquired gasoline. If less than 5% of X's gross receipts are derived from the resale of the acquired gasoline, then X may either allocate its gross receipts between the gross receipts derived from the gasoline refined by X within the United States and the gross receipts derived from the resale of the acquired gasoline, or X may treat all of its gross receipts derived from the sale of the refined gasoline as DPGR. If X's gross receipts attributable to the gasoline refined by X within the United States constitute less than 5% of X's total gross receipts, then X may either allocate its gross receipts between the gross receipts derived from the gasoline refined by X within the United States and the gross receipts derived from the resale of the acquired gasoline, or X may treat all of its gross receipts derived from the sale of the refined gasoline as non-DPGR.

Multiple-year transactions. Reg. § 1.199-1(e) prescribes rules for taxpayers who use a percentage of completion method and/or who receive advance payments with respect to their activities.

Advance Payments. If a taxpayer recognizes and reports gross receipts from advance payments or other similar payments on a Federal income tax return for a taxable year, then the taxpayer's use of historical data in making an allocation of gross receipts from the transaction between DPGR and non-DPGR may constitute a reasonable method. If a taxpayer makes allocations using historical data, and subsequently updates the data, then the taxpayer must use the more recent or updated data, starting in the taxable year in which the update is made.

Percentage of completion method. A taxpayer using a percentage of completion method under Code Sec. 460 must determine the ratio of DPGR and non-DPGR using a reasonable method that is satisfactory to the Secretary based on all of the facts and circumstances that accurately identifies the gross receipts that constitute DPGR.

Examples illustrating the rules for multiple-year transactions is set forth below:

Example 7-35: On December 1, 2009, X, a calendar year accrual method taxpayer, sells for $100 a one-year computer software maintenance agreement that provides for (i) computer software updates that X expects to produce in the United States, and (ii) customer support services. At the end of 2009, X uses a reasonable method based on all of the facts and circumstances to allocate 60% of the gross receipts ($60) to the computer software updates and 40% ($40) to the customer support services. X treats the $60 as DPGR in 2009. At the expiration of the one-year agreement on November 30, 2010, no computer software updates are provided by X. Because X used a reasonable method based on all of the facts and circumstances to identify gross receipts as DPGR, X is not required to make any adjustments to its 2009 Federal income tax return (for example, by amended return) or in 2010 for the $60 that was properly treated as DPGR in 2009, even though no computer software updates were provided under the contract.

Example 7-36: X manufactures automobiles within the United States and sells 5-year extended warranties to customers. The sales price of the warranty is based on historical data that determines what repairs and services are performed on an automobile during the 5-year period. X sells the 5-year warranty to Y for $1,000 in 2010. Under X's method of accounting, X recognizes warranty revenue when received. Using historical data, X concludes that 60% of the gross receipts attributable to a 5-year warranty will be derived from the sale of parts (QPP) that X manufactures within the United States, and 40% will be derived from the sale of purchased parts X did not manufacture and non-qualifying services. X's method of allocating its gross receipts with respect to the 5-year warranty between DPGR and non-DPGR is a reasonable method that is satisfactory to the Secretary based on all of the facts and circumstances. Therefore, X properly treats $600 as DPGR in 2010.

> *Tax Pointer:* Because the Code Sec. 199 deduction is inversely proportional to the amount of expenses which must be offset against domestic production gross receipts, taxpayers will carefully review allocations being made to these expenses, so as to arrive at the maximum deduction possible.

.06 Domestic Production Gross Receipts (DPGR)

Code Sec. 199(c)(4) prescribes that the term "domestic production gross receipts" (DPGR) means the gross receipts of the taxpayer which are derived from:

   (a) any lease, rental, license, sale, exchange, or other disposition of:

      (i) qualifying production property (QPP) which was manufactured, produced, grown, or extracted (MPGE) by the taxpayer in whole or in significant part within the United States,

      (ii) any qualified film produced by the taxpayer, or

      (iii) electricity, natural gas, or potable water produced by the taxpayer in the United States,

   (b) construction performed in the United States, or

   (c) engineering or architectural services performed in the United States for construction projects in the United States.

> *Tax Pointer 1:* Reg. § 1.199-3(i)(4)(i)(A) states that except for construction and engineering/architectural services, the domestic production activities deduction is not available with respect to the performance of services. Accordingly, professional service companies, such as lawyers, will not qualify for the deduction because they are selling their services, despite the fact that they provide a tangible item such as a legal document.

> *Tax Pointer 2:* Reg. § 1.199-3(i)(9) provides that DPGR do not include gross receipts derived from non-operating mineral interests—for example, interests other than operating mineral interests within the meaning of Reg. § 1.614-2(b) and Reg. § 1.199-3(p) states that DPGR do not include guaranteed payments to a partner under Code Sec. 707(c).

> *Tax Pointer 3:* For tax years beginning before June 1, 2006, Reg. § 1.199-3's regulatory rules did not apply; instead the earlier proposed reliance regulations applied, except that the proposed reliance regulations did not have any equivalent to the rule regarding guaranteed payments for partners.

¶722.06

Definition of Gross Receipts (GR). Reg. § 1.199-3(c)(3) provides that the definition of gross receipts (GR) includes:

- Total sales (net of returns and allowances) and all amounts received for services;

- Any income from investments and from incidental or outside sources. For example, gross receipts include interest (including original issue discount and tax-exempt interest within the meaning of Code Sec. 103), dividends, rents, royalties, and annuities, regardless of whether the amounts are derived in the ordinary course of the taxpayer's trade or business; and

- Gross receipts are not reduced by cost of goods sold (CGS) or by the cost of property sold if such property is described in Code Sec. 1221(a)(1), (2), (3), (4), or (5).

Reg. § 1.199-3(c)(3) provides in pertinent part that GR do not include:

- Except to the extent of gain recognized, gross receipts derived from a nonrecognition transaction, such as a Code Sec. 1031 exchange;

- Amounts received by the taxpayer with respect to sales tax or other similar state and local taxes if, under the applicable state or local law, the tax is legally imposed on the purchaser of the good or service and the taxpayer merely collects and remits the tax to the taxing authority. If, in contrast, the tax is imposed on the taxpayer under the applicable law, then gross receipts include the amounts received that are allocable to the payment of such tax; and

- Amounts received in repayment of a loan or similar instrument (for example, a repayment of the principal amount of a loan held by a commercial lender).

Tax Pointer 4: While Reg. § 1.199-3(c) permits the inclusion in gross receipts of items not derived in the ordinary course of the taxpayer's trade or business such as interest, Reg. § 1.199-8(c)(1) appears to prohibit the inclusion of those types of items in computing the domestic production activities deduction because it states that Reg. § § 1.199-1 through 1.199-9 are applied by taking into account only items that are attributable to the actual conduct of a trade or business.

Reg. § 1.199-3(d)(1) requires that a taxpayer determine whether GR qualify as DPGR on an item-by-item basis. Thus, determining GR on a division-by-division, product-line-by-product-line, or transaction-by-transaction basis will not qualify. The regulations prescribe that to determine an "item" taxpayers must engage in a two part test geared to the taxpayer's normal course of business: does the taxpayer offer the property in the taxpayer's normal course of business? If so, the item qualifies. If not, is any component of the property offered in the ordinary course of business? If so, the component qualifies.

An example from Reg. § 1.199-3(d)(4) will illustrate:

Example 7-37: Q manufactures leather and rubber shoe soles in the United States. Q imports shoe uppers, which are the parts of the shoe above

¶722.06

the sole. Q manufactures shoes for sale by sewing or otherwise attaching the soles to the imported uppers. Q offers the shoes for sale to customers in the normal course of Q's business. Because Q did not manufacture the "uppers," this is not an "item" for DPGR. However, because Q manufactures the soles, the soles count as a "component," and thus they can be used to determine DPGR.

Hedging transactions. Reg. § 1.199-3 (i) (3) (i) prescribes that hedging can be considered DPGR providing:

> the risk being hedged relates to QPP described in Code Sec.1221 (a) (1) or relates to property described in Code Sec. 1221 (a) (8) consumed in an activity giving rise to DPGR, and provided that the transaction is a hedging transaction within the meaning of Code Sec.1221 (b) (2) (A) and Reg. § 1.1221-2 (b) and is properly identified as a hedging transaction in accordance with Reg. § 1.1221-2 (f). If this occurs, then
>
> (A) In the case of a hedge of purchases of property described in Code Sec. 1221 (a) (1), gain or loss on the hedging transaction must be taken into account in determining CGS;
>
> (B) In the case of a hedge of sales of property described in Code Sec. 1221 (a) (1), gain or loss on the hedging transaction must be taken into account in determining DPGR; and
>
> (C) In the case of a hedge of purchases of property described in Code Sec.1221 (a) (8), gain or loss on the hedging transaction must be taken into account in determining DPGR.

Lease income. Reg. § 1.199-3 (l) (ii) states that the financing and interest components of a lease of QPP or a qualified film are considered to be derived from the lease of such QPP or qualified film. However, any portion of the lease income that is attributable to services or non-qualified property generally is not derived from the lease of QPP or a qualified film.

Income substitutes (Business interruption insurance, government subsidies, etc). Reg. § 1.199-3 (l) (iii) states that the proceeds from business interruption insurance, governmental subsidies, and governmental payments not to produce are treated as gross receipts derived from the lease, rental, license, sale, exchange, or other disposition to the extent that they are substitutes for gross receipts that would qualify as DPGR.

Related persons. Reg. § 1.199-3 (b) (2) prescribes however that gross receipts derived from the license of QPP to a related person for reproduction and sale, exchange, lease, rental, or sublicense to an unrelated person for the ultimate use of the unrelated person may qualify as DPGR.

Manufacturing, Producing, Growing or Extracting (MPGE) for QPP. Reg. § 1.199-3 (e) (1) states that the

> term "MPGE" includes manufacturing, producing, growing, extracting, installing, developing, improving, and creating QPP; making QPP out of scrap, salvage, or junk material as well as from new or raw material by processing, manipulating, refining, or changing the form of an article, or by combining or assembling two or more articles; cultivating soil, raising livestock, fishing, and mining minerals. The term MPGE also includes storage, handling, or other processing activities (other than transportation activities) within the United

¶722.06

States related to the sale, exchange, or other disposition of agricultural products, provided the products are consumed in connection with or incorporated into the MPGE of QPP, whether or not by the taxpayer. Pursuant to Reg. § 1.199-3(f)(1), the taxpayer must have the benefits and burdens of ownership of the QPP under Federal income tax principles during the period the MPGE activity occurs in order for gross receipts derived from the MPGE of QPP to qualify as DPGR.

Reg. § 1.199-3(e)(2) and (3) prescribe special rules for installations and packaging, repacking, labeling and minor assembly of items.

- *Packaging, repackaging, labeling, or minor assembly.* If a taxpayer packages, repackages, labels, or performs minor assembly of QPP and the taxpayer engages in no other MPGE activity with respect to that QPP, the taxpayer's packaging, repackaging, labeling, or minor assembly does not qualify as MPGE with respect to that QPP.

- *Installing.* If a taxpayer installs QPP and engages in no other MPGE activity with respect to the QPP, the taxpayer's installing activity does not qualify as an MPGE activity. However, if the taxpayer installs QPP and the taxpayer has the benefits and burdens of ownership of the QPP under Federal income tax principles during the period the installing activity occurs, then the portion of the installing activity that relates to the QPP is an MPGE activity.

The following examples are set forth to illustrate application of the rules:

Example 7-38: Z engages in MPGE QPP within the United States. The following activities are performed by Z as part of the MPGE of the QPP while Z has the benefits and burdens of ownership under Federal income tax principles: materials analysis and selection, subcontractor inspections and qualifications, testing of component parts, assisting customers in their review and approval of the QPP, routine production inspections, product documentation, diagnosis and correction of system failure, and packaging for shipment to customers. Because Z MPGE the QPP, these activities performed by Z are part of the MPGE of the QPP.

Example 7-39: X purchases automobiles from unrelated persons and customizes them by adding ground effects, spoilers, custom wheels, specialized paint and decals, sunroofs, roof racks, and similar accessories. X does not manufacture any of the accessories. X's activity is minor assembly and is not an MPGE activity.

Definition of "by the taxpayer". To qualify for a Code Sec. 199 deduction, the MPGE must be done "by the taxpayer." Reg. § 1.199-3(f)(1) defines "by the taxpayer" to mean the one who " has the benefits and burdens of ownership" of the property during the period the activity occurs. Consequently, if one taxpayer performs a qualifying activity pursuant to a contract with another party, then only the taxpayer that has the benefits and burdens of ownership of the QPP, qualified film, or utilities under Federal income tax principles during the period in which the qualifying activity occurs is treated as engaging in the qualifying activity. To deal with members of an expanded affiliated group (EAG), activities involving qualifying in-kind partnerships as defined by Reg. § 1.199-3T(i)(7), activities involving EAG

¶722.06

partnerships, sub-contractors and government contracts, Reg. § 1.199-3(f)(2) and (3) provide special rules. An example will illustrate the basic rules defining "by the taxpayer:"

> ***Example 7-40:*** X designs machines that it uses in its trade or business. X contracts with Y, an unrelated person, for the manufacture of the machines. The contract between X and Y is a fixed-price contract. The contract specifies that the machines will be manufactured in the United States using X's design. X owns the intellectual property attributable to the design and provides it to Y with a restriction that Y may only use it during the manufacturing process and has no right to exploit the intellectual property. The contract specifies that Y controls the details of the manufacturing process while the machines are being produced; Y bears the risk of loss or damage during manufacturing of the machines; and Y has the economic loss or gain upon the sale of the machines based on the difference between Y's costs and the fixed price. Y has legal title during the manufacturing process and legal title to the machines is not transferred to X until final manufacturing of the machines has been completed. Based on all of the facts and circumstances, Y has the benefits and burdens of ownership of the machines under Federal income tax principles during the period the manufacturing occurs and, as a result, Y is treated as the manufacturer of the machines.

MPGE activity takes must be "in whole or in significant part" within the United States. Reg. § 1.199-3(g)(1) prescribes that to obtain a Code Sec. 199 deduction, the QPP must be manufactured, produced, grown or extracted by the taxpayer "in significant part" within the United States. A taxpayer will satisfy this requirement by either the "substantial in nature" or the "safe harbor" tests discussed below.

Substantial in nature test. Reg. § 1.199-3(g)(2) states that QPP will be treated as manufactured, produced, grown or extracted by the taxpayer in significant part within the United States if, based on all of the facts and circumstances, the manufacturing, production, growth, or extraction activity (the "qualified manufacturing activity") performed by the taxpayer in the United States is substantial in nature. The facts and circumstances taken into account in making this determination include the relative value added by, and relative cost of, the taxpayer's qualified manufacturing activity in the United States, the nature of the property, and the nature of the qualified manufacturing activity that the taxpayer performs in the United States. As to the manufacture, production, growth, or extraction of a key component of qualifying production property, this does not, in itself, meet the substantial-in-nature requirement with respect to the qualifying production property.

"In significant part" safe harbor. Reg. § 1.199-3(g)(3) provides a mathematical safe harbor to determine if qualifying production property will be treated as manufactured, produced, grown or extracted by the taxpayer in significant part within the United States geared to the taxpayer's direct labor and overhead to manufacture, produce, grow, or extract that property within the United States. Specifically, if the taxpayer's direct labor and overhead account for either:

¶722.06

(1) 20% or more of the taxpayer's cost of goods sold for the property; or

(2) in a transaction without cost of goods sold (for example, a lease, rental, or license), 20% or more of the taxpayer's unadjusted depreciable basis in the property. "Unadjusted depreciable basis" means per Reg. § 1.199-3(g)(3)(ii) "the basis of property for purposes of Code Sec. 1011 without regard to any adjustments described in Code Sec. 1016(a)(2) and Code Sec. 1016(a)(3)." Further, Reg. § 1.199-3(g)(3)(ii)(A) and (B) provides that the adjusted depreciable basis does not reflect the reduction in basis for: any portion of the basis the taxpayer properly elects to treat as an expense under Code Sec. 179 or 179C, or any adjustments to basis provided by other provisions of the Code and regulations (for example, a reduction in basis by the amount of the disabled access credit pursuant to Code Sec. 44(d)(7)).

Examples illustrating the rules are set forth below:

Example 7-41: X purchases gemstones and precious metal from outside the United States and then uses these materials to produce jewelry within the United States by cutting and polishing the gemstones, melting and shaping the metal, and combining the finished materials. X's MPGE activities are substantial in nature. Therefore, X has MPGE with respect to the jewelry because of the large amount of work done in the United States.

Example 7-42: X operates an automobile assembly plant in the United States. In connection with such activity, X purchases assembled engines, transmissions, and certain other components from Y, an unrelated person, and X assembles all of the component parts into an automobile. X also conducts stamping, machining, and subassembly operations, and X uses tools, jigs, welding equipment, and other machinery and equipment in the assembly of automobiles. On a per-unit basis, X's selling price and costs of such automobiles are as follows:

Selling price	$2,500
Cost of goods sold:	
Material—Acquired from Y:	$1,475
Direct labor and overhead:	$ 325
Total cost of goods sold:	$1,800
Gross profit:	$ 700
Administrative and selling expenses:	$ 300
Taxable income:	$ 400

Although X's direct labor and overhead are less than 20% of total CGS ($325/$1,800, or 18%), X is not within the "in significant part" safe harbor, the activities conducted by X in connection with the assembly of an automobile are substantial in nature taking into account the nature of X's activity and the relative value of X's activity. Therefore, X's automobiles will be treated as MPGE in significant part by X within the United States.

Example 7-43: X is a retailer within the United States that sells cigars and pipe tobacco that X purchases from an unrelated person. While being displayed and offered for sale by X, the cigars and pipe tobacco age on X's shelves in a room with controlled temperature and humidity. Although X's cigars and pipe tobacco may become more valuable as they age, the gross receipts derived by X from the sale of the cigars and pipe tobacco are non-DPGR because the aging of the cigars and pipe tobacco while being displayed and offered for sale by X does not qualify as an MPGE activity that is substantial in nature.

Definition of the United States. To obtain a Code Sec. 199 deduction, the MPGE activity must be "in whole or in significant part" within the United States. Reg. § 1.199-3(h) defines the term "United States" as including the 50 states, the District of Columbia, the territorial waters of the United States, and the seabed and subsoil of those submarine areas that are adjacent to the territorial waters of the United States and over which the United States has exclusive rights, in accordance with international law, with respect to the exploration and exploitation of natural resources. The term United States does not include possessions and territories of the United States or the airspace or space over the United States and these areas.

Construction activities performed in the United States. Reg. § 1.199-3(m)(1)(i) prescribes that to obtain a Code Sec. 199 deduction for "construction," the taxpayer must be engaged at the time the taxpayer constructs the real property in a construction trade or business on a regular and ongoing basis. In the case of a new construction trade or business Reg. § 1.199-3(m)(1)(ii) states that "in the case of a newly-formed trade or business or a taxpayer in its first taxable year, the taxpayer is considered to be engaged in a trade or business on a regular and ongoing basis if the taxpayer reasonably expects that it will engage in a trade or business on a regular and ongoing basis."

Reg. § 1.199-3(m) defines "construction" broadly. Thus, the following activities will constitute "construction:"

Generally. Activities performed in connection with a project to erect or substantially renovate real property, including activities performed by a general contractor or that constitute activities typically performed by a general contractor; for example, activities relating to management and oversight of the construction process such as approvals, periodic inspection of the progress of the construction project, and required job modifications. Reg. § 1.199-3(m) (5) defines "substantially renovate" to mean the renovation of a major component or substantial structural part of real property that materially increases the value of the property, substantially prolongs the useful life of the property, or adapts the property to a new or different use.

Tangential services. Activities constituting construction do not include tangential services such as hauling trash and debris, and delivering materials, even if the tangential services are essential for construction. However, if the taxpayer performing construction also, in connection with the construction project, provides tangential services such as delivering materials to the construction site and removing its construction debris, then the gross receipts derived from the tangential services are DPGR.

Other construction activities. Improvements to land that are not capitalizable to the land (for example, landscaping) and painting are activities constituting construction only if these activities are performed in connection with other activities (whether or not by the same taxpayer) that constitute the erection or substantial renovation of real property. Services such as grading, demolition (including demolition of structures under Code Sec. 280B), clearing, excavating, and any other activities that physically transform the land are activities constituting construction only if these services are performed in connection with other activities (whether or not by the same taxpayer) that constitute the erection or substantial renovation of real property. A taxpayer engaged in these activities must make a reasonable inquiry or a reasonable determination as to whether the activity relates to the erection or substantial renovation of real property in the United States. Construction activities also include activities relating to drilling an oil or gas well and mining and include any activities the cost of which are intangible drilling and development costs within the meaning of Reg. § 1.612-4 or development expenditures for a mine or natural deposit under Code Sec. 616.

Administrative support services. If the taxpayer performing construction activities also provides, in connection with the construction project, administrative support services (for example, billing and secretarial services) incidental and necessary to such construction project, then these administrative support services are considered construction activities.

Exceptions. The lease, license, or rental of equipment, for example, bulldozers, generators, or computers, for use in the construction of real property is not a construction activity. The term construction does not include any activity that is within the definition of engineering and architectural services under Code Sec. 199.

Reg. § 1.199-3(m)(1)(i) provides further clarification of the term "construction" by stating that a ""trade or business that is considered construction under the NAICS means a construction activity under the two-digit NAICS code of 23 and any other construction activity in any other NAICS code provided the construction activity relates to the construction of real property such as NAICS code 213111 (drilling oil and gas wells) and 213112 (support activities for oil and gas operations)...Tangible personal property (for example, appliances, furniture, and fixtures) that is sold as part of a construction project is not considered real property [for construction purposes]. In determining whether property is real property, the fact that property is real property under local law is not controlling. Conversely, property may be real property even though under local law the property is considered tangible personal property." Thus, infrastructure items such as sidewalks, power lines, sewers, cable, wiring, etc. qualify as construction.

Receipts derived from construction. To receive a Code Sec. 199 deduction from construction activities, Reg. § 1.199-3(m)(6)(i) details that generally, DPGR derived from the construction of real property performed in the United States includes the proceeds from the sale, exchange, or other disposition of real property constructed by the taxpayer in the United States (whether or not the property is

¶722.06

sold immediately after construction is completed and whether or not the construction project is completed). DPGR derived from the construction of real property includes compensation for the performance of construction services by the taxpayer in the United States. DPGR derived from the construction of real property includes gross receipts derived from materials and supplies consumed in the construction project or that become part of the constructed real property, assuming all the requirements of this section are met. Additionally, Reg. § 1.199-3(m)(6)(ii) provides that DPGR includes gross receipts from any qualified construction warranty, provided it is furnished in connection with the constructed real property in the normal course of the taxpayer's business and: (A) The price for the construction warranty is not separately stated from the amount charged for the constructed real property; and (B) The construction warranty is neither separately offered by the taxpayer nor separately bargained for with customers (that is, the customer cannot purchase the constructed real property without the construction warranty).

Reg. § 1.199-3(m)(6)(iii) excludes from the computation of DPGR those gross receipts derived from the sale, exchange, or other disposition of real property acquired by the taxpayer even if the taxpayer originally constructed the property. In addition, DPGR derived from the construction of real property does not include generally gross receipts from the lease or rental of real property constructed by the taxpayer, or gross receipts derived from the sale or other disposition of land (including zoning, planning, entitlement costs, and other costs capitalized to the land). However, Reg. § 1.199-3(m)(6)(iv) provides special rules to allow a taxpayer to allocate gross receipts between those realized on the sale, exchange or disposition of real property constructed by the taxpayer and those from sale, exchange or disposition of land.

Examples illustrating the rules are set forth below:

Example 7-44: A, who is in the trade or business of construction under NAICS Code 23 on a regular and ongoing basis, purchases a building in the United States and retains B, an unrelated person, to oversee a substantial renovation of the building. Although not licensed as a general contractor, B performs general contractor level work and activities relating to management and oversight of the construction process such as approvals, periodic inspection of the progress of the construction project, and required job modifications. B retains C (a general contractor) to oversee day-to-day operations and hire subcontractors. C hires D (a subcontractor) to install a new electrical system in the building as part of that substantial renovation. The amounts that B receives from A for construction services, the amounts that C receives from B for construction services, and the amounts that D receives from C for construction services qualify as DPGR. The gross receipts that A receives from the subsequent sale of the building do not qualify as DPGR because A did not engage in any activity constituting construction even though A is in the trade or business of construction. The results would be the same if A, B, C, and D were members of the same EAG under Reg. § 1.199-7(a).

Example 7-45: X, who is engaged in the trade or business of construction under NAICS Code 23 on a regular and ongoing basis, constructs housing that is classified as real property. On June 1, 2007, X pays $50,000,000 and acquires 1,000 acres of land that X will develop as a new housing development. In November 2007, after the expenditure of $10,000,000 for entitlement costs, X receives permits to begin construction. After this expenditure, X's land costs total $60,000,000. The development consists of 1,000 houses to be built on half-acre lots over 5 years. On January 31, 2012, the first house is sold for $300,000. Construction costs for each house are $170,000. Common improvements consisting of streets, sidewalks, sewer lines, playgrounds, clubhouses, tennis courts, and swimming pools that X is contractually obligated or required by law to provide cost $55,000 per lot. The common improvements of $55,000 per lot include $30,000 in land costs underlying the common improvements.

Pursuant to Reg. § 1.199-3(m)(6)(iv)'s safe harbor rules, X calculates the basis for each house sold as $195,000 (total costs of $255,000 ($170,000 in construction costs plus $55,000 in common improvements (including $30,000 in land costs) plus $30,000 in land costs for the lot), which are reduced by land costs of $60,000). X calculates the DPGR for each house sold by taking the gross receipts of $300,000 and reducing that amount by land costs of $60,000 plus a percentage of $60,000. As X acquired the land on June 1, 2007, for each house sold on the land between January 31, 2012, and June 1, 2012, the percentage reduction for X is 5% because X has held the land for not more than 60 months from the date of acquisition. Thus, X's DPGR for each house is $237,000 ($300,000 - $60,000 - $3,000) with costs for each house of $195,000 ($255,000 - $60,000). For each house sold on the land between June 2, 2012 and June 1, 2017, the percentage reduction for X is 10% because X has held the land for more than 60 months but not more than 120 months from the date of acquisition. Thus, of the $300,000 of gross receipts, X's DPGR for each house is $234,000 ($300,000 - $60,000 - $6,000) with costs for each house of $195,000 ($255,000 - $60,000).

> *Tax Pointer:* Care must be exercised by taxpayers who utilize the cash basis. For instance, the Tax Court has held that asphalt, concrete, and flooring contractors were deemed to provide services rather than selling and installing merchandise.[156]

Engineering and architectural services similar to construction activities. Code Sec. 199(c)(4)(c) prescribes that gross receipts derived from engineering or architectural services performed in the United States for a construction project are DPGR. Reg. § 199-3(n)(1) provides generally that to qualify, the taxpayer must be engaged in a trade or business (but not necessarily its primary, or only, trade or business) that is considered engineering or architectural services for purposes of the NAICS, for example NAICS codes 541330 (engineering services) or 541310 (architectural services), on a regular and ongoing basis at the time the taxpayer performs the engineering or architectural services. In the case of a newly-formed trade or business or a taxpayer in its first taxable year, a taxpayer is considered to

---

[156] *Jim Turin & Sons, Inc. v. Comm.*, TC Memo 1998-223; *Galedrige Construction, Inc. v. Comm.*, TC Memo 1997-240 (asphalt)—*RACMP Enterprises, Inc. v. Comm.*, 114 TC 211 (2000); *Vandra Bros. Construction Co., Inc. v. Comm.*, TC Memo 2000-233 (concrete)—*Smith v. Comm.*, TC Memo 2000-353 (flooring).

be engaged in a trade or business on a regular and ongoing basis if the taxpayer reasonably expects that it will engage in a trade or business on a regular and ongoing basis. DPGR include gross receipts derived from engineering or architectural services, including feasibility studies for a construction project in the United States, even if the planned construction project is not undertaken or is not completed.

Reg. § 199-3(n)(2) and (3) defines engineering and architectural services:

Engineering services. Engineering services in connection with any construction project include any professional services requiring engineering education, training, and experience and the application of special knowledge of the mathematical, physical, or engineering sciences to those professional services such as consultation, investigation, evaluation, planning, design, or responsible supervision of construction (for the purpose of assuring compliance with plans, specifications, and design) or erection, in connection with any construction project.

Architectural services. Architectural services in connection with any construction project include the offering or furnishing of any professional services such as consultation, planning, aesthetic and structural design, drawings and specifications, or responsible supervision of construction (for the purpose of assuring compliance with plans, specifications, and design) or erection, in connection with any construction project.

With respect to administrative support services, if the taxpayer performing engineering or architectural services also provides administrative support services (for example, billing and secretarial services) incidental and necessary to such engineering or architectural services, then Reg. § 199-3(n)(4) details that these administrative support services are considered engineering or architectural services. However, Reg. § 199-3(n)(5) states that engineering or architectural services do not include postconstruction services such as annual audits and inspections.

Reg. § 199-3(n)(6) provides a *de minimis* exception for DPGR, to wit: If less than 5 percent of the total gross receipts derived by a taxpayer from engineering or architectural services performed in the United States for a construction project are derived from services not relating to a construction project (for example, the services are performed outside the United States or in connection with property other than real property), then the total gross receipts derived by the taxpayer may be treated as DPGR from engineering or architectural services performed in the United States for the construction project. In the case of gross receipts derived from engineering or architectural services that are received over a period of time (for example, an installment sale), Reg. § 199-3(n)(6)'s *de minimis* exception is applied by taking into account the total gross receipts for the entire period derived (and to be derived) from engineering or architectural services. For consistency, if a taxpayer treats gross receipts as DPGR under this de minimis exception, then the taxpayer must treat the gross receipts recognized in each taxable year consistently as DPGR.

Agricultural products. Reg. § 1.199-3(e) states that domestic production gross receipts include gross receipts of a taxpayer derived from any sale, exchange or other disposition of agricultural products with respect to which the taxpayer performs storage, handling or other processing activities (other than transportation activities) within the United States, provided such products are consumed in connection with, or incorporated into, the manufacturing, production, growth or extraction of qualifying production property (whether or not by the taxpayer).

Examples illustrating this provision are set forth below:

Example 7-46: A, B, and C are unrelated persons and are not cooperatives to which Part I of subchapter T of the Code applies. B grows agricultural products in the United States and sells them to A, who owns agricultural storage bins in the United States. A stores the agricultural products and has the benefits and burdens of ownership under Federal income tax principles of the agricultural products while they are being stored. A sells the agricultural products to C, who processes them into refined agricultural products in the United States. The gross receipts from A's, B's, and C's activities are DPGR from the MPGE of QPP.

Example 7-47: The facts are the same as in the above example except that B grows the agricultural products outside the United States and C processes them into refined agricultural products outside the United States. The gross receipts derived by A from its sale of the agricultural products to C are DPGR from the MPGE of QPP within the United States. B's and C's respective MPGE activities occur outside the United States and, therefore, their respective gross receipts are non-DPGR.

Food and beverages. Code Sec. 199(c)(4)(B) prescribes some exceptions to the definition of "gross receipts" detailed in Code Sec. 199(c)(4)(A), to wit, the sale of food and beverages prepared by the taxpayer at a retail establishment. Reg. § 1.199-3(o)(1) provides some clarification and guideline for this exception in terms of the definition of a retail establishment.

A retail establishment is defined as tangible property (both real and personal) owned, leased, occupied, or otherwise used by the taxpayer in its trade or business of selling food or beverages to the public at which retail sales are made. In addition, a facility that prepares food and beverages for take out service or delivery is a retail establishment (for example, a caterer). If a taxpayer's facility is a retail establishment, then, for purposes of Code Sec. 199(c)(4), the taxpayer may allocate its gross receipts between the gross receipts derived from the retail sale of the food and beverages prepared and sold at the retail establishment (that are non-DPGR) and gross receipts derived from the wholesale sale of the food and beverages prepared and sold at the retail establishment. Wholesale sales are defined as food and beverages held for resale by the purchaser. The exception for sales of certain food and beverages also applies to food and beverages for non-human consumption. A retail establishment does not include the bonded premises of a distilled spirits plant or wine cellar, or the premises of a brewery (other than a tavern on the brewery premises).

Reg. § 1.199-3(o)(2) provides a "safe harbor", to wit: A taxpayer may treat a facility at which food or beverages are prepared as not being a retail establishment if less than 5 percent of the gross receipts derived from the sale of food or beverages at that facility during the taxable year are attributable to retail sales.

Examples illustrating the provisions regarding food and beverage establishments are set forth below:

> **Example 7-48:** X buys coffee beans and roasts those beans at a facility in the United States, the only activity of which is the roasting and packaging of coffee beans. X sells the roasted coffee beans through a variety of unrelated third-party vendors and also sells roasted coffee beans at X's retail establishments. At X's retail establishments, X prepares brewed coffee and other foods. To the extent that the gross receipts of X's retail establishments are derived from the sale of coffee beans roasted at the facility, the receipts are DPGR. To the extent the gross receipts of X's retail establishments are derived from the retail sale of brewed coffee or food prepared at the retail establishments, the receipts are non-DPGR. However, X must allocate part of the receipts from the retail sale of the brewed coffee as DPGR to the extent of the value of the coffee beans that were roasted at the facility and that were used to brew coffee.

> **Example 7-49:** Y operates a bonded winery within the United States. Bottles of wine produced by Y at the bonded winery are sold to consumers at the taxpaid premises. The bonded premises is not considered a retail establishment and is treated as separate and apart from the taxpaid premises, which is considered a retail establishment. Accordingly, the wine produced by Y in the bonded premises and sold by Y from the taxpaid premises is not considered to have been produced at a retail establishment, and the gross receipts derived from the sales of the wine are DPGR.

> **Tax Pointer 5:** The 2004 Economic Report of the President illustrates the difficulty in terms of defining "manufacturing activities." The Report noted that mixing water and concentrate to produce soft drinks is generally classified as "manufacturing," but when the activity occurs at a snack bar, it is considered a "service." Specifically, the Report asks the rhetorical question: "When a fast-food restaurant sells a hamburger, is it providing a service, or is it combining inputs to manufacture a product?"

.07 Qualified Production Property (QPP)

Code Sec. 199(c)(5) defines QPP as:

(a) tangible personal property,

(b) any computer software, and

(c) any property described in Code Sec. 168(f)(4).

Congress did not define the term "QPP." Reg. § 1.199-3(j) provides assistance to define the term QPP, to wit:

Tangible personal property in general. Reg. § 1.199-3(j)(1)(i) states that the term tangible personal property is any tangible property other than land, real property and any property described in Reg. § 1.199-3(j) (3) and(4), (k)(1), or (l). Additionally, tangible personal property generally also includes any gas, chemical, and similar property, for example, steam, oxygen, hydrogen, and nitrogen. Property

¶722.07

such as machinery, printing presses, transportation and office equipment, refrigerators, grocery counters, testing equipment, display racks and shelves, and neon and other signs that are contained in or attached to a building constitutes tangible personal property. Generally, computer software, sound recordings, and qualified films are not treated as tangible personal property regardless of whether they are affixed to a tangible medium. However, the tangible medium to which such property may be affixed (for example, a videocassette, a computer diskette, or other similar tangible item) is tangible personal property.

Intangible property. Reg. § 1.199-3(j)(1)(iii) details that the term tangible personal property does not include property in a form other than in a tangible medium. For example, mass-produced books are tangible personal property, but neither the rights to the underlying manuscript nor an online version of the book is tangible personal property. The preamble to these regulations provided some further definition by stating that some business information reports may qualify as QPP; for example, business information reports published by the taxpayer in books that qualify as QPP.

Computer software and sound recordings. Reg. § 1.199-3(j)(3) contains detailed provisions to define these terms.

>*Tax Pointer 1:* In an earlier guidance from the IRS, Notice 2005-14 § 4.04(8)(b),[157] detailed that the term "QPP" is derived primarily from Reg. § 1.48-1(c). However, Notice 2005-14 § 4.04(8)(b) references Reg. § 1.263A-(2)(ii) in terms of defining "QPP." Reg. § 1.263A-2(a)(2) defines "tangible personal property" to include films, sound recordings, videotapes, books, and other similar property embodying words, ideas, concepts, images, or sounds. "Other similar property" means intellectual or creative property for which, as costs are incurred in producing the property, it is intended, or reasonably likely, that a tangible medium in which the property is embodied will be mass-distributed in a form that is not substantially altered. Further, the Section 263A regulations prescribe that "tangible personal property" does not include tangible items provided incident to services, such as documents prepared by attorneys.

>While the basic principles of Section 263A may be helpful in defining "tangible personal property," they are not conclusive. For instance, the Section 263A regulations define books as "tangible personal property."

Related persons. Code Sec. 199(c)(7)(A) prescribes that for purposes of determining DPGR, gross receipts derived from property leased, licensed, or rented by the taxpayer for use by a related person is not DPGR. Code Sec. 199(c)(7)(B) details that for purposes of defining a "related person," a person shall be treated as related to another person if such persons are treated as a single employer under subsection (a) or (b) of Code Sec. 52 or subsection (m) or (o) of Code Sec. 414, except that determinations under subsections (a) and (b) of Code Sec. 52 shall be made without regard to Code Sec. 1563(b).

---

[157] 2005-7 IRB 498.

Tax Pointer 2: Code Sec. 52(a) and (b) treats employees of 50% "commonly controlled businesses" as employees of a single employer for purposes of the work opportunity credit, with "commonly controlled businesses" being defined by Code Sec. 1563. Code Sec. 414(m) and (o) treats all employees of all members of an affiliated service group as employees of a single employer for purposes of specified retirement plan qualification provisions, and for purposes of the specified fringe benefit plan rules.

Reg. § 1.199-3(b)(2) prescribes however that gross receipts derived from the license of QPP to a related person for reproduction and sale, exchange, lease, rental, or sublicense to an unrelated person for the ultimate use of the unrelated person may qualify as DPGR. Similarly, the license of computer software to a related person for reproduction and sale, exchange, lease, rental or sub-license to an unrelated person for the ultimate use of such unrelated person is not treated as excluded property by reason of the license to the related person.

.08 Definition and Special Rules

Code Sec. 199(d) contains special rules and definitions for the application of Code Sec. 199(a).

Affiliated groups. Code Sec. 199(d)(4) prescribes special rules for affiliated groups, to wit:

(a) *In General.* All members of an expanded affiliated group shall be treated as a single corporation for purposes of Code Sec. 199.

(b) *Expanded Affiliated Group.* For purposes of Code Sec. 199, the term "expanded affiliated group" means an affiliated group as defined in Code Sec. 1504(a), determined:

(i) by substituting "50 percent" for "80 percent" each place it appears, and

(ii) without regard to paragraphs (2) and (4) of Code Sec. 1504(b).

(c) *Allocation of Deduction.* Except as provided in regulations, the deduction under Code Sec. 199(a) shall be allocated among the members of the expanded affiliated group in proportion to each member's respective amount (if any) of qualified production activities income.

.09 Pass-Through Entities

Code Sec. 199(d)(1) prescribes that a Code Sec. 199 deduction is available to pass-through entities, including S corporations, partnerships, estates and trusts. However, there are special rules for agricultural and horticultural cooperatives. Code Sec. 199's deduction is applied at the S corporate shareholder, partner, or similar level. Specifically, Code Sec. 199(d)(1) prescribes that:

(a) *In General.* In the case of an S corporation, partnership, estate or trust, or other pass-through entity:

(i) subject to the provisions of paragraphs (2) and (3), Code Sec. 199 shall be applied at the shareholder, partner, or similar level, and

¶722.09

(ii) the Secretary shall prescribe rules for the application of Code Sec. 199, including rules relating to:

  (I) restrictions on the allocation of the deduction to taxpayers at the partner or similar level, and

  (II) additional reporting requirements.

Code Sec. 199(d)(1)(B) prescribes that Code Sec. 199(b)(2)'s W-2 limitation on the amount of deduction is applied first at the entity level, but the deduction itself is determined at the shareholder, partner, or similar level. Similarly, Code Sec. 199(d)(1)(B) prescribes that notwithstanding Code Sec. 199(d)(1)(A)(i), for purposes of applying Code Sec. 199(b), a shareholder, partner, or similar person which is allocated qualified production activities income from an S corporation, partnership, estate, trust, or other pass-through entity shall also be treated as having been allocated W-2 wages from such entity in an amount equal to such person's allocable share of such wages.

.10 S Corporations

Reg. § 1.199-5T covers passthrough entities, providing separate sections to cover partnerships, S corporations, estates and trusts, etc. Reg. § 1.199-5T(c) deals with S corporations providing specificity for the uniqueness of S corporations.

Code Sec. 199 deduction determination at shareholder level. Reg. § 1.199-5T(c)(1)(i) provides that the Code Sec. 199 deduction of an S corporation is determined at the shareholder level. As a result, each shareholder must compute its deduction separately. The Code Sec. 199 deduction will have no effect on the basis of a shareholder's stock in an S corporation. Each shareholder generally is allocated, in accordance with Code Sec. 1366, her, his or its pro rata share of S corporation items (including items of income, gain, loss, and deduction), CGS allocated to such items of income, and gross receipts included in such items of income, even if the shareholder's share of CGS and other deductions and losses exceeds DPGR, and regardless of the amount of the shareholder's share of the W-2 wages of the S corporation for the taxable year. Generally, to determine his, her or its Code Sec. 199 deduction for the taxable year, the shareholder aggregates his, her or its pro rata share of such items, to the extent they are not otherwise disallowed by the Code, with those items it incurs outside the S corporation (whether directly or indirectly) for purposes of allocating and apportioning deductions to DPGR and computing its QPAI.

Determination at entity level. Reg. § 1.199-5T(c)(1)(ii) generally prescribes that an S corporation can calculate a shareholder's share of QPAI and W-2 wages at the entity level, instead of allocating, in accordance with Code Sec. 1366, the shareholder's pro rata share of S corporation items (including items of income, gain, loss, and deduction) and the shareholder's allocable share of wages. If an S corporation does calculate QPAI at the entity level, then:

(A) Each shareholder is allocated its share of QPAI and W-2 wages from the S corporation, which are combined with the shareholder's QPAI and W-2 wages from other sources, if any;

(B) For purposes of computing QPAI, a shareholder does not take into account the items from such an S corporation (for example, a shareholder does not take into account items from such an S corporation in determining whether a threshold or *de minimis* rule applies or when the shareholder allocates and apportions deductions in calculating its QPAI from other sources);

(C) A shareholder generally does not recompute his, her or its share of QPAI from the S corporation using another method; however, the shareholder might have to adjust his, her or its share of QPAI from the S corporation to take into account certain disallowed losses or deductions, or the allowance of suspended losses or deductions; and

(D) A shareholder's share of QPAI from an S corporation may be less than zero.

Disallowed losses or deductions. Reg. § 1.199-5T(c)(2) provides generally that losses or deductions of the S corporation that otherwise would be taken into account in computing the shareholder's Code Sec. 199 deduction for a taxable year are taken into account in that year only if and to the extent the shareholder's pro rata share of the losses or deductions from all of the S corporation's activities is not disallowed by Code Secs. 465, 469, or 1366(d), or any other provision of the Code. If only a portion of the shareholder's share of the losses or deductions is allowed for a taxable year, a proportionate share of those allowable losses or deductions that are allocated to the S corporation's qualified production activities, determined in a manner consistent with Code Secs. 465, 469, and 1366(d), and any other applicable provision of the Code, is taken into account in computing the QPAI and the wage limitation of Code Sec. 199(d)(1)(A)(iii) for that taxable year. To the extent that any of the disallowed losses or deductions are allowed in a later taxable year, the shareholder takes into account a proportionate share of those losses or deductions in computing its QPAI for that later taxable year. Losses or deductions of the S corporation that are disallowed for taxable years beginning on or before December 31, 2004, are not taken into account in a later taxable year for purposes of computing the shareholder's QPAI or the wage limitation of Code Sec. 199(d)(1)(A)(iii) for that taxable year, regardless of whether the losses or deductions are allowed for other purposes.

Shareholder's share of wages. Under Code Sec. 199(d)(1)(A)(iii), a S corporation shareholder's share of wages of the S corporation for purposes of determining the shareholder's W-2 wage limitation equals the shareholder's allocable share of those wages. Generally, the S corporation must allocate the paragraph (e)(1) wages among the shareholders in the same manner it allocates wage expense among those shareholders. The shareholder then must add his, her or its share of wages from the S corporation to the shareholder's wages from other sources, if any, and then must determine the portion of those wages allocable to DPGR to compute the shareholder's W-2 wages. Reg. § 1.199-2T(e)(2) details the method for the computation of W-2 wages and the proper allocation of such wages to DPGR.

Transition rule for definition of W-2 wages and for W-2 wage limitation. If an S corporation and any of its shareholders have different taxable years, only one of which begins on or before May 17, 2006, the definition of W-2 wages of the S corporation and the Code Sec. 199 (d) (1) (A) (iii) limitation on W-2 wages from that S corporation is determined under the law applicable to S corporations based on the beginning date of the S corporation's taxable year. Thus, for example, for the short taxable year of an S corporation beginning after May 17, 2006, and ending in 2006, a shareholder's share of W-2 wages from the S corporation is determined under Code Sec. 199 (d) (1) (A) (iii) for taxable years beginning after May 17, 2006, even if that shareholder's taxable year began on or before May 17, 2006.

> ***Tax Pointer:*** If an S corporation is composed of two or more individual shareholders and one receives greater compensation than the other, this greater compensation will not cause the shareholder to have a larger W-2 wage allocation due to the fact that the shareholder only receives his or her allocable share of the wages. Thus, if there are two shareholders in an S corporation, a 1% and 99% shareholder, the 1% shareholder is paid $100,000 in salary and there are no other Code Sec. 199 deductions, the shareholder would only be allocated 1% of the wage allocation and the 99% shareholder the balance even though the shareholder has not performed any work.

Practical application of Code Sec. 199. The IRS Statistics of Income Bulletin (Winter 2004) details that S corporations are a very popular vehicle, with 2004 projections indicating that the number of S corporations will grow at an average annual percentage of 3.45 percent for 2004 through 2010. In 2004, the projection is that there will be 3,486,400 Forms 1120S filed. The IRS, in IR-2005-76, announced that two million S corporations reported net income of $250,000,000,000 in 2002, with about one million S corporations reporting losses of approximately $63,000,000,000. Further, almost 60 percent of all corporate tax returns filed in 2002 were by S corporations. However, Code Sec. 199's manufacturing deduction geared to income will probably cause more S corporations to be formed, for the simple reason that in an S corporation, income can be manipulated through shareholder employee salaries. *J. Radtke*[158] and its ilk only require that S corporation shareholder employees take "a reasonable salary," with case law to define this term. While there is a fifty percent limit regarding the amount of Code Sec. 199 deduction geared to wages, it is obvious that calculators will be grinding to determine the maximum tax benefit for S corporate shareholder employees, keeping in mind that if a shareholder employee's wages are too low, this might affect retirement plan contributions and social security benefits. If it appears that this Code Sec. 199 deduction will yield a big deduction, then S corporations will probably aggressively reduce shareholder employees' salaries to a minimum to maximize this deduction, taking the balance of the profits as a distribution self-employment tax-free, as sustained in *P.B. Ding.*[159]

If the Code Sec. 199 deduction has no effect, given the nebulous concept of the Radtke standard of "reasonable compensation," the S corporation still may keep shareholder employee salaries low to take advantage of profit distributions being self-employment tax-free.

---

[158] CA-7, 90-1 USTC ¶ 50,113, 895 F.2d 1196.

[159] 74 TCM 708, Dec. 52,269(M), TC Memo. 1997-435. Aff'd, CA-9, 2000-1 USTC ¶ 50,137, 200 F3d 587.

¶722.10

While it is difficult to project from the IRS Statistics of Income Bulletin the number of S corporations who would be classified as manufacturers for Code Sec. 199 purposes, it is probable that a significant amount exists, given the broad definition of "manufacturers" and "production activities." Consequently, given such a large number of S corporation returns, it is doubtful if IRS can effectively audit this "reasonable compensation" loophole generated in Code Sec. 199.

Form 8903. Taxpayers use Form 8903 to obtain Code Sec. 199's deduction.

.11 Trade or Business Requirements

Code Sec. 199(d)(5) prescribes that Code Sec. 199 can only be applied by taking into account items which are attributable to the actual conduct of a trade or business.

> *Tax Pointer:* The Code Sec. 199 deduction applies only to items attributable to "actual conduct of a trade or business." Code Sec. 179 and Code Sec. 274 prescribe that their deduction is geared to "active conduct" of a trade or business. Clarification will have to be provided to see if these types of expenses are Code Sec. 199 deductions to arrive at qualified income, or if they are excluded.

.12 Application to Individuals

Code Sec. 199(d)(2) prescribes that for individuals, Code Sec. 199(a)(1)(B)'s "taxable income" limitation does not apply; rather, it is AGI. Further, Code Sec. 199(d)(2)(A) prescribes that for purposes of applying the AGI limitation, AGI shall be determined:

(a) after application of Code Sec. 86, Code Sec. 135, Code Sec. 137, Code Sec. 219, Code Sec. 221, Code Sec. 222 and Code Sec. 469, and

(b) without regard to this section.

.13 Alternative Minimum Tax

Code Sec. 199(d)(6) prescribes that Code Sec. 199's deduction is allowed against AMT. The deduction in computing alternative minimum taxable income is determined by reference to the lesser of the qualified production activities income (as determined for the regular tax) or the alternative minimum taxable income (in the case of an individual, adjusted gross income as determined for the regular tax) without regard to this deduction.

.14 Add-Backs

Effective for taxable years beginning after December 31, 2004, Code Sec. 246(b)(1) is amended to prescribe that any deduction taken by a corporation will, in addition to the other items, have to add back to compute the taxable income limitation on a corporation's dividends received deduction, the Code Sec. 199 deduction.

For individuals who take a Code Sec. 199 deduction on their Form 1040, Schedule C, various Code provisions, such as Code Sec. 219(g)(3)(ii) (deduction for contributions to IRAs) and Code Sec. 222(b)(2)(C)(i) (deduction for qualified

¶722.14

higher education expenses) prescribe that the Code Sec. 199 deduction must be added back to determine the amount of the deduction, exclusion, etc.

¶ 723 Deferred Compensation Plans

The Internal Revenue Service has issued final regulations under Code Sec. 409A; however, it is beyond the scope of this book to set forth a discussion of them. The reader is respectfully directed to consult these regulations when reading the material set forth below.

.01 Definition of "Deferred Compensation Plan"

Deferred compensation plans allow employees to defer receipt of wages and bonuses until some future years when the employee may be in a lower tax bracket (i.e., retired), and thus pay lower income tax on the compensation when it is received. There are qualified deferred compensation plans such as plans formed under Code Sec. 401 (profit-sharing plans, Code Sec. 401(k) plans, etc.), and non-qualified plans. Non-qualified compensation plans (NQCPs) are utilized by employers with key employees or with shareholder employees because the NQCPs do not have to meet the stringent requirements imposed for qualified plans as set forth in Code Sec. 401 et seq. Accordingly, NQCPs can discriminate and not have to cover a broad base of employees—rather, only key executive and shareholder employees can be covered. NQCPs are not as difficult to establish as qualified plans because they do not have to be approved by the IRS and the Department of Labor; however, NQCPs must meet certain requirements:

(1) The deferred compensation arrangement between the employee and his or her employer must be entered into before the compensation is earned by the employee;

(2) The amount of the deferred compensation must not be available to the employee until the agreed-upon future date or event (e.g., the employee's retirement or satisfaction of an employment contract); and

(3) The amount of the deferred compensation must not be secured.

Notwithstanding the above rules, Congress believed that many non-qualified deferred compensation arrangements allowed improper deferral of income. Executives often used arrangements that would allow deferral of income, but also provide security of future payment and control over amounts deferred. For example, non-qualified deferred compensation arrangements often contained provisions that allow participants to receive distributions upon request, subject to forfeiture of a minimal amount (i.e., a "haircut" provision [e.g., forfeit ten percent of the amount of the distribution]).

With rabbi trusts,[160] the trust or fund could be located in a foreign jurisdiction, making it difficult or impossible for creditors to reach the assets.

While the general tax principles governing deferred compensation are well established, the determination whether a particular arrangement effectively allows deferral of income was generally made on a facts and circumstances basis. There

---

[160] Private IRS Letter Ruling 8113107 (12/3/80).

was limited specific guidance with respect to common deferral arrangements. Congress believed that it is appropriate to provide specific rules regarding whether deferral of income inclusion should be permitted.

Congress believed that certain arrangements that allow participants inappropriate levels of control or access to amounts deferred should not result in deferral of income inclusion. Also, Congress believed that certain arrangements, such as offshore trusts, which effectively protect assets from creditors, should be treated as funded and not result in deferral of income inclusion.

To effect control over NQCPs, Code Sec. 409A(d)(1) defines an "NQCP" as any plan that provides for the deferral of compensation other than a qualified employer plan or any bona fide vacation leave, sick leave, compensatory time, disability pay, or death benefit plan. A qualified employer plan means a qualified retirement plan, tax-deferred annuity, simplified employee pension, and SIMPLE. A qualified governmental excess benefit arrangement (Code Sec. 415(m)) is a qualified employer plan. An eligible deferred compensation plan (Code Sec. 457(b)) is also a qualified employer plan under the provision. A tax-exempt or governmental deferred compensation plan that is not an eligible deferred compensation plan is not a qualified employer plan. The application of the provision is not limited to arrangements between an employer and employee. Note: Code Sec. 409A(d)(1)'s provisions do not apply to a plan meeting the requirements of Code Sec. 457(e)(12) if the plan was in existence as of May 1, 2004, was providing nonelective deferred compensation described in Code Sec. 457(e)(12) on such date, and is established or maintained by an organization incorporated on July 2, 1974. If the plan has a material change in the class of individuals eligible to participate in the plan after May 1, 2004, the provision applies to compensation provided under the plan after the date of such change.

For purposes of Code Sec. 409A(d)(6), it is not intended that the term "nonqualified deferred compensation plan" include an arrangement taxable under Code Sec. 83 providing for the grant of an option on employer stock with an exercise price that is not less than the fair market value of the underlying stock on the date of grant if such arrangement does not include a deferral feature other than the feature that the option holder has the right to exercise the option in the future. Additionally, Code Sec. 409A(d)(6) is not intended to change the tax treatment of incentive stock options meeting the requirements of Code Sec. 422 or options granted under an employee stock purchase plan meeting the requirements of Code Sec. 423.

It is intended that the provision does not apply to annual bonuses or other annual compensation amounts paid within 2 1/2 months after the close of the taxable year in which the relevant services required for payment have been performed.

Reg. § 1.409A-1 et seq. sets forth an example as to the operation of the two-and-one-half-month period, to wit: an employer with a calendar year taxable year who on November 1, 2006 awards a bonus so that the employee is considered to have a legally binding right to the payment as of November 1, 2006, will not be considered to have provided for a deferral of compensation if, in accordance with the terms of

¶723.01

the bonus plan, the amount is paid or made available to the employee on or before March 15, 2007. An employer with a September 1 to August 31 taxable year who on November 1, 2006 awards a bonus so that the employee is considered to have a legally binding right to the payment as of November 1, 2006, will not be considered to have provided for a deferral of compensation if, in accordance with the terms of the bonus plan, the amount is paid or made available to the employee on or before November 15, 2007.

Likewise, Reg. § 1.409A-1 et seq. prescribes that Code Sec. 409A is not to apply for amounts actually or constructively received by the service provider within a short period following the lapse of a substantial risk of forfeiture. The exception is intended to address multi-year compensation arrangements, where the right to the compensation is or may be earned over multiple years but is payable at the end of the earning period. For example, a three-year bonus program requiring the performance of services over three years and entitling the service provider to a payment within a short specified period following the end of the third year generally would not constitute a deferral of compensation.

.02 Code Sec. 409A's Provision to Curtail Abuse with Deferred Compensation Plans

To curb abuse with NQCPs, Code Sec. 409A(a)(1)(B)(i) prescribes that there will be an immediate taxation of NQCPs which fail Code Sec. 409A's rules.

In addition to current income inclusion, Code Sec. 409A(a)(1)(B)(i) prescribes that interest at the underpayment rate plus one percentage point is imposed on the under-payments that would have occurred had the compensation been includable in income when first deferred, or if later, when not subject to a substantial risk of forfeiture. The amount required to be included in income is also subject to a 20-percent additional tax to whom the requirements of the provision are not met. For example, suppose a plan covering all executives of an employer (including those subject to Code Sec. 16(a) of the Securities and Exchange Act of 1934) allows distributions to individuals subject to Code Sec. 16(a) upon a distribution event that is not permitted under the provision. The individuals subject to Code Sec. 16(a), rather than all participants of the plan, would be required to include amounts deferred in income and would be subject to interest and the 20-percent additional tax. (Note: Due to Code Sec. 409A's enactment date, these consequences apply to amounts deferred after October 22, 2004.)

.03 Plans Covered by Code Sec. 409A

Examples of plans which would be covered by Code Sec. 409A are equity incentive plans that provide grants of deferred stock units; restricted stock units; Stock Appreciation Rights (SARS); discounted stock options; employment and consulting agreements. By definition, a severance plan is subject to Code Sec. 409A. Plans which would be exempt are defined in Code Sec. 409A(d)(2), and they include Code Sec. 401(k) plans; bona fide vacation plans; sick leave plans; Health Savings Accounts (HSAs); death benefit plans; compensatory time plans; qualified retirement plans; disability payment plans; etc. Notice 2005-1, Q&A (3) prescribes that Code Sec. 409A may apply to arrangements between a service recipient and an independent contractor, or arrangements between a partner and a partnership.

    Tax Pointer: Because Code Sec. 409A can apply to employment agreements, brokerage situations, consulting agreements, etc., care should be exercised when drafting these agreements for key employees and shareholder-employees in closely-held S corporations so as not to run afoul of the regulatory provision.

    Code Sec. 409A(a)(1) prescribes that if at any time during a taxable year a non-qualified deferred compensation plan fails to meet the requirements of paragraphs (2), (3) (regarding acceleration of benefits) and (4) (regarding elections), or is not operated in accordance with such requirements, all compensation deferred under the plan for the taxable year and all preceding taxable years shall be includable in gross income for the taxable year to the extent not subject to a substantial risk of forfeiture and not previously included in gross income.

    Code Sec. 409A(a)(1)(A)(ii) states that the provision regarding failures applies only with respect to all compensation deferred under the plan for participants with respect to whom the failure relates.

    Tax Pointer: Normally, under Code Sec. 404(a)(5) and Reg. § 1.404-12(b)(2), an employer is entitled to a deduction for the tax year where the employee includes income received from a NQCP. Presumably, if a plan violates Code Sec. 409A, and a participant has to include income before it would normally be paid, then this acceleration would likewise accelerate the employer's income tax deduction for the amount included.

.04 Stock Appreciation Rights

    Reg. § 1.409A-1(b)(5) prescribes that SARS will not be subject to Code Sec. 409A if (1) the value of the stock the excess over which the right provides for payment upon exercise (the SAR exercise price) may never be less than the fair market value of the underlying stock on the date the right is granted, (2) the stock of the service recipient subject to the right is traded on an established securities market, (3) only such traded stock of the service recipient may be delivered in settlement of the right upon exercise, and (4) the right does not include any feature for the deferral of compensation other than the deferral of recognition of income until the exercise of the right. In addition, until further guidance is issued, a payment of stock or cash pursuant to the exercise of a stock appreciation right (or economically equivalent right), or the cancellation of such a right for consideration, where such right is granted pursuant to a program in effect on or before October 3, 2004 will not be treated as a payment of a deferral of compensation subject to the requirements of Code Sec. 409A if: (1) the SAR exercise price may never be less than the fair market value of the underlying stock on the date the right is granted, and (2) the right does not include any feature for the deferral of compensation other than the deferral of recognition of income until the exercise of the right.

    Further, Reg. § 1.409A-1(b)(5) prescribes that if a SAR has a fixed payment date, it will generally comply with Code Sec. 409A.

¶723.04

.05 Partnership Transactions

Notice 2005-1,[161] Q&A (7) and proposed Code Sec. 409A regulations prescribe that taxpayers may treat an issuance of a profits interest in connection with the performance of services that is properly treated under applicable guidance as not resulting in inclusion of income by the service provider at the time of issuance, as also not resulting in the deferral of compensation. Similarly, taxpayers may treat an issuance of a capital interest in connection with the performance of services in the same manner as an issuance of stock, i.e., subject to the same rules regarding stock options, etc.

.06 Distributions

Code Sec. 409A(a)(2)(A) prescribes that compensation deferred in a NQCP cannot be distributed earlier than certain events.

Separation from service. Code Sec. 409A(a)(2)(A)(i) prescribes that in the case of a "specified employee" who separates from service, distributions may not be made earlier than six months after the date of the separation from service or upon death. "Specified employees" are "key employees" of a publicly-traded corporation. "Key employees" are defined in Code Sec. 416(i) and generally include officers having annual compensation greater than $130,000 (adjusted for inflation and limited to 50 employees), five percent owners, and one percent owners having annual compensation from the employer greater than $150,000.

Disabled. Code Sec. 409A(a)(2)(A)(ii) prescribes that a participant is considered disabled if he or she (i) is unable to engage in any substantial gainful activity by reason of any medically determinable physical or mental impairment which can be expected to result in death or can be expected to last for a continuous period of not less than 12 months; or (ii) is, by reason of any medically determinable physical or mental impairment which can be expected to result in death or can be expected to last for a continuous period of not less than 12 months, receiving income replacement benefits for a period of not less than three months under an accident and health plan covering employees of the participant's employer.

Death.

Specified time. Code Sec. 409A(a)(2)(A)(iv) prescribes that it is permissible to pay benefits at specified times detailed in the NQCP. Amounts payable at a specified time or pursuant to a fixed schedule must be specified under the plan at the time of deferral. Amounts payable upon the occurrence of an event are not treated as amounts payable at a specified time. For example, amounts payable when an individual attains age 65 are payable at a specified time, while amounts payable when an individual's child begins college are payable upon the occurrence of an event.

Change in control. Code Sec. 409A(a)(2)(A)(v) prescribes that distributions upon a change in the ownership or effective control of a corporation, or in the ownership of a substantial portion of the assets of a corporation, may only be made to the extent provided by the Secretary. The Conference Committee Reports state

---

[161] IRB 2005-2.

¶723.05

that it is intended that the Secretary use a similar, but more restrictive, definition of change in control as is used for purposes of the golden parachute provisions of Code Sec. 280G consistent with the purposes of the provision. The provision requires the Secretary to issue guidance defining change of control within 90 days after October 22, 2004.

> *Tax Pointer:* The Service issued regulations under Code Sec. 280G defining "Golden Parachute Payments," detailing when a change of ownership of a corporation occurs for purposes of the Golden Parachute Payment rules, when there is a change of effective control of the corporation, etc.

Unforeseeable emergency. In the case of an unforeseeable emergency, Code Sec. 409A(a)(2)(A)(vi) permits distributions from an NQCP. An "unforeseeable emergency" is defined as a severe financial hardship to the participant: (1) resulting from an illness or accident of the participant, the participant's spouse, or a dependent (as defined in Code Sec. 152(a)); (2) loss of the participant's property due to casualty; or (3) other similar extraordinary and unforeseeable circumstances arising as a result of events beyond the control of the participant. The amount of the distribution must be limited to the amount needed to satisfy the emergency plus taxes reasonably anticipated as a result of the distribution. Distributions may not be allowed to the extent that the hardship may be relieved through reimbursement or compensation by insurance or otherwise, or by liquidation of the participant's assets (to the extent such liquidation would not itself cause a severe financial hardship).

Prohibition on acceleration of distributions. Code Sec. 409A(a)(3) prescribes that no accelerations of distributions may be allowed. The Conference Committee Reports prescribe that in general, changes in the form of distribution that accelerate payments are subject to the rule prohibiting acceleration of distributions. However, it is intended that the rule against accelerations is not violated merely because a plan provides a choice between cash and taxable property if the timing and amount of income inclusion is the same regardless of the medium of distribution. For example, the choice between a fully taxable annuity contract and a lump-sum payment may be permitted. It is also intended that the Secretary provide rules under which the choice between different forms of actuarially equivalent life annuity payments is permitted.

The Conference Committee Reports detail that it is intended that the Secretary will provide other, limited, exceptions to the prohibition on accelerated distributions, such as when the accelerated distribution is required for reasons beyond the control of the participant and the distribution is not elective. For example, it is anticipated that an exception could be provided if a distribution is needed in order to comply with Federal conflict of interest requirements or a court-approved settlement incident to divorce. The Conference Committee Reports detail that it is intended that Treasury regulations provide that a plan would not violate the prohibition on accelerations by providing that withholding of an employee's share of employment taxes will be made from the employee's interest in the non-qualified deferred compensation plan.

¶723.06

- Treasury regulations provide that a plan would not violate the prohibition on accelerations by providing for a distribution to a participant to pay income taxes due upon a vesting event subject to Code Sec. 457(f), provided that such amount is not more than an amount equal to the income tax withholding that would have been remitted by the employer if there had been a payment of wages equal to the income includable by the participant under Code Sec. 457(f).

- Treasury regulations provide that a plan would not violate the prohibition on accelerations by providing for automatic distributions of minimal interests in a deferred compensation plan upon permissible distribution events for purposes of administrative convenience. For example, a plan could provide that upon separation from service of a participant, account balances less than $10,000 will be automatically distributed (except in the case of specified employees).

.07 Election Rules

Code Sec. 409A(a)(4) prescribes the means for individuals to elect to defer compensation. Code Sec. 409A(a)(4) sets forth the following requirements:

Initial elections. Code Sec. 409A(a)(4) requires that a plan must provide that compensation for services performed during a taxable year may be deferred at the participant's election only if the election to defer is made no later than the close of the preceding taxable year, or at such other time as provided in Treasury regulations. Code Sec. 409A(a)(4)(B) prescribes that in the first year that an employee becomes eligible for participation in a non-qualified deferred compensation plan, the election may be made within 30 days after the date that the employee is initially eligible. In the case of any performance-based compensation based on services performed over a period of at least 12 months, such election may be made no later than six months before the end of the service period. It is not intended that the provision override the constructive receipt doctrine, as constructive receipt rules continue to apply. It is intended that the term "performance-based compensation" will be defined by the Secretary to include compensation to the extent that an amount is: (1) variable and contingent on the satisfaction of preestablished organizational or individual performance criteria and (2) not readily ascertainable at the time of the election. For the purposes of Code Sec. 409A(a)(4), it is intended that performance-based compensation may be required to meet certain requirements similar to those under Code Sec. 162(m), but would not be required to meet all requirements under that section. For example, it is expected that the Secretary will provide that performance criteria would be considered preestablished if it is established in writing no later than 90 days after the commencement of the service period, but the requirement of determination by the compensation committee of the board of directors would not be required. It is expected that the Secretary will issue guidance providing coordination rules, as appropriate, regarding the timing of elections in the case when the fiscal year of the employer and the taxable year of the individual are different. It is expected that Treasury regulations will not permit any election to defer any bonus or other compensation if the timing of such election would be inconsistent with the purposes of the provision.

¶723.07

The time and form of distributions must be specified at the time of initial deferral. A plan could specify the time and form of payments that are to be made as a result of a distribution event (e.g., a plan could specify that payments upon separation of service will be paid in lump sum within 30 days of separation from service) or could allow participants to elect the time and form of payment at the time of the initial deferral election. If a plan allows participants to elect the time and form of payment, such election is subject to the rules regarding initial deferral elections under the provision. It is intended that multiple payout events are permissible. For example, a participant could elect to receive 25 percent of their account balance at age 50 and the remaining 75 percent at age 60. A plan could also allow participants to elect different forms of payment for different permissible distribution events. For example, a participant could elect to receive a lump-sum distribution upon disability, but an annuity at age 65.

Under Code Sec. 409A(a)(4), a plan may allow changes in the time and form of distributions subject to certain requirements.

Subsequent elections. A non-qualified deferred compensation plan may allow a subsequent election to delay the timing or form of distributions only if: (1) the plan requires that such election cannot be effective for at least 12 months after the date on which the election is made; (2) except in the case of elections relating to distributions on account of death, disability or unforeseeable emergency, the plan requires that the additional deferral with respect to which such election is made is for a period of not less than five years from the date such payment would otherwise have been made; and (3) the plan requires that an election related to a distribution to be made upon a specified time may not be made less than 12 months prior to the date of the first scheduled payment. It is expected that in limited cases, the Secretary will issue guidance, consistent with the purposes of the provision, regarding to what extent elections to change a stream of payments are permissible. The Secretary may issue regulations regarding elections with respect to payments under nonelective, supplemental retirement plans.

.08 Funding Rules

Code Sec. 409A(b) establishes rules to curtail abuse re: funding.

Foreign trusts. Code Sec. 409A(b)(1) prescribes that in the case of assets set aside (directly or indirectly) in a trust (or other arrangement determined by the Secretary) for purposes of paying non-qualified deferred compensation, such assets are treated as property transferred in connection with the performance of services under Code Sec. 83 (whether or not such assets are available to satisfy the claims of general creditors) at the time set aside if such assets (or trust or other arrangement) are located outside of the United States or at the time transferred if such assets (or trust or other arrangement) are subsequently transferred outside of the United States. Any subsequent increases in the value of, or any earnings with respect to, such assets are treated as additional transfers of property. Interest at the underpayment rate plus one percentage point is imposed on the underpayments that would have occurred had the amounts set aside been includable in income for the taxable year in which first deferred or, if later, the first taxable year not subject to a substantial risk of forfeiture. The amount required to be included in income is also subject to an additional 20-percent tax.

It is expected that the Secretary will provide rules for identifying the deferrals to which assets set aside are attributable, for situations in which assets equal to less than the full amount of deferrals are set aside. Code Sec. 409A(b) does not apply to assets located in a foreign jurisdiction if substantially all of the services to which the non-qualified deferred compensation relates are performed in such foreign jurisdiction. Code Sec. 409A(b) is specifically intended to apply to foreign trusts and arrangements that effectively shield from the claims of general creditors any assets intended to satisfy non-qualified deferred compensation arrangements. The Secretary has authority to exempt arrangements from the provision if the arrangements do not result in an improper deferral of U.S. tax and will not result in assets being effectively beyond the reach of creditors.

Triggers upon financial health. Code Sec. 409A(b)(2) states that a transfer of property in connection with the performance of services under Code Sec. 83 also occurs with respect to compensation deferred under a non-qualified deferred compensation plan if the plan provides that upon a change in the employer's financial health, assets will be restricted to the payment of non-qualified deferred compensation. An amount is treated as restricted even if the assets are available to satisfy the claims of general creditors. For example, the provision applies in the case of a plan that provides that upon a change in financial health, assets will be transferred to a rabbi trust.

The transfer of property occurs as of the earlier of when the assets are so restricted or when the plan provides that assets will be restricted. It is intended that the transfer of property occurs to the extent that assets are restricted or will be restricted with respect to such compensation. For example, in the case of a plan that provides that upon a change in the employer's financial health, a trust will become funded to the extent of all deferrals, all amounts deferred under the plan are treated as property transferred under Code Sec. 83. If a plan provides that deferrals of certain individuals will be funded upon a change in financial health, the transfer of property would occur with respect to compensation deferred by such individuals. Code Sec. 409A(b)(2) is not intended to apply when assets are restricted for a reason other than change in financial health (e.g., upon a change in control) or if assets are periodically restricted under a structured schedule and scheduled restrictions happen to coincide with a change in financial status. Any subsequent increases in the value of, or any earnings with respect to, restricted assets are treated as additional transfers of property. Interest at the underpayment rate plus one percentage point is imposed on the underpayments that would have occurred had the amounts been includable in income for the taxable year in which first deferred or, if later, the first taxable year not subject to a substantial risk of forfeiture. The amount required to be included in income is also subject to an additional 20-percent tax.

¶723.08

.09 Other Rules

Code Sec. 409A(b)(4) prescribes that any interest imposed is treated as interest on an underpayment of tax. Income (whether actual or notional) attributable to non-qualified deferred compensation is treated as additional deferred compensation and is subject to the provision. Code Sec. 409A(c) prescribes that Code Sec. 409A is not intended to prevent the inclusion of amounts in gross income under any provision or rule of law earlier than the time provided in the provision. Any amount included in gross income under Code Sec. 409A is not required to be included in gross income under any provision of law later than the time provided in Code Sec. 409A. Code Sec. 409A also does not affect the rules regarding the timing of an employer's deduction for non-qualified deferred compensation.

.10 Aggregation Rules

Under Code Sec. 409A(d)(6), except as provided by the Secretary, employer aggregation rules apply. It is intended that the Secretary issue guidance providing aggregation rules as are necessary to carry out the purposes of Code Sec. 409A(d)(6). For example, it is intended that aggregation rules would apply in the case of separation from service so that the separation from service from one entity within a controlled group, but continued service for another entity within the group, would not be a permissible distribution event. It is also intended that aggregation rules would not apply in the case of change in control so that the change in control of one member of a controlled group would not be a permissible distribution event for participants of a deferred compensation plan of another member of the group.

.11 Reporting Requirements

Amounts required to be included in income under the provision are subject to reporting and Federal income tax withholding requirements. Amounts required to be includable in income are required to be reported on an individual's Form W-2 (or Form 1099) for the year includable in income.

The provision also requires annual reporting to the IRS of amounts deferred. Such amounts are required to be reported on an individual's Form W-2 (or Form 1099) for the year deferred even if the amount is not currently includable in income for that taxable year. It is expected that annual reporting of annual amounts deferred will provide the IRS greater information regarding such arrangements for enforcement purposes. It is intended that the information reported would provide an indication of what arrangements should be examined and challenged. Under Code Sec. 409A, the Secretary is authorized, through regulations, to establish a minimum amount of deferrals below which the reporting requirement does not apply. The Secretary may also provide that the reporting requirement does not apply with respect to amounts of deferrals that are not reasonably ascertainable. It is intended that the exception for amounts not reasonably ascertainable only apply to non-account balance plans and that amounts be required to be reported when they first become reasonably ascertainable. For this purpose, it is intended that the exception be similar to that under Reg. § 31.3121(v)(2)-1(e)(4).

¶723.11

.12 Effective Date

The provisions of Code Sec. 409A are effective for amounts deferred in taxable years beginning after December 31, 2004. Earnings on amounts deferred before the effective date are subject to the provision to the extent that such amounts deferred are subject to the provision.

Amounts deferred in taxable years beginning before January 1, 2005, are subject to the provision if the plan under which the deferral is made is materially modified after October 3, 2004. The addition of any benefit, right or feature is a material modification. The exercise or reduction of an existing benefit, right, or feature is not a material modification. For example, an amendment to a plan on November 1, 2004, to add a provision that distributions may be allowed upon request if participants are required to forfeit 10 percent of the amount of the distribution (i.e., a "haircut") would be a material modification to the plan so that the rules of the provision would apply to the plan. Similarly, accelerating vesting under a plan after October 3, 2004, would be a material modification. A change in the plan administrator would not be a material modification. As another example, amending a plan to remove a distribution provision (e.g., to remove a "haircut") would not be considered a material modification.

Operating under the terms of a deferred compensation arrangement that complies with current law and is not materially modified after October 3, 2004, with respect to amounts deferred before January 1, 2005, is permissible, as such amounts would not be subject to the requirements of the provision. For example, subsequent deferrals with respect to amounts deferred before January 1, 2005, under a plan that is not materially modified after October 3, 2004, would not be subject to Code Sec. 409A. However, there is no inference that all subsequent deferral elections under plans that are not materially modified are permissible under present law. No inference is intended that all deferrals before the effective date are permissible under present law. It is expected that the IRS will challenge pre-effective date deferral arrangements that do not comply with present law.

For purposes of the effective date, an amount is considered deferred before January 1, 2005, if the amount is earned and vested before such date. To the extent there is no material modification after October 3, 2004, present law applies with respect to vested rights.

No later than 60 days after October 22, 2004, the Secretary shall issue guidance providing a limited period of time during which a non-qualified deferred compensation plan adopted before December 31, 2004, may, without violating the requirements of the provision relating to distributions, accelerations, and elections be amended (1) to provide that a participant may terminate participation in the plan, or cancel an outstanding deferral election with respect to amounts deferred after December 31, 2004, if such amounts are includable in income of the participant as earned, or if later, when not subject to a substantial risk of forfeiture, and (2) to conform with the provision with respect to amounts deferred after December 31, 2004. It is expected that the Secretary may provide exceptions to certain requirements of the provision during the transition period (e.g., the rules regarding timing of elections) for plans coming into compliance with the provision. Moreover, it is

¶723.12

expected that the Secretary will provide a reasonable time, during the transition period but after the issuance of guidance, for plans to be amended and approved by the appropriate parties in accordance with this provision.

.13 Planning Opportunities with Deferred Compensation Situations

The recent case of *Love*[162] offers an interesting planning opportunity coordinated with an ESOP. For a discussion of *Love*, see ¶ 1507.03.

---

[162] TC Memo 2012-166.

Chapter 8

Corporate Income Taxes

¶ 801 Corporate Tax Liabilities

An S corporation can be liable for income tax (at the *corporate* level) for the following: built-in gains, general business credit recapture, passive investment income, and LIFO inventory recapture. All four of the income taxes imposed on an S corporation occur only after a C corporation has switched to an S corporation or an S corporation has acquired a C corporation.

¶ 802 Built-In Gains Tax

.01 Background and Net Recognized Built-in Gains

Background. Congress recognized a problem shortly after creating S corporations in 1958—that corporations could use the S status to avoid double taxation, particularly with the capital gains tax. Example 8-1 illustrates the type of abuse that Congress was concerned about in changing the law.

> ***Example 8-1:*** A C corporation, Jacobi Inc., foreseeing large capital gains in the following year, adopted the S status for that tax year, passing the capital gains and distributing money equal to the capital gains to its shareholders. The next year, Jacobi Inc. terminated its S election and continued to conduct business. By adopting the C-S-C approach, the corporation avoided any capital gains tax at the C level and was able to pass its gains to its shareholders.

To prevent such tax avoidance, Congress in 1966 imposed a tax on built-in gains by adopting Code Sec. 1378. When the Subchapter S Revision Act of 1982 was adopted, Code Sec. 1378 became Code Sec. 1374. Code Sec. 1374 has been modified several times since then with its purpose (as was its predecessor's) being to impose tax hurdles on C corporations converting to S status with appreciated assets.

Net recognized built-in gains. Any net recognized built-in gain that the S corporation has for a tax year is taxed at the highest corporate rate, currently 35 percent.[1] The tax applies to built-in gains recognized during a recognition period. For taxable years before 2009 the recognition period was the ten-year period beginning on the date the C corporation converted to S status; then it was changed to 7 years for 2009 and 2010 (i.e., the "recognition period"). For tax years beginning in 2011, Code Sec. 1374's recognition period is the five-year period beginning with the first day of the first tax year for which the corporation was an S corporation. The "net recognized built-in gain" is defined as the lesser of (1) the amount that would be the S corporations's taxable income if only recognized built-in gain and loss were taken into account or (2) the corporation's taxable income for the tax year computed with the modification listed in Code Sec. 1375(b)(1)(B).[2]

> *Example 8-2:* Grayson Inc., a calendar-year, cash-basis C corporation, converts to S status on January 1, 2005. At the time of conversion, it has only one asset, a piece of land with a basis of $100 and a fair market value of $300. Two years after conversion, Grayson Inc. sells the land for $700. Grayson Inc. will pay a tax under Code Sec. 1374 on $200 of the gain ($300 − $100), passing the gain, net of the tax paid, to its shareholders. With a built-in gains rate of 35%, the shareholders will receive their allocation of the net gain after tax, $130 ($200 − (.35 × $200)), plus their allocation of the remainder of the gain, $400 ($700 − $300).

The key to understanding Code Sec. 1374 is "recognized built-in gain." If there is no recognized built-in gain, then there is no tax on disposition of the C corporation assets. Thus, in Example 8-2, if the land was sold for $100 or less during the five-year period beginning January 1, 2005, there would be no recognized built-in gain. Alternatively, if Grayson Inc. in Example 8-2 was able to wait and sell its appreciated land in 2011, it would not be subject to any Code Sec. 1374 taxation. Selling a C corporation asset for its book value at the time of conversion may be unrealistic, however. Fortunately, there are ways to minimize (and in some instances, avoid entirely) the built-in gains tax.[3]

The Code provides rules for determining recognized built-in gain (and recognized built-in loss) and for determining built-in income (and deduction) items. Any gain recognized by an S corporation during the recognition period is presumed to be a recognized built-in gain unless the S corporation shows that it did not hold the asset on the first day of the recognition period or there was no appreciation at the time of the conversion.[4] Similar rules apply to any loss recognized during the recognition period.[5] Gain or loss recognized may come from sales or exchanges.[6] A gain or loss resulting from transactions other than sales or exchanges is also taken into account under the built-in income (and deduction) rules (e.g., distribution of appreciated property to shareholders).

---

[1] Code Sec. 1374(a)-(b). The corporate tax rate is designated in Code Sec. 11(b).

[2] Code Sec. 1374(d)(2).

[3] See tax-planning discussion at ¶ 802.18.

[4] Code Sec. 1374(d)(3).

[5] Code Sec. 1374(d)(4).

[6] IRS regulations for Code Sec. 1374(d)(3) and (4).

¶802.01

The built-in gains tax is not a subjective tax depending on the taxpayer's motive; rather, it is a mechanical tax geared to statutory definitions.[7] Any item of income or deduction properly taken into account by an S corporation during the recognition period is recognized built-in gain or loss if the item is attributable to periods before the recognition period.[8] Under the regulations, an S corporation's items of income or deduction generally are treated as recognized built-in gain or loss if the item would have been taken into account before the recognition period by a taxpayer using the accrual method. The accrual method is used because valuing items of income and deduction on the first day of the recognition period would be unduly burdensome both for S corporations, many of which are small businesses, and the IRS.

The regulations also adopt special rules for determining recognized built-in gain and loss in the case of (1) positive and negative income adjustments under Code Sec. 481(a), (2) cancellation of indebtedness income and bad debt deductions, (3) income and deductions reported under the completed contract method, (4) income from sales or exchanges reported under the installment method, and (5) the distributive share of partnership items of income, gain, loss, and deduction.

Revocation and re-election of S corporate status. When Code Sec. 1374 was amended in the Tax Reform Act of 1986 to prescribe a ten-year measuring period for Code Sec. 1374 instead of a three-year one, Congress provided a transitional rule in the Technical and Miscellaneous Act of 1988 (TAMRA) for C corporations that made an election to be an S corporation before January 1, 1989. In *Colorado Gas Compression, Inc. v. Comm,*[9] the Court reviewed a unique situation involving the transition rule. The C corporation elected S status during the transition period in 1988, and then revoked the election on December 1, 1989. Subsequently, the C corporation re-elected S status effective January 1, 1994. The corporation sold assets during the years 1994 through 1996. The Court held that the 1998 election was made during the transition period when Code Sec. 1374's three-year rule applied.

The Service, in response to this decision, promulgated Reg. § 1.1374-8 and Reg. § 1.1374-10 to provide that the S corporation's most recent election, not an earlier election which had been revoked or terminated, is to be utilized to determine the measuring period for Code Sec. 1374's rules. Under Reg. § 1.1374-8 and Reg. § 1.1374-10, the corporation in *Colorado* would have been held to a ten-year measuring period under Code Sec. 1374, not the three-year one, as the Court decided. It remains to be seen what effect Reg. § 1.1374-8 and Reg. § 1.1374-10 will have on future Court decisions on this point.

---

[7] *Warrensburg Board & Paper Corp.,* 77 TC 1107, Dec. 38,424 (1981) (former Code Sec. 1378 applied to gain from insurance recovery; taxpayer's motivation was irrelevant).

[8] Code Sec. 1374(d)(5). The Treasury Department and the IRS intend no inference regarding rules they may adopt in other regulations, such as under Code Secs. 382(h)(6) and 384(c)(1)(B), which contain language similar to Code Sec. 1374(d)(5).

[9] 2004-1 USTC ¶ 50,213 (10th Cir. 2004).

.02 Comparison to the Passive Investment Income Tax

It is possible for an S corporation to be subject to both the built-in gains tax and the passive investment income tax.[10] However, the chance of being liable for both taxes is rare since the passive investment income tax cannot be imposed unless the S corporation has C corporation earnings and profits and the S corporation has passive investment income.[11] The built-in gains tax will be imposed whether or not there are C corporation earnings and profits.

.03 Computing the Built-In Gains Tax

To compute the built-in gains tax, Reg. § 1.1374-1(a) prescribes that the tax imposed on the income of an S corporation by Code Sec. 1374(a) for any tax year during the 5-year recognition period is computed using the following four steps:

(1) Determine the net recognized built-in gain of the corporation for the tax year under Code Sec. 1374(d)(2) and Reg. § 1.1374-2.

(2) Reduce the net recognized built-in gain (but not below zero) by any net operating loss and capital loss carryforward allowed under Code Sec. 1374(b)(2) and Reg. § 1.1374-5.

(3) Compute a tentative tax by applying the rate of tax determined under Code Sec. 1374(b)(1) for the tax year to the amount determined under (2).

(4) Compute the final tax by reducing the tentative tax (but not below zero) by any credit allowed under Code Sec. 1374(b)(3) and Reg. § 1.1374-6.

Tax Pointer: The current 5 year recognition period for Code Sec. 1374 is geared to "taxable years." So, if a June 30th fiscal year C corporation converts to an S corporation and adopts under Code Sec. 444 a 10/31 fiscal year for its year of operation (for a discussion of Code Sec. 444, see ¶ 502.04), and then after the first full fiscal year of operation terminates its October 31st fiscal year to operate under a calendar year; the S corporation will be able to shorten the 5 year recognition period to 4 calendar years as illustrated below

7/1/y1–10/31/y1	1st year of recognition
11/1/y1-10/31/y2	2nd year of recognition
11/1/y2-12/31/y2	3rd year of recognition
1/1/y3-12/31/y3	4th year of recognition
1/1/y4-12/31/y4	5th year of recognition

.04 Determining Net Recognized Built-In Gain

To compute the net recognized built-in gain for Step 1 above, Reg. § 1.1374-2 prescribes in general that the term "net recognized built-in gain" for any tax year is the least of

---

[10] Code Secs. 1374 and 1375. See ¶ 802.19 for more details.   [11] See further discussion at ¶ 804.02.

- the corporation's taxable income determined by using the rules applying to C corporations and considering only its recognized built-in gain, recognized built-in loss, and recognized built-in gain carryover (pre-limitation amount);

- the corporation's taxable income determined by using all rules applying to C corporations as modified by Code Sec. 1375(b)(1)(B) (taxable income limitation); and

- the amount by which its net unrealized built-in gain exceeds its net recognized built-in gain for all prior taxable years (net unrealized built-in gain limitation).

.05 Determining Net Unrealized Built-In Gain

Reg. §1.1374-3(a) defines the term "net unrealized built-in gain" generally as the total of the following:

(1) The amount that would be the amount realized if, at the beginning of the first day of the recognition period (generally the effective date of the S election), the corporation had remained a C corporation and had sold all its assets at fair market value to an unrelated party that assumed all its liabilities; *decreased by*

(2) any liability of the corporation that would be included in the amount realized on the sale, but only if the corporation would be allowed a deduction on payment of the liability (accounts payable of a cash-basis C corporation); *decreased by*

(3) the aggregate adjusted bases of the corporation's assets at the time of the sale; *increased or decreased by*

(4) the corporation's Code Sec. 481 adjustments that would be taken into account on the sale;[12] and *increased by*

(5) any recognized built-in loss that would not be allowed as a deduction under Code Secs. 382,[13] 383,[14] or 384[15] on the sale.

Example 8-3, taken from Reg. §1.1374-3(b), illustrates how to compute the net unrealized built-in gain.

> **Example 8-3:** *Net unrealized built-in gain.* Marco, a calendar-year C corporation using the cash method, elects to become an S corporation on January 1, 2000. On December 31, 1999, Marco has assets and liabilities as follows:

---

[12] That is, the income to be realized caused by the corporation changing from cash to accrual.

[13] Code Sec. 382 covers limitation on net operating loss carryforwards.

[14] Code Sec. 383 covers special limitations on certain excess credits, etc.

[15] Code Sec. 384 covers limitation on use of preacquisition losses to offset built-in gains.

Assets	Fair Market Value	Basis
Factory	$ 500,000	$900,000
Accounts receivable	300,000	0
Goodwill	250,000	0
Total	$1,050,000	$900,000

Liabilities	Amount
Mortgage	$ 200,000
Accounts payable	100,000
Total	$ 300,000

Further, Marco must include a total of $60,000 in taxable income in 2000, 2001, and 2002 under Code Sec. 481(a).

If, on December 31, 1999, Marco sold all its assets to a third party that assumed all its liabilities, Marco's amount realized would be $1,050,000 ($750,000 cash received + $300,000 liabilities assumed). Thus, Marco's net unrealized built-in gain is determined as follows:

Amount realized	$1,050,000
Deduction allowed	(100,000)
Bases of Marco's assets	(900,000)
Code Sec. 481 adjustments	60,000
Net unrealized built-in gain	$ 110,000

Appraisals when a C corporation converts to S status. The regulations do not address how to value the assets at the time of converting from C status to S status. However, unless the corporation can demonstrate that there was no appreciation in the assets at the time of the conversion, any gain recognized during the 10-year period will be subject to the built-in gains tax.[16] Thus, to prevent any adverse tax results from occurring, the S corporation should arrange for an appraisal at the time of acquiring C corporation assets. Whether the assets are acquired from a C status to S status conversion or through a reorganization,[17] a valuation of the assets will determine the amount of unrecognized built-in gain at the time of conversion (i.e., the fair market value of the asset(s) less book value). To be safe, depending on the nature and size of the asset(s), the S corporation may want to obtain more than one appraisal and then average the appraisals to further document that the fair market value is true and correct.

---

[16] Code Sec. 1374(d)(3).

[17] See ¶ 1211 for a discussion on reorganizations.

¶802.05

.06 Income Recognition Events

Recognized built-in gains and losses result not only from sales or exchanges of assets but also from other income-recognition events such as the collection of accounts receivable by a cash-basis corporation.[18]

Accounts receivable. Example 8-4, adapted from Reg. § 1.1374-4(b)(3), illustrates Congress's concern regarding accounts receivable when an C corporation converts to S status.

Example 8-4: Accounts receivable. Billings is a C corporation using the cash method that elects to become an S corporation effective January 1, 2010. On January 1, 2010, Billings has $50,000 of accounts receivable for services rendered before that date. On that date, the accounts receivable have a fair market value of $40,000 and an adjusted basis of $0. In 2010, Billings collects $50,000 on the accounts receivable and includes that amount in gross income. Under Reg. § 1.1374-4(b)(1), the $50,000 included in gross income in 2010 is recognized built-in gain because it would have been included in gross income before the beginning of the recognition period if Billings had been an accrual-method taxpayer. However, if Billings instead disposes of the accounts receivable for $45,000 on July 1, 2010, in a transaction treated as a sale or exchange for federal income tax purposes, Billings would have recognized built-in gain of $40,000 on the disposition.

To avoid the built-in gains tax that arises on accounts receivable when a C corporation converts to S status, the S corporation could consider "zeroing out" taxable income by taking deductions (e.g., giving salary to shareholder-employees).[19]

Accrual-method rules. The following two tests from Reg. § 1.1374-4(b) may be applied for reporting income, expense, etc.

(1) *Income items.* Any item of income properly taken into account during the recognition period is recognized built-in gain if the item would have been properly included in gross income before the beginning of the recognition period by an accrual-method taxpayer (disregarding any method of accounting for which an election by the taxpayer must be made unless the taxpayer actually used the method when it was a C corporation). The accrual method of accounting requires that income is to be reported pursuant to Code Sec. 446 when pursuant to the "all events" test: (1) all events have occurred that fix the taxpayer's right to receive the income; and (2) the amount can be determined with reasonable accuracy. In *Houchin v. Commissioner,*[20] there was a lawsuit resulting in a settlement agreement involving a C corporation which converted to an S on January 1, 1999. The settlement agreement was signed on December 21, 1998 and it provided that "This Settlement Agreement shall become effective immediately upon execution by all the Settling Parties." The settlement agreement was effective by December 31, 1998 and the C corporation—

---

[18] Reg. § 1.1374-4(a)-(h).

[19] See ¶ 802.18 for further discussion.

[20] TC Memo 2006-119.

now an S—received the check for the settlement agreement on January 4, 1999. The court held that the "all events" test was satisfied in 1998; thus, the corporation could report the income in 1998 as C corporate income and not in 1999 as S corporate income subject to Code Sec. 1374.

(2) *Deduction items.* Any item of deduction properly taken into account during the recognition period is recognized built-in loss if the item would have been properly allowed as a deduction against gross income before the beginning of the recognition period to an accrual-method taxpayer (disregarding any method of accounting for which an election by the taxpayer must be made unless the taxpayer actually used the method when it was a C corporation). In determining whether an item would have been properly allowed as a deduction against gross income by an accrual-method taxpayer, Code Sec. 461(h)(2)(C) and Reg. § 1.461-4(g) do not apply (relating to liabilities for tort, worker's compensation, breach of contract, violation of law, rebates, refunds, awards, prizes, jackpots, insurance contracts, warranty contracts, service contracts, taxes, and other liabilities).

Contingent liabilities, deferred payment liabilities, and deferred prepayment income. Examples 8-5, 8-6, and 8-7, adapted from Reg. § 1.1374-4(b)(3), illustrate how to determine the tax on capital gains for contingent liabilities, deferred payment liabilities, and deferred prepayment income.

Example 8-5: *Contingent liability.* Micron is a C corporation using the cash method that elects to become an S corporation effective January 1, 2010. In 2009, a lawsuit was filed against Micron claiming $1,000,000 in damages. In 2010, Micron loses the lawsuit, pays a $500,000 judgment, and properly claims a deduction for that amount. Under Reg. § 1.1374-4(b)(2), the $500,000 deduction allowed in 2010 is not recognized built-in loss because it would not have been allowed as a deduction against gross income before the beginning of the recognition period if Micron had been an accrual-method taxpayer (even disregarding Code Sec. 461(h)(2)(C) and Reg. § 1.461-4(g)).

Example 8-6: *Deferred payment liabilities.* Sexton is a C corporation using the cash method that elects to become an S corporation on January 1, 2010. In 2009, Sexton lost a lawsuit and became obligated to pay $150,000 in damages. Under Code Sec. 461(h)(2)(C), this amount is not allowed as a deduction until Sexton makes payment. In 2010, Sexton makes payment and properly claims a deduction for the amount of the payment. Under Reg. § 1.1374-4(b)(2), the $150,000 deduction allowed in 2010 is recognized built-in loss.

Example 8-7: *Deferred prepayment income.* Wixom is a C corporation using the accrual method that elects to become an S corporation effective January 1, 2010. In 2009, Wixom received $2,500 for services to be rendered in 2010, and properly elected to include the $2,500 in gross income in 2010 under Rev. Proc. 71-21, 1971-2 CB 549. Under Reg. § 1.1374-4(b)(1), the $2,500 included in gross income in 2010 is not recognized built-in gain because it would not have been included in gross income before the beginning of the recognition period by an accrual-method taxpayer using the method that Wixom actually used before the beginning of the recognition period.

.07 Inventory

The fair market value of the inventory of an S corporation on the first day of the recognition period equals the amount that a willing buyer would pay a willing seller for the inventory in a purchase of all the S corporation's assets, by a buyer that expects to continue to operate the S corporation's business.[21] The buyer and seller are presumed not to be under any compulsion to buy or sell and to have reasonable knowledge of all relevant facts.

The Preamble to the final Code Sec. 1374 regulations recognized that clarification and direction had to be furnished for the valuation of inventory. The Preamble stated that the buyer and seller are presumed not to be under any compulsion to buy or sell and to have reasonable knowledge of all relevant facts. Relevant facts include the following:

- Replacement cost of the inventory

- Expected retail selling price of the inventory

- Seller's incentive to demand a price for the inventory that would compensate for and provide a fair return for expenditures the seller incurred to obtain, prepare, carry, and dispose of the inventory before the sale of the business

- Buyer's incentive to pay a price for the inventory that would compensate for and provide a fair return for similar expenditures the buyer expects to incur after the sale of the business

It is expected that the value of an S corporation's inventory as determined under the final regulations will generally be less than its anticipated retail price, but greater than its replacement cost.

As to valuation, the Preamble to the proposed Code Sec. 1374 regulations stated the following:

> Rev. Proc. 77-12, 1977-1 C.B. 569, provides guidance for valuing inventory where the assets of a business are purchased for a lump sum or the stock of a corporation is purchased and the corporation liquidates under former section 334(b)(2). The Treasury Department and the IRS are considering whether Rev. Proc. 77-12 should be modified to (1) provide guidance for valuing inventory for purposes of sections 336, 338, 1060, and 1374, and (2) incorporate the principles of relevant case law such as *Knapp King-Size Corp. v. United States,* 527 F.2d 1392 (Ct. Cl. 1975), and *Zeropack Company v. Commissioner,* T.C. Memo 1983-652.

> ***Tax Pointer:*** Despite the difficulty determining the appropriate valuation of inventory, the final regulations do not prescribe any safe harbors for S corporations.

---

[21] Reg. § 1.1374-7(a).

.08 Discharge of Indebtedness and Bad Debts

S corporations may have built-in gains from the discharge of indebtedness or built-in losses from bad debts if such items arise from a debt owed by or to an S corporation at the beginning of the recognition period.[22]

.09 Completion of Contract

Any item of income properly taken into account during the recognition period under the completed-contract method[23] (where the corporation began performance of the contract before the beginning of the recognition period) is recognized built-in gain if the item would have been included in gross income before the beginning of the recognition period under the percentage-of-completion method.[24] Any similar item of deduction is recognized built-in loss if the item would have been allowed against gross income before the beginning of the recognition period under the percentage-of-completion method.

.10 Installment Sales

To cover installment sales situations, Reg. §1.1374-4(h)(1) prescribes the following:[25]

> If a corporation sells an asset before or during the [5-year] recognition period and reports the income from the sale using the installment method under section 453 during or after the recognition period, that income is subject to tax under section 1374.

Thus, a corporation cannot defer the built-in gains tax by selling an asset during the 5-year recognition period under the installment method and having the gain reported after the expiration of the recognition period. If the corporation sold an asset using the installment method prior to conversion, but the installment period runs through the recognition period, Reg. §1.1374-4(h) prescribes that the corporation must compute the gain which would have been subject to Code Sec. 1374 as if the corporation had elected out of the installment method.

> **Example 8-8:** Yuma is a C corporation that elects to become an S corporation on January 1, 2006. On that date, Yuma owns an office building with a fair market value of $150,000 and an adjusted basis of $90,000. In 2006, Yuma sells the office building for $150,000 on the installment method. The installment note provides for a market rate of interest to be paid annually with the principal amount due in 2012, the first year after the 5-year recognition period. Because Yuma does not elect out of the installment method,[26] the $60,000 gain from the sale is not recognized until payment is received in 2012. Although the gain is not recognized until after the 5-year recognition period expires, it will be subject to the built-in gains tax because the sale occurred during the recognition period.

If income is reported under the installment method for a tax year under the 5-year recognition period, the S corporation's Code Sec. 1374 attributes may be

---

[22] Reg. §1.1374-4(f).
[23] Reg. §1.451-3(d).
[24] Reg. §§1.451-3(c) and 1.1374-4(g).

[25] Reg. §1.1374-4(h) adopts Notice 90-27, 1990-1 CB 336.
[26] Code Sec. 453(d).

¶802.08

used to the extent allowed in determining the built-in gains tax.[27] When an asset is sold using an installment sale basis under Code Sec. 453, Code Sec. 1374(d)(7)(E) states that the treatment of the payments are determined by the tax year in which the sale is made. However, the S corporation's recognized loss for a tax year after the recognition period (that would have been recognized built-in loss if it had been recognized in the recognition period) may not be used in determining the built-in gains tax.

.11 Partnership Transactions

The drafters of the built-in gains regulations wrote them to prevent a C corporation, prior to converting to S status, from avoiding or limiting its built-in gains tax by transferring appreciated assets to a partnership and having the partnership sell the appreciated assets. Since the partnership would sell the assets, not the S corporation, no built-in gains tax would be realized on the sale.

Regulations pertaining to partnership interests. Partnership interests that are held by a C corporation when it converts to an S corporation and that receive a transfer of appreciated assets after the conversion date do not keep the S corporation from paying the built-in gains tax.[28] An S corporation must "look through" its partnership interest and treat its distributive share of its partnership's items as recognized built-in gain or loss (to the extent that its distributive share would have been treated as recognized built-in gain or loss had the items originated in and been taken into account directly by the S corporation). "Look-through" rules are generally limited to the built-in gain or built-in loss inherent in the partnership interest itself. If the S corporation disposes of the partnership interest during the recognition period, the amount treated as recognized built-in gain or loss in the disposition is adjusted to take into account amounts treated as recognized built-in gain or loss under the look-through rules. The look-through rules do not apply in cases where the S corporation owns an interest in a partnership with a value less than $100,000 or a less-than-10-percent interest in the partnership's capital and profits. Also, a special rule applies to taxpayers (not otherwise subject to the built-in gains regulations) who contribute property to a partnership to avoid the built-in gains tax. As discussed below, an elaborate tracking system is required so that at the time of converting from C to S status, the amount of built-in gain can be calculated.

Four-part test. Reg. § 1.1374-4(i)(1) prescribes a four-part test to tax partnership transactions. If an S corporation owns a partnership interest at the beginning of the recognition period or transfers property to a partnership in a transaction to which Code Sec. 1374(d)(6) applies during the recognition period, the S corporation determines the effect on its net recognized built-in gain from its distributive share of partnership items as follows:

(1) Apply the rules of Code Sec. 1374(d) to the S corporation's distributive share of partnership items of income, gain, loss, or deduction included in income or allowed as a deduction under the rules of subchapter K to determine the extent to which it would have been treated as recognized

---

[27] Reg. § 1.1374-4(h)(4). [28] Reg. § 1.1374-4(i).

built-in gain or loss if the partnership items had originated in and been taken into account directly by the S corporation (partnership 1374 items).

(2) Determine the S corporation's net recognized built-in loss without partnership 1374 items.

(3) Determine the S corporation's net recognized built-in gain with partnership 1374 items.

(4) If the amount computed under Step 3 exceeds the amount computed under Step 2, the excess (as limited by Reg. § 1.1374-4(i)(2)(i)) is the S corporation's partnership recognized built-in gain (RBIG), and the S corporation's net recognized built-in gain is the sum of the amount computed under Step 2 *plus* the partnership RBIG. If the amount computed under Step 2 exceeds the amount computed under Step 3, the excess (as limited by Reg. § 1.1374-4(i)(2)(i)) is the S corporation's partnership recognized built-in loss (RBIL), and the S corporation's net recognized built-in gain is the remainder of the amount computed under Step 2 *minus* the partnership RBIL.

Examples 8-9 and 8-10, adapted from Reg. § 1.1374-4(i)(8), illustrate the general application of Reg. § 1.1374-4(i)(1).

> **Example 8-9:** *Pre-conversion partnership interest.* Canup is a C corporation that elects to become an S corporation on January 1, 2007. On that date, Canup owns a 50% interest in partnership Peta, and Peta owns (among other assets) Goldencrown with a basis of $25,000 and a value of $45,000. In 2007, Peta buys Silvercrown for $50,000. In 2010, Peta sells Goldencrown for $55,000 and recognizes a gain of $30,000 of which $15,000 is included in Canup's distributive share. Peta also sells Silvercrown in 2010 for $42,000 and recognizes a loss of $8,000 of which $4,000 is included in Canup's distributive share. Under Reg. § 1.1374-4(i)(1), and Code Sec. 1374(d)(3), Canup's $15,000 gain is presumed to be recognized built-in gain and thus treated as a partnership 1374 item, but this presumption is rebutted if Canup establishes that Peta's gain would have been only $20,000 ($45,000 – $25,000) if Goldencrown had been sold on the first day of the recognition period. In such a case, only Canup's distributive share of the $20,000 built-in gain, $10,000, would be treated as a partnership 1374 item. Under Reg. § 1.1374-4(i)(1) and Code Sec. 1374(d)(4), Canup's $4,000 loss is not treated as a partnership 1374 item because Peta did not hold Silvercrown on the first day of the recognition period.

> **Example 8-10:** *Post-conversion contribution.* Domer is a C corporation that elects to become an S corporation on January 1, 2005. On that date, Domer owns (among other assets) Roost Haven with a basis of $100,000 and a value of $200,000. On January 1, 2005, when Roost Haven has a basis of $100,000 and a value of $200,000, Domer contributes Roost Haven to partnership Philco for a 50% interest in Philco. On January 1, 2011, Philco sells Roost Haven for $300,000 and recognizes a gain of $200,000 on the sale ($300,000 – $100,000). Domer is allocated $100,000 of the gain under Code Sec. 704(c), and another $50,000 for its 50% share of the remainder, for a total of $150,000. Under Reg.

¶802.11

§ 1.1374-4(i)(1) and Code Sec. 1374(d)(3), if Domer establishes that Philco's gain would have been only $100,000 ($200,000 – $100,000) if Roost Haven had been sold on the first day of the recognition period, Domer would treat only $100,000 as a partnership 1374 item.

.12 Limitations on Partnership Recognized Built-In Gains and Losses

The following limitations on recognized built-in gains (RBIG) and recognized built-in losses (RBIL) are from Reg. § 1.1374-4(i)(2):

   (i) *Partnership RBIG.* An S corporation's partnership RBIG for any taxable year may not exceed the excess (if any) of the S corporation's RBIG limitation over its partnership RBIG for prior taxable years. The preceding sentence does not apply if a corporation forms or avails of a partnership with a principal purpose of avoiding the tax imposed under section 1374.

   (ii) *Partnership RBIL.* An S corporation's partnership RBIL for any taxable year may not exceed the excess (if any) of the S corporation RBIL limitation over its partnership RBIL for prior taxable years.

Reg. § 1.1374-4(i)(4) defines RBIG and RBIL limitations as follows:

   (A) The amount that would be the amount realized if, at the beginning of the first day of the recognition period, the corporation had remained a C corporation and had sold its partnership interest (and any assets the corporation contributed to the partnership during the recognition period) at fair market value to an unrelated party; decreased by

   (B) The corporation's adjusted basis in the partnership interest (and any assets the corporation contributed to the partnership during the recognition period) at the time of the sale referred to in [Reg. § 1.1374-4(i)(4)(i)(A)]; and increased or decreased by

   (C) The corporation's allocable share of the partnership's section 481(a) adjustments at the time of the sale referred to in [Reg. § 1.1374-4(i)(4)(i)(A)].

Reg. § 1.1374-4(i)(4)(ii) prescribes that if the recognized built-in gain or loss is a positive amount under Reg. § 1.1374-4(i), the S corporation has a "RBIG limitation" equal to that amount and a RBIL limitation of $0. However, if the result is a negative amount, the S corporation has a "RBIL limitation" equal to that amount and a RBIG limitation of $0.

Examples 8-11 through 8-14, adapted from Reg. § 1.1374-4(i)(8), illustrate the operation of Reg. §§ 1.1374-4(i)(2) and (4).

   Example 8-11: *RBIG limitation of $100,000 or $50,000.* Franco is a C corporation that elects to become an S corporation on January 1, 2010. On that date, Franco owns a 50% interest in partnership Zoom with a RBIG limitation of $100,000 (i.e., the difference between the partner's basis in its capital and the fair market value of the partnership assets) and a RBIL limitation of $0. Zoom owns (among other assets) Gemstone with a basis of $50,000 and a value of $200,000. In 2010, Zoom sells Gemstone for $200,000 and recognizes a gain of $150,000 of which $75,000 is included in Franco's distributive share and treated as a partnership 1374 item. Franco's net recognized built-in gain for 2010 computed without partnership 1374 items is $35,000 and with partnership 1374 items is $110,000. Thus, Franco has a partnership RBIG of $75,000 except as limited under Reg. §1.1374-4(i)(2)(i). Because Franco's RBIG limitation is $100,000, Franco's partnership RBIG of $75,000 is not limited and Franco's net recognized built-in gain for the year is $110,000 ($35,000 + $75,000) (thereby leaving $25,000 of unrealized built-in gains remaining). However, if Franco had an RBIG limitation of $50,000 instead of $100,000, Franco's partnership RBIG would have been limited to $50,000 under Reg. §1.1374-4(i)(2)(i) and Franco's net recognized built-in gain would be $85,000 ($35,000 + $50,000).

Example 8-12: *RBIL limitation of $60,000 or $40,000.* Granger is a C corporation that elects to become an S corporation on January 1, 2010. On that date, Granger owns a 50% interest in partnership Proship with a RBIG limitation of $0 and a RBIL limitation of $60,000. Proship owns (among other assets) Truckload with a basis of $225,000 and a value of $125,000. In 2010, Proship sells Truckload for $125,000 and recognizes a loss of $100,000 of which $50,000 is included in Granger's distributive share and treated as a partnership 1374 item. Granger's net recognized built-in gain for 2010 computed without partnership 1374 items is $75,000 and with partnership 1374 items is $25,000. Thus, Granger has a partnership RBIL of $50,000 for the year except as limited under Reg. §1.1374-4(i)(2)(ii). Because Granger's RBIL limitation is $60,000, Granger's partnership RBIL for the year is not limited and Granger's net recognized built-in gain for the year is $25,000 ($75,000 – $50,000). However, if Granger had a RBIL limitation of $40,000 instead of $60,000, Granger's partnership RBIL would be limited to $40,000 under Reg. §1.1374-4(i)(2)(ii) and Granger's net recognized built-in gain for the year would be $35,000 ($75,000 – $40,000).

Example 8-13: *RBIG limitation of $0.* Handee is a C corporation that elects to become an S corporation on January 1, 2010. Handee owns a 50% interest in partnership Mitts with a RBIG limitation of $0 and a RBIL limitation of $25,000. In 2010, Mitt's partnership 1374 items are ordinary income of $25,000 and capital gain of $75,000. Handee itself has recognized built-in ordinary income of $40,000 and recognized built-in capital loss of $90,000. Handee's net recognized built-in gain for 2010 computed without partnership 1374 items is $40,000 and with partnership 1374 items is $65,000 ($40,000 + $25,000). Thus, Handee's partnership RBIG is $25,000 for the year except as limited under Reg. §1.1374-4(i)(2)(i). Because Handee's RBIG limitation is $0, Handee's partnership RBIG of $25,000 is limited to $0 and Handee's net recognized built-in gain for the year is $40,000.

Example 8-14: *RBIL limitation of $0.* Indigo is a C corporation that elects to become an S corporation on January 1, 2010. Indigo owns a 50% interest in partnership Perfecto with a RBIG limitation of $60,000 and a RBIL limitation of $0. In 2010, Perfecto's partnership 1374 items are ordinary income of $25,000 and capital loss of $90,000. Indigo itself has recognized built-in ordinary income of $40,000 and recognized built-in capital gain of $75,000. Indigo's net recognized built-in gain for 2010 computed without partnership 1374 items is $115,000 ($40,000 + $75,000) and with partnership 1374 items is

$65,000 ($40,000 + $25,000). Thus, Indigo's partnership RBIL is $50,000 for the year except as limited under Reg. § 1.1374-4(i)(2)(ii). Because Indigo's RBIL limitation is $0, Indigo's partnership RBIL of $50,000 is limited to $0 and Indigo's net recognized built-in gain for the year is $115,000.

Gain and loss on property contributed to the partnership. The "ceiling rule," for purposes of the built-in gains tax only, is prescribed by Reg. § 1.1374-4(i)(6) as:

> [A]n S corporation's section 704(c) gain or loss amount with respect to any asset is not reduced during the recognition period, except for amounts treated as recognized built-in gain or loss with respect to that asset under [Reg. § 1.1374-4(i)].

Example 8-15, adapted from Reg. § 1.1374-4(i)(8), illustrates the application of the "ceiling rule."

> **Example 8-15:** *Code Sec. 704(c) case.* Jamco is a C corporation that elects to become an S corporation on January 1, 2007. On that date, Jamco contributes Asset 1, 5-year property with a value of $40,000 and a basis of $0, and an unrelated party contributes $40,000 in cash, each for a 50% interest in partnership Kings. The partnership adopts the traditional method under Reg. § 1.704-3(b). If Kings sold Asset 1 for $40,000 immediately after it was contributed by Jamco, Kings' $40,000 gain would be allocated to Jamco under Code Sec. 704(c). Instead, Asset 1 is sold by Kings in 2010 for $36,000 and Kings recognizes gain of $36,000 ($36,000 – $0) on the sale. However, because book depreciation of $8,000 per year has been taken on Asset 1 in 2007, 2008, and 2009, Jamco is allocated only $16,000 of Kings' $36,000 gain (($40,000 – (3 × $8,000) = ($16,000 – $0)) under Code Sec. 704(c). The remaining $20,000 of Kings' $36,000 gain ($36,000 – $16,000) is allocated 50% to each partner under Code Sec. 704(b). Thus, a total of $26,000 ($16,000 + $10,000) of Kings' $36,000 gain is allocated to Jamco. However, under Reg. § 1.1374-4(i)(6), Jamco treats $36,000 as a partnership 1374 item on Kings' sale of Asset 1.

.13 Partnership Dispositions and Small Interests

Disposition of partnership interest. Reg. § 1.1374-4(i)(3) prescribes the following:

> If an S corporation disposes of its partnership interest, the amount that may be treated as recognized built-in gain may not exceed the excess (if any) of the S corporation's RBIG limitation over its partnership RBIG during the recognition period. Similarly, the amount that may be treated as recognized built-in loss may not exceed the excess (if any) of the S corporation's RBIL limitation over its partnership RBIL during the recognition period.

Example 8-16, adapted from Reg. § 1.1374-4(i)(8), illustrates the application of the rules pertaining to the disposition of a partnership interest.

> **Example 8-16:** *Disposition of partnership interest.* Kimmer is a C corporation that elects to become an S corporation on January 1, 2007. On that date, Kimmer owns a 50% interest in partnership Photops with a RBIG limitation of $200,000 and a RBIL limitation of $0. Photops owns (among other assets) Stark with a basis of $20,000 and a value of $140,000. In 2007, Photops sells Stark for

¶802.13

$140,000 and recognizes a gain of $120,000 of which $60,000 is included in Kimmer's distributive share and treated as a partnership 1374 item. Kimmer's net recognized built-in gain for 2007 computed without partnership 1374 items is $95,000 and with partnership 1374 items is $155,000. Thus, Kimmer has a partnership RBIG of $60,000. In 2010, Kimmer sells its entire interest in Photops for $350,000 and recognizes a gain of $250,000. Under Reg. § 1.1374-4(i)(3), Kimmer's recognized built-in gain on the sale is limited by its RBIG limitation to $140,000 ($200,000 – $60,000).

Disposition of distributed partnership asset. Reg. § 1.1374-4(i)(7) addresses the situation where the partnership holding built-in gain property distributes this "built-in gain" partnership asset to the S corporation partner:

> If on the first day of the recognition period an S corporation holds an interest in a partnership that holds an asset and during the recognition period the partnership distributes the asset to the S corporation that thereafter disposes of the asset, the asset is treated as having been held by the S corporation on the first day of the recognition period and as having the fair market value and adjusted basis in the hands of the S corporation that it had in the hands of the partnership on that day.

Example 8-17, adapted from Reg. § 1.1374-4(i)(8), illustrates the application of the "distributed partnership asset" rule.

> ***Example 8-17:*** *Disposition of distributed partnership asset.* Linus is a C corporation that elects to become an S corporation on January 1, 2007. On that date, Linus owns a 50% interest in partnership Scaper, and Scaper owns (among other assets) Gro with a basis of $20,000 and a value of $40,000. On January 1, 2007, Scaper distributes Gro to Linus, when Gro has a basis of $20,000 and a value of $50,000. Under Code Sec. 732(a)(1), Linus has a transferred basis of $20,000 in Gro. On January 1, 2010, Linus sells Gro for $60,000 and recognizes a gain of $40,000. Under Reg. § 1.1374-4(i)(7) and Code Sec. 1374(d)(3), Linus has recognized built-in gain from the sale of $20,000, the amount of built-in gain in Gro on the first day of the recognition period.

Small partnership interest. In an effort to provide some ameliorative relief from the tracing rules of Reg. § 1.1374-4(i)(1), Reg. § 1.1374-4(i)(5)(i) generally provides a $100,000 exclusionary rule by prescribing that Reg. § 1.1374-4(i)(1)

> does not apply to a taxable year in the recognition period if the S corporation's partnership interest represents less than 10 percent of the partnership's capital and profits at all times during the taxable year and prior taxable years in the recognition period, and the fair market value of the S corporation's partnership interest as of the beginning of the recognition period is less than $100,000.

Further, Reg. § 1.1374-4(i)(5)(ii) provides a rule for contribution of assets:

> [I]f the S corporation contributes any assets to the partnership during the recognition period and the S corporation held the assets as of the beginning of the recognition period, the fair market value of the S corporation's partnership interest as of the beginning of the recognition period is determined as if the assets were contributed to the partnership before the beginning of the recognition period (using the fair market value of each contributed asset as of the beginning of the recognition period). The contribution does not affect whether

¶802.13

[Reg. § 1.1374-4(i)(5)(i)] applies for taxable years in the recognition period before the taxable year in which the contribution was made.

In addition, Reg. § 1.1374-4(i)(5)(iii) prescribes that the de minimis rule of Reg. § 1.1374-4(i)(5)(i) will not apply if a "corporation forms or avails of a partnership with a principal purpose of avoiding the tax imposed under section 1374" (i.e., an anti-abuse rule). An example illustrating the anti-abuse rule would be if a corporation owns interests in multiple partnerships each with a fair market value of less than $100,000.

.14 Computing the Net Recognized Built-in Gain

C corporation income. For the unanswered questions regarding the computation of C corporation income (for purposes of Reg. § 1.1374-2(a)(1) and (2)), Reg. §§ 1.1374-2 through 1.1374-9 provide some details for the computation of tax.[29] Unfortunately, the regulations do not provide complete guidance. For instance, Reg. § 1.1374-2(a)(1) prescribes that one of the bases for built-in gains tax is the S corporation's "taxable income determined by using all rules applying to C corporations." Unfortunately, the regulations provide no guidance as to how to compute the "C taxable income." The S corporation is left to figure out how this figure is determined. Two questions come to mind.

(1) While it is easy to add back items passed through, such as charitable contributions, dividends, etc., what does one do with the various elections made at the shareholder level?[30]

(2) Suppose one shareholder made the election but the others did not. For dividends, does the corporation obtain a dividends-received credit? For charitable contributions, suppose, on recomputation, the charitable contribution limit for C corporation purposes is exceeded?

Allocation rules, recognized built-in gain carryover, and accounting methods. The computation of the built-in gains tax depends on the recognized built-in gain, recognized built-in loss, recognized built-in gain carryover, and taxable income of the corporation (the "pre-limitation amount"). Reg. § 1.1374-2(b)-(d) provides some guidance.

(b) *Allocation rule.* If an S corporation's pre-limitation amount for any taxable year exceeds its net recognized built-in gain for that year, the S corporation's net recognized built-in gain consists of a ratable portion of each item of income, gain, loss, and deduction included in the pre-limitation amount.

(c) *Recognized built-in gain carryover.* If an S corporation's net recognized built-in gain for any taxable year is equal to its taxable income limitation, the amount by which its pre-limitation amount exceeds the taxable income limitation is a recognized built-in gain carryover included in its pre-limitation amount for the succeeding taxable year. The recognized built-in gain carryover consists of that portion of each item of income, gain, loss, and deduction not included in the S corporation's net recognized built-in gain for the year the carryover arose, as determined under [Reg. § 1.1374-2(b)].

---

[29] Reg. § 1.1374-1.   [30] Reg. § 1.1363-1(c)(2).

¶802.14

(d) *Accounting methods.* In determining its taxable income for pre-limitation amount and taxable income limitation purposes, a corporation must use the accounting method(s) it uses for tax purposes as an S corporation.

Example 8-18, adapted from Reg. § 1.1374-2(e), illustrates the application of the rules under Reg. § 1.1374-2.

> **Example 8-18:** *Net recognized built-in gain.* Minot is a calendar-year C corporation that elects to become an S corporation on January 1, 2009. Minot has a net unrealized built-in gain of $50,000 and no net operating loss or capital loss carryforwards. In 2009, Minot has a pre-limitation amount of $20,000, consisting of ordinary income of $15,000 and capital gain of $5,000, a taxable income limitation of $9,600, and a net unrealized built-in gain limitation of $50,000. Therefore, Minot's net recognized built-in gain for 2009 is $9,600 because that is the least of the three amounts described in Reg. § 1.1374-2(a). Under Reg. § 1.1374-2(b), Minot's net recognized built-in gain consists of recognized built-in ordinary income of $7,200 ($15,000 × ($9,600 ÷ $20,000)) and recognized built-in capital gain of $2,400 ($5,000 × ($9,600 ÷ $20,000)). Under Reg. § 1.1374-2(c), Minot has a recognized built-in gain carryover to 2010 of $10,400 ($20,000 – $9,600), consisting of $7,800 ($15,000 – $7,200) of recognized built-in ordinary income and $2,600 ($5,000 – $2,400) of recognized built-in capital gain.

.15 Deductions and Credits

Loss carryforwards. Because the built-in gains tax is geared to C corporation assets, Code Sec. 1374(b)(2) and the regulations, in particular Reg. § 1.1374-5, provide that C corporation net operating losses (NOLs) and capital loss carryforwards are generally deductible in computing the S corporation's net recognized built-in gains.

An S corporation's net operating loss and capital loss carryforwards from C years are allowed as deductions against its net recognized built-in gain.[31] However, any other carryforwards, such as charitable contribution carryforwards under Code Sec. 170(d)(2), are not allowed as deductions against net recognized built-in gain.

Example 8-19, adapted from Reg. § 1.1374-5(b), illustrates how to use net operating loss carryovers as a deduction.

> **Example 8-19:** *Code Sec. 382 limitation.* Nines is a C corporation that has an ownership change under Code Sec. 382(g)(1) on January 1, 2006. On that date, Nines has a fair market value of $500,000, NOL carryforwards of $400,000, and a net unrealized built-in gain under Code Sec. 382(h)(3)(A) of $0. Assume Nines' Code Sec. 382 NOL limitation under Code Sec. 382(b)(1) is $40,000. Nines elects to become an S corporation on January 1, 2010. On that date, Nines has NOL carryforwards of $240,000 (having used $160,000 of its pre-change net operating losses in its four preceding tax years) and a Code Sec. 1374 net unrealized built-in gain of $250,000. In 2010, Nines has net recognized built-in gain of $100,000. Under Reg. § 1.1374-5, Nines may use

---

[31] Reg. § 1.1374-5.

¶802.15

$40,000 of its NOL carryforwards as a deduction against its $100,000 net recognized built-in gain, because Nines' Code Sec. 382 limitation is $40,000.

Credits and credit carryforwards. Reg. § 1.1374-6, following Code Sec. 1374(b)(3), prescribes that certain credits are allowed against the built-in gains tax. The general rule of Reg. § 1.1374-6(a) states:

> The credits and credit carryforwards allowed as credits against the section 1374 tax under section 1374(b)(3) are allowed only to the extent their use is allowed under the rules applying to C corporations. Any other credits or credit carryforwards, such as foreign tax credits under section 901, are not allowed as credits against the section 1374 tax.

Reg. § 1.1374-6(b) does impose some limitations on how much credit can be applied:

> The amount of business credit carryforwards and minimum tax credit allowed against the section 1374 tax are subject to the limitations described in section 38(c) and section 53(c), respectively, as modified by [Reg. § 1.1374-6(b)]. The tentative tax determined under [Reg. § 1.1374-1(a)(3)] is treated as the regular tax liability described in sections 38(c)(1) and 53(c)(1), and as the net income tax and net regular tax liability described in section 38(c)(1). The tentative minimum tax described in section 55(b) is determined using the rate of tax applicable to corporations and without regard to any alternative minimum tax foreign tax credit described in that section and by treating the net recognized built-in gain determined under § 1.1374-2, modified to take into account the adjustments of sections 56 and 58 applicable to corporations and the preferences of section 57, as the alternative minimum taxable income described in section 55(b)(2).

Examples 8-20 and 8-21, adapted from Reg. § 1.1374-6(c), illustrate the application of the provisions applying to credits and credit carryforwards.

Example 8-20: Business credit carryforward. Ocho is a C corporation that elects to become an S corporation on January 1, 2010. On that date, Ocho has a $500,000 business credit carryforward from a C year and Asset 1 with a fair market value of $400,000, a basis for regular tax purposes of $95,000, and a basis for alternative minimum tax purposes of $150,000. In 2010, Ocho has net recognized built-in gain of $305,000 from selling Asset 1 for $400,000. Thus, Ocho's tentative tax under Reg. § 1.1374-1(a)(3) and regular tax liability under Reg. § 1.1374-6(b) is $106,750 ($400,000 – $95,000 = $305,000 × .35). Also, Ocho's tentative minimum tax determined under Reg. § 1.1374-6(b) is $47,000 ($400,000 – $150,000 = $250,000 – $15,000 [$40,000 corporate exemption amount – $25,000 phase-out = $15,000] = $235,000 × .20 [assuming a 20% tax rate]). Thus, the business credit limitation under Code Sec. 38(c) is $59,750 ($106,750 – $47,000 [the greater of $47,000 or $20,438 (.25 × $81,750 ($106,750 – $25,000 = $81,750))]= $59,750). As a result, Ocho's Code Sec. 1374 tax is $47,000 ($106,750 – $59,750) for 2010 and Ocho has $440,250 ($500,000 – $59,750) of business credit carryforwards for succeeding tax years.

Example 8-21: Minimum tax credit. Crowe is a C corporation that elects to become an S corporation on January 1, 2010. On that date, Asset 1 has a fair market value of $5,000,000, a basis for regular tax purposes of $4,000,000, and a basis for alternative minimum tax purposes of $4,750,000. Crowe also has a minimum tax credit of $310,000 from 1995. Crowe has no other assets, no net operating or capital loss carryforwards, and no business credit carryforwards. In 2010, Crowe's only transaction is the sale of Asset 1 for $5,000,000. Therefore, Crowe has net recognized built-in gain in 2010 of $1,000,000 ($5,000,000 – $4,000,000) and a tentative tax under Reg. § 1.1374-1(a)(3) of $350,000 ($1,000,000 × .35). Also, Crowe's tentative minimum tax determined under Reg. § 1.1374-6(b) is $47,000 ($5,000,000 – $4,750,000 = $250,000 – $15,000 [$40,000 corporate exemption amount – $25,000 phase-out = $15,000]= $235,000 × .20 [assuming a 20% tax rate]). Thus, Crowe may use its minimum tax credit in the amount of $303,000 ($350,000 – $47,000) to offset its Code Sec. 1374 tentative tax. As a result, Crowe's Code Sec. 1374 tax is $47,000 ($350,000 – $303,000) in 2010 and Crowe has a remaining minimum tax credit attributable to years for which Crowe was a C corporation of $7,000 ($310,000 – $303,000).

.16 Transfer of Assets from C Corporations to S Corporations

When an S corporation acquires assets in a reorganization under Code Sec. 368 (i.e., a merger), any C assets are segregated and looked through for built-in gains at the time of the reorganization. That built-in gain and any gain if the assets are disposed of during the five-year recognition period are subject to the built-in gains tax.[32] Reg. § 1.1374-8(b) prescribes the following:

(b) *Separate determination of tax.* For purposes of the tax imposed under section 1374(d)(8), a separate determination of tax is made with respect to the assets the S corporation acquires in one section 1374(d)(8) transaction from the assets the S corporation acquires in another section 1374(d)(8) transaction and from the assets the corporation held when it became an S corporation. Thus, an S corporation's section 1374 attributes when it became an S corporation may only be used to reduce the section 1374 tax imposed on dispositions of assets the S corporation held at that time. Similarly, an S corporation's section 1374 attributes acquired in a section 1374(d)(8) transaction may only be used to reduce a section 1374 tax imposed on dispositions of assets the S corporation acquired in the same transaction.

For income, Reg. § 1.1374-8(c) prescribes that if only one Code Sec. 1374(d)(8) group has recognized built-in gain for a tax year, then all income is to be allocated to this group for purposes of the tax computation. The regulation specifically states:

(c) *Taxable income limitation.* For purposes of [Reg. § 1.1374-8(a)], an S corporation's taxable income limitation under § 1.1374-2(a)(2) for any taxable year is allocated between or among each of the S corporation's separate determinations of net recognized built-in gain for that year (determined without regard to the taxable income limitation) based on the ratio of each of those determinations to the sum of all of those determinations.

Example 8-22, adapted from Reg. § 1.1374-8(d), illustrates the rules of the built-in gains tax with respect to a merger and the taxable income limitations.

Example 8-22: *Allocation of taxable income limitation.* Quax is a C corporation that elects to become an S corporation effective January 1, 2009. The assets Quax holds when it becomes an S corporation have a net unrealized

---

[32] Code Sec. 1374(d)(8).

built-in gain of $5,000. Quax has no loss carryforwards, credits, or credit carryforwards. On January 1, 2010, Zeno (an unrelated C corporation) merges into Quax in a transaction to which Code Sec. 368(a)(1)(A) applies. Zeno has no loss carryforwards, credits, or credit carryforwards. The assets Quax acquired from Zeno are subject to tax under Code Sec. 1374 and have a net unrealized built-in gain of $80,000.

In 2010, Quax has a pre-limitation amount on the assets it held when it became an S corporation of $15,000, a pre-limitation amount on the assets Quax acquired from Zeno of $15,000, and a taxable income limitation of $10,000. However, because the assets Quax held on becoming an S corporation have a net unrealized built-in gain of $5,000, its net recognized built-in gain on those assets is limited to $5,000 before taking into account the taxable income limitation. Quax's taxable income limitation of $10,000 is allocated between the assets Quax held on becoming an S corporation and the assets Quax acquired from Zeno for purposes of determining the net recognized built-in gain from each pool of assets. Thus, Quax's net recognized built-in gain on the assets Quax held on becoming an S corporation is $2,500 ($10,000 × ($5,000 ÷ $20,000)). Quax's net recognized built-in gain on the assets Quax acquired from Zeno is $7,500 ($10,000 × ($15,000 ÷ $20,000)). Therefore, Quax has a Code Sec. 1374 tax of $3,500 (($2,500 + $7,500) × .35 [assuming a 35% tax rate]) for its 2010 tax year.

Qualified subchapter S subsidiaries (QSubs). The built-in gains tax can also arise on QSub transactions.[33] For a separate determination of tax, Reg. § 1.1361-4(b)(1) prescribes the following:

> [I]f a C corporation elects to be treated as an S corporation and makes a QSub election (effective the same date as the S election) with respect to a subsidiary, the liquidation occurs immediately before the S election becomes effective, while the S electing parent is still a C corporation.

Tax Pointer: Under Code Sec. 1374(d)(8), there can be duplicative recognition of built-in gain transactions with QSUBs. Reg. § 1.1374-3(b) and (c) prescribes the adjustments required to eliminate the duplicative treatment. For a discussion of Reg. § 1.1374-3(b), see ¶ 1405.06.

.17 Anti-Stuffing Rules

To prevent attempts to avoid the built-in gains tax by "stuffing" (i.e., contributing) "loss assets" to a C corporation prior to conversion to S status, Reg. § 1.1374-9 provides the following:

> If a corporation acquires an asset before or during the recognition period with a principal purpose of avoiding the tax imposed under section 1374, the asset and any loss, deduction, loss carryforward, credit, or credit carryforward attributable to the asset is disregarded in determining the S corporation's pre-limitation amount, taxable income limitation, net unrealized built-in gain limitation, deductions against net recognized built-in gain, and credits against the section 1374 tax.

---

[33] See discussion at Chapter 14.

.18 Tax Planning

To overcome Code Sec. 1374's built-in gains tax, there are various means that can be employed to limit or eliminate the tax effect. Basically, these procedures are developed from a simple reading of Code Sec. 1374.

Allocation of assets. If a C corporation's assets are disposed of other than in the ordinary course of business (e.g., a sale of assets in bulk), an allocation of the sales price should be made to reduce or eliminate the amount of built-in gain.

> *Example 8-23:* Widgman Inc. is a calendar-year C corporation engaged in manufacturing widgets in leased premises. On January 1, 2010, it converts to S status. At the time it converts to S status, Widgman has several Code Sec. 1374 assets it uses in the manufacturing process, and the built-in gain is $600,000 ($1,000,000 fair market value of the machinery at the time of conversion – $400,000 adjusted basis). Billie Brady is the sole shareholder of Widgman and devotes all her time to the business. One year after conversion to S status, Mo Jenkins approaches Brady to buy Widgman's manufacturing business for $1,100,000. The parties enter into a contract for $1,100,000 with the following allocation negotiated at arm's length and reported on Form 8594: Code Sec. 1374 assets are to be stated at book value at the time of sale, and Brady will enter a covenant not to compete and a consulting agreement for the difference; the allocation will be one-half to the covenant not to compete and the remaining half to the consulting agreement. Accordingly, no built-in gains tax is due.

With respect to the allocation, one might consider using a salary approach to reduce the gain in the year of sale. IRS Letter Ruling 8609052 (December 2, 1985) should be consulted on using a salary approach to temper the effects under the built-in gains tax. In IRS Letter Ruling 8609052, the payment of a bonus to a shareholder-employee in a Code Sec. 337 liquidation did not affect the liquidation.

Zero-out income. The built-in gains tax is computed on the lower of the built-in gain or taxable income. The S corporation's taxable income is recomputed as a C corporation as a basis for tax.[34] By definition, if there is no taxable income, then there is no built-in gains tax to pay. However, the Committee Reports to the 1986 tax legislation also contain a pitfall that must be carefully watched to avoid difficulty. In a nutshell, the Committee Reports state that if the S corporation is successful in preventing tax under the new Code Sec. 1374 in the first year the tax arises, it must continue to have no taxable new Code Sec. 1374 income for the remainder of the 5-year recognition period; otherwise, Code Sec. 1374 will tax the corporate income.

> *Example 8-24:* Dr. Adams incorporated her practice as Dr. Adams P.C. in 1989 as a cash-basis, calendar-year C corporation. On January 1, 2005, Dr. Adams P.C. elects S status, and at the time of conversion has $50,000 of accounts receivables and $10,000 of accounts payable (the $10,000 represents

---

[34] Code Sec. 1374(d)(2)(A)(ii).

expenses incurred, but not paid at the time of conversion to S status). Dr. Adams P.C. will have $40,000 of Code Sec. 1374 "net recognized built-in gain."

Example 8-25: Assume the same facts as in Example 8-24, except that in the 2005 tax year, Dr. Adams P.C. was paid a salary of $40,000 that zeroed out the Code Sec. 1374 income so no tax is due. In 2006, Dr. Adams P.C. earned $25,000 of income, so the corporation will pay Code Sec. 1374 tax on $25,000 leaving $15,000 remaining for Code Sec. 1374 tax. If, however, Dr. Adams P.C. had no taxable income until the year 2011, it appears that the $40,000 net receivable income will never be taxed under Code Sec. 1374.

In certain industries it may not be possible to "zero out" the Code Sec. 1374 income with payment of salaries. For instance, in the real estate industry, salaries to landlords are limited. For a discussion of what is a reasonable salary for landlords, see *S & B Realty Co.*[35] and *Chevy Chase Motor Co., Inc.*[36]

Tax Pointer: Salaries paid to shareholder-employees to reduce the built-in gains tax could be deemed unreasonable under C corporation standards due to the fact that the built-in gains tax is geared to a predecessor C corporation's history, not to the S corporation.

Like-kind exchanges. Because no gain is recognized on a like-kind exchange, a corporation may consider exchanging built-in gain property in a qualified like-kind exchange, rather than selling it, in order to avoid payment of the built-in gains tax. However, it should be noted than under Code Sec. 1374(d)(6), the property received in the like-kind exchange will be treated as if it were owned on the date of the conversion to S status (having both the basis and holding period of the built-in gain property for which it was exchanged), so that a subsequent sale of this property within the 5-year recognition period will also trigger liability for the built-in gains tax.

Leases with an option to sell. If the Code Sec. 1374 assets can be leased as well as sold, a corporation should initially pursue a lease of the assets rather than dispose of them. However, if the S corporation has earnings and profits from its C years, then a problem may be generated under Code Secs. 1362(d) and 1375 on the lease income received.[37] Additionally, a simple lease transaction may not satisfy the lessee's or the lessor's nontax objectives. It may be necessary for the lessee to have an option to buy the assets at the end of the lease term.

A simple reading of Code Sec. 1374 indicates that by having the option exercised at the end of the recognition period, there should be no built-in gains tax. However, it might be argued that an option is akin to an installment sale situation, and since Reg. § 1.1374-4(h)(1)[38] taxes installment sales whether completed during or after the end of a recognition period, then likewise, Code Sec. 1374 should tax the sale under the option whenever it occurs. Because of this possibility, the corporation may consider a lengthy lease (e.g., fifty years). Also, there is a question of how to treat the option payment, assuming that one is made at the time the lease

---

[35] *S & B Realty Co.,* 54 TC 863, Dec. 30,073 (Acq.).

[36] *Chevy Chase Motor Co., Inc.,* 36 TCM 942, Dec. 34,517(M), TC Memo. 1977-227.

[37] See ¶ 804 for details.

[38] See ¶ 802.10 for further discussion.

and option agreement is signed. Under normal tax principles, the option produces no taxable income.

Use C corporation graduated rates of taxation. As discussed at ¶ 802.01, built-in gains are taxed at the highest corporate tax rate, currently 35 percent;[39] the graduated rates do not apply. If a C corporation, prior to electing S status, was to sell its potential Code Sec. 1374 assets, converting them to cash, then the corporation could avail itself of the graduated C corporation tax rates rather than pay the highest rate as an S corporation.

Utilizing a partnership to avoid Code Sec. 1374. To avoid Code Sec. 1374's current 5 year recognition period, the S corporation may decide to establish a partnership with a would-be buyer of the built-in-gain assets with the S corporation transferring in the built-in gain assets into the partnership and the would-be buyer, cash, notes, etc. Then the partnership would operate the property. Such a situation occurred with Chief Counsel Advice 201324013 (6/14/2013); however, the Advice treated the establishment of the partnership as a disguised sale under Code Sec. 707(a)(2)(B) causing the S corporation to bear tax under Code Sec. 1374.

.19 Passive Investment Income Tax and the Built-in Gains Tax

As discussed in ¶ 804.02, if a C corporation converts to S status but does not dispose of its C earnings and profits in a timely manner, it can incur taxes on both its passive investment income (Code Sec. 1375) and built-in gains (Code Sec. 1374). To prevent taxation of the same income under both Code Secs., the Code provides that passive income does not include built-in gains (or losses) recognized during the 10-year recognition period.[40]

.20 Reporting the Built-In Gains Tax

Example 8-26 illustrates how to compute the built-in gains tax using Form 1120S, Schedule D (2012).

Example 8-26: CranStone Inc., a calendar-year C corporation formed in 1980, converted to S status on January 1, 2012. At the time of conversion, the corporation had one asset, Bog Vista, raw land that it bought in 1989 for $10,000. On January 1, 2012, Bog Vista was appraised at $100,000. On February 1, 2012, CranStone Inc. sold Bog Vista to a third party for $100,000. CranStone Inc.'s taxable income for 2012 was $100,000. Code Sec. 1374's tax rate is 35%. CranStone Inc. has no net operating loss carryforwards at the time it converts to S status nor credits permitted under Code Sec. 1374(b)(3).

Line 16:	Excess of recognized built-in gains over recognized built-in losses ($100,000 – $10,000) .	$90,000
Line 17:	Taxable income (attach computation schedule)	100,000
Line 18:	Net recognized built-in gain. Enter the smallest of line 16, line 17, or line 6 of Schedule B	90,000
Line 19:	Code Sec. 1374(b)(2) deduction	0

---

[39] Code Sec. 11(b).   [40] Code Sec. 1375(b)(4).

¶802.19

Line 20:	Subtract line 19 from line 18. If zero or less, enter -0- here and on line 23	90,000
Line 21:	Enter 35% of line 20	31,500
Line 22:	Business credit and minimum tax credit carryforwards under Code Sec. 1374(b)(3) from C corporation years	0
Line 23:	Tax. Subtract line 22 from line 21 (if zero or less, enter -0-). Enter here and on Form 1120S, page 1, line 22b	$31,500

Example 8-27: Assume the same facts as in Example 8-26, except that CranStone Inc.'s taxable income was $15,000 instead of $100,000, due to the fact that CranStone Inc. paid its shareholder-employees a bonus on December 31, 2012, of $85,000. CranStone Inc.'s tax would be $5,250 (.35 × $15,000).[41]

.21 Estimated Tax Payments

If an S corporation is liable for the built-in gains tax, it must make estimated tax payments.[42]

.22 Premium Payment for an Asset; Use of Minority Discount for Code Sec. 1374 Tax Computation

In *Ringgold Telephone Company*, it was held that the full sales price of an asset subject to Code Sec. 1374 was not required for purposes of computing built-in gain. The facts which lead to this result were as follows: An S corporation that was previously taxed as a C corporation disposed of one of its assets, a minority partnership interest during Code Sec. 1374's taxing period for $5,220,423. Relying on its accounting firm, Taxpayer valued the partnership interest at $2,600,000 claiming unique circumstances, namely, that the purchase price may have exceeded fair market value because the buyer wanted to discourage other partners in the partnership from exercising their right of first refusal with respect to such interest. The court valued the interest for Code Sec. 1374 purposes, using its own analysis, at $3,727,142. In reaching its decision, the court noted that the IRS conceded that "a minority discount is appropriate in valuing that interest."[43]

¶ 803 General Business Credit Recapture

A prior-year general business credit recapture may apply if a corporation claimed general business credits on a prior year's corporation income tax return before it became an S corporation.[44] If the S corporation makes an early disposition of the property, the S corporation, and not its shareholders, will be liable for payment of the tax. The corporation must complete Form 4255, "Recapture of Investment Credit," and include the tax in the total amount to be entered in the tax section on page 1 of Form 1120S.

---

[41] For a discussion of the use of salary to zero-out income and reduce Code Sec. 1374's tax, see ¶ 802.18.

[42] Code Sec. 6655.

[43] TC Memo 2010-103.

[44] Reg. § § 1.47-2 and 1.47-4(a)(1).

When a C corporation elects S corporation status, the election itself does not trigger the recapture of general business credit on any assets for which the C corporation previously claimed a credit. However, if the S corporation makes an early disposition of its predecessor's assets, it, not the shareholders, will pay the tax on the recapture, and file Form 4255.[45]

Estimated tax payments. An S corporation is required to make estimated tax payments for any general business credit recapture.[46]

¶ 804 Excess Net Passive Income Tax

.01 Passive Investment Income Coming from a C Corporation

An S corporation can have 100 percent of its income from passive investment income (e.g., being the landlord under a triple net lease).[47] However, an S corporation that has accumulated earnings and profits from a C corporation (as predecessor or due to a reorganization) will find itself punished by the possible loss of S status and the excess net passive income tax.[48] While the termination rules of Code Secs. 1362(d)(3) and 1375 operate on similar terms to Code Sec. 469's passive income and loss rules,[49] they do act differently. For instance, Code Sec. 469 classifies dividend income as "portfolio income"[50] and thus not "tainted," while Code Secs. 1362(d)(3) and 1375 always classify dividend income as passive.[51] Likewise, there may be a similarity between Code Secs. 1362(d)(3) and 1375 and the personal holding company rules for C corporations at Code Sec. 543; however, they also act differently. Thus, if a C corporation composed of 20 individual shareholders actively operates an office building, apartment house, and so on as a landlord, providing cleaning services, trash removal, etc., it will not be taxed as a personal holding company under Code Sec. 543. Yet, let this same corporation convert to an S corporation and have one dollar of earnings and profits from C corporation status, and it will find itself subject to the onerous provisions of Code Secs. 1362(d)(3) and 1375.

Although the reasons have changed slightly for punishing an S corporation under Code Secs. 1362(d)(3) and 1375, the basic reason for penalizing the S shareholders is to insure that the S corporation distributes any C corporation earnings and profits.

> **Example 8-28:** Logan Inc., a C corporation, is formed in 2000 to engage in the architectural drafting business. In 2002, it elects S status when it has $10 of earnings and profits. In 2009, more than six years after it elects S status and while it is still showing $10 of earnings and profits, it has passive investment income in excess of 25% of its gross receipts from rents it receives by leasing personal property without rendering significant services. Logan Inc. must pay an income tax on its passive investment income at the highest rate of 35%.[52]

---

[45] Code Sec. 1371(d)(2).

[46] *Ibid.*

[47] Code Sec. 1363(a).

[48] Code Secs. 1362(d)(3) and 1375. For further discussion, see ¶ 1204.

[49] See further discussion at ¶ 911 et seq.

[50] See further discussion at ¶ 911.06.

[51] See further discussion at ¶ 804.06 and ¶ 804.02.

[52] Code Sec. 11(b) specifies the top corporate tax rate for C corporations in 2001 is 35 percent. Code Sec. 1375.

Tax Pointer: If an S corporation does not have earnings and profits from prior years as a C corporation, Code Sec. 1362 will not apply and the S corporation will not be penalized for having passive investment income.[53]

.02 Taxation of Excess Net Passive Income

The excess net passive income tax is imposed on the income of an S corporation for the tax year when it has (1) accumulated earnings and profits at the close of the tax year from a C corporation (either as a predecessor or due to a reorganization) and (2) passive investment income that totals more than 25 percent of gross receipts.[54] Passive investment income is defined as income, net of related expenses, from the following sources: (1) rents, (2) royalties, (3) interest, (4) dividends, and (5) annuities.

Tax Pointer 1: If an S corporation has earnings and profits at the end of each tax year for three consecutive years, and passive investment income totaling more than 25 percent of gross receipts, then the S corporation's election will be terminated at the end of the third consecutive year.

Before a tax on excess net passive income can be imposed, four tests have to be satisfied in the tax year in question; namely, the S corporation must have all of the following:

(1) Accumulated earnings and profits at the close of the tax year[55]

(2) Passive investment income that is more than 25 percent of gross receipts[56]

(3) Net passive income[57]

(4) Taxable income for the year[58]

Passive activity losses and credits. Code Secs. 1375 and 1362 just deal with the effect of passive investment income at the corporate level,[59] not how it is characterized at the individual level. If a corporation is subject to the excess net passive income tax, a shareholder could also be subject to the rules regarding the characterization of the income. An example would be a C corporation that converts to S status and is engaged in certain rental situations that are considered passive activities (e.g., triple net leases).[60]

Tax Pointer 2: St. Charles Investment Co.[61] held that when a closely held C corporation which was engaged in the real estate business converted to S status and then began to dispose of its real estate holdings, the S corporation could deduct the suspended passive activity losses on its tax returns. While the Court felt that the S corporation shareholders were receiving a windfall in that

---

[53] Code Secs. 1362(d)(3)(A) or 1375.

[54] Code Sec. 1375. See ¶1204.01 for a definition of "accumulated earnings and profits" and a discussion of reorganization.

[55] Code Sec. 1375(a)(1). See ¶1204.01 for a definition of "accumulated earnings and profits."

[56] Code Sec. 1375(a)(2).

[57] Code Sec. 1375(b)(2). See ¶804.10 for a definition of "net passive income."

[58] Code Sec. 1375(b)(1)(B). See ¶804.12 for the definition of "taxable income."

[59] Passive income from rents, royalties, interest, dividends, annuities, and income from the sales or exchanges of stocks or securities.

[60] Code Sec. 469 and 469(c)(2).

[61] *St. Charles Investment Co.*, CA-10, 2000-2 USTC ¶50,840, 232 F3d 773.

the shareholders were able to offset income with losses arising from a different taxpayer (i.e., the former C corporation), the Court felt that Code Sec. 469(b) overrode Code Sec. 1371(b)(1). For a discussion of *St. Charles Investment Co.*, see ¶ 404.08.

.03 Rents

Rents. While rents are included in the term "passive investment income," neither Code Sec. 1362 or 1375 defines the term.[62] Consequently, rent is defined by the courts and the IRS. The IRS's definition of "rent" is "amounts received for the use of, or right to use, property (whether real or personal) of the corporation."[63]

Real property. The term "rents" includes amounts received for the use of, or right to use, real property (i.e., real estate) of the corporation. Reg. § 1.1362-2 states that the term "rents"[64]

> does not include rents derived in the active trade or business of renting property. Rents received by a corporation are derived in an active trade or business of renting property only if, based on all the facts and circumstances, the corporation provides significant services or incurs substantial costs in the rental business. Generally, significant services are not rendered and substantial costs are not incurred in connection with net leases. Whether significant services are performed or substantial costs are incurred in the rental business is determined based upon all the facts and circumstances including, but not limited to, the number of persons employed to provide the services and the types and amounts of costs and expenses incurred (other than depreciation).

As seen in the above definition, if the S corporation renders significant services to the occupants as well as services other than those customarily rendered by a landlord (e.g., providing maid service), the S corporation, even though it might have 100 percent real estate rental income, will not be subject to the excess net passive income tax or termination of its S status.[65] However, the demarcation line as to what is prohibited passive investment income and what is not, is not easy to define. It also should be noted that, under prior law, the classification tests were more rigid than under present law. Thus, if an S corporation can satisfy the standards under the prior law, it should automatically pass under current law.

Consider the following rulings on passive investment income pertaining to real property under the prior law:

- Operating a motel did not produce passive investment income "rents" because of the services involved, so the S corporation kept its S status. However, renting an entire motel to one party under a 1-year lease caused an S corporation to lose its status,[66] and renting vacation bungalows caused an S corporation to lose its election.[67]

- Renting tennis and handball courts to players; providing them with locker room, parking facilities, lessons, and so on;[68] and charging fees for an attendant parking lot[69] did not cause an S corporation to lose its S status.

---

[62] Code Secs. 1362(d)(3)(C)(i) and 1375(b)(2).
[63] Reg. § 1.1362-2(c)(5)(ii)(B) *(1)*.
[64] Reg. § 1.1362-2(c)(5)(ii)(B) *(2)*.
[65] Code Secs. 1375 and 1362(d)(3).

[66] Rev. Rul. 78-307, 1978-2 CB 222.
[67] *M. Feingold,* 49 TC 461, Dec. 28,840.
[68] Rev. Rul. 76-48, 1976-1 CB 265.
[69] IRS Letter Ruling 7907059 (November 16, 1978).

- Renting out an owned shopping mall may or may not cause an S corporation to lose its S status. IRS Letter Rulings 8921039 (February 23, 1989), 8904012 (October 26, 1988), and 8906035 (November 12, 1988) sustained an S election, but *McIlhinney*[70] did not. However, renting and operating a mobile home park did not cause the loss of an S election.[71]

> **Tax Pointer 1:** If there are not sufficient services provided in renting real property, the passive investment income from the rent may cause the S corporation to lose its S election.[72]

> **Tax Pointer 2:** In contrast, a C corporation engaged in real estate rentals can be exonerated from personal holding tax[73] if it can show that 50 percent or more of its adjusted ordinary gross income and dividends paid for the tax year equal or exceed the amount, if any, by which the corporation's nonrent-personal-holding-company income for the year exceeds 10 percent of its ordinary gross income.

Personal property. When renting personal property, the same factors as in renting real property apply, such as the amount of "significant services" provided by the corporation, the number of people employed to provide the services, etc. If the services are significant, then the rental income will not be classified as passive investment income. S corporations have not lost their S status from renting housewares,[74] clothes,[75] golf carts,[76] motion pictures,[77] short-and long-term leases for motorcars,[78] aircraft,[79] warehousing, and so on while providing services. Services should usually revolve around the type of work performed. For example, in the case of leasing aircraft, amounts received by an S corporation from the lease of an aircraft while not providing a pilot, fuel, or oil will constitute passive income, but amounts received from a full-service charter will not.[80]

> **Tax Pointer 3:** Before switching to S status, the C corporation, if it is involved with rental activities concerning personal property, should check the cases and rulings to determine if its rental activities will constitute passive investment income. If it appears that passive investment income will be generated, and that this income will exceed 25 percent of its gross receipts, then the S corporation should seek means to provide significant services to renters or to distribute its earnings and profits to its shareholders.

Who provides the services? Either the landlord S corporation or independent contractors hired by the landlord S corporation may provide the services. Basically, there is no problem as to who renders the services; they just must be significant.[81]

---

[70] *J.J. McIlhinney,* 39 TCM 554, Dec. 36,463(M), TC Memo. 1979-473. Aff'd, CA-3 (unpublished opinion 1/19/81).

[71] IRS Letter Ruling 7718007 (February 1, 1977).

[72] The regulations have an all-or-nothing test.

[73] Code Sec. 543(b)(3).

[74] Rev. Rul. 64-232, 1964-2 CB 334.

[75] Rev. Rul. 65-83, 1965-1 CB 430.

[76] *Ibid.*

[77] Rev. Rul. 75-349, 1975-2 CB 349.

[78] Rev. Rul. 65-40, 1965-1 CB 429 (short-term leasing).

[79] Rev. Rul. 81-197, 1981-2 CB 166.

[80] *Ibid.*

[81] IRS Letter Ruling 8211103 (December 21, 1981).

¶804.03

Produced film rents. For purposes of an S corporation's passive investment income, produced film rents are not included in the definition of rents.[82]

Income from leasing self-produced tangible property. Rents, for purposes of an S corporation's passive investment income, do not include compensation, however designated, for the use of, or right to use, any real or tangible personal property developed, manufactured, or produced by the S corporation if during the tax year the taxpayer is engaged in substantial development, manufacturing, or production of real or tangible personal property of the same type.[83]

.04 Royalties

As is the case with "rents," "royalties" are not defined by statute. Reg. § 1.1362-2(c)(5)(ii)(A) *(1)*, states the following:

> *Royalties* means all royalties, including mineral, oil, and gas royalties, and amounts received for the privilege of using patents, copyrights, secret processes and formulas, good will, trademarks, tradebrands, franchises, and other like property. The gross amount of royalties is not reduced by any part of the cost of the rights under which the royalties are received or by any amount allowable as a deduction in computing taxable income.

Royalties derived in the ordinary course of a trade or business. Reg. § 1.1362-2(c)(5)(ii)(A) *(2)* states the following:

> *Royalties* does not include royalties derived in the ordinary course of a trade or business of franchising or licensing property. Royalties received by a corporation are derived in the ordinary course of a trade or business of franchising or licensing property only if, based on all the facts and circumstances, the corporation—
>
> (i) Created the property; or
>
> (ii) Performed significant services or incurred substantial costs with respect to the development or marketing of the property.

Copyright, mineral, oil and gas, and active business computer software royalties. Reg. § 1.1362-2(c)(5)(ii)(A) *(3)* states the following:

> *Royalties* does not include copyright royalties, nor mineral, oil and gas royalties if the income from those royalties would not be treated as personal holding company income under sections 543(a)(3) and (a)(4) if the corporation were a C corporation; amounts received upon disposal of timber, coal, or domestic iron ore with respect to which the special rules of sections 631(b) and (c) apply; and active business computer software royalties as defined under section 543(d) (without regard to paragraph (d)(5) of section 543).

Example 8-29, adapted from Reg. § 1.1362-2(c)(6), illustrates the rule for royalties.

> ***Example 8-29:*** In 2004, Score Corporation has gross receipts of $75,000. Of this amount, $5,000 is from royalty payments with respect to Trademark A, $8,000 is from royalty payments with respect to Trademark B, and $62,000 is gross receipts from operations. Score created Trademark A, but Score did not

---

[82] Reg. § 1.1362-2(c)(5)(ii)(B) *(3)*. Definition of produced film rents at Code Sec. 543(a)(5).

[83] Reg. § 1.1362-2(c)(5)(ii)(B) *(4)*.

create Trademark B or perform significant services or incur substantial costs with respect to the development or marketing of Trademark B.

Because Score created Trademark A, the royalty payments with respect to Trademark A are derived in the ordinary course of Score's business and are not included within the definition of *royalties* for purposes of determining Score's passive investment income. However, the royalty payments with respect to Trademark B are included within the definition of *royalties* for purposes of determining Score's passive investment income. Score's passive investment income for the year is $8,000, and Score's passive investment income percentage for the taxable year is 10.67% ($8,000 ÷ $75,000). This does not exceed 25% of Score's gross receipts and consequently the three-year period described in Code Sec. 1362(d)(3) does not begin to run.

Royalties for the broadcast rights to athletic events. Payments received by an S corporation for broadcast rights to athletic events will not terminate S corporation status.[84]

.05 Interest

Reg. § 1.1362-2(c)(5)(ii)(D) *(1)* states the following:

> *Interest* means any amount received for the use of money (including tax-exempt interest and amounts treated as interest under sections 483, 1272, 1274, or 7872).

However, interest on an obligation acquired in the ordinary course of an S corporation's trade or business from the sale of inventory-type goods is excluded from consideration.[85] Consequently, C corporations converting to S corporation status with accumulated earnings and profits should consider how much interest will be earned during each tax year, lest interest earned during the year together with the other five types of income exceed 25 percent of gross receipts.[86] Further, if the C corporation has bonds that produce tax-exempt income there is no exemption for them. Tax-exempt interest is included in gross receipts for this purpose.[87] Consequently, the C corporation, prior to conversion to S status, should consider disposing of these securities.

Lending, financing, and other businesses engaged in the ordinary course of a business of securing mortgages, dealing in property, purchasing or discounting accounts receivable, notes or installment obligations are not subject to the excess net passive income tax rules[88] on the interest generated from these business activities.[89]

Tax Pointer 1: Since interest from installment sales[90] arising from a sale other than in the ordinary course of business is included in determining the

[84] Rev. Rul. 71-407, 1971-2 CB 318.

[85] Code Sec. 1362(d)(3)(C)(ii). An example where interest was excluded is found in IRS Letter Ruling 8515056 (January 14, 1985) where a corporation developed and sold lots on an installment basis charging interest on the financing.

[86] The 25-percent-of-gross-receipts test presumably includes Code Secs. 1273 and 1283 interest in its determination.

[87] Code Secs. 1362(d)(3) and 1375.

[88] *Ibid.*

[89] Code Sec. 1362(d)(3)(C)(iii) and Reg. § 1.1362-2(c)(5)(iii)(B).

[90] Code Sec. 453.

25-percent-of-gross-receipts test, care should be taken not to exceed the 25 percent test by generating too much interest from having too much principal financed for too long a time.

Tax Pointer 2: The fact that interest is unavoidable has no effect on disallowance. An S corporation lost its status because of interest received from a condemnation award.[91] The S corporation had to accept the interest on the award in order to be compensated for the governmental taking (i.e., condemnation).

Tax Pointer 3: Interest expense may not be used to reduce interest income.[92]

.06 Dividends

While an S corporation can be a shareholder in a C corporation, dividends received from a C corporation are passive investment income.[93] The dividends are composed of the following three categories:[94]

(1) Any distribution of property made by a corporation to its shareholders out of earnings and profits from its current tax year or from earnings and profits accumulated after February 18, 1913.[95]

(2) Amounts included in gross income that are related to foreign personal holding company income taxed to U.S. shareholders.[96]

(3) Consent dividends made to avoid the personal holding company tax[97] or improper accumulation of surplus.[98]

Tax Pointer: Before a C corporation converts to S status, it should review its investment portfolio to determine the effect that dividends will have on passive investment income. The corporation may decide to change its portfolio to acquire low-dividend stocks; however, if the C corporation sells the stocks after converting to S status, the capital gains realized from the sales may also constitute passive investment income.[99]

.07 Annuities

Reg. § 1.1362-2(c)(5)(ii)(E) defines the term "annuities" as

the entire amount received as an annuity under an annuity, endowment, or life insurance contract, if any part of the amount would be includible in gross income under section 72.

.08 Gross Receipts

Once the tainted items of passive investment income have been determined for the S corporation, it is necessary to perform a computation to see if these items exceed 25 percent of gross receipts for purposes of the excess net passive income

---

[91] IRS Letter Ruling 7727027 (April 9, 1977).

[92] *M. Llewellyn,* 70 TC 370, Dec. 35,177.

[93] This is not true if an S corporation meets the conditions of Code Sec. 1362(d)(3)(E). See further discussion at ¶ 1409.02.

[94] Reg. § 1.1362-2(c)(5)(ii)(C).

[95] Code Sec. 316.

[96] Code Sec. 551.

[97] Code Sec. 543.

[98] Code Sec. 565.

[99] See further discussion at ¶ 804.02.

¶804.06

tax and possible termination of S status. The term "gross receipts" is defined by Reg. § 1.1362-2(c)(4) to mean

> the total amount received or accrued under the method of accounting used by the corporation in computing its taxable income and is not reduced by returns and allowances, cost of goods sold, or deductions.

Additionally, Reg. § 1.1362-2(c)(4)(iii) excludes the following items from gross receipts:

> (A) Amounts received in nontaxable sales or exchanges except to the extent that gain is recognized by the corporation on the sale or exchange; or
>
> (B) Amounts received as a loan, as a repayment of a loan, as a contribution to capital, or on the issuance by the corporation of its own stock.

Tax Pointer: Because Code Secs. 1031, 351, and 721 exchanges are exempt, careful planning can be used to avoid taxation. Instead of having to sell capital assets, an S corporation may go into a partnership or an LLC with the prospective buyer and set up partnership allocations to achieve desired results.

Long-term contracts. Example 8-30, adapted from Reg. § 1.1362-2(c)(6), explains the rules for long-term contracts.

Example 8-30: Long-term contract reported on percentage-of-completion method. Wink Corporation, an S corporation, has a long-term contract as defined in Reg. § 1.451-3(b) for which it reports income according to the percentage-of-completion method as described in Reg. § 1.451-3(c)(1). The portion of the gross contract price that corresponds to the percentage of the entire contract that has been completed during the tax year is included in Wink's gross receipts for the year.

Installment sales. A corporation, which regularly sells personal property on the installment plan, elects to report its taxable income from the sale of property (other than a capital asset or stock or securities) on the installment method in accordance with Code Sec. 453. The installment payments actually received in a given tax year by the corporation are included in gross receipts for that year.[100]

.09 Net Passive Income

Code Sec. 1375(b)(2) defines "net passive income" as the S corporation's passive investment income, reduced by the deductions allowable that are directly connected with the production of such income (other than deductions allowable under Code Sec. 172 and part VIII of subchapter B).

Code Sec. 1375 does not define the term "directly connected." However, Reg. § 1.1375-1(b)(3)(i) defines "directly connected" generally to mean having a proximate and primary relationship to the income. Expenses, depreciation, and similar items attributable solely to such income qualify for deduction.

Reg. § 1.1375-1(b)(3)(ii) prescribes the following:

---

[100] For an example on installment sales, see Reg. § 1.1362-2(c)(6), Example 3.

If an item of deduction is attributable . . . in part to passive investment income and in part to income other than passive investment income, the deduction shall be allocated between the two types of items on a reasonable basis. The portion of any deduction so allocated to passive investment income shall be treated as proximately and primarily related to such income.

.10 Excess Net Passive Income

The excess net passive income tax is imposed on the lower of "taxable income" or "excess net passive income."[101] Reg. § 1.1375-1(b)(1) defines "excess net passive income" with the following formula:

$$\text{ENPI} \quad = \quad \text{NPI} \quad \times \quad \frac{\text{PII} - (.25 \times \text{GR})}{\text{PII}}$$

Where:

ENPI	=	excess net passive income
NPI	=	net passive income (defined at ¶ 804.10)
PII	=	passive investment income (defined at ¶ 802.02)
GR	=	gross receipts (defined at ¶ 804.09)

Example 8-31 illustrates the computation of excess net passive income.

Example 8-31: For the year, Sharps, an S corporation in the widget business with $1 of earnings and profits from a predecessor C corporation, has the following income and expenses:

Dividends	$500
Interest	100
Brokerage fees incurred in earning the dividends and interest	150
Widget income	200
Widget expense	75
Passive investment income (PII) (500 + 100)	600
Net passive income (NPI) (500 + 100 – 150)	450
Gross receipts (GR) (200 + 500 + 100)	800

$$\text{ENPI} \quad = \quad \$450 \quad \times \quad \frac{\$600 - (.25 \times \$800)}{\$600} \quad \text{or} \quad \$300$$

For the year, Sharps has excess net passive income of $300.

.11 Taxable Income

If an S corporation has no taxable income,[102] it cannot be liable for the excess net passive income tax.[103] If it does have taxable income, but its taxable income is

---

[101] Reg. § 1.1375-1(b).

[102] Taxable income as computed under Code Sec. 63(a).

[103] Code Sec. 1375(b)(1)(B).

¶804.10

less than its excess net passive income,[104] the taxable income will be subject to the excess net passive income tax.

.12 Rate of Tax

The rate of tax is the highest corporation rate specified in Code Sec. 11(b) (currently 35 percent).[105]

.13 Computing the Excess Net Passive Income Tax

An S corporation has to satisfy all of the following four elements for the excess net passive income tax to be imposed:[106]

    (1) Accumulated earnings and profits at the end of the tax year

    (2) Passive investment income that totals more than 25 percent of the S corporation's gross receipts

    (3) Net passive investment income

    (4) Taxable income

If these four elements are satisfied, the S corporation is taxed on the lower of its taxable income[107] or its excess passive net income.[108] A simple means is found by using the worksheet in the Instructions for Form 1120S shown in Example 8-32. Note that there is no official form to compute this tax as is the case with the built-in gains tax.

> **Example 8-32:** Klein Inc. is a corporation engaged in the rental of buildings without providing significant services. At the end of its first year as an S corporation (December 31, 2010), it has the following: $10 of accumulated earnings and profits from its years as a C corporation, $100,000 of rental income, $20,000 of management fees expense, $5,000 of real estate taxes, $8,000 of utilities, and $17,000 of other operating expenses. Klein Inc. will pay an excess net passive income tax of $13,125, computed as follows:
>
> 1. Enter gross receipts for the tax year (see Code Sec. 1362(d)(3)(B) for gross receipts from the sale of capital assets) $100,000
> 2. Enter passive investment income as defined in Code Sec. 1362(d)(3)(C) 100,000
> 3. Enter 25% of line 1 (If line 2 is less than 3, stop here. You are not liable for this tax.) 25,000
> 4. Excess passive investment income—Subtract line 3 from line 2 75,000
> 5. Enter deductions directly connected with the production of income on line 2 (see Code Sec. 1375(b)(2)) ($20,000 + $5,000 + $8,000 + $17,000) 50,000
> 6. Net passive income—Subtract line 5 from line 2 50,000

---

[104] See ¶ 804.10 for definition of excess net passive income.

[105] Code Sec. 1375(a).

[106] Code Sec. 1375. See previous discussion at ¶ 804.02.

[107] Taxable income as computed under Code Sec. 1374(d).

[108] Code Sec. 1375(a) and (b)(1)(B).

7. Divide amount on line 4 by amount on line 2	75%
8. Excess net passive income—Multiply line 6 by line 7 . . .	37,500
9. Enter taxable income [$100,000 – ($20,000 + $5,000 + $8,000 + $17,000)]	50,000
10. Enter smaller of line 8 or line 9	37,500
11. Excess net passive income tax—Enter 35% of line 10. Enter here and on line 22a, page 1, Form 1120S	$ 13,125

Credits. Only the credit for federal tax on gasoline and special fuels can reduce the net passive income tax.[109]

Coordination with any built-in gains. If an S corporation has gain that would result in both a built-in gains tax and excess net passive income tax[110] Code Sec. 1375(b)(4) states that

> the amount of passive investment income shall be determined by not taking into account any recognized built-in gain or loss of the S corporation for any taxable year in the recognition period.

Example 8-33: Blarney Inc. is a C corporation with $1 of earnings and profits. On January 1, 2010, it converted from C status to S status, with cash and one asset: appreciated stock in Caledonia Inc., cost basis $10, fair market value at conversion, $100. On March 1, 2010, Blarney Inc. sold the stock for $150. Under Code Sec. 1374, Blarney Inc. has gain of $90 ($100 – $10); under Code Sec. 1375, Blarney Inc. has passive investment income of $140 ($150 – $10) from the sale of stock or securities. Code Sec. 1374 will tax $90 of the gain, and the remaining gain of $50 ($140 – $90) will be included to determine Blarney Inc.'s gross receipts to see if it is liable for tax under Code Sec. 1375 and the corporation's possible loss of election under Code Sec. 1362(d).

Estimated tax payments. An S corporation, if it is liable for the excess net passive income tax, must pay estimated tax payments.[111]

.14 Obtaining a Waiver of the Excess Net Passive Income Tax

To receive a waiver, the S corporation must show to the satisfaction of the IRS all of the following:[112]

- It used good faith and diligence to determine that it did not have accumulated earnings and profits

- How it learned of its mistake

- What steps it will take to distribute the earnings and profits

The request for a waiver must be made in the form of a ruling request and all the accumulated earnings and profits have to be distributed by the date the waiver is to become effective.[113]

---

[109] Code Sec. 34's credit prescribed in Code Sec. 1375(c).
[110] See also discussion at ¶ 802.19.
[111] Instructions for Form 1120S.

[112] Code Sec. 1375(d) and Reg. §1.1375-1(d)(2) prescribe grounds for the waiver of Code Sec. 1375's tax.
[113] Reg. §1.1375-1(d)(2).

¶804.14

Example 8-34: Ludwig Inc., a C corporation, converted to S status on January 1, 2008. Before converting to S status, Ludwig Inc. distributed all its earnings and profits to its shareholders as a dividend so that on January 1, 2008, Ludwig Inc.'s books showed zero for earnings and profits. Ludwig Inc., on electing S status, engaged in 100% passive investment income activities. In 2009, the IRS commenced an audit on Ludwig Inc. when it was a C corporation. When the audit was concluded in 2010, the IRS found that Ludwig Inc. had earnings and profits. Unless the corporation obtains relief under Code Sec. 1375(d), it may be liable for the net passive income tax under Code Sec. 1375(a); if it is liable for the tax for three consecutive years, its S election will be terminated under Code Sec. 1362(d)(3)(D).

.15 Reducing Pass-Through Passive Investment Income

As was the case with the built-in gains tax, the excess net passive income tax reduces the amount of the pass-through to the shareholders.[114]

Example 8-35: Assume the same facts as in Example 8-32. The amount of passive investment that is taxed to the shareholders is $86,875 ($100,000 – $13,125).

Tax Pointer: If the S corporation had passive investment income of several different types, the tax would have been allocated proportionately to the various types of passive investment income.

.16 Reducing Earnings and Profits

If an S corporation has earnings and profits, instead of distributing the earnings after the election, the S corporation can earmark (providing all shareholders who receive a distribution in the tax year elect to do so) that the distributions be from accumulated earnings and profits and be considered a dividend to the extent thereof.[115] Example 10-19 at ¶ 1004.03 illustrates the distribution election; for a sample form to make the election, see Appendix 3.

Until all the earnings and profits are distributed by this route, the shareholders will be liable for the excess net passive income tax; if the S corporation is liable for this tax for three consecutive years, the S election will be terminated.[116]

Tax Pointer 1: As discussed in ¶ 1004.03, there are tax reasons for distributing accumulated earnings and profits other than to eliminate a problem under Code Secs. 1375 and 1362(d)(3).

Tax Pointer 2: Code Sec. 1(h)(11) provides that dividends received by an S corporation shareholder after 2002 and before 2013 are eligible for a special tax rate of 5 percent for individuals in the 10 percent-15 percent bracket, and then a maximum of 15 percent thereafter. Thus, because of the favorable tax rates, shareholders have an incentive to distribute S corporation earnings and profits, thereby eliminating the problem under Code Sec. 1375 and Code Sec.

---

[114] Code Sec. 1366(f)(3).
[115] Code Sec. 1368(e)(3).
[116] Code Sec. 1362(d)(3).

1362(d)(3). Dividends can likewise be used to offset interest expense. For a discussion of the rules, see ¶ 702.

Elimination of all earnings and profits attributable to pre-1983 years. The Small Business Jobs Protection Act of 1996 provided that if a corporation was an S corporation for its first taxable year beginning after December 31, 1996, the accumulated earnings and profits of the corporation as of the beginning of that year were reduced by the accumulated earnings and profits (if any) accumulated in a taxable year beginning before January 1, 1983, for which the corporation was an electing small business corporation under Subchapter S.

Congress provided in the Small Business and Work Opportunity Tax Act of 2007 ("SBWOTA") for taxable years beginning after May 25, 2007 in the case of any corporation which was not an S corporation for its first taxable year beginning after December 31, 1996, the accumulated earnings and profits of the corporation as of the beginning of the first taxable year beginning after May 25, 2007 is reduced by the accumulated earnings and profits (if any) accumulated in a taxable year beginning before January 1, 1983, for which the corporation was an electing small business corporation under Subchapter S.

.17 Tax Planning

Introduction. The excess net passive income tax and termination of S status is basically a mechanical proposition—either the S corporation meets the statutory criteria for the adverse results or it does not. In a particular tax year, an S corporation could avoid the tax (and not have the year counted for termination purposes) by increasing its gross receipts and income from nonpassive investment sources so that it will fail the 25-percent-of-gross-receipts test for passive investment income. One way an S corporation could increase its receipts is by selling its inventory.

Tax Pointer 1: By definition, the IRS could increase or decrease an S corporation's gross receipts by reallocation under Code Sec. 482 and/or the assignment-of-income doctrine.

Tax Pointer 2: When an S corporation is a partner or a member of an LLC, it includes, for purposes of gross receipts, the S corporation's share of the partnership or LLC gross receipts rather than the S corporation's distributive share of partnership income.[117]

Example 8-36: Avilon Inc., an S corporation, is a 50% general partner in DriveThru Co., a partnership engaged in a retailing venture. In 2010, DriveThru Co. reported the following: gross receipts from operations, $400,000; deductions, $350,000; net income, $50,000. Thus, Avilon Inc.'s share of DriveThru Co.'s income is $25,000; however, for purposes of Code Secs. 1375 and 1362(d)(3), the S corporation includes gross receipts of $200,000 (50% × $400,000). Alternatively, the S corporation could distribute its accumulated earnings and profits, maintaining its S election under Code Sec. 1368(e)(3).[118]

---

[117] Rev. Rul. 71-455, 1971-2 CB 318.   [118] See ¶ 804.16 for more information.

¶804.17

Reduction of taxable income. If an S corporation does not have any taxable income,[119] then no excess net passive income tax can be imposed. If an S corporation's taxable income is less than excess net passive income, then tax is imposed on taxable income. There are various ways to reduce or eliminate taxable income. One logical means is to make sales on the installment method (spreading the income out over a number of years)[120] rather than receiving the income all in one year. However, the S corporation should have adequate security to ensure the continued collection of an installment sale. The S corporation could also use nontaxable sales or exchanges, establish a retirement plan, accelerate expenses, or defer the recognition of income. An S corporation could also increase expenses by giving salaries to shareholder-employees.

>   *Tax Pointer 3:* Salaries paid to shareholder-employees to reduce taxable income may be deemed unreasonable under C corporation standards because the excess net passive income tax is geared toward the predecessor C corporation's history.

>   *Tax Pointer 4:* Even though an S corporation might be successful in eliminating the excess net passive income tax by eliminating taxable income, the S corporation could still lose its S election because the S corporation is not required to have any taxable income under Code Sec. 1362.[121]

>   *Tax Pointer 5:* The built-in gains tax uses the S corporation's taxable income as a basis for taxation. Accordingly, the S corporation should consider using installment sales, like-kind exchanges, leases with an option to buy, and similarly structured dispositions to minimize current-year taxable income.[122]

Reduction of net passive income. If net passive income can be eliminated (i.e., by raising gross receipts from nonpassive investment income above 25 percent), then no tax will be incurred, and a counting year for S status termination will be eliminated. Another means to reduce net passive income is to plan for passive investment income. Instead of an S corporation acquiring stock that produces high dividends, it should acquire stock that has a great chance of appreciation and low dividends. Also, acceleration of expenses that arise with passive investment income (such as stock brokerage fees) could help to reduce net passive income. Installment selling of stock on listed exchanges, however, is not available.[123]

Distribute accumulated earnings and profits. If accumulated earnings and profits are eliminated,[124] then the excess net passive income tax and loss of S status rules do not apply. An S corporation should consider distributing earnings and profits, because once the accumulated earnings and profits are eliminated from the corporate books, the S corporation no longer has to worry about passive investment income.

---

[119] Code Sec. 63(a).

[120] On December 17, 1999, Congress severely limited the use of the installment sale method. See the discussion at ¶ 1208.05 for the Congressional limitations and the means to limit the effect of the restrictions on installment sales.

[121] Code Sec. 1362(d)(3)'s test.

[122] For further discussion of there suggestions, see ¶ 802.18.

[123] Code Sec. 453(k).

[124] See discussion at ¶ 609.03.

Tax Pointer 6: Code Sec. 1(h)(11) provides that dividends received by an S corporation shareholder after 2002 and before 2013 are eligible for a special tax rate of 5 percent for individuals in the 10 percent-15 percent bracket, and then a maximum of 15 percent thereafter. Thus, because of the favorable tax rates, shareholders have an incentive to distribute S corporation earnings and profits, thereby eliminating the problem under Code Sec. 1375 and Code Sec. 1362(d)(3). Dividends can likewise be used to offset interest expense. For a discussion of the rules, see ¶ 702.

Dispose of assets generating passive investment income. While at first blush, disposition of assets generating passive investment income (e.g., stocks, bonds, etc.) may be seen as a reasonable means to solve the taxation of excess net passive income and loss of S status, in reality, if a disposition is not properly structured, adverse tax results could occur.[125]

Elimination of all earnings and profits attributable to pre-1983 years. The Small Business Jobs Protection Act of 1996 provided that if a corporation was an S corporation for its first taxable year beginning after December 31, 1996, the accumulated earnings and profits of the corporation as of the beginning of that year were reduced by the accumulated earnings and profits (if any) accumulated in a taxable year beginning before January 1, 1983, for which the corporation was an electing small business corporation under Subchapter S.

Congress provided in the Small Business and Work Opportunity Tax Act of 2007 for taxable years beginning after May 25, 2007 in the case of any corporation which was not an S corporation for its first taxable year beginning after December 31, 1996, the accumulated earnings and profits of the corporation as of the beginning of the first taxable year beginning after May 25, 2007 is reduced by the accumulated earnings and profits (if any) accumulated in a taxable year beginning before January 1, 1983, for which the corporation was an electing small business corporation under Subchapter S.

¶ 805 S Corporations That Do Not Have Excess Net Passive Income

.01 S Corporations Without Earnings and Profits

An S corporation can have no current earnings and profits[126] and will not have accumulated earnings and profits if it has been an S corporation its entire existence, never was involved with a C corporation that had earnings and profits created by merger, and was not formed as a product of a tax-free division under Code Secs. 312(b) and 355 or otherwise. When an S corporation is without earnings and profits, the excess net passive income tax or possible loss of S status cannot take effect.

---

[125] See discussion at ¶ 802.01 regarding dispositions of assets. Also, for tax planning in regards to built-in gains situations, see ¶ 802.18.

[126] By definition of Code Secs. 1362(d)(3) and 1375.

.02 S Corporations Without Rents, Royalties, Interest, Dividends, and Annuities

If an S corporation does not have passive income from the six areas including rents, royalties, interest, dividends, annuities, and sales or exchanges of stocks or securities,[127] it will not have difficulty with the excess net passive income tax or possible loss of S status.[128]

> **Example 8-37:** Lebo Inc. was formed January 1, 1995, and elected S status on that date. Since inception, it has only engaged in manufacturing activities. Lebo is not subject to the excess net passive income tax nor will it lose its S status due to excess passive income.

.03 C Corporations That Convert to S Status Without Earnings and Profits

A C corporation that converts to S status and has no earnings and profits will never be plagued with the excess net passive income tax or possible loss of S status because of it.[129] A C corporation operating at a loss would not have earnings and profits.[130]

.04 S Corporations Without Taxable Income or Net Passive Investment Income

An S corporation that does not have taxable income or net passive investment income[131] cannot be subject to the excess net passive income tax.

¶ 806 LIFO Inventory Recapture

When a C corporation that maintains its inventories under LIFO converts to S status, it must recapture the excess of the inventory's value using a FIFO cost flow assumption over its LIFO value as of the close of its last tax year as a C corporation (or the "LIFO recapture amount").[132] The tax that will be generated by the inclusion in income of the LIFO recapture amount is payable in four equal installments with the first installment to be paid on or before the due date of the corporate tax return (without regard to extensions) for the corporation's last year as a C corporation. The three remaining installments are due on the due date of the corporation's tax returns for the three succeeding tax years (without regard to extensions). No interest is payable on these installments if they are paid by the respective due dates.

> **Tax Pointer:** C corporation net operating losses can be used, subject to certain restrictions, against the LIFO recapture amount.[133]

The LIFO recapture amount is the excess of the inventory's value using FIFO over its LIFO value at the close of the corporation's last year as a C corporation.[134] If

---

[127] Code Sec. 1362(d)(3)(B).

[128] Code Secs. 1375 and 1362(d)(3).

[129] Code Secs. 1362(d)(3) and 1375. See discussion throughout ¶ 804.

[130] The tax consequences of a C corporation converting to S status with net operating losses are discussed at ¶ 802.15 and ¶ 404.08.

[131] See definition of these terms at ¶ 804.11 and ¶ 804.09.

[132] Code Sec. 1363(d), added in the Tax Reform Act of 1987.

[133] Rev. Proc. 94-61, 1994-2 CB 775.

[134] Code Sec. 1363(d)(3).

the corporation uses the retail method for valuing inventories under LIFO, that method will be used to make FIFO valuation.

> *Example 8-38:* Traylor Inc., which uses LIFO, converts from a C corporation to S status on January 1, 2010. At the time of conversion, the corporation had the following inventory records:

Opening inventory: (1,000 units at $5)	$ 5,000
Purchases: (2,000 units at $7)	14,000
Sales: (2,000 units at $8)	16,000
Ending inventory: (1,000 units at $5)	5,000

The FIFO ending inventory would be $7,000 ($7 × 1,000 units). The LIFO recapture amount is $2,000 ($7,000 − $5,000).

.01 Means to Abate LIFO Inventory Recapture

In the area of S corporations, many times form applies over substance. Such is the case with Code Sec. 1363(d). This was demonstrated in the case of *Coggin Automotive Corporation v. Comm.*[135] To understand *Coggin*, one must have some understanding of partnership taxation. As a general rule under Code Sec. 721, the transfer of property to a partnership in exchange for partnership interest is tax-free, similar to Code Sec. 351 with corporations. Thus, if LIFO inventory was transferred by partners to a partnership, there would be no recognition of the transfer.[136] However, if inventory is held by a partnership or an LLC classified as a partnership for tax purposes, when a C corporate partner converts to an S status, the company must recognize LIFO recapture and pay tax thereon as if it held the inventory directly.[137] In *Coggin*, taxpayer was a C corporation holding company which held majority interest in five C corporate auto dealerships; the auto dealerships utilized the LIFO inventory method. Taxpayer had no inventory. In order to provide ownership incentives to managers at the dealerships, obtain greater flexibility than afforded in a corporate format, and to accomplish estate tax planning, Luther Coggin, the majority owner of the taxpayer, restructured operations by taking the following actions: (a) six separate S corporations were established by Luther and his brothers; (b) six limited partnerships were formed, with each S corporation contributing cash to a newly-formed limited partnership in return for a one percent general partnership interest; (c) each of the taxpayer's subsidiaries contributed assets and liabilities of the dealership to the limited partnership in exchange for a limited partnership interest and the partnership utilized the LIFO method for reporting their inventories; (d) taxpayer then liquidated each subsidiary into itself, and then elected S status, with the taxpayer now becoming a limited partner in each of these limited partnerships.

The court held that Code. Sec. 1363(d) did not apply, because while the taxpayer satisfied the first part of Code Sec. 1363(d) because it elected S status, it did not satisfy the second part, because it did not utilize LIFO to report its inventories in the year prior to conversion. In reaching its decision, the Court noted

---

[135] 115 TC 349; *rev'd*, 2002-1 USTC ¶ 50,448 (11th Cir. 2002).

[136] Private IRS Letter Ruling 200123035.

[137] TAM 9716003.

¶806.01

that it felt that the aggregate concept of partnership taxation applied, which treated each partner as owning an undivided interest in the interests and activities of the partnership; not the entity concept, which would determine taxation based on each partner's transactions. Applying the aggregate concept, since the taxpayer had no inventories, the Court felt that Code Sec. 1363(d) did not apply.

In reaching its decision, the Court acknowledged that its decision created a loophole, but that "such a loophole is not [the Court's]to close, but must rather be closed or cured by Congress." The Court also acknowledged situations where loopholes had been sanctioned by the courts, citing *Brown Group v. Comm.*[138], and *Petroleum Corp. of Texas, Inc. v. U.S.*[139] In *Brown*, it was held that a corporate partner's share of income earned by a foreign limited partnership was not foreign-based company income under the former Code Sec. 956(d)(3), and subject to Sub Part F income. The Court held that Sub Part F will only apply to the partnership if the partnership controls the foreign corporation. Additionally, the Court felt that while a loophole was created, there was a valid business reason for the partner-ship—namely, to give managers business incentives to continue with the business enterprise.

> *Tax Pointer:* Caution is indicated when utilizing holding companies to avoid Code Sec. 1363(d) taxation—there must be a valid business purpose established for the holding company.

The Service, in response to *Coggin*, issued Reg. § 1.1363-2(b) to repudiate the decision.

Reducing taxable income in the last year of C corporation's status. Code Sec. 1363(d) LIFO recapture's tax is geared to taxable income of the C corpora-tion's last year before converting to S Status. So if the C corporation before converting to S status reduces its taxable income, this has a direct proportion on the tax which has to be paid on conversion. An easy means to reduce taxable income is to declare salaries, bonuses, etc. keeping in mind that the IRS could challenge these increases in salaries as "unreasonable." However, an examination of recent cases, such as *Menard*,[140] in which a CEO's 17 million dollar bonus paid to him by his wholly owned C corporation deductible illustrates that there is great flexibility in utilizing compensation as a means to adjust income.

.02 Penalties and Interest for Failure to Pay Code Sec. 1363(d)'s Tax Timely

Code Secs. 6601 and 6651 impose interest and penalties for late payment(s) of Code Sec. 1363(d)'s LIFO recapture tax. Notice 2003-4[141] prescribes that a late payment of one installment will not cause an acceleration of the due date for the remaining installments. However, Code Sec. 6662 prescribes that the company may be liable for an accuracy-related penalty if the S corporation omits payment of Code Sec. 1363(d)'s tax.

---

[138] CA-8, 96-1 USTC ¶ 50,055 (8th Cir. 1996), 77 F3d 217. Vac'g 104 TC 105, Dec. 50,436 (1997) (Nonacq.).
[139] 91-2 USTC ¶ 50,417 (5th Cir. 1991).

[140] 2009-1 USTC ¶ 50,270 (7th Cir. 2009).
[141] 2000-3 IRB 24.

.03 Sole Proprietorship Can Exclude LIFO Recapture under Code Sec. 1363(d) on Conversion to S Corporation

IRS Letter Ruling 201010026 (Nov. 20, 2009) held that a proprietorship which uses the LIFO inventory method when it converts to an S corporation is not subject to Code Sec. 1363(d) on conversion to an S corporation. In reaching its holding, the Service stated: "Our literal reading of Code Sec. 1363(d) in this case does not thwart congressional intent. Congress enacted a related provision, Code Sec. 1374, to tax an S corporation on the built-in gains attributable to the period when it was a C corporation. Code Sec. 1374 applies, however, only to built-in gains recognized during the first 10 years of the corporation's existence as an S corporation ('10-year recognition period'). Because of the mechanics of the LIFO inventory method, the built-in gains from LIFO inventories will not be fully recognized until the taxpayer experiences a decrement in every inventory layer that existed on the date the C corporation elected to be an S corporation. It is possible, even likely, that the S corporation will not experience a decrement in any of these inventory layers during the 10-year recognition period and, thus, will escape taxation under Code Sec. 1374 altogether. This result gives an S corporation using the LIFO inventory method a tax-based competitive advantage over an S corporation using the FIFO inventory method. To counter this result, Congress enacted Code Sec. 1363(d), which prevents an S corporation from avoiding the taxation of any built-in gains attributable to LIFO inventories held when it was a C corporation. . . . We do not believe Congress intended Code Sec. 1363(d) to apply when avoidance of the built-in gain rules of Code Sec. 1374 is not possible and, thus, cannot be one of the goals of the corporation's election to be an S corporation. The existence of built-in gain subject to Code Sec. 1374 is not possible in this case for the same reasons that Code Sec. 1363(d) literally does not apply to the facts of this case."

Chapter 9

Basis, Losses, and Passive Loss Rules

Chapters 6 and 7 discuss how to determine S corporation income and expense as well as which items pass through to shareholders as separately stated items. This chapter discusses how those items are allocated among shareholders, how and when they are reported on the shareholders' returns, and how they affect the shareholders' bases in stock and debt. Before discussing basis, it is important to note when a shareholder recognizes income and losses.

¶ 901 When a Shareholder Recognizes Income and Losses

All items of income, gain, loss, credits, and deductions that pass through to S corporation shareholders are to be allocated on a per-share, per-day basis.[1] Those items of income, loss, etc. are to be reported by the shareholders in each shareholder's tax year that includes the last day of the S corporation's tax year.[2] Two categories of income pass through to the shareholders: (1) separately stated items (e.g., capital gains and losses, Code Sec. 1231 gains and losses, charitable contributions) and (2) nonseparately stated items (i.e., Form 1120S, page 1, line 21).[3]

---

[1] Code Sec. 1377(a)(1).
[2] Code Sec. 1366(a)(1).

[3] See ¶ 602 and ¶ 603 for more discussion.

.01 Taxable Year of Inclusion

When determining how much income, loss, etc. should be reported by an S shareholder, consider whether the S shareholder held the stock for the entire year or only part of the year.

Stock held the entire year. If an S shareholder remains a shareholder for the entire year, the items of income, loss, etc. are multiplied by the stock percentage of the shareholder and are reported to the shareholder on Schedule K-1 of Form 1120S.[4]

Example 9-1: Carrots Inc., a calendar-year S corporation, is owned by two shareholders, sisters Doris and Elaine Cole, who own 50 shares each. They have both held their stock interest for the entire year of 2004. In 2004, Carrots Inc., has ordinary income of $60,000 (Form 1120S, page 1, line 21). Doris and Elaine would each report $30,000 of income for the year 2004.

Stock held part of the year. Initially, it should be noted that a sale of stock will have no effect on the amount of the S corporation's income or loss for the year. Determining how much of each item of income, loss, etc. each shareholder reports involves three steps:

(1) Divide the item by the number of days in the S corporation's tax year (this figure is the daily amount of the item).

(2) Multiply the daily amount of the item by the percentage of stock owned by the shareholder on that day (this figure is the shareholder's daily part of the daily amount of the items).

(3) Total the shareholder's daily parts of the daily amount of the item (this figure is the shareholder's pro rata share of the item for the tax year).

Example 9-2 illustrates a shorthand version of how the three-part test works.

Example 9-2: Assume the same facts as in Example 9-1, except that Elaine sells 25 of her shares in Carrots Inc. 90 days before the end of the year to Frank Zelder. Zelder is a qualified S shareholder. The shareholders will report the $60,000 of corporate income as follows:

Step 1

Shareholder	Percentage of Stock Owned	Percentage of Year Stock Was Owned	Percentage of Stock for Year Owned
Doris Cole	50 %	100.0 %	50.000 %
Elaine Cole	50	75.3 *	37.650
Elaine Cole	25	24.7 **	6.175
Frank Zelder	25	24.7	6.175
			100.000 %

*275/365

**90/365

[4] Code Sec. 1377(a)(1).

¶901.01

ifﬁifﬁ

Basi

Step 2

Shareholder	Total Amount of Income		Shareholder's Pro Rata Share
Doris Cole	(50% × $60,000)	=	$30,000
Elaine Cole	((37.65% + 6.175%) × $60,000)	=	26,295
Frank Zelder	(6.175% × $60,000)	=	3,705
Total		=	$60,000

Tax Pointer: If there is a qualifying disposition of stock, the S corporation can elect to treat the S corporation's tax year as two separate years, the first ending on the day the qualifying disposition occurs.[5] In Example 9-2, Elaine Cole's transfer of stock to Frank Zelder will qualify for such an election.[6]

.02 Closing the S Corporation's Books

Disposition of shareholder's entire interest in an S corporation. If a shareholder's entire interest in an S corporation is sold or terminated during the S corporation's tax year and the corporation and all affected shareholders agree, the S corporation may elect to have the corporation's tax year consist of two separate tax years for the affected shareholders, the first of which ends at the close of the day on which the shareholder's entire interest in the S corporation is sold or terminated.[7] Closing the S corporation's tax year allows for a more precise allocation of the S corporation's income, loss, etc. among the shareholders. If the election under Code Sec. 1377(a)(2) is not made, the selling shareholder determines his or her share of S corporation income, loss, etc. using the daily allocation method described previously. Note that since income or loss passed through from the S corporation affect the computation of tax basis, the selling shareholder will not be able to compute gain or loss to be recognized on sale of the stock until receipt of the Schedule K-1 from the S corporation summarizing the shareholder's share of all items of S corporation income, gain, loss, and deduction.

---

[5] Reg. § 1.1368-1(g).

[6] For a discussion of the election under Reg. § 1.1368-1(g), see ¶ 1208.02.

[7] Code Sec. 1377(a)(2) and Reg. § 1.1377-1(b)(1).

¶**901.02**

Tax Pointer: Closing the S corporation books pursuant to Code Sec. 1377(a)(2) prevents the surviving shareholder(s) from manipulating the books (e.g., compare Example 9-3 to Example 9-4).

Death of a shareholder. When a shareholder dies before the end of the S corporation's tax year, his or her share of the corporation's income, loss, etc. for the period up to and including the date of death is included on the shareholder's final tax return.[8] Income attributable to the decedent's shares for the period beginning on the first day after the date of death through the end of the S corporation's tax year is reported by the estate (or, if settled, the beneficiaries') income tax return.

Example 9-3: Michael Moore is a 50% shareholder of Bloom Inc., a calendar-year S corporation making widgets. Moore dies September 30; as of September 30, the S corporation earned $60,000, with $30,000 allocated to Moore. However, on December 31, the last day of Bloom Inc.'s tax year, a number of Bloom Inc.'s customers paid their bills, and Bloom Inc. earned a total of $240,000 for the year ($120,000 being allocated to Moore). Accordingly, $90,000 of income ($120,000 × (9 months ÷ 12 months)) must be reported on Moore's final return.

Election to close the books at shareholder's death. A shareholder whose interest in the S corporation terminates can close the S corporation books on his or her termination.[9] Because death is a termination event,[10] the estate of a deceased shareholder has to make a determination as to which is better: using the date of death to determine income taxes, or electing to close the S corporation books at the date of death.

Example 9-4: Assume the same facts as in Example 9-3, except that Moore's estate elects to close the books as of Moore's death on September 30, thereby resulting in only $30,000 of income being allocated to Moore on his final Form 1040 (the actual income earned to date of death); however, his estate must report $90,000 of income ($120,000 – $30,000 of income earned for the period October 1-December 31).

As Example 9-4 illustrates, closing the books at the shareholder's death can, in certain circumstances, shift significant amounts of tax liability from the decedent's final return to the income tax return of the estate, or vice versa. Due to the sharp progressivity of the income tax rates for estates, retaining as much income on the decedent's final return as possible is often desirable. Not only can this reduce the overall income tax burden on the income passed through from the S corporation, it may also reduce the taxable value of the estate since income taxes owed on the decedent's final return are a liability of the estate.

Of course, when the decedent's final return is subject to the highest individual marginal tax rate (currently 35 percent), it may be desirable to shift the tax liability to the estate rather than the decedent's final return. Careful planning is often necessary before making the election to terminate the S corporation's tax year.

---

[8] Code Sec. 1366(a)(1) and Reg. § 1.1377-1(a)(2)(ii).
[9] Code Sec. 1377(a)(2), see discussion at ¶ 1208.02.
[10] Reg. § 1.1377-1(b)(4).

In either case, consideration must be given to any liquidity concerns that may arise when a substantial amount of S corporation income passes through to the decedent or his or her estate. It may be wise to include a provision in the shareholders' agreement requiring the corporation to make a certain minimum level of cash distributions of income to shareholders to cover taxes, or to redeem some or all of the decedent's stock in these situations.

Other events that can terminate an S corporation's tax year.

Qualifying dispositon of less than 100 percent interest. Reg. § 1.1368-1(g)(2) allows the S corporation to elect to close its tax year on the occurrence of any of the following events:[11]

- Disposition by a shareholder or shareholders of 20 percent or more of the *outstanding* stock of the corporation during any 30-day period (whether or not such disposition completely terminiates the shareholder's interest)

- Redemption by the corporation of 20 percent or more of its outstanding stock during any 30-day period

- Issuance by the S corporation of stock equal to or greater than 25 percent of its previously outstanding stock during any 30-day period

Termination of S status. Under Code Sec. 1362(e), the S corporation's tax year ends upon the termination, inadvertent or otherwise, of its S election. In such cases, however, the S corporation does *not* close its books and records as it does when it voluntarily elects to close its year. Rather, Code Sec. 1362(e)(2) requires that the corporation's income, loss, deduction, etc. be allocated on a pro rata daily basis between the two short years (the S corporation year and the subsequent regular corporation year).

An exception to the pro rata daily allocation requirement applies if 50 percent or more of the S corporation's stock is sold or exchanged during the termination year. In such cases, the corporation can *elect* to close its books and records as of the date of the termination of its election and determine its income in each short year using its normal method of accounting.[12] Such an election has consequences exactly like those associated with the elections discussed above under Code Sec. 1377(a)(2) and Reg. § 1.1368-1(g)(2).

.03 Elections That Affect Income, Expenses, and Losses

Elections that affect the computation of items derived from an S corporation are generally made by the corporation except for the two elections that are made separately by each shareholder.[13] These two shareholder-level elections are: deduction and recapture of certain mining exploration expenditures[14] and the election to claim a deduction or credit for income taxes paid to foreign countries and U.S. possessions.[15]

---

[11] See Reg. § 1.1368-1(g)(2) and discussion at ¶ 1208.02.
[12] See Reg. § 1.1362-3(b)(3) and the discussion at ¶ 1207 et seq.
[13] Code Sec. 1363(c)(2).
[14] Code Sec. 617.
[15] Code Sec. 901.

.04 Year Items Are Included

It is possible that an S corporation could have a tax year different from its shareholders.[16] The items of income, loss, etc. are required to be reported in the tax year by the S shareholder that includes the last day of the S corporation year.[17] For example, assume that an S corporation is on a permitted fiscal year of October 31, 2004, and the S shareholders are calendar-year taxpayers. The S corporation items of income, loss, etc. for the fiscal year ended October 31, 2004, are reported on the S shareholders' tax returns for 2004.

¶ 902 Basis—The Road Map

S corporation losses and deductions that pass through to shareholders are deductible by the shareholders to the extent that the shareholders have basis in stock and loans to the S corporation.[18] Accordingly, it is important to determine how to compute basis so that if losses occur, the S corporation shareholders can deduct them on their tax returns. Basis is divided into two components: (1) basis from corporate stock that a shareholder owns and (2) basis from shareholder loans to the corporation.

.01 Importance of Basis

Basis for an S corporation shareholder is composed of two segments—stock basis and debt. Basis allows a shareholder to determine at any given time if money has been made or lost on his, her, or its investment.

> **Example 9-5:** Karl Taylor formed Amber Inc., a qualified S corporation, on January 1, 1998, contributing property with a tax basis of $100,000 and a fair market value of $215,000 in exchange for 100 percent of Amber Inc.'s stock. In the first six years of Amber Inc.'s existence, it reported total net taxable income of $365,000. Karl received no distributions from the corporation and made no additional contributions of cash or property. On January 1, 2004, Karl sold all of his Amber Inc. stock to an unrelated buyer for $580,000. Thus, his total profit from his Amber Inc. investment over the six-year period was $480,000 ($580,000 selling price *less* $100,000 tax basis of property contributed at formation). Of this amount, $365,000 represents the income earned by Amber Inc. and already taxed on Karl's pervious years' tax returns. Since this income reported in previous years increased Karl's stock basis (to $465,000), he will recognize only $115,000 gain on the sale of his stock ($580,000 – $465,000).

A shareholder cannot deduct losses in excess of basis. Thus, it is essential to know a shareholder's basis to maximize the deduction(s) for losses.[19] Knowledge of basis also allows a shareholder to take advantage of certain situations involving S corporation operations and find a means for altering the normal order of basis adjustments to obtain desired tax results.[20]

---

[16] See discussion at ¶ 501, ¶ 502.03, and ¶ 502.04.

[17] The rules of Code Sec. 1366(a)(1); see description at ¶ 601.

[18] Code Sec. 1366(d).

[19] See ¶ 903.05 for details.

[20] For an example of such a situation, see ¶ 904.

Knowledge of basis in S corporation stock also allows a shareholder to determine if he, she, or it will have a gain on receipt of a distribution from an S corporation, or just a return of capital. If an S corporation shareholder receives a distribution in excess of his or her stock basis, then the shareholder will recognize capital gain.[21] This same situation may also occur when a shareholder lends money to the corporation.[22]

.02 Statute of Limitations Overstatement of Basis Is 3 Years

Code Sec. 6501(e)(1)(A) prescribes that if a taxpayer omits from gross income an amount properly includible therein and such amount is in excess of 25 percent of the amount of gross income stated in the return, the statute of limitations for assessment is 6 years instead of the normal 3 year period as set forth in Code Sec. 6501(a). However, if an S corporate shareholder overstates basis, then the Code Sec. 6501(a)'s 3 year statute of limitation controls.[23]

¶ 903 Stock Basis

.01 Original Basis

A shareholder can acquire stock in an S corporation in various ways. The shareholder can make a capital contribution under Code Sec. 351; he or she can purchase stock, receive it by gift or inheritance, etc. Determining the shareholder's initial stock basis will differ depending on how the stock is acquired.

Capital contribution under Code Sec. 351. When a shareholder forms a corporation and elects S status at the earliest possible point,[24] the shareholder acquires basis in stock equal to the basis of the property contributed plus any gain recognized on the contribution. It is beyond the scope of this book to detail the rules of Code Sec. 351 and how they apply to S corporations; however, the following should be noted:

- No gain or loss will be recognized on the transfer of property to the S corporation solely in exchange for its stock, providing the transferor(s) of the property is (are) in control of the corporation immediately after the transfer.[25] "Control" for this purpose means ownership of at least 80 percent of the combined voting power of the stock entitled to vote, and at least 80 percent of each class of non-voting stock.[26]

- The transferor's basis in stock received in an S corporation is equal to the adjusted basis of the property transferred, increased by any gain recognized, and decreased by the fair market value of any boot received.[27]

Example 9-6: In 2004, Dennis White forms Tipper Inc., a corporation that elects S status, reporting its income, loss, etc. on a calendar-year basis.

[21] Code Sec. 1368(b)(2).

[22] See Example 9-20 for illustration.

[23] *Home Concrete & Supply LLC v. U.S.*, 2012-1 USTC ¶ 50,315 (USSC 2012), *accord; Beard v. Comm.*, TC Memo 2009-184 (overstatement of basis is not an omission of gross income for purposes of Code Sec. 6501(e)(1)(A)).

[24] Pursuant to Code Sec. 1362(b).

[25] Code Sec. 351.

[26] Code Sec. 368(c).

[27] Code Sec. 358(a)(1).

White is the only shareholder, contributing $100,000 in cash for all of the stock of Tipper Inc. White's original basis in his S corporation stock is $100,000.

Example 9-7: Assume the same facts as in Example 9-6, except that White contributes Copperhead, vacant land that cost White $65,000 but is now worth $100,000. White's basis in his stock is $65,000; similarly Tipper Inc.'s basis in Copperhead is $65,000.

Stock acquired by gift. Under Code Sec. 1015, a taxpayer's basis in property acquired by gift is generally equal to the donor's basis in such property immediately prior to the gift. Thus, a shareholder acquiring stock in an S corporation by gift generally takes an initial tax basis in the stock equal to the donor's basis, adjusted of course for any income, loss, etc. passed through to the donor for the period(s) preceding the gift.[28]

Example 9-8: Clara Hand was the sole sharholder of Majors Inc., a qualified S corporation, until June 30, 2010, when she gave half of her Majors Inc. stock to her grandson, Chester. As of January 1, 2010, Clara's basis in her Majors Inc. stock was $125,000. For the year 2010, the corporation reported net taxable income of $80,000, and no separately stated items. At June 1, Chester's basis in the stock received from Clara was $82,500 (Clara's $62,500 tax basis in the 50 percent interest transferred to Chester, plus $20,000 of the income passed through to these shares for the period January 1 through June 30).

An exception to the carryover basis rule of Code Sec. 1015 applies if the value of the property is less than the donor's tax basis at the date of the gift. In such cases, the transferee's basis in the gifted property is limited to its value at the date of the gift.[29]

Stock acquired by inheritance. When S corporation stock is received by inheritance rather than by gift, Code Sec. 1014 provides that the recipient's tax basis in such stock is equal to its fair market value at the decedent's date of death (or the alternate valuation date six months after the date of death if applicable). Note that under Code Sec. 1014, although the beneficiaries of S corporation stock take a fair market value basis in the shares received, the S corporation itself is not affected; its basis in its assets remains unchanged. Consequently, the shareholders will be required to recognize taxable income upon the sale or distribution of appreciated S corporation property, while no income or gain would be recognized on the sale of some or all of the inherited stock.[30]

Stock acquired by purchase. The basis of stock acquired by purchase is its cost.[31] If a shareholder uses a note to acquire stock, then the interest expense that the purchaser incurs has to be allocated. Initially, a shareholder incurs investment

---

[28] See ¶ 1124 for a discussion of this point. See also ¶ 1109.07 for a discussion of the use of minority and lack of control discounts to determine the value of the gifted stock.

[29] See Code Sec. 1015 and the regulations thereunder to determine the tax consequences when a donee re-

ceives depreciated property that subsequently appreciates in value and is sold or otherwise disposed of by the donee.

[30] See ¶ 1124.02 for a discussion of this point.

[31] Code Sec. 1012.

¶903.01

interest expense.[32] Then, an additional classification has to be made[33] if the investment is passive under the passive activity rules (likewise, a determination has to be made to see if a shareholder is at risk).[34] An example will illustrate how a shareholder determines his, her, or its cost basis in the stock.

>*Example 9-9:* Laurie Harris in 2010 buys all the stock of Mars Inc. for $100,000 from Richard Rowe, a stranger, paying all cash. Harris' basis in Mars Inc.'s stock is $100,000.

>*Example 9-10:* Assume the same facts as in Example 9-9, except Harris paid for the stock by issuing a note from her corporation for $100,000 to Rowe, with interest being paid pursuant to the applicable federal rates on the unpaid balance of principal. Harris' basis in her stock is $100,000.

Stock acquired by issuing notes. If an individual issues his, her, or its personal note to the S corporation in exchange for stock, the shareholder will have zero basis in the stock because no property or money was exchanged. When the note is paid, basis will be increased by the amount of the payment.[35]

>*Example 9-11:* Assume the same facts as in Example 9-10, except Harris acquired the stock from the corporation, issuing her own personal note for the stock. Harris' basis in her stock is zero.

Stock basis when a C corporation elects S status. When a C corporation elects S status, the shareholder's basis in the S corporation stock at the time of the election will be the same as his, her, or its basis in the C corporation stock prior to the election.[36]

>*Example 9-12:* Lois O'Reilly is the sole shareholder of Green Inc., a C corporation. She acquired her stock in 1997 for $50,000. On January 1, 2010, Green Inc. elects S status. At the time of the election, the C corporation has earnings and profits of $75,000. O'Reilly's basis in her S corporation stock on January 1, 2010, is $50,000.

Stock received for services. S corporations sometimes compensate shareholders for services rendered by issuing them additional shares of stock. If this occurs, the service provider must report as compensation the fair market value of the stock,[37] and the S corporation will be entitled to a deduction in the same amount. The service provider's basis in the stock will generally be equal to the amount of compensation included in gross income.[38] If the stock is paid to the service provider as an organization expense (e.g., the S corporation, instead of paying its lawyer in cash for forming the corporation, pays him or her with S corporation stock), then the corporation must capitalize an amount equal to the value of the stock transferred; it can elect to amortize this amount under Code Sec. 248.

---

[32] Code Sec. 163(d)(1). For a general discussion of the investment interest rules, see ¶ 702.

[33] Pursuant to Code Sec. 469.

[34] Code Sec. 465. For a related discussion of the at-risk rules, see ¶ 710.

[35] Rev. Rul. 81-187, 1981-2 CB 167.

[36] Code Sec. 1371(a).

[37] Reg. § 1.83-1(a).

[38] Reg. § 1.83-4(b).

Stock received in a reorganization. A shareholder's basis in stock received in a reorganization is generally equal to the basis of the stock exchanged, increased by any gain recognized, and decreased by the amount of money and fair market value of property received.[39]

> ***Example 9-13:*** Jack Larsen is the sole shareholder of Glen Inc., a calendar-year S corporation with 100 shares. On January 1, 2010, Glen Inc. merges with Brook Inc. to form Glenbrook Inc. Larsen's basis in his Glen Inc. shares is $20,000. Larsen exchanges his 100 shares of stock for 50 shares of Glenbrook Inc.; Larsen's basis in Glenbrook Inc. is $20,000.

Stock received in a Code Sec. 355 transaction.[40] A shareholder receiving stock in a tax-free spin-off, split-off, or split-up under Code Sec. 355 must allocate a portion of his or her basis in existing shares to the newly received shares obtained in the Code Sec. 355 transaction. This allocation is generally based on the relative fair market values of the new shares received and the old shares retained (if any).[41]

> ***Example 9-14:*** Taurus Inc., an S corporation, has one shareholder, Ray York, and a 100% subsidiary. On January 1, 2010, Taurus Inc. distributes all of the stock of the subsidiary to its shareholder York pursuant to a Code Sec. 355 spin-off. York's basis in his Taurus stock at the time of the spin-off is $50,000. At the time of the spin-off, the subsidiary's stock is worth $100,000, and York's Taurus stock is worth $300,000. York's basis in the subsidiary is $12,500 (($100,000 ÷ $400,000) × $50,000), and York's basis in his Taurus stock is $37,500 ($50,000, York's basis in Taurus Inc. *less* $12,500, York's basis in the subsidiary).

Shareholder's basis in stock vs. corporation's basis in its assets. At formation, the shareholders' aggregate basis in their stock will generally be equal to the corporation's net tax basis in its assets (i.e., basis in assets net of debt). Moreover, because S corporation income, losses, etc. pass through to shareholders and increase or decrease their stock basis, this equality between stock basis (outside basis) and asset basis (inside basis) will frequently be maintained until there is a change in ownership of some or all of the S corporation's outstanding stock. Unlike partnerships and LLCs, an S corporation cannot adjust its basis in assets when the makeup of its shareholders changes. Thus, the sale or bequest of shares in the S corporation will disrupt the balance between the S corporation's inside basis in its assets and the shareholders' outside bases in their stock. Moreover, any disruption is generally permanent.

> ***Example 9-15:*** Jennifer Canby formed an S corporation several years ago with a cash contribution of $100,000. Over the years, she withdrew all income generated by the corporation so that both its basis in its assets and Jennifer's basis in her stock remained $100,000. This year, she sold all her stock in the corporation to an unrelated buyer for $280,000. The new shareholder's basis in the stock acquired will be $280,000; the S corporation's basis

---

[39] Code Sec. 358(a)(1). ¶ 1211 discusses reorganizations such as mergers and consolidations.

[40] ¶ 1211.05 discusses Code Sec. 355 transactions (i.e., a split-off, spin-off, or split-up).

[41] Code Sec. 358(b).

in its assets will still be $100,000, and the corporation will still list the shareholder's stock basis on Form 1120S, Schedule L, at $100,000.

.02 Adjustments to Stock Basis

In the course of an S corporation's life, a shareholder's basis in stock could increase or decrease by a number of factors: S corporation operations, distributions,[42] and/or additional capital contributions.[43] The following are adjustments that are made to the basis of S corporation stock during the life of the S corporation.

Annual adjustments to basis. A shareholder makes the following adjustments annually to his, her, or its stock basis.[44]

Increase in basis. Stock basis is increased annually by the shareholder's share of the following:

(1) Separately stated items of income (capital gains, Code Sec. 1231 gains, tax-exempt interest, etc.)[45]

(2) Nonseparately stated items of income (S corporation ordinary income found on Form 1120S, page 1, line 21)[46]

(3) Excess of the deduction for depletion over the basis of the property subject to depletion

Decrease in basis. The decreases to a shareholder's stock basis[47] beginning on or after August 8, 1998,[48] are as follows:

(1) Initially, by distributions that are not includible in the shareholder's income.[49] Items in this category would be distributions of items that have already been taxed to the shareholder (e.g., distributions from the accumulated adjustments account (AAA), of from previously taxed income (PTI)).[50]

(2) Then by the shareholder's share of the following:

(a) Corporate expenditures not deductible in computing taxable income and not properly chargeable to a capital account (e.g., fines and penalties)[51]

(b) The amount of the shareholder's deductions for depletion of oil and gas wells under Code Sec. 611[52]

(c) Separately stated items of loss and deduction (e.g., capital losses, tax-exempt expenses, Code Sec. 1231 losses)[53]

---

[42] See Chapters 6 and 7.

[43] ¶ 903.02 et seq. detail what occurs if a shareholder acquires additional stock by gift, inheritance, etc.

[44] Code Sec. 1367(a).

[45] Code Sec. 1367(a)(1)(A). (See ¶ 602 for discussion.)

[46] Code Sec. 1367(a)(1)(B). (See ¶ 603 for discussion.)

[47] Code Sec. 1367(a)(2)(A)-(E).

[48] Reg. § 1.1367-1(f). For tax years beginning before 1997, there was a different order for distribution. How-

ever, discussion is only made for the current rules. If an amended return has to be filed for 1996 or prior years, consult the prior law.

[49] Code Sec. 1367(a)(2)(A).

[50] See Chapter 10 for a discussion of these topics.

[51] Code Sec. 1367(a)(2)(D).

[52] Code Sec. 1367(a)(2)(E).

[53] Code Sec. 1367(a)(2)(B). See ¶ 602 and Chapter 7 for discussion.

(d) Nonseparately computed loss (this is the shareholder's share of "taxable loss" on Form 1120S, page 1, line 21)[54]

Tax Pointer: For tax years beginning on or after August 18, 1998, Reg. § 1.1367-1(f) requires that adjustments be made in the order specified above. These changes make it more probable that distributions to shareholders will be tax free; the old rules, under which losses were recognized before distributions, allowed the loss to be deductible but made the distribution taxable.

Code Sec. 50's effect on basis. A shareholder's basis is increased by the recapture of general business credits when the recapture is accompanied by a corresponding addition to an S corporation asset's basis.[55] Likewise, an asset's basis is required to be reduced when general business credits cause such a reduction.[56] General business credits include investment tax credit (including the energy and rehabilitation credit), the targeted jobs credit, the low income housing credit, alcohol fuel credit, and incremental research credit.[57]

Requirements for basis changes. There can be no increase in basis for items of separately and nonseparately stated items of income unless such amounts are included in the gross income of the shareholder on the shareholder's tax return.[58]

.03 Timing of Basis Adjustments

Adjustments to the basis of a shareholder's stock are determined as of the close of the corporation's tax year, and the adjustments generally are effective as of that date.[59] However, if a shareholder disposes of stock during the corporation's tax year, the adjustments with respect to that stock are effective immediately prior to the disposition.

Adjustment for nontaxable item. An adjustment for a nontaxable item is determined for the tax year in which the item would have been includible or deductible under the corporation's method of accounting for federal income tax purposes if the item had been subject to federal income taxation.[60]

Termination of S corporation's tax year. If an election is made under Code Sec. 1377(a)(2) (terminating the corporation's tax year when a shareholder's interest terminates) or under Reg. § 1.1368-1(g)(2) (terminating the corporation's year when a qualifying disposition occurs), the tax year is deemed to consist of separate tax years, the first of which ends at the close of the day on which either the shareholder's interest terminates or a qualifying disposition occurs.[61]

.04 Adjustment for Noncapital, Nondeductible Expenses

Expenses of the corporation not properly chargeable to a capital account and not deductible in computing its taxable income (noncapital, nondeductible expenses) nonetheless reduce the shareholders' bases in their stock. Nondeductible,

---

[54] Code Sec. 1367(a)(2)(C). See ¶ 603 and Chapter 7 for discussion.

[55] Code Sec. 50(a)(1).

[56] Code Sec. 50(c)(1).

[57] Code Sec. 38(b).

[58] Code Sec. 1367(b)(1).

[59] Reg. § 1.1367-1(d)(1).

[60] Reg. § 1.1367-1(d)(2).

[61] Reg. § 1.1367-1(d)(3).

noncapitalizable expenditures include only those items for which no loss or deduction is allowable and do not include items for which the deduction is deferred to a later tax year.[62] Examples of noncapital, nondeductible expenses include (but are not limited to) the following: illegal bribes, kickbacks, and other payments not deductible under Code Sec. 162(c); fines and penalties not deductible under Code Sec. 162(f); expenses and interest relating to tax-exempt income under Code Sec. 265; losses for which the deduction is disallowed under Code Sec. 267(a)(1); the portion of meals and entertainment expenses disallowed under Code Sec. 274; and the two-thirds portion of treble damages paid for violating antitrust laws not deductible under Code Sec. 162.[63] For purposes of an educational IRA, presumably, corporate contributions for an educational IRA will be classified as a nondeductible, noncapital expense.[64]

> *Tax Pointer:* In terms of Code Sec. 274, recently, in *Sutherland Lumber Southwest, Inc.*,[65] a corporation was allowed to deduct its entire costs in supplying a jet for vacation travel for employees, and was not limited to the amount the employee would recognize as fringe benefit income. Congress eliminated this tax break in 2004 by enacting Code Sec. 274(e)(2).

.05 Decrease in Shareholder's Basis—The Spillover Rule

The basis of a shareholder's stock is decreased by an amount equal to the shareholder's pro rata portion of the pass-through items and distributions attributable to that stock,[66] determined on a per-share, per-day basis.[67] If the amount attributable to a share exceeds its basis, the excess is applied to reduce (but not below zero) the remaining bases of all other shares of stock in the corporation owned by the shareholder in proportion to the remaining basis of each of those shares.[68] For an example of the operation of this spillover rule, see Example 9-16.

Losses in excess of basis. A shareholder can only deduct losses from S corporation activities to the extent of his, her, or its basis in S corporation stock and debt.[69] If a shareholder does not have sufficient basis in stock and debt to take a loss from S corporation activities, the shareholder can carry the loss forward indefinitely during the S corporation's life (and, in a limited manner, during the post-termination period).[70]

Basis can never be negative. An S corporation shareholder's basis in stock or debt can never be negative.[71]

---

[62] Code Sec. 1367(a)(2)(D).

[63] Reg. § 1.1367-1(c)(2). Note that in the recent case of *S.P. DiLeonardo,* 79 TCM 1820, Dec. 53,836(M), TC Memo. 2000-120, a trust beneficiary was allowed to deduct her litigation costs even though the Court found her lawsuit frivolous, made in bad faith, made for the sole purpose to harass, etc. It remains to be seen how this case will apply in the S corporation area of frivolous lawsuits.

[64] For a discussion of corporate contributions to an educational IRA, see ¶ 1128.

[65] *Sutherland Lumber Southwest, Inc.*, 114 TC 197, Dec. 53,817, aff'd per curiam, CA-8, 2000-2 USTC ¶ 50,503, 255 F3d 495, acq. IRB 2002-6.

[66] Code Sec. 1367(a)(2).

[67] Code Sec. 1377(a).

[68] Reg. § 1.1367-1(c)(3).

[69] Code Sec. 1366(d)(1).

[70] Code Sec. 1366(d)(2).

[71] Code Sec. 1367(a)(2). For a discussion of the post-termination period, see ¶ 912.

.06 Elective Ordering Rules for Stock Basis Adjustments

The annual adjustments to basis are detailed in ¶ 903.02. However, Reg. § 1.1367-1(g) prescribes that a shareholder can change the normal ordering rules by filing an election with the IRS. Specifically, a shareholder can elect to reduce stock basis by having separately and nonseparately stated losses[72] deducted before nondeductible, noncapital expenses and oil and gas depletion.[73] The election under Reg. § 1.1367-1(g) should be made after an analysis is conducted of the basis account to determine which approach is better for the shareholder(s)—the normal ordering rules or the elective rules.

Making the election. A shareholder makes the election by attaching a statement to the shareholder's timely filed original or amended return electing the alternative ordering rules and stating that the shareholder agrees to carryover any noncapital, nondeductible expenses to the succeeding taxable year(s).[74] Once a shareholder makes an election under this paragraph, the shareholder must continue to use the alternative ordering rules in future tax years unless the shareholder receives the permission of the Commissioner to change back.

.07 Examples of Adjustments to Stock Basis

Examples 9-16 through 9-19 illustrate how to make adjustments to stock basis.

Example 9-16: On December 31, 2008, Albert Getz owns 50 shares of stock with an adjusted basis of $6 per share in Corporation Berlin. On December 31, 2008, Getz purchases for $400 an additional 50 shares of stock with an adjusted basis of $8 per share. Thus, Getz holds 100 shares of stock for each day of the 2009 tax year. For Berlin's 2009 tax year, Getz's pro rata share of the amount of items described in Code Sec. 1367(a)(1)(A) (relating to increases in basis of stock) is $300, Getz's pro rata share of the amount of the items described in Code Sec. 1367(a)(2)(B) (relating to decreases in basis of stock attributable to items of loss and deduction) is $300, and Getz's pro rata share of the amount of the items described in Code Sec. 1367(a)(2)(D) (relating to decreases in basis of stock attributable to noncapital, nondeductible expenses) is $200. Berlin makes a distribution to Getz in the amount of $100 during 2009.

Following the ordering rules of Code Sec. 1367, Getz first increases the basis of each share of stock by $3 ($300 ÷ 100 shares) and then decreases the basis of each share by $1 ($100 ÷ 100 shares) for the distribution. Getz next decreases the basis of each share by $2 ($200 ÷ 100 shares) for the noncapital, nondeductible expenses, and then decreases the basis of each share by $3 ($300 ÷ 100 shares) for the items of loss. Thus, on January 1, 2010, Getz has a basis of $3 per share in the original 50 shares ($6 + $3 – $1 – $2 – $3) and a basis of $5 per share in the second 100 shares ($8 + $3 – $1 – $2 – $3).[75]

Example 9-17: Assume the same facts as in Example 9-16, except that Getz's tax basis in the additional 50 shares purchased on December 31, 2008,

---

[72] Items 2(c) and 2(d) at ¶ 903.02.
[73] Items 2(a) and 2(b) at ¶ 903.02.

[74] Reg. § 1.1367-1(g).
[75] Example 9-16 was adapted from Reg. § 1.1367-1(h).

is $100, or $2 per share, rather than $400. Upon receipt of the Schedule K-1 for 2009, Getz first increases the basis of each of these shares by $3, then decreases the basis of each share by $1, as above. Getz then decreases the basis of each share by $2 for the noncapital, nondeductible expenses before decreasing them for the loss items. Since his remaining basis in the additional 50 shares is only $2 per share, he cannot apply the full $3 per share loss against these shares. The $1 excess is therefore applied against the tax basis of the original 50 shares. Thus, at the beginning of year 2010, Getz's basis in the original 50 shares will be $2 per share ($6 + $3 – $1 – $2 – $3 – $1), and his basis in the additional 50 shares purchased on December 31, 2008, will be $0 per share ($2 + $3 – $1 – $2 – $2).

Example 9-18: Jenna Inc. is a calendar-year S corporation with one shareholder, Carl Kim. In 2010, Jenna Inc. reported the following items on its tax return (no distributions were made during the year):

Capital stock	$10,000 *
Ordinary income (Form 1120S, page 1) . .	6,000
Charitable contributions	600
Penalty	200

*Kim's cost basis for the stock

Kim's basis is computed as follows:

Basis, beginning of the year		$10,000
Increases:		
Ordinary income		6,000
Decreases:		
Penalty	($200)	
Charitable contributions	(600)	800
Basis, end of year		$15,200

Example 9-19: Assume the same facts as in Example 9-18, except that instead of having income of $6,000, Jenna reported a loss of $6,000. Kim's basis for 2010 would be $3,200 computed as follows:

Basis, beginning of the year		$10,000
Decreases:		
Penalty	($ 200)	
Charitable contributions . .	(600)	
Loss	(6,000)	6,800
Basis, end of year		$ 3,200

¶903.07

.08 Restoration of a Shareholder's Stock Basis

Assuming that a shareholder's basis is reduced to zero by losses and distributions, a shareholder has two means to increase stock basis: (1) by not taking any distributions for items that increase basis (e.g., capital gains, ordinary income, etc.), leaving the money generated by these transactions in the corporation, and paying the tax on these items of income, gain, etc. from personal funds; or (2) by contributing additional money or property for additional stock. If basis is not increased, the shareholder's deductions for future S corporation losses may be limited.

¶ 904 Debt Basis

.01 Use of Loans to Deduct Losses

A shareholder is allowed to deduct losses from S corporation operations against his or her basis in loans to the corporation after stock basis is reduced to zero.[76] In other words, a shareholder has flexibility in establishing basis for taking losses from S corporation operations—using either stock or a combination of stock and debt. If a shareholder's stock basis is zero, then instead of making a capital contribution, the shareholder can just lend money or property to the corporation to create basis for taking losses.

Proposed Regs. §§ 1.108-7, 1.1366-0, 1.1366-2, 1.1366-5, 1.1367-1 and 1.1367-3 prescribe that only bona fide shareholder loans create basis in the S corporation. In an effort to eliminate disputes, the IRS has issued proposed regulations to clarify when "certain loan transactions involving multiple parties, including back-to-back loan transactions, create shareholder basis of indebtedness...." In that context, the proposed regulations noted "[a] limited number of court decisions have allowed shareholders to increase basis of indebtedness as a result of incorporated pocket-book transactions. See *Yates v. Comm'r*, T.C. Memo. 2001-280; *Culnen v. Comm'r*, T.C. Memo. 2000-139. Under these proposed regulations, an incorporated pocket-book transaction increases basis of indebtedness only where the transaction creates a bona fide creditor-debtor relationship between the shareholder and the borrowing S corporation."

The "proposed regulations only address whether a shareholder has basis of indebtedness for purposes of Code Sec. 1366(d)(1)(B) and do not address how to determine the basis of the shareholder's stock in the S corporation for purposes of Code Sec. 1366(d)(1)(A). Therefore, these proposed regulations leave unchanged the conclusion found in published guidance that a shareholder of an S corporation does not increase basis in stock for purposes of Code Sec. 1366(d)(1)(A) upon the contribution of the shareholder's own unsecured demand promissory note to the corporation. Rev. Rul. 81-187 (1981-2 CB 167). This conclusion is consistent with published guidance and case law in the partnership context that the contribution of the partner's own note will not increase such partner's basis in its partnership interest under Code Sec. 722. Rev. Rul. 80-235 (1980-2 CB 229); *Oden v. Comm'r*, T.C. Memo. 1981-184, aff'd without published opinion, 679 F.2d 885 (4th Cir. 1982)

---

[76] Code Sec. 1367(b)(2).

(because the partner incurred no cost in making the note, the partner's basis in the note to him was zero)." (But see *S. Lessinger*, CA-2, 89-1 USTC ¶ 9254, 872 F2d 519, *Rev'g* 85 TC 824, Dec. 42,489 (shareholder's personal note contributed on incorporation prevented a recognition of gain on incorporation under Code Sec. 357(c)). See also *D.J. Peracchi*, CA-9, 98-1 USTC ¶ 50,374, 143 F3d 487. *Rev'g and rem'g* 72 TCM 2830, Dec. 51,305(M), TC Memo. 1996-191 (unsecured note contributed in a Code Sec. 351 exchange held as corporate property to avoid the imposition of Code Sec. 357(c)). The proposed regulations set forth the 4 examples below to illustrate the operation of the rules:

> *Example 1:* **Shareholder loan transaction.** A is the sole shareholder of S, an S corporation. S received a loan from A. Whether the loan from A to S constitutes bona fide indebtedness from S to A is determined under general Federal tax principles and depends upon all of the facts and circumstances. If the loan constitutes bona fide indebtedness from S to A, A's loan to S increases A's basis of indebtedness. The result is the same if A made the loan to S through an entity that is disregarded as an entity separate from A under Reg. § 301.7701-3.

> *Example 2:* **Guarantee.** A is a shareholder of S, an S corporation. In 2013, S received a loan from Bank. Bank required A's guarantee as a condition of making the loan to S. Beginning in 2014, S could no longer make payments on the loan and A made payments directly to Bank from A's personal funds until the loan obligation was satisfied. For each payment A made on the note, A obtains basis of indebtedness. Thus, A's basis of indebtedness is increased during 2014 to the extent of A's payments to Bank pursuant to the guarantee agreement.

> *Example 3:* **Back-to-back loan transaction.** A is the sole shareholder of two S corporations, S1 and S2. S1 loaned $200,000 to A. A then loaned $200,000 to S2. Whether the loan from A to S2 constitutes bona fide indebtedness from S2 to A is determined under general Federal tax principles and depends upon all of the facts and circumstances. If A's loan to S2 constitutes bona fide indebtedness from S2 to A, A's back-to-back loan increases A's basis of indebtedness in S2.

> *Example 4:* **Loan restructuring through distributions.** A is the sole shareholder of two S corporations, S1 and S2. In March 2013, S1 made a loan to S2. In December 2013, S1 assigned its creditor position in the note to A by making a distribution to A of the note. Under local law, after S1 distributed the note to A, S2 was relieved of its liability to S1 and was directly liable to A. Whether S2 is indebted to A rather than S1 is determined under general Federal tax principles and depends upon all of the facts and circumstances. If the note constitutes bona fide indebtedness from S2 to A, the note increases A's basis of indebtedness in S2.

¶904.01

.02 Distributions and Debt

Excess distributions received from the S corporation cannot be applied against debt; distributions can only be applied against stock basis.[77]

> **Example 9-20:** Brian Reed starts a calendar-year S corporation on January 1, 2010, named Enluck Inc. Reed establishes the capitalization of the corporation with $10,000 of stock and a $40,000 loan to the corporation. Enluck Inc. breaks even its first year, has no separately stated items of income, etc., and on December 31, 2010, distributes $25,000 to Reed, its sole shareholder. The result is that Reed has $15,000 of capital gain ($25,000 – $10,000); the $40,000 of debt basis remains unchanged. If Reed had used the $25,000 to repay the debt, there would have been no capital gain and his debt basis would have been reduced to $15,000.

.03 Types of Shareholder Debt—Written Note and Open Account

A shareholder could lend money or property to an S corporation in two forms—by a written note or by open account (e.g., just writing a check to the corporation, which the corporation records as a loan from the shareholder). The Internal Revenue Service issued Reg. §1.1367-2(a)(2) in an effort to eliminate loopholes created by the use of open account debt effective after October 17, 2008. For a discussion of the regulation see ¶ 904.14.

> **Tax Pointer:** If possible, all loans by shareholders to the S corporation should be in a written form.

.04 Consequences of Using Debt

Debt as a second class of stock. In some cases, debt can create a second class of stock thereby causing a termination of S corporation status. However, Congress created a safe harbor for so-called "straight" debt to alleviate this concern.[78] Accordingly, shareholders should proceed carefully with debt to avoid a termination of S corporation status.

Straight debt. Code Sec. 1361(c)(5) provides that straight debt will not be treated as a second class of stock. To qualify as straight debt, all of the following requirements must be satisfied:[79]

- The debt must be written and must constitute an unconditional promise by the borrower to pay a sum certain on a specified date or on demand.

- The debt must require the payment of interest at a rate, and on payment dates, that are not contingent on profits, the borrower's discretion, etc.

- The debt must not be convertible into stock.

- The creditor must be an individual other than a nonresident alien, an estate, a qualified trust, or a person actively and regularly engaged in the business of lending money.

---

[77] See Chapter 10 for discussion of distributions.
[78] Code Sec. 1361(c)(5). See discussion at ¶ 208.
[79] Code Sec. 1361(c)(5)(B).

Shareholders planning on making loans to a corporation that does not meet these requirements should exercise caution; reclassification of the debt as stock will generally result in termination of the corporation's S status effective as of the date of issuance of the debt.

.05 Debt and Shareholder Loans for Taking Losses

After a shareholder's stock basis is reduced to zero, then any excess of loss generated is then applied to reduce (but not below zero) the basis of any indebtedness of the S corporation to the shareholder held by the shareholder at the close of the corporation's tax year.[80] Any such indebtedness that has been satisfied by the corporation, or disposed of or forgiven by the shareholder, during the tax year is considered not held by the shareholder at the close of that year and, therefore, is not subject to basis reduction.

Shareholder terminates interest in the corporation. If a shareholder terminates his, her, or its interest in the corporation (e.g., by sale of the stock interest) during the tax year, excess losses are applied to any indebtedness of the S corporation held by the shareholder immediately prior to the termination of the shareholder's interest in the corporation.[81] If a shareholder continues to hold the debt of the corporation, the shareholder becomes a simple creditor of the corporation with the debt; there is no opportunity to restore basis.

Multiple indebtedness. If a shareholder holds more than one indebtedness at the close of the corporation's tax year or, if applicable, immediately prior to the termination of the shareholder's interest in the corporation, a reduction in basis is applied to each indebtedness in the same proportion that the basis of each indebtedness bears to the aggregate bases of the indebtedness to the shareholder.[82]

Example 9-21, adapted from Reg. § 1.1367-2(e), illustrates a reduction in basis of debt.

> **Example 9-21:** Alan Anderson has been the sole shareholder in Corporation Sandpiper since 1995. In 2005, Anderson loans Sandpiper $1,000 (Debt 1), which is evidenced by a ten-year promissory note in the face amount of $1,000. In 2008, Anderson loans Sandpiper $5,000 (Debt 2), which is evidenced by a demand promissory note. On December 31, 2008, the basis of Anderson's stock is zero and the loss in excess of stock basis is $5,000; accordingly, the basis of Debt 1 has been reduced to $0; and the basis of Debt 2 has been reduced to $1,000. On January 1, 2009, Anderson loans Sandpiper $4,000 (Debt 3), which is evidenced by a demand promissory note. For Sandpiper's 2009 taxable year, the S corporation has a loss of $4,000 and makes no payments to Anderson on any of the loans during 2009.
>
> The $4,000 excess of loss and deduction items is applied to reduce the basis of each indebtedness in proportion to the basis of that indebtedness over the aggregate bases of the indebtedness to the shareholder (determined

---

[80] Reg. § 1.1367-2(b)(1).
[81] Reg. § 1.1367-2(b)(2). See also ¶ 1208.

[82] Reg. § 1.1367-2(b)(3).

immediately before any adjustment is effective for the taxable year[83]). Thus, the basis of Debt 2 is reduced in an amount equal to $800 ($4,000 excess × ($1,000 basis of Debt 2 ÷ $5,000 total basis of all debt)). Similarly, the basis of Debt 3 is reduced in an amount equal to $3,200 ($4,000 × ($4,000 ÷ $5,000)). Accordingly, on December 31, 2009, Anderson's basis in his stock is zero and his bases in the three debts are as follows:

	1/1/2008 Basis	12/31/2008 Reduction	1/1/2009 Basis	12/31/2009 Reduction	1/1/2010 Basis
Debt 1	$1,000	$1,000	$ 0	$ 0	$ 0
Debt 2	5,000	4,000	1,000	800	200
Debt 3			4,000	3,200	800

What constitutes debt. Because of the importance of debt, there have been a number of cases, rulings, and so on, defining the term. Initially, case law holds that debt means debt owed by the corporation to the shareholder, not to a third party.

Guarantee of shareholders. Generally, the case law indicates that the guarantee of corporate debt will not increase basis. However, Rev. Rul. 70-50[84] prescribes that when the shareholder makes a payment under the guarantee, basis is increased by the amount of the payment.[85] A variation of the guarantee occurs when a shareholder substitutes his, her, or its note for a guarantee of a corporate debt. Rev. Rul. 75-144[86] holds that a shareholder's substitution of his own note for his corporation's note to a bank, which then released the corporation from its liability, resulted in basis to the shareholder equal to the face of the note. In regard to a situation that will not generate basis, Rev. Rul. 69-125[87] prescribes that debt does not include loans made by a partnership composed of the shareholders.

How debt value is determined for Code Sec. l367(b) (2) (A). A shareholder's debt basis will generally be cost.[88] However, if the debt is generated in a Code Sec. 351 exchange, then the debt will be recorded at its fair market value. If the S corporation is on the accrual method and is indebted to a shareholder, then under general tax principles, the shareholder has basis in this debt to the extent the shareholder includes the items generating the debt in income.

Debt for losses not created when a shareholder issues his, her, or its own note. If a shareholder issues his, her, or its own note to acquire stock, it will not create basis for any purposes; money or property must be transferred. Likewise, if a shareholder has acquired stock by contributing money or property and then issues his, her, or its own note to the corporation in an attempt to acquire basis for taking losses, this personal note, regardless of its form, will not create basis pursuant to Rev. Rul. 81-187.[89] Instead, property or money must be lent to the corporation to create basis.

---

[83] Code Sec. 1367(b)(2)(A) (i.e., distributions of accumulated adjustments account (AAA) and previous taxable income (PTI) discussed at ¶ 1003 and ¶ 1005.

[84] Rev. Rul. 70-50, 1970-1 CB 178.

[85] But see *E.M. Selfe,* CA-11, 86-1 USTC ¶ 9115, 778 F2d 769, which held that a shareholder who guaranteed a corporate debt is entitled to a factual determination as to whether this debt is eligible for basis for S corporation basis purposes.

[86] Rev. Rul. 75-144, 1975-1 CB 277.

[87] Rev. Rul. 69-125, 1969-1 CB 207.

[88] Code Sec. 1012.

[89] Rev. Rul. 81-187, 1981-2 CB 167.

Treatment of open account debt between an S corporation and its shareholders. For a discussion of this area, see ¶ 904.14.

.06 Restoration of Debt Basis

Unlike stock, a shareholder cannot restore debt basis by contributing money or property. Rather, the shareholder's basis in debt can be restored only[90] by applying subsequent years' profits. In subsequent years, the shareholder's basis in debt will be restored by the amount by which the shareholder's pro rata share of the items described in Code Sec. 1367(a)(1)[91] exceed the items described in Code Sec. 1367(a)(2)[92] for the tax year. These restoration rules apply only to indebtedness held by a shareholder as of the beginning of the tax year in which the net increase arises. The reduction in basis of indebtedness must be restored before any net increase is applied to restore the basis of a shareholder's stock in an S corporation. In no event may the shareholder's basis in indebtedness be restored above the face value of such indebtedness.

Multiple indebtedness. If a shareholder holds more than one indebtedness as of the beginning of a corporation's tax year, any net increase is applied first to restore the reduction of basis in any indebtedness repaid (in whole or in part) in that tax year to the extent necessary to offset any gain that would otherwise be realized on the repayment.[93] Any remaining net increase is applied to restore each outstanding indebtedness in proportion to the amount that the basis of each outstanding indebtedness has been reduced and not restored. Examples 9-22 through 9-26, adapted from Reg. § 1.1367-2(e) illustrate.

> **Example 9-22:** *Restoration of basis of indebtedness.* The facts are the same as in Example 9-21. On July 1, 2010, Sandpiper completely repays Debt 3, and, for Sandpiper's 2010 tax year, the corporation earns $4,500 of net income that was not distributed to the shareholder. The "net increase" is applied first to restore the bases in the debts held on January 1, 2010, before any of the net increase is applied to increase Anderson's basis in his shares of Sandpiper's stock. The net increase is applied to restore first the basis in indebtedness repaid in 2010. Any remaining net increase is applied to restore the bases of the outstanding debts in proportion to the amount that each of these outstanding debts have been reduced previously and not restored. As of December 31, 2010, the total reduction in Anderson's debts held on January 1, 2010, equals $9,000. Thus, the basis of Debt 3 is restored by $3,200 (the amount of the previous reduction) to $4,000. Anderson's basis in Debt 3 is treated as restored immediately before that debt is repaid. Accordingly, Anderson does not realize any gain on the repayment. The remaining net increase of $1,300 ($4,500 – $3,200) is applied to restore the bases of Debt 1 and Debt 2. As of December 31, 2010, the total reduction in these outstanding debts is $5,800 ($9,000 – $3,200). The basis of Debt 1 is restored in an amount equal to $224 ($1,300 × ($1,000 ÷ $5,800)). Similarly, the basis in Debt 2 is restored in an amount equal

---

[90] Code Sec. 1367(b)(2)(B) and Reg. § 1.1367-2(c)(1).
[91] Income items and excess deduction for depletion.

[92] Losses; deductions; noncapital, nondeductible expenses; certain oil and gas depletion deductions; and certain distributions.
[93] Reg. § 1.1367-2(c)(2).

to $1,076 ($1,300 × ($4,800 ÷ $5,800). On December 31, 2010, Anderson's basis in his S stock is zero, and his bases in the two remaining debts are as follows:

Original Basis	Amount Reduced	1/1/2010 Basis	Amount Restored	12/31/2010 Basis
$1,000	$1,000	$ 0	$ 224	$ 224
5,000	4,800	200	1,076	1,276

Example 9-23: *Full restoration of basis in indebtedness when debt is repaid in part during the tax year.* Claire Klein is the sole shareholder in Symmetry Corp. since 1995. In 2009, Klein loans Symmetry $1,000. Symmetry issues its note to Klein in the amount of $1,000, of which $950 is payable on March 1, 2010, and $50 is payable on March 1, 2011. On December 31, 2009, Klein's basis in all her shares of Symmetry stock is zero, and her basis in the note has been reduced to $900 because the corporation had a loss of $100. For 2010, Symmetry Corp. had $300 of ordinary income that was not distributed to the shareholder. Because Klein's basis of indebtedness was reduced in a prior tax year for the $100 loss, the net increase for 2001 is applied to restore this reduction. The restored basis cannot exceed the adjusted basis of the debt as of the beginning of the first day of 2010, excluding prior adjustments under Code Sec. 1367, or $1,000. Therefore, $100 of the $300 net increase is applied to restore the basis of the debt from $900 to $1,000 effective immediately before the repayment on March 1, 2010. The remaining net increase of $200 increases Klein's basis in her stock, with Klein reporting $300 of net income on personal Form 1040 for 2010, based on Symmetry Corp.'s Form 1120S, K-1.

Example 9-24: Assume the same facts as in Example 9-23, except Symmetry Corp. distributed the entire $300 of net income to Klein. Klein's basis in her stock would still stay at zero, and her debt would remain at $900. Klein would report $300 of net income from Symmetry Corp. on her personal Form 1040 for 2010, and $50 income from partial repayment of the loan ($950 – $900).

Example 9-25: Assume the same facts as in Example 9-23, except Symmetry Corp. distributed only $200 of the net income. Klein's basis in her stock would remain at zero, and her debt basis would be increased to $1,000. Klein would report $300 of net income from Symmetry Corp. on her personal Form 1040 for 2010; $200 from the distribution, and $100 from the undistributed portion pursuant to Symmetry Corp.'s Form 1120S, K-1.

Example 9-26: Assume the same facts as in Example 9-24, except Symmetry Corp. distributed $2,000 to Klein. Klein would report the $300 of net income from Symmetry Corp., and because she had no basis in her stock, she would report a $1,700 capital gain ($2,000 – $300) because she received a distribution in excess of her stock basis (which was zero at the end of the tax year). She will also recognize a $50 gain on the partial repayment of the indebtedness.

¶904.06

Open account debt. The Internal Revenue Service has revised Reg. § 1.1367-2(a)(2) to prescribe special rules for restoration of debt basis for open account debt. For a discussion of this area, see ¶ 904.14.

.07 Date When Basis Adjustments of Debt Are Effective

The amounts of the adjustments to basis of indebtedness are determined as of the close of the corporation's tax year, and the adjustments are generally effective as of the close of the corporation's tax year.[94] However, if the shareholder is not a shareholder in the corporation at that time, these adjustments are effective immediately before the shareholder terminates his or her interest in the corporation. If a debt is disposed of or repaid in whole or in part before the close of the tax year, the basis of that indebtedness is restored, effective immediately before the disposition or the first repayment on the debt during the tax year.

Effect of election under Code Sec. 1377(a)(2) or Reg. § 1.1368-1(g)(2). If an election is made under Code Sec. 1377(a)(2) (to terminate the year in the case of the termination of a shareholder's interest) or under Reg. § 1.1368-1(g)(2) (to terminate the year in the case of a qualifying disposition), the tax year of the S corporation is deemed to consist of separate tax years, the first of which ends at the close of the day on which the shareholder either terminates his or her interest in the corporation or disposes of a substantial amount of stock, whichever the case may be.

Open account debt. The Internal Revenue Service has revised Reg. § 1.1367-2(a)(2) to prescribe special rules for adjustments regarding open account debt. For a discussion of this area, see ¶ 904.14.

.08 Tax Planning with Repayment of Debt

There are tax-planning opportunities for restoration of debt basis and repayment of debt. There are also tax traps for the unwary, so that shareholders of the S corporation should proceed carefully, because if debt is repaid by the S corporation, there may not be any debt basis for the purpose of taking S corporation losses.

Payment of shareholder's debt. When an S corporation repays a shareholder's debt, no gain or loss is generally recognized by the corporation. However, if the S corporation pays the debt with property, gain (but not loss) will be recognized in an amount equal to the difference between the corporation's basis in the property and its fair market value (which will give rise to gain being passed through to the shareholders pursuant to Code Sec. 1366 *et seq.*).[95]

As to the shareholder, a taxable transaction will result upon the repayment of the debt by the corporation, depending upon whether or not the debt is evidenced by a note. If the debt is evidenced by a note,[96] the retirement of a "debt instrument"[97] is treated as an exchange that will generally create capital gains. However, if the debt is not evidenced by a note, the income generated on its collection

---

[94] Reg. § 1.1367-2(d)(1).
[95] Reg. § 1.1001-2 and Rev. Rul. 70-271, 1970-1 CB 166.

[96] Code Sec. 1271(a)(1).
[97] See Code Sec. 1275(a)(1) for the definition of a "debt instrument."

because no debt instrument exists is treated as ordinary income.[98] Accordingly, to be safe, all loans by shareholders to the S corporation should be evidenced by written note(s).

Open account debt. The Internal Revenue Service has revised Reg. § 1.1367-2(a)(2) to prescribe special rules regarding open account debt. For a discussion of this area, see ¶ 904.14.

.09 Distributions to Reduce Stock Basis but Not Debt

Distributions only reduce stock basis; there is no reduction of debt basis.[99] For an illustration of this point, see Example 9-26.

.10 Loan from Related Entities

As a rule, loans from a related entity to an S corporation to give a shareholder basis for purposes of deducting losses are not sustained. Examples of loans from related entities which have been struck down are: partnerships (*Frankel*);[100] estates (*Prashker*);[101] trusts (*Fear*);[102] and corporations (*Burnstein*).[103] Accordingly, to be safe, if a shareholder of an S corporation plans to utilize a related entity from which to borrow money with which to establish basis, extreme formality should be followed, in that the shareholder should: (a) first take the money out of the related entity by means of a recognized transaction such as a dividend, compensation, or a loan secured by adequate security with the loan bearing interest; (b) deposit the check in the shareholder's bank and wait for it to clear; and (c) after the check clears, either lend the funds to the S corporation, taking back a note bearing interest, and/or make a capital contribution.

> **Tax Pointer:** The IRS may, notwithstanding the formality outlined above, strike down the back-to-back loans, claiming that the shareholder has not made a true economic outlay. For an example of such a situation, see Technical Advice Memorandum 9403003 (September 23, 1999) and *Oren*.[104] But *Bolding*,[105] did sustain a back-to-back loan transaction.

Notwithstanding the above, there are cases where loans from related entities have been sustained. *Culnen*[106] is an example; it is discussed at ¶ 205.05. In *Yates*,[107] a loan was sustained to give an S shareholder basis, even though not all the formalities for the loan were established. In *Yates*, the husband (H) owned Adena (A), an S corporation. To protect his assets, H formed Fox Trot (FT), another S corporation. Until September 1, 1994, H was the sole owner of FT; then, for the

---

[98] See, e.g., *B. Barr*, 39 TCM 834, Dec. 36,714(M), TC Memo. 1980-3 (payment of an open account debt generated ordinary income not capital gains).

[99] Code Sec. 1368(b) and (c).

[100] *E.J. Frankel*, 61 TC 343, Dec. 32,250 (1973) aff'd without published opn., CA-3, 506 F2d 1051 (1974) (loan by a partnership to an S corporation did not increase basis for shareholders).

[101] *R.M. Prashker*, 59 TC 172, Dec. 31,583 (S corporation's debt to estate not recognized for purposes of establishing basis).

[102] *D.D. Fear*, 57 TCM 306, Dec. 45,665(M), TC Memo. 1989-211 (loan from a trust to an S corporation not recognized to create basis for the shareholder).

[103] *S.P. Burnstein*, 47 TCM 1100, Dec. 40,997(M), TC Memo. 1984-74 (loan from brother S corporation to sister S corporation not recognized to create basis for shareholder who owned both corporations).

[104] *D.G. Oren*, Dec. 54,811(M), 84 TCM 50, TC Memo. 2002-172 (loans by brother-sister corporation to S corporation not deemed loans to create basis for shareholders because there was no actual economic outlay).

[105] *D.E. Bolding*, CA-5, 97-2 USTC ¶ 50,554, 117 F3d 270.

[106] *D.J. Culnen*, 79 TCM 1933, Dec. 53,856(M), TC Memo. 2000-139, rev'd and rem'd on other grounds, CA-3, 2002-1 USTC ¶ 50,200.

[107] *C.E. Yates*, 82 TCM 805, Dec. 54,523(M), TC Memo. 2001-280.

¶904.09

period September 1, 1994 through December 31, 1996, H transferred stock ownership to his wife (W). A was profitable during the years in question; however, due to bank loan restrictions, A was restricted in terms of dividends that A could make to H. However, A could lend money to H without restriction. Because H traveled extensively, he had his accountant (CPA) write checks, post entries, and then confer with H afterwards to determine if the posting was correct. Beginning October 1, 1994, with respect to the transfer of funds from A to FT, they "were posted as either distributions or loans from A to H, and as either capital contributions from H to FT." CPA recorded in A's books the 1995 transfer of funds from A to FT as accounts payable (i.e., loans) from petitioners. The Court sustained the transfers to W's basis in FT for purposes of taking losses, stating "the uncontradicted and credible testimony of Mr. Yates established that Mr. Yates made gifts to Mrs. Yates of the subsequent transfers from A. Mr. Yates, however, skipped the step of having A transfer such funds to him, depositing funds into petitioners' joint account, and then have Mrs. Yates write a check to FT. Accordingly, these transfers increased Mrs. Yates' basis in FT."

.11 Loans Must Have Economic Reality

If a loan does not have economic reality, the IRS will strike it down, giving the shareholder no basis for the transaction. This was illustrated in *Pike*,[108] where taxpayers borrowed money from a tax shelter promoter to contribute to an S corporation to establish basis; then, the S corporation lent money back to the promoter.

.12 Risk in Shareholder Loans

While shareholder loans provide basis for taking losses in an S corporation, there are also risks inherent for shareholders over and above the risks detailed in ¶ 904.01–.11. For instance, if there is more than one shareholder in the S corporation, and one shareholder lends proportionately more than his, her or its shareholder percentage, then there is no economic benefit to the shareholder-creditor of the S corporation, except that the loan will enable the shareholder to deduct more losses due to S corporation operations. An example will illustrate.

> **Example 9-27:** Debra and Robert are equal shareholders in an S corporation, each contributing $10,000 to acquire the stock in the corporation. During its first taxable year, the S corporation grosses $100,000 of income. Robert develops severe cash-flow problems because he is going to graduate school, so Debra lends $100,000 to the corporation to keep it afloat. At the end of the year, the S corporation lost $120,000, with $60,000 of loss being allocated to each shareholder (50% × $120,000). Debra is penalized economically, since she receives no economic benefit for the remainder of her loan (to wit, $50,000 [$100,000 of loan less $50,000 of loan basis utilized to take the $60,000 of loss]). Instead, Debra should have negotiated with Robert, requiring him to transfer some of his stock to her so that she would have received a proper return for her economic risk. So, if Debra owned 90% of the stock, in the first

[108] *S.J. Pike*, 78 TC 822, Dec. 39,037, aff'd without published opn., CA-9, 732 F2d 164 (1984).

year of operation, Debra would have been able to deduct $90,000 worth of loss ($10,000 from her stock and $80,000 from her loan), leaving only $20,000 unutilized.

.13 Imputation of Interest

When loans are made to a corporation, there is always the danger that the IRS will impute interest under Code Secs. 7872 and 1274. ¶ 1114 discusses some of the problems. Recently, in *Rountree Cotton Co., Inc.*,[109] the Court, in a case of first impression, imputed interest to the shareholders of a corporation in connection with a below-market loan made by the corporation to entities involving the shareholders of the corporation and other family members, none of whom had a controlling interest in the corporation. The facts of *Rountree* are as follows.

The taxpayer, a cotton brokerage business which had a principal place of business in Las Cruces, New Mexico, was owned by members of a family and the estate of a deceased family member; however, none of the family members had a controlling interest in the corporation. In its 1994 fiscal year, the taxpayer made interest-free loans to six partnerships. All of the partners in these partnerships were members of the same family; however, not all of the partners were also shareholders in the taxpayer. Notwithstanding, the Court held that Code Sec. 7872 applies to impute interest income at the AFR rate for the foregone interest on the entire amount of the loans (under Code Sec. 7872, a corporation making a below-market-interest loan is treated as if it had received the foregone interest and paid it to the shareholders as a nondeductible dividend). Reg. § 1.7872-4(d)(1) prescribes that interest foregone on loans from the corporation to shareholders is treated as distribution from the S corporation.

.14 Treatment of Open Account Debt between an S Corporation and its Shareholders

In *Brooks v. Comm.*,[110] a shareholder made a series of open account advances to his corporation receiving repayments during the same year. To accomplish these loans to his corporation, the shareholder borrowed money from his bank. The net effect of these open account transactions was that in one taxable year the shareholder was able to use the borrowings for basis to take losses. In the subsequent year, when the corporation had sufficient funds, it repaid the advances to the shareholder who in turn repaid the bank. At the end of this subsequent year, the shareholder realized that under Code Sec. 1367 that he would have gain because the corporation had insufficient profits to restore basis to his debt account; so he advanced more funds to his corporation through open advances by borrowing money from his bank thereby preventing any gain recognition. At the same time, the additional advances allowed him to have basis to take losses for this subsequent year. The court held under former Reg. § 1.1367-2(a)(2)(i) "that the basis of the open account indebtedness is properly computed by netting at the close of the year advances of open account debt during the year and repayments of open account debt during the year."

---

[109] *Rountree Cotton Co., Inc.*, 113 TC 422, Dec. 53,659, aff'd CA-10, 2001-1 USTC ¶ 50,316.

[110] TC Memo 2005-2004.

In an effort to narrow the definition of open account debt and to modify the rules for adjustments of basis in indebtedness for the more narrowly defined open account debt, the Internal Revenue Service promulgated Reg. § 1.1367-2(a)(2) et seq. effective after October 17, 2008.

Reg. § 1.1367-2(a)(2) defines "'open account debt' to mean shareholder advances not evidenced by separate written instruments and repayments on the advances, the aggregate outstanding principal of which does not exceed $25,000 of indebtedness of the S corporation to the shareholder at the close of the S corporation's taxable year." Reg. § 1.1367-2(a)(2)(ii) prescribes that "if the shareholder advances not evidenced by a separate written instrument, net of repayments, exceeds an aggregate outstanding principal amount of $25,000 at the close of the S corporation's taxable year, for any subsequent taxable year the aggregate principal amount of that indebtedness is treated in the same manner as indebtedness evidenced by a separate written instrument . . . "

Reg. § 1.1367-2(d)(2) prescribes that "[a]ll advances and repayments on open account debt . . . during the S corporation's taxable year are netted at the close of the S corporation's taxable year to determine the amount of any net advance or net repayment. The net advance or net repayment is combined with the outstanding aggregate principal balance of the existing open account debt and that amount is carried forward to the beginning of the subsequent taxable year as the outstanding aggregate principal amount of the open account debt . . . However, if the shareholder in the S corporation is not a shareholder of the S corporation at the close of the S corporation's taxable year, such advances and repayments on open account debt are netted, and the basis of that indebtedness is restored under Reg. § 1.1367-2(c) effective immediately before the shareholder terminates his or her interest in the S corporation. If any open account debt is disposed of before or upon the close of the taxable year, the disposition is effective at the close of the S corporation's taxable year, and all advances and repayments are netted immediately prior to the disposition and the basis of that indebtedness is restored under Reg. § 1.1367-2(c), effective at the close of the S corporation's taxable year."

Examples illustrating Reg. § 1.1367-2(a)(2)'s rules are set forth below:

Example 9-28: Treatment of open account debt. **Part A:** A and B have been the two shareholders in Corporation S since 2000. As of the end of the 2008 taxable year, the bases of A's and B's stock are both zero. On June 1, 2009, A advances S $16,000, which is not evidenced by a written instrument. On August 1, 2009, B advances S $22,000, which is not evidenced by a written instrument. Both the $16,000 advance and the $22,000 advance are open account debt and remain outstanding at those amounts during 2009. There is no net increase under Reg. § 1.1367-2(c) for 2009. At the close of the 2009 taxable year, A's open account debt does not exceed $25,000. A therefore carries forward to the beginning of the 2010 taxable year the $16,000 as open account debt. At the close of the 2009 taxable year, B's open account debt does not exceed $25,000. B therefore carries forward to the beginning of the 2010 taxable year the $22,000 as open account debt.

¶904.14

Part B: Assume the same facts as in Part A of this example. On December 31, 2009, A's basis in the open account debt is reduced under Reg. § 1.1367-2(b) to $8,000. On April 1, 2010, S repays A $4,000 of the open account indebtedness. On September 1, 2010, A advances S an additional $1,000, which is not evidenced by a written instrument. There is no net increase under Reg. § 1.1367-2(c) in year 2010. The $4,000 April repayment S makes to A and A's $1,000 September advance are netted to result in a net repayment of $3,000 for the taxable year on A's $16,000 open account debt carried forward from 2009. Because there is no net increase in 2010, no basis of indebtedness is restored for the 2010 taxable year, and A realizes $1,500 of income on the $3,000 net repayment at the close of the 2010 taxable year. At the close of the 2010 taxable year, A's open account debt does not exceed $25,000. The net repayment of $3,000 for the taxable year on A's $16,000 open account debt carried forward from 2009 leaves A with an open account debt of $13,000 to carry forward as open account debt to the beginning of the 2011 taxable year.

Example 9-29: Treatment of shareholder indebtedness not evidenced by a written instrument which exceeds $25,000. The facts are the same as in Example 9-28 in addition to which, on February 1, 2011, S repays $5,000 of the open account debt and on March 1, 2011, A advances S $20,000, which is not evidenced by a written instrument. At the close of the 2010 taxable year, A has an open account debt of $13,000 to carry forward as open account debt to the beginning of the 2011 taxable year. The 2011 advances and repayments are netted to result in a net advance of $15,000 on A's $13,000 open account debt carried forward from 2010, increasing A's open account debt to $28,000 as of the close of the 2011 taxable year. Because A's open account debt exceeds $25,000, for any subsequent taxable year the $28,000 indebtedness will be treated in the same manner as indebtedness evidenced by a separate written instrument for the purposes of this section. Because there is no net increase in 2011, no basis of indebtedness is restored for the 2011 taxable year.

Tax Pointer 1: If Prop. Reg. § 1.1367-2 is issued in final form in the same format as proposed, tremendous bookkeeping will be required to keep track of open account borrowings from shareholders, especially so as to avoid the difficulties of the $10,000 threshold. For the unsophisticated, open account advances could become a trap for the unwary. To avoid difficulty, shareholders when making advances might consider utilizing the capital account. While bookkeeping is still required, there is no danger of crossing the $10,000 threshold. However, this utilization of the capital account will still not solve lines of credit advances and repayments. If the S corporation has C corporation earnings and profits, care must be practiced so as not to create a dividend when making distributions from the capital account, especially if the corporation has an insufficient accumulated adjustment account. For a discussion of the accumulated adjustment account, see Chapter 10.

Tax Pointer 2: To prevent ordinary income treatment from occurring on repayment of open account debt where gain will result (i.e., where debt basis has not been restored by the end of the year), shareholders should consider only making loans to the corporation by means of written notes. In this way, if a repayment results in taxable gain, the gain will be capital pursuant to Code Sec. 1271(a)(1) and case law. (See, e.g. *B. Barr*,[111] (payment of an open account debt generated ordinary income not capital gains). For further discussion of this point, see ¶ 904.08.)

¶ 905 Determination of a Shareholder's Share of Items

.01 Separately Stated Items

Each shareholder must take into account separately the shareholder's pro rata share of any item of income (including tax-exempt income), loss, deduction, or credit of the S corporation that if separately taken into account by any shareholder could affect the shareholder's tax liability for that tax year differently than if the shareholder did not take the item into account separately.[112] The separately stated items of the S corporation include, but are not limited to, the following:[113]

(i) The corporation's combined net amount of gains and losses from sales or exchanges of capital assets grouped by applicable holding periods, by applicable rate of tax, and by any other classification that may be relevant in determining the shareholder's tax liability;

(ii) The corporation's combined net amount of gains and losses from sales or exchanges of property described in Code Sec. 1231 (relating to property used in the trade or business and involuntary conversions), grouped by applicable holding periods, by applicable rate of tax, and by any other classification that may be relevant in determining the shareholder's tax liability;

(iii) Charitable contributions, grouped by the percentage limitations of Code Sec. 170(b) (i.e., 20%, 30% and 50% charities), paid by the corporation within the tax year of the corporation;

(iv) The taxes described in Code Sec. 901 that have been paid (or accrued) by the corporation to foreign countries or to possessions of the United States;

(v) Each of the corporation's separate items involved in the determination of credits against tax allowable under part IV of subchapter A (Code Sec. 21 and following) of the Internal Revenue Code, except for any credit allowed under Code Sec. 34 (relating to certain uses of gasoline and special fuels);

(vi) Each of the corporation's separate items of gains and losses from wagering transactions (Code Sec. 165(d)); soil and water conservation expenditures (Code Sec. 175); deduction under an election to expense certain depreciable business expenses (Code Sec. 179); medical, dental, etc., expenses (Code Sec. 213); the additional itemized deductions for individuals provided in part VII of subchapter B (Code Sec. 212 and following)

---

[111] 39 TCM 83, Dec. 36,714(M), TC Memo, 1980-3.   [113] *Ibid.*
[112] Reg. § 1.1366-1(a)(2).

of the Internal Revenue Code; and any other itemized deductions for which the limitations on itemized deductions under Code Secs. 67 or 68 applies;

(vii) Any of the corporation's items of portfolio income or loss, and expenses related thereto, as defined under Code Sec. 469;

(viii) The corporation's tax-exempt income. For purposes of subchapter S, tax-exempt income is income that is permanently excludible from gross income in all circumstances in which the applicable provision of the Internal Revenue Code applies. For example, Reg. § 1.1366-1(a)(2)(viii) provides that income that is excludible from gross income under Code Sec. 101 (certain death benefits) or Code Sec. 103 (interest on state and local bonds) is tax-exempt income, while income that is excludible from gross income under Code Sec. 108 (income from discharge of indebtedness)[114] or Code Sec. 109 (improvements by lessee on lessor's property) is not tax-exempt income;

(ix) The corporation's adjustments described in Code Secs. 56 and 58, and items of tax preference described in Code Sec. 57; and

(x) Any item identified in guidance (including forms and instructions) issued by the Commissioner as an item required to be separately stated.

.02 Nonseparately Stated Items of Income or Loss

After determining the separately stated items of income, gain, loss, etc., each shareholder is required to take into account the shareholder's pro rata share of the nonseparately computed income or loss of the S corporation.[115] Nonseparately computed income or loss is determined by aggregating all S corporation items of income, gain, loss, and deductions not required to be separately stated.

.03 Separate Activities Requirement

An S corporation must report, and each shareholder must take into account in the shareholder's return, the shareholder's pro rata share of an S corporation's items of income, loss, deduction, or credit (separately and nonseparately) for each of the corporation's activities as defined by Code Sec. 469 on an activity-by-activity basis.[116]

.04 Aggregation of Deductions or Exclusions and Their Limitations

Generally shareholders are required to aggregate their separate deductions or exclusions with their pro rata shares of the S corporation's separately stated deductions or exclusions in determining the amount of their allowable deduction or exclusion, such as the Code Sec. 179 expense.[117]

Example 9-30: In 2004, Corporation Merkel, an S corporation, purchases and places in service Code Sec. 179 property costing $10,000. Corporation Merkel elects to expense the entire cost of the property. Shareholder Al Park

---

[114] For a discussion of discharge of indebtedness income, see ¶ 610.

[115] Reg. § 1.1366-1(a)(3).

[116] Reg. § 1.1366-1(a)(4).

[117] Reg. § 1.1366-1(a)(5).

owns 50 percent of the stock of Corporation Merkel. Park's pro rata share of this item after Corporation Merkel applies the Code Sec. 179(b) limitations is $5,000. Because the aggregate amount of Park's pro rata share and separately acquired Code Sec. 179 expense may not exceed $100,000 plus the inflation adjustment (the aggregate maximum cost that may be taken into account under Code Sec. 179(a) for the applicable tax year), Park may elect to expense up to $95,000 of separately acquired Code Sec. 179 property that is purchased and placed in service in 2004, subject to the limitations of Code Sec. 179(b).

Treasury Decision 8852 (December 21, 1999), in discussing the example that Example 9-28 is adapted from, states the following:

> The example is intended to illustrate that a shareholder may expense only up to the amount allowable under section 179 in any given year regardless of whether the property is owned individually or through an S corporation. The example is not intended to imply that a shareholder must elect to expense property held in an S corporation before it can expense any separately acquired property. However, once an S corporation elects to expense property under section 179, a shareholder will generally elect to expense personal property only to the extent the shareholder's pro rata share of the corporation's section 179 expense does not exceed the shareholder's individual limitation under section 179(b).

.05 Determination of a Shareholder's Tax Liability

An S corporation must report, and a shareholder is required to take into account in the shareholder's return, the shareholder's "pro rata share," whether or not distributed, of the S corporation's items of income, loss, deduction, or credit.[118] A shareholder's pro rata share is determined in accordance with the provisions of Code Sec. 1377(a) and the regulations thereunder. The shareholder takes these items into account in determining the shareholder's taxable income and tax liability for the shareholder's tax year with or within which the tax year of the corporation ends. If the shareholder dies (or if the shareholder is an estate or trust and the estate or trust terminates) before the end of the tax year of the corporation, the shareholder's pro rata share of these items is taken into account on the shareholder's final return.

Characterization of items constituting pro rata share of income, loss, deduction, credit, etc. A shareholder must report his, her, or its pro rata share of income, loss, deduction, credit, etc. Generally the character of any item of income, loss, deduction, or credit is determined by the S corporation and retains that character in the hands of the shareholder.[119] For example, if an S corporation has capital gain on the sale or exchange of a capital asset, a shareholder's pro rata share of that gain will also be characterized as a capital gain regardless of whether the shareholder is otherwise a dealer in that type of property. Similarly, if an S corporation engages in an activity that is not for profit (Code Sec. 183), a shareholder's pro rata share of the S corporation's deductions will be characterized as not for profit. Also, if an S corporation makes a charitable contribution to a qualified charitable organization, a shareholder's pro rata share of the S corporation's charitable contribution will be characterized as made to a qualified organization.

---

[118] Code Sec. 1366(a)(1) and Reg. §1.1366-1(a)(1).   [119] Reg. §1.1366-1(b)(1).

Exceptions to the recharacterization rules.

Dealer property. If an S corporation is formed or availed of by any shareholder or group of shareholders for a principal purpose of selling or exchanging contributed property that in the hands of the shareholder or shareholders would not have produced capital gain if sold or exchanged by the shareholder or shareholders because they were dealers, then the gain on the sale or exchange of the property recognized by the corporation is not treated as a capital gain.[120]

There is no time period as in partnerships or two-or-more-person limited liability companies for cleansing dealer-tainted property.[121] When the courts have faced the issue of dealer taint prior to the adoption of the recent regulations under Code Sec. 1366, shareholders have won some victories.[122]

Contribution of capital loss property. If an S corporation is formed or availed of by any shareholder or group of shareholders for a principal purpose of selling or exchanging contributed property that in the hands of the shareholder or shareholders would have produced capital loss if sold or exchanged by the shareholder or shareholders, then the loss on the sale or exchange of the property recognized by the corporation is treated as a capital loss to the extent that, immediately before the contribution, the adjusted basis of the property in the hands of the shareholder or shareholders exceeded the fair market value of the property.[123] However, note that there is no statutory authority for the provision in Reg. § 1.1366-1(b)(3). Consequently, it is foreseeable that litigation will develop to challenge Reg. § 1.1366-1(b)(3).

Gross income of a shareholder. Generally where it is necessary to determine the amount or character of the gross income of a shareholder, the shareholder's gross income includes the shareholder's pro rata share of the gross income of the S corporation.[124] The shareholder's pro rata share of the gross income of the S corporation is the amount of gross income of the corporation used in deriving the shareholder's pro rata share of S corporation taxable income or loss.

Net operating loss deduction of a shareholder. To determine a net operating loss deduction under Code Sec. 172, a shareholder of an S corporation must take into account the shareholder's pro rata share of items of income, loss, deduction, or credit of the corporation.[125] In determining under Code Sec. 172(d)(4) the nonbusiness deductions allowable to a shareholder of an S corporation (arising from both corporate sources and any other sources), the shareholder separately takes into account the shareholder's pro rata share of the deductions of the corporation that are not attributable to a trade or business and combines this amount with the shareholder's nonbusiness deductions from any other sources. The shareholder also separately takes into account the shareholder's pro rata share of the gross income of the corporation not derived from a trade or business and combines this amount with the shareholder's nonbusiness income from all other sources.

---

[120] Reg. § 1.1366-1(b)(3).
[121] See Code Sec. 724.
[122] See ¶ 606 for a discussion of this area.

[123] Reg. § 1.1366-1(b)(3).
[124] Reg. § 1.1366-1(c)(1).
[125] Reg. § 1.1366-1(e).

Items affecting a shareholder's basis. The following three items can affect basis.

No pass-through of Code Sec. 34 credit. There is no pass-through to S corporation shareholders of any credit allowable under Code Sec. 34 (certain uses of gasoline and special fuels).[126]

Reduction in pass-through for tax imposed on built-in gains under Code Sec. 1374. If a tax is imposed on an S corporation under Code Sec. 1374 for any tax year of the S corporation, the amount of the tax imposed is treated as a loss sustained by the S corporation during the tax year and reduces the amount of pass-through items.[127] The character of the deemed loss is determined by allocating the loss proportionately among the recognized built-in gain items giving rise to the tax and attributing the character of each recognized built-in gain item to the allocable portion of the loss.

Reduction in pass-through for tax imposed on excess net passive income. If a tax is imposed on an S corporation under Code Sec. 1375 for any tax year of the S corporation, each item of passive investment income is to be reduced by an amount that bears the same ratio to the amount of the tax as the amount of the item bears to the total net passive investment income for that tax year.[128]

¶ 906 Limitations on Losses and Deductions

For a shareholder to deduct losses, whether separately stated or not, the shareholder must have sufficient basis in stock and debt.[129] The total amount of loss and deduction that an S corporation shareholder can claim in an S corporation's tax year cannot exceed the sum of (1) the adjusted basis of the shareholder's stock and (2) the shareholder's adjusted basis in S corporation debt.[130] A shareholder may want to dispose of some stock, notwithstanding that there are suspended losses. Reg. § 1.1366-2(a)(5) details what occurs with suspended losses if a shareholder does not dispose of his, her or its entire stock interest.[131]

.01 Carryover of Disallowance

The net amount of losses and deductions allocated to a shareholder for a tax year that is in excess of the sum of (1) the adjusted basis of the shareholder's stock in an S corporation and (2) any indebtedness of the S corporation to the shareholder is not allowed for the tax year.[132] However, any disallowed loss or deduction is treated as incurred by the corporation in the corporation's first succeeding tax year, and subsequent tax years, with respect to a shareholder to the extent that the shareholder's adjusted basis of stock or indebtedness exceeds zero. Unused losses may be carried forward in this manner indefinitely.

> **Tax Pointer:** See ¶ 906.04 for a discussion of the treatment of suspended losses where, pursuant to Code Sec. 1041(a), stock which has such losses are transferred from one spouse to the other.

---

[126] Reg. § 1.1366-4(a).
[127] Reg. § 1.1366-4(b).
[128] Reg. § 1.1366-4(c).
[129] Code Sec. 1366(d)(1).

[130] Reg. § 1.1366-2(a)(1).
[131] For a discussion of Reg. § 1.1366-2(a)(5), see ¶ 1124.01.
[132] Reg. § 1.1366-2(a)(2).

.02 Determination of Basis for Taking Losses

A shareholder cannot deduct losses in excess of basis in stock and debt.[133] The procedure to determine both stock basis and debt basis is detailed below.

Stock basis. A shareholder generally determines tax basis in stock for deducting losses by taking into account only increases in basis under Code Sec. 1367(a)(1) (income, nonseparately computed income items and excess depletion) for the tax year and decreases in basis under Code Sec. 1367(a)(2)(A), (D), and (E) (relating to distributions, noncapital, nondeductible expenses, and certain oil and gas depletion deductions) for the tax year.[134] In determining this loss limitation amount, the shareholder disregards decreases in basis under Code Sec. 1367(a)(2)(B) and (C) (for losses and deductions, including losses and deductions previously disallowed) for the tax year. However, if the shareholder has in effect for the tax year an election under Reg. § 1.1367-1(g) to decrease basis by items of loss and deduction prior to decreasing basis by noncapital, nondeductible expenses and certain oil and gas depletion deductions, the shareholder also disregards decreases in basis under Code Sec. 1367(a)(2)(D) and (E).[135]

Debt basis. A shareholder determines the shareholder's adjusted basis in indebtedness of the corporation for purposes of taking losses and deductions without regard to any adjustment for distributions for the tax year.[136] Prop. Reg. § 1.1367-2(a)(2) prescribes special rules regarding open account debt and when recognition of losses and deductions can occur. For a discussion of this area, see ¶ 904.14.

Allocation procedures when losses exceed stock and debt basis. If a shareholder's separately and/or nonseparately stated losses from the S corporation exceed the shareholder's basis in stock and debt, then the limitation on losses must be allocated among the shareholder's pro rata share of each loss or deduction.[137] The shareholder cannot, for example, deduct his or her entire share of S corporation charitable contributions and defer his or her share of S corporation capital losses.

Unused corporate losses carry over indefinitely. If a shareholder cannot deduct S corporation losses due to inadequate basis in stock and debt, the loss is carried over until one of three events occur: (1) the shareholder dies; (2) the shareholder disposes of his, her or its stock by sale, or an individual shareholder disposes of the stock by gift; or (3) the S election is terminated (however, a shareholder can take losses during the post-termination transition period (PTTP) on stock).[138]

Any loss or deduction allocated to a shareholder is personal to the shareholder and cannot in any manner be transferred to another person.[139] If a shareholder transfers some but not all of the shareholder's stock in the corporation, the amount of any of the shareholder's loss or deduction is not reduced and the transferee does

---

[133] Code Sec. 1366(d)(1).

[134] Reg. § 1.1366-2(a)(3)(i). See discussion at ¶ 903.02.

[135] See ¶ 903.06 for further discussion of this point.

[136] Reg. § 1.1366-2(a)(3)(ii). See discussion at ¶ 904.05.

[137] Reg. § 1.1366-2(a)(4).

[138] Code Sec. 1366(d)(2). See ¶ 912 for a discussion of the post-termination transition period.

[139] Reg. § 1.1366-2(a)(5).

not acquire any portion of the disallowed loss or deduction. If a shareholder transfers all of the shareholder's stock in the corporation, any unused loss or deduction is permanently lost.

>*Tax Pointer:* See ¶ 906.04 for the special rules regarding suspended losses for divorced couples.

.03 Effect of Liquidations, Reorganizations, and Corporate Separations on Carryover of Losses

Chapter 12 discusses liquidations, reorganizations, and separations. If a shareholder has unused losses, the following special rules apply to their carryover.

Liquidations and reorganizations. If a corporation acquires the assets of an S corporation in a transaction to which Code Sec. 381(a) applies (relating to the carryover of tax attributes in a merger or reorganization), any unused loss or deduction with respect to a shareholder of the distributor or transferor S corporation is available to that shareholder as a shareholder of the acquiring corporation.[140] Thus, where the acquiring corporation is an S corporation, a loss or deduction of a shareholder of the distributor or transferor S corporation disallowed prior to or during the tax year of the transaction is treated as incurred by the acquiring S corporation with respect to that shareholder if the shareholder is a shareholder of the acquiring S corporation after the transaction. Where the acquiring corporation is a C corporation, a post-termination transition period arises the day after the last day that an S corporation was in existence and the rules discussed at ¶ 912 apply with respect to any shareholder of the acquired S corporation that is also a shareholder of the acquiring C corporation after the transaction.

Corporate separations. If an S corporation transfers a portion of its assets constituting an active trade or business to another corporation in a tax-free reorganization under Code Sec. 368(a)(1)(D), and immediately thereafter the stock and securities of the controlled corporation are distributed in a tax-free spin-off, split-off, or split-up under Code Sec. 355, any unused loss or deduction for a shareholder of the distributing S corporation immediately before the transaction is allocated between the distributing corporation and the controlled corporation for the shareholder.[141] The amount of unused loss or deduction allocated to the distributing (or controlled) corporation for the shareholder is an amount that bears the same ratio to each item of unused loss or deduction as the value of the shareholder's stock in the distributing (or controlled) corporation bears to the total value of the shareholder's stock in the distributing and controlled corporations, in each case as determined immediately after the distribution.

.04 Transfer of Suspended Losses Incident to Divorce

Code Sec. 1366(d)(2) was amended for taxable years beginning after December 31, 2004 to prescribe that if S corporate stock is transferred pursuant to a marital break-up under Code Sec. 1041(a), and there are suspended losses or distributions with respect to the stock received by the transferee, any suspended losses or deduction in terms of this stock will be treated as incurred by the S

---

[140] Reg. § 1.1366-2(c)(1).

[141] Reg. § 1.1366-2(c)(2).

corporation in the succeeding taxable year. Thus, if the transferee has basis due to undistributed S corporate income, the transferee can take the losses to the extent of the undistributed income allocated to the transferee's stock, assuming that all of the conditions are satisfied. (Under prior law, any suspended losses on transferred stock would be lost forever.)

> *Tax Pointer 1:* The amendment to Code Sec. 1366(d)(2) did not detail what would occur if the transferring shareholder kept some of the S corporate stock. Presumably, the transferee spouse would receive his or her pro rata share of any suspended losses.

> *Tax Pointer 2:* Not detailed is how the transferee-spouse recognizes the suspended losses, if the losses arose because of a passive activity, or the transferor-spouse was a "passive" shareholder under Code Sec. 469's rules.

¶ 907   Creating Basis So That Current Losses Can Be Deducted

.01   *Methods of Creating Basis*

While Code Sec. 1366(d)(2) allows S corporation losses to be carried over if a shareholder has insufficient basis in stock and/or debt, obviously, as a general rule, it is better to deduct S corporation losses currently rather than defer them. Thus, care should be taken to review the S corporation books prior to the end of the tax year to determine if it is operating at a gain or loss, and if it is operating at a loss, to determine if the shareholders have enough basis in their stock and/or debt to take the loss.

If there is not sufficient basis, the shareholders can undertake several steps to correct the problem; for example, if there is sufficient time, try to generate additional income to counteract the loss or contribute funds or property before the end of the year to establish basis. Alternatively, cut expenses to reduce the amount of loss to the extent of the shareholder's basis in stock and debt. As to the second alternative, care must be exercised. Initially, the shareholder(s) may not have the funds to "pump into" the S corporation to take the losses. Thus, the shareholders may wish to "cut their losses" and leave the S corporation in limbo or terminate the S election, thereby creating a C corporation with future net operating losses (i.e., it will incur losses in C years) that can be marketed as a "loss corporation." Assuming that the shareholders have the funds and the desire to place them in the S corporation, the question to resolve is how to make this additional input-loan or acquire additional stock. The shareholders may wish to be creditors rather than just mere shareholders and lend money to the corporation to obtain basis. However, being the creditor of an S corporation could cause adverse tax consequences.

Case law. Case law provides some interesting examples of creativity to create basis. In *Maguire v. Commissioner*,[142] there was a family brother sister S corporation situation; one, a car dealership, where the majority ownership was owned by Mom and Dad and was not profitable; the other, a car loan company, where the majority interest was owned by the son and was profitable. The profitable S corporation financed the sales of the car dealership. The profitable corporation distributed its

---

[142] TC Memo 2012-160.

car financing loans to the shareholders. The parents contributed the receivables to the car company. However, there was still a shortfall. So, the son loaned his parents accounts receivable by means of a note which they in turn contributed to the car dealership to create basis for purposes of taking losses in this S corporation. The court sustained this means for the parents to create stock basis for purposes of deducting losses.

.02 Maintaining Accurate Records

It is critical that the shareholder maintain accurate records of basis. Because a shareholder is required to take separately and nonseparately stated loss items into basis at the end of the S corporation's tax year,[143] it is essential that the shareholder know his, her, or its basis before the end of the corporation's tax year.[144] Accordingly, good tax planning would dictate that a shareholder should undertake a stock and debt analysis in sufficient time before the year end so that if there are going to be S corporation losses for the year, the shareholder will know it.

¶ 908 Preparer Penalties

In an effort to curb tax abuse, Congress amended Code Sec. 6694 to provide, effective for tax returns due after December 21, 2007 that the term "income tax return preparer" is changed to "tax return preparer;" thus preparers of estate and gift tax, employment tax, and excise tax returns, and returns of exempt organizations are subject to tax return preparer penalties.

Code Sec. 6694 also altered the standards of conduct that must be met to avoid imposition of the penalties for preparing a return with respect to which there is an understatement of tax. First, the provision replaces the realistic possibility standard for undisclosed positions with a requirement that there be a reasonable belief that the tax treatment of the position was more likely than not the proper treatment. The provision replaces the not-frivolous standard accompanied by disclosure with the requirement that there be a reasonable basis for the tax treatment of the position accompanied by disclosure.

The provision also increases the first-tier penalty from $250 to the greater of $1,000 or 50 percent of the income derived (or to be derived) by the tax return preparer from the preparation of a return or claim with respect to which the penalty is imposed. The provision increases the second-tier penalty from $1,000 to the greater of $5,000 or 50 percent of the income derived (or to be derived) by the tax return preparer.

If the tax return preparer can show that he or she acted in good faith and can show good cause, Code Sec. 6694(a)(3) prescribes that Code Sec. 6694's penalty will not apply.

In *Papermaster*,[145] a tax return preparer (a CPA and an attorney) had a preparer penalty imposed against him for negligence when he deducted an S corporation

---

[143] Code Sec. 1366(a)(1) and Reg. § 1.1366-1(a)(1).

[144] See *D.J. Sauvigne*, 30 TCM 123, Dec. 30,649(M), TC Memo. 1971-30 (taxpayer unable to deduct a loss because he could not prove his basis).

[145] *M. Papermaster*, DC Wis., 81-1 ustc ¶ 9217. Aff'd CA-7 (unpublished order No. 80-1612, 6/25/82).

loss in excess of the shareholder's basis in stock in violation of Code Sec. 1374(c). If a tax return preparer commits fraud in the preparation of the return, *Vincent Allen*[146] a case of first impression, holds that there is an *unlimited* (emphasis added) statute of limitation for collection of tax and interest on the fraudulent return from the taxpayer, not the regular three year limitation period. In reaching its decision, the court stated:

> Taxpayers are charged with the knowledge, awareness, and responsibility for their tax returns. The taxpayer, not the preparer, has the ultimate responsibility to file his or her return and pay the tax due. This duty cannot generally be avoided by relying on an agent. We do not find it unduly burdensome for taxpayers to review their returns for items that are obviously false or incorrect. It is every taxpayer's obligation. Taxpayer cannot hide behind an agent's fraudulent preparation of his returns and escape paying tax . . . The Commissioner has just as much need for an extended limitations period to investigate and examine taxpayers who sign and allow to be filed returns that greatly overstate expenses or include fictitious expenses whether the fraud was committed by the taxpayer or the taxpayer's preparer. To find otherwise would allow a taxpayer to receive the benefit of a fraudulent return by hiding behind the preparer. Taxpayers whose returns are fraudulent owing to fraud committed by the preparers would escape their tax liability if the Commissioner were unable to identify or investigate the fraud within the normal 3-year period. (Citations omitted)

¶ 909 Alternative Minimum Tax (AMT) Effect on Basis

An S corporation is not liable for alternative minimum tax.[147] However, the corporation may pass through to shareholders items of S corporation activity that are subject to AMT, such as MACRS depreciation. Accordingly, to prevent problems, separate basis records should be maintained for AMT purposes and for regular tax purposes to assist a shareholder in computing his, her, or its income tax.

¶ 910 Applying Losses to Basis

The basis rules of Code Sec. 1366 that limit the deduction of losses to the amount of shareholder's basis are applied first before the application of Code Sec. 165(g) and Code Sec. 166(d) to any tax year of the shareholder in which the stock or debt of the S corporation becomes worthless.[148] If stock, which is a capital asset, becomes worthless during the tax year, the loss is a capital loss.[149] If a non-business bad debt[150] becomes worthless, the loss is a capital loss.[151]

> *Example 9-31:* Robb Inc., a calendar-year S corporation, has one shareholder, Darren Robb. Robb's beginning basis in stock in 2010 is $10,000. During 2010, Robb Inc. has an operating loss of $8,000 and goes bankrupt. The loss for Darren Robb is computed as follows:

---

[146] 128 TC No. 4.

[147] Code Sec. 56(g)(6).

[148] Code Sec. 1367(b)(3).

[149] Code Sec. 165(g). But see Code Sec. 1244 which allows losses on the sale or worthlessness of qualified small business stock to be deducted as ordinary losses

(up to $50,000 per year for unmarried taxpayers, $100,000 for married taxpayers).

[150] A nonbusiness bad debt is any debt other than one created or acquired in a taxpayer's trade or business, or one involving loss proximately related to the trade or business in which the taxpayer is engaged when the debt becomes worthless.

[151] Code Sec. 166(d).

Stock basis before loss	$10,000
Deductible net operating loss	8,000
Stock basis	2,000
Capital loss due to stock becoming worthless .	2,000
Stock basis	$ 0

S corporation shareholders cannot pick and choose when they want to deduct losses. If they have basis at the time the S corporation incurs a loss, the shareholders must deduct the losses at that time; they cannot defer recognition.[152]

¶ 911 Passive Income and Losses

.01 Introduction

The thrust of the Tax Reform Act of 1986 was to prevent taxpayers from using either net losses from passive activities or credits arising from passive activities to offset income attributable to other, nonpassive activities. To accomplish this objective, Congress adopted or amended a number of provisions, with one major provision being Code Sec. 469, "Passive Activity Losses and Credits Limited," which is effective for tax years beginning after December 31, 1986.

While it is beyond the scope of this book to provide a detailed discussion of Code Sec. 469, a brief general discussion as it applies to S corporations and its shareholders is given below.

Code Sec. 469 prescribes that a loss from a passive activity (a PAL) cannot be deducted against other types of income such as wages, interest, and dividends; the losses are generally deductible only against income from other passive activities.

.02 Definition of Passive Activity

Code Sec. 469(c)(1) defines a "passive activity" as (1) "any activity which involves the conduct of any trade or business where the taxpayer does not materially participate" and (2) a "rental activity" regardless of whether the taxpayer materially participates. Code Sec. 469(c)(2) excludes a working interest in oil and gas property. The Internal Revenue Code does not define "activity"; rather, Code Sec. 469(l)(1) prescribes that the regulations define the term.[153]

.03 Definition of Activity

A taxpayer's trade or business activities and rental activities must be grouped for purposes of applying the passive activity loss and credit limitation rules of Code Sec. 469.[154] A taxpayer's activities include those conducted through C corporations that are subject to Code Sec. 469, S corporations, and partnerships.

---

[152] *Barnes*, TC Memo 2012-80, *aff'd*, 2013-1 ¶ 50,267 (DC Cir. 2013).

[153] Code Sec. 469(l) prescribes that the regulations are to define a number of such terms, such as "material participation," what items of gross income are to be in-cluded in the computation of passive income or loss, etc. Consult Code Sec. 469(l) to determine what items are defined by the regulations.

[154] Reg. § 1.469-4(a).

Trade or business activities. Trade or business activities are activities (other than rental activities), that

- involve the conduct of a trade or business (within the meaning of Code Sec. 162);

- are conducted in anticipation of the commencement of a trade or business; or

- involve research or experimental expenditures that are deductible under Code Sec. 174 (or would be deductible if the taxpayer adopted the method described in Code Sec. 174(a)).[155]

Generally the determination of whether an activity is passive or nonpassive is done at the S corporation shareholder level. However, there are certain activities (namely, real estate) where the determination in part is made at the corporate level.[156]

Method for determining activities. A determination has to be made as to what an "activity" is. Two tests are used—the appropriate economic unit test and the facts and circumstance test.[157]

Tax Pointer: To determine an "activity," a shareholder is at a crossroads. To determine if a shareholder materially participates by counting hours (see Tests 1, 3, and 4 discussed at ¶ 911.04), it is better to group activities as one. However, if a shareholder wants to recognize unused PALs on disposal of an activity, it would be easier if the activities were separated.

Appropriate economic unit test. One or more trade or business activities or rental activities may be treated as a single activity if the activities constitute an appropriate economic unit for the measurement of gain or loss for purposes of Code Sec. 469.[158]

Facts and circumstances test. A facts and circumstances test to determine an activity is provided in the regulations.[159] Basically, the grouping of activities depends upon all the relevant facts and circumstances. A taxpayer may use any reasonable method of applying the relevant facts and circumstances in grouping activities. The factors listed below from Reg. § 1.469-4(c)(2) (not all of which are necessary for a taxpayer to treat more than one activity as a single activity) are given the greatest weight in determining whether activities constitute an appropriate economic unit for the measurement of gain or loss.

  (i) Similarities and differences in types of trades or businesses;

 (ii) The extent of common control;

(iii) The extent of common ownership;

 (iv) Geographical location; and

  (v) Interdependencies between or among the activities (for example, the extent to which the activities purchase or sell goods between or among

---

[155] Reg. § 1.469-4(b)(1).
[156] Temp. Reg. § 1.469-2T(e)(1).
[157] Reg. § 1.469-4(c)(1) and (2).

[158] Reg. § 1.469-4(c)(1).
[159] Reg. § 1.469-4(c)(2).

themselves, involve products or services that are normally provided together, have the same customers, have the same employees, or are accounted for with a single set of books and records).

Example 9-32: Charlie Crane has a significant ownership interest in a bakery and a movie theater at a shopping mall in Baltimore and in a bakery and a movie theater in Philadelphia. In this case, after taking into account all the relevant facts and circumstances, there may be more than one reasonable method for grouping Crane's activities. For instance, depending on the relevant facts and circumstances, the following groupings may or may not be permissible: a single activity; a movie theater activity and a bakery activity; a Baltimore activity and a Philadelphia activity; or four separate activities. Moreover, once Crane groups these activities into appropriate economic units, Reg. § 1.469-4(e) requires Crane to continue using that grouping in subsequent tax years unless a material change in the facts and circumstances makes it clearly inappropriate.

Example 9-33: Bonnie Blake, an individual, is a shareholder in a business that sells nonfood items to grocery stores (S corporation Loomworks). Blake also is a shareholder in a S corporation that owns and operates a trucking business (S corporation Quester). The two S corporations are under common control. The predominant portion of Quester's business is transporting goods for Loomworks, and Quester is the only trucking business in which Blake is involved. Blake appropriately treats Loomwork's wholesale activity and Quester's trucking activity as a single activity.

Restraints on grouping certain activities. A rental activity may not be grouped with a trade or business activity unless the activities being grouped together constitute an appropriate economic unit as defined in Reg. § 1.469-4(d)(1):

(A) The rental activity is insubstantial in relation to the trade or business activity;

(B) The trade or business activity is insubstantial in relation to the rental activity; or

(C) Each owner of the trade or business activity has the same proportionate ownership interest in the rental activity, in which case the portion of the rental activity that involves the rental of items of property for use in the trade or business activity may be grouped with the trade or business activity.

Examples 9-34 through 9-36 illustrate the limitation of Reg. § 1.469-4(d)(1).

Example 9-34: Harriet and Walter Moore are married and file a joint return. Harriet is the sole shareholder of an S corporation that conducts a grocery store trade or business activity. Walter is the sole shareholder of an S corporation that owns and rents out a building. Part of the building is rented to Harriet's grocery store trade or business activity (the grocery store rental). The grocery store rental and the grocery store trade or business are not insubstantial in relation to each other. Because they file a joint return, Harriet and Walter Moore are treated as one taxpayer for purposes of Code Sec. 469.

¶911.03

Therefore, the sole owner of the trade or business activity (taxpayer Harriet-Walter Moore) is also the sole owner of the rental activity. Consequently, each owner of the trade or business activity has the same proportionate ownership interest in the rental activity. Accordingly, the grocery store rental and the grocery store trade or business activity may be grouped together into a single trade or business activity.

Example 9-35: Attorney Dick Dome is a sole practitioner in Boise, Idaho. Dome also wholly owns residential real estate in Boise that Dome rents to third parties. Dome's law practice is a trade or business activity. The residential real estate is a rental activity and is insubstantial in relation to Dome's law practice. Under the facts and circumstances, the law practice and the residential real estate do not constitute an appropriate economic unit for grouping activities. Therefore, Dome may not treat the law practice and the residential real estate as a single activity.

Example 9-36: Taxpayers Dunn, Eaton, Fleming, Golden, and Hooks are doctors who operate separate medical practices. Dunn invested in a tax shelter several years ago that generates passive losses, and the other doctors intend to invest in real estate that will generate passive losses. The five taxpayer doctors form a partnership to engage in the trade or business of acquiring and operating X-ray equipment. In exchange for equipment contributed to the partnership, they receive limited partnership interests. The partnership is managed by a general partner selected by the taxpayers; the taxpayers do not materially participate in its operations. Substantially all of the partnership's services are provided to the taxpayers or their patients, roughly in proportion to the doctors' interests in the partnership. Fees for the partnership's services are set at a level equal to the amounts that would be charged if the partnership were dealing with the taxpayers at arm's length and are expected to assure the partnership a profit. The taxpayers treat the partnership's services as a separate activity from their medical practices and offset the income generated by the partnership against their passive losses.

For each of the taxpayers, the taxpayer's own medical practice and the services provided by the partnership constitute an appropriate economic unit, but the services provided by the partnership do not separately constitute an appropriate economic unit. Moreover, a principal purpose of treating the medical practices and the partnership's services as separate activities is an attempt to create passive income when none existed before. Accordingly, the taxpayers are required to treat their medical practices and their interests in the partnership as a single activity, regardless of whether the separate medical practices are conducted through C corporations subject to Code Sec. 469, S corporations, partnerships, or sole proprietorships.

Tax Pointer: For cases where a grouping has been sustained, see the discussion at ¶ 911.10.

Grouping real property rentals and personal property rentals prohibited. An activity involving the rental of real property and an activity involving the rental of personal property may not be treated as a single activity (other than personal

¶911.03

property provided in connection with the real property or real property provided in connection with the personal property).[160]

Grouping activities on Form 8582. An S corporation must group or separate its passive activities pursuant to the rules provided in Reg. § 1.469-4(c)(1) and (2).[161] An S corporation shareholder, upon receipt of the S corporation's Form 1120S, K-1 is then required to group the S corporation's activities with the shareholder's own activities and other activities reflected on K-1s received from other pass-through entities (e.g., other S corporations, partnerships, etc.) (the shareholders do this grouping on Form 8582). Additionally, an activity that a taxpayer conducts through a C corporation subject to Code Sec. 469 may be grouped with another activity of the taxpayer, but only for purposes of determining whether the taxpayer materially or significantly participates in the other activity.[162]

Consistency requirements for grouping of passive activities. Once a taxpayer has grouped activities in a tax year to determine the application of the passive activities, the taxpayer may not regroup these activities in subsequent tax years unless the original grouping was clearly inappropriate, or there has been a material change in facts and circumstances that makes the original grouping inappropriate.[163]

Activities conducted by limited partners and limited entrepreneurs. Rules are provided in the regulations for grouping of activities where activities are conducted by limited partners and limited entrepreneurs in tax-shelter activities.[164] A "limited entrepreneur" is defined as a person who has an interest in an enterprise other than as a limited partner who does not actively participate in the management of such enterprise.[165]

.04 Material Participation

A passive activity is one where the taxpayer does not materially participate.[166] When a shareholder materially participates in an activity to make the income or loss for that activity "active," then the taxpayer can deduct the loss in the tax year incurred. If the loss is "passive," then the loss can only be deducted against passive income from that or other passive activities.[167]

The determination of whether each item of S corporation income or loss reported on the shareholder's Form 1120S, K-1 is passive or active is made according to the participation of the shareholder in the activity(ies) that generated such item, with the determination geared to the S corporation's tax year, not the tax year of the shareholder.[168]

Example 9-37: Andrea Brown, a calendar-year individual, is a shareholder in a S corporation that has a tax year ending January 31. During its tax

---

[160] Reg. § 1.469-4(d)(2).

[161] Reg. § 1.469-4(d)(5).

[162] Reg. § 1.469-4(d)(5)(ii). See ¶ 911.10 for a discussion of the tax-planning possibilities with respect to grouping activities.

[163] Reg. § 1.469-4(e). See ¶ 911.10 for a discussion of the tax-planning possibilities with respect to grouping activities.

[164] Reg. § 1.469-4(d)(3).

[165] Code Sec. 464(e).

[166] Code Sec. 469(c). Real estate activities are generally considered passive regardless of the level of participation by the taxpayer, subject to certain exceptions, namely Code Sec. 469(c)(7).

[167] Code Sec. 469(h).

[168] Temp. Reg. § 1.469-2T(e)(1).

year ending on January 31, 2000, the S corporation engages in a single trade or business activity. For the period from February 1, 1999, through January 31, 2000, Brown does not materially participate in this activity. In Brown's calendar-year 2000 return, Brown's distributive share of the S corporation's gross income and deductions from the activity must be treated as passive activity gross income and passive activity deductions without regard to Brown's participation in the activity from February 1, 2000, through December 31, 2000.

Tests to determine material participation. A shareholder is deemed to materially participate if the individual satisfies one of the following seven tests described in Reg. § 1.469-5T.

  (1) **500-hour test.** The individual participates in the activity for more than 500 hours during such year.

  (2) **Substantially all test.** The individual's participation in the activity for the tax year constitutes substantially all of the participation in such activity of all individuals (including individuals who are not owners of interests in the activity) for such year.

  (3) **100-hour test.** The individual participates in the activity for more than 100 hours during the tax year, and such individual's participation in the activity for the tax year is not less than the participation in the activity of any other individual (including individuals who are not owners of interests in the activity) for such year).

  (4) **Significant participation test.** The activity is a significant participation activity (within the meaning of paragraph (c) of this section) for the tax year, and the individual's aggregate participation in all significant participation activities during such year exceeds 500 hours. *Gregg*[169] allowed a taxpayer, utilizing this test, to group activities arising from his C corporation with activities from his LLC, where he was a passive member, to deduct losses in a taxable year. While *Gregg* dealt with an LLC for purposes of applying the significant participation test, it should be equally applicable to a situation involving a C corporation and an S corporation, with the S corporation being substituted for the LLC in the *Gregg* situation.

  (5) **5-out-of-10-year test.** The individual materially participated in the activity for any five tax years (whether or not consecutive) during the ten tax years that immediately precede the tax year.

  (6) **Personal service activity test.** The activity is a personal service activity and the individual materially participated in the activity for any three tax years (whether or not consecutive) preceding the tax year.

  (7) **Facts and circumstances test.** Based on all of the facts and circumstances, the individual participates in the activity on a regular, continuous, and substantial basis during such year.

---

[169] *S.A. Gregg*, DC Ore., 2001-1 USTC ¶ 50,169.

¶911.04

For examples illustrating the application of the above tests, see Examples 9-35 through 9-42.

Personal service activity test. An activity constitutes a personal service activity if such activity involves the performance of the following personal services described in Reg. § 1.469-5T(d):

(1) The fields of health, law, engineering, architecture, accounting, actuarial science, performing arts, or consulting; or

(2) Any other trade or business in which capital is not a material income-producing factor.

Significant participation activity test. An individual is treated as significantly participating in this activity for a tax year if and only if the individual participates in the activity for more than 100 hours during such year.[170]

Facts and circumstances test. Certain conditions that will affect the ability of a shareholder to be deemed to materially participate under this test include:[171]

- *Certain management activities.* An individual's services performed in the management of an activity shall not be taken into account in determining whether such individual is treated as materially participating in such activity for the tax year for the "facts and circumstances test" unless, for such tax year—

  (A) No person (other than such individual) who performs services in connection with the management of the activity receives compensation described in Code Sec. 911(d)(2)(A) in consideration for such services; and

  (B) No individual performs services in connection with the management of the activity that exceed (by hours) the amount of such services performed by such individual.

- *Participation less than 100 hours.* If an individual participates in an activity for 100 hours or less during the tax year, such individual shall not be treated as materially participating in such activity for the tax year under the "facts and circumstances test."

Work done by a spouse. For any person who is a married individual (within the meaning of Code Sec. 7703) for the tax year, any participation by such person's spouse in the activity during the tax year (without regard to whether the spouse owns an interest in the activity and without regard to whether the spouses file a joint return for the tax year) shall be treated as participation by such person in the activity during the tax year.[172]

Participation.

S corporation shareholders who are investors. If an S corporation shareholder is classified as an investor in the S corporation, generally work done by an individual in the individual's capacity as an investor in an activity shall not be treated as

---

[170] Temp. Reg. § 1.469-5T(c)(2).
[171] Temp. Reg. § 1.469-5T(b)(2)(ii) and (iii).
[172] Temp. Reg. § 1.469-5T(f)(3).

participation in the activity for purposes of Code Sec. 469 unless the individual is directly involved in the day-to-day management or operations of the activity.[173] Generally that work done by an individual in the individual's capacity as an investor is an activity described in Reg. § 1.469-5T(f)(2)(ii)(B) that includes:

(1) Studying and reviewing financial statements or reports on operations of the activity;

(2) Preparing or compiling summaries or analyses of the finances or operations of the activity for the individual's own use; and

(3) Monitoring the finances or operations of the activity in a nonmanagerial capacity.

Accordingly, if an S corporation shareholder is deemed an investor who does not participate in the day-to-day affairs of the S corporation, then the shareholder will be able to deduct losses as they are incurred, providing the shareholder has basis to deduct the losses. As to the converse, if the S corporation has income, the investor shareholder will not be able to offset passive losses for other activities against this S corporation income.

Work done by shareholders. Generally any work done by an individual (without regard to the capacity in which the individual does the work) in connection with an activity in which the individual owns an interest at the time the work is done shall be treated for purposes of Code Sec. 469 as participation of the individual in the activity.[174] Work done in connection with an activity shall not be treated as participation in the activity, according to Reg. § 1.469-5T(f)(2)(i), if:

(A) Such work is not of a type that is customarily done by an owner (i.e. a shareholder) of such an activity; and

(B) One of the principal purposes for the performance of such work is to avoid the disallowance, under Code Sec. 469 and the regulations thereunder, of any loss or credit from such activity.

Means to prove participation. The extent of an individual's participation in an activity may be established by any reasonable means. Contemporaneous daily time reports, logs, or similar documents are not required if the extent of such participation may be established by other reasonable means (e.g., salary paid on so many hours worked).[175] Reasonable means for purposes of this paragraph may include but are not limited to the identification of services performed over a period of time and the approximate number of hours spent performing such services during such period, based on appointment books, calendars, or narrative summaries.

Examples of material participation. Examples 9-38 through 9-45 illustrate the application of the tests to determine material participation in an activity. They are adapted from Reg. § 1.469-5T(k) and Reg. § 1.469-5.

> ***Example 9-38:*** Alex Day, a calendar-year individual, owns 50% of the stock of Plenty, an S corporation. Carl Dexa owns the remaining stock in Plenty. Plenty has a single activity, a restaurant, which is a trade or business

---

[173] Temp. Reg. § 1.469-5T(f)(2)(ii)(A).
[174] Reg. § 1.469-5(f)(1).

[175] Temp. Reg. § 1.469-5T(f)(4).

¶911.04

activity. During the tax year, Day works for an average of 30 hours per week in connection with Plenty's restaurant activity. Under the 500-hour test, Day is treated as materially participating in the activity for the tax year because Day participates in the restaurant activity during such year for more than 500 hours.

Example 9-39: The facts are the same as in Example 9-36, except that Plenty's restaurant activity is to be managed by Dexa, and Day's work in the activity is performed pursuant to an employment contract between Day and Plenty. Work done by Day in connection with the activity in any capacity is treated as participation in the activity by Day. Accordingly, the conclusion is the same as in Example 9-36.

Example 9-40: Brad Bowman, an individual, is employed full-time as a carpenter. Bowman also owns an interest in an S corporation that is engaged in a van conversion activity, which is a trade or business activity. Bowman and Eric Clark, the other shareholder, are the only participants in the activity for the tax year. The activity is conducted entirely on Saturdays. Each Saturday throughout the tax year, Bowman and Clark work for eight hours in the activity. Although Bowman does not participate in the activity for more than 500 hours during the tax year, under the 100-hour test, Bowman is treated for such year as materially participating in the activity because Bowman participates in the activity for more than 100 hours during the tax year, and Bowman's participation in the activity for such year is not less than the participation of any other person in the activity for such year.

Example 9-41: Joan Carson, an individual, is employed full time as an accountant. Carson also owns interests in a restaurant and a shoe store. The restaurant and shoe store are both trade or business activities conducted through S corporations, and are properly treated as separate activities. Each activity has several full-time employees. During the tax year, Carson works in the restaurant activity for 400 hours and in the shoe store activity for 150 hours. Both the restaurant and shoe store activities are significant participation activities of Carson for the tax year. Accordingly, since Carson's aggregate participation in the restaurant and shoe store activities during the tax year exceeds 500 hours, Carson is treated under the significant participation test as materially participating in both activities.

Example 9-42: In 1995, Joe Duke, an individual, acquires stock in an S corporation engaged in a trade or business activity. For every tax year from 1995 through 1999, Duke is treated as materially participating in the activity, because Duke passed the material participation tests. Duke retires from the activity at the beginning of 2000, and would not be treated as materially participating in the activity for 2000 and subsequent tax years if material participation were required in those years. However, under the 5-out-of-10-year test, Duke is treated as materially participating in the activity for tax years 2000 through 2005 because he materially participated in the activity for five tax years during the ten tax years that immediately precede each of those years. Under the 5-out-of-10-year test, Duke is not treated as materially participating

¶911.04

in the activity for tax years beginning after 2005 because for those years Duke has not materially participated in the activity for five of the last ten immediately preceding tax years.

Example 9-43: The facts are the same as in Example 9-40, except that Duke does not acquire any stock in the S corporation until 1996. Duke is not treated as participating in the activity for any tax year prior to 1996 because Duke does not own an interest in the activity for any such tax year. Accordingly, Duke materially participates in the activity for only four tax years prior to 2000, and Duke is not treated under the 5-out-of-10-year test as materially participating in the activity for 2000 or subsequent tax years.

Example 9-44: Jane Engle, a married individual filing a separate return for the tax year, is employed full time as an attorney. Engle also owns an interest in a professional football team that is a trade or business activity. Engle does no work in connection with this activity. Engle anticipates that for the tax year, Engle's deductions from the activity will exceed Engle's gross income from the activity and that, if Engle does not materially participate in the activity for the tax year, part or all of Engle's passive activity loss for the tax year will be disallowed. Accordingly, Engle pays Engle's spouse, Dave, to work as an office receptionist in connection with the activity for an average of 15 hours per week during the tax year. Any participation in the activity by Engle's spouse is treated as participation in the activity by Engle. However, the work done by Dave, Engle's spouse, is not treated as participation in the activity because work as an office receptionist is not work of a type customarily done by an owner of a football team, and one of Engle's principal purposes for paying her spouse, Dave, to do this work is to avoid the disallowance of Engle's passive activity loss. Accordingly, Engle is not treated as participating in the activity for the tax year.

Example 9-45: Brian Fisher, an individual, owns an interest in an S corporation that feeds and sells cattle. The managing shareholder of the S corporation periodically mails Fisher a letter setting forth certain proposed actions and decisions with respect to the cattle-feeding operation. Such actions and decisions include, for example, what kind of feed to purchase, how much to purchase, and when to purchase it, how often to feed cattle, and when to sell cattle. The letters explain the proposed actions and decisions, emphasize that taking or not taking a particular action or decision is solely within the discretion of Fisher and other shareholders, and ask Fisher to indicate a decision with respect to each proposed action by answering certain questions. The managing shareholder receives a fee that constitutes earned income (within the meaning of Code Sec. 911(d)(2)(A)) for managing the cattle-feeding operation. Fisher is not treated as materially participating in the cattle-feeding operation.

Fisher's only participation in the cattle-feeding operation is to make certain managerial decisions. Such management services are not taken into account in determining whether the taxpayer is treated as materially participating in the activity for a tax year under the facts and circumstances test if any

¶911.04

other person performs services in connection with the management of the activity and receives compensation described in Code Sec. 911(d)(2)(A) for such services. Therefore, Fisher is not treated as materially participating for the tax year in the cattle-feeding operation.

.05 Rental Activities Classified as Passive Activity

Definition of "rental activity." A rental activity is generally treated as a passive activity.[176] An activity is a rental activity for a tax year generally if the following from Reg. § 1.469-1T(e)(3)(i) are true:

(A) During such tax year, tangible property held in connection with the activity is used by customers or held for use by customers; and

(B) The gross income attributable to the conduct of the activity during such taxable year represents (or, in the case of an activity in which property is held for use by customers, the expected gross income from the conduct of the activity will represent) amounts paid or to be paid principally for the use of such tangible property (without regard to whether the use of the property by customers is pursuant to a lease or pursuant to a service contract or other arrangement that is not denominated a lease).

Exceptions to definition of rental activity. An activity involving the use of tangible property is not a rental activity for a tax year if *any* of the following tests from Reg. § 1.469-1T(e)(3)(ii) are satisfied for such tax year:

(1) **7-days-or-less test.** The average period of customer use for such property is seven days or less.

(2) **30-days-or-less test.** The average period of customer use for such property is 30 days or less, and significant personal services are provided by or on behalf of the owner of the property in connection with making the property available for use by customers.

(3) **Extraordinary personal service test.** Extraordinary personal services are provided by or on behalf of the owner of the property in connection with making such property available for use by customers (without regard to the average period of customer use).

(4) **Incidental test.** The rental of such property is treated as incidental to a nonrental activity of the taxpayer.

(5) **Customarily available test.** The taxpayer customarily makes the property available during defined business hours for nonexclusive use by various customers.

(6) **Related-party test.** The provision of the property for use in an activity conducted by a partnership, S corporation, or joint venture in which the taxpayer owns an interest is not a rental activity.

It is beyond the scope of this book to provide a detailed description of rental activities due to their specialized nature. Accordingly, Code Sec. 469 and its

---

[176] Code Sec. 469(c)(2).

¶911.05

regulations should be consulted; however, note the following with regard to the related-party test.

Related-party test. If the taxpayer owns an interest in a partnership, S corporation, or joint venture conducting an activity other than a rental activity, and the taxpayer provides property for use in the activity in the taxpayer's capacity as an owner of an interest in such partnership, S corporation, or joint venture, the provision of such property is not a rental activity.[177] Thus, if a partner contributes the use of property to a partnership, none of the partner's distributive share of partnership income is income from a rental activity unless the partnership is engaged in a rental activity. In addition, a partner's gross income attributable to a payment described in Code Sec. 707(c) is not income from a rental activity under any circumstances. The determination of whether property used in an activity is provided by the taxpayer in the taxpayer's capacity as an owner of an interest in a partnership, S corporation, or joint venture shall be made on the basis of all of the facts and circumstances.

Examples of rental activities. Examples 9-46 through 9-50 illustrate when an activity is classified as a rental activity, and thus passive, and when it is not.

Example 9-46: Dean Young is engaged in an activity of leasing photocopying equipment. The average period of customer use for the equipment exceeds 30 days. Pursuant to the lease agreements, skilled technicians employed by Young maintain the equipment and service malfunctioning equipment for no additional charge. Service calls occur frequently (three times per week on average) and require substantial labor. The value of the maintenance and repair services (measured by the cost to Young of employees performing these services) exceeds 50 percent of the amount charged for the use of the equipment. Under these facts, services performed by individuals are provided in connection with the use of the photocopying equipment, but the customers' use of the photocopying equipment is not incidental to their receipt of the services. Therefore, under the extraordinary personal services test, extraordinary personal services are not provided in connection with making the photocopying equipment available for use by customers, and the activity is a rental activity.

Example 9-47: The facts are the same as in Example 9-46, except that the average period of customer use for the photocopying equipment exceeds seven days but does not exceed 30 days. Under these facts, significant personal services (under the 30-days-or-less test) are provided in connection with making the photocopying equipment available for use by customers, and the activity is not a rental activity.

Example 9-48: Kathy Patel is engaged in an activity of transporting goods for customers. In conducting the activity, Patel provides tractor-trailers to transport goods for customers pursuant to arrangements under which the tractor-trailers are selected by Patel, may be replaced at the sole option of Patel, and are operated and maintained by drivers and mechanics employed by

---

[177] Temp. Reg. § 1.469-1T(e)(3)(vii).

¶911.05

Patel. The average period of customer use for the tractor-trailers exceeds 30 days. Under these facts, the use of tractor-trailers by the taxpayer's customers is incidental to their receipt of personal services provided by Patel. Accordingly, the services performed in the activity satisfy the extraordinary personal services test, and the activity is not a rental activity.

Example 9-49: Jim East is engaged in an activity of owning and operating a residential apartment hotel. For the tax year, the average period of customer use for apartments exceeds seven days but does not exceed 30 days. In addition to cleaning public entrances, exits, stairways, and lobbies, and collecting and removing trash, East provides a daily maid and linen service at no additional charge. All of the services other than maid and linen service are excluded services (under the 30-days-or-less test), because such services are similar to those commonly provided in connection with long-term rentals of high-grade residential real property. The value of the maid and linen services (measured by the cost to East of employees performing such services) is less than 10 percent of the amount charged to tenants for occupancy of apartments. Under these facts, neither significant personal services (under the 30-days-or-less test) nor extraordinary personal services (for the extraordinary personal services test) are provided in connection with making apartments available for use by customers. Accordingly, the activity is a rental activity.

Example 9-50: Glen Foster operates a golf course. Some customers of the golf course pay greens fees upon each use of the golf course, while other customers purchase weekly, monthly, or annual passes. The golf course is open to all customers from sunrise to sunset every day of the year except certain holidays and days on which Foster determines that the course is too wet for play. Foster thus makes the golf course available during prescribed hours for nonexclusive use by various customers. Accordingly, under the customarily available test, Foster is not engaged in a rental activity, without regard to the average period of customer use for the golf course.

Grouping of rental activities. A rental activity may not be grouped with a trade or business activity unless either the rental activity is insubstantial in relation to the trade or business activity or vice-versa.[178] Reg. § 1.469-9(e)(3)(i) prescribes that a taxpayer who develops real estate, constructs buildings, and owns an interest in real estate, cannot group the rental real estate with either the development or the construction activity.

Election to treat all interest in real estate as a single rental real estate activity. If a taxpayer is engaged in the real estate business as defined by Code Sec. 469(c)(7)(B) (hereafter a "qualifying taxpayer"), the regulations generally require that the qualifying taxpayer may make an election to treat all of the taxpayer's interests in rental real estate as a single rental real estate activity.[179] The case of *Krukowski*[180] illustrates the danger of not grouping passive activities. In *Krukowski*, the taxpayers owned two rental buildings. One housed a health club wholly owned

---

[178] Neither Code Sec. 469 nor its regulations define "substantiality" or the lack thereof.

[179] Reg. § 1.469-9(g)(1).

[180] *T.P. Krukowski*, CA-7, 2002-1 USTC ¶ 50,219, 279 F3d 547.

by the husband, and the other housed a law firm where the husband was president and sole shareholder. All the husband's earned income came from the law firm. The couple charged rent for the space being rented, with the taxpayers reporting $175,149 of passive income from the law firm building, and a passive loss of $69,100 from the health club building. The couple netted the passive loss with the passive income without filing the election pursuant to Reg. § 1.469-4(c)(1). The Court struck down the netting, stating that because the taxpayers did not elect to treat the rental activities as a single activity on their 1994 income tax return, they cannot now claim that the activity should be grouped as a single activity because of this dispute.

Interests in real estate held by an S corporation. Generally a qualifying taxpayer's interest in rental real estate held by a partnership or an S corporation is treated as a single interest in rental real estate if the pass-through entity grouped its rental real estate as one rental activity.[181] If the pass-through entity grouped its rental real estate into separate rental activities under Reg. § 1.469-4(d)(5), each rental real estate activity of the pass-through entity will be treated as a separate interest in rental real estate of the qualifying taxpayer. However, the qualifying taxpayer may elect under Reg. § 1.469-9(g) to treat all interests in rental real estate, including the rental real estate interests held through pass-through entities, as a single rental real estate activity.

Qualifying taxpayer holding a 50-percent-or-greater interest in a pass-through entity. If a qualifying taxpayer owns, directly or indirectly, a fifty-percent-or-greater interest in the capital, profits, or losses of a pass-through entity for a tax year, each interest in rental real estate held by the pass-through entity will be treated as a separate interest in rental real estate of the qualifying taxpayer, regardless of the pass-through entity's grouping of activities under Reg. § 1.469-4(d)(5).[182] However, the qualifying taxpayer may elect under Reg. § 1.469-9(g) to treat all interests in rental real estate, including the rental real estate interests held through pass-through entities, as a single rental real estate activity.

Interests held in tiered pass-through entities. A special rule for real estate applies to holdings involving tiered pass-through entities, namely, if a pass-through entity owns a fifty-percent-or-greater interest in the capital, profits, or losses of another pass-through entity for a tax year, each interest in rental real estate held by the lower-tier entity will be treated as a separate interest in rental real estate of the upper-tier entity, regardless of the lower-tier entity's grouping of activities under Reg. § 1.469-4(d)(5).[183]

.06 Portfolio Income

Income and expense derived from standard investment activities are classified as "portfolio" income and expense and may not be offset by passive losses even though the taxpayer does not materially participate in either the portfolio activity or the passive activity. Portfolio income includes gross income from interest, dividends, annuities, or royalties, other than those derived in the taxpayer's ordinary

---

[181] Reg. § 1.469-9(h)(1). Care must be practiced in grouping activities. See e.g., *Carlos*, 123 TC No. 16 discussed at ¶ 911.10.

[182] Reg. § 1.469-9(h)(2).

[183] Reg. § 1.469-9(h)(3).

trade or business (e.g., as a securities dealer).[184] Portfolio expenses are those expenses (other than interest) "clearly and directly allocable" to portfolio income.[185] In addition, gains or losses attributable to the sale or disposition of assets generating portfolio income or held for investment will be classified as portfolio income (or loss).

Return on working capital. Any income, gain, or loss that is attributable to an investment of working capital shall be treated as *not* derived in the ordinary course of a trade or business (i.e., as portfolio income or loss).

Tax Pointer: Although passive losses cannot be deducted against portfolio income, investment interest expense can. Thus, classification of S corporation income as portfolio income, rather than as income from a trade or business, may be beneficial to shareholders.

Specific definitions of portfolio income. Specific definitions regarding what is included in portfolio income are provided in Reg. § 1.469-2T(c)(3)(i) and (ii):

- Dividends on S corporation stock within the meaning of Code Sec. 1368(c)(2) (i.e., dividends from earnings and profits from a predecessor C corporation)

- Gross income derived in the ordinary course of a trade or business. Specifically included in the definition of "gross income derived in the ordinary course of a trade or business" are:

  (A) Interest income on loans and investments made in the ordinary course of a trade or business of lending money;

  (B) Interest on accounts receivable arising from the performance of services or the sale of property in the ordinary course of a trade or business of performing such services or selling such property, but only if credit is customarily offered to customers of the business;

  (C) Income from investments made in the ordinary course of a trade or business of furnishing insurance or annuity contracts or reinsuring risks underwritten by insurance companies;

  (D) Income or gain derived in the ordinary course of an activity of trading or dealing in any property if such activity constitutes a trade or business;

  (E) Royalties derived by the taxpayer in the ordinary course of a trade or business of licensing intangible property;

  (F) Amounts included in the gross income of a patron of a cooperative (within the meaning of Code Sec. 1381(a), without regard to paragraph (2)(A) or (C) thereof) by reason of any payment or allocation to the patron based on patronage occurring with respect to a trade or business of the patron; and

  (G) Other income identified by the Commissioner as income derived by the taxpayer in the ordinary course of a trade or business.

---

[184] Code Sec. 469(e)(1). [185] *Ibid.*

Self-charged interest. If a passive S corporation shareholder lends money to an S corporation, the interest income received by the shareholder is portfolio income; however, the corporation's interest expense is a passive deduction. To alleviate this position of dichotomy, Proposed Reg. § 1.469-7(a)(1) provides that

   (i) certain interest income resulting from these lending transactions may be treated as passive activity gross income;

  (ii) certain deductions for interest expense that is properly allocable to such interest income are treated as passive activity deductions; and

 (iii) the passive activity gross income and passive activity deductions resulting from this treatment must be allocated among the taxpayer's activities.

Self-charged management fees. In *Hillman*,[186] the Court addressed the situation of self-charged management fees involving pass-through entities. Regulations under Code Sec. 469 are silent as to the treatment of management fees rendered by the shareholder of an S corporation which is engaged in passive activities. The facts in *Hillman* are as follows.

The taxpayer, during the years in question, owned 93.43 percent of the stock of an S corporation (SMC) which provided management services to 90 partnerships (general and limited) and S corporations where the taxpayer owned an interest. The general partner of each of the limited partnerships was either a taxpayer, an upper-tier partnership, or S corporation in which the taxpayer had an interest. The taxpayer's participation was over 500 hours in SMC's real estate management activities; however, the taxpayer did not participate in the activities of the pass-through entities. The taxpayer deducted the total amounts of the management fee expenses of the pass-through entities, which were charged by SMC against the income the taxpayer received from SMC for providing these management services to the pass-through entities. The regulations are silent as to the treatment of self-charged management fees; however, for self-charged interest, the Committee Reports to Code Sec. 469 prescribe a wash (income earned from the interest by the taxpayer is not treated as portfolio income; rather, it is deemed passive, and it is washed against the passive interest expense from the pass-through entity). The Court reversed the Tax Court and remanded the case, holding that the management fees in this instance earned by SMC are not passive income. On remand, the Tax Court,[187] following the mandate of the appellate court, reluctantly refused to sustain the taxpayer's alternative argument to deduct the management fees.

Interest expense on shareholder's loans allocated amongst activities. Generally if interest expense arises from a passive activity, the interest expense will be treated as a deduction attributable to a passive activity.[188] The regulations state that to determine the activity to which the interest expense is attributable, the taxpayer must trace the disbursement of the debt proceeds.[189] Accordingly, with respect to interest, if an S corporation is engaged in both rental activities (e.g.,

---

[186] *D.H. Hillman*, CA-4, 2001-1 ustc ¶ 50,354, 250 F3d 228.

[187] *D.H. Hillman*, 118 TC 323, Dec. 54,711.

[188] Temp. Reg. § 1.163-8T(a)(4)(i)(B).

[189] Temp. Reg. § 1.163-8T(a)(3).

¶911.06

being a landlord) as well as engaged in a trade or business (e.g., operating a store), and the S corporation incurs debt, an allocation of proceeds must be made to determine the tax treatment for the interest expense arising with both activities. Then, a shareholder determination must be made; if the shareholder is passive, the interest arising from the trade or business will be classified as passive; if the shareholder is active, no such classification will be required.

.07 Tax Treatment of Passive Losses and Credits

A loss arising from a passive activity is deductible against net income arising from passive activities.[190] Generally, losses and credits that are not deductible for a particular tax year (because there is no passive income to offset them) are carried forward indefinitely, and allowable as deductions against passive income from any source in future years.[191] When a taxpayer disposes of his, her, or its entire interest in a passive activity in a taxable transaction (e.g., an S corporation shareholder sells his, her, or its interest), the unused passive losses can be applied against the taxpayer's "active" income in the year of disposition.[192] Examples 9-51 and 9-52 illustrate.

> **Example 9-51:** Restaurant Inc. was formed on January 1, 2009, as a calendar-year S corporation composed of two equal shareholders—two brothers, Abe and Milt Rosen. Abe lives in New York, and Milt lives in San Diego, California, where Restaurant Inc. has its only restaurant. Milt is the chef as well as the only officer of the corporation; Abe is an active, rich attorney, basically assuming a passive role in the corporation (not participating in any activity such as choice of menu, etc. Accordingly, under Code Sec. 469, his stock interest is deemed "passive." Abe's capital contribution is $100,000; Milt's capital contribution is $1,000. For 2009, Restaurant Inc. lost $20,000, of which $10,000 is allocable to each shareholder. Abe and Milt have no passive income from any passive activities in 2009. The tax results for Abe and Milt are as follows: Abe has adequate basis to deduct the $10,000 of loss from Restaurant Inc.; however, because he is a passive investor in the S corporation, he cannot deduct any of the $10,000 loss in 2009. (Note, however, that the loss will still reduce his basis in his stock.) Milt, who is the chef and only corporate officer, is deemed to materially participate in the activities, but can only deduct $1,000 of the loss because he has only $1,000 of basis; accordingly, he will carry forward $9,000 of losses until he has basis to deduct the loss.

> **Example 9-52:** Assume the same facts as in Example 9-49. In 2010, Abe is still a "passive" investor for purposes of Code Sec. 469, while Milt's interest is "active." Restaurant Inc. earns $50,000, none of which is distributed to the shareholders. Abe and Milt will each report $25,000 of income from the restaurant, paying the tax thereon. Abe's basis will increase to $115,000 ($90,000 + $25,000), and on the Form 8582, he will now deduct the $10,000 of passive loss from 2009 that he could not previously deduct because he now has passive income to offset the loss. Milt's basis will be $16,000 ($1,000 − loss of

---

[190] Code Sec. 469.
[191] Code Sec. 469(b).
[192] Code Sec. 469(g).

$10,000) + $25,000)). Milt will now be able to deduct the $9,000 of carryforward loss as an "active loss."

Passive activity credit. Credits arising from passive activities are allowable to the extent that the "sum of the credit from all passive activities allowable for the taxable year" exceeds "the regular tax liability of the taxpayer for the taxable year allocable to all passive activities."[193] With respect to real estate activities, the Code requires the application of certain credits (e.g., the low-income housing credit).[194] Generally, unused credits can be carried forward indefinitely.

Disposition of a passive activity. Upon the disposition of a taxpayer's entire interest in a passive activity (to an unrelated party), he or she is allowed to deduct the full amount of previously suspended passive activity losses (PALs) attributable to that activity.[195] These losses are deductible in full without regard to the taxpayer's passive income from other activities. The Code requires, however, that the losses must be applied agains net income or gain from other passive activities before being applied against the taxpayer's trade or business or portfolio income for the year of disposition.[196] The effect of this requirement is to crowd out losses incurred in other passive activities during that year; those losses will only be deductible to the extent passive income from other sources exceeds the passive loss carryforward attributable to the terminated passive activity.

Disposition of S corporation stock. The disposition of S corporation stock is a disposition of an interest in each of the S corporation activities—real estate, portfolio, and trade or business.[197]

Installment sales for disposition of a passive activity. If an S corporation shareholder uses an installment sale to dispose of his, her, or its corporation stock, suspended losses are allowed in the ratio of gain recognized each year to total gain.[198]

Disposition of S corporation stock to a related party. If a taxpayer transfers an interest in a passive activity to a related party as defined by Code Sec. 267(b) or Code Sec. 707(b) (i.e., a family member) other than by gift, suspended PALs are carried forward by the transferor and deductible against passive income from other passive activities of the transferor.[199] When the related-party transferee disposes of the activity to an unrelated third party, then the transferor will recognize the remaining suspended PALs. Note that abandonment by the transferee will constitute a fully taxable disposition.

Disposition of a passive activity by gift. If a shareholder disposes of a passive activity by gift (i.e., a passive S corporation shareholder makes a gift of the S corporation stock), the transfer is not a disposition triggering recognition of the suspended PALs; rather, the basis of the transferred interest is increased by the amount of the losses.[200]

---

[193] Code Sec. 469(d)(2).
[194] Code Sec. 469(i).
[195] Code Sec. 469(g).
[196] Code Sec. 469(g)(1)(A).

[197] Temp. Reg. §1.469-2T(c)(3).
[198] Code Sec. 469(g)(3).
[199] Code Sec. 469(g)(1)(B)
[200] Code Sec. 469(j)(6).

¶911.07

Death of a taxpayer. On the death of a taxpayer, suspended PALs can be recognized in the year of death to the extent that they exceed the amount by which decedent's basis is increased by Code Sec. 1014.[201]

Disposition of a passive activity resulting in a capital loss. If the disposition of the passive activity (i.e., a shareholder sells his, her, or its stock) results in a capital loss, the rules of Code Sec. 1211 et seq. apply; the capital loss is deductible to the extent of capital gains plus $3,000 in the year of disposition, with the unused losses carried over to future years free of PAL limitations.[202] Code Sec. 1211 does not restrict the deductibility of the passive loss carryforward under Code Sec. 469(g). Note that Code Sec. 1244 treatment may be available, however, to convert the capital loss to an ordinary loss.

Carryover of PALs on termination of S status. When S corporation status is terminated, shareholders' suspended PALs continue as such and can only be offset against C corporation passive income if the C corporation conducts the same passive activities.[203] A special rule for closely held C corporations (other than personal service corporations) allows a deduction for passive losses against C corporation active income.[204] It is unclear what happens if the C corporation disposes of the passive activity after termination, however.

.08 Closely Held C Corporations

A closely held C corporation receives special tax treatment with respect to PALs, namely, the ability to deduct PALs against the C corporation's passive activity gross income and the corporation's net active (but not portfolio) income for the tax year.[205] To be classified as a closely held C corporation, it must, at any time during the last half of its tax year, have 50 percent of its stock owned directly or indirectly by and for not more than five individuals.[206]

Closely held C corporations electing S status. In *St. Charles Investment Co.*,[207] a shareholder of an S corporation could deduct suspended Code Sec. 469 passive activity losses arising from C corporation years in the year that the S corporation disposed of the activity that gave rise to the losses. The facts which gave rise to this decision are as follows.

On January 1, 1991, a closely held C corporation that was engaged in a real estate rental business elected S status. At the time of its election, the corporation had suspended passive losses arising from its rental activities. In 1991, during its first year as an S corporation, the corporation disposed of the passive activities, with the S corporation deducting on its tax return the suspended passive activity losses. The Court held that Code Sec. 469(b) overrides Code Sec. 1371(b)(1) (the prohibition on an S corporation from carrying forward any C activities to the S corporation). In reaching its decision, the Court noted that the shareholders of the corporation were receiving a windfall, in that the shareholders were able to offset

---

[201] Code Sec. 469(g)(2).

[202] Reg. § 1.469-2(d)(2)(ix).

[203] Reg. § 1.469-1(f)(4).

[204] Code Sec. 469(e)(2).

[205] Code Sec. 469(a)(2)(B).

[206] Code Sec. 542(a)(2).

[207] *St. Charles Investment Co.*, CA-10, 2000-2 USTC ¶ 50,840, 232 F3d 773.

income with losses arising from a different taxpayer (i.e., the former C corporation).[208]

.09 Casualty Losses Are Not Subject to Passive Activity Loss Limitations

Casualty losses arising from storms, fires, theft, etc. are deductible pursuant to the casualty loss rules, and are not hampered by the PAL rules.[209]

.10 Material Participation of a Trustee for Purposes of Satisfying Code Sec. 469

Code Sec. 469 prescribes for purposes of making an activity "active" rather than "passive" for purposes of deducting losses there has to be material participation. In the case of a trust, *Mattie K. Carter Trust v. U.S.*,[210] "material participation" by a trustee of a testamentary trust engaged in a ranching business was determined by addressing the activities of the trust through its fiduciaries, employees, and agents, and could not be decided by evaluating only the activities of the trustee. However, IRS Letter Ruling 201029014 (Jul. 24, 2010) held that a trust may only have "active" participation in a business for Code Sec. 469 purposes if only the trustee materially participates.[211].

.11 Tax Planning under the Passive Activity Loss Rules

The area of passive activities is a complex and difficult one. Planning, because of these complexities, also becomes difficult; however, certain ground rules become readily evident. Code Sec. 469's slant is to create disallowable passive losses while at the same time creating active or portfolio income that cannot be offset by PALs. Classification of activities is critical in order to plot future courses of action. If there will be difficulty satisfying the participation test, then activities should be combined; but if there will be PALs on disposition of the activity, it may be beneficial to segregate them rather than join them.

Converting to S status provides unique planning opportunities. For instance, in *St. Charles Investment Co.*,[212] as more fully discussed at ¶ 911.08, shareholders of an S corporation were allowed to deduct suspended Code Sec. 469 passive activity losses arising from C corporation years in the year that the S corporation disposed of the activity which gave rise to the losses.

Gregg[213] presents a very interesting case where a taxpayer was able to group activities so that his active participation in a C corporation allowed him to group them with his passive activities in an LLC where he was a member. *Gregg* dealt with an LLC acting as a passthrough entity similar to the way an S corporation would in these circumstances. The facts in *Gregg* are as follows.

The taxpayer, during 1994, was a 60 percent owner in Ethix Corporation, a C corporation that provided consulting, marketing, networking, business services,

---

[208] But see Technical Advice Memorandum 9628002 (October 10, 1995), which stated that suspended passive activity losses of a C corporation that converted to an S could not be recognized subsequently by the S corporation.

[209] Temp. Reg. § 1.469-2T.

[210] 2003-1 USTC ¶ 50,418, (Apr. 11, 2003).

[211] *Accord*, Technical Advise Memorandum 200733023 (Aug. 17, 2007).

[212] *St. Charles Investment Co.*, CA-10, 2000-2 USTC ¶ 50,840, 232 F3d 773.

[213] *S.A. Gregg*, DC Ore., 2001-1 USTC ¶ 50,169.

¶911.09

etc. to the health care industry. Capital was not a material income-producing factor for Ethix's business operations. Ethix served physicians, insurance companies, and managed health care companies. On November 4, 1994, the date the taxpayer husband sold his stock in Ethix, he formed Cadaja, LLC in the state of Oregon, filing a partnership tax return for the short period. Cadaja performed basically the same services as Ethix, but instead of dealing with the field of traditional medicine, it concentrated on alternative medicine.

The taxpayer, who was the sole financier, brought in two other members to the LLC who brought nothing, no cash or property, but their know-how. These individuals, Capelli and Fleming, worked at least 40 hours per week for Cadaja in 1994, and received a salary of $75,000. The taxpayer husband, who was the sole member of Cadaja, worked approximately 100 hours during 1994 and did not receive any compensation for the services he provided.

Capital was not a material income-producing factor for Cadaja, and Cadaja incurred a loss for the period of November 4, 1994–December 31, 1994 of $230,723, which the taxpayer reported as ordinary loss. The Court sustained the taxpayer's loss as ordinary, citing the following.

The Court felt that the taxpayer's membership interest in the LLC should be judged as a general partner under the § 469 regulations, not to the higher standard of limited partner. If the taxpayer was deemed a limited partner, then for the taxpayer to take the losses from the LLC as ordinary, he would have to meet tests (1), (5), or (6) of Reg. § 1.469-5T(a)(1)-(7); however, if the taxpayer's membership interest in the LLC was deemed as a general partner, then the taxpayer's participation for deduction of the loss as ordinary would be that he could satisfy any of the tests (1)-(7).

The Court felt, based on state law, that Reg. § 1.469-5T(e)(3)(i)(B), which prescribes that the taxpayer's interest would be deemed a limited partnership, was "obsolete," because "the limited liability statutes create a new type of business entity that is materially distinguishable from a limited partnership." In reaching its decision, the Court noted that LLC members retain liability protection regardless of the level of participation in the management of the LLC, but a limited partner in a limited partnership under state law cannot, by definition, participate in management.

The Court felt that the 500-hour test set forth in Reg. § 1.469-5T(a)(1) could not be prorated to satisfy the 500-hour test. The Court acknowledged that the 500-hour test was unfair for businesses that have a short initial first year, but felt that Reg. § 1.469-5T(a), which had a standard of strict compliance, had to comply. As to the other tests under Reg. § 1.469-5T(a)(2)-(3), (5)-(7), these would not apply. As to the significant participation standard under Reg. § 1.469-5T(a)(4), the Court lumped the taxpayer's participation in Ethix, where he worked at least 40 hours per week on a continuous basis from January 1, 1994–November 4, 1994, with his participation in the LLC, even though there was no common ownership between the two other than the fact that the taxpayer owned more than 50 percent of each entity at two different times. In reaching its decision, the Court stated that "no rules or regulations require that activities be grouped [to] occur at the same time."

Further, the Court felt that the grouping provisions of Reg. § 1.469-4T, which applied to the taxable years before 1992, provided useful insights into grouping activities in professional services, such as those involving health or consulting. The Court reached this conclusion even though Reg. § 1.469-4 was to apply to taxable years after 1992, not Reg. § 1.469-4T.

Accordingly, the Court felt that the taxpayer could group his activities in Ethix and the LLC as a single activity to determine whether he materially participated in the activities of the LLC in the taxable year 1994. Based on this reasoning, the Court held that the taxpayer's loss for 1994 had to be ordinary.

Besides *Gregg*, other cases should be noted; two favorable and one not. In *Schumacher v. Comm.*,[214] the taxpayer owned ninety percent of PFC, an S corporation engaged in flight training, aircraft rental, charter service, and aircraft sales. PFC's general manager owned the remaining ten percent of the S corporation, receiving his stock interest in exchange for future services. The taxpayer decided that PFC needed additional equipment. Rather than have the general manager who did not contribute any capital to PFC, own 10 percent of the equipment, taxpayer decided to purchase the equipment himself and lease it to PFC. PFC had operating losses. The court held that the activities, pursuant to Reg. § 1.469-4(d)(1)(A) could be grouped, and were active, allowing the taxpayer to deduct the losses, and combine them with the losses for the S corporation, PFC (the court did not comment on the status of PFC; however, the tenor of the decision was that PFC was active).

In reaching its decision, the court felt that the most significant fact in the case was that the taxpayer created and operated the leasing activity solely for PFC's benefit. In furtherance of this goal, taxpayer spent very little time conducting the affairs of the leasing activity in comparison with the very substantial amount of time and effort expended by the taxpayer in carrying on PFC's business. The leasing activity was intended to, and in fact did, provide a service solely to PFC, with the purpose being to enhance PFC's ability to generate business, maintain PFC's viability as an ongoing concern, and possibly enabling PFC to become profitable in the future (not to provide an income stream independently from PFC). The court also held that the leasing activity was "insubstantial" in relationship to the PFC activities.

> **Tax Pointer:** Based on the reasoning of *Schumacher*, a taxpayer should be able to engage in leasing items to the taxpayer's company, with any losses generated in the leasing activity to be deemed "active." Examples of such a situation would be a trucker who rents trucks to his trucking company; doctors who rent diagnostic equipment to their own company, etc.

In *Al Assaf*[215], taxpayer losses arising from a building which taxpayers owned and leased to lawyers was deemed deductible under Reg. § 1.469-1T(e)(3)(ii)'s extraordinary service exception. The taxpayer wife, a lawyer, and her husband, a doctor (as well as a full-time professor) were equal members in an LLC which owned an office building where each of them practiced their profession. However,

---

[214] TC Summary Opn. 2003-96.   [215] TC Memo 2005-14.

the LLC's principal activity was providing legal support to attorneys, such as providing paralegal services, computers with legal research capabilities, conference rooms, a file room, client intake, phone and message answering services, document filing, typing, dictation, case referrals, scheduling depositions, court reporters, and making travel arrangements. Also, the company offered the husband's expert consulting services as a physician.

> **Tax Pointer:** The Court, in sustaining the taxpayer's losses in *Al Assaf* allowed post-event testimony rather than contemporaneous diaries, log books, etc. to prove participation.

In *Carlos*[216], taxpayers who owned and rented two commercial real estate properties to two separate wholly-owned S corporations in which they materially participated could not treat their combined net income from the two properties as non-passive self-rental income. Instead, the income from the income-generating property was treated as a self-rental, and thus excluded from the passive activity loss computation pursuant to Reg. § 1.469-2(f)(6). The loss generated by the second property where no rent was charged was treated as separate passive loss.

¶ 912 Post-Termination Transition Period (PTTP)

When the S status of a corporation terminates and it becomes a C corporation, it is basically governed by C corporation rules regarding distributions. However, if certain conditions are met, the corporation can make tax-free distributions of the accumulated adjustments account (AAA) to the shareholders,[217] and if there are suspended losses, they can be taken on the last day of any PTTP to the extent of a shareholder's then-existing basis, subject to the at-risk rules of Code Sec. 465.[218]

.01 Distributions

If a C corporation distributes money with respect to its stock during a PTTP, the distribution shall be (1) received free by the shareholder to the extent of the predecessor S corporation's AAA balance as of the date of termination of S status[219] and (2) reduce the shareholder's basis in stock. For these provisions to apply, the recipient of the distribution must have been a shareholder of the S corporation at the time of the termination of S status.[220]

> **Tax Pointer:** In the event that the C corporation has inadequate funds, it should consider borrowing money to accomplish this tax-free distribution.

.02 Time Limit

The three PTTPs defined in Code Sec. 1377(b)(1) are the following:

(A) the period beginning on the day after the last day of the corporation's last taxable year as an S corporation and ending on the later of—

    (i) the day which is 1 year after such last day, or

    (ii) the due date for filing the return for such last year as an S corporation (including extensions),

---

[216] 123 TC No. 16.

[217] The accumulated adjustments account (AAA) is discussed at ¶ 1003.01.

[218] Code Sec. 1371(e) and Code Sec. 1366(d)(3).

[219] Code Sec. 1371(e)(1).

[220] Reg. § 1.1377-2(b).

(B) the 120-day period beginning on the date of any determination pursuant to an audit of the taxpayer which follows the termination of the corporation's election and which adjusts a subchapter S item of income, loss, or deduction of the corporation arising during the S period (as defined in Code Sec. 1368(e)(2)), and

(C) the 120-day period beginning on the date of a determination that the corporation's election under Code Sec. 1362(a) had terminated for a previous taxable year.

A definition of "determination" for purposes of Code Sec. 1377(b)(1)(B) and (C), is

- a determination as defined in Code Sec. 1313(a), or
- an agreement between the corporation and the Secretary that the corporation failed to qualify as an S corporation.[221]

.03 Recognition of Suspended Losses

A shareholder cannot take losses without basis in either stock or debt. If the S corporation terminates, a shareholder is generally allowed to recognize suspended losses on the last day of any PTTP for a shareholder's stock (not debt).[222] A shareholder is allowed to increase his, her, or its stock basis if the amount of the loss carryforwards at the date of termination of S status exceed a shareholder's basis in stock.[223] Since the Code requires that loans cannot be used during the PTTP to absorb losses, a shareholder may consider converting debt to stock during the PTTP to create stock basis.[224]

.04 At-Risk Rules

If a shareholder increases his, her, or its basis during the PTTP by contributing money or property, presumably, this will increase the amount that the shareholder has at risk under Code Sec. 465 to allow a shareholder to deduct the losses.[225]

[221] Code Sec. 1377(b)(2)(B).
[222] Code Sec. 1366(d)(3).
[223] Code Sec. 1366(d)(3)(B).
[224] Code Sec. 1366(d)(3)(B).
[225] Code Sec. 1366(d)(3)(D).

Chapter 10

Distributions and the Accumulated Adjustments Account

¶ 1001 S Corporations—With and Without Earnings and Profits

While Chapters 6, 7, and 9 discuss how shareholders are taxed on S corporation income and when they recognize it, this chapter completes the picture, discussing the tax consequences when an S corporation makes distributions to its shareholders. Since an S corporation is a pass-through entity, its income is not taxed at the corporate level. Instead, S corporation income is passed through to the shareholders and taxed to them on their individual tax returns. And because S corporation income is taxed to the shareholders, a shareholder can withdraw previously taxed income without further tax.[1]

The tax consequences of an S corporation distribution depend on whether the corporation distributes cash or other property, whether it has accumulated earnings and profits (E&P) remaining from prior years as a regular corporation, and whether it has undistributed but previously taxed income (PTI) from S corporation tax years prior to 1983. If the corporation distributes only cash to its shareholders, and has no E&P from prior C corporation years, the tax consequences to the shareholders are relatively straightforward. Change the distribution to appreciated property, add E&P and/or PTI,[2] however, and the consequences become increasingly complex.

.01 Distributions Are Dividends Under State Law

Any distribution from a profitable S corporation to a shareholder is treated as a dividend under the state law where the S corporation is incorporated. As such, the

---

[1] Code Sec. 1368.   [2] See ¶ 1005 for a definition of PTI.

formalities for dividend declaration under state law and compliance with state law must be followed by S corporations, just like C corporations.

.02 Types of Distributions Covered

The ordering distribution rules of Code Sec. 1368 apply to any distribution of "property" made by an S corporation on its stock. "Property" is defined as money, securities, and property other than stock in the distributing corporation, or the right to acquire stock.[3]

> ***Tax Pointer:*** If appreciated property is distributed to shareholders, then a gain must be recognized by the corporation that passes through and is taxable to the shareholders.[4] If depreciated property is distributed to a shareholder, then Code Sec. 311(a) prescribes that there is no recognition of loss. Accordingly, the corporation should sell the depreciated property, recognize the loss, and then distribute the cash to the shareholder, thereby creating a deductible loss situation.

> **Failed stock redemption.** A stock redemption is not a distribution, but rather the purchase by a corporation of its own stock. If the redemption is qualified, as defined in Code Secs. 302(b) and 303, it will be subject to the same rules and will have the same tax consequences as a stock redemption by a regular corporation. Redemptions that do not satisfy the requirements of Code Secs. 302(b) and 303 (i.e., nonqualified redemptions) are treated as distributions and will be subject to the distribution provisions of Code Sec. 1368(a) (if the corporation is a qualified S corporation).

¶ 1002 S Corporations Without Earnings and Profits

An S corporation without earnings and profits could be created in a number of ways:

(1) It could be created at any time and be an S corporation *de novo* (i.e., make an S corporation election on Form 2553 for its first tax year).

(2) It could have been a C corporation without any earnings and profits that converted to S status (a C corporation without earnings and profits at the time of conversion could be created in any number of ways, such as distributing all its earnings and profits as dividends just prior to the S election, operating always at a loss, etc.).

(3) It could have been an S corporation that acquired C corporation earnings and profits in a merger and then distributed all the earnings and profits as a taxable dividend to the shareholders from the C corporation earnings.

(4) It could have been a C corporation that had earnings and profits at the time of conversion to S status and declared a dividend to remove the earnings and profits from the corporation.

---

[3] Code Sec. 317(a).   [4] Code Sec. 311(b).

.01 Rules for Distribution

A two-tier system is established for distributions for an S corporation without earnings and profits.[5] First, distributions are tax free to the extent of shareholder's basis in the stock of the S corporation; second, if the distribution exceeds the adjusted basis of the stock, such excess shall be treated as gain from the sale or exchange of property (i.e., capital gain).

Changes to basis. In terms of priority, basis increases and decreases for stock under Code Sec. 1367 occur before the distribution rules of Code Sec. 1368 apply.[6] Accordingly, before determining the tax treatment of any S corporation distributions, the basis of the shareholder's stock is increased by the shareholder's distributive share of items of S corporation income and the excess of the deduction for depletion *over* the basis of the property subject to depletion.[7]

The following order is used for reduction of basis:[8]

(1) Distributions that were not includible in the income of the shareholder

(2) Any items of S corporation loss or deduction (fines and penalties)[9]

(3) Oil and gas depletion deduction[10]

(4) Any loss for separately stated items (capital loss, Code Sec. 1231 loss)[11]

(5) Nonseparately stated items (a loss from S corporation trade or business)[12]

Distributions from an S corporation without E&P are tax free to the extent of the shareholder's adjusted stock basis. The shareholder must recognize capital gain to the extent the distribution exceeds the adjusted basis of his or her stock. The gain will be long term or short term, depending upon the holding period of the shareholder's stock.[13]

Example 10-1: Crawford Inc., a calendar-year S corporation, is composed of one shareholder, Bert Crawford, and was formed on January 1, 2009, with Crawford Inc. making its S election effective as of January 1, 2009. Bert Crawford, a bachelor, contributed $10,000 for the stock interest in the S corporation. At the end of Crawford Inc.'s first year of operation, it had ordinary income (Form 1120S, page 1) of $30,000. Bert materially participated in Crawford Inc. During the year, Crawford Inc. made a distribution to Bert of $46,000. The tax consequences (determined at the end of the S corporation year) are as follows:

Bert reports taxable income of $30,000 increasing his stock basis by $30,000 to $40,000 ($10,000 original basis + $30,000 income). Bert receives the first $40,000 of the distribution tax free, reducing his stock basis to zero. The remaining $6,000 is taxed as a capital gain.

---

[5] Code Sec. 1368(b).
[6] Code Sec. 1368(d)(1).
[7] Reg. § 1.1368-1(e).
[8] Reg. § 1.1368-1(e).
[9] Code Sec. 1367(a)(2)(D).

[10] Code Sec. 1367(a)(2)(E).
[11] Code Sec. 1367(a)(2)(B).
[12] Code Sec. 1367(a)(2)(C).
[13] Code Sec. 1368(b).

Example 10-2: Assume the same facts as in Example 10-1 except that at the end of 2009, Crawford Inc. has ordinary income of $12,000 and tax-exempt income of $18,000. The tax results are as follows:

Bert had taxable income of $12,000 increasing his stock basis to $22,000. The nontaxable income further increases Bert's basis to $40,000 ($10,000 + $12,000 + $18,000). Bert's basis is reduced tax free by $40,000, and $6,000 is taxed as a capital gain.

Example 10-3: Assume the same facts as in Example 10-1, except that Crawford Inc. does not distribute $46,000 to Bert until 2010. Accordingly, Bert will still report $30,000 in income and have basis increased by $30,000. The tax consequences to Bert of the $46,000 distribution in 2010 will depend upon whether Crawford Inc. earns a profit or a loss in 2010. Assuming that Bert's basis did not change in 2010 (i.e., Crawford Inc. broke even, had no separately stated items, etc.), the $46,000 distribution will cause Bert to recognize a $6,000 capital gain, just as in Example 10-2; this gain will not be recognized, however, until 2010.

Example 10-4: Jensen Inc. is a calendar-year S corporation having one shareholder, Gwen Jensen, who materially participates in the corporation. Jensen Inc. was formed on January 1, 2010, and Gwen's initial contribution to Jensen Inc. was $10,000. During 2010, Jensen Inc. made a distribution of $2,000 to Gwen. At the end of 2010, Jensen Inc. had ordinary income of $7,000. Gwen reports $7,000 of income for 2010, increasing her basis to $17,000. The $2,000 distribution is tax free to Gwen, and Gwen's stock basis as of December 31, 2010, is $15,000 ($10,000 + $7,000 − $2,000).

Example 10-5: Assume the same facts as in Example 10-4, except that Jensen Inc. is a calendar-year C corporation and that Gwen's father, Fritz, who owned all the stock, died on December 31, 2009, leaving all his stock to his daughter, Gwen. The stock in Jensen Inc. was valued on Fritz's estate tax return, Form 706, at $100,000. Gwen, as the sole shareholder of Jensen Inc., elected S status for the corporation on January 1, 2010. At the time of the S election, Jensen Inc. had no earnings and profits, having distributed them prior to Fritz's death. Gwen, for 2010, will report $7,000 of income on her personal Form 1040, receiving the distribution tax free. Her basis at the end of 2010 will be $105,000 ($100,000 + $7,000 − $2,000).

Example 10-6: Assume the same facts as in Example 10-5, except that Jensen Inc. distributed $90,000 to Gwen in 2010. Gwen would report $7,000 of income, increasing her basis to $107,000. The distribution will be tax free, reducing her stock basis to $17,000 ($107,000 − $90,000).

Tax Pointer: It is important to note that Schedule L, where this distribution is reported in part, will show the basis of Gwen's stock that she inherited from her father at its original cost, not the $100,000 in inherited value.

Example 10-7: Assume the same facts as in Example 10-6, except that Jensen Inc., instead of distributing $2,000 to Gwen in 2010, distributes vacant land that Jensen Inc. bought in 1998 for investment. The land has a cost basis to Jensen Inc. at the time of distribution of $500 and a fair market value of $2,000. The result to Gwen is that she recognizes $7,000 of income, and $1,500 of capital gain ($2,000 – $500) reported as a separately stated item. Gwen increases the basis in her stock from $100,000 to $108,500 ($100,000 + $7,000 + $1,500) pursuant to Code Sec. 1367(a)(1)(A) and (B) ($7,000 by Code Sec. 1367(a)(1)(B) and $1,500 per Code Sec. 1367(a)(1)(A)). The distribution then reduces her basis to $18,500 ($108,500 – $90,000).

.02 Timing of Distributions

The tax consequences of a distribution to an S corporation shareholder are determined at the end of the corporation's tax year.[14] Thus, if a shareholder receives money or property from the corporation during its tax year, the shareholder will not know its status for tax purposes until the end of the tax year.

> **Example 10-8:** Micky Laine is the sole shareholder of Mist Inc., a calendar-year S corporation. Laine's basis in his stock as of January 1, 2010, is $10,000. Mist Inc. elected S status on January 1, 1999, the date of its formation. On January 1, 2010, Mist Inc. distributes $100,000 in cash to Laine. For the tax year ending December 31, 2010, Mist Inc. broke even from its business operations; it had no separately stated items of gain, loss, no depletion, etc. Mist Inc., as of January 1, 2010, also made a killing of $1,000,000 in the stock market; however, on December 31, 2010, it lost $1,000,000 due to a bad trade. Laine, on his personal tax return for 2010, will report $90,000 of long-term capital gain on Schedule D (pursuant to Code Sec. 1368(b)(2)) ($10,000 stock basis – $100,000 of distribution = $90,000 of money distributed in excess of basis).

> **Tax Pointer:** A distribution is taken into account on the date made by the corporation, regardless of whether the distribution is treated as received by the shareholder under his or her method of accounting.[15]

.03 Fiscal-Year S Corporations

An S corporation could have a tax year different from that of its shareholders. However, the tax consequences of a distribution cannot be determined until the end of the S corporation's tax year.[16]

> **Example 10-9:** Sarla Inc., an S corporation formed on January 1, 2009, has a fiscal year ending October 31, 2009. Sarla Inc. has one shareholder, Ben Johnson, an individual whose stock basis on November 1, 2009, is $10,000. On December 31, 2009, Sarla Inc. makes a distribution to Johnson of $25,000. The $25,000 distribution will have no effect on Johnson's Form 1040 for 2009; rather, it will be reported on Johnson's 2010 return when Sarla Inc.'s Form 1120S is computed.

---

[14] Reg. § 1.1368-1(c).

[15] Reg. § 1.1368-1(b).

[16] Code Sec. 1368(d)(1).

.04 Distribution Rules and Debt

Note that the Code Sec. 1368 distribution rules apply only to distributions of stock, not to payments on debt. So, assuming stock basis is reduced to zero by S corporation losses or distributions, future distributions will generate capital gain for the shareholder even if he, she, or it has basis in S corporation debt.

Example 10-10: *2007.* Farmway Inc. is a calendar-year S corporation having one shareholder, Ben Miller, a bachelor who materially participates in Farmway's business activities. It has no earnings or profits. For the year ending December 31, 2007, its records indicate the following:

Stock basis, January 1, 2007	$10,000
Miller's loan to Farmway Inc., January 1, 2007	4,000
Distribution to Miller, July 1, 2007	8,000
Ordinary income for 2007 (Form 1120S, page 1)	15,000

2008. In 2008, Fairway Inc. reported a loss of $20,000 on Form 1120S, page 1, and on January 1, 2008, made a distribution of $2,000 to Miller.

2009. In 2009, Fairway Inc. had ordinary income of $23,000, and on December 31, 2009, Fairway Inc. made a distribution of $27,000 to Miller. The tax results are reported as follows:

2007	Stock	Debt	Total
Basis, January 1, 2007	$10,000	$4,000	$14,000
Ordinary Income	15,000	—	15,000
Distribution	(8,000)	—	(8,000)
Basis, December 31, 2007	$17,000	$4,000	$21,000

2008	Stock	Debt	Total
Basis, January 1, 2008	$17,000	$4,000	$21,000
$2,000 distribution*	(2,000)	—	(2,000)
$20,000 loss:			
Stock	(15,000)	—	(15,000)
Debt	—	(4,000)	(4,000)
Basis, December 31, 2008	$0	$0	$0

2008	Stock	Debt	Total
Loss carryforward, Code Sec. 1366(d)(2) ..	$ 1,000	—	$ 1,000

*Pursuant to Reg. § 1.1367-1(f), the shareholder accounts for the distribution before reducing stock basis by his distributive share of nondeductible and deductible S corporation losses.

2009	Stock	Debt	Total
Basis, January 1, 2009	$ 0	$ 0	$ 0
$23,000 ordinary income:			
Applied to restore debt .	—	4,000	4,000
Applied to stock	19,000	—	19,000
$27,000 distribution	(27,000)	—	(27,000)
Capital gain, Code Sec. 1368(b)(2)	8,000	—	8,000
Basis, December 31, 2009	$ 0	$4,000	$4,000

Note: Miller's loss carryforward under Code Sec. 1366(d)(2) was not used in 2009, and so is carried forward to 2010. The capital gain recognized on receipt of the distribution is long term since Miller's holding period for the S corporation stock dates to at least January 1, 2007.

.05 Share-by-Share Basis

In the course of an S corporation's existence, S corporation stock could be sold, given away, etc. Accordingly, basis must be tracked for each share. To do so, the shareholder must maintain adequate records to track basis and to determine the tax effects of distributions.

Example 10-11: Mary Marshall and Nicole Marshall, mother and daughter, are equal shareholders in Melody Inc., a calendar-year S corporation. On December 31, 2010, Mary died. At the time of her death, her stock had a fair market value of $10,000; Nicole's basis in her stock was $1,000. Mary bequeathed her 50% interest in Melody Inc. to her daughter Nicole. For 2010, Melody Inc. broke even and had no transactions other than distributing $5,000 to the shareholders, or $2,500 to Nicole for her 50% interest, and $2,500 to Nicole for the stock she received from her mother. Reg. § 1.1367-1(c)(3) prescribes the following result, with Nicole not recognizing any gain on the distribution:

Nicole's Share	Basis	Distribution	Excess	Basis After Distribution
Original shares	$ 1,000	$(2,500)	$ 1,500	$ 0
Inherited shares	10,000	(2,500)	(1,500)	6,000

¶ 1003 Earnings and Profits—Maintenance of AAA Account

If an S corporation has earnings and profits either because they arose from a reorganization[17] or from a predecessor C corporation, the distribution rules become more complex. The tax consequences associated with the distribution will depend on whether it is deemed to come from income generated by the S corporation or from the E&P accumulated during the prior C corporation years. Adding to this complexity is the fact that Congress adopted the Subchapter S Revision Act of 1982 (SSRA) that created a new corporate level account, the accumulated adjustments account (AAA). Prior to the SSRA of 1982, the S corporation had an account called "previously taxed income" (PTI) that was basically a personal account to each shareholder.[18] The following sections of this paragraph (¶ 1003) provide a road map for understanding the interaction of earnings and profits on distributions, the elimination of earnings and profits to avoid complexity, and the operation of the AAA.

.01 Accumulated Adjustments Account (AAA)

An S corporation is a pass-through entity with income taxed at one level, the shareholder's level, rather than taxed at both the corporate and shareholder levels, as with C corporations. The AAA is a corporate account of the S corporation that generally reflects the accumulated, undistributed net income for the corporation's post-1982 years.[19] (Corporations formed prior to 1983 use the previously taxed income (PTI) account.) Because the AAA is a corporate-level account, it is not affected by transfers of stock by sale or gift. The AAA is affected by redemptions, however.

.02 AAA Required Only if Earnings and Profits

An S corporation is required to only maintain the AAA to determine the tax effect of distributions during S years and the post-termination transition period. An S corporation without accumulated earnings and profits does not need to maintain the AAA in order to determine the tax effect of distributions. Nevertheless, if an S corporation without accumulated earnings and profits engages in certain transactions to which Code Sec. 381(a) applies, such as a merger into an S corporation with accumulated earnings and profits, the S corporation must be able to calculate its AAA at the time of the merger to determine the tax effect of post-merger distributions. Therefore, it is recommended that the AAA be maintained by all S corporations.[20] IRS Letter Ruling 9046036 prescribes that an S corporation formed

---

[17] Reorganizations are discussed in detail at ¶ 1211.
[18] See ¶ 1005 for a discussion of PTI.

[19] 2012 Instructions for Form 1120S, U.S. Income Tax Return for an S Corporation.
[20] 2012 Instructions for Form 1120S, U.S. Income Tax Return for an S Corporation.

de novo, which by definition would not have any earnings and profits, was required to maintain an AAA account.

.03 Maintaining the AAA

The AAA, as defined by Code Sec. 1368(e), is maintained and computed in a manner similar to, but not identical with, the manner in which Code Sec. 1367 computes basis. The AAA starts with a zero balance on the first day of an S corporation's first tax year beginning after 1982.[21] Reg. § 1.1368-2(a) requires that it be adjusted for subsequent S corporation operations as follows:

Increases to the AAA. The accumulated adjustments account is increased each year by[22]

(1) separately stated items that increase the S corporation's *taxable* income;

(2) S corporation nonseparately computed income; and

(3) the excess of deductions for depletion over the basis of property subject to depletion (except for oil and gas property, the basis of which has been allocated to shareholders under Code Sec. 613A(c)(11)).

Decreases to the AAA. The accumulated adjustments account is decreased each year by[23]

(1) separately stated items of loss or deduction, other than expenses attributable to nontaxable income;

(2) S corporation nonseparately computed loss; and

(3) nondeductible expenditures of the corporation not properly chargeable to a capital account (other than expenses attributable to nontaxable income and federal income taxes attributable to prior C corporation years).

In addition, AAA is decreased by S corporation distributions *deemed to originate from AAA*. It is important to note that the AAA can be reduced below zero by items of S corporation loss or deduction (including nondeductible expenditures not chargeable against capital), but it *cannot* be reduced below zero by distributions to shareholders.[24]

Losses in excess of basis decrease AAA. The negative adjustment to AAA for S corporation losses is not limited to the amount that a shareholder is allowed to deduct under the basis rules of Code Sec. 1366(d)(1).[25] Example 10-12, adapted from Reg. § 1.1368-3, Example 2, will illustrate:

Example 10-12: Corporation Saline, an S corporation, has no earnings and profits as of January 1, 2009, the first day of its 2009 tax year. Saline's sole shareholder, Alfred West, holds 10 shares of Saline stock with a basis of $1 per share as of that date. On March 1, 2009, Saline makes a distribution of $38 to West. For Saline's 2009 tax year, West's pro rata share of the amount of the items described in Code Sec. 1367(a)(1) (capital gain, ordinary income, etc.) is $50. West's pro rata share of the amount of the items described in Code Sec.

[21] Code Sec. 1368(e)(1)(A).
[22] Reg. § 1.1368-2(a)(2).
[23] Reg. § 1.1368-2(a)(3).
[24] Reg. § 1.1368-2(a)(3)(iii).
[25] Reg. § 1.1368-2(a)(3)(ii).

1367(a)(2)(B) through (D) (relating to decreases in basis of stock for items other than distributions) is $26, $20 of which is attributable to capital losses and $6 of which is attributable to a fine.

The positive adjustments to the basis of West's stock in Saline are made before the distribution rules of Code Sec. 1368 are applied. Thus, West's basis per share in the stock is $6 ($1 + ($50 ÷ 10)) before taking into account the distribution. The basis of West's stock is decreased by distributions that are not includible in West's income. The amount of the distribution that is attributable to each share of West's stock is $3.80 ($38 distribution ÷ 10 shares). Thus, West's basis per share in the stock is $2.20 ($6.00 – $3.80), after taking into account the distribution. The basis of each share of West's stock in Saline after taking into account the distribution, $2.20, is decreased by $.60 ($6 fine ÷ 10 shares). Thus, West's basis per share after taking into account the nondeductible, noncapital expenses is $1.60 (capital loss ÷ 10 shares). Next, the shareholder takes a deduction for the capital losses. However, basis may not be reduced below zero. Therefore, the basis of each share of West's stock is reduced to zero. As of January 1, 2010, West has a basis of $0 in his shares of Saline stock. The $.40 loss ($2.00 – $1.60 deduction) in excess of West's basis in each of his shares of S stock is treated as incurred by the corporation in the succeeding tax year with respect to West. Although West was allowed to deduct only $2.20 per share of flow-through losses from Saline, Saline's AAA is reduced by the full $2.60 per share loss. AAA will not be adjusted next year when (and if) West claims a deduction for the $.40-a-share carryforward under Code Sec. 1366(d).

.04 AAA Can Be Decreased Below Zero

Generally, the AAA can be decreased below zero[26] (note, however, that stock basis cannot be reduced below zero[27]). Once the AAA is negative, it can only be increased by the items detailed in Reg. § 1.1368-2(a)(2) (income from the S corporation operations, capital gains, etc.).[28] Shareholder contributions have no effect on AAA.

.05 Distributions and the AAA

After all the adjustments have been made, the AAA is reduced (but not below zero) by any distribution to shareholders.[29]

.06 Example of Maintaining the AAA

The operation of the AAA is shown in Example 10-13.

Example 10-13: Apex Inc., a calendar-year S corporation, has one shareholder, John Howe. For 2010, its first year of operation, Apex Inc. had the following:

---

[26] Reg. § 1.1368-2(a)(3)(ii).
[27] Code Sec. 1367(a)(2).
[28] Code Sec. 1368(e)(1).
[29] Reg. § 1.1368-2(a)(3)(i) and (iii).

Ordinary income from operations	$219,000
Loss from real estate operation	(3,000)
Interest income	4,000
Dividend income	16,000
Charitable contributions	(24,000)
Code Sec. 179 depreciation expense	(3,000)
Work opportunity credit	6,000
Nondeductible expense (reduction in salaries for work opportunity credit)	(6,000)
Cash distributions to shareholders	65,000

Apex Inc.'s AAA as of December 31, 2010, is $138,000, computed as follows:

1. Balance at beginning of year	$ 0
2. Ordinary income	219,000
3. Other additions (interest $4,000 + dividend $16,000)	20,000
4. Other reductions (real estate loss $3,000 + charitable contribution $24,000 + Code Sec. 179 depreciation $3,000 + nondeductible expense $6,000*)	(36,000)
5. Combine lines 1 through 4	203,000
6. Distributions	65,000
7. Balance at end of tax year (subtract line 6 from 5)	$138,000

*AAA is properly adjusted for $6,000 nondeductible wages. These are not attributable to tax-exempt income.

.07 Distributions in Excess of the AAA

Generally if there is more than one distribution during the corporation's tax year, and the total amount of distributions exceeds the AAA at the end of the tax year, an allocation must be made to determine what portion of the distribution will be a nontaxable distribution of the AAA, and what portion will not.[30] The nontaxable, AAA portion of each distribution is determined by multiplying the balance of the AAA at the close of the current tax year by a fraction, the numerator of which is the amount of each distribution and the denominator of which is the amount of all distributions made during the tax year.[31]

---

[30] Reg. § 1.1368-2(b).   [31] Reg. § 1.1368-2(b)(2).

Example 10-14: Grayson Inc., a calendar-year S corporation, has $10,000 in the AAA as of the end of its first tax year 2010. The following distributions were made to Grayson Inc.'s shareholders during 2010: $12,500 on June 30, and $12,500 on December 31, for total distributions of $25,000. Because the total distributions from the AAA exceed the balance of the AAA at the end of the year by $15,000 ($25,000 – $10,000), 40% ($10,000 ÷ $25,000) will be deemed nontaxable; accordingly, $5,000 of each distribution is a nontaxable distribution of the AAA (40% × $12,500).

.08 AAA Adjustment for Redemptions of Stock

Redemptions of corporate stock by a shareholder could be treated as dividends or afforded capital gains treatment, depending on whether the redemption meets the requirements of Code Sec. 302(b) or Code Sec. 303. If a redemption is not qualified, then the proceeds received by the shareholders are subject to the rules applicable to S corporation distributions. If the redemption is qualified under Code Sec. 302(b) or Code Sec. 303, then the AAA is adjusted by an amount equal to the ratable share of the AAA (positive or negative) attributable to the reduced stock.[32]

Example 10-15: MuShu Inc., a calendar-year S corporation, has ten equal shareholders, each owning 10% of the stock. As of December 31, 2010, MuShu Inc. has AAA of $1,000. On that date, MuShu Inc. redeems the entire stock holding of Bin Ho, one of the shareholders, in a qualified redemption under Code Sec. 302(b). MuShu Inc. must reduce its AAA by $100 (10% × $1,000). (If the corporation has earnings and profits, the previously taxed income (PTI) account and the other adjustments account (OAA)[33] must be adjusted as well.)

Example 10-16: Assume the same facts as in Example 10-15, except that MuShu Inc.'s AAA had a deficit balance of $1,000. MuShu Inc. must reduce its AAA by $100, leaving it with AAA of ($900).

Example 10-17: Jardine Inc., a calendar-year S corporation, has AAA of $500 at the end of its 2010 tax year. Jardine Inc. has two shareholders, Marcus Hall and Manny Palmas, who are not related. They each own 50 shares. Jardine Inc. redeems 10 shares of Hall's stock for $500; however, the redemption does not qualify for capital gains treatment under Code Sec. 302(b) or Code Sec. 303. Jardine Inc.'s AAA is reduced to zero, allowing Hall to treat the entire $500 as a nontaxable distribution from the AAA.

Tax Pointer: As Example 10-17 illustrates, with proper tax planning, desired results can be obtained. Example 10-17 also illustrates that the AAA can be a trap.

Ordinary and redemption distributions. In any year in which a corporation makes one or more ordinary distributions and makes one or more redemption distributions, the AAA of the corporation is adjusted first for any ordinary distributions and then for any redemption distributions.[34]

[32] Reg. § 1.1368-2(d).
[33] See ¶ 1006 for a definition of OAA.
[34] Reg. § 1.1368-2(d)(1)(i).

.09 AAA in Reorganizations and Separations

An S corporation acquiring the assets of another S corporation in a reorganization under Code Sec. 368(a)(1) will succeed to and merge its AAA (whether positive or negative) with the AAA (whether positive or negative) of the distributor or transferor S corporation as of the close of the date of distribution or transfer.[35] Thus, the AAA of the acquiring corporation after the transaction is the sum of the AAAs of both corporations prior to the transaction.

.10 Life Insurance Proceeds Do Not Increase AAA

An S corporation may want to purchase life insurance on a shareholder, a key employee, etc. The reason why the S corporation would want to insure a shareholder's life is to fund a redemption of the shareholder's stock at the shareholder's death.[36] While Code Sec. 101 will exempt the proceeds from income tax for the shareholders and the corporation, it will not increase AAA. Furthermore, Reg. § 1.1368-2(a)(3)(i)(C)(2) indicates that the premiums paid for the life insurance policy(ies) do not reduce AAA.

¶ 1004 Earnings and Profits

The AAA is only relevant if the S corporation has earnings and profits. For S corporations formed after 1982, the general order of distributions is:[37]

(1) AAA earnings

(2) Earnings and profits

(3) Stock basis

(4) Capital gains for anything in excess of the first three categories

Note that tax-exempt income (and related expenses) of the S corporation are not reflected in its AAA. These items are reflected in shareholder basis; however, under the above ordering rules, they can be distributed to the shareholders only after the S corporation has distributed all of its E&P.

> **Tax Pointer:** Because increases to AAA also increase the shareholders' bases in their S corporation stock, distributions from AAA reduce both AAA and stock basis. Thus, although a distribution from AAA will generally not trigger recognition of gain to any shareholder, it will reduce stock basis, increasing the likelihood that subsequent distributions may be partially or wholly taxable to shareholders.

.01 Definition of Earnings and Profits

By definition, an S corporation does not have earnings and profits; rather, an S corporation acquires earnings and profits from a predecessor or with respect to a reorganization.[38] The Small Business Jobs Protection Act of 1996 provided that if a corporation was an S corporation for its first taxable year beginning after December 31, 1996, the accumulated earnings and profits of the corporation as of the begin-

---

[35] Reg. § 1.1368-2(d)(2).

[36] See discussion at ¶ 1125 for the various forms of life insurance ownership and the tax consequences following therefrom.

[37] For S corporations formed before 1983, an additional S corporation account for "previously taxed income" (PTI) must be considered. See ¶ 1005.

[38] Code Sec. 1371(c)(1).

ning of that year were reduced by the accumulated earnings and profits (if any) accumulated in a taxable year beginning before January 1, 1983, for which the corporation was an electing small business corporation under Subchapter S.

Congress now provides for taxable years beginning after May 25, 2007 in the case of any corporation which was not an S corporation for its first taxable year beginning after December 31, 1996, the accumulated earnings and profits of the corporation as of the beginning of the first taxable year beginning after May 25, 2007 is reduced by the accumulated earnings and profits (if any) accumulated in a taxable year beginning before January 1, 1983, for which the corporation was an electing small business corporation under Subchapter S.

.02 Order Required for Distributions of Earnings and Profits

If the S corporation has earnings and profits,[39] distributions have tax consequences as follows:

(1) Distributions are tax free to the extent of the AAA.[40]

(2) The remainder of the distribution is then taxable as a dividend to the extent of the S corporation's earnings and profits.[41]

(3) The next portion of the distribution is tax free to the extent of the shareholder's basis in stock of the S corporation.[42]

(4) Finally, the remaining distribution generates taxable gain (capital gain) to the extent the distribution exceeds the basis in stock.[43]

Earnings and profits are reduced by the amount of dividends to the shareholders (see (2) above)[44] and have to be adjusted for stock redemptions and partial liquidations occurring under Code Sec. 302[45] as well as Code Sec. 368 reorganizations and Code Sec. 355 transactions.[46] Earnings and profits must be reduced by any recapture tax for which the S corporation would be liable under Code Sec. 47 for the recapture of investment tax credit.[47]

> **Example 10-18:** Zeus Inc., a calendar-year S corporation, has one shareholder, Eileen Nelson. Zeus Inc.'s AAA was ($20,000) (deficit) on January 1, 2009, and Nelson's basis in her Zeus stock was $40,000. Zeus Inc. also had $30,000 in accumulated earnings and profits from prior years as a C corporation. For its 2009 tax year, Zeus Inc. reported taxable net profits of $12,000, and no separately stated items. The company distributed $8,500 to Nelson. Because S corporation profits were not sufficient to increase Zeus Inc.'s AAA above zero (AAA will be ($8,000) after adjustment for the current year's profits), no portion of the distribution to Nelson will be deemed to originate from AAA. Accordingly, the entire $8,500 distribution will be taxed as a dividend, reducing Zeus Inc.'s E&P to $21,500. It will have AAA at January 1, 2010, of ($8,000) (deficit balance), and Nelson's stock basis will still be $40,000.

---

[39] Code Sec. 1368(c).

[40] Code Sec. 1368(c)(1).

[41] Code Sec. 1368(c)(2).

[42] Code Sec. 1368(b)(1).

[43] Code Sec. 1368(b)(2).

[44] Code Sec. 1371(c)(3).

[45] See ¶ 1209 for discussion of redemptions and partial liquidations.

[46] See ¶ 1211 for discussion of reorganizations and transactions.

[47] Code Sec. 1371(d)(3).

Tax Pointer: For earnings and profits which exist in an S Corporation for periods for taxable years beginning before January 1, 1983 there exist special rules regarding inclusion. See ¶ 1004.01 for a discussion of these rules.

.03 Election to Bypass the AAA

The shareholders of an S corporation can make an election to reduce earnings and profits of the S corporation before taking a distribution from the AAA. The shareholders may consider this when owing a tax under Code Sec. 1375 (tax on excess passive income) or loss of election under Code Sec. 1362(d)(3). See Appendix 3 for a sample form to make this election. Example 10-19 illustrates the operation of the election under Code Sec. 1368(e)(3):

> *Example 10-19:* Quantum Inc., a calendar-year S corporation is composed of two shareholders, Bob and Jack McCoy, brothers. In 2010, Quantum Inc. makes a distribution to the two brothers of $10,000 each. On December 31, 2010, before giving effect to the distributions, Quantum Inc.'s earnings and profits account is $20,000, its AAA is $35,000, and the shareholders' bases are $40,000 (aggregate). The brothers, because the corporation will face a tax under Code Sec. 1375 for passive investment income,[48] decide to file an election under Code Sec. 1368(e)(3) regarding the $20,000 distribution. The effect of the election will be to reduce the $20,000 of earnings and profits to zero and thus prevent the imposition of tax under Code Sec. 1375. The brothers would realize ordinary income of $20,000 from the dividend. If they had not made the election under Code Sec. 1368(e)(3), the $20,000 would have been a nontaxable distribution from the AAA, reducing AAA to $15,000 and their aggregate stock basis to $20,000.

Reasons to make a Code Sec. 1368(e)(3) election. An S shareholder could find him-, her-, or itself in a situation where Code Sec. 1375 and Code Sec. 1362(d)(3) have no effect, yet the shareholder wants to make a Code Sec. 1368(e)(3) election to incur a dividend rather than have a tax-free distribution under the AAA. A shareholder may prefer a dividend distribution, for example, if the shareholder has a substantial personal net operating loss in the tax year that cannot otherwise be used. Alternatively, the shareholder may need investment income for purposes of the investment interest expense limitation of Code Sec. 163(d).[49] In such cases, an election under Code Sec. 1368(e)(3) would reduce the S corporation's E&P without increasing the shareholder's individual tax liability.

> *Example 10-20:* Assume the same facts as in Example 10-19, except the S corporation is not facing a tax under Code Sec. 1375. The shareholders, because of Code Sec. 163(d), have excess investment interest expense of $10,000 each. They file the Code Sec. 1368(e)(3) election to have $10,000 distributed to them in 2010 as a dividend. Due to their excess investment interest expense, the dividend will not increase their tax liability; yet E&P will be eliminated, preventing the corporation from encountering future problems with the tax on excess passive income.

---

[48] See ¶ 804 for discussion of passive investment income.

[49] See ¶ 702 for discussion of interest expense.

> ***Tax Pointer:*** If the S corporation does not completely distribute the earnings and profits in the first year it elects under Code Sec. 1368(e)(3) and wants to make the election in a different year, it must file the election form again and obtain the necessary consents.

¶ 1005 Distributions of Previously Taxed Income (PTI)

.01 Distribution Rules

If an S corporation was in existence prior to the Subchapter S Revision Act of 1982, it could have previously taxed income (PTI). It is beyond the scope of this book to offer a detailed discussion of PTI; however, the following should be noted. PTI represents taxable income of an S corporation prior to January 1, 1983, that was not distributed to the shareholders. PTI is a personal item to the shareholders—it is not transferable as is the AAA. Under prior law, PTI increased the basis of stock just as AAA does under current law.

For distributions of PTI, Code Sec. 1368 does not specifically address this point. However, the Instructions for Form 1120S include distribution rules. If the S corporation does not have earnings and profits, the distribution from the S corporation is made in the following order:

(1) AAA

(2) PTI

(3) Nontaxable return of capital to the extent of remaining basis

(4) Taxable disposition of stock

If the S corporation has earnings and profits as well as PTI, the order of distribution is as follows:

(1) AAA

(2) PTI

(3) Dividend to the extent of earnings and profits

(4) Nontaxable return of capital to the extent of remaining basis

(5) Taxable disposition of stock

Example 10-21: Bryce Inc., a calendar-year S corporation, is composed of one shareholder, Jane Bryce. Bryce Inc. was incorporated in 1978. In 2010, before any distributions, Bryce Inc. has the following items on its balance sheet: AAA, $5,000; PTI, $10,000. Jane's stock basis is $1,500. In 2010, Bryce Inc. distributed a total of $17,000 to Jane—$8,000 in June and $9,000 in October. The tax treatment is as follows:

Source of Distribution	Distribution	Nontaxable	Taxable Distribution Capital Gains
Total distribution	$ 17,000		
From the AAA	(5,000)	$ 5,000	
Balance	$ 12,000		
From PTI	(10,000)	10,000	
Balance	$ 2,000		
From stock basis	1,500	1,500	
Balance	$ 500		
Capital gains	(500)		$500
Total	$ 0	$16,500	$500

Example 10-22: Manny Davis has been a shareholder in an S corporation since 1978. At the end of 2010, before any distributions, Davis's stock basis is $15,500. This $15,500 basis is divided as follows:

1.   AAA . . . . $ 5,000
2.   PTI   10,000
3.   Capital contribution under Code Sec. 351 . .   500

                                                   $15,500

During 2010, Davis received distributions of $8,000 in June and $9,000 in October from the S corporation. Davis's share of earnings and profits of the S corporation was $500. The tax consequences of the distribution are as follows:

Source of Distribution	Distribution	Nontaxable	Dividend	Taxable Distribution Capital Gains
Total distribution . .	$ 17,000			
From the AAA	(5,000)	$ 5,000		
Balance	$ 12,000			
From PTI	(10,000)	10,000		
Balance	$ 2,000			
From earnings and profits	(500)		$500	
Balance	$ 1,500			
From balance of stock basis	(500)	500		
Balance	$ 1,000			

¶1005.01

Source of Distribution	Distribution	Nontaxable	Dividend	Taxable Distribution Capital Gains
Gain from a sale or exchange	1,000			$1,000
Total	$ 0	$15,500	$500	$1,000

Since the distributions of $17,000 exceed the balance in the AAA at the close of the tax year, the $5,000 must be allocated proportionately between the June distribution of $8,000 and the October distribution of $9,000, or $2,353 and $2,647 respectively. At year end, Davis's basis in his stock is $0 because his beginning adjusted basis in the stock was $15,500, and $15,500 of the distributions is treated as a return of his basis in the stock. Also, in addition to his share of the separately stated items and the nonseparately computed income, Davis must report a $500 dividend and a $1,000 long-term capital gain on his personal income tax return as a result of the distributions.

.02 Election to Bypass the PTI Account

An S corporation with PTI can elect to bypass the PTI account for distributions similar to the means to bypass the AAA for distributions of earnings and profits.[50] In the bypass election, an S corporation can bypass the AAA to have distributions from PTI, or can bypass both the AAA and PTI and have the distribution made from earnings and profits only.

¶ 1006 Other Adjustments Account (OAA)

Tax-exempt income and any expense related to it do not increase or decrease the AAA; however, tax-exempt income increases basis and tax-exempt expense decreases basis.[51]

Tax-exempt income and expense is reported on Form 1120S, Schedule M, and for distribution purposes it is reported on Schedule M-2, column (b)—Other adjustments account. The consequence of tax-exempt income and expense to an S corporation is that if it is not careful, the distribution could cause a taxable dividend to occur if the S corporation has earnings and profits.

Example 10-23: Veda Inc. is an S corporation that has ordinary income of $5,000 at the end of its tax year, which increases the AAA to $5,000. It also reported tax-exempt income from a state bond of $12,000, and has earnings and profits of $7,000 from prior years as a C corporation. During the S corporation tax year, $6,000 is distributed to the shareholders. Of the $6,000 received by the shareholders, the first $5,000 will be treated as a tax-free distribution from AAA. However, because the S corporation's tax-exempt interest income does not increase AAA, the next $1,000 received by the shareholders will be taxable as dividend income. At the end of the year, the

---

[50] Reg. § 1.1368-1(f)(2)(ii). See discussion of election to bypass the AAA at ¶ 1004.03.

[51] Code Sec. 1368(e)(1). See ¶ 903.02 for a discussion of stock-basis adjustments.

shareholders' stock bases will be increased by $12,000 ($5,000 ordinary income + $12,000 tax-exempt income – $5,000 distribution from AAA). The balance in the AAA going into the next year will be zero, and the balance in E&P will be $6,000 ($7,000 beginning balance – $1,000 dividend distribution).

¶ 1007 S Corporation's Payments on Behalf of Its Shareholders

When a shareholder's S corporation makes payments on behalf of a shareholder, such as paying a shareholder's business expenses, the question arises how to characterize it—is it a loan or a distribution. The answer is fact intensive. *Prewitt v. Commissioner*[52] held that the S corporate shareholder could deduct on his individual return expenses paid by the S corporation on his behalf in connection with an insurance business where the amounts claimed had not been deducted by the S corporation. The payments were made by the S corporation to satisfy debts of the shareholder's other business and were necessary to protect the shareholder's insurance business. The Court classified the payments to the shareholder as loan.

---

[52] TC Memo 1995-487.

Chapter 11

Income and Estate Tax Planning

¶ 1101 Tax Planning

An S corporation has restricted income and estate tax planning opportunities that Congress has imposed. For example, only certain trusts are permitted to be shareholders in an S corporation. Notwithstanding, there are still numerous ways to use S corporations in income and estate tax planning. The most useful ways are discussed in this chapter.

¶ 1102 Providing Funds for the Elderly or Other Relatives

An S corporation can be used to enhance the funds provided by an adult child for his or her parents (or vice versa).

> **Example 11-1:** Marvin Dunn's parents, Alvin and Harriet, are retired, but both are under the age of 62. Dunn, because of his high income, is in the 35% bracket. Thus, it costs him $100 to give his parents $75. If Dunn made his parents shareholders in his S corporation, the middleman, Uncle Sam, would be eliminated and Dunn would effectively be able to give more money to his parents since the money would go directly to them from the S corporation. Dunn's parents would pay tax on their S shareholder income at their low tax bracket rate of 15% instead of Marvin's high bracket of 35% thereby providing them with more funds (i.e., 20% (35% − 15%) times whatever funds are paid to the parents from the S corporation).

> **Tax Pointer 1:** Code Sec. 1366(e) requires that shareholders in a family-owned S corporation must be fairly compensated for services rendered, and/or capital provided, to the S corporation. Thus, family members working or otherwise providing services for the S corporation must be paid a reasonable salary for their efforts, which reduces S corporation income that can be allocated to family members. Likewise, shareholders providing capital (e.g., allowing the S corporation to use shareholder-owned equipment) must be fairly compensated before allocating residual income to other family members.

> **Tax Pointer 2:** Field Service Advice 200143004 (July 5, 2001), discussed at ¶ 1126.01, refused to recognize an S corporation established by a mother where the corporate assets were cash, Treasury bills and municipal bonds, prescribing that when the mother transferred S corporation stock to her children utilizing minority discounts, her sole purpose was to reduce federal taxes. The IRS felt that the S corporation had no business purpose and was formed solely as a conduit for planned family giving using Code Sec. 2503(b)'s annual exclusion.

Kiddie Tax. Code Sec. 1(g) provides special rules (generally referred to as the "kiddie tax") for the net unearned income of certain children. Generally, the kiddie tax applies where: (1) (a) the child is under-age 18, regardless of whether his or her earned income equals more than one-half of his or her support; or (b) the child turns 18, or if a full-time student turns 19-23, before the end of the applicable year, and the child's earned income for the tax year does not exceed one-half of his or her support; (2) the child has at least one living parent at the close of the tax year;

(3) the child doesn't file a joint return for the tax year; and (4) the child has more than the inflation-adjusted prescribed amount of unearned income that triggers the kiddie tax.

Reg. § 1.152-1(a)(2)(i) defines support:

> The term "support" includes food, shelter, clothing, medical and dental care, education, and the like. Generally, the amount of an item of support will be the amount of expense incurred by the one furnishing such item. If the item of support furnished an individual is in the form of property or lodging, it will be necessary to measure the amount of such item of support in terms of its fair market value.

Cases under case law defining support incorporate a person's lifestyle, not necessarily "necessities" so that the definition includes parochial high school, college, summer camp, bicycle repairs, vacations, etc. Accordingly, case law should be consulted to determine which items are deemed support and which are not.

In terms of tax planning, a number of situations can be followed:

1. Parents can no longer flip to kids in college gifts of appreciated property to pay college expenses; thus students have to take out student loans to be repaid when they reach age 24, cashing in the appreciated property at that time. However, it is impossible to predict what the capital gain rate will be at that time.

2. Any child who is a beneficiary of a qualified disability trust (as defined in Code Sec. 642(b)(2)(C)(ii)), any amount included in the income of such child under Code Secs. 652 and 662 during a taxable year shall be considered earned income of such child for such taxable year.

3. Scholarships received by a student at a Code Sec. 170(b)(1)(A)(ii) educational institution are not counted as support.

4. Parents who have a business can hire their children to work for them and pay them reasonable compensation with this compensation being taxed at the child's tax rates, and if the child earns more than one-half of his or her support for the year, then the child will not be subject to kiddie tax on unearned income.

5. Parents of children who are subject to the kiddie tax rules should consider means to avoid tax such as making the children stockholders in a family business which produces little or no cash dividends, purchasing tax exempt bonds or Series EE savings bonds to defer the interest reporting.

¶ 1103 Retirement Plans and Fringe Benefits

Since the enactment of the Employee Retirement Income Security Act of 1974 (ERISA), the area of retirement planning has become an extremely complex area with jurisdiction for enactment resting in two principal areas: the Department of Labor and the Internal Revenue Service. ERISA has been amended a number of times, with the latest being the Pension Protection Act of 2006 (PPA). It is beyond the scope of this book to provide a comprehensive discussion of the area, rather just a brief overview of some of the pertinent areas which would apply to S corporations.

Generally, the rules regarding retirement plans for S corporations are similar to the ones for C corporations; however, Code Sec. 1372 treats S corporations as partnerships for this purpose. Code Sec. 1372 permits S corporations to establish fringe benefits for their shareholder-employees, but subject to the limitations imposed on partnerships. Thus, S corporations can establish retirement plans, Code Sec. 401(k) plans, etc.

An S corporation can establish retirement plans and fringe benefits for its employees, although there are restrictions on the amounts that can be contributed on behalf of 2-percent-or-more shareholder-employees.[1] Nonetheless, retirement plans may be the only option for shareholder-employees to accumulate funds tax free.

> **Tax Pointer:** The IRS can attack retirement benefits of a shareholder-beneficiary for unpaid taxes.[2] For a case illustrating such a situation, see *Sawaf.*[3]

The Economic Growth and Tax Relief Reconciliation Act of 2001 (EGTRRA) and the Job Creation and Worker Assistance Act of 2002 (JCWA) substantially enhanced the planning possibilities with retirement plans for S corporation shareholder-employees. It is beyond the scope of this book to present a detailed analysis of EGTRRA and JCWA; however, several areas are discussed. For a complete analysis, the provisions of EGTRRA and JCWA should be consulted.

In terms of the planning possibilities caused by EGTRRA and JCWA, the following illustration is set forth.

> **Example 11-2:** Assume that Tom, age 26, a consultant, is debating how to operate. He is debating whether to operate as a self-employed individual utilizing a one-taxpayer LLC, or as a corporation. Tom earns a net of $100,000 from his consulting income after self-employment tax. Tom established a Code Sec. 401(k) plan and a profit-sharing plan. Tom can contribute $11,000 to the Code Sec. 401(k) plan (additional contribution if the consultant is age 50 or older this year), and then $20,000 to the profit-sharing plan, due to the change fostered by the Economic Growth and Tax Relief Reconciliation Act of 2001, in that the contribution to the profit-sharing plan is not reduced by the salary reduction pay-in for the Code Sec. 401(k) plan. If Tom signs the consulting agreement, has his corporation sign the consulting agreement with the business who is paying for the consulting services, and Tom takes a salary from the corporation, the results become even more dramatic, because the corporation's contribution to the profit-sharing plan is *not* limited by the 20% pay-in requirement for self-employed individuals. Thus, utilizing the $100,000 of compensation illustration discussed previously, the profit-sharing plan contribution is 25% of compensation, or $25,000, and the Code Sec. 401(k) plan contribution is $11,000, or a total of $36,000; the contributions would be $37,000 if the salaried individual is age 50 or over this year.

---

[1] See Code Sec. 1372 which treats S corporations as partnerships for this purpose.

[2] Code Sec. 401(a)(13).

[3] *A.H. Sawaf,* CA-6, 96-1 USTC ¶ 50,063, 74 F3d 119.

¶1103

.01 Contributions to Retirement Plans

S corporations can make contributions to retirement plans pursuant to the rules regarding Keogh plans. As such, the contributions are geared to compensation, not profits distributed to shareholder-employees. Consequently, while pursuant to ¶ 716.03, distributions to shareholder-employees are not subject to self-employment tax—they provide no benefit for a shareholder-employee who wishes to utilize a retirement plan for income and estate tax planning purposes.

.02 Employee Stock Ownership Plan Trusts

As Chapter 15 illustrates, ESOPs offer an income-tax-free means to transfer ownership from the owners of a company to the employees. The ESOP is an evolving concept with new cases and rulings emerging daily. One interesting planning possibility involves an S corporation acquiring a building partly leased to an ESOP sponsor.[4] The acquired building, as illustrated in Example 11-3, is considered a qualified replacement property for stock that the ESOP sponsor sold to the ESOP.[5]

> **Example 11-3:** Celtic Inc. is owned equally by shareholders and brothers William, James, and Daniel O'Neill. Celtic Inc. established an ESOP, and on January 30, 2003, each brother sold 11% of Celtic Inc. stock to the ESOP in a transaction that qualified under Code Sec. 1042(b), leaving each brother owning 22.3% of Celtic Inc.'s stock. The three brothers, on or before January 30, 2004, will each reinvest the proceeds from the sale to the ESOP in qualified replacement property under Code Sec. 1042. Their plan is to form a new corporation, Shamrock Inc., that will elect S status, and they will reinvest all or part of the proceeds from the ESOP transaction in Shamrock Inc. within the 12-month reinvestment period prescribed under Code Sec. 1042. Celtic Inc. leases some space in a building owned by Jim Yarrow. Shamrock Inc. intends to buy the building from Yarrow. Notwithstanding the fact that the three O'Neill brothers still control Celtic Inc., owning 67%, the acquisition of Shamrock Inc. stock by the O'Neills will constitute qualified replacement property.

.03 Contributions to Individual Retirement Accounts (IRAs)

Reg. § 1.219-1(c)(1) prescribes that salary received by an S corporation shareholder-employee is compensation for purposes of contributions to an IRA; however, S corporation earnings distributed to a shareholder under Code Sec. 1366(a) is not compensation for IRA purposes. However, Code Sec. 219(g) imposes an adjusted gross income (AGI) limitation if the shareholder-employee is an active participant in a retirement plan with respect to the taxpayer's IRA contributions, prescribing that no contribution will be permitted if the shareholder-employee's AGI for 2010 is $56,000 for a single person and $89,000 for joint returns. For purposes of the computation of AGI, it includes a shareholder-employee's S corporation distributions.

---

[4] For a discussion of ESOPs, see Chapter 15. See also Michael Schlesinger, "How Far Does Small Business Act Go in Extending ESOP Benefits to S Corporations?," *Journal of Taxation*, Vol. 89, No. 6 at 361 (June 1997).

[5] IRS Letter Rulings 9801053-055 (October 8, 1997).

Catch-up contributions. If a shareholder-employee is over 50 during the shareholder-employee's taxable year, the individual, pursuant to Code Sec. 219(b)(5)(B) will be able to make annually $1,000 catch-up contributions over and above his or her regular IRA contribution. Code Sec. 219(b)(5)(B)'s catch-up contributions are not tied to a shareholder working during the taxable year; he or she just has to have an IRA established for previous employment.

Tax Pointer: The Bankruptcy Abuse Prevention and Consumer Protection Act of 2005 (BAPCPA) provides various limitations with respect to tax planning using these vehicles. The reader should consult ¶ 1103.15 for a discussion of this topic.

.04 Credits for Establishing a Retirement Plan

To encourage small employers to establish retirement plans, Congress, per Code Sec. 45E, Code Sec. 38(b)(14), Code Sec. 39(d)(10), and Code Sec. 196(c)(10), provides a nonrefundable income tax credit for 50 percent of the administrative and retirement-education expenses for any small business that adopts a new qualified defined benefit or defined contribution plan (including a Code Sec. 401(k) plan), SIMPLE plan, or simplified employee pension (SEP). The credit applies to 50 percent of the first $1,000 in administrative and retirement-education expenses for the plan for each of the first three years of the plan (Code Sec. 45E(a)).

The credit, which is limited to $500 in any tax year, is available to an employer that did not employ, in the preceding year, more than 100 employees who receive compensation at least equal to $5,000 per year. Per Code Sec. 45E(e)(1), in order for an employer to be eligible for the credit, the plan must cover at least one nonhighly compensated employee.[6] In addition, if the credit is for the cost of a payroll deduction IRA arrangement, the arrangement must be made available to all employees of the employer who have worked with the employer for at least three months.

The credit is a general business credit. Code Sec. 45E(b) prescribes that the maximum credit is $500 for the first credit year and for the two taxable years immediately following the first credit year. The 50 percent of qualifying expenses that are effectively offset by the tax credit are not deductible; the other 50 percent of the qualifying expenses (and other expenses) are deductible to the extent permitted under present law. An example will illustrate.

Example 11-4: Alpha, Inc., an S corporation with 20 employees who has never offered a retirement plan for its employees, adopts one for full-time employees in 2007, incurring plan-related costs of $1,500 in 2007; $2,300 in 2008; and $2,400 in 2009. Alpha, Inc. can deduct a credit of $500 in each of the three years: 2007, 2008, and 2009. Alpha, Inc. can deduct as a business expense under Code Sec. 162: $1,000 in 2007 ($1,500 minus $500); $1,800 in 2008; and $1,900 in 2009.

---

[6] Congress did not define in Code Sec. 45E(d)(1)(B) who is a "highly compensated employee." Presumably, Code Sec. 414(q)'s definition will apply.

¶1103.04

.05 Rollovers of Retirement Plan and IRA Distributions

Under prior law, taxpayers were permitted the rollover of funds from a tax-favored retirement plan to another tax-favored retirement plan. The rules that applied depended on the type of plan involved. Similarly, the rules regarding the tax treatment of amounts that are not rolled over depended on the type of plan involved. Congress, to provide further incentives for individuals to continue to accumulate funds for retirement, amended various Code sections effective for distribution after December 31, 2001.

General provisions. The law has been amended to provide that eligible rollover distributions from qualified retirement plans, Code Sec. 403(b) annuities (primarily for employees of public schools and certain tax-exempt organizations), and governmental Code Sec. 457 plans generally can be rolled over to any of such plans or arrangements.[7]

Similarly, distributions from an IRA generally are permitted to be rolled over into a qualified plan, Code Sec. 403(b) annuity, or governmental Code Sec. 457 plan. The direct rollover and withholding rules are extended to distributions from a governmental Code Sec. 457 plan, and such plans are required to provide the written notification regarding eligible rollover distributions.

The rollover notice (with respect to all plans) is required to include a description of the provisions under which distributions from the plan to which the distribution is rolled over may be subject to restrictions and tax consequences different than those applicable to distributions from the distributing plan. Qualified plans, Code Sec. 403(b) annuities, and Code Sec. 457 plans would not be required to accept rollovers.

Some special rules apply in certain cases. A distribution from a qualified plan is not eligible for capital gains or averaging treatment if there was a rollover to the plan that would not have been permitted under prior law. Thus, in order to preserve capital gains (i.e., for those individuals born before 1936) and averaging treatment for a qualified plan distribution that is rolled over, the rollover would have to be made to a "conduit IRA" as under present law, and then rolled back into a qualified plan. Amounts distributed from a Code Sec. 457 plan are subject to the early withdrawal tax to the extent the distribution consists of amounts attributable to rollovers from another type of plan. Code Sec. 457 plans are required to separately account for such amounts.

In order to accept rollovers of after-tax contributions, a qualified plan must separately track the contributions and earnings generated thereon. IRAs are not required to separately track after-tax contributions. Code Sec. 401(a)(31)(B) prescribes that a qualified plan must separately permit direct trustee-to-trustee rollovers of after-tax contributions to an IRA or to a qualified plan if the IRA and/or plan have separate accounts to track the taxable portion of the distribution. However, as discussed *infra*, after-tax contributions may not be rolled over from an IRA

---

[7] Hardship distributions from governmental Code Sec. 457 plans would be considered eligible rollover distributions.

to a qualified plan, unless the individual's IRA combined amount contains a taxable amount at least as much as the nontaxable amount being rolled over.

> *Tax Pointer 1:* The "rollover" amendments are not mandatory. They only apply if qualified plans, Code Sec. 457 plans, etc., permit rollovers to occur.

> *Tax Pointer 2:* The Bankruptcy Abuse Prevention and Consumer Protection Act of 2005 (BAPCPA) provides various limitations with respect to tax planning using these vehicles. The reader should consult ¶ 1103.15 for a discussion of this topic.

> *Tax Pointer 3:* An employer's and trustee's failure to disclose adverse tax consequences of an early retirement program was deemed a breach of fiduciary duties under ERISA; however, despite fiduciary breach, no remedy is available to the participants under ERISA.[8]

> *Tax Pointer 4:* From a tax planning perspective, a rollover from an IRA to a retirement plan is not a wise idea, because there are more benefits to an IRA participant than a participant in a retirement plan. For instance, the individual in an IRA can direct the investment strategy of the IRA; this will be impossible in a retirement plan unless the participant is also a trustee.

Direct rollovers from eligible retirement plans to Roth IRAs. Code Sec. 408A(e) has been amended effective for distributions made after December 31, 2007 to allow distributions from tax-qualified retirement plans, tax-sheltered annuities, and governmental 457 plans to be rolled over directly trustee to trustee from such plan into a Roth IRA, subject to the present law rules that apply to rollovers from a traditional IRA into a Roth IRA. For example, a rollover from a tax-qualified retirement plan into a Roth IRA is includible in gross income (except to the extent it represents a return of after-tax contributions), and the 10-percent early distribution tax does not apply. Similarly, an individual with AGI of $100,000 or more could not roll over amounts from a tax-qualified retirement plan directly into a Roth IRA.

.06 Notice of Significant Reduction in Plan Benefit Accruals

Under prior law, the Internal Revenue Code did not require any notice concerning a plan amendment that provides for a significant reduction in the rate of future benefit accrual.

Congress believed that employees were entitled to meaningful disclosure concerning plan amendments that may result in reductions of future benefit accruals; in particular, conversion of traditional defined benefit plans to "cash balance" plans. Congress also believed that any disclosure requirements applicable to plan amendments should strike a balance between providing meaningful disclosure and avoiding the imposition of unnecessary administrative burdens on employers, and that this balance may best be struck through the regulatory process with an opportunity for input from affected parties.

In addition, Congress understood that there were other issues in addition to disclosure that have arisen with respect to the conversion of defined benefit plans

---

[8] *Farr v. U.S. West Communications, Inc.*, 151 F3d 908 (9th Cir. 1998). Cert. denied, 120 SCt 935 (1/18/00).

¶1103.06

to cash balance or other hybrid plans, particularly situations in which plan participants did not earn any additional benefit under the plan for some time after
conversion (called a "wear away").

Code Sec. 4980F(e)(2) authorizes the Secretary of the Treasury to provide a
simplified notice requirement or an exemption from the notice requirement for
plans with less than 100 participants and to allow any notice required under the
provision to be provided by using new technologies. Code Sec. 4980F(g) and Code
Sec. 4980F(e)(2)(B) also authorize the Secretary to provide a simplified notice
requirement or an exemption from the notice requirement if participants are given
the option to choose between benefits under the new plan formula and the old plan
formula. In such cases, the provision would have no effect on the fiduciary rules
applicable to pension plans that may require appropriate disclosure to participants,
even if no disclosure is required under the provision.

Code Sec. 4980F(e)(1) prescribes that the plan administrator is required to
provide this notice to each affected participant, each affected alternate payee, and
each employee organization representing affected participants. For purposes of the
provision, Code Sec. 4980F(f)(1) prescribes that an affected participant or alternate
payee is a participant or alternate payee whose rate of future benefit accrual may
reasonably be expected to be significantly reduced by the plan amendment.

Code Sec. 4980F(e)(3) prescribes that, except to the extent provided by
Treasury regulations, the plan administrator is required to provide the notice within
a reasonable time before the effective date of the plan amendment. The provision
permits a plan administrator to provide any notice required under the provision to a
person designated in writing by the individual to whom it would otherwise be
provided.

Code Sec. 4980F(b)(1) imposes on a plan administrator that fails to comply
with the notice requirement an excise tax equal to $100 per day per omitted
participant and alternate payee. However, Code Sec. 4980F(c) prescribes that:

(a) no excise tax is imposed during any period during which any person
subject to liability for the tax did not know that the failure existed and
exercised reasonable diligence to meet the notice requirement;

(b) no excise tax is imposed on any failure if any person subject to liability for
the tax exercised reasonable diligence to meet the notice requirement
and such person provides the required notice during the 30-day period
beginning on the first date such person knew, or exercising reasonable
diligence would have known, that the failure existed;

(c) if the person subject to liability for the excise tax exercised reasonable
diligence to meet the notice requirement, the total excise tax imposed
during a taxable year of the employer would not exceed $500,000; and

(d) in the case of a failure due to reasonable cause and not to willful neglect,
the Secretary of the Treasury is authorized to waive the excise tax to the
extent that the payment of the tax would be excessive relative to the
failure involved.

¶1103.06

For plan amendments taking effect on or after June 7, 2001, Code Sec. 4980F is established to provide as follows.

Code Sec. 4980F prescribes that the plan administrator of a defined benefit pension plan or a money purchase pension plan furnish a written notice concerning a plan amendment that provides for a significant reduction in the rate of future benefit accrual, including any elimination or reduction of an early retirement benefit or retirement-type subsidy. The plan administrator is required to provide in this notice, in a manner calculated to be understood by the average plan participant, sufficient information (as defined in Treasury regulations) to allow participants to understand the effect of the amendment.

.07 Borrowing from a Retirement Plan

S corporation shareholder participants in qualified retirement plans (not SEPs or SIMPLE plans) can borrow from the plans. For a discussion of borrowing from a plan, see ¶ 1302.06.

.08 Employer Deduction for Code Sec. 529 Plans

Individuals can establish Code Sec. 529 plans to save for college education expenses for themselves and members of their families.[9] S corporations, on behalf of the employees, can establish employer-sponsored payroll deduction Code Sec. 529 savings plans for their employees so that the employee can amass funds for college.

Code Sec. 529(f) prescribes that the Treasury has regulatory authority to enact regulations to remedy abuse which is occurring in Code Sec. 529 Plans. Examples of the abuse are that taxpayers may seek to avoid gift and generation skipping transfer taxes by establishing and contributing to multiple qualified tuition program accounts with different designated beneficiaries (using the provision of Code Sec. 529 that permits a contributor to contribute up to five times the annual exclusion amount per donee in a single year and treat the contribution as having been made ratably over five years), with the intention of subsequently changing the designated beneficiaries of such accounts to a single, common beneficiary and distributing the entire amount to such beneficiary without further transfer tax consequences. Taxpayers also may seek to use qualified tuition program accounts as retirement accounts with all of the tax benefits but none of the restrictions and requirements of qualified retirement accounts. The provision grants the Secretary broad regulatory authority to clarify the tax treatment of certain transfers and to ensure that qualified tuition program accounts are used for the intended purpose of saving for higher education expenses of the designated beneficiary, including the authority to impose related recordkeeping and reporting requirements. Code Sec. 529(f) also authorizes the Secretary to limit the persons who may be contributors to a qualified tuition program and to determine any special rules for the operation and Federal tax consequences of such programs if such contributors are not individuals.

[9] For a discussion of Section 529 Plans, see Michael Schlesinger, "Tax Planning for Children's Education," *Journal of Practical Estate Planning*, 4 (2009): 17.

¶1103.07

.09 Employer-Provided Educational Assistance

Code Sec. 127 prescribes that an employer can provide up to $5,250 of payments for education of an employee which the employee can exclude from gross income. The payments can be for tuition, fees, books, supplies, etc. While courses do not have to be job-related, there are limitations. For instance, Reg. § 1.127-2(c)(3) prescribes that courses involving sports, games or hobbies are not covered unless they involve the employer's business, or are required as part of a degree program. With respect to Code Sec. 127 plans for S corporation share-holder-employees, Code Sec. 127(b)(2) and (3) imposes restrictions on them, such as not allowing these plans to be discriminatory in favor of employees who are "highly compensated employees" within the meaning of Code Sec. 414(q), or their dependents. Code Sec. 127(b)(3) prescribes that not more than five percent of the amounts paid or incurred by the employer for educational assistance during the year may be provided for the class of individuals who are shareholders or owners (or their spouses or dependents), each of whom (on any day of the year) owns more than five percent of the stock or of the capital or profits interest in the employer.

> **Tax Pointer:** The Bankruptcy Abuse Prevention and Consumer Protection Act of 2005 (BAPCPA) provides various limitations with respect to tax planning using these vehicles. The reader should consult ¶ 1103.15 for a discussion of this topic.

.10 Child Care and Dependent Care Services Provided by the Employer

Code Sec. 129 provides that an employer (i.e., an S corporation) can provide certain child and dependent care service for employees, with the result that the amount provided is excluded from the employee's income. However, the maximum that can be excluded is $5,000 ($2,500 in the case of a married couple filing separate tax returns) per year. Further, the employer's plan cannot discriminate in favor of the highly compensated employees or their dependents, and not more than 25 percent of the amounts paid or incurred by the employer during the year can be provided to a 5-percent-or-more shareholder, the shareholder's spouse or dependents.[10]

.11 Code Sec. 401(k) Plans

In a Code Sec. 401(k) plan, employer contributions are not included as income for the employee participant, because the employee has the option of taking the contribution in cash or having it paid to a plan (these plans are called "elective contribution plans"). Alternatively, the contribution could coincide with a salary reduction plan. Code Sec. 401(k) plans where there is an option to take cash or leave the money in the plan are called cash or deferred arrangements (CODAs). Code Sec. 401(k) plans must generally be part of a profit-sharing or stock benefit plan. As such, the Code Sec. 401(k) plan must satisfy generally the requirements of Code Sec. 401 plans, such as limits on deferrals, service requirements, etc.

---

[10] For a case discussing the application of Code Sec. 129, *see Frank Settimo*, TC Memo 2006-261 (Day care expenses paid by S corporation for shareholder's minor children's day-care expenses disallowed).

> *Tax Pointer:* For taxable years after December 31, 2001, Congress prescribes a credit to the employer for establishing retirement plans. For a discussion of this credit, see ¶ 1103.04.

Automatic enrollment in Code Sec. 401(k) plans. In the PPA Congress made a number of changes to Code Sec. 401(k) plans effective for years beginning after December 31, 2007. One key provision is that Code Sec. 401(k) plans can provide that elective contributions will be made for a participant unless he or she affirmatively elects otherwise. Plans with these features are often referred to as "automatic enrollment" or "negative election" plans.

.12 SIMPLE Retirement Plans

SIMPLE IRAs. If an employer has 100 or fewer employees who receive at least $5,000 of compensation from the employer for the preceding year, an employer (i.e., an S corporation) can establish a SIMPLE retirement plan. For an employer to establish a SIMPLE retirement plan, the employer cannot have any other employer-sponsored retirement plan except for a collectively bargained plan for covered employees.

A SIMPLE plan can be of two types: an IRA established for each participant, or a SIMPLE Code Sec. 401(k) plan. The advantage to a SIMPLE plan is that it is not subject to nondiscrimination standards and other qualification rules applicable to qualified plans. In a SIMPLE IRA, elective contributions must be permitted. Specifically, Code Sec. 408(p)(2)(A)(ii) prescribes that each eligible employee must elect to have the employer make payments, either: (1) directly to the employee in cash; or (2) by contributing a percentage of compensation to a SIMPLE IRA account. Contributions are limited to a maximum of $6,000 for any calendar year subject to an increase for cost of living. The $6,000 deferral may be matched by an employer contribution dollar for dollar.

SIMPLE Code Sec. 401(k) plan. A SIMPLE Code Sec. 401(k) plan is like a SIMPLE IRA plan. Accordingly, the rules for top-heavy plans do not apply. As to the contributions for each employee, the maximum is $6,000 per taxable year, plus a cost of living increase. An employer is required to match dollar for dollar the employee's contributions, equal to three percent of the employee's compensation, unless the employer exercises a "nonelective contribution" plan. Code Sec. 401(a)(17) prescribes that an employer satisfies the nonelective contribution formula by making contributions equal to two percent of the compensation for each employee who is eligible to participate.

> *Tax Pointer:* The Bankruptcy Abuse Prevention and Consumer Protection Act of 2005 (BAPCPA) provides various limitations with respect to tax planning using these vehicles. The reader should consult ¶ 1103.15 for a discussion of this topic.

.13 Simplified Employee Pension (SEP) Plans

Another plan an S corporation can establish for its employees is a simplified employee pension (SEP) plan, where the employer contributes to the IRAs of its employees, with IRAs typically being separate accounts in a group IRA. Unlike

SIMPLE IRAs, the employer's annual contribution cannot exceed the lesser of 15 percent of the participant's compensation, or $30,000. If the employer contributes an excess, the employee is generally taxed for the excess contribution.

.14 Travel and Entertainment Expenses

Sutherland Lumber Southwest, Inc.,[11] a case in which the IRS acquiesced, states that for purposes of Code Sec. 274, a corporation is allowed the entire cost of supplying corporate items, such as jets, boats, residences, etc. to shareholder-employees; not the amount of the compensation that the employee recognizes pursuant to Reg. § 1.61-21(g). Congress, however, effective for transactions after October 22, 2004, closed this major loophole by enacting Code Sec. 274(e)(2). Notice 2005-45[12] provides guidance regarding the deduction limits for personal use of an airplane.

The Notice prescribes a formula which is complex; however, for purposes of calculating the amount of disallowed expenses on aircraft, the business must take into account all of the expenses of maintaining and operating the aircraft, even the costs of on-board refreshments. The rules apply equally to leased and chartered aircraft. In terms of coverage, the rules apply to owners, employees or partners who are "specified individuals," with a "specified individual" being an officer, director, or more than ten-percent owner of a corporation taxed under Subchapters C or S, or a personal service corporation. For partnerships, "specified individuals" include any partner holding more than a ten-percent equity interest in the partnership, a general partner, officer, or managing member of a partnership. "Specified individuals" also include a director or officer of a tax-exempt entity, with related entities being grouped together as are spouses or family members.

Prop. Reg. § 1.274-9 et seq. have simplified the computation for nondeductible miles such as for charitable activities. The reader should consult the Proposed Regulation for guidance.

.15 Bankruptcy Abuse Prevention and Consumer Protection Act of 2005 (BAPCPA) as it Affects Retirement Accounts, Code Sec. 529 Plans, and CESAs

The Bankruptcy Abuse Prevention and Consumer Protection Act of 2005 (BAPCPA) was enacted to curb bankruptcy abuses, but it also expands bankruptcy protections previously available for a debtor's retirement funds. Bankruptcy Code Sec. 522(b) provides a new federal exemption for retirement funds held in several types of tax-favored plans which applies to cases begun after October 17, 2005.

Debtors achieve bankruptcy protection by claiming either an exclusion of items from the bankruptcy estate, or exemption. If retirement funds qualify for exclusion, they are never included as part of the bankruptcy estate and turned over to the bankruptcy trustee; if the exclusion does not apply, the funds become part of the estate, but are shielded from creditor claims if an exemption applies. *Patterson v. Shumate*[13] prescribes that a debtor's interest in a plan that is covered by ERISA,

---

[11] *Sutherland Lumber Southwest, Inc.*, 114 TC 197, Dec. 53,817, aff'd per curiam, CA-8, 2001-2 USTC ¶ 50,503, 255 F3d 495, acq. IRB 2002-6.

[12] IRB 2005-24.

[13] 504 US 753.

and meets ERISA's requirements, is excluded from the bankruptcy estate if the plan is a trust. However, the exclusion does not apply to a debtor's interest in an IRA, a SEP-IRA, a Code Sec. 403(b) plan, or a Code Sec. 457 plan. Plans which cover sole proprietors, partners, and sole shareholders of a business and their spouses who wish not to have any common law employees are not governed by ERISA; accordingly, under the prior law scheme, these plans are not excluded from the bankruptcy estate unless state law provides to the contrary.

Bankruptcy exemption. Bankruptcy Code Sec. 522(d)(10)(E), which is not affected by the BAPCPA, generally provides an exemption for debtor's rights to receive funds held in a stock bonus, pension, profit-sharing, annuity, or similar plan or arrangement, providing the payment is (a) unaccounted illness, disability, death, age, or length of service, and (b) reasonably necessary for the support of the debtor or his dependents. *Rousey v. Jacoway*[14] prescribed that funds in a traditional IRA satisfy the "on account of" requirement for the Bankruptcy Code Sec. 522(d)(10)(E) exemption.

Bankruptcy Code Sec. 522 prescribes that all debtors in bankruptcy obtain an exemption for retirement assets in a fund or account that is exempt from taxation under Code Sec. 401 (including qualified defined benefit and defined contribution plans including Code Sec. 401(k) plans), Code Sec. 403 (including qualified annuity plans and tax-sheltered Code Sec. 403(b) annuities), Code Sec. 408 (including traditional IRAs, SEP-IRAs, and SIMPLE IRAs), Code Sec. 408(a) (Roth IRAs), Code Sec. 414 (qualified governmental plans), Code Sec. 457 (deferred compensation plans of state or local governments or tax-exempt organizations), and Code Sec. 501(a) (specified types of organizations which are exempt from federal income tax).

Bankruptcy Code Sec. 522's exemption now covers plans which cover only working owners that have no common law employees, providing the plan is tax-qualified. However, Bankruptcy Code Sec. 522(m) prescribes that for assets in a traditional IRA or Roth IRA, the aggregate value of the asset which may qualify for exemption cannot exceed one million dollars for an individual debtor. However, for purposes of computing this one-million-dollar cap, rollover contribution pursuant to Code Sec. 402(c), Code Sec. 402(e)(6), Code Sec. 403(a)(4), Code Sec. 403(a)(5), and Code Sec. 403(b)(8) and the earnings therefrom are excluded. Additionally, this one-million-dollar cap will be adjusted for inflation, and may be increased if the interests of justice so require. In terms of the rollovers, the exemption applies whether the tax-free rollover occurs due to a direct trustee-to-trustee transfer, or is an eligible rollover distribution.

> ***Information Pointer:*** While *Rousey v. Jacoway* protects traditional IRA rollovers, rollovers to Roth IRAs may not be protected due to their unique format, until October 17, 2005, unless state laws already protect them (items which make Roth IRAs unique include no tax or penalty on withdrawals from IRAs up to the amount of after-tax contributions, and no required distribution rules).

---

[14] 2005-1 USTC ¶ 50,258.

¶1103.15

.16 Rollovers of Retirement Accounts by Non-Spouse Beneficiaries

Code Sec. 402(c)(11) provides effective for distributions after December 31, 2006 that benefits of a beneficiary other than a surviving spouse may be transferred directly to an IRA by means of a trustee-to-trustee transfer. The IRA is treated as an inherited IRA of the nonspouse beneficiary thereby allowing the beneficiary to use his or her life expectancy for distributions from the IRA with payments to start the year after the decedent's death. The provision applies to amounts payable to a beneficiary under a qualified retirement plan, Code Sec. 401(k), governmental Code Sec. 457 plan, or a tax-sheltered annuity. To the extent provided by the Secretary, the provision applies to benefits payable to a trust maintained for a designated beneficiary to the same extent it applies to the beneficiary.

> *Tax Pointer 1:* Code Sec. 402(c)(11) will no longer require life partners, children, etc. to take lump sum payments or payments over a maximum of a 5 year period on the death of the decedent.

> *Tax Pointer 2:* Code Sec. 402(c)(11) applies only to employer-provided securities, not to existing IRAs.

> *Tax Pointer 3:* Bankruptcy creditors can reach an inherited IRA per Code Sec. 408(e)(1) because inherited IRAs remain titled in the name of the original owner for the benefit of the beneficiary; thus the account balance is not the beneficiary's retirement funds.[15] But see *Nessa*,[16] which held that an inherited IRA is exempt from creditor attack under the Bankruptcy Code.

Notice 2007-7,[17] provides some clarification with respect to the operation of this Code provision, to wit:

Nonspousal rollovers optional. A qualified plan does not have to provide non-spousal rollovers; they are optional. (Q&A 14 and 15). Q&A 14 prescribes that if the plan offers direct rollovers to nonspouse beneficiaries of some, but not all, participants, the rollovers must be offered on a nondiscriminatory basis because pursuant to the nondiscrimination rules of Code Sec. 401(a)(4), the opportunity to make a direct rollover is a benefit, right, or feature that is subject.

Direct rollovers of the IRA. Q&A 13 states that the IRA must be established in a manner that identifies it as an IRA with respect to a deceased individual and also identifies the deceased individual and the beneficiary, for example, "Tom Smith as beneficiary of John Smith."

Qualified plan Required Minimum Distribution (RMD) is not eligible for rollover. Q&A 17 and 18 prescribe that an RMD which the decedent should have taken from the qualified plan under Code Sec. 401(a)(9) but didn't, is not eligible for a rollover.

Q&A (c)(2), describes a special rule that is an exception to the general rule in Q&A 19 discussed below. If, under a plan, the 5-year rule applies for determining required minimum distributions, a nonspouse designated beneficiary may, never-

---

[15] *In re Chilton*, BC-DC-TX, 2010-1 USTC ¶ 50,275, 426 BR 612.

[16] Bktcy. App. Panel,105 AFTR 2d ¶ 2010-724 (8th Cir 2010).

[17] 2007-5 IRB.

theless, treat the plan as using the life expectancy rule provided the rollover into the IRA is made prior to the end of the year following the year of the participant's death. Thus, despite a plan provision for the 5-year rule, the nonspouse designated beneficiary is permitted to treat the plan as using the life expectancy rule both for determining the amount eligible for rollover and for determining the required minimum distributions under the IRA, but only if the rollover is made prior to the end of the year following the year of the participant's death. For example, if a participant in a Section 401(k) plan dies in 2007 before his required beginning date and under the plan the 5-year rule applies for determining required minimum distributions, the participant's nonspouse designated beneficiary is permitted to roll over the deceased participant's entire account balance into an IRA in 2007 and take required minimum distributions from the IRA under the life expectancy rule. If the account balance is rolled over in 2008, the amount eligible for rollover must be reduced by the amount of the required minimum distribution for 2008, determined using the life expectancy rule. After 2008, the nonspouse designated beneficiary may still roll over funds from the Section 401(k) plan, but would have to take required minimum distributions from the IRA under the 5-year rule. No amount can be rolled over after 2011.

Post rollover RMDs from recipient IRA. Q&A describes the general rule for determining required minimum distributions in the case of a nonspouse beneficiary rollover. It provides that the rules for determining required minimum distributions under a plan with respect to a nonspouse designated beneficiary also apply to an IRA. If a participant dies before his or her required beginning date, the required minimum distributions for purposes of determining the amount eligible for rollover with respect to a nonspouse designated beneficiary are determined under either the 5-year rule described in Section 401(a)(9)(B)(ii) or the life expectancy rule described in Section 401(a)(9)(B)(iii).

.17 Investment Advice and Prohibited Transaction Exemptions

Under present law, ERISA and the Code prohibit certain transactions between an employer-sponsored retirement plan and a disqualified person (referred to as a "party in interest" under ERISA). Under ERISA, the prohibited transaction rules apply to employer-sponsored retirement plans and welfare benefit plans. Under the Code, the prohibited transaction rules apply to qualified retirement plans and qualified retirement annuities, as well as individual retirement accounts and annuities (IRAs), health savings accounts (HSAs), Archer MSAs, and Coverdell education savings accounts.

Disqualified persons include a fiduciary of the plan, a person providing services to the plan, and an employer with employees covered by the plan. For this purpose, a fiduciary includes any person who (1) exercises any authority or control respecting management or disposition of the plan's assets, (2) renders investment advice for a fee or other compensation with respect to any plan moneys or property, or has the authority or responsibility to do so, or (3) has any discretionary authority or responsibility in the administration of the plan.

¶1103.17

Prohibited transactions include (1) the sale, exchange or leasing of property, (2) the lending of money or other extension of credit, (3) the furnishing of goods, services or facilities, (4) the transfer to, or use by or for the benefit of, the income or assets of the plan, (5) in the case of a fiduciary, any act that deals with the plan's income or assets for the fiduciary's own interest or account, and (6) the receipt by a fiduciary of any consideration for the fiduciary's own personal account from any party dealing with the plan in connection with a transaction involving the income or assets of the plan. However, certain transactions are exempt from prohibited transaction treatment, for example, certain loans to plan participants.

Under ERISA, the Secretary of Labor may assess a civil penalty against a person who engages in a prohibited transaction, other than a transaction with a plan covered by the prohibited transaction rules of the Code. The penalty may not exceed five percent of the amount involved in the transaction for each year or part of a year that the prohibited transaction continues. If the prohibited transaction is not corrected within 90 days after notice from the Secretary of Labor, the penalty may be up to 100 percent of the amount involved in the transaction. Under the Code, if a prohibited transaction occurs, the disqualified person who participates in the transaction is subject to a two-tier excise tax. The first level tax is 15 percent of the amount involved in the transaction. The second level tax is imposed if the prohibited transaction is not corrected within a certain period and is 100 percent of the amount involved.

Effective with respect to investment advice provided after December 31, 2006, ERISA Sec. 408(b) and (g) and Code Sec. 4975(d)(15) and (16) have been amended and Code Sec. 4975(f)(8) has been added to provide a new category of prohibited transaction exemption in connection with the provision of investment advice through an "eligible investment advice arrangement" to participants and beneficiaries of a defined contribution plan who direct the investment of their accounts under the plan and to beneficiaries of IRAs. (The portions of the provision relating to IRAs apply to HSAs, Archer MSAs, and Coverdell education savings accounts; references to IRAs include such other arrangements as well.) If the requirements under the provision are met, the following are exempt from prohibited transaction treatment: (1) the provision of investment advice; (2) an investment transaction (i.e., a sale, acquisition, or holding of a security or other property) pursuant to the advice; and (3) the direct or indirect receipt of fees or other compensation in connection with the provision of the advice or an investment transaction pursuant to the advice. The prohibited transaction exemptions provided under the provision do not in any manner alter existing individual or class exemptions provided by statute or administrative action.

The PPA Committee Reports detail that the Secretary of Labor, in consultation with the Secretary of the Treasury, are directed to determine, based on certain information to be solicited by the Secretary of Labor, whether there is any computer model investment advice program that meets the requirements of the provision and may be used by IRAs. The determination is to be made by December 31, 2007. If the Secretary of Labor determines there is such a program, the exemptions described above apply in connection with the use of the program with respect to

¶1103.17

IRA beneficiaries. If the Secretary of Labor determines that there is not such a program, such Secretary is directed to grant a class exemption from prohibited transaction treatment (as discussed below) for the provision of investment advice, investment transactions pursuant to such advice, and related fees to beneficiaries of such arrangements.

Eligible investment advice arrangements. Code Sec. 4975(f)(8)(B) provides that the exemptions provided under this prohibited exemption provision for invest-ment advice apply in connection with the provision of investment advice by a fiduciary adviser under an eligible investment advice arrangement. An eligible investment advice arrangement is an arrangement (1) meeting certain require-ments (discussed below) and (2) which either (a) provides that any fees (including any commission or compensation) received by the fiduciary adviser for investment advice or with respect to an investment transaction with respect to plan assets do not vary depending on the basis of any investment option selected, or (b) uses a computer model under an investment advice program as described below in connection with the provision of investment advice to a participant or beneficiary. In the case of an eligible investment advice arrangement with respect to a defined contribution plan, the arrangement must be expressly authorized by a plan fiduci-ary other than (1) the person offering the investment advice program, (2) any person providing investment options under the plan, or (3) any affiliate of (1) or (2).

Investment advice program using computer model. If an eligible invest-ment advice arrangement provides investment advice pursuant to a computer model, Code Sec. 4975(f)(8)(C) requires that the model must (1) apply generally accepted investment theories that take into account the historic returns of different asset classes over defined periods of time, (2) use relevant information about the participant or beneficiary, (3) use prescribed objective criteria to provide asset allocation portfolios comprised of investment options under the plan, (4) operate in a manner that is not biased in favor of any investment options offered by the fiduciary adviser or related person, and (5) take into account all the investment options under the plan in specifying how a participant's or beneficiary's account should be invested without inappropriate weighting of any investment option. An eligible investment expert must certify, before the model is used and in accordance with rules prescribed by the Secretary, that the model meets these requirements. The certification must be renewed if there are material changes to the model as determined under regulations. For this purpose, an eligible investment expert is a person who meets requirements prescribed by the Secretary and who does not bear any material affiliation or contractual relationship with any investment adviser or related person.

In addition, if a computer model is used, the only investment advice that may be provided under the arrangement is the advice generated by the computer model, and any investment transaction pursuant to the advice must occur solely at the direction of the participant or beneficiary. This requirement does not preclude the participant or beneficiary from requesting other investment advice, but only if the request has not been solicited by any person connected with carrying out the investment advice arrangement.

¶1103.17

Audit requirements. In the case of an eligible investment advice arrangement with respect to a defined contribution plan, Code Sec. 4975(f)(8)(E) prescribes that an annual audit of the arrangement for compliance with applicable requirements must be conducted by an independent auditor (i.e., unrelated to the person offering the investment advice arrangement or any person providing investment options under the plan) who has appropriate technical training or experience and proficiency and who so represents in writing. The auditor must issue a report of the audit results to the fiduciary that authorized use of the arrangement. In the case of an eligible investment advice arrangement with respect to IRAs, an audit is required at such times and in such manner as prescribed by the Secretary of Labor.

Notice requirements. Code Sec. 4975(f)(8)(F) provides that before the initial provision of investment advice, the fiduciary adviser must provide written notice (which may be in electronic form) containing various information to the recipient of the advice, including information relating to: (1) the role of any related party in the development of the investment advice program or the selection of investment options under the plan; (2) past performance and rates of return for each investment option offered under the plan; (3) any fees or other compensation to be received by the fiduciary adviser or affiliate; (4) any material affiliation or contractual relationship of the fiduciary adviser or affiliates in the security or other property involved in the investment transaction; (5) the manner and under what circumstances any participant or beneficiary information will be used or disclosed; (6) the types of services provided by the fiduciary adviser in connection with the provision of investment advice; (7) the adviser's status as a fiduciary of the plan in connection with the provision of the advice; and (8) the ability of the recipient of the advice separately to arrange for the provision of advice by another adviser that could have no material affiliation with and receive no fees or other compensation in connection with the security or other property. This information must be maintained in accurate form and must be provided to the recipient of the investment advice, without charge, on an annual basis, on request, or in the case of any material change.

Any notification must be written in a clear and conspicuous manner, calculated to be understood by the average plan participant, and sufficiently accurate and comprehensive so as to reasonably apprise participants and beneficiaries of the required information. The Secretary is directed to issue a model form for the disclosure of fees and other compensation as required by the provision. The fiduciary adviser must maintain for at least six years any records necessary for determining whether the requirements for the prohibited transaction exemption were met. A prohibited transaction will not be considered to have occurred solely because records were lost or destroyed before the end of six years due to circumstances beyond the adviser's control.

Other requirements. In order for the exemption to apply, Code Sec. 4975(f)(8)(G) provides that the following additional requirements must be satisfied: (1) the fiduciary adviser must provide disclosures applicable under securities laws; (2) an investment transaction must occur solely at the direction of the recipient of the advice; (3) compensation received by the fiduciary adviser or affiliates in connection with an investment transaction must be reasonable; and (4) the terms of the investment transaction must be at least as favorable to the plan as an arm's length transaction would be.

Fiduciary adviser. Code Sec. 4975(f)(8)(j)(i) defines "fiduciary adviser" as a person who is a fiduciary of the plan by reason of the provision of investment advice to a participant or beneficiary and who is also: (1) registered as an investment adviser under the Investment Advisers Act of 1940 or under State laws; (2) a bank, a similar financial institution supervised by the United States or a State, or a savings association (as defined under the Federal Deposit Insurance Act), but only if the advice is provided through a trust department that is subject to periodic examination and review by Federal or State banking authorities; (3) an insurance company qualified to do business under State law; (4) registered as a broker or dealer under the Securities Exchange Act of 1934; (5) an affiliate of any of the preceding; or (6) an employee, agent or registered representative of any of the preceding who satisfies the requirements of applicable insurance, banking and securities laws relating to the provision of advice. A person who develops the computer model or markets the investment advice program or computer model is treated as a person who is a plan fiduciary by reason of the provision of investment advice and is treated as a fiduciary adviser, except that the Secretary may prescribe rules under which only one fiduciary adviser may elect treatment as a plan fiduciary. "Affiliate" means an affiliated person as defined under Section 2(a)(3) of the Investment Company Act of 1940. "Registered representative" means a person described in Section 3(a)(18) of the Securities Exchange Act of 1934 or a person described in Section 202(a)(17) of the Investment Advisers Act of 1940.

Fiduciary rules. Subject to certain requirements, an employer or other person who is a plan fiduciary, other than a fiduciary adviser, is not treated as failing to meet the fiduciary requirements of ERISA, solely by reason of the provision of investment advice as permitted under the provision or of contracting for or otherwise arranging for the provision of the advice. This rule applies if: (1) the advice is provided under an arrangement between the employer or plan fiduciary and the fiduciary adviser for the provision of investment advice by the fiduciary adviser as permitted under the provision; (2) the terms of the arrangement require compliance by the fiduciary adviser with the requirements of the provision; and (3) the terms of the arrangement include a written acknowledgement by the fiduciary adviser that the fiduciary adviser is a plan fiduciary with respect to the provision of the advice.

The provision does not exempt the employer or a plan fiduciary from fiduciary responsibility under ERISA for the prudent selection and periodic review of a fiduciary adviser with whom the employer or plan fiduciary has arranged for the provision of investment advice. The employer or plan fiduciary does not have the duty to monitor the specific investment advice given by a fiduciary adviser. The provision also provides that nothing in the fiduciary responsibility provisions of ERISA is to be construed to preclude the use of plan assets to pay for reasonable expenses in providing investment advice.

¶1103.17

.18 Modification of the Rules Regarding Hardship Situations and Unforeseen Financial Emergencies

Distributions from a qualified cash or deferred arrangement (a "Code Sec. 401(k) plan"), a tax-shelter annuity, Code Sec. 457 plan, or nonqualified deferred compensation plan subject to Code Sec. 409A can not be made prior to the occurrence of one or more specified events. In the case of a Code Sec. 401(k) plan or tax-sheltered annuity, one event upon which distribution is permitted is the case of a hardship. Similarly, distributions from Code Sec. 457 plans and nonqualified deferred compensation plans subject to Code Sec. 409A may be made in the case of an unforeseeable emergency. Effective on August 17, 2006, the Secretary of the Treasury pursuant to Pension Protection Act (PPA) Sec. 826 is directed to revise the rules for determining whether a participant has had a hardship or unforeseeable emergency to provide that if an event would constitute a hardship or unforeseeable emergency under the plan if it occurred with respect to the participant's spouse or dependent, such event shall, to the extent permitted under the plan, constitute a hardship or unforeseeable emergency if it occurs with respect to a beneficiary under the plan. The provision requires that the revised rules be issued within 180 days after August 17, 2006.

.19 One-Participant Retirement Plan Exempt from Filing Form 5500 (the Annual Report) if the Plan's Assets Are $250,000 or Less

PPA Sec. 1103(a)(1) provides that generally effective for plan years beginning after 2006, one-participant retirement plans with assets of $250,000 or less as of the close of the plan year need not file an annual return (Form 5500) for that year.

PPA Sec. 1103(a)(2) defines a "one-participant retirement plan" as a retirement plan with respect to which the following requirements are met: on the first day of the plan year covered only one individual (or the individual and the individual's spouse) and the individual owned 100 percent of the plan sponsor (whether or not incorporated), or the plan covered only one or more partners (or partners and their spouses) in the plan sponsor. Additionally, the plan meets the minimum coverage requirements of Code Sec. 410(b) without being combined with any other plan of the business that covers the employees of the business; the plan:(I) does not provide benefits to anyone except the individual (and the individual's spouse) or the partners (and their spouses); (II) does not cover a business that is a member of an affiliated service group, a controlled group of corporations, or a group of businesses under common control; and (III) does not cover a business that uses the services of leased employees (within the meaning of Code Sec. 414(n)). Act Code Sec. 1103(a)(2) states that the term "partner" includes a 2-percent shareholder (as defined in Code Sec. 1372(b) of such Code) of an S corporation.

.20 Simplified Annual Filing Requirements for Plans with Fewer than 25 Participants

PPA Sec. 1103(b) provides that in the case of plan years beginning after December 31, 2006, the Secretary of the Treasury and the Secretary of Labor shall provide for the filing of a simplified annual return for any retirement plan which

¶1103.20

covers less than 25 participants on the first day of a plan year and which meets the requirements described in Act Sec. 1103(a)(2).

.21 Computing High-Three Year Average Compensation for Benefit Limitation Purposes

Under present law, annual benefits payable to a participant under a defined benefit pension plan generally may not exceed the lesser of (1) 100 percent of average compensation for the participant's high three years, or (2) $175,000 (for 2006). The dollar limit is reduced proportionately for individuals with less than 10 years of participation in the plan. The compensation limit is reduced proportionately for individuals with less than 10 years of service. For purposes of determining average compensation for a participant's high three years, the high three years are the period of consecutive calendar years (not more than three) during which the participant was both an active participant in the plan and had the greatest aggregate compensation from the employer.

Code Sec. 415(b)(3) has been amended, effective for years beginning after December 31, 2005 to provide that for purposes of determining average compensation for a participant's high three years, the high three years are the period of consecutive calendar years (not more than three) during which the participant had the greatest aggregate compensation from the employer.

.22 Conversion of Traditional IRAs and Qualified Retirement Plans to Roth IRAs

Starting this year, pursuant to Code Sec. 408A(c) anyone, regardless of income or filing status, can convert a traditional IRA or qualified retirement benefits to a Roth IRA. However, income taxes must be paid now on the amount converted rather than deferring taxes until such amounts are withdrawn. However, Code Sec. 408A(c)(3)(B) prescribes that a taxpayer can spread the resulting income over two years, 2011 and 2012, effectively allowing deferral of the tax on the conversion. Alternatively, Code Sec. 408A(e)(i)(I) allows a taxpayer to elect to report all of the income from the conversion in 2010. Income from conversions made after 2010 must be reported in full in the year in which the conversions are made; there is no deferral rule for conversions after 2010.

If the converted account has only pre-tax contributions, then it is fully includible in gross income. So if the IRA has been funded by tax-deductible contributions, any conversion of the funds in the IRA results in full inclusion in income. If the account has been funded with both deductible and nondeductible contributions, then only a portion of the converted amount is included in gross income.

For example, if a person has a single traditional IRA of $25,000 to which he had made a nondeductible contribution of $5,000, then 80 percent of the conversion, or $20,000, is taxable, with 20 percent representing after-tax contributions to the traditional IRA and is not taxed. The value of amounts in all nondeductible IRAs is taken into account in determining the tax on the conversion, even if some or all of the nondeductible IRAs are not converted.

¶1103.21

There is no 10 percent penalty on conversion income even though the individual is under age 59½, as long as the funds remain in the Roth IRA for at least five years. The fact that the traditional IRA being converted was a rollover made within 12 months does not bar the conversion of this account to a Roth IRA. If a portion of the account required to be distributed for the year is a required minimum distribution (RMD), no conversion is allowed; only amounts in the account after RMDs can be converted. Thus, if there is a traditional IRA with $30,000 and the RMD for 2010 is $1,000, the maximum amount that can be converted in 2010 is $29,000.

Annual contributions. Code Sec. 408A(c)(2) states that an individual can make a conversion and an annual contribution to a Roth IRA. For 2010, the contribution limit remains $5,000, with the "catch up" contribution of an additional $1,000 for those age 50 or older by the end of the year. There are modified adjusted gross income (MAGI) limits on eligibility to make annual contributions to a Roth IRA. Accordingly, full contributions are allowed for 2010 for singles with MAGI up to $105,000 and for joint filers with MAGI up to $167,000. Partial contributions are allowed for singles with MAGI between $105,000 and $120,000, and for joint filers with MAGI between $167,000 and $177,000.

Estimated taxes. If conversions are made, then estimated taxes should be made to cover the tax liability to avoid estimated tax penalties.

State income taxes. State law has to be consulted to determine if income taxes have to be paid in addition to federal income taxes on the conversion.

Roth 401(k) Plans. Code Sec. 402A prescribes that 401(k) plans and 403(b) plans (but not SIMPLE plans, SARSEPs, or 457 plans) are authorized (but not required) to incorporate a "qualified Roth contribution program," pursuant to which participants may make an irrevocable election to have all or a portion of their elective deferrals to the plan designated as after-tax "Roth contributions." The participant is subject to income tax (as well as FICA and Medicare payroll taxes) on the contributions at the time of deferral and the contribution is reported on the participant's W-2 Form in the year of the contribution. The Roth 401(k) contributions do not reduce a participant's taxable income. However, "qualified distributions" from a designated Roth account are not included in adjusted gross income nor are they subject to income tax.

¶ 1104 Social Security Benefits

.01 Utilizing a Family S Corporation to Provide Social Security Benefits

Social Security is a complex area. For instance, there is the 20/40 rule. 42 USC § 423(c)(1); 20 CFR § 404.130(b) which requires that an applicant above the age of 31 must work twenty of the previous forty quarters (i.e., five of the last ten years) to qualify for SSDI ("the 20/40 Rule"). The case of *Collier v. Barnhart* illustrates this point.[18] In *Collier*, a female who contracted ALS (Lou Gehrig's disease) was denied Social Security Disability Insurance (SSDI) and medicare benefits because she did not have the required recent work history under the 20/40 rule. 42 USC § 423(c)(1); 20 CFR § 404.130(b) requires that an applicant above the age of 31 must

---

[18] 473 F. 3d 444 (2nd Cir. 2007).

have worked twenty of the previous forty quarters (i.e., five of the last ten years) to qualify for SSDI ("the 20/40 Rule"). Collier did not have a recent work history as she left the paid workforce in 1994, upon the birth of her first child. Collier continued to be a stay-at-home mother through the birth of her second and third children; she states that "she always intended to return to the workforce," but wanted "to be a full-time mother while her children were young." For fifteen consecutive years beforehand, however, from 1979 through 1994, petitioner had worked outside the home and, during that time, she and her employers contributed over $40,000 in Social Security and Medicare taxes. Collier claimed that her rights to due process and equal protection were violated as the 20/40 rule discriminated against women, who are more likely to leave the workforce to parent full-time. The court held there was not denial of due process or equal protection in that the statute is gender-neutral on its face even though the court acknowledged that the 20/40 Rule has a disproportionate impact on women returning to the work force. The court felt it was up to Congress to change the law rather than the court.

To avoid the consequences of *Collier*, namely the 20/40 rule, individuals may want to be employed by a family corporation. For instance, if Mrs. Collier's husband owned an S corporation, he could have put her on the payroll to assist him with operations of the company.

.02 Earned Income from an S Corporation and Social Security

If an individual draws Social Security at 62 and is under full retirement age for the entire year, the taxpayer's Social Security benefit is reduced by $1 for every $2 earned above the annual limit. For 2013, that limit is $15,120. In S corporations, there have been mixed decisions on whether a shareholder who still works for the S corporation but receives distributions on his or her shares but no salary has earned income to disqualify the shareholder from Social Security benefits. In *Ludeking v. Finch*,[19] an S corporate shareholder who worked on average 30 to 35 hours a week received distributions from his S corporation but no salary had the S corporate distributions characterized as earned income rather than a "dividend." Thus, he lost his Social Security benefits. But in *Gardner v. Hall*,[20] an S corporate shareholder who worked only several hours each week in the family S corporation but received no salary was entitled to his Social Security benefits. In *Gardner*, the shareholder's wife drew a salary which was deposited into a joint bank account with her husband and the Social Security Administration claimed that ½ of her salary was his "earned income" because he had the right to draw from the joint bank account. The Court refused to reallocate the wife's salary; thus, the husband received full salary.

¶ 1105 Income Distributions Not Subject to Self-Employment Tax

As noted in ¶ 1001.01, a shareholder's distributive share of S corporation income is not earned income for federal tax purposes. This is true whether or not the income is distributed to the shareholder. Accordingly, S corporation *pass-*

---

[19] 421 F2d.499 (8th Cir. 1970).   [20] 366 F2d. 132 (10th Cir. 1966).

through income is not subject to the self-employment tax.[21] The characterization of S corporation pass-through income is a significant advantage of the S corporation form of organization relative to partnerships.

> *Tax Pointer 1:* Shareholders must carefully weigh the choice between salaries and pass-through income. While salaries are subject to the payroll tax, and pass-through income is not, nonearned income does not accrue Social Security benefits for its recipients. Any portion of an S corporation income distribution that is not subject to the self-employment tax will not accrue benefits under the Social Security Act. Likewise, S corporation income distributions do not count as compensation for computing an employee's contribution formula in a retirement plan.

> *Tax Pointer 2:* *Radtke*[22] requires a shareholder to take a reasonable salary.

> *Tax Pointer 3:* While the Department of the Treasury is recommending new legislation to correct the abuse caused by shareholder-employees failure to take a reasonable salary, Congress has yet to pass a law. Deputy Inspector General for audit, Pamela J. Gardner, reported on May 20, 2005 that 36,000 one-owner S corporations with profits of $100,000 or more paid no payroll taxes on profits; 40,000 S corporations with profits in the $50,000-$100,000 range paid no payroll taxes on the profits because no salary was taken. Accordingly, the Department of the Treasury is recommending that Congress close this loophole by subjecting to employment taxes all operating gains of S corporations that accrue to more than fifty-percent owners and their relatives.

¶ 1106 Shareholders' Agreement

.01 Protection Against Termination of S Corporation Status

An S corporation can voluntarily revoke its status if more than 50 percent of the corporation's shareholders consent to the revocation. However, it is possible for one shareholder, even if he, she, or it is not a 50-percent-or-more shareholder, to terminate an S election. The method is simple—all the shareholder has to do to break the S corporation election is to transfer his, her, or its stock to an entity that is not a permitted shareholder (e.g., a C corporation controlled by a shareholder who is a nonresident alien).[23] Therefore, to protect against this contingency, a shareholders' agreement should be established containing language to guard against inadvertent termination. For example, a repurchase agreement providing the corporation the right of first refusal when a shareholder wishes to sell shares will provide a means to prevent the transfer of shares to nonqualified shareholders.[24] A shareholders' agreement will not be considered to create a second class of

---

[21] *P.B. Ding,* 74 TCM 708, Dec. 52,269(M), TC Memo. 1997-435. Aff'd, CA-9, 2000-1 USTC ¶ 50,137, 200 F3d 587 (S corporation pass-through of income deemed not self-employment income).

[22] *J. Radtke,* CA-7, 90-1 USTC ¶ 50,113, 895 F2d 1196. Aff'g 89-2 USTC ¶ 9466, 712 FSupp 143.

[23] For an example of how this can be done, see discussion at ¶ 1203.01 on *T.J. Henry Associates, Inc.,* 80 TC 886, Dec. 40,110 (Acq.).

[24] See, e.g., IRS Letter Ruling 199935035 (June 4, 1999) where an S corporation status was maintained even though minority shareholders transferred stock to nonpermitted shareholders in violation of the shareholders' agreement.

stock,[25] providing that the valuation for the stock is between book value and fair market value.[26] Also, the shareholders' agreement can limit transfers of stock only to taxpayers who would qualify as S corporation shareholders (e.g., only resident aliens, no C corporations, etc.).

.02 Stock Transfers

Normally, when taxpayers gather together to form and operate an S corporation, they do not want a shareholder to bring in strangers who may not share their vision for the S corporation. By adopting a shareholders' agreement, the shareholders can provide an orderly means to control transfers. For instance, the shareholders' agreement should provide that a shareholder wishing to sell stock must offer it first to the other shareholder(s), thereby insuring that the original group of shareholders will continue. (See an example of such language at Appendix 4, Shareholders' Agreement.)

.03 Stock Price Establishment

When a shareholder transfers stock, either because the shareholder dies, wants to leave, etc., the shareholder wants a reasonable price for the stock. Unless there is a shareholders' agreement establishing a price for the stock, litigation will likely arise because of different perspectives—the buyer will try to use a formulation that produces a low valuation for the stock, and the seller will try to produce a high valuation. By including a formula for the stock in the shareholders' agreement (with the method of valuation agreed upon when the S corporation commences operations), stock price disputes can be avoided. Note that the price for S corporation stock has to be between book value and fair market value to prevent termination of the S status; however, a family transaction is to be valued at fair market value.[27] Various means can be used to accomplish this valuation. For instance, a certificate of value (an appraisal valuation based on the book value of the corporation) or a multiple-of-earnings approach can be used. Determination of the appropriate method to be used depends on the particular business in which the S corporation is engaged. Case law dealing with estate tax and shareholders' agreements may help determine the proper valuation method for the respective business. (See an example of valuation language at Appendix 5, Disposition of Stock Upon Shareholder's Death.)

.04 Allowing Parents or Others Control

Parents. Frequently, S corporations are established for family ventures; however, the parents want to retain control of the corporation until their respective deaths. A shareholders' agreement can provide protection for these parents by prescribing that all the shareholders will vote their stock for particular officers and directors (i.e., the parents) as the sole officers and directors. Thus, children will be relegated to serving only in the role of shareholders, without any effective voting control. Of course, shareholders do have certain rights, whether they are voting or

---

[25] See, e.g., IRS Letter Ruling 8411057 (December 13, 1983).

[26] Reg. § 1.1361-1(l)(2)(iii)(A). See also ¶ 208.02 on what is a second class of stock. (Fair market value must be used in all instances for the valuation of family transfers; otherwise, gift tax will be imposed per Code Sec. 2701 et seq.)

[27] *Ibid.*

¶1106.02

nonvoting shareholders: for example, they have the right to sue the controlling shareholders (i.e., the parents) for waste of corporate assets.

Others. Frequently, an individual with insubstantial assets (e.g., an inventor) needs others to help him or her develop a business product; however, this individual (and shareholder) wants to keep control. So the individual has the other shareholders agree that he or she will be the sole officer and director, subject to the derivative action for waste.

.05 Resolving Disputes Among Shareholders

It is probable that during the normal life of an S corporation, disputes will arise among shareholders. Under our present system of jurisprudence, disputes among shareholders can, unless an agreement provides otherwise, be resolved in a court of law, which at times can be a slow, cumbersome, and expensive process. Consequently, the shareholders can prescribe a faster means to resolve difficulties, such as arbitration, and/or requiring the loser to pay the costs of litigation, and/or arbitration including attorneys' fees and costs. (See an example of such language at Appendix 6, Resolution of Disputes.)

.06 Minimum Distribution of Earnings

When an S corporation has income or gain from its operations, it has a choice of distributing its income or retaining it. If the S corporation distributes all its income, gain, etc. from operations, then the shareholders have a source of funds to pay their respective income taxes due on the income. If the S corporation decides not to distribute any of its income because it needs the funds earned during the year to finance its growth or maintain itself, then the shareholders have a problem in that they do not have any current distribution of income to finance their tax liabilities. (Of course, their stock basis is increased, but increase in basis does not pay taxes.) To alleviate this situation, the shareholders can provide in the shareholders' agreement for a minimum distribution of income to pay their taxes. (See such a provision at Appendix 7, Minimum Distribution.)

Shareholder deadlock. Shareholders may also want a minimum distribution provision in case of a voting deadlock, or where there are minority shareholders who might be adversely affected if current income, gain, etc. were not distributed to pay taxes.

> **Example 11-5:** Ansel Inc. is composed of two individual shareholders, Irene Carr and Laurie Levin, who each own 50% of the S corporation. Carr is independently wealthy, and Levin lives on her salary. In its first year of operations, Ansel Inc. earns $1,000,000 of income, or $500,000 for each shareholder. Carr and Levin, at the end of Ansel Inc.'s first tax year, convene a meeting to decide if they should distribute the income or retain it. Carr votes to retain the income, claiming that the S corporation needs the million dollars to finance internal growth; Levin, who has no independent means to pay taxes on income of $500,000, wants a minimum distribution of funds from the S corporation to pay the tax generated on the income. Because the shareholders are deadlocked, the income cannot be distributed, and Levin then moves for judicial dissolution under state law. However, pending the court's decision

¶1106.06

concerning judicial dissolution, there will be no distribution of funds, so Levin will be required to file her income tax return and incur penalties if she fails to pay her tax on the $500,000 pass-through income on time.

   Tax Pointer 1: A taxpayer who has no funds to pay his or her taxes may not want to file a tax return. However, under current tax law, individuals should always file their tax returns even when they cannot pay their taxes because it is a crime not to file a tax return. It is not a crime, however, to file a tax return and not pay the taxes owed, providing the tax return filed is correct. Of course, the IRS will assess penalties and interest, and institute collection proceedings to obtain the taxes owed.

   When there is a deadlock between shareholders on a vote (e.g., a split between two 50 percent shareholders), other adverse situations can develop. For instance, in Example 11-5, if Carr was the president of the corporation, she could fire Levin. Levin, who is dependent on her salary to support herself (pending distribution of S corporation profits), would face a complete cut-off of funds until a judicial review could be made of the corporate deadlock and the termination of her employment. Levin could request that the board of directors review her termination of employment, but because Carr could vote to sustain her presidential decision, Levin's only practical recourse, other than selling her stock to Carr or deferring to Carr, is to hope that a court will reverse Carr's decision. However, a reverse of Carr's decision is not likely given that anyone can be fired for cause in a split over a corporation's operation.

   Tax Pointer 2: To avoid being cut-off from funds through a termination as described above, Levin, on formation of the corporation, should be named president, if at all possible.

   Benefit to minority shareholders. An S corporation's minimum distribution provisions will only benefit a minority shareholder, never a majority shareholder. When forming an S corporation, or when new shareholders join an S corporation, the majority shareholders may not want to cede control over distribution of income since that control could be a very powerful weapon for them. A minimum distribution provision places limits on that power.

   Effects of insolvency. An S corporation, like other business enterprises, cannot render itself insolvent by distributing income to its shareholders. Thus, if an S corporation adopts a minimum distribution provision in its shareholders' agreement, the provision has to provide that the S corporation cannot be rendered insolvent by the distribution.

.07 Removing an Undesirable Shareholder

   Goodwill is usually a very important commodity to S corporation operations. In order to preserve this goodwill, a shareholders' agreement can prescribe that shareholders who commit crimes such as moral turpitude or who malpractice in a professional situation (e.g., an accountant charged with tax evasion) can be removed. (For an example provision that removes a shareholder when moral turpitude occurs, see Appendix 8, Events Requiring Transfer of Stock.)

¶1106.07

.08 Requiring Best Efforts and Covenant Not to Compete

Best efforts. When businesses form, the shareholders, as a rule, want all shareholders to use their best efforts to cause the venture to succeed. However, it is possible that one shareholder may be involved in other ventures, and thus cannot direct his or her best efforts to the S corporation venture (e.g., a shareholder wants to do volunteer work or teach part time at a university). By having a best efforts clause in the S corporation shareholders' agreement, the other shareholders can eliminate a shareholder if the shareholder will not put forth his or her best efforts. (See example language at Appendix 9, Best Efforts Language.)

Covenant not to compete. In addition to a best efforts clause, and perhaps as a supplement thereto, the shareholders' agreement can provide a covenant not to compete. The covenant requires that during a shareholder's tenure, and for a reasonable period after tenure, he or she will not directly or indirectly compete with the corporation within a certain geographic area. A reasonable geographic area restriction can cover any area where the corporation does the bulk of its business or is planning to develop a new market. After the shareholder leaves, the covenant can basically maintain the restrictions about competition that existed during the shareholder's tenure, but under an imposed time period that will not be considered as anticompetitive. State law(s) where the S corporation will be operating should also be consulted for what is a reasonable covenant. Also, the tax effect of the covenant should be assessed.[28] (See a sample covenant restriction at Appendix 10, Covenant Not to Compete Language.)

.09 Ensuring Books Will Close on Sale or Transfer of Stock

When a shareholder terminates an interest in an S corporation, there are two methods to report the S corporation income, loss, etc. for the period prior and after the S shareholder's termination of interest.

(1) If no election has been made to terminate the tax year under Code Sec. 1377(a)(2), the S corporation's items of income, loss, etc. will be allocated on a per-share, per-day basis, which could produce skewed results not in control of the terminating shareholder.[29]

(2) If the books are closed on the terminating event, then the terminating shareholder is in control of the situation; namely, at the time of termination, it can be determined whether or not the S corporation has incurred loss, gain, etc.

Consent of affected shareholders. The election to close the books on a terminating event, however, requires the consent of all the affected shareholders.[30] An affected shareholder is (1) any shareholder whose interest is terminated and (2) all shareholders to whom such shareholder has transferred shares during the tax year. If, however, the shareholder has transferred shares to the corporation, then the term "affected shareholder" includes all persons who are shareholders during the tax year. Previously, Code Sec. 1377(a)(2) required the consent of *all* the

---

[28] See Michael Schlesinger, "A Covenant Not to Compete Can Provide Tax Savings to Buyer," *Taxation for Accountants,* Vol. 44, No. 2 at 96 (February 1990).

[29] Code Sec. 1377(a)(1).
[30] Code Sec. 1377(a)(2).

shareholders, not just the affected ones. However, because it is difficult to predict who will be an affected shareholder and to ensure that this consent will occur, the shareholders' agreement can provide that at the request of the terminating shareholder all of the affected shareholders will consent to closing the books. (See an example of such language at Appendix 11, Closing S Corporation Books on Sale of S Corporation Stock.)

Income in respect of a decedent. When a shareholder dies, due to the S corporation's method of accounting, all income may not have been earned at the time of the shareholder's death. Thus, Code Sec. 691 will apply to dictate the treatment for tax purposes. Physically closing the books on the date of death of shareholder would be the simpler method since there is no guesswork where items belong.

.10 Appreciated Property

In drafting shareholders' agreements, it is important to note the effect of appreciated property.

> *Example 11-6:* Harry Rubble and Bob Kahn, two individuals who are not related, start Rubicon Inc., contributing $10 each for stock. They elect S status for the corporation. Rubicon Inc. uses the $20 to buy land, which becomes the corporation's sole asset. The corporation engages in no other activity but holding the land. Rubble and Kahn, at the time the corporation is established, enter into a cross-purchase agreement that states they will each buy each other's stock interest during life and at death, funding the purchase at death with life insurance. Twenty years after corporate formation, Rubicon Inc. is worth $1,000,000 due to the appreciation of the land. Kahn, pursuant to the shareholders' agreement, at Rubble's request, purchases Rubble's stock for $500,000, increasing Kahn's basis in the S corporation to $500,010 ($10, Kahn's original basis + $500,000 from the stock purchase). Kahn, as sole owner of the S corporation, causes the S corporation to sell the land for $1,000,000 to recover the funds used to buy out Rubble. Kahn recognizes gain of $999,980 ($1,000,000 proceeds – $20 cost basis [characterization of the gain as long term or Code Sec. 1231 depends on the corporate activity]), and pays the tax due. Assume a tax rate of 20% on the sale, and assume that the entire $1,000,000 was all gain (i.e., the $20 cost basis will be discounted to zero for purposes of the calculation). Kahn would realize only $300,000 as net proceeds from the transactions ($1,000,000 – $200,000 tax (20% × $1,000,000) – $500,000 to pay Rubble for Rubble's stock).[31]

If the cross-purchase agreement in Example 11-6 had provided that the $500,000 that Kahn paid Rubble be reduced by one-half of the taxes to be paid on the sale, a more equitable result would have developed.

> *Tax Pointer 1:* Shareholders should provide in their agreement that the purchase price incorporate the tax effect of the sale of shareholder interest.

---

[31] However, discounts for tax effect are only recognized for C corporations. For a discussion of this point, see Tax Pointer 3 in this section, ¶ 1106.10.

¶1106.10

That way the remaining or surviving shareholder(s) will not face an onerous tax bill.

Example 11-7: Assume the same facts as in Example 11-6, except that the tax effect of the sale of the corporate asset, the land, is to be computed as of the date the stock is transferred. Assume the tax rate is 20% and the tax is $200,000; the cross-purchase agreement provides that the purchase price for the stock is to be reduced by one-half the tax that the corporation would realize on the date of sale, assuming that the corporation disposed of the land for its fair market value as of the date of sale. Thus, Kahn would not pay Rubble $500,000; Kahn would pay Rubble only $400,000 ($500,000 − (.5 × $200,000, the tax on the sale)). If Rubicon Inc. sold the land on the date Kahn bought Rubble's interest, Kahn would realize net proceeds of $400,000 ($1,000,000 − $200,000 tax on the sale of the land) − $400,000 paid to Rubble for Rubble's share)). Note that there is an inherent problem in discounting the purchase price in that Kahn is under no compulsion to sell the land. He could hold the land forever.

Tax Pointer 2: Partnerships and limited liability companies (LLCs) do not need such tax compensation provisions in their agreements. Rather, if a partnership or LLC made an election pursuant to Code Sec. 754, then there would be an immediate step-up in the basis of the partnership or LLC assets to fair market value at the time of sale.[32] t

Tax Pointer 3: Case law should be consulted prior to incorporating the tax language inserted into the shareholders' agreement to ensure that it is recognized in the shareholders' jurisdiction. See *Eisenberg,*[33] which sustained a discount for tax liability when assets are sold or the C corporation is liquidated. Although *Eisenberg* applied only to a C corporation, arguably, the logic of the decision should apply to S corporations.

.11 Cross-Purchase vs. Redemption Agreements

A question often asked is what type of shareholders' agreement should be used for an S corporation—a cross-purchase or redemption agreement? Normally, unless the number of shareholders is too large, a cross-purchase agreement is recommended because a shareholder can increase basis by purchasing stock. However, if there are accumulated earnings and profits on the corporate books from C corporation years or a merger with a C corporation, a redemption agreement may be preferred since a pro rata amount of the earnings and profits will be removed by the departing shareholder's redemption. This option alleviates for the surviving shareholders any future problems with the tax on excess passive income, potential termination of the S election, and characterization of distributions as dividends. Of course, the redemption provisions of Code Sec. 302(a) and/or Code Sec. 303 must be satisfied for this reduction in earnings and profits to occur.

---

[32] The basis increase is only for such portion of the partnership's or LLC's assets attributable to the ownership interest sold. See ¶ 1304.03 for a brief discussion of Code Sec 754.

[33] *I. Eisenberg,* CA-2, 98-2 USTC ¶ 60,322, 155 F3d 50. Rev'g and rem'g 74 TCM 1046, Dec. 52,321(M), TC Memo. 1997-483.

A cross-purchase agreement requires the remaining shareholders of a corporation to purchase the departing shareholder's stock, because the departing shareholder died, reached retirement age, etc. The advantage of a cross-purchase agreement is that when the remaining shareholders purchase the stock, their stock basis[34] is increased by the purchase price. In contrast, if a redemption agreement is utilized to acquire a departing shareholder's stock interest, there is no change in the remaining shareholders' basis, since the S corporation's assets are being utilized to fund the acquisition. One difficulty in utilizing a cross-purchase agreement to purchase a departing shareholder's stock is that the remaining shareholders may not have sufficient assets to purchase the departing shareholder's stock, with the result being that the corporation may have to increase the compensation to the remaining shareholders to fund the acquisition. In contrast, with a redemption agreement, the S corporation could have the assets, thereby not causing difficulties for the remaining shareholders.

If life insurance is utilized to assist in funding the purchase price of a decedent's stock interest in a cross-purchase agreement, as discussed at ¶ 1125, there will not be a problem with AAA with respect to the insurance proceeds. An example will illustrate the discussion above.

> *Example 11-8:* Karen and Phil, who are not married to each other, are equal shareholders in KP, Inc., an S corporation. When KP, Inc. was formed in 1990, Karen and Phil contributed $100 each to acquire their stock. Every year, because of their cash needs, the shareholders distribute all the profits to themselves. Thus, their stock basis in 2004 remains at $100 each—their original capital contribution. However, KP, Inc. has been very successful; consequently, each of the shareholders' stock is worth $500,000. Karen wants to leave. If Phil buys Karen's stock, he will be the sole shareholder of the corporation, having a basis of $500,100 per Code Sec. 1012 for purposes of taking losses, distributions, etc. However, he will have to use after-tax dollars to make the purchase. If the corporation were to redeem Karen's stock (see discussion at ¶ 1209), after-tax dollars or funds borrowed by the corporation would have to be used. However, Phil's basis would still remain at $100, since it is the corporation purchasing the stock.

> *Tax Pointer:* Consulting agreements, goodwill, and covenants not to compete could be used to accomplish favorable tax results in addition to the buyout of the shareholder. For a discussion of consulting agreements and covenants not to compete, see Michael Schlesinger, "Consider Consulting and Non-Compete Agreements When Selling a Business," *Practical Tax Strategies,* Vol. 68, No. 5 at 260 (May 2002).

.12 Effect of Code Sec. 409A on Shareholder and Redemption Agreements

As the discussion at ¶ 723 details, shareholder and redemption agreements are subject to Code Sec. 409A. At this stage, it is difficult to project what effect Code Sec. 409A will have on these types of agreements; however, it is probable that certain language will affect the agreements, such as Code Sec. 409A's distribution

---

[34] For a discussion of stock basis, see ¶ 903.01.

provisions detailing when an individual is disabled, when there will be a change of control, allowing a shareholder to accelerate payments, etc. Accordingly, the reader should consult ¶ 723, as well follow the developments under Code Sec. 409A.

¶ 1107 S Corporations Can Have an 80-Percent-or-More C Corporation and Wholly-Owned Subsidiaries

For tax years beginning after December 31, 1996, Congress has prescribed that S corporations can have different trades or businesses operate in different corporate entities, whether or not they are organized through a parent-subsidiary corporation or brother-sister arrangements.[35]

Likewise, an S corporation can operate different trades or businesses using one-member limited liability companies (LLCs).[36] By using a subsidiary or one-member LLC format, an S corporation limits its liability—only its subsidiary LLC assets are exposed to creditors; its parent's assets are not.

¶ 1108 Partner in a Partnership or Member in a Limited Liability Company (LLC)

The tax provisions applicable to partnerships differ from those applicable to S corporations. Because of the differences, S corporations may want to be a partner in a partnership or a member in an LLC.[37] For an example of when an S corporation was a partner in a partnership, see *Selig*.[38]

.01 Reasons to Be a Partner or a Member

A partnership is allowed to allocate its income among its partners in a manner that may be inconsistent with their interests in capital, providing the allocation has substantial economic effect.[39] In contrast, S corporations can basically only distribute income in two ways: distributions pursuant to stock interest or by means of salary to its shareholder-employees.[40]

> **Example 11-9:** Alan Larsen, an inventor of a widget, approaches Bruce Montgomery, a wealthy investor, for help in developing his invention. Larsen proposes that they be 50-50 owners in an S corporation. Montgomery has no objections to the 50-50 split. However, Montgomery would like to be compensated for the $1,000,000 that he will invest in the corporation. Montgomery invests his $1,000,000 by giving a loan to the S corporation, and each shareholder puts in $5 for a 50% stock interest in the corporation. At the end of the first year, the S corporation incurred a loss of $1,000,000. Because Montgomery and Larsen are 50-50 shareholders, each will receive a $500,000 loss on their Forms 1120S K-1. Because Larsen only has $5 of basis, he cannot realistically deduct the loss. While Montgomery has $500,005 of basis because

---

[35] See Chapter 14 for a discussion of subsidiaries.

[36] See ¶ 1307 for a discussion of one-member LLCs.

[37] For further discussion, see ¶ 1304 and ¶ 1307. Also see Michael Schlesinger, *Essential Facts: Limited Liability Companies,* Boston: Warren, Gorham & Lamont, Inc. (1995).

[38] *A.H. Selig,* CA-7, 84-2 USTC ¶ 9696, 740 F2d 572. Aff'g 83-2 USTC ¶ 9442, 565 FSupp 524 (a partnership involving the Milwaukee Brewers, which was a limited partnership, having the Milwaukee Brewers Baseball Club, Inc., an S corporation, as a partner).

[39] Code Sec. 704.

[40] For an example illustrating the tax benefits of LLCs, see ¶ 1304.03.

of his loan to the corporation, he cannot obtain the full tax benefit from his $1,000,000 investment.

Example 11-10: Assume the same facts as in Example 11-9, except Larsen and Montgomery form an LLC. Further, the LLC operating agreement provides that the first $1,000,000 loss is to be allocated to Montgomery, along with all profits until he recovers any loss on his $1,000,000 loan. If Montgomery materially participates in the LLC, he can write off a $1,000,000 loss in the first year of the LLC, clearly giving him a $500,000 benefit over an S corporation format.

S corporations sustained as partners. The IRS in a series of Private Letter Rulings has sustained S corporations as partners in the following situations:

- A law practice partnership containing several incorporated lawyers was recognized as a partnership.[41]

- An S corporation in the investment banking business that sold half of its assets to a C corporation, which then entered into a partnership with the S corporation, had that relationship sustained.[42]

- An S corporation and a new C corporation (controlled by a minority shareholder of the S corporation) entered into a partnership to operate retail stores. The partnership that contained various formulae to allocate the income under Code Sec. 704 was recognized for tax purposes.[43]

- A partnership formed by an S corporation and a C corporation that intended to elect S status was recognized because the business purpose for the partnership was to consolidate and simplify management of certain manufacturing operations.[44]

¶ 1109 Estate and Gift Tax Planning

.01 Estate Tax

When an S shareholder dies, general tax principles allow the stock basis of the deceased shareholder to be stepped up to the fair market value at the time of death or the alternate valuation date, six months after death.[45] An S shareholder's estate can become a shareholder in his or her S corporation. Example 11-11 illustrates the effect that death will have on an S corporation:

Example 11-11: Pam Silvers is the sole shareholder of Amerika Inc., an S corporation. Amerika Inc. has one asset, a piece of land, and at the time of Silver's death, Silver's stock basis is zero because of all of the losses passed through to her from Amerika Inc.'s operations. Amerika Inc.'s only asset, the land, is worth $300,000 at Silver's death. For estate tax valuation on Form 706, Silver's stock is valued at $300,000. Silver leaves all her Amerika stock to her

---

[41] IRS Letter Ruling 8823027 (March 8, 1988).

[42] IRS Letter Ruling 8711020 (January 15, 1986).

[43] IRS Letter Ruling 8804015 (October 28, 1987).

[44] IRS Letter Ruling 9050021 (September 14, 1990).

[45] Code Sec. 1014. Code Secs. 2518(b), 2662, and 6018 provide that for estates of decedents dying after Decem-

ber 31, 2009, and before December 17, 2010, the due date for (1) filing an estate tax return, (2) paying the estate tax, and (3) making a disclaimer of an interest in property passing by reason of the decedent's death, is not earlier than nine months after December 17, 2010.

brother, Dick. Dick's basis in the stock will be $300,000; this is the basis he would use when he sells the stock or takes losses in Amerika Inc. from operations.

The Tax Relief, Unemployment Insurance Reauthorization and Job Creation Act of 2010. Congress made extensive changes in the estate and gift tax laws to provide great planning opportunities for the small closely held family S corporation. It is beyond the scope of this book to provide an extensive discussion of the area, except to note the following:

- Code Secs. 2010 and 2631 provide that the amount of the estate tax exemption and generation-skipping tax exemption is five million dollars per individual for the years 2010, 2011 and 2012 subject to an inflation adjustment in 2012.

- Code Secs. 2010, 2631 and 6018 provide that the $5 million estate tax exclusion is made portable between spouses for decedents dying after 2010, but not the generation-skipping tax exemption.

- Code Secs. 2001(c) and 2502(a) provide that the top estate and gift tax rate is 35% in 2010, 2011, and 2012.

- Code Secs. 2010(c) and 2631(c) for estates of decedents dying, and generation-skipping transfers, after 2009 and before 2013, the generation-skipping transfer (GST) tax was reinstated retroactively to the beginning of 2010; however for transfers in 2010 only, the tax rate for GST tax purposes is zero. For 2011, the GST exemption is the same as the estate tax exemption ($5 million indexed for inflation after 2011). Further, the GST exemption may be allocated to a trust created or funded in 2010.

- Code Sec. 1014 *et seq.* provides that for estates of decedents dying in 2010 and thereafter, property passing by the estate will receive a stepped-up basis equal to the property's fair market value on the date of the decedent's death (or on an alternate valuation date). Estate tax will be due on any property not exempt subject to a maximum taxation of 35 percent. However, for estates of decedents dying in 2010 "modified carryover basis" rules for property can be elected by the estate pursuant to Code Sec. 1014 *et seq.* Under the modified carryover basis rules: (a) the basis of property acquired from a decedent (increased by allocable dollar allowances) is the lesser of the property's adjusted basis in the hands of the decedent, or its fair market value on the date of the decedent's death; and (b) no estate tax is due.

- Code Sec. 2505(a)(1) provides that the gift tax exemption is unified with estate tax exemption for gifts made after 2010, namely up to a maximum of $5 million but stays unchanged at $1 million for gifts made in 2010.

Extension of time to pay estate tax. The due date for payment of estate tax can be extended if the original due date will cause undue hardship.[46] An "undue hardship" means more than an inconvenience to the taxpayer. It must appear that substantial financial loss (e.g., loss due to the sale of property at a sacrifice price)

---

[46] Code Sec. 6161.

will result to the taxpayer by having to pay on the original due date vs. an extended due date.[47] If a market exists, the sale of property at its current market price is not ordinarily considered as resulting in an undue hardship.

.02 Estate Tax Planning Is Limited

Estate tax planning for an S corporation is limited. For instance, while S corporations can have employee stock ownership plans (ESOPs), Congress has imposed a number of restrictions for S corporations that don't exist for C corporations.[48] Another limitation is that an S corporation can only have two classes of stock—voting and nonvoting; in contrast, an LLC, partnership, and C corporation can have various classes of ownership; preference as to distributions, liquidation rights, convertible debentures; etc.[49] S corporations can only have 100 shareholders (the maximum number used to be only 10); in contrast, an LLC, partnership, and C corporation can have any number of owners—10, 20, 100, or 1,000. Also, an S corporation can only have certain shareholders (i.e., no nonresident aliens); in contrast, an LLC, partnership, and C corporation can have anyone as a shareholder, partner, or member.

.03 Code Sec. 2036 as It Applies to Closely-Held Family S Corporations

Code Sec. 2036 is an estate tax provision which provides that the value of the gross estate shall include the value of all property to the extent of any interest therein of which the decedent has at any time made a transfer (except in case of a bona fide sale for an adequate and full consideration in money or money's worth), by trust or otherwise, under which he (or she) has retained for his (or her) life or for any period not ascertainable without reference to his (or her) death for any period which does not in fact end before his (or her) death:

(a)(1) The possession or enjoyment of, or the right to the income from, the property, or

(a)(2) The right, either alone or in conjunction with any person, to designate the persons who shall possess or enjoy the property or the income therefrom.

Code Sec. 2036 is equally applicable to S corporations and partnerships; notwithstanding, the Internal Revenue Service has been focusing its attention on family partnerships, due to their favorable planning possibilities in contrast to S corporations. *The Estate of Strangi v. Comm.*[50] (hereinafter referred to as *"Strangi II"*) is illustrative of the approach being utilized by the Tax Court to deal with Code Sec. 2036 vis-a-vis family businesses. *Strangi II* utilized Code Sec. 2036(a)(1) and (2) to attack a family partnership where minority discounts were used for estate planning purposes.[51]

The facts in *Strangi II* are as follows: Ninety-eight percent of decedent's wealth, including decedent's residence, was transferred to the Strangi Family

---

[47] Reg. § 1.6161-1(b).

[48] For a discussion of S corporation ESOPs, see Chapter 15.

[49] See discussion at ¶ 208.01.

[50] TC Memo 2003-145, *aff'd* 2005-2 USTC ¶ 60,506 (5th Cir. 2005). This case was due to the remand of 115 TC

478, Dec. 54,135. For a detailed discussion of *Strangi II*, see Michael Schlesinger, *Family Businesses: The Impact of Strangi II*, Tax Practice & Procedure at 15, March 2004.

[51] For a discussion of minority discounts, see ¶ 1109.07.

Limited Partnership (SFLP). Stranco, Inc. (Stranco), was a corporation formed to be the managing partner, which owned one percent of the partnership, and was owned 47 percent by the decedent, with the balance owned equally by four of the decedent's children, with these children subsequently transferring 0.25 percent to a charity so that the charity owned one percent of Stranco. The charity was the McLennan County Community College (MCCC). One of decedent's children, Mrs. Gulig, was married to Michael J. Gulig, Esq. Decedent gave Michael a general power of attorney prior to his death. The decedent, as a limited partner, owned 99 percent of the limited partnership, with Stranco owning the remaining one percent as the managing partner. As a limited partner in SFLP, decedent did not have any right to exercise managerial authorities. Stranco and SFLP were established pursuant to the Fortress Family Plan (Fortress). The decedent was required to pay rent to SFLP for the residence he transferred to SFLP, but instead of rent being paid, rent was accrued on SFLP's books, with SFLP reporting income for the rent and the rent accrual being paid three years after decedent's death.

SFLP covered various expenditures for the decedent, such as paying for the back surgery of decedent's caretaker, and on decedent's death in 1994, paying nearly $40,000 for funeral expenses; in 1995 and 1996, $65,000 of decedent's expenditures, as well as paying $3,187,800 for decedent's federal and state inheritance taxes. SFLP accounted for these payments as "advances to partners."

About seventy-five percent of the assets contributed by decedent was cash and securities. The Stranco shareholder agreement provided that decedent and his four children would be the sole directors, with each agreeing to reelect themselves or a nominee at each annual meeting.

Code Sec. 2036(a)(1). Prior to *Strangi II*, the Internal Revenue Service has been able to strike down family partnerships in technical grounds. For instance, in *Estate of Schauerhomer*,[52] where the Court, under Code Sec. 2036(a), struck down the family partnership because the decedent deposited the family limited partnership income directly into his checking account, co-mingling it with his income from other sources. In *Estate of Reichardt*,[53] the family partnership was struck down again because the decedent co-mingled the assets with his own. The difference between *Reichardt and Schauerhomer* was that an accountant in *Reichardt* tried at year-end to separate the family partnership transactions from the personal ones. Additionally, the decedent paid no rent with respect to residence transferred into the family partnership. In *Estate of Harper*,[54] the Court felt that Code Sec. 2036(a) would apply, because there was a five-month delay in doing the necessary paperwork to establish the family limited partnership. Additionally, there was a three-month delay by the partnership to set up the bank account and obtain a tax identification number.

In *Strangi II*, the Court utilized *Schauerhomer*, *Reichardt* and *Harper* to pick apart the family partnership, in that SFLP was really a pocket-book for the dece-

---

[52] 73 TCM 2855, Dec. 52,061(M), TC Memo. 1997-242.   [54] 83 TCM 1641, Dec. 54,745(M), TC Memo. 2002-121.
[53] 114 TC 144 (2000).

dent, paying his personal expenses, letting him accrue rent rather than pay for it on a monthly basis, etc. As the Court stated:

> The SFLP/Stranco arrangement... [bore]greater resemblances to one man's estate plan than to any sort of arm's-length, joint enterprise.

Digging deeper, the Court stated:

> [T]he crucial characteristic is that virtually nothing beyond formal title changed in decedent's relationship to his assets. Mr. Gulig managed decedent's affairs both before and after the transfer. Decedent's children did not obtain a meaningful economic stake in the property during decedent's life. They raised no objections or concerns when large sums were advanced for expenditures of decedent or his estate, thus implying an understanding that decedent's access thereto would not be restricted.

Accordingly, the Court felt that "the preponderance of the evidence establishes that decedent retained possession of, enjoyment of, or the right to income from the property transferred within the meaning of section 2036(a)(1)."

Code Sec. 2036(a)(2). The Tax Court, relying on *Byrum*[55] struck down this family partnership, even though the Court recognized that:

- The decedent, as a minority shareholder of Stranco, was without the ability to elect a majority of directors, thus retaining even less control than was present in *Byrum*; and

- Under the Texas Limited Partnership Act (TRLPA), Tex. Rev. Civ. Stat. Ann. art. 6132a-1, sec. 3.03 (Vernon Supp. 2003), a limited partner expressly does not participate in control of the business of a partnership by virtue of acting as an officer, director, or stockholder of a corporate general partner.

The Court found that the family partnership violated Code Sec. 2036(a)(2) because the partnership did not utilize the "independent trustee" concept of *Byrum* to prevent misuse of the partnership assets and income. In reaching its decision, the Court noted the estate's argument that the managing partner, Stranco, owed the family partnership fiduciary responsibility, and that the charity MCCC was independent, and as such, was subject to the jurisdiction of the Attorney General of the State of Texas. The Court picked apart these two arguments by stating:

> As regards fiduciary obligations of Stranco and its directors, these duties, too, have little significance in the present context. Although Stranco would owe a fiduciary duty to SFLP and to the limited partners, decedent owned the sole, 99-percent limited partnership interest. The rights to designate traceable to decedent through Stranco cannot be characterized as limited in any meaningful way by duties owed essentially to himself. Nor do the obligations of Stranco directors to the corporation itself warrant any different conclusion. Decedent held 47 percent of Stranco, and his own children held 52 of the remaining 53 percent. Intrafamily fiduciary duties within an investment vehicle simply are not equivalent in nature to the obligations created by the *Byrum*... scenario.

* * *

> With respect to the role of MCCC, *Byrum*... affords no basis for permitting outcomes under Code Sec. 2036(a)(2) to turn on factors amounting to no more

---

[55] For a discussion of *Byrum*, see ¶ 1304.03.

than window dressing. A charity given a gratuitous one-percent interest would not realistically exercise any meaningful oversight.

In reaching its decision, the Court implied that a different result might occur if the partnership was an "active" one, like *Byrum*, rather than a passive one, like *Strangi*. The Court stated:

> Another element stressed by [*Byrum*] was the manner in which the flow of funds allegedly under Mr. Byrum's control would be subject to economic and business realities consequent upon the status of the relevant corporations as typical small operating enterprises. Earnings and dividends of a small operating company could be affected by, inter alia, changes in products, in competition, or in industry regulation and outlook; use of funds for replacement of plant and equipment or for growth and expansion; and the need to retain sufficient earnings for working capital. These complexities do not apply to SFLP or Stranco, which held only monetary or investment assets.

Finally, the Court, utilizing prior precedent, namely *Harper*, stated that there was no consideration for the transfer:

> First, no *bona fide* sale, in the sense of an arm's-length transaction, occurred in connection with decedent's transfer of property to SFLP and Stranco. Mr. Gulig, as decedent's attorney in fact, prepared the arrangement using Fortress materials in absence of any meaningful negotiation or bargaining with other anticipated interest-holders. He determined how the entities would be structured and operated, what property would be contributed, and what interests various parties would obtain therein. Hence, decedent essentially stood on both sides of the transaction, a fact unchanged by the manner in which the Strangi children opted to join after the substantive decisions had been made.
>
> Second, full and adequate consideration does not exist where, as here, there has been merely a "recycling" of value through partnership or corporate solution... As we recently explained in *Harper*:
>
> to call what occurred here a transfer for consideration within the meaning of Code Sec. 2036(a), much less a transfer for an adequate and full consideration, would stretch the exception far beyond its intended scope. In actuality, all decedent did was to change the form in which he held his beneficial interest in the contributed property. *** Without any change whatsoever in the underlying pool of assets or prospect for profit, as, for example, where others make contributions of property or services in the interest of true joint ownership or enterprise, there exists nothing but a circuitous "recycling" of value. We are satisfied that such instances of pure recycling do not rise to the level of a payment of consideration. To hold otherwise would open Code Sec. 2036 to a myriad of abuses engendered by unilateral paper transformations.

* * *

> Decedent contributed more than 99 percent of the total property placed in the SFLP/Stranco arrangement and received back an interest the value of which derived almost exclusively from the assets he had just assigned. Furthermore, the SFLP/Stranco arrangement patently fails to qualify as the sort of functioning business enterprise that could potentially inject intangibles that would lift the situation beyond mere recycling. We therefore hold that decedent did not engage in any transfer for consideration upon the creation and funding of SFLP and Stranco. Accordingly, the estate is entitled to no exception to the treatment mandated by Code Sec. 2036(a).

¶1109.03

In reading the *Strangi II* Court's holding under Code Sec. 2036(a)(2), based on *Byrum*, one may feel that the Court was somewhat "shooting from the hip" in its analysis, and that on appeal, or in another court's decision, the Court's position regarding Code Sec. 2036(a)(2) may be reversed or severely limited. In analyzing the Court's approach, initially, it is to be noted that it has reversed a whole line of private rulings[56] which held that an individual, as a general managing partner in a family partnership, could control partnership assets without these assets being included in the individual's estate under Code Sec. 2036(a)(2). Also, the Court ignored *Old Colony Trust Co. v. U.S.*,[57] which stated that "no aggregation of purely administrative powers [retained by the grantor] can meet the government's amorphous test of 'sufficient dominion and control' so as to be equated with ownership."

Since *Strangi II*, there have been several decisions with their results being multi-faceted in terms of the application of Code Sec. 2036 to family partnerships. *Stone III Estate*[58] sustained a family partnership where the children were represented by counsel. Likewise, in *Kimbell, Sr.*,[59] Code Sec. 2036 was found inapplicable to a family partnership. However, in *Turner*,[60] Code Sec. 2036 was held to apply.

Recently, there have been several cases where Code Sec. 2036(a) was found not to apply. One is *Estate of Black*,[61] where stock transferred by a decedent to a family limited partnership (FLP) was not includible in the decedent's gross estate under Code Sec. 2036(a) because the transfer was a bona fide sale for adequate and full consideration. Some of the factors which influenced the court ruling was the fact that the decedent created an FLP in order to consolidate and protect his stock holdings in an insurance company, namely by preventing his grandsons from selling their shares of stock and protecting his son's shares from potential claims incident to divorce. In reaching its decision the court noted that the use of trusts to "[hold]an untraded portfolio of marketable securities weighs negatively," and that it was not engaged in an active trade or business, but felt that it could not "blindly" strike down the partnership. The court also noted that "[A] family limited partnership that does not conduct an active trade or business may nonetheless be formed for a legitimate and significant nontax reason" citing *Estate of Schutt*.[62]

Planning for S Corporations under Code Sec. 2036. *New S Corporations.* Applying *Strangi II* to the formation of a new family S corporation, clearly, to avoid the Court's view of Code Sec. 2036(a)(2), taxpayers will have to follow certain procedures to ensure safety.

(1) Some independence must be established for the children's interest to be recognized in the family S corporation to prevent the imposition of Code Sec. 2036. For instance, one can have the children represented by an attorney to negotiate their rights as S corporate shareholders. The family S corporation can no longer be a situation where a parent's attorney prepares the shareholders agreement for the children and other family

---

[56] Private IRS Letter Rulings 9026021, 9131006, 9310039, 9332006, 9415007, and 9546006.

[57] 70-1 USTC ¶ 12,667 (1st Cir. 1970).

[58] TC Memo 2003-309, Dec. 55,341 (M).

[59] CA-5, 2004-1 USTC ¶ 60,486, 371 F.3d 257.

[60] CA-3, 2004-2 USTC ¶ 60,489, 382 F.3d 367.

[61] 133 TC No 15.

[62] TC Memo. 2005-126.

members to sign; there must be negotiations between parents and family members, with each party represented by counsel.

(2) Where possible, establish that an independent person will operate the S corporation.

(3) If the assets in the family S corporation are investment-type situations, then have a professional manager operate the S corporation to invest these assets to limit recycling of value as set forth in *Harper*[63] and its ilk.

(4) Have children contribute their own assets and expertise to the S corporation—do not have them assume a passive role.

(5) Utilize an operating business if possible to fund the S corporation rather than passive assets.

(6) Have a non-family member as an S corporate shareholder, with this non-family member owning a significant interest in the S corporation. In *Byrum*, more than a majority of the individuals by number (not by vote) were involved with Mr. Byrum in the business entities.

(7) If an individual (i.e., a parent) is establishing a family S corporation, ensure that the individual has sufficient assets on which to live independently of any distributions and/or loans from the family S corporation.

(8) Observe formalities with respect to establishing the family S corporation immediately upon formation, such as opening a bank account, obtaining a federal identification number, establishing a set of books, etc.

Existing S Corporations. As to existing family S corporations which closely resemble *Strangi II* situations where virtually all of the parents' wealth is contributed to the family S corporation, advice is difficult, because there is no final determination at this time as to *Strangi II*'s analysis under Code Sec. 2036(a)(2). Further, whatever approach is decided, naturally, there will be tax consequences which will follow. One easy suggestion is to dissolve the family S corporation. A second would be to sell the donor's interest in the family S corporation. Giving away the offending interest to the children is also an approach.

.04 Trusts

The following six trusts can qualify as shareholders in an S corporation.[64]

Tax Pointer 1: Before setting up an S corporation trust for family members, it is wise to examine all of the alternatives and their advantages. Often a qualified subchapter S trust (QSST)[65] or an electing small business trust (ESBT)[66] may have more limitations due to statutory provisions than a trust established for a limited liability company (LLC), which has no statutory limitations.[67]

Qualified subchapter S trusts (QSSTs). For individuals other than surviving spouses, a QSST may prove invaluable in keeping S corporation stock out of a

---

[63] 83 TCM 1641, Dec. 54,745(M), TC Memo. 2002-121.

[64] See Chapter 3 for more discussion on each trust.

[65] QSSTs are discussed in detail at ¶ 307.

[66] ESBTs are discussed in detail at ¶ 306.

[67] LLCs are discussed in detail at ¶ 1304 and ¶ 1307.

beneficiary's hands (i.e., the corpus) while still providing income to that beneficiary from S corporation operations.

> *Example 11-12:* Alice Olson, a widow and the sole shareholder in an S corporation, has two children: Mary, who acts responsibly, and Bob, who has a drug habit. Alice fears that if she gives the stock in her S corporation to Bob, he will sell the stock to raise cash for drugs. However, if Alice transfers the stock in her S corporation to a QSST and lists its beneficiary as Bob, she can instruct that no corpus be distributed during Bob's life, only income. In this way, Alice does not help Bob maintain or increase his drug usage. Alice, as controlling shareholder, can also regulate the income flowing to Bob's QSST through her salary (i.e., taking all the S corporation income as salary so that the QSST realizes no income).

Of course, if a controlling shareholder were to prevent income from flowing to shareholders of an S corporation, the shareholders (i.e., in Example 11-12, Bob, the beneficiary of the QSST) could request the trustee sue the corporation for corporate waste because the controlling shareholder is taking too much salary. Also, when games are played with salary, the rules of Code Sec. 1366(e) may be breached and a reallocation of income may occur.

Qualified terminal interest property (QTIP) trust. This testamentary trust allows a married individual to care for his or her surviving spouse without giving the surviving spouse control of the S corporation or other businesses. In a QTIP trust,[68] the income from the S corporation is left to the surviving spouse during his or her lifetime, and the corpus (i.e., the S corporation stock) is left to the original spouse's children (children of a prior marriage) at the surviving spouse's death.

> *Tax Pointer 2:* State law may allow a surviving spouse to elect against a testamentary QTIP trust thereby defeating the deceased spouse's wishes. If the surviving spouse elects against a QTIP trust, he or she obtains an outright bequest thereby giving him or her a shareholder position vis-à-vis the remaindermen (i.e., the children of a prior marriage). Potentially this surviving spouse could then become a divisive force in S corporation operations.

> *Tax Pointer 3:* QTIP trusts, like all trusts, in effect rule from the grave. Aside from monetary planning, consideration should be given to the surviving spouse's feelings—often his or her good memories may be tainted by the appearance that the decedent refused to trust him or her.

Electing small business trusts (ESBTs). An ESBT,[69] in contrast to a QSST, allows the trustee of the trust discretion in distributing income and/or corpus to a beneficiary. However, in exchange for this discretion, Code Sec. 1361(e) exacts a stiff price—the ESBT must pay tax on the trust's income at the highest individual tax rate, with no graduated income tax rate to apply. Thus, in reality, the only beneficiaries of this trust can be individuals in the highest income tax bracket.

Voting trusts. Voting trusts allow a shareholder (e.g., a parent) to control the votes of the other shareholders (e.g., his or her children) by requiring that the

---

[68] QTIPs are discussed in detail at ¶ 304.   [69] ESBTs are discussed in detail at ¶ 306.

shareholders place their stock in a trust where the trustee votes the stock. Voting trusts are established under state law and, as a rule, cannot stay in existence perpetually (usually the life span is ten years, subject to renewal). However, control may be easier if a shareholder's agreement is used since the agreement can be perpetual and cover other events as well, such as transition at death, disability, etc.[70]

Grantor trusts. A grantor trust is allowed to be a shareholder of an S corporation, provided that the grantor is an individual, not a nonresident alien, and treated as owning all of the trust. A grantor of a grantor trust qualifying as an S corporation shareholder can retain (1) the right to revoke the trust; (2) a reversionary power in the trust; and (3) certain administrative rights normally designated to the trustee, such as the right to decide to distribute income or accumulate it for the grantor, the grantor's spouse, or both. And/or the grantor can control beneficial enjoyment of the corpus or income.

Because of all the powers that grantor trusts have, they become invaluable for S corporation planning. A classic example of a grantor trust is the revocable *inter vivos* trust or living trust, which is often used as an estate-planning device to minimize estate probate of assets.

Trusts owned by the beneficiary (Code Sec. 678 trusts). A Code Sec. 678 trust owned by a beneficiary (a person other than the grantor) is allowed to be a shareholder of an S corporation, provided that the beneficiary is an individual and not a nonresident alien.

A Code Sec. 678 trust allows a donor gift-giving flexibility in that the donee (i.e., the beneficial owner) can elect or not elect to be an S corporation shareholder. Practically, this means that the donor is not "ruling from the grave." To illustrate, assume a parent establishes a Code Sec. 678 trust for a child and places C corporation stock in it. Under this scenario, the child can decide to elect S status.

.05 Other Considerations

S corporation election after the death of a shareholder. An estate can make an S election for a corporation after the death of a shareholder even if the corporation was never an S corporation during the life of the shareholder.[71] However, all shareholders of the S corporation, including the personal representative of the estate, must consent to the election during the first two and one-half months of the S corporation's first tax year.[72] It is not clear if an estate of a nonresident alien can be a shareholder since a nonresident alien cannot be a shareholder.[73] Also, a foreign trust is specifically excluded from being a shareholder.[74]

One level of taxation. An estate may want to elect S status after the death of a shareholder to provide a flow of income that will be subject to only one level of taxation. The tax effect of such a decision is illustrated in Example 11-13.

---

[70] For a discussion of voting trusts, see ¶ 305.

[71] Reg. § 1.1362-6(b)(2)(iii).

[72] Code Sec. 1362(b)(2)(B)(ii).

[73] Code Sec. 1361(b)(1)(C).

[74] Code Sec. 1361(c)(2).

Example 11-13: Ted Fox was the sole shareholder of Bucktown Inc., a calendar-year C corporation that owned income-producing property. In 2000, a triple net lease on a prime piece of property was calculated to produce $1,000,000 income each year for Bucktown Inc. for the next five years. While Fox was alive, he withdrew the net earnings from the C corporation ($1,000,000 a year). Fox died on January 1, 2004, survived by his wife, Janis, and three children. His entire estate was left to his wife, and his estate elected S corporation status to provide her an income stream at one level of taxation.

Tax Pointer: Whenever a C corporation converts to S status, adverse tax results may occur due to the interplay of Code Sec. 1374 (built-in gains tax), Code Sec. 1375 (tax on excess passive income), and Code Sec. 1362(d) (termination of S election if corporation has excess passive income in three consecutive years). Accordingly, the three sections should be consulted.[75]

Contributing appreciated property to an S corporation. Unwarranted tax results could occur if appreciated property is contributed to an S corporation since it can be converted from capital gain to ordinary income property.

Example 11-14: Abe Henkel, an 80-year-old widower with two children, is an art collector who decides to fulfill a lifetime dream by establishing an art gallery. Henkel establishes Colorama Inc. He then contributes paintings to Colorama Inc. that cost him $20,000 but have a current fair market value of $1,000,000, taking back all of the stock in Colorama Inc. in return. Henkel elects S status for the corporation. Shortly thereafter, while the paintings are still worth $1,000,000 and none have been sold, Henkel dies. On his estate tax return, the estate reports the stock is worth $1,000,000, the fair market value of the paintings. His children, who received the stock of Colorama Inc. from his estate, desire to obtain the paintings from the corporation for their own use. Because Henkel's art collection became inventory at the time of incorporation, Colorama Inc. has a serious tax problem. If Colorama Inc. sells the paintings for $1,000,000, the children will realize $980,000 of ordinary income ($1,000,000 – $20,000 cost basis). If the proceeds of $1,000,000 are distributed to the children, their basis will become $1,980,000 in Colorama Inc. stock ($1,000,000 stock basis + $980,000 of gain) – $20,000 of cash)). Since the corporation has no assets at this juncture, the children could liquidate the corporation. Upon liquidation, if the children have no capital gains to offset the $980,000 capital loss, then the children will only be permitted to take $3,000 of capital loss each year pursuant to the Internal Revenue Code, and any unused losses will expire at their death. Alternatively, the children could require the corporation to distribute the paintings to them. Since a distribution is treated as a sale, however, the children would realize $980,000 of ordinary income and have the same liquidation problem just discussed.[76]

Utilizing non-voting stock in estate planning for family and trusted employees. In estate planning for S corporation shareholders, use of nonvoting stock

---

[75] See Chapter 8 for a discussion of these three statutory provisions.

[76] Code Sec. 311. See ¶ 608 for a discussion of property distributed to shareholders.

can successfully accomplish family objectives. IRS Letter Ruling 9022045 (March 6, 1990), parts of which were adapted in Example 11-15, illustrates the use of nonvoting stock.

> *Example 11-15:* Greg Amato owns all the stock (voting and nonvoting) of Viva Inc., an S corporation. Amato has four children: Tony, a son, and three daughters, Mara, Jenna, and Elsa. Tony works for Viva Inc. While Amato is living, he does not want to give Tony any stock for fear of alienating his daughters. Amato also has a trusted employee, Ed Shumann, whom he wants to reward for being so loyal. Again, while Amato is living, he does not want to give Schumann any stock. Thus, Amato's last will and testament becomes the means for giving Viva Inc. stock as desired.
>
> In the will, Amato left all the voting stock to Tony, his son, and to his three daughters he left 95% of the nonvoting stock to be divided equally among those surviving him. To protect against his daughters ever transferring the nonvoting stock to anyone else, such as a son-in-law through a divorce settlement, Amato imposed stipulations in his will that a daughter parting with any of her stock must sell the stock to the corporation for its fair market value at the time of redemption. As to employee Schumann, Amato gave him 5% of the remaining nonvoting stock to reward him for his faithful performance, subject to the same transferability restrictions and conditions imposed upon his daughters. Furthermore, to prevent difficulties, additional restrictions were imposed on Schumann's stock: (1) Schumann may only keep the stock while still employed by Viva Inc. and (2) if Schumann leaves Viva Inc. to enter into a competing business within a certain geographical area within a certain period of time, then Schumann will forfeit his stock redemption proceeds as well.

The restrictions imposed in Example 11-15 by Amato's will did not create a second class of stock, which would cause the S corporation to lose its S election. Instead, Amato was able to accomplish a major goal: maintaining family control of the business. By using a will, he can easily change it if one of his children or trusted employee anger him, striking out the provision for that beneficiary. However, if stock had been issued to that same individual during Amato's life, he would be forced to buy that individual out, which could prove costly as well as lead to lawsuits. By using the will format, Amato is able to provide funds for his daughters, assuming that the business generates profits, but at the same time, allow Tony to run the business without fear of being outvoted by his sisters. Of course, Tony, by controlling the company, can prevent any earnings from flowing to his sisters by increasing salaries, expending funds, etc., but his sisters always have the rights of shareholders such as inspection, derivative suits, etc. to protect themselves. One of the disadvantages of using a will is that there is no means to bequeath the stock to after-born grandchildren.

It may be wondered why in Example 11-15 a shareholders' agreement was not used to accomplish Amato's objectives. The simple reason is that a shareholders' agreement is not effective while there is only one shareholder. Additionally, Amato did not want to give, transfer, or sell the stock in the S corporation during his lifetime to his children or the trusted employee, preferring to keep his options

¶1109.05

open. Thus, since there were no other individuals Amato wanted as shareholders, a shareholders' agreement would not have be effective.

Redemption agreements.[77] Rather than do a sales agreement between shareholders, or grant a permitted shareholder an option on S corporation stock, a shareholder may desire to enter into an agreement of redemption with the S corporation.

Avoiding the alternative minimum tax (AMT). When a redemption agreement is funded with life insurance, it may be advisable in estate planning to convert from C status to S status during the life of the shareholder. Depending on the circumstances, the death of the shareholder and the collection of the insurance proceeds could generate AMT. If an S election is in effect, then the AMT is obviated since there will be no AMT generated by collection of the proceeds. Alternatively, the shareholders could change the shareholders' agreement to incorporate a cross purchase agreement (i.e., shareholder(s) purchases the stock from the selling shareholder) rather than a redemption agreement, but there may be a problem with the transfer of the policies based on the various insurance provisions in the Code.

.06 Postmortem Estate Tax Planning

Occasionally, a will leaving S corporation stock is drafted in such a way that the bequest will cause the S corporation election to terminate. This situation could occur if a bequest of S corporation stock is made to a nonresident alien, or any other nonpermitted shareholder pursuant to Code Sec. 1361. One way to solve this dilemma is to not make this bequest immediately; instead, keep the estate of the deceased shareholder open because an estate is a permissible shareholder. While the estate is open, the estate can pursue various approaches to solve this problem. One approach might be to redeem the stock intended for the nonresident alien beneficiary thereby preserving the S election by converting the stock to cash. Another alternative might be to sell the S corporation assets and then distribute the net proceeds to the shareholders. As to how long an estate can be kept open, see Rev. Rul. 76-23.[78] See also IRS Letter Ruling 7951131 (September 24, 1979) where the IRS refused to rule, claiming a fact question, that an estate could be kept open pending a federal estate tax audit without becoming a trust and *Old Virginia Brick Co., Inc.*[79] where an estate that began in 1941 consented to S corporation status in 1959 and lost its S corporation election since the estate terminated and was succeeded by a testamentary trust.

Postmortem qualification for certain trusts. In the event that the decedent's will bequeaths S corporation stock to a trust that would be an ineligible S corporation shareholder, the S corporation election will not terminate for a period of two years from the date that the stock is transferred to the ineligible trust.[80] Thus, the S corporation will have two years to take the necessary steps to solve its problem with the ineligible trust by either redeeming the ineligible trust's shares or

---

[77] See ¶ 1209 for a discussion of redemptions.
[78] Rev. Rul 76-23, 1976-1 CB 264.

[79] *Old Virginia Brick Co., Inc.*, CA-4, 66-2 USTC ¶ 9708, 367 F2d 276. Aff'g 44 TC 724, Dec. 27,532, (1965).
[80] Code Sec. 1361(c)(2)(A).

liquidating them. Consequently, if a will prescribes that an ineligible testamentary trust is to become an S corporation shareholder, the estate, in conjunction with the S corporation, has a tremendous amount of time to solve the problem: (1) the period that the estate stays open as such and does not establish the ineligible testamentary trust and (2) the two-year period beginning on the date the stock is transferred to the trust.

Code Sec. 303 redemptions. A Code Sec. 303 redemption used after a decedent's death can remove funds tax free from an S corporation. See ¶ 1209.05 for a discussion of these redemptions.

.07 Discounts to Reduce Gift Taxes on Stock Transfers

Minority and lack of control discounts. One of the prime reasons for using an S corporation when estate planning for families is the availability of a minority and lack of control discount. Two significant cases, *LeFrak*[81] (30 percent minority discount sustained on a transfer of a real estate interest to family members in a partnership) and *Mandelbaum*[82] (30 percent minority discount sustained on transfers of S corporation stock) establish the fact that a parent can transfer a minority interest in S corporation stock to a child, taking a minority and lack of control discount. The amount of discount is still being determined by the courts; however, the two cases mentioned above and a number of others have sustained a 30 percent discount. What this means is that a parent can both reduce an estate and also pass income to the donee. The IRS in *Tax Advise Memorandum 200443032* struck down a situation where a corporation transferred assets to a newly-formed limited partnership, followed by the pro rata distribution of the partnership interests to its shareholders with discounts being taken, due to the fact that no partnership interest could control the partnership. The IRS held that under Code Sec. 311(b) the corporation was deemed to sell the assets in their entirety for their fair market value; thus no discounts were available.

> **Example 11-16:** Joe Tanner, a parent, owns 100% of the stock in Deeds Inc., an S corporation that owns vacant land worth $1,000,000. The land's cost basis to Deeds Inc. is $0; thus, whatever the S corporation sells the land for will be 100% gain. Joe transfers 10% of the stock to his daughter, Ann Tanner. The 10% stock transferred to her is worth $100,000 since Deeds Inc.'s sole asset is the land worth $1,000,000; however, by applying a 30% minority and lack of control discount, the valuation for gift tax purposes is $70,000. Assume that, the day after the transfer, Deeds Inc. sells the land; Ann would realize $100,000 of gain, which she would be entitled to receive as a 10% shareholder, but her father, Joe, would not report the gain and also would have the proceeds excluded from his estate.

> **Tax Pointer 1:** Field Service Advice 200143004 (July 5, 2001), discussed at ¶ 1126.01, refused to recognize an S corporation established by a mother where the corporate assets were cash, Treasury bills and municipal bonds,

---

[81] *S. LeFrak*, 66 TCM 1297, Dec. 49,396(M), TC Memo. 1993-526.

[82] *B. Mandelbaum*, 69 TCM 2852, Dec. 50,687(M), TC Memo. 1995-255. Aff'd, CA-3, 96-2 USTC ¶ 60,240, 91 F3d 124.

prescribing that when the mother transferred S corporation stock to her children utilizing minority discounts, her sole purpose was to reduce federal taxes. The IRS felt that the S corporation had no business purpose and was formed solely as a conduit for planned family giving using Code Sec. 2503(b)'s annual exclusion.

Discount for tax liability on appreciated assets. *Eisenberg*[83] permitted a discount for potential future tax liability on a gift of C corporation stock, ruling that the corporation would pay tax on the "gain on the distribution of appreciated property to its shareholders irrespective of whether the gain occurred in a liquidating or nonliquidating context." Arguably, *Eisenberg* should apply equally to an S corporation, but the question has not yet been addressed.[84]

Non-voting stock. As discussed at ¶ 208.01, an S corporation can have two classes of stock—voting and non-voting. For valuation purposes, a discount might be considered for non-voting stock because it is limited by design—i.e., the shareholders are not permitted to vote on corporate matters. In terms of valuation, Code Sec. 2703(b)(3) states that gifts of non-voting stock are not affected by Code Sec. 2701 et seq. Care must be practiced with issuing non-voting stock, in that the holder of same, while restricted on voting, still has rights under state law to bring a derivative action for corporate waste. An example of such a derivative action would be where, in a small, closely-held family S corporation, children who are the recipients of the non-voting stock may sue the parents who hold the voting stock because they are taking compensation which the children believe is excessive.

> *Tax Pointer 2:* For an example of utilizing non-voting stock in family estate planning, see IRS Letter Ruling 9022045 discussed at ¶ 1109.05.

> *Tax Pointer 3:* Before using a discount for transferred appreciated assets, check what discount has been permissible under current case law.

Code Sec. 2701-04 indicates that gifts of minority interest may qualify for minority discount without the application of Code Sec. 2701 *et seq.* For a discussion of Code Sec. 2701-04, see ¶ 1120.

.08 Burden of Proof Regarding Valuation of Gifts—Code Sec. 7491

In 1998, Congress provided, pursuant to Code Sec. 7491(a), that if a taxpayer produces credible evidence in a civil proceeding and meets other statutory thresholds, the burden of proof on the factual issues will be shifted to the IRS. In *Dailey*,[85] a taxpayer was able to shift the burden of proof to the IRS on the question of valuation in connection with gifts by a parent of interest in a family business to children.

---

[83] *I. Eisenberg*, CA-2, 98-2 USTC ¶ 60,322, 155 F3d 50. Rev'g and rem'g 74 TCM 1046, Dec. 52,321(M), TC Memo. 1997-483.

[84] The *Eisenberg* court specifically excluded S corporations by *dicta* in sustaining a discount for taxes; however, it is submitted that the logic of the decision still applies.

[85] *E.M. Dailey Est.*, 82 TCM 710, Dec. 54,506(M), TC Memo. 2001-263.

.09 Minority Discounts Allowed for Gift Transfer of Interest in a Family Business Even if the Family Business Assets Are Marketable Securities or Non-Income-Producing Assets

In the field of partnership taxation, minority discounts involving marketable securities and non-income-producing assets for gift tax purposes in connection with transfers of interest in a family business to children of the partners were sustained. For example, in *Knight*,[86] a husband and wife created a family partnership with their two unmarried children, with assets valued at approximately $2,000,000. The parents' ranch with mineral rights and the children's residence where they were living rent-free were transferred to the partnership (the residences represented approximately 24 percent of the partnership assets). Trusts were established for the children, with each trust owing 44.6 percent of the partnership units; however, neither the children nor their trust participated in the management of the partnership. The partnership kept no records, prepared no annual reports, and had no employees. The Court sustained the partnership for gift tax purposes, permitting a 15 percent discount with respect to transfers of partnership interest, claiming that if the partnership was validly formed under state law, it was valid for gift tax purposes. The Court also rejected the IRS's attempt to strike down the partnership under Code Sec. 2704(b) because the restrictions imposed by the partnership (i.e., a lack of withdrawal rights by the limited partners and the 50-year term of the partnership) was no more restrictive than state law. By definition, the principles of these cases apply to S corporations.

In *Strangi*,[87] a partnership was established two months before the decedent's death by his attorney in fact (his son-in-law). The partnership assets had a value of approximately $9.8 million, of which roughly 75 percent of the assets was either cash or securities. Further, the partnership basically followed the Fortress Plan established by the Fortress Financial Group, Inc. One part of the Fortress Plan included the utilization of establishing a charity as a partner. The Court refused to apply Code Sec. 2703(a)(2) to prevent minority discounts on transfers of the partnership interest to family members. Further, the Court sustained a 31 percent discount for minority interest and lack of marketability, exactly what the IRS's expert witness stated was a proper discount. However, as the textual discussion at ¶ 1109.03 details, the *Strangi* Court, utilizing Code Sec. 2036, looks with great disdain at family businesses where passive assets are the bulk of the assets; rather, the Court prefers active businesses to be utilized where there will be such problems as cash flow with respect to operations of the business. Further, the Court wants business plans to be developed with the assets, not just continuing the status quo.

.10 Reciprocal Gifts

The courts frown on reciprocal gifts. *Sather*[88] is a good illustration of the IRS's position in this area. In *Sather*, A, B, C and D were brothers. A, B and C were

---

[86] *I.F. Knight*, 115 TC 506, Dec. 54,136.

[87] *A. Strangi Est.*, 115 TC 478, Dec. 54,135, *aff'd* 2005-2 USTC ¶ 60,506 (5th Cir. 2005).

[88] *L.L. Sather*, 78 TCM 456, Dec. 53,548(M), TC Memo. 1999-309. Aff'd and rev'd on penalties, CA-8, 2001-1 USTC ¶ 60,409, 251 F3d 1168.

married, and each married couple had three children. D was not married and had no children. A, B, C and D and A, B and C's wives owned R, an S corporation, a family-owned candy distribution business. On advice of counsel, because the brothers and their respective spouses wanted to pass the S corporation stock to the next generation to minimize tax consequences, each brother and their wives made a transfer of S corporation stock to their own children, and gifts to each of their nieces and nephews on the same date in equal amounts, utilizing the annual exclusion pursuant to Code Sec. 2503(b), thereby allowing each donor to claim nine annual exclusions (three for their own children and six for their nieces and nephews). On the same date, the unmarried brother made gifts of S corporation stock in equal amounts to his three brothers, his sisters-in-law, and his nine nieces and nephews. The taxpayer's accountant, who had been employed by the IRS and was previously a partner in the tax department of a major accounting firm, prepared all the returns at issue and advised the brothers to make the reciprocal transfers. The Court struck down the reciprocal gifts, however. Because the brothers relied on their accountant with respect to the gifts, they were not held liable for the accuracy-related penalty. Notwithstanding, two of the brothers' wives who did not appear at the trial and had not submitted any evidence as to how the returns were prepared, were found to be liable for the accuracy-related penalty.

¶ 1110 Private Annuities and *Cain* Redemptions

Private annuities. A private annuity is one planning device used to reduce estate taxes. Basically, the mechanics of the annuity are that an individual (e.g., a parent) transfers assets to another individual (e.g., a child) in return for the child's promise to support the parent for the parent's life according to actuarial formulas and tables. Example 11-17 illustrates the tax effect of an annuity.

> **Example 11-17:** Arthur Church, a widower, is a 50% shareholder in an S corporation, Aries Inc. The other shareholder of Aries Inc. is Bob Church, Arthur's son. Arthur's estate is composed mainly of stock in Aries Inc., which is worth in excess of $675,000. To reduce his taxable estate, Arthur, in 2003, enters into a private annuity with his daughter, Dorothy Reed, a permitted S corporation shareholder, funding the annuity with some of his S corporation stock. By setting up the annuity, Arthur reduces his estate to $500,000. Shortly after entering into the annuity with his daughter, Arthur dies in a plane crash in 2004. Because Arthur's estate is below $675,000, there will be no estate tax against it. Also, Dorothy will acquire the annuity contract's stock in Aries Inc. free of estate tax.

Cain redemptions. As an alternative to a private annuity, a *Cain*[89] redemption can also reduce estate taxes. In *Cain,* the decedent redeemed, without reservation or contingency, stock in a family-owned corporation for $150,000. The corporation was to pay $6,000 at the time the stock was transferred and $1,000 per month for 12 years or until the decedent's death, whichever occurred first. The $1,000 monthly payments were made according to a note that was payable without interest, except that any installment that became delinquent would carry 6 percent interest from the

---

[89] *R.L. Cain,* 37 TC 185, Dec. 25,119 (Acq.).

scheduled date of payment until it was actually paid. At the time the decedent died, the balance of the unpaid note was $44,135.

The *Cain* court sustained the stock redemption and excluded the balance of the unpaid note, $44,135, from the decedent's estate. Thus, like an annuity, the family was able to reduce the decedent's estate tax. However, as an advantage over an annuity (and similar to an installment sale), an interest deduction was created for the buyer (i.e., the corporation). Thus, when there is corporate stock that can be redeemed, the *Cain* redemption is an alternative for accomplishing estate-planning objectives.[90]

> *Tax Pointer 1:* The IRS turns a skeptical eye toward sales between related parties. Because the seller and the buyer do not have adversarial interests as would be the case if the parties were not related, it may be difficult to convince the IRS that the selling price reflected the true value of the S corporation stock sold. Accordingly, family members should go to some length to document the value of the S corporation prior to entering into a private annuity or *Cain* redemption.

> *Tax Pointer 2:* Prop. Reg. § 1.72-6 and Prop. Reg. § 1.1001-1 are effective generally for transactions entered into after October 18, 2006 that would knock out the income tax advantages of selling appreciated property in exchange for a private annuity. The proposed regulations would do this by causing the property seller's gain to be recognized in the year the annuity is created rather than as payments are received. Thus, caution should be practiced before entering into a private annuity until resolution of these proposed regulations occurs.

¶ 1111 Gift Tax

A shareholder during life may decide to reduce his or her holdings by making gifts of S corporation stock and taking advantage of the $10,000 annual exclusion (indexed for inflation) as prescribed in Code Sec. 2503(b) and the unified credit of Code Sec. 2010, or just on general principles. Care must be exercised when gifts are made with S corporation stock to ensure the requirements of Code Sec. 1361 are not breached (i.e., the stock will not be transferred to nonpermitted shareholders and the numerical limit of 100 shareholders will not be exceeded). Further, if a shareholders' agreement is in place, then the gift of S corporation stock must comply with the terms of that agreement.

> *Tax Pointer:* An S corporation should discount gifts for lack of control and minority status when computing the gift tax associated with a gift of S corporation stock.[91]

Code Sec. 2001(f) states that if a gift is adequately disclosed on the gift tax return and the gift tax statute of limitations has expired, the IRS cannot revalue the donor's gift when computing estate tax liability of the decedent on the donor's death.

---

[90] See ¶ 1209 for further discussion of redemptions. [91] See ¶ 1109.07 for a discussion of gift tax discounts.

The Tax Relief, Unemployment Insurance Reauthorization and Job Creation Act of 2010. Congress made extensive changes in the estate and gift tax laws to provide great planning opportunities for the small closely held family S corporation. It is beyond the scope of this book to provide an extensive discussion of the area. Please see discussion of the changes made to gift taxation at ¶ 1109.

¶ 1112 Sale of an S Corporation

.01 Introduction

Sometimes during an S corporation's history, its shareholders may want to sell the business. Prior to the Tax Reform Act of 1986, the shareholders had a number of choices to accomplish their objectives. Now that the 1986 Reform Act has eliminated a one-level Code Sec. 337 liquidation, S shareholders basically have two choices when selling the business—sale of assets at the corporate level or sale of the corporation's stock.

.02 Sale of Assets

If the S election has been effective since inception of the corporation, then sale of the business assets at the corporate level becomes an easy undertaking, and any gain or loss from the sale of assets are passed through to the shareholders following the rules of Code Sec. 1366. Because assets are being sold instead of stock, a buyer should be easily found since there is little risk to assume when purchasing assets, and the buyer obtains a fair market value basis for the assets, a benefit that is not available unless the buyer uses Code Sec. 338, a very complicated and expensive situation.[92]

C corporation assets. If an S corporation has C corporation assets acquired in a merger or a spin-off, or from prior years as a C corporation, selling its assets becomes complicated because of Code Sec. 1374 (the built-in gains tax).[93] Shareholders in such a situation will probably give serious consideration to selling stock when selling the corporate business.

Excluding certain assets. When a business is being sold, the purchaser may not want all of its assets (e.g., shareholder-employee's car, desks, obsolete equipment). Alternatively, the S corporation may not want to sell certain assets (e.g., cash, accounts receivable). Because of these excluded assets, the S corporation shareholders, instead of selling, may liquidate the corporation and sell off the unwanted assets or keep certain assets in corporate name and sell off unwanted assets, determining which option creates the better tax effect.[94] (Keeping assets in corporate name may not be viable if the S corporation is in a state that does not recognize S corporation status and imposes a minimum franchise tax.)

.03 Sale of Stock

Because of the risk a buyer takes on when purchasing S corporation stock, it may be difficult to sell it, let alone sell it at a fair price. However, in certain

---

[92] Code Sec. 338 and the risks in purchasing stock are discussed at ¶ 1208.04.

[93] Code Sec. 1374 and the built-in gains tax are discussed at ¶ 802.

[94] See removing assets from sale at ¶ 1208.06 and tax-planning opportunities at ¶ 1208.04.

circumstances, the sale of S corporation stock may be the only viable alternative to dispose of a business.[95]

.04 Reorganizations, Mergers, and Recapitalizations

Rather than pursue the sale of S corporation assets or stock in a taxable transaction, shareholders may consider the tax-free reorganization sections under Code Sec. 368.[96]

¶ 1113 Small Business Stock Election (Code Sec. 1244)

If a Code Sec. 1244 election is not in effect for S corporation stock, then upon the stock's sale or liquidation of the corporation, any loss will have to be reported by the shareholder as a capital loss. However, if there is a Code Sec. 1244 election in effect for S corporation stock, then an ordinary loss can be taken. That loss is limited to a maximum of $50,000 each year if the shareholder is single and $100,000 if the shareholder is married and files a joint return.[97] There are a number of requirements for S corporation stock to qualify for the small business stock election (e.g., estates and trusts do not qualify for Code Sec. 1244 treatment[98]).

> *Tax Pointer:* For specific situations facing an S corporation shareholder, review the numerous requirements of Code Sec. 1244.

¶ 1114 Below-Market Loans

Code Sec. 7872 was enacted to deal with below-market loans—loans where inadequate interest is being charged. In the context of S corporations, below-market loans could arise in two situations: loans from shareholders to the S corporation and loans from the S corporation to shareholders.

.01 Loans from a Shareholder

By definition, if a shareholder makes a below-market loan to an S corporation, he, she, or it will be considered to have made a contribution to capital for the amount of the below-market loan interest. The shareholder's basis will increase by the same amount. On the other side, the corporation will be considered to have made an interest payment to the shareholder for the amount of interest that is below market, causing the shareholder to report interest income in the same amount. However, the shareholder will be able to offset some or all (depending on his or her stock interest) of this interest income by the corporation's interest deduction for the deemed payment to the shareholder.[99]

> *Tax Pointer:* Interest should be charged when shareholder loans are made to a corporation. In *Hoffman,*[100] the payment of corporate expenses by the shareholders with their own personal funds was treated as a loan to the corporation (for which interest was imputed) rather than classfied as a capital contribution.

---

[95] See ¶ 1208 for a discussion of selling stock interests. See also Chapter 15 for a discussion of selling stock to an ESOP.

[96] See a discussion of reorganizations at ¶ 1211.

[97] Code Sec. 1244(b).

[98] Code Sec. 1244(d)(4).

[99] Proposed Reg. § 1.7872-4(d)(1).

[100] *F.R. Hoffman Est.,* 78 TCM 898, Dec. 53,644(M), TC Memo. 1999-395.

.02 Loans to a Shareholder

Two types of loans from an S corporation to a shareholder attract special attention: a below-market loan and a compensation-related loan.[101] Basically, a lending transaction between an S corporation and a shareholder will be a wash; however, adverse tax consequences could possibly develop if the shareholder's accumulated adjustments account has a zero balance at the time the below-market or compensation-related loan occurs,[102] and the corporation has E&P.[103]

¶ 1115 Conversion of S Corporation to C Corporation and/or Form 1040, Schedule C Sole Proprietorship

.01 Conversion of S Corporation to C Corporation

It may be advantageous for an S corporation to convert to C corporation status (e.g., closely held C corporations can offset ordinary income against passive losses[104]). Because there are various advantages offered to C corporations, S corporation status should be periodically reviewed to see if it is still best to continue as one.

.02 Transforming S Corporation Earnings to a Form 1040, Schedule C Sole Proprietorship

The recent case of *Cibotti*[105] illustrates creativity. Taxpayer was a 33.3% shareholder of Liberty Mortgage ("Liberty"), an S corporation (the other two-thirds was held by members of a family unrelated to Taxpayer). Taxpayer was the largest shareholder of Liberty and its president; however, Taxpayer did not perform any services as an officer of Liberty. Taxpayer on his tax return reported wages received from Liberty, but claimed business expense deductions relating to his work with Liberty on Form 1040, Schedule C such as mileage. The court sustained Taxpayer's filing of Form 1040, Schedule C by noting "An 'officer of a corporation who as such does not perform any services or performs only minor services and who neither receives nor is entitled to receive, directly or indirectly, any remuneration is considered not to be an employee of the corporation.' Sec. 31.3121(d)-1(b), Employment Tax Regs. Therefore, we conclude that Taxpayer is not considered an employee of Liberty Mortgage simply because he was the president." In addition, when the court discussed the independent contractor factors stated: "The record reflects that Liberty Mortgage did not have control over or dictate Taxpayer's hours of business, total hours, route, office location, or methods of obtaining clients. Taxpayer obtained the majority of his clients through personal contacts in the military and the IPA. Taxpayer did not have an office at Liberty Mortgage, and his only interactions with Liberty Mortgage centered around a weekly meeting and the payment of commissions. Liberty Mortgage did not supervise or control the manner or the means by which Taxpayer sold mortgages; therefore this factor indicates independent contractor status."

[101] Code Sec. 7872.

[102] Proposed Reg. § 1.7872-4(d)(1).

[103] For a case imputing interest to a shareholder where loans were made by a corporation to entities where the shareholders were not controlling shareholders of the lender, see ¶ 904.13.

[104] See discussion at ¶ 911.08.

[105] TC Summ. Opn. 2012-21.

¶ 1116 Audit Procedures for S Corporations

.01 *Introduction*

Audit procedures for S corporations have evolved over time. Originally, the audit of an S corporation was a procedure basically involving an individual S corporation shareholder and the IRS. This simple shareholder audit procedure, however, became cumbersome and inefficient, resulting in a settlement with one shareholder that was not binding on the other shareholder(s) of the S corporation. Congress, in an effort to improve efficiency, adopted unified audit procedures. However, for tax years beginning after 1996, Congress decided that the unified audit procedures were too complex for S corporations when there were a limited number of shareholders. Thereafter, they adopted a much simpler procedure, incorporating the rules for filing an S corporation return.[106]

.02 *Rules for Filing an S Corporation Return*

A general rule requires that an S corporation shareholder treat a subchapter S item (on the shareholder's return) in a manner consistent with the treatment of that item on the corporate return.[107] A "subchapter S item" is defined as any item of an S corporation that is more appropriately determined at the corporate level than at the shareholder level.[108] In other words, for administrative expediency, the S corporation shareholder is required to report items of income, expense, gain, etc. in the same manner as the corporation does. If the shareholder feels that the corporation's treatment of a subchapter S item is incorrect, then the shareholder has to notify the IRS by means of a statement identifying the inconsistency.[109] Form 8082 is used for this purpose.

If a shareholder does not notify the IRS of an inconsistency (i.e., reporting the item differently than the S corporation without notifying the IRS of the inconsistency), the IRS can make an adjustment to the shareholder's return[110] to conform the shareholder's return to the corporate return just as it would adjust a return for mathematical or clerical errors.[111] The IRS makes adjustments for mathematical or clerical errors by assessing a tax deficiency to which the taxpayer has no right to petition the Tax Court for review. Further, the shareholder does not have the right to demand an abatement of the assessment.[112] Accordingly, the consequences are severe to an S corporation shareholder if the shareholder adopts inconsistent treatment to Form 1120S without giving the IRS proper notice of the inconsistency. Further, a shareholder may be penalized for noncompliance.[113] Unfortunately, the imposition of a penalty is not clear. Code Sec. 6037(c)(5) prescribes an "addition to tax in the case of a shareholder's negligence in connection with, or disregard of, the requirements of this section, see Part II of subchapter A of chapter 68."

Part II of subchapter A of chapter 68 refers to the accuracy-related penalties found in Code Secs. 6662-6664. However, it is unclear from a simple statutory reading of Code Secs. 6662-6664 with Code Sec. 6037(c)(5) exactly what penalties

---

[106] Code Sec. 6037.
[107] Code Sec. 6037(c)(1).
[108] Code Sec. 6037(c)(4).
[109] Code Sec. 6037(c)(2).

[110] Code Sec. 6037(c)(3).
[111] Code Sec. 6213(b)(1).
[112] Code Sec. 6037(c)(3).
[113] Code Sec. 6037(c)(5).

will be imposed because Code Sec. 6037(c)(5) provides penalties for negligence and disregard while the penalties imposed in Code Secs. 6662-6664 apply to substantial understatements of tax. The question to be asked is: If a shareholder is inconsistent in reporting, will the shareholder be liable for just substantial understatement penalties or will negligence penalties be imposed as well?

.03 Not Filing an S Corporation Return

If an S corporation does not file an income tax return, the shareholder is required to notify the IRS of the nonfiling[114] in the same manner as for an inconsistent item.[115] Thus, a shareholder who does not receive Schedule K-1 from the S corporation must notify the IRS that his or her personal return does not include S corporation items or contains estimates that are inconsistent with information reported by the S corporation (because no such information was reported).

.04 Burden of Proof—Code Sec. 7491(a)

In 1998, Congress provided, pursuant to Code Sec. 7491(a), that if a taxpayer produces credible evidence in a civil proceeding plus meets some other statutory thresholds, the burden of proof on the factual issues will be shifted to the IRS. Recently, in *Dailey*,[116] a taxpayer was able to shift the burden of proof to the IRS on the question of valuation in connection with gifts by a parent of interest in a family business to children.

¶ 1117 Shareholder Debt—Pros and Cons

Pros. Debt between a shareholder and an S corporation is a primary reason for electing S corporation status.[117] If a shareholder's debt is evidenced by a written note, then when the note is repaid and when basis is zero, capital gain will result.[118] However, if the debt is an open account, that is, just a book entry, then ordinary income will result.

> **Tax Pointer:** S shareholders lending money to their S corporation should do so by means of a note to make sure any gain recognized on repayment is taxed as capital gain rather than ordinary income. If open account debt occurs, the regulations issued under Code Sec. 1367 detail that extensive bookkeeping is required to determine when any loss can be recognized and ordinary income generated on repayment of the loan. (See ¶ 904.14.)

Cons. There are also risks in the use of shareholder loans to an S corporation. For instance, the debt could create a second class of stock,[119] and unused losses or deductions that are in existence when the S election terminates can only be applied against stock basis, not loans.[120]

---

[114] Code Sec. 6037(c)(2)(A)(i)(II).

[115] Code Sec. 6037(c)(2)(A)(i)(I).

[116] *E.M. Dailey Est.*, 82 TCM 710, Dec. 54,506(M), TC Memo. 2001-263.

[117] See ¶ 208.05 for a discussion of debt in S corporations.

[118] Code Sec. 1271(a)(1). See discussion of repayment of debt at ¶ 904.08.

[119] See discussions at ¶ 208.

[120] Code Sec. 1366(d)(3). See discussion at ¶ 912 on termination of S status.

.01 Shareholder's Debt Can Prevent Gain

Code Sec. 357(c) states that, as a general rule, gain is recognized to the extent that liabilities are assumed by a corporation in a transfer to a controlled corporation pursuant to Code Sec. 351 when the liabilities exceed the total of the adjusted basis in the hands of the transferee shareholder of the properties transferred.

> **Example 11-18:** Assume that Hanna Brach, a sole proprietor, incorporates her business, taking back all the stock. At the time of incorporation and transfer of the assets to the corporation, Brach's liabilities from the business exceeded the assets by $50,000. Brach will be taxed on a $50,000 gain on incorporation.

However, in the case of *Lessinger*,[121] the court held that when the shareholder furnished a personal note on incorporation that gave the amount that liabilities were in excess of basis, the shareholder prevented a recognition of gain on incorporation under Code Sec. 357(c). The *Lessinger* case, of course, calls into question Rev. Rul. 81-187,[122] whether or not furnishing a personal note will increase basis. However, Proposed Reg. § 1.465-22(a) appears to have addressed this point by stating that a note payable will not be deemd an amount at risk until "such time as the proceeds of the note are actually devoted to the activity."

¶ 1118 Tax-Exempt Bonds and Stocks

.01 Tax-Exempt Bonds

At first blush, it may appear that because an S corporation generally passes income through to its shareholders, there should be no problem in having the S corporation hold tax-exempt bonds. However, on several grounds, this belief is dangerous. If the shareholders of the S corporation will have a problem under Code Sec. 1411, having the corporation own tax-exempt bonds is not a problem since by definition, the tax exempt interest earned from the bonds is not net investment income. See ¶ 1604.02 for further discussion of this subject.

- An S corporation owning tax-exempt bonds when it has earnings and profits could lead to a recharacterization of the tax-exempt income as taxable (due to the penalty tax on excess passive income).[123]

- If tax-exempt bonds are in excess of book value and they are distributed, shareholders will realize a gain on the distribution equal to the difference between the bonds' fair market value at the time of distribution and the S corporation's basis in them.[124]

- When an S corporation liquidates under Code Sec. 331, its shareholders will have to report gain on the difference between the bonds' fair market value and the basis the shareholders have in S corporation stock.

---

[121] *S. Lessinger,* CA-2, 89-1 USTC ¶ 9254, 872 F2d 519. Rev'g 85 TC 824, Dec. 42,489. See also *D.J. Peracchi,* CA-9, 98-1 USTC ¶ 50,374, 143 F3d 487. Rev'g and rem'g 72 TCM 2830, Dec. 51,305(M), TC Memo. 1996-191 (unsecured note contributed in a Code Sec. 351 exchange held as corporate property to avoid the imposition of Code Sec. 357(c)).

[122] Rev. Rul. 81-187, 1981-2 CB 167.

[123] See discussion at ¶ 1006.

[124] Code Sec. 311(b). See discussion at ¶ 608.

.02 Stock and Securities

Stock and securities also pose a problem for S corporation shareholders. As with tax-exempt bonds, when an S corporation liquidates under Code Sec. 331, its shareholders will have to report gain on the difference between the stock and securities' fair market value and the basis the shareholders have in S corporation stock.

¶ 1119 Family S Corporation Rules

.01 Introduction

Significant tax planning can be done in family situations through S corporations using trusts or the Uniform Transfers to Minors Act (UTMA). However, Congress was concerned that tax abuse would occur in family S corporations, so it specifically applied the family partnership rules of Code Sec. 704(e) to S corporations in Code Sec. 1366(e). Besides the family partnership rules of Code Sec. 704(e), the IRS has other weapons in its arsenal to prevent abuse. Field Service Advice 200143004 (July 5, 2001) indicates that the IRS will attack a family-owned S corporation if the IRS feels that the corporation has no business purpose and is established only to act as a conduit for gift-giving by a family member utilizing minority discounts to reduce federal taxes.

.02 Origin of Rules

The origins of the present-day family S corporation rules, Code Sec. 1366(e), are case law and the field of partnerships. In fact, Code Sec. 1366(e) duplicates the partnership provisions of Code Sec. 704(e). Accordingly, for ease of discussion, the perspective shall be from the partnership provisions.

.03 Operation of Rules

If a family member of one or more of the S corporation's shareholders performs services, or furnishes capital, for the S corporation without receiving reasonable compensation, the IRS has the power to adjust those items to reflect their fair market value.[125] Consideration will be given to all the facts and circumstances, including the amount that ordinarily would be paid in order to obtain comparable services or capital from a non-family member.[126] In addition, if a family member of one or more of the S corporation's shareholders holds an interest in a pass-through entity (i.e., a partnership, S corporation, trust, or estate) that performs services, or furnishes capital, for the S corporation without receiving reasonable compensation, the IRS Commissioner shall make adjustments to the pass-through entity and the corporation to reflect the value of those items.[127] The term "family of any shareholder" includes only the shareholder's spouse, ancestors, lineal descendants, and any trust for the primary benefit of any of these persons.[128]

> ***Example 11-19:*** The stock of an S corporation, Mason Inc., is owned 50 percent by Fred Mason and 50 percent by Ted Mason, the minor son of Fred. For the tax year, Mason Inc. has items of taxable income equal to $70,000.

---

[125] Code Sec. 1366(e).
[126] Reg. § 1.1366-3.
[127] Code Sec. 1366(e).
[128] *Ibid.*

Compensation of $10,000 is paid by the corporation to Fred for services rendered during the tax year, and no compensation is paid to Ted, who rendered no services. Based on all the relevant facts and circumstances, reasonable compensation for Fred's services would be $30,000. At the discretion of the IRS, up to an additional $20,000 of Mason Inc.'s $70,000 taxable income may be allocated to Fred as compensation for services rendered. If the IRS allocates $20,000 of Mason Inc.'s taxable income to Fred as compensation for his services, Mason Inc.'s taxable income would be reduced by $20,000 to $50,000, of which Fred and Ted each would be allocated $25,000. Fred would also report $30,000 as compensation.

Example 11-20: The stock of an S corporation, HoCho Inc., is owned by Al Berman and Ben Eagle. During the tax year, HoCho Inc. paid a partnership for its services; however, Berman's spouse is a partner in that partnership. Consequently, if HoCho Inc. did not reasonably compensate the partnership for its services, then the IRS, at its discretion, may make adjustments to those items based on all the relevant facts and circumstances.

.04 Parental Support Obligations

Besides satisfying Code Sec. 1366(e)'s rules, parents have to be careful in the operation of an S corporation not to violate another rule, using a device (i.e., a trust) to relieve them of support obligations. For a case discussing this concept, see *Braun.*[129]

.05 Establishing and Operating a Family S Corporation

The decision to establish a family S corporation involves consideration of a number of variables. However, key concepts have emerged over the years based on a reading of the cases involving Code Sec. 704(e)'s family partnership rules, which help to establish recognition of the family enterprise. As such, a written S corporation agreement should be used that fully describes (1) management, voting, and participation of the donee-shareholder; (2) capital contributions; (3) what occurs on death, disability, divorce, etc.; (4) how S corporation income is to be divided, reflecting that donee capital is not to receive more distributions than donor capital; (5) reasonable compensation for the services of the donor shareholder; and (6) a means to ensure the filing of tax returns. Further, the donee-shareholder should be held out to the public as a shareholder, such as allowing the donee-shareholder to sign checks and reflecting the donee-shareholder on leases, insurance contracts, etc.

Operating agreements. Operating agreements for an S corporation, whether the S corporation is a family business or not, are critical, in that they solve problems before they arise during normal business situations. Operating agreements are more critical for family businesses because of the added pressure that arises after business hours at family celebrations, family activities, etc. Two situations that also

---

[129] *F.C. Braun, Jr.,* 48 TCM 210, Dec. 41,250(M), TC Memo. 1984-285 (parents' support obligations for children included private high school and college).

stress family businesses are death and divorce. Example 11-21 illustrates how operating agreements in family S corporations can resolve problems in advance.

> *Example 11-21:* Jan and Larry Gardner want to establish a family S corporation for real estate ownership with their unmarried children. The Gardners are concerned that their children may later marry the "wrong" person and subsequently become divorced. To prevent an "ex-in-law" from receiving a shareholder interest and thereby staying involved in operating the family S corporation, the Gardners prescribe in their family S corporation operating agreement that, in the event of a divorce or legal separation of a shareholder, the shareholder must sell his or her interest to the other share-holders for fair market value. By inserting this provision, there is no chance that an ex-in-law will stay involved in the family S corporation. The difficulty, however, is that two people are really removed from the business enterprise: the in-law and the child. The Gardners, however, rationalize that it is better to remove a child than to have an ex-in-law question business decisions and potentially destroy the family business.

Allocating income, loss, etc. to a family shareholder. The question often asked is: How much income, loss, etc. can be allocated to a family shareholder and still have the family S corporation recognized? Two cases in family S corporation rules are relevant to this question. In the first, *Trucks, Inc.,*[130] the court refused to reallocate income from a family S corporation to a family shareholder when that shareholder worked less than 10 hours each year for the corporation. In the second, *Davis,*[131] an orthopedic surgeon formed two corporations in connection with his practice: one to carry out physical therapy and the other to perform X-rays. Davis made gifts of 90% of the stock to his children (all minors at the time), keeping 10% of it for himself. Both corporations elected S status. Each corporation owned equipment, employed other people, and paid no salary to Davis (he worked less than 20 hours per year for the corporations). The court refused to allocate income on Dr. Davis' referral of work to these two corporations since he had never received fees for referring work to unrelated physical therapists and radiologists. However, in *Westbrook,*[132] a salary paid to a son from the sole shareholder's S corporation was disallowed as excessive.

The uniform transfers to minors act (UTMA). Because a minor can obtain stock in an S corporation on reaching majority, the donor may want to use a trust to designate the age the minor may be vested in the stock (e.g., one-half of the stock at 25 years of age and the balance at 30).[133] Alternatively, the donor may want to use a shareholders' agreement to control disposition of the stock (e.g., no transfer of stock without the consent of the other shareholders, etc.).

---

[130] *Trucks, Inc.,* DC Neb., 84-1 USTC ¶ 9418, 588 FSupp 638. Aff'd on other issue, CA-8, 85-2 USTC ¶ 9461, 763 F2d 339.

[131] *E.D. Davis,* 64 TC 1034, Dec. 33,419.
[132] TC Memo 1993-634.
[133] For a discussion of trusts, see Chapter 3.

¶1119.05

.06 Buyout of a Family Member

A family will most likely structure a buyout of a parent as a stock sale by the parent to the child, coupled with a consulting agreement.[134] By doing a stock sale, the parent will realize capital gains on the sale, and the consulting agreement will allow the S corporation to rapidly write off a portion of the purchase price as a business deduction. A parent could also sell a customer list[135] or other Code Sec. 197 assets to the corporation, providing the parent owned them, producing capital gain for the parent. The difficulty with the sale of Code Sec. 197 assets to a corporation is that the corporation has to amortize the purchase price over fifteen years, even though the asset(s) may have a shorter life. Thus, it is preferable to allocate a large portion of a stock purchase price to a consulting agreement even though the parent will realize ordinary income and self-employment tax.

> **Example 11-22:** Joe Crain, the owner of Crain Inc., an S corporation, wants to pass his Crain Inc. stock ownership to his only child with little after-tax dollars. Therefore, Crain obtains a consulting agreement with Crain Inc. for three years for 90% of the consideration of $100,000. Crain Inc. can deduct $90,000 ($30,000 per year) for the agreement, and Crain's daughter, JoEllen Crain, is only required to pay $10,000 for the stock.

In a closely held family S corporation, a departing shareholder (i.e., a parent) could enter into a covenant not to compete with the corporation, with the tax allocation to the covenant not to compete being sustained.[136] However, the covenant not to compete must have economic reality to be sustained. To illustrate, in *Kalamazoo Oil Co.*,[137] the Court refused to sustain a covenant not to compete that a shareholder entered into with his corporation while still a shareholder.

¶ 1120 Special Valuation Rules (Code Secs. 2701-2704)

.01 Introduction

In 1986, Congress implemented Code Sec. 2036(c) to tax wealth transfers from one family generation to another. However, in the Omnibus Budget Reconciliation Act of 1990 (Reconciliation Act) (P.L. 101-508), Congress retroactively repealed Code Sec. 2036(c) to the date of its enactment (December 17, 1987). In its place, Congress established Code Secs. 2701-2704, which take a different approach to taxing family transfers. The aim of the Reconciliation Act was to establish a more accurate gift tax valuation when a gift is made among certain family members.

Code Secs. 2701-2704 are not specific to S corporations. However, because S corporations could involve various formats involving family members (e.g., a family limited liability company, subsidiaries of S corporations where family members are shareholders together with the S corporation), it is important to have some

---

[134] The tax aspects of a stock purchase are discussed at ¶ 1208.04.

[135] See *Martin Ice Cream Co.*, 110 TC 189, Dec. 52,624.

[136] For an example of such a situation, see *D.L. Chiapetti*, 71 TCM 2778, Dec. 51,294(M), TC Memo. 1996-183. For a discussion of covenants not to compete,

see Michael Schlesinger, "Consider Consulting and Non-Compete Agreements When Selling a Business," *Practical Tax Strategies*, Vol. 68, No. 5 at 260 (May 2002).

[137] *Kalamazoo Oil Co.*, CA-6, 82-2 USTC ¶ 9695, 693 F2d 618, aff'g 42 TCM 304, Dec. 38,036 (M), TC Memo. 1981-344.

knowledge as to the operation of the rules. To develop an overall perspective of these rules, planning opportunities are discussed in ¶ 1120.02–¶ 1120.05.

.02 Transfers of Interests

If an individual transfers an interest in a corporation or partnership to (or for the benefit of) an "applicable family member," special rules apply to determine whether the transfer creates a gift and if so, to determine the gift's value.[138] To value the property, established gift tax principles are followed initially (i.e., if a C corporation has common and preferred stock, and the common stock is transferred, the value of the common stock is arrived at by subtracting the value of the preferred stock from the value of the common stock). However, Code Sec. 2701 et seq. describe other computational methods that should also be used (e.g., establishing a minimum value for a junior equity interest).

Definition of family members. A "family member" is (1) the transferor's spouse, (2) a lineal descendant of the transferor or the transferor's spouse, and (3) the spouse of any such descendant.[139]

Attribution rules. The attribution rules consider an individual to hold an interest in a corporation or partnership even when the interest is held *indirectly* (e.g., through a corporation, partnership, trust, or other entity).[140] If a transfer results in an indirectly held interest no longer being held by an individual, the transfer must be considered a transfer *by* the individual.[141]

> **Example 11-23:** Edgewood Inc., an S corporation, owns 25% of the stock of a C corporation subsidiary, Brickman Inc., and John Walker owns 50% of Edgewood Inc. When Edgewood Inc. sells all its stock in Brickman Inc. to Chris Walker, John's son, the sale is considered a transfer by John to Chris of 12.5% of Brickman Inc.'s stock.

> **Tax Pointer 1:** The attribution rules apply whether a family member holds 1% or 100% of an entity.[142]

Definition of a transfer. Code Secs. 2701-2704 provide various definitions as to what a transfer is. Code Sec. 2701(e)(5) provides that "except as provided in the regulations, a contribution to capital or a redemption,[143] recapitalization,[144] or other change in the capital structure of a corporation or partnership shall be treated as a transfer of an interest in such entity" if the taxpayer or an applicable family member receives a retained interest in such entity whose value would be affected by the new rules. However, Code Sec. 2701(e)(5) does not apply to any change in capital structure "if the interest in the entity held by the transferor, applicable family member, and members of the transferor's family are substantially identical before and after the transaction." For example, the 1990 Committee Reports to the Reconciliation Act provide that Code Sec. 2701(e)(5) does not apply to a "recapitalization not involving a contribution to capital if all shareholders hold substantially

---

[138] Code Sec. 2701(a).
[139] Code Sec. 2701(e)(1).
[140] Code Sec. 2701(e)(3).
[141] *Ibid.*

[142] *Ibid.*
[143] Redemptions are discussed at ¶ 1209.
[144] Recapitalizations are discussed at ¶ 1211.06.

¶1120.02

identical interests both before and after the recapitalization." Additionally, the 1990 Committee Reports to the Reconciliation Act provide that Code Sec. 2701(e)(5) will not "apply to a change in the corporate name." However, Code Sec. 2701(e)(5) prescribes, and the 1990 Committee Reports to the Reconciliation Act ordain, that "the addition of capital to an existing partnership or corporation would result in the application of these rules only to the extent of the contribution."

Examples 11-24 and 11-25, adapted from the 1990 Committee Reports to the Reconciliation Act, illustrate the application of Code Sec. 2701(e)(5).

> *Example 11-24:* A mother and her daughter, Martha and Kelly Hart, together own all the common shares in their corporation, Hartland Inc. Martha, the mother, redeems her common shares for preferred stock. The valuation rules of Code Sec. 2701 apply to Martha's preferred stock and will determine whether or not her redemption of the common shares is considered a gift to her daughter, Kelly.

> *Example 11-25:* A father and his son, Mark and Brad Wilson, form a partnership to which each contributes capital. The father, Mark, receives a preferred interest while the son, Brad, receives a residual interest. Code Sec. 2701 applies in determining whether, and the extent to which, the father's capital contribution constitutes a gift.

Applicable retained interests. The following transfers of interest will incur taxation:

- Liquidations, puts, calls, and conversion rights[145]
- Distribution rights[146]
- Bundled rights

Liquidation, put, call, and conversion rights. A liquidation, put, call, or conversion right, or any similar right, is defined as a right which, exercised or not exercised, affects the value of a transferred interest.[147] The value of a liquidation, put, call, or conversion right to a gift transfer is treated as $0[148] unless the right must be exercised at a specific time and at a specific amount.[149] Example 11-26, adapted from Example 1 of the 1990 Conference Committee Report to the Reconciliation Act, illustrates the application of these rights.

> *Example 11-26:* Joe McNamara retains cumulative preferred stock in a transaction to which an applicable retained interest applies. His yearly stock dividends total $100, and the stock may be redeemed at any time after two years for $1,000. Under the conference agreement, the value of McNamara's cumulative preferred stock is the lesser of (1) the present value of two years of $100 dividends plus the present value of the redemption for $1,000 in year two or (2) the present value of $100 paid every year in perpetuity. If the present values were substantially identical, the stock would receive that value.

---

[145] Code Sec. 2701(b)(1)(B).
[146] Code Sec. 2701(b)(1)(A).
[147] Code Sec. 2701(c)(2)(A).

[148] Code Sec. 2701(a)(3)(A).
[149] Code Sec. 2701(c)(2)(B)(i).

The liquidation, put, call, and conversion rights do not include retained rights that are of

- the same class,
- proportionately the same, or
- subject to a later tax.[150]

Same class rights. Code Sec. 2701 does not apply if the retained interest is of the same class as the transferred interest.[151] As the 1990 Senate Committee Report to the Reconciliation Act states:

> [u]nder this exception, [Code Sec. 2701] does not affect the valuation of a gift of common stock if the transferor only retains rights of that class of common stock. Likewise, [Code Sec. 2701] does not affect the valuation of a gift of a partnership interest if all interests in the partnership share equally in all items of income, deduction, loss and gain in the same proportion (i.e., straight-up allocations).

The IRS may, by regulation, treat a retained interest as two or more separate interests.[152] The 1990 Conference Committee Report to the Reconciliation Act states:

> [s]uch treatment would allow value to be accorded to the participating feature of a participating preferred interest pursuant to the exception for retained interests that are of the same class as the transferred interests.

Examples 11-27 and 11-28, adapted from Examples 3 and 4 from the 1990 Conference Committee Report to the Reconciliation Act, illustrate this rule.

Example 11-27: Jan Jones owns all the stock in a corporation. One class of stock is entitled to dividends each year of (1) $100 and (2) half of all dividends over $100; the second class of stock is entitled to the other half of all dividends over $100. Jones retains the first class of stock, but gives the second class to her son, Doug. The first class of stock is two instruments: one, an instrument bearing a preferred right to dividends of $100 (the preferred right is cumulative); the other, an instrument bearing the right to half the annual dividends over $100, which would fall within the exception for retained interests of the same class as the transferred interest.

Example 11-28: Ken Swift and his daughter, Jenny Swift, enter into a partnership with Ken contributing $1 million to partnership capital and Jenny nothing. Under the terms of the partnership agreement, Ken is to receive the first $1 million in net cash receipts and is thereafter to share equally in distributions with Jenny. Ken's retained interests consist of two interests: (1) a distribution right to $1 million and (2) a 50 percent partnership interest. Ken could elect to treat the first interest as a right to receive qualified payments at specified amounts and times; the second interest would fall within the exception for retained interests of the same class as the transferred interest.

Proportionately the same rights. Code Sec. 2701 will not apply to a retained interest if it is of a class proportionately the same as the transferred interest, but for

---

[150] Code Sec. 2701(c)(2)(C).
[151] Code Sec. 2701(c)(2)(C)(i).
[152] Code Sec. 2701(e)(7).

¶1120.02

nonlapsing differences in voting power (or, in the case of a partnership, nonlapsing differences with management, limitations, and liability).[153] Nonlapsing limitations on liability are permitted only if the transferor or applicable family member does not have the right to alter the transferee's liability. The 1990 Conference Committee Report to the Reconciliation Act states that this exception

> would apply . . . if the retained and transferred interests consisted of two classes of common stock, which shared in all distributions, liquidation or other rights in a two-to-one ratio. It would not apply to a partnership with both a general and limited partner if one partner had a preference with respect to distributions.

Thus, a transfer of nonvoting S corporation stock coupled with a retention of voting stock in the S corporation would be covered by this exception. The 1990 Conference Committee Report to the Reconciliation Act goes on to provide that

> [e]xcept as provided in Treasury regulations, a right that lapses by reason of Federal or State law generally will be treated as nonlapsing under this exception. The conferees contend, however, that Treasury regulations may give zero value to rights which lapse by reason of Federal or State law that effectively transfer wealth that would not pass in the absence of a specific agreement. Such regulations could, for example give zero value to a management right that lapses by reason of the death of a partner under the Uniform Partnership Act as adopted in a State, if the decedent had waived in the partnership agreement the right to be redeemed at fair market value under that Act.

Rights subject to a later tax. Code Sec. 2701 does not apply to a right to convert into a fixed number (or a fixed percentage) of the shares of the same class as the transferred stock if such rights are nonlapsing, subject to proportionate adjustment for splits, combinations, reclassifications, and similar changes in the capital stock, and adjusted for accumulated dividends not paid on a timely basis.[154] The 1990 Senate Committee Report to the Reconciliation Act states that

> [a] similar exception applies to rights in partnerships. This exception is provided because the full appreciated value of such right will be subject to later transfer tax.

Market quotations. Although not an exception listed at Code Sec. 2701(c)(2)(C), Code Sec. 2701(a)(1) excludes from taxation any transfer where market quotations are readily available as of the date of transfer on an established securities market.

Distribution rights. "Distribution rights" are defined as any right to a distribution from a corporation of its stock, or a distribution from a partnership of a partner's interest in the partnership.[155] Exceptions to the definition of distribution rights, include any right to (1) a junior equity interest (defined below), (2) any liquidation, put, call, or conversion right, or (3) any right to receive a guaranteed payment of a fixed amount.[156] A retained distribution right that is noncumulative or lacks a preference on liquidation is valued at $0 if the transferor and applicable family members control the entity.[157] "Control" is defined as the holding of at least

---

[153] Code Sec. 2701(c)(2)(C)(ii), (iii) and (iv).
[154] Code Sec. 2701(c)(2)(C)(i).
[155] Code Sec. 2701(c)(1)(A).

[156] Code Sec. 2701(c)(1)(B).
[157] Code Sec. 2701(b)(1)(A).

50 percent by vote or value of the stock of a corporation. To determine control, an individual is considered to hold any interest held by his or her brothers, sisters, or lineal descendants. Examples 11-29 through 11-31, adapted from Examples 2-4 of the 1990 Senate Committee Report to the Reconciliation Act, illustrate distribution rights.

> **Example 11-29:** Helen May, a mother holding all the common and preferred stock in Elfin Inc., sells half of her common stock to her son, Jeff May. The preferred stock is cumulative and can be put to Elfin Inc. for its par value. In determining whether there is a gift and the amount of the gift, the determinations of whether cumulative dividends can reasonably be paid is made without regard to Helen's control, the put right is valued at $0, and the retained rights under the common stock are valued as under present law.

> **Example 11-30:** Assume the same facts as in Example 11-29, except that the mother, Helen, does not have control over Elfin Inc. In determining whether there is a gift and the amount of the gift, the put right is valued at $0. The right to distributions and the retained rights under the common stock are valued as under present law.

> **Example 11-31:** Frank Holt owns 25 shares of the 100 outstanding shares of noncumulative preferred stock in Mora Inc. Frank's father, George Holt, owns the remaining 75 shares of the noncumulative preferred stock in Mora Inc. Frank owns all of the 100 outstanding shares of common stock in Mora Inc. Frank gives 10 shares of the common stock to his son, Ryan. The noncumulative preferred stock of both Frank and George would be given a value of $0 in determining the amount of the gift Frank gave his son, Ryan. Thus, the gift would be the same amount as if Mora Inc. had only 100 shares of common stock outstanding.

Bundled rights. "Bundled rights" are defined as

> a retained interest that confers (1) a liquidation, put, call, or conversion right, and (2) a distribution right that consists of the right to receive a qualified payment [defined below]is valued on the assumption that each right is exercised in a manner resulting in the lowest value for all such rights.[158]

The term "qualified payment" is defined as "a dividend payable on a periodic basis and at a fixed rate under cumulative preferred stock (or a comparable payment under a partnership agreement)" with a "fixed rate . . . bearing a fixed relationship to a specified market rate."[159] Additionally, a transferor or applicable family member may elect not to treat the dividend under the preferred stock (or comparable payment) as a qualified payment: "if the transferor [makes]such an election, unpaid amounts on cumulative preferred interest [will] not be subject to the compounding rules . . . . [Further], [a] transferor or applicable family member may elect to treat any other distribution right as a qualified payment to be paid in the amounts and at the times specified in the election."[160]

---

[158] 1990 Conference Committee Report to the Reconciliation Act.

[159] *Ibid.*
[160] *Ibid.*

The election to treat distribution rights as qualified payments cannot be inconsistent with the legal instrument underlying the right. Accordingly, the transferor cannot elect to treat a distribution right as a right to receive a qualified payment in excess of the amounts that could actually be received under the instrument. For example, a transferor cannot elect to value a noncumulative right to $100 per year on the assumption that it would pay $110 per year.

> **Example 11-32:** Carl Huff and his daughter, Dana Huff, are partners in a partnership to which Carl contributes an existing business. Carl is entitled to 80 percent of the net cash receipts of the partnership until he receives $1 million, after which time he and Dana both receive 50 percent of the partnership's cash flow. Carl's liquidation preference equals $1 million. The retained right to $1 million is valued at $0, unless Carl elects to treat it as a right to receive qualified payments in the amounts, and at the times, specified in the election. If Carl elects such treatment, amounts not paid at the times specified in the election become subject to the compounding rules.

Junior equity interest. A "junior equity interest" is defined as common stock or any partnership interest "under which the rights as to income and capital are junior to the rights of all other classes of equity interest."[161] The term "equity interest" means stock or any interest as a partner, as the case may be.

To value a junior equity interest, it must have a minimum value on transfer.[162] That minimum

> shall in no event be valued at an amount less than the value which would be determined if the total value of all the junior equity interest in the entity were equal to 10% of the sum of (i) the total value of all of the equity interest in such entity, plus (ii) the total amount of indebtedness of such entity to the transferor (or an applicable family member).[163]

Tax treatment of transfers. Code Sec. 2701(d) provides for taxation on the transfers discussed above in certain situations. There is to be an increase made in taxable gifts or the taxable estate of a transferor who retained cumulative preferred stock (or comparable partnership interest) that is valued under the rules dealing with bundled rights.[164] However, exceptions for certain spousal transfers and limitations on the amount of increase that could be made for taxable gifts or the taxable estate.[165] The amount of increase that could be made to the taxable gifts or the taxable estate is the excess of

> (i) the value of the qualified payments payable during the period beginning on the date of the transfer . . . and ending on the date of the taxable event determined as if (I) all such payments were paid on the date payment was due, and (II) all such payments were reinvested by the transferor as the date of payment and the yield equal to the discount rate used in determining the value of the applicable retained interest described at [Code Sec. 2701(a)(1)], over (ii) the value of such payments paid during such period computed[166] [on the basis of when such payments were actually paid] . . . . [Furthermore, a] grace period

---

[161] Code Sec. 2701(a)(4)(B).
[162] Code Sec. 2701(a)(4)(A).
[163] *Ibid.*

[164] Code Sec. 2701(d)(1). Bundled rights fall under Code Sec. 2701(a)(3)(B).
[165] Code Sec. 2701(d)(2) and (3).
[166] Code Sec. 2701(d)(2)(A).

[when] any payment of any distribution during the four-year period beginning on its due date shall be treated as having been made on such due date.[167]

The taxable event that triggers taxation under Code Sec. 2701 is detailed at Code Sec. 2701(d)(3)(A). There are three events:

(i) the death of the transferor if the retained interest conferring the distribution rights is includible in the estate of the transferor;

(ii) the lifetime transfer of the applicable retained interest; and

(iii) at the election of the taxpayer, the payment of any qualified payment after the grace period set forth in Code Sec. 2701(d)(2)(C) discussed previously.

For spousal transfers, the retained interest is transferred to the transferor's spouse, and the transfer is exempted from taxation by the marital deduction, or the spouse pays consideration for the transfer; the transferor is not subject to taxation.[168] Instead, the spouse is treated as the transferor and the adjustment occurs when a taxable event occurs to the spouse.[169]

A cap is placed on the amount of increase.[170] Basically, the amount of unpaid dividends and interest subject to subsequent transfer tax equals the excess of (1) the fair market values of equity interest that are junior to any retained preferred interests at the date of the later transfer over (2) such values as of the date of the prior transfer of the junior interest multiplied by the fraction described in Code Sec. 2701(d)(2)(B)(ii). This fraction is determined immediately before the later transfer. The numerator of the fraction is the number of shares of preferred interest held by the transferor; the denominator is the number of shares of the same class of preferred stock. Additionally, a similar rule is applicable for partnerships. The 1990 Conference Committee Report to the Reconciliation Act states that "this limitation applies with respect to each class of preferred held by the transferor or applicable family member." Example 11-36, adapted from Example 5 of the 1990 Conference Committee Report to the Reconciliation Act, illustrates how the cap provisions work.

> **Example 11-33:** A corporation, JinHa, has four classes of stock. Class A is entitled to the first $10 of dividends each year; Class B is entitled to the second $10 of dividends each year; Class C is entitled to the third $10 of dividends each year; and Class D is entitled to all dividends in excess of those paid to Classes A, B, and C. Classes A, B, and C all have cumulative rights to dividends. In a transaction to which the provision applies, Harvey Kamen gives his daughter, Barbra, stock in Classes A and C while retaining stock in Class B. Class D is owned by an unrelated party. Dividends are not paid on the Class C stock and several years later Harvey dies holding the Class B stock. The cap on future amounts subject to transfer tax equals the excess of the fair market value of stock in Classes C and D at the date of Harvey's death over such value at the date of the gift multiplied by a fraction equal to the percentage of Class B stock held by Harvey.

[167] Code Sec. 2701(d)(2)(C).
[168] Code Sec. 2701(d)(3)(B).
[169] Code Sec. 2701(d)(3)(B)(iii).
[170] Code Sec. 2701(d)(2)(B).

Special rules apply for family members.[171] Basically, if an applicable family member owns cumulative preferred stock (or a comparable partnership interest) that was taken into account in valuing the original transfer by the transferor, the family member is treated in the same manner as the transferor for purposes of the increase in value rules given in Code Sec. 2701(d). In other words, if a taxable event for an applicable family member occurs, it will be subject to the increase rule.

> *Example 11-34:* Carlos Inc. is composed of the following shareholders: Frank Carlos, who owns all the common stock, and his father Hector Carlos, who owns cumulative preferred stock. The preferred stock carries a liquidation right. Frank transfers all his common stock to his son, Sam. The value of the gift to Sam is the value of the entire company less the value of rights retained by Frank and Hector, determined using the rule for bundled rights. Carlos Inc. declares no dividends on the stock for five years. Hector dies a widower, transferring his preferred stock to his girlfriend, Marisa. The preferred stock is includible in Hector's estate determined under general principles of tax law, but increased to reflect the value as computed by Code Sec. 2701(d)(2).

In a termination, under the increase rule, the termination of any interest is treated as a transfer.[172] How a retained interest is valued under Code Sec. 2701 for the generation-skipping tax, etc., Code Sec. 2701(e)(6) provides for the method of adjustment. The effective date for the Code Sec. 2701 rules applies to the transfer of certain interests in corporations and partnerships after October 8, 1990. Furthermore, for property transferred before October 9, 1990, the failure to exercise a right of conversion, pay dividends, or exercise other rights specified in the regulations is not treated as a subsequent transfer.

> *Tax Pointer 2:* The IRS has issued regulations under Code Sec. 2701; they should be consulted in a review of this area of law.

.03 Buy-Sell Agreements and Options

Congress, in an effort to control family transfers and buy-sell agreements, adopted Code Sec. 2703 effective for agreements and options entered into or granted after October 8, 1990. Likewise, if an agreement that was entered into before October 8, 1990, is substantially modified, the rules under Code Sec. 2703 will apply. Code Sec. 2703(a) states that the value of any property for transfer tax purposes is to be determined without regard to

    (1) any option, agreement, or other right to acquire or use the property at a price less than the fair market value of the property (without regard to such option, agreement, or right) or

    (2) any restriction on the right to use or sell such property

unless the option, agreement, right, or restriction meets the three requirements as set forth at Code Sec. 2703(b). The three requirements are:

---

[171] Code Sec. 2701(d)(4).

[172] Code Sec. 2701(d)(5).

¶1120.03

(1) it is a bona fide business arrangement;

(2) it is not a device to transfer . . . property to members of the decedent's family for less than full and adequate consideration in money or money's worth; and

(3) the terms are comparable to similar arrangements entered into by persons in an arm's-length transaction.

With respect to the three requirements, the following should be noted:

- The 1990 Senate Committee Report to the Reconciliation Act advises that the restrictions of Code Sec. 2703 apply to any restriction, however created. Thus, the restrictions could apply to the capital structure of the partnership as contained in the partnership agreement, or they could be found in the articles of incorporation, the corporate bylaws, or shareholders' agreement.

- For the provisions of Code Sec. 2703(b)(1) and (2), the 1990 Senate Committee Report to the Reconciliation Act provides that these two provisions are independent tests. As the 1990 Senate Committee Report to the Reconciliation Act stated:

  The mere showing that the agreement is a bona fide business arrangement would not give the agreement estate tax effect if other facts indicate that the agreement is a device to transfer property to members of the decedents [decedent's] family for less than full and adequate consideration. In making this clarification, it adopts the reasoning of *Saint Louis County Bank v. United States*[173] and rejects the suggestion of other cases that the maintenance of family control standing alone assures the absence of a device to transfer wealth.

- In determining whether the agreement is reached at arm's length (required by Code Sec. 2703(b)(3)), the 1990 Senate Committee Report to the Reconciliation Act provides that a number of factors have to be considered, such as

  the expected term of the agreement, the present value of the property, its expected value at the time of exercise, and consideration offered for the option. It is not met simply by showing isolated comparables, but requires a demonstration of the general practice of unrelated parties. Expert testimony would be evidence of such practice. In unusual cases where comparables [are] difficult to find because the taxpayer owns a unique business, the taxpayer can use the comparables from similar businesses.

Additionally, the 1990 Senate Committee Report to the Reconciliation Act provides that Code Sec. 2703 still does not change the present law requirement that an agreement have lifetime restrictions in order to be binding at death.

Tax Pointer: In *Strangi,*[174] the Court refused to apply Code Sec. 2703(a)(2) to prevent minority discounts on transfers of the partnership interest to family members. Further, the Court sustained a 31 percent discount for

[173] *St. Louis County Bank, Exr.,* CA-8, 82-1 USTC ¶ 13,459, 674 F2d 1207.

[174] *A. Strangi Est.,* 115 TC 478, Dec. 54,135. *Aff'd,* 2005-2 USTC ¶ 60,506 (5th Cir. 2005).

minority interest and lack of marketability, exactly what the IRS's expert witness stated was a proper discount. However, the Court struck down the arrangement utilizing Code Sec. 2036. For a discussion of *Strangi* as it affects family planning, see ¶ 1109.03.

Changes to a shareholders agreement. IRS Letter Ruling 201313001 stated that changes to a shareholders agreement where the installment payment obligation was lengthened and interest rate increased was not a taxable event.

.04 Lapsing Rights and Restrictions

Code Sec. 2704 was enacted to overturn the results and reasoning of *Harrison*.[175] In *Harrison*, a father and his two sons entered into a limited partnership with the father contributing assets to the partnership for a 1 percent general partnership interest and a 77.8 percent limited partnership interest. The two sons contributed assets to the partnership in return for separate 10.6 percent general partnership interests. The father's combined partnership interests were worth $59,476,523 on creation of the partnership and the sons' $7,981,351. The partnership agreement provided, *inter alia,* that each general partner had the right to dissolve the partnership during life, but this right expired at death. At the father's death, the IRS argued that the limited partnership interest was worth $59,555,020, the value that could be obtained if the father had caused the partnership to liquidate just before his death. Pursuant to the partnership agreement, the father's estate valued the limited partnership interest at $33,000,000, claiming that the limited partnership interest standing by itself without a right to dissolution had a limited value. The court ruled in favor of the father's estate and valued the interest at $33,000,000.

If there is a lapse of any voting or liquidation right in a corporation or partnership, and the individual holding such right immediately before the lapse, and members of such individual's family hold, both before and after the lapse control of the entity, the lapse of the voting or liquidation right will result in a transfer by gift or inclusion in the gross estate.[176] The amount of the transfer (or inclusion) is the value of all interest in the entity held by the transferor immediately before the lapse (determined as if the voting and liquidation rights were nonlapsing) over the value of such interests immediately after the lapse.[177]

> **Example 11-35:** Gary Olson and his son, Ken Olson, control a corporation. Gary's stock has a voting right that lapses on his death. Under the conference agreement, Gary's stock is valued for federal estate tax purposes as if the voting right were nonlapsing.

> **Example 11-36:** John Gibson and his son, Brian Gibson, each own general and limited interests in a partnership. The general partnership interest carries with it the right to liquidate the partnership; the limited partnership interest has no such right. The liquidation right associated with the general partnership interest lapses after ten years. Under the conference agreement, there is a gift at the time of the lapse equal to the excess of (1) the value of

---

[175] *D.J. Harrison, Jr., Est.,* 52 TCM 1306, Dec. 43,609(M), TC Memo. 1987-8.

[176] Code Sec. 2704.
[177] Code Sec. 2704(a)(2).

John's partnership interests determined as if he held the right to liquidate over (2) the value of such interests determined as if he did not hold such right.

Code Sec. 2704(b) gives certain rules regarding restrictions. The 1990 Conference Committee Report to the Reconciliation Act states that

> any restriction that effectively limits the ability of a corporation or partnership to liquidate is ignored in valuing a transfer among family members if
>
> (1) the transferor and family members control the corporation or partnership, and
>
> (2) the restriction either lapses after the transfer or can be removed by the transferor or members of his family, either alone or collectively.

Example 11-37, adapted from the 1990 Conference Committee Report to the Reconciliation Act, illustrates the application of this rule.

Example 11-37: Gina Harris and her son, Michael Harris, are partners in a two-person partnership. The partnership agreement provides that the partnership cannot be terminated. Gina dies and leaves her partnership interest to her daughter, Jennifer. As the sole partners, Jennifer and Michael acting together could remove the restriction on partnership termination. Under the conference agreement, the value of Gina's partnership interest in her estate is determined without regard to such restriction. Such value would be adjusted to reflect any appropriate fragmentation discount.

"Control" is defined the same as control in Code Sec. 2701(b)(2), i.e., holding before the transfer at least 50 percent (by vote or value) the stock of a corporation. Family members are defined under Code Sec. 2704(c)(2) to mean a spouse, ancestor, or lineal descendant of such individual (or spouse), any brother or sister of the individual, and any spouse of any individual described previously. Additionally, the attribution rules given in Code Sec. 2701(e)(3) apply. The effective date for the restrictions is October 8, 1990.

Tax Pointer: In *Knight*,[178] the IRS, utilizing Code Sec. 2704(b), attempted to strike down a family partnership created where there were restrictions placed on family members who were limited partners. The Court refused to strike down the partnership, sustaining it instead, because it was validly formed under state law. The Court, in reaching its decision, sustained the partnership, even though approximately 24 percent of the partnership assets were the children's residence where they were living rent-free. The Court, however, rejected the taxpayers' minority discounts. Instead, discounts of only 15 percent were sustained.

.05 Trusts and Term Interest in Property

Code Sec. 2702 provides rules to determine whether a transfer of an interest in a trust to a member of the transferor's family is a gift, and if so, the amount of the gift. To determine whether a gift is made or not, Code Sec. 2702(a)(1) prescribes that the value of the remainder interest is to be subtracted from the value of the

---

[178] *I.F. Knight*, 115 TC 506, Dec. 54,136.

¶1120.05

entire property to determine the value of the transferred interest. Code Sec. 2702(a)(2) prescribes that the value of any interest retained by the transferor or an applicable family member is to be $0, unless the interest is a "qualified interest." Code Sec. 2702(b) defines a "qualified interest" as (1) a right to receive fixed amounts payable at least annually, (2) a right to receive amounts payable at least annually which are a fixed percentage of the trust's assets (determined annually), or (3) a noncontingent remainder interest if all the other interests in the trust are qualified payments. To determine the value of a qualified interest, Code Sec. 2702(a)(2)(B) requires that it shall be determined according to Code Sec. 7520.

Two exceptions apply.[179] If the transfer is of a trust's interest in a residence to be used as a personal residence by persons holding term interests in the trust,[180] or if the transfer is incomplete the provisions of Code Sec. 2702 will not apply. An incomplete transfer exists, according to Code Sec. 2702(a)(3)(B), when the transfer "would not be treated as a gift whether or not consideration was received for such transfer." The pertinent part of the 1990 Senate Committee Report to the Reconciliation Act explains the application of these rules.

> Thus, a person who makes a completed transfer of nonresidential property in trust and retains (1) the right to the income of the trust for a term of years and (2) a reversionary right [or a testamentary general power of appointment with respect] to trust corpus is treated as making a transfer equal to the value of the whole property. The same result obtains if the transferor retains (1) the right to both income and appreciation for a term of years plus (2) a testamentary general power of appointment over trust corpus for that period. In contrast, the creation of a trust, the only interests in which are an annuity for a term of years and a noncontingent remainder interest, is valued under present law.

> **Tax Pointer:** Besides the exclusion of a principal residence from the gift tax, a secondary residence, including a vacation home, could also qualify for the exception.[181]

Code Sec. 2702(c) provides for the inclusion of certain situations that are not trusts. For instance, the retention of a term interest [defined below] (including a life estate) in property is treated like the retention of an interest in a trust.[182] Accordingly, if a father retains a term interest in property and makes a present gift of the remainder interest to his son, no consideration is made of the father's retention of the term interest; rather, the gift is computed on the entire value of the property. A joint purchase by two or more members of the same family (with members of the family defined pursuant to Code Sec. 2704(c)(2)) is to be treated as an acquisition of the entire property by the holder of the term interest, followed by a transfer of the remainder interest.[183] Thus, the term purchaser is treated as making a gift to the remainder purchaser of an amount equal to the value of the property reduced by the amount paid by the remainder person.

A "term interest" is defined as a "life interest in property, or an interest in property for a term of years."[184] A special rule applies to a term interest in tangible property where the nonexercise of the term-holder's rights do not substantially

[179] Code Sec. 2702(a)(3).
[180] Code Sec. 2702(a)(3)(A)(ii).
[181] Ibid.
[182] Code Sec. 2702(c)(1).
[183] Code Sec. 2702(c)(2).
[184] Code Sec. 2702(c)(3).

affect the value of the property passing to the remaindermen.[185] In this case, the value of the term interest is the amount for which the taxpayer establishes that the interest could be sold to an unrelated third party. Such an amount is determined under the Treasury tables, but by reference to market norms, taking into account the illiquidity of such interest. For example, the rule could apply to the joint purchase of a painting or undeveloped real estate (the value of which primarily reflects future development potential). On the other hand, the rule would not apply to a joint purchase of depletable property. The 1990 Senate Committee Report to the Reconciliation Act provides that regulations to be issued by the IRS will give illustrations. The effective date of the provisions under Code Sec. 2702 apply after October 8, 1990.

¶ 1121 Innocent Spouse Doctrine

In *Dynamic Energy, Inc.,*[186] an ex-wife of a shareholder did not have the right to litigate innocent spouse relief in Tax Court when the court was reviewing an audit of the S corporation. In *Reser,*[187] however, innocent spouse status was sustained for a personal injury lawyer who was involved with her husband in an S corporation that brokered large real estate projects.

> **Tax Pointer:** For a detailed discussion of the Innocent Spouse Doctrine, see Michael Schlesinger, "Innocent Spouse Relief: A Roadmap to Understanding the Maze Created by Code Sec. 6015," *Journal of Tax Practice and Procedure*, Vol. 4, No. 2 at 19 (May 2002).

Code Sec. 6015(f) does not contain any restrictions as to when it can be brought. Notwithstanding, the Internal Revenue Service maintains that the same statute of limitations which applies to relief sought under Code Sec. 6015(b) and (c) applies to any relief sought under Code Sec. 6015(f).[188]

¶ 1122 Effect of Death on Unused Losses

In the normal course of the operation of an S corporation, a shareholder could have insufficient basis to deduct losses for S corporation operations.[189] A loss in excess of basis could arise if the S corporation borrows money from a third party (i.e., a bank). If a shareholder dies before being able to use these unused losses, the loss is lost forever.[190]

> **Example 11-38:** Art Jensen forms ArtWay Inc. in 2003, electing S status on formation. Jensen acquires all the stock for $500, and, in ArtWay Inc.'s first year of operation, the S corporation borrows $10,000 from a bank. ArtWay Inc. files its tax return on a calendar-year basis, and at the end of its first tax year, ArtWay Inc. had a loss of $10,000. Jensen, who only has $500 of basis in the

---

[185] Code Sec. 2702(c)(4).

[186] *Dynamic Energy, Inc.,* 98 TC 48, Dec. 47,942.

[187] *R.J. Reser,* CA-5, 97-1 USTC ¶ 50,416, 112 F3d 1258. Aff'g in part and rev'g in part 70 TCM 1472, Dec. 51,032(M), TC Memo. 1995-572.

[188] *See Hall,* 135 TC No. 19, Reg. §1.6015-5(b)(1), which provides that a spouse must request equitable relief under Code Sec. 6015(f) no later than two years

from the first collection activity against the spouse, held invalid; thus there is no time limit on request for equitable innocent spouse relief under Code Sec. 6015. *Lantz,* 132 TC No. 8 reached the same conclusion but it was reversed and remanded at *Lantz,* 2010-1 USTC ¶ 50,446, (Jun. 8, 2010).

[189] See Chapter 9 for a discussion of basis and losses.

[190] Code Sec. 1366(d)(2).

stock, can only deduct $500, carrying forward $9,500 ($10,000 of loss – $500 of basis). Jensen dies on January 1, 2004, at the commencement of ArtWay Inc.'s next tax year. Because Jensen died before he had basis to deduct the losses suspended by Code Sec. 1366(d)(2), the $9,500 of nondeductible losses are lost forever.

Tax Pointer: Code Sec. 469 passive losses are treated differently than other losses. Specifically, suspended passive losses remaining when a taxpayer dies are allowed to the extent they exceed the step up in basis the property receives because of the shareholder's death.[191]

¶ 1123 Income in Respect of a Decedent (IRD)

It is beyond the scope of this book to provide a detailed description of income in respect of a decedent (IRD). However, note the following points.

Income accrued to decedent. IRD are items of income that accrued to a decedent during his or her lifetime, but were not includible in the decedent's income before his or her death. To illustrate, assume an S corporation shareholder-employee is paid on a weekly basis, but dies on Tuesday of a work week. Two days of salary (i.e., Monday and Tuesday) would constitute IRD.[192]

Income accrued to beneficiary. IRD is includible in the income of the person entitled to receive it, with the person who includes IRD income allowed a tax deduction for the estate tax attributable to the items of IRD.[193] For individuals dying after August 20, 1996, if a beneficiary acquires S corporation stock from a decedent, the beneficiary must treat as IRD the decedent's pro rata portion of any corporate income that would have been IRD if the income had been acquired directly from the decedent.[194] A deduction under Code Sec. 691(c) will be allowed for the estate tax attributable to the item of IRD.[195] Further, the beneficiary's basis in the stock acquired from the decedent is reduced by the portion of the value of the stock that is attributable to items consisting of IRD. When a shareholder dies, due to the S corporation's method of accounting, all income may not have been earned at the time of the shareholder's death. Thus, Code Sec. 691 will apply to dictate the treatment for tax purposes. Physically closing the books on the date of death of shareholder would be the simpler method since there is no guesswork where items belong. For a discussion of closing of the S corporate books and the election to be made, see ¶ 1106.09.

¶ 1124 Gifted Stock Basis

.01 Donee's Basis in Gifted Stock

A donee's basis in S corporation stock received as a gift is generally equal to the basis of the stock in the hands of the donor.[196] The donee's basis is increased by the amount of the gift tax attributable to the appreciation of the property at the time of the gift.[197] The donee's basis for taking a loss is equal to the lesser of the donor's

---

[191] Code Sec. 469(g)(2).
[192] Code Sec. 691.
[193] *Ibid.*
[194] Code Sec. 1367(b)(4).

[195] Code Sec. 1367(b)(4)(B).
[196] Code Sec. 1015(a).
[197] Code Sec. 1015(d)(6).

basis or the fair market value of the property at the time of making the gift.[198] However, a shareholder cannot take losses in excess of a shareholder's basis in his or her stock.[199] Presumably, for purposes of taking losses, the donee's basis will be the lower of Code Sec. 1015(a)'s basis, or Code Sec. 1366(d)(1)'s.

Carryover of unused losses. If a shareholder has suspended losses because of insufficient basis, the shareholder cannot use them until the shareholder has sufficient basis.[200] Reg. § 1.1366-2(a)(5) states that if a shareholder makes a gift of stock when there are suspended losses due to having inadequate basis, the donee will receive stock with a zero basis, with the loss carryforwards, since they are personal to the donor, being lost forever.

Reg. § 1.1366-2(a)(5) also prescribes that "if a shareholder transfers some but not all of the shareholder's stock in the corporation, the amount of any disallowed loss or deduction . . . is not reduced, and the transferee does not acquire any portion of the disallowed loss or deduction." Unclear, however, is the treatment of stock vis-a-vis the losses. An example will illustrate.

> **Example 11-39:** Alvin is the sole owner of Alvin, Inc., a calendar-year S corporation since inception. Alvin, Inc. commenced operations on January 1, 2002, borrowing $300,000 from a bank, with Alvin acquiring all 100 shares of capital stock of the corporation for $100,000. At the end of its first year of operation, Alvin, Inc. lost $300,000, with Alvin deducting $100,000 of loss equal to his basis, carrying forward $200,000. On January 1, 2002, Alvin plans to make a gift of 25% of the stock to his daughter-in-law, Laurie. Under Code Sec. 1366(d) and Reg. § 1.1366-2(a)(5), it is unclear if $50,000 of the suspended loss is to be allocated on a share-by-share basis (i.e., 25% of the $200,000) to Laurie's shares, or lost forever, because Alvin, at the time he made the gift, had no basis to take the loss, with Laurie having zero basis on her shares; or, does Alvin retain $200,000 of suspended losses allocated to his 75 shares?

> **Tax Pointer:** To resolve all doubt as to the utilization of the suspended losses, if Alvin in Example 11-39 lent money to Alvin, Inc. on January 1, 2002, and/or made a capital contribution of $200,000 to Alvin, Inc., then Alvin could deduct the entire $200,000 of suspended losses.

In terms of utilization of the losses by the donor shareholder, assuming a shareholder does not dispose of his or her entire stock interest, this could only occur if basis is generated for the donor shareholder in the corporation. An example where basis could be generated is the S corporation earns income and does not distribute same.

Gain vs. loss basis in gifted stock. Under Code Sec. 1015, the donee's tax basis in S corporation stock received as a gift from another shareholder differs depending on whether the stock is subsequently sold for a gain or a loss. If the donee subsequently sells the stock for an amount that exceeds the donor's tax basis in the stock just prior to the gift, the donee recognizes gain equal to the difference between the selling price and the donor's tax basis (i.e., the donee takes

---

[198] Code Sec. 1015(a).

[199] Code Sec. 1366(d)(1).

[200] Code Sec. 1366(d)(2).

a carryover basis in the stock). If instead the donee sells the property for less than the donor's date-of-gift tax basis, the donee's recognized loss is equal to the excess of the stock's *fair market value* at the date of the gift over the proceeds of sale (i.e., the donee's basis is deemed to be the fair market value of the stock at the date of the gift rather than its carryover basis). If the selling price is between the fair market value and tax basis of the stock at the date of the gift, the donee recognizes neither gain or loss.

> *Example 11-40:* Jason Moore, who has stock basis of $10,000 in his Jason Inc. S corporation stock, gives the stock to his daughter, Marcy, when the stock is worth $1,000. Marcy subsequently sells the stock for $5,000. Marcy reports no gain or loss on the sale since the stock price is between the donor's basis and its fair market value at the time of the gift.

.02 Beneficiary's Basis in S Corporation Stock

Shareholders receiving their stock as an inheritance take a tax basis in such stock equal to its fair market value at the date of death, or the alternate valuation date according to Code Sec. 2032.[201] Income in respect to a decedent has an impact on stock basis pursuant to Code Sec. 1367(b)(4)(B).[202]

¶ 1125 Life Insurance

.01 Tax Aspects of Life Insurance

An S corporation can insure the lives of its shareholders, key employees, etc. Code Sec. 101 prescribes that the proceeds received from life insurance are tax-free to the corporation. As discussed at ¶ 905.01, life insurance proceeds received by the corporation on the death of an insured corporate individual increases the S corporation shareholder's stock basis, but as discussed at ¶ 1003.10, life insurance proceeds do not increase the accumulated adjustments account (AAA). Despite these limitations on AAA, life insurance can be used for redemption of a deceased shareholder's interest, utilizing in part Code Sec. 303. The danger for the S corporation arises if it has accumulated earnings and profits from its operations as a C corporation, and/or a merger with a C corporation, in that a distribution of proceeds for the redemption on death funding the acquisition with life insurance proceeds could be deemed a dividend if the procedures of the Code are not satisfied for a deceased shareholder.

In terms of the treatment of the premiums paid for the life insurance, there are three types of insurance: term, cash surrender value, and split dollar. Split dollar is discussed at ¶ 1125.04. As to premiums for term insurance, the premiums should reduce a shareholder's basis. However, if the policy is one which has a cash surrender value element in it, then Code Sec. 1367(a)(2)(D) may preclude a deduction to basis, due to the fact that a premium could be classified as a nondeductible but capitalized expenditure, or, alternatively, to the extent the premiums exceed the increase in the cash surrender value of the policy.

---

[201] Code Sec. 1014(a).

[202] See ¶ 1123 for a discussion of income in respect of a decedent.

.02 Utilization of Life Insurance for Redemptions of Shareholder's Capital Stock—Interest at Death

¶ 1106.11 and ¶ 1209 discuss the tax aspects of redemption of a shareholder's stock interest at death. A corporation may decide to fund the redemption of the acquisition of a shareholder's stock at death with life insurance. Besides the problems with life insurance discussed in ¶ 1125.01, there are also practical problems in utilizing life insurance for redemptions. One primary problem is ensuring that the life insurance proceeds are equal to the redemption agreement price to be paid for the decedent's stock at death. If the proceeds from the insurance policy(ies) are too little, then the corporation has to fund the difference, placing restrictions on its cash, depending upon the terms of the redemption. If the proceeds of the life insurance policy(ies) are in excess of the redemption price, then the corporation has the right to retain them, making a profit on a shareholder's death.

To prevent either type of situation from occurring, the redemption should set forth procedures to minimize these occurrences—particularly to minimize the cash needs of the corporation to fund the redemption at death. One means is to provide in the redemption agreement that, periodically (i.e., every two years), a determination will be made of the value of the corporation, and if the corporation has grown substantially, the shareholders will obtain additional life insurance. The difficulty with this approach is that the value of the corporation could subsequently decrease; then, the shareholders are faced with the situation they were trying to minimize— namely, the S corporation having insurance proceeds in excess of the redemption price and no increase in AAA. Also, one or more of the shareholders could become uninsurable, or the premium(s) from the insurance could be prohibitive. While periodic review to monitor the financial net worth of the corporation may not provide a perfect solution to the problems outlined above, the review has the potential to minimize the situation.

Alternatively, if the life insurance policies are substantially in excess of the net worth of the S corporation, the shareholders may decide to terminate the redemption agreement, opting instead to create a cross-purchase agreement,[203] and transferring the life insurance to the shareholders to cross-insure themselves. However, there is a problem with this transfer: the transfer for value provision under Code Sec. 101.

.03 Cross-Purchase Agreements Utilizing Life Insurance

As discussed at ¶ 1003.10, life insurance proceeds do not increase AAA. Consequently, in a redemption situation of a decedent's stock funded by life insurance if there are life insurance proceeds in excess of the redemption price, the remaining shareholders have a problem to remove the excess proceeds from the corporation. In contrast, if a cross-purchase agreement funded by life insurance is utilized, then no difficulty can arise with AAA, since the proceeds are already in the remaining shareholders' hands without any involvement of the corporation.

---

[203] For a discussion of cross-purchase agreements, see ¶ 1106.11.

¶1125.02

.04 Split Dollar Life Insurance

In a split dollar life insurance plan, the employer (i.e., an S corporation) pays a part of the premium for life insurance equal to the increase in the cash surrender value of the policy, and the employee (i.e., a shareholder-employee) pays the rest of the premium. On the death of the employee, the proceeds are divided into two parts—one part payable to the company to allow it to recover its outlays for the premiums, with the employee's beneficiary(ies) receiving the balance of the proceeds. IRS Letter Rulings 9309046 (December 9, 1992) and 9735006 (May 20, 1997) provide that split dollar life insurance for S corporation shareholders does not create a second class of stock, providing the S corporation is reimbursed for the premiums paid.

In Notice 2002-8,[204] the IRS outlined a proposed revamping of split dollar life insurance to be published in proposed regulations. Notice 2002-8 divides split dollar life insurance arrangements into two segments. If the employer is formally designated as the owner of the policy, then the benefits provided to the employee are treated as providing a current economic benefit (i.e., current life insurance protection), and taxable to the employee under Code Sec. 61. A transfer of the life insurance contract to the employee is taxed under Code Sec. 83. The proposed regulations will not treat an employer as having made a transfer of a portion of the cash surrender value of a life insurance contract to an employee for purposes of Code Sec. 83 solely because the interest or other earnings credited to the cash surrender value of the contract cause the cash surrender value to exceed the portion thereof payable to the employer.

If the employee is formally designated as the owner of the policy, then the premiums paid by the employer are treated as a series of loans by the employer to the employee, with the employee obligated to repay the employer, whether out of contract proceeds or otherwise. The loans are subject to original discount or below market loan rules. If the employee is not obligated to repay the premiums paid by the employer, then such amounts are treated as compensation income to the employee at the time the premiums are paid by the employer. Furthermore, the same principles are expected to govern the federal tax treatment of split-dollar life insurance arrangements in other contexts, including arrangements that provide benefits in gift and corporation-shareholder contexts. The IRS has issued tables for valuing life insurance protection. For split-dollar life insurance arrangements entered into before the publication of the final regulations, before the effective date of future guidance and before January 28, 2002, the IRS has issued guidance as to how to handle these situations in terms of taxation.

.05 Purchasing Life Insurance from a Qualified Retirement Plan

Frequently, corporations purchase life insurance on a shareholder-employee participant in the plan. Since life insurance basically only generates value when the insured dies, the corporation may want to purchase the plan's life insurance policy on the shareholder-employee. If this occurs, the full cash surrender value must be paid for the policy; no discount can be taken for surrender charges.[205]

---

[204] Notice 2002-8, IRB 2002-4, 398.   [205] *Matthies v. Comm.*, 134 TC No. 6.

¶ 1126 Conversion of an S Corporation to an LLC to Obtain Partnership Taxation Benefits

As discussed at ¶ 1304, a two or more member LLC currently offers more tax planning opportunities than an S corporation due to the nature of partnership taxation. Consequently, the shareholders of a corporation may decide to convert the S corporation to an LLC to obtain these benefits. There are two basic methods to effect this conversion: first, keeping the S corporation alive, which is basically a tax-free proposition; and second, liquidating and dissolving the S corporation, which is a taxable event.

.01 Keeping the S Corporation Alive and Having Family Members or Others as Members in the LLC

Reg. § 1.701-2(d) discussed at ¶ 202.01, illustrates that an S corporation can form an LLC with another taxpayer, even if the taxpayer is not a permitted S corporation shareholder. On formation of the LLC, the members would make their respective capital contributions tax-free to the LLC pursuant to Code Sec. 721, with the S corporation transferring its assets, and the other members contributing theirs. At the end of each taxable year, the non-S corporation members would, respectively, report their income, loss, etc. arising from the LLC, with the S corporation member acting as a conduit to its shareholders. If the S corporation was subject to taxation under Code Secs. 1374 and 1375, the S corporation would pay tax on the income received from the LLC under these provisions before reporting the LLC income, expense, etc. to its shareholders. It is beyond the scope of this book to present a detailed explanation of the interplay of an S corporation and an LLC; however, the following should be noted as an example of how the combination of LLC and S corporation taxation would work.

> **Example 11-41:** Mom and Dad are advanced in years, and have two grown children, Laura and Dave. Laura and Dave each have two children. Mom and Dad formed an S corporation, Antique, Inc., a number of years ago. In 2002, Mom and Dad (who each own 50% of Antique, Inc.) are faced with the following situation: They have zero basis in their stock; yet the corporation is worth $2,000,000. They want to utilize their respective Code Sec. 2001 unified credit amounts and their respective Code Sec. 2503(b) annual exclusion to make gifts to their family. They propose utilizing a family LLC, having the S corporation act as a managing member, but having their children assuming a role in the operation of the LLC. Mom and Dad form the LLC with Antique, Inc. being one member and Laura and Dave, or trusts for their benefit, as the other members. The following is one possible scenario.
>
> (1) From an estate planning perspective, the LLC will be sustained. In *Knight*,[206] the Court stated that as long as a family partnership is validly formed under state law, it will be recognized for tax purposes.
>
> (2) If non-income-producing assets are contributed as a capital contribution, minority discounts will apply for gift tax purposes. In *Knight*,[207]

---

[206] *I.F. Knight*, 115 TC 506, Dec. 54,136.   [207] *Ibid.*

houses where the donee's children were living rent-free were contributed to a family partnership. The Court sustained discounting with respect to these assets. Likewise, discounting was permitted with respect to marketable securities that were transferred to the partnership.

(3) If members are considered limited partners in the LLC, then, pursuant to Proposed Reg. §1.1402(a)-2(h), they are not subject to self-employment tax. Thus, the members could decide that the LLC be a managed one, with Antique, Inc. being the manager. The result is that the other members (i.e., the children) would not incur self-employment tax on the income from the LLC, providing the provisions of Proposed Reg. §1.1402(a)-2(h)(2) are followed (i.e., the child does not participate in the LLC's trade or business for more than 500 hours during the taxable year). In terms of Antique, Inc.'s operation as a manager, any income allocated to it, subject to the family partnership rules of Code Sec. 704(e), can be passed to Mom and Dad as shareholder-employees utilizing the combination of distributions and reasonable salary, subject to the *Radke*[208] standard.[209]

(4) Mom and Dad, on establishing the LLC, could set up trusts for the children and grandchildren, free of the limitations of ESBTs and QSSTs as discussed at ¶306.04 and ¶307.04, thereby providing greater income and estate tax planning possibilities.

(5) As discussed at ¶1304.03, in particular at Example 13-10, LLC income and deductions can be allocated easily among the members, including the establishment of a profits interest to distribute profits to one member.

A "profits interest" means that a member of an LLC is entitled to a certain percentage of the profits for a prescribed portion of a taxable year. To illustrate, when an associate becomes a partner at a law firm, the associate is usually awarded a profits interest, since the associate does not have to make a capital contribution to become a partner. By holding a profits interest, the associate receives a portion of the income.[210]

Allocation of income and deductions in an LLC, unlike in an S corporation which has to rely on salaries, can easily be changed by the LLC, with the only proviso being that the allocations made have to have substantial economic effect. To illustrate one scenario utilizing an S corporation-managed LLC, the following example is set forth.

---

[208] For a discussion of *J. Radke*, see ¶716.02 and ¶716.03.

[209] *Thompson*, 2009-2 USTC ¶50,501 (Ct. Cl. 2009) holds that possession of an LLC interest where the LLC is classified as a partnership for tax purposes is not presumptively passive under Code Sec. 469(h)(2)'s "limited partner rule;" thus losses can be deducted without having them reclassified *ab initio* as "passive".

[210] Rev. Proc. 93-27, 1993-2 CB 343, provides that the creation of a profits interest will not be deemed a taxable event if certain events do not occur. See also Private Letter Ruling 200329001 which provides further guidance regarding profits interests.

Example 11-42: Assume the same facts as in Example 11-41, except that Mom and Dad, because they are already in such a high tax bracket, do not want any income from the LLC allocated to them in the year 2003. Yet, they want to control the LLC for the year 2003 and for the foreseeable future. Because Laura and Dave are of advanced years, they want to enjoy their lives, and thus have planned to take a year-long cruise commencing January 1, 2003. To provide for management of the family LLC, they grant their children a profits interest in the LLC for the year 2003, to be split evenly by them providing they achieve a certain profit level, with the concept to be reviewed again as of January 1, 2004, depending on how successful the LLC is for the year 2003. While this type of profit arrangement could be done by an S corporation with salaries being payable to the children, the general rules of taxation frown upon such a situation, in that salaries are to remain a constant, and not to go up and down depending upon the profits of the venture.

Tax challenges to the LLC family partnership. It is foreseeable that the IRS could challenge and attack the family LLC as outlined in Examples 11-44 and 11-45. The IRS has a number of arrows in its quiver to attack family situations such as this. For instance, it may challenge the family LLC utilizing the broad anti-abuse rule set forth in Reg. § 1.701-2(b) which states: "If a partnership is formed or availed of in connection with a transaction a principal purpose of which is to reduce substantially the present value of the partners' aggregate federal tax liability in a manner that is inconsistent with the intent of subchapter K, the Commissioner can recast the transaction for federal tax purposes, as appropriate to achieve tax results that are consistent with the intent of subchapter K, in light of the applicable statutory and regulatory provisions and the pertinent facts and circumstances."

In Field Service Advice 200149019 (August 31, 2001), the IRS used (in what appears to be a case of first impression in a partnership situation) Code Sec. 482 and assignment of income principles to strike down a partnership composed of a C corporation and an S corporation owned by the same taxpayer, where the partnership was established to divest taxable income from one of the corporations to the other.

Field Service Advice 200143004 (July 5, 2001) attacked a family-owned S corporation, saying that the corporation should be ignored for gift tax purposes, because the corporation had no business purpose. The corporation's assets were cash, Treasury notes, and 12 tax-free municipal bonds. The corporation elected S status, and after attaining appraisals for the stock, the sole shareholder, a mother, transferred stock in the S corporation to her children, utilizing discounts for lack of control and marketability. The IRS stated that the reason the S corporation should be disregarded for gift tax purposes is that it functioned as a mere conduit for planned family giving and was formed for the sole purpose of reducing federal tax. Obviously, the reasoning of Field Service Advice 200143004 could easily apply to partnership situations involving S corporations and family members. But see *Pierre*[211] where the step transaction doctrine was applied to collapse a taxpayer's

---

[211] TC Memo, 2010-106.

¶1126.01

simultaneous gifts and sales into two gifts of 50 percent interests in a family limited liability company (LLC) since both sales and gifts were done solely to avoid gift tax; notwithstanding discounts for lack of marketability and control were basically sustained.

.02 Liquidation of the S Corporation to Form an LLC

Liquidation of the S corporation as discussed at ¶ 1210 is a taxable event for the shareholders of the S corporation. Accordingly, if the shareholders pursue the liquidation approach to form the LLC, this could prove very expensive for the shareholders compared to maintaining the S corporation and having it form an LLC in conjunction with other taxpayers such as family members. There are various methods to liquidate the S corporation to form the LLC:

(1) liquidation of the S corporation followed by the shareholders contributing the S corporation's net liquidation proceeds to the LLC;

(2) the S corporation forms the LLC, transfers to it its net assets in exchange for a membership interest that the corporation distributes to its shareholders in a complete liquidation;

(3) the shareholders form an LLC and contribute their stock to the LLC, with the LLC liquidating the S corporation; and

(4) merger of the corporation into an LLC with the LLC surviving. An example will illustrate the liquidation of the S corporation followed by the formation of the LLC.

Example 11-43: Concept, Inc., a calendar-year S corporation from inception, is owned equally by two individuals, Ted and Janice. Concept, Inc., after the corporation has been in existence for five years, decides on January 1, 2002 to liquidate, with Ted and Janice to utilize the assets from the liquidation to form an LLC. Concept's sole asset is a piece of land having a fair market value, based on appraisals, of $250,000 and a cost basis of $100,000; Ted's and Janice's stock basis is zero. Upon liquidation, the corporation will realize a gain of $150,000 ($250,000 – $100,000), which per Code Sec. 1366(a) must be reported by each shareholder in the amount of $75,000 each ($150,000 × 50%) on their respective personal tax returns. Ted's and Janice's stock basis, per Code Sec. 1367(a), is increased to $75,000 (zero basis + the $75,000 of income generated by liquidation). Ted and Janice then must calculate gain or loss realized on the redemption of their stock. Each realizes a gain of $50,000, computed as follows: $125,000 (one-half of the fair-market value of the land received on liquidation) – $75,000 basis = $50,000 of capital gain. Ted and Janice now form the LLC, with each contributing their 50% interest in the land formerly owned by the corporation, which has a value to each of $125,000. Pursuant to Code Sec. 721, neither Ted, Janice nor the LLC recognize any gain on the transfer of the assets to the LLC. Code Sec. 722 prescribes that Ted and Janice will take a basis in their membership interest equal to the basis that he or she had in the land transferred to the LLC (i.e., $125,000 each), with the LLC, pursuant to Code Sec. 723, taking a basis in the land contributed by the members to the LLC of $250,000. Code Sec. 1223(2) prescribes that the LLC's holding period for the contributed asset includes the members' holding periods for the contributed assets.

.03 Analysis of the Liquidation of an S Corporation Followed by the Establishment of an LLC

In Example 11-43, Ted and Janice were able to form the LLC at a tax cost to each of them in the amount of $125,000 ($75,000 of gain realized by the corporation transferring the assets on liquidation to Ted and Janice respectively, plus $50,000 of gain realized on the redemption of the shareholder's stock on liquidation). Results would differ depending on the stock basis of the shareholders. To illustrate, assume in Example 11-43 that Ted and Janice each had a basis of $150,000 in their stock at the time of liquidation. Then Ted and Janice would receive a net capital loss of $25,000 followed by the establishment of the LLC, computed as follows: original stock basis of $100,000 plus corporate gain on liquidation of $75,000 equals $225,000; Ted and Janice each receive land worth $125,000; thus, the net loss is $25,000 ($225,000 less $125,000 equals $100,000 loss less $75,000 of gain equaling a net loss of $25,000).

> **Tax Pointer:** To minimize the economic effects set forth in this paragraph, the taxpayers, if they have capital gains arising on the liquidation of the S corporation, may want to accelerate transactions which will generate capital loss. Alternatively, if they have capital loss being generated on the liquidation of the S corporation, then they may want to accelerate transactions which will produce capital gains.

.04 Transfer Taxes on Liquidation

Foreseeably, there could be state and local transfer taxes imposed on the asset transfers to create the LLC, such as a franchise tax on liquidation. Consequently, state and local tax laws have to be reviewed to see if there are other alternatives to accomplish the transfer of the corporate assets to an LLC, such as having the corporation form an LLC first; then have the corporation contribute its assets and liabilities to the LLC in exchange for a membership interest, followed by the S corporation distributing the LLC membership interest to the shareholders in complete liquidation. While the result may be the same as in Example 11-43 for Ted and Janice for federal tax purposes, depending on state law, the alternative set forth above may produce no state transfer taxes, thus saving them money.

On January 23, 2006, final regulations regarding mergers and consolidations were issued dealing in part with LLCs, etc. ¶ 1211.02 should be consulted for the various means by which mergers and consolidations can be accomplished.

.05 Merger of the Corporation into the LLC, with the LLC the Survivor

Assume that the state where the S corporation is located permits a merger and/or consolidation of an S corporation into an LLC. By using this approach, state and local transfer taxes may be saved or severely reduced. To illustrate, assume that the S corporation was formed under Delaware law, and the LLC is formed under Delaware law. Concept, Inc. in Example 11-43, instead of liquidating, could merge into the LLC, transferring all its assets to the LLC. On the date of the

¶1126.03

merger, the corporation is liquidated and ceases to exist, and, pursuant to Code Secs. 331 and 336(a), the liquidation is a taxable event to both the shareholders and the corporation, producing the same $125,000 of taxable income to each shareholder, as detailed in Example 11-43. Pursuant to Code Sec. 1012, Ted's and Janice's individual basis in their LLC membership interest is equal to the fair market value of the land transferred: $125,000. Alternatively, if Antique, Inc. wanted to operate as a partnership or as a taxpayer LLC classified as a partnership for state purposes and an S corporation for federal tax purposes, the S corporation could do an F reorganization as discussed at ¶ 1211.08 to accomplish this objective.

¶ 1127 Tax Structured Transactions; Liability Protection

The field of S corporations is a very structured area, where many times form prevails over substance. For instance, Code Sec. 1361(b)(1)(C) prohibits nonresident aliens from being shareholders, but if the S corporation forms a partnership with the nonresident alien, the corporation election, as detailed at ¶ 202.01, will not be terminated, and the partnership will not be deemed abusive under Reg. § 1.704-2's partnership anti-abuse regulations. The recent case of *United Parcel Service of America*[212] details a situation where the Court found that a tax-structured transaction was not a sham, but one that had economic substance. The facts in *United Parcel Service* were as follows.

UPS originally provided excess value insurance on packages over $100. UPS formed Overseas Partners, Ltd. (OPL) in Bermuda as a reinsurer, distributing the stock of OPL as a taxable dividend to UPS's shareholders. UPS entered into a contract with National Union (NU) to insure packages where UPS customers purchased insurance to cover excess coverage (UPS only insured packages up to $100). NU entered into a reinsurance transaction with OPL where NU would remit 100 percent of the premiums collected less losses paid, commissions and other related expenses, with OPL to assume any risk of loss if NU could not cover the loss. UPS, however, had a duty to carefully monitor shipments where excess value insurance was purchased. As to OPL being required to actually reinsure NU, the Court observed that the chances were slim. Nevertheless, the Court sustained the transaction, because (1) UPS lost the income stream produced by the excess value insurance premiums; (2) OPL was an independent entity; and (3) UPS had a right to alter its loss protection program, even though the result was that the insurance business operated similarly to the format it operated in previously.

In reaching its decision sustaining the creation and operation of OPL, the Court noted that there may often be no tax-independent reason for a taxpayer to choose between different ways of structuring a transaction, but that does not mean that the taxpayer lacks a business purpose for a method which reduces taxes. As an example, the Court cited the manner in which to raise funds for a business—either to borrow, which produces deductible interest—or sale of equity, which yields nondeductible dividends.[213]

---

[212] *United Parcel Service of America*, CA-11, 2001-2 USTC ¶ 50,475, 254 F3d 1014.

[213] For an example of another tax-structured transaction which was sustained, see *IES Industries*, CA-8, 2001-2 USTC ¶ 50,471, 253 F3d 350 (tax structured transaction with ADRs which involved approximately $26,000,000 in tax plus interest, sustained). But see *Winn-Dixie Stores, Inc.*, CA-11, 2001-2 USTC ¶ 50,495, 254 F3d 1313 (sham

.01 Codification of Economic Substance Doctrine and Imposition of Penalties

Code Sec. 7701 details that after March 31, 2010 a transaction is treated as having economic substance only if (1) the transaction changes in a meaningful way (apart from Federal income taxes) the taxpayer's economic position, and (2) the taxpayer has a substantial purpose (apart from Federal income taxes) for entering into the transaction. State and local income tax effects are treated in the same manner as Federal income tax effects. Favorable financial accounting treatment is not taken into account if the benefit arises from a reduction of Federal income taxes.

In the case of individuals, Code Sec. 7701(o)(5)(B) states that in the case of an individual, the provision applies only to transactions entered into in connection with a trade or business or an activity engaged in for the production of income.

A 20 percent penalty (increased to 40 percent if the transaction is not adequately disclosed on the tax return) applies to the disallowance of claimed tax benefits by reason of a transaction lacking economic substance. No exceptions, including the reasonable cause rules, to the penalty are available.

Tax Pointer 1: The economic substance doctrine can apply in a criminal case. See *United States v. Pfaff,*[214] where the court instructed the jury that the government was required to establish lack of economic substance to the transactions ("tax shelters") which required the government to prove beyond a reasonable doubt both "that the relevant taxpayer had no business purpose for engaging in the transaction apart from creating the tax deduction" and "that there was no reasonable possibility that the transaction would result in a profit."

Tax Pointer 2: The Committee Reports to Code Sec. 7701 state that "[t]he provision is not intended to alter the tax treatment of certain basic business transactions that, under longstanding judicial and administrative practice are respected, merely because the choice between meaningful economic alternatives is largely or entirely based on comparative tax advantages. Among these basic transactions are (1) the choice between capitalizing a business enterprise with debt or equity; (2) a U.S. person's choice between utilizing a foreign corporation or a domestic corporation to make a foreign investment; (3) the choice to enter a transaction or series of transactions that constitute a corporate organization or reorganization under subchapter C; and (4) the choice to utilize a related-party entity in a transaction, provided that the arm's length standard of section 482 and other applicable concepts are satisfied. Leasing transactions, like all other types of transactions, will continue to be analyzed in light of all the facts and circumstances. (Citation of authorities omitted.)"

(Footnote Continued)

transaction doctrine applied to deny interest and fee deductions on corporate-owned life insurance policy loans).

[214] 2010-2 USTC ¶ 50,586 (2nd Cir. 2010).

¶1127.01

Tax Pointer 3: The IRS has issued Notice 2010-62[215] which states:

1. in Part B that the IRS will not issue a private letter ruling or determination letter on whether the economic substance doctrine is relevant to any transaction or whether any transaction complies with the requirements of Code Sec. 7701(o).

2. under Accuracy Related Penalties, if a transaction lacking economic substance is a reportable transaction, then for Code Sec. 6662(i)(2)'s purposes, adequate disclosure requirement will be satisfied only if the taxpayer makes adequate disclosure, in particular the disclosure requirements under the Code Sec. 6011 regulations. However, for a "reportable transaction" a taxpayer will not meet the disclosure requirements under the Code Sec. 6011 regulations if only attaching Form 8275, Disclosure Statement, or Form 8275-R, Regulation Disclosure Statement, to an original or qualified amended return.

.02 Liability Protection

While an S corporation by definition provides liability protection, shareholders may want additional protection from creditors by creating a chain of entities to own the stock such as having a grantor trust own a single member limited liability company which in turn owns the S corporate stock. Such an ownership situation was approved in IRS Letter Ruling 200339026 (June 23, 2003).

¶ 1128 S Corporation Can Make Contributions to Educational IRAs

Code Sec. 530 prescribes that taxpayers can establish educational IRAs to pay educational expenses of a designated beneficiary. The contribution limit is $2,000 for the beneficiary, and pursuant to Code Sec. 530(c)(1), there is a threshold limit for a taxpayer making a contribution (i.e., a married couple is precluded from making a contribution to an educational IRA if their adjusted gross income is in excess of $220,000). However, for taxable years beginning after December 31, 2001, Code Sec. 530(c)(1) provides that corporations are permitted to make contributions to educational IRAs for a beneficiary, regardless of the income of the corporation during the year of the contribution. The IRS has issued no guidance as to how an S corporation is to treat any contribution. Presumably, the S corporation would treat the contribution as a noncapital nondeductible expense, deductible from a shareholder's basis pursuant to Code Sec. 1367(a)(2)(D).[216] It remains to be seen if a corporation can discriminate in terms of making contributions, i.e., can a corporation make a contribution for S corporation shareholder-employees only, or must it make contributions for all its employees?

In terms of tax planning, it is to be noted that the contributions toward an educational IRA are not tax-deductible for the contributor. Educational IRAs only allow for contributed funds to grow tax-free providing they are used for educational expense. Further, Code Sec. 4973 imposes a six percent excise tax on excess

---

[215] 2010-40 IRB.

[216] See ¶ 903.02 and ¶ 903.04 for discussion of this area.

contributions to educational IRAs; accordingly, assuming a parent's adjusted gross income is below the threshold cutoff amount, the parent cannot make a $2,000 educational IRA contribution in a taxable year for a beneficiary, and then have his or her S corporation make an identical $2,000 for the beneficiary. Consequently, coordination has to occur with respect to any contributions for an educational IRA to prevent the six percent excise tax.

¶ 1129 Tax Credit for Employer-Provided Child Care Facilities

To provide a tax credit to employers for supporting child care and child care resources, Code Sec. 45F provides that pursuant to Code Sec. 45F(a), taxpayers receive for purposes of Code Sec. 38 tax credit equal to 25 percent of qualified expenses for employee child care and 10 percent of qualified expenses for child care resource and referral services. Code Sec. 45F(b) prescribes that the maximum total credit that may be claimed by a taxpayer cannot exceed $150,000 per year.

Code Sec. 45F(c)(1) prescribes that qualified child care expenses include costs paid or incurred:

(1) to acquire, construct, rehabilitate or expand property that is to be used as part of the taxpayer's qualified child care facility;[217]

(2) for the operation of the taxpayer's qualified child care facility, including the costs of training and certain compensation for employees of the child care facility, and scholarship programs; or

(3) under a contract with a qualified child care facility to provide child care services to employees of the taxpayer.

Code Sec. 45F(c)(2) states that to be a qualified child care facility, the principal use of the facility must be for child care (unless it is the principal residence of the taxpayer), and the facility must meet all applicable state and local laws and regulations, including any licensing laws. A facility is not treated as a qualified child care facility with respect to a taxpayer unless:

(1) it has open enrollment to the employees of the taxpayer;

(2) use of the facility (or eligibility to use such facility) does not discriminate in favor of highly compensated employees of the taxpayer (within the meaning of Code Sec. 414(q)); and

(3) at least 30 percent of the children enrolled in the center are dependents of the taxpayer's employees, if the facility is the principal trade or business of the taxpayer.

Code Sec. 45F(c)(3)(a) specifies that qualified child care resource and referral expenses are amounts paid or incurred under a contract to provide child care resource and referral services to the employees of the taxpayer. Code Sec. 45F(c)(3)(b) sets forth a nondiscrimination rule, to wit: Qualified child care services and qualified child care resource and referral expenditures must be provided

---

[217] In addition, a depreciation deduction (or amortization in lieu of depreciation) must be allowable with respect to the property, and the property must not be part of the principal residence of the taxpayer or any employee of the taxpayer.

(or be eligible for use) in a way that does not discriminate in favor of highly compensated employees of the taxpayer (within the meaning of Code Sec. 414(q)).

Code Sec. 45F(f)'s no double benefit rules prescribe that any amounts for which the taxpayer may otherwise claim a tax deduction are reduced by the amount of these credits. Similarly, if the credits are taken for expenses of acquiring, constructing, rehabilitating, or expanding a facility, the taxpayer's basis in the facility is reduced by the amount of the credits.

Code Sec. 45F(d) sets forth recapture rules, to wit: Credits taken for the expenses of acquiring, constructing, rehabilitating, or expanding a qualified facility are subject to recapture for the first 10 years after the qualified child care facility is placed in service. The amount of recapture is reduced as a percentage of the applicable credit over the 10-year recapture period.

Code Sec. 45F(d)(2) sets forth the following table for the reduction:

If the recapture event occurs in:	The applicable recapture percentage is:
Years 1-3	100
Year 4	85
Year 5	70
Year 6	55
Year 7	40
Year 8	25
Years 9 and 10	10
Year 11 and thereafter	0

Recapture takes effect if the taxpayer either ceases operation of the qualified child care facility or transfers its interest in the qualified child care facility without securing an agreement to assume recapture liability for the transferee.

> **Tax Pointer:** Before undertaking this credit, taxpayers should take a survey to determine the cost of child care facilities in the employer's geographic area.

¶ 1130 Travel and Entertainment Expenses

Code Sec. 274 disallows deductions attributable to certain types of travel, entertainment expense, and gifts. While Code Sec. 274 and its regulations do not discuss S corporations directly, there have been a number of cases applying the statute to S corporations. Recently, in *Sutherland Lumber Southwest, Inc.*,[218] a corporation was allowed to deduct its entire costs in supplying a jet for vacation travel for employees, with the employer not limited to the amount that an employee would recognize as fringe benefit income. Congress amended *Sutherland* by enacting Code Sec. 274(e)(2). For a discussion of Code Sec. 274(e)(2), see ¶ 706.03.

---

[218] *Sutherland Lumber Southwest, Inc.*, 114 TC 197, Dec. 53,817, aff'd per curiam CA-8, 2001-2 USTC ¶ 50,503, 255 F3d 495, acq. IRB 2002-6.

Chapter 12

Changes to S Corporations

¶ 1201 Termination and Revocation of S Status

An S corporation can lose its S status in any of three ways:

(1) It may voluntarily revoke its S status.[1]

(2) It may inadvertently terminate its status by failing one of the statutory standards (e.g., acquiring 101 or more shareholders).[2]

(3) It may inadvertently terminate its status if it has passive investment income that exceeds 25 percent of its gross receipts for each of three consecutive tax years, but only if it has accumulated earnings and profits at the end of each of the three consecutive tax years.[3]

When an S corporation revokes or inadvertently terminates its S status, the S corporation becomes a C corporation on the date of revocation or termination, reporting its income as such.

When termination occurs other than at the beginning or end of the S corporation's tax year, the tax year is split between the short S tax year and the short C tax year. Adverse tax consequences can arise from termination of the S election if proper planning does not take place.

[1] Code Sec. 1362(d)(1). See discussion at ¶ 1202.
[2] Code Sec. 1362(d)(2). See discussion at ¶ 1203.
[3] Code Sec. 1362(d)(3). See discussion at ¶ 1204.

In some instances, the IRS can waive inadvertent terminations.[4] And even if deliberate, there is a procedure for reelection of S status after termination.[5]

¶ 1202 Voluntary Revocation of S Status

An S corporation can voluntarily revoke its S status.[6] Shareholders of the corporation holding more than one-half of the issued and outstanding shares of stock (including nonvoting shares) on the date of revocation must consent to such revocation, and the corporation must file a statement that it is revoking its S corporation election.[7]

There is no official form for the revocation, but an example of an unofficial form is found in Appendix 12, Notice of Revocation of Subchapter S Election. The following must be included in a valid statement of revocation:[8]

- The statement must be signed by any person authorized to sign the corporate tax return,[9] and it must be filed with the IRS service center where the election was properly filed.

- Attached to the statement of revocation must be a statement of consent to the revocation signed by each consenting shareholder showing the number of issued and outstanding shares of stock (including nonvoting stock) that is held by each such shareholder at the time the revocation is made.

Tax Pointer 1: Care must be exercised in revoking S status. On one hand, there are a number of IRS Letter Rulings that state that once an S corporation files its statement of revocation, the IRS will not allow it to be rescinded.[10] On the other hand, the regulations provide a means to rescind the revocation before it becomes effective.[11]

Tax Pointer 2: If an S corporation voluntarily revokes its S status,[12] it cannot seek relief from the IRS by asking that the termination be waived as inadvertent.[13]

Tax Pointer 3: An S corporation's written notation on the top of its final return was sufficient to put the IRS on notice of the revocation of its S election.[14]

.01 Reasons for Revoking S Status

There are many tax and nontax reasons for revoking S status. For nontax reasons, an S corporation may want corporations and partnerships as shareholders, or it may want more than 100 shareholders.

Tax Pointer: As an alternative to revocation, the S corporation could form a partnership with any nonpermitted shareholder(s).

---

[4] Code Sec. 1362(f). See discussion at ¶ 1205.
[5] Code Sec. 1362(g). See discussion at ¶ 1206.
[6] Code Sec. 1362(d)(1).
[7] Reg. § 1.1362-6(a)(3).
[8] Reg. § 1.1362-6(a)(3).
[9] Code Sec. 6037.

[10] See, e.g., IRS Letter Rulings 8336033 (June 6, 1983) and 8336014 (June 1, 1983).
[11] Reg. § 1.1362-6(a)(4).
[12] Code Sec. 1362(d)(1).
[13] Code Sec. 1362(f)(1).
[14] IRS Letter Ruling 9750036 (September 11, 1997).

A prime tax reason for electing S status is to pass start-up losses directly through to the shareholders. Once the S corporation is profitable, there may be tax reasons to discontinue S status (e.g., to take advantage of lower corporate income tax rates and the dividends-received deduction[15]). The passive loss rules[16] offer another reason for revoking S status, in that a closely held C corporation, unlike an S corporation, can offset passive losses against active income.[17]

.02 Effective Date of Revocation

Various dates can be chosen for revoking S status. For instance, a revocation made on or before the 15th day of the third month of an S corporation tax year is retroactive and in effect for the entire tax year, and thus, there would not be any S corporation year.[18] However, a revocation made after the fifteenth day of the third month of the S corporation tax year will cause the revocation to be effective on the first day of the following tax year.[19]

Overriding the above revocation specifications is Code Sec. 1362(d)(1)(D)'s general statement that

> If the revocation specifies a date for revocation which is on or after the day on which the revocation is made, the revocation shall be effective on and after the date so specified.

Thus, shareholders holding more than 50 percent of an S corporation's stock could elect a date of revocation to be the date the revocation is made or any date thereafter.

Example 12-1: Anatom Inc., an S corporation, is formed on January 1, 2010, and has one shareholder, Paula Price. Anatom Inc. files its tax return on a calendar-year basis. On February 15, 2010, Price, the sole shareholder, decides to revoke the S corporation status. Anatom Inc. will file as a calendar-year C corporation for 2010.

Example 12-2: Assume the same facts as in Example 12-1, but Price revokes the S status on April 1, 2010, not specifying when the revocation will go into effect. Anatom Inc. will file as an S corporation for 2010, but as of January 1, 2011, it will file as a C corporation.

Example 12-3: Assume the same facts as in Example 12-2, but in filing the revocation on April 1, 2010, Price specifies that the revocation shall go into effect on July 1, 2010. The effect is that Anatom Inc. will be an S corporation for a six-month period, January 1 to June 30, 2010, and a C corporation for the rest of its life unless it reelects S status. Further, Anatom Inc. will file two short returns: one as an S corporation from January 1 to June 30, 2010, and the other as a C corporation from July 1 to December 31, 2010.

Tax Pointer 1: Filing Form 1120 instead of Form 1120S may be determined by the IRS as a sufficient statement to cause a revocation of S status,

---

[15] Code Sec. 243.
[16] Code Sec. 469.
[17] Code Sec. 469(a)(2)(B).

[18] Code Sec. 1362(d)(1)(C)(i).
[19] Code Sec. 1362(d)(1)(C)(ii).

especially if the corporation has only one shareholder.[20] The revocation, however, will not be effective until the year of filing (or the following taxable year if filed after the 15th day of the third month).

    Tax Pointer 2: A 50-percent-or-more shareholder can cause a revocation of S status by transferring more than 50 percent of the corporation's stock to another shareholder who refuses to consent to S status.[21]

.03 Rescinding an Intentional Revocation

The shareholders of an S corporation opting for revocation may wish to change their minds before the revocation's effective date. Unfortunately, there is no specific statutory authority allowing an S corporation to rescind an intentional revocation. However, if action is taken before the intentional revocation date, that revocation can be rescinded and S status will remain.[22]

.04 Effect of Bankruptcy on Revocation

By definition, an S corporation can go bankrupt and revoke its S status. However, if the S corporation revokes its S status to become a C corporation, then in bankruptcy, taxes on any taxable transaction are paid by the corporation; they are not passed through to the corporate shareholders to pay. This revocation could have enormous tax consequences. For instance, in *The Majestic Star Casino, LLC v. Barden Development, Inc.*,[23] a case involving a QSUB, the court held that S corporation status is not a property right; thus, creditors cannot object if the S corporation shareholders revoke S status. The result was that approximately 2.26 million dollars of estimated income tax was not paid to the Indiana Department of Revenue for 2010 by the shareholders on revocation. The court in reaching its decision acknowledged *In re Trans-Line West, Inc.*[24] and its ilk, but stated that it "decline[d] to follow the rationale of Trans-Line West and its progeny, and we conclude that S-corp status is not 'property' within the meaning of the Code."

.05 Revocation and Re-Election of S Corporation Status

A C corporation could elect S status, then revoke it, and subsequently re-elect it, selling the S corporate assets, with the question being the operation of Code Sec. 1374 in terms of the sale of the assets. The Department of the Treasury promulgated Reg. §1.1374-8 and -10 to address this point. For a discussion of the temporary regulations, see ¶ 802.01.

¶ 1203 Failure to Remain an S Corporation

Electing S corporation status is not a one-time event; it is a status that needs to be continually monitored. Once an S corporation fails to meet one of the require-

---

[20] *A.N. Hoffman,* 47 TC 218, Dec. 28,193 (1966). Aff'd, per curiam, CA-5, 68-1 USTC ¶ 9284, 391 F2d 930, but see *F.E. Poulter,* 26 TCM 1092, Dec. 28,659(M), TC Memo. 1967-220. Aff'd, per curiam, CA-4, 68-2 USTC ¶ 9477, 397 F2d 415.

[21] *T.J. Henry Associates, Inc.,* 80 TC 886, Dec. 40,110. Acq., 1984-1 CB 2 where a father, a principal shareholder in an S corporation, transferred stock to himself as custo-

dian for his four children, and as such a custodian, he refused to consent to continue the S status thereby terminating the S election.

[22] Reg. §1.1362-6(a)(4). See also IRS Letter Ruling 9003029 (October 24, 1989).

[23] 2013-1 USTC ¶ 50,338 (3rd Cir. 2013).

[24] 203 B.R. 653, 97-1 USTC ¶ 50,252 (Bankr. ED Tenn. 1996) S status a property right.

ments to be an S corporation,[25] the corporation will lose its S status. In such cases, the inadvertent termination is effective as of the date of the terminating event.[26]

> **Example 12-4:** Gormly Inc. is a calendar-year S corporation. On July 1, 2010, it acquired a nonresident alien as a shareholder, Gloria Fuentes, thereby terminating its S status on July 1, 2010.

Because Gormly Inc. in Example 12-4 ceased to be an S corporation on a date other than the beginning or end of its tax year, it will be forced to file two tax returns: one for the period from January 1 to June 30, 2010, on Form 1120S, and one for the period from July 1 to December 31, 2010, on Form 1120. Thereafter, unless Gormly Inc. can show that its termination was inadvertent[27] or it applies for reelection,[28] it will file a Form 1120 for the rest of its existence.

.01 Rules for Termination

An S election may be terminated[29] either intentionally or inadvertently. An example of an intentional termination[30] is given in *T.J. Henry Associates, Inc.*[31] while an inadvertent termination could arise under many circumstances, one example being when a S corporation fails to keep track of the number of its shareholders and thus has 101 shareholders at one juncture instead of 100. A corporation can take steps to prevent terminating events from occurring by entering into a shareholders' agreement with its shareholders forbidding certain events, such as transferring stock to ineligible shareholders. (See Appendix 4, Shareholders' Agreement, for example language as well as ¶ 1106 for a discussion.) Of course, should a terminating event occur, shareholders may follow procedures to regain the election.[32]

.02 Notification of Termination of S Status

When an S election terminates because the requirements to be an S corporation are no longer being met (e.g, the corporation has 101 shareholders or its QSST failed to make a proper election),[33] the corporation is required to attach to its return for that year a notification that a termination has occurred and the date of termination.[34] However, the IRS has not developed any official form for notification of the termination. Accordingly, a corporation needs to develop its own form (see an example form at Appendix 12, Notice of Revocation of Subchapter S Election) or it may just put a notification on top of its final S corporation return.[35]

---

[25] Code Sec. 1361 requirements are discussed at ¶ 204 (e.g., ineligible shareholders such as nonresident aliens and partnerships).

[26] Code Sec. 1362(d)(2)(B).

[27] Code Sec. 1362(f).

[28] Code Sec. 1362(g).

[29] Code Sec. 1362(d)(2).

[30] Code Sec. 1362(d)(2) rather than under Code Sec. 1362(d)(1).

[31] *T.J. Henry Associates, Inc.,* 80 TC 886, Dec. 40,110. Acq., 1984-1 CB 2 where a father, a principal shareholder in an S corporation, transferred stock to himself as custodian for his four children and as such a custodian refused to consent to continue the S status thereby terminating the S election.

[32] Code Sec. 1362(f) or (g). See discussion at ¶ 1205 and ¶ 1206.

[33] Code Sec. 1361(b).

[34] Reg. § 1.1362-2(b)(1).

[35] IRS Letter Ruling 9750036 (September 11, 1997).

¶ 1204 More than 25 Percent of Gross Receipts from Passive Investment Income

One danger in operating an S corporation with earnings and profits from a C corporation is that the S corporation could incur a penalty tax if more than 25 percent of its gross receipts are from passive investment income.[36] The other danger is that if the S corporation for three consecutive years has earnings and profits and more than 25 percent of its gross receipts from passive investment income, it can lose its S status.[37] The S status would terminate on and after the first day of the first tax year beginning after the third consecutive year in which the S corporation has excessive passive investment income.[38]

On losing an S status, the following should be noted:

- If any part of the termination test is not met (e.g., during one of the three consecutive years, gross receipts are *less* than 25 percent of passive investment income), the S status will not be lost.[39]

- To prevent an inadvertent termination, steps should be taken to remove subchapter C earnings and profits from the corporation.[40]

Example 12-5: HamOil Inc. converted to S status on January 1, 2001, having one shareholder, Rita Croft. At the time of its conversion, it had $1 of subchapter C earnings and profits. In its first two years of operation as an S corporation, its gross receipts consisted of 100% of passive investment income. HamOil Inc. paid the Code Sec. 1375 penalty tax on its passive investment income for the two years involved. In year three, HamOil Inc. had no passive investment income. HamOil Inc. will not lose its S status under Code Sec. 1362(d)(3)(A)(i) because, even though it has subchapter C earnings and profits, it did not have passive investment income exceeding 25% of gross receipts for three consecutive years. Thus, the three-year counting period commences again, starting from the fourth year of its operation.

.01 Definition of C Corporation Earnings and Profits

For an S corporation to be taxed on passive investment income[41] or to lose its S status,[42] it must have accumulated earnings and profits at the close of each of three consecutive tax years. Earnings and profits[43] are defined as

> the earnings and profits of any corporation, including the S corporation or an acquired or predecessor corporation, for any period with respect to which an election under section 1362(a) (or under section 1372 of prior law) was not in effect. The subchapter C earnings and profits of an S corporation are modified as required by section 1371(c).[44]

Tax Pointer: For earnings and profits which exist in an S Corporation for periods for taxable years beginning before January 1, 1983 there exist special rules regarding inclusion. See ¶ 1004.01 for a discussion of these rules.

---

[36] Code Sec. 1375. See ¶ 804 et seq. for a discussion of excess net passive income tax.

[37] Code Sec. 1362(d)(3)(A)(i).

[38] Code Sec. 1362(d)(3)(A)(ii).

[39] Code Sec. 1362(d)(3).

[40] See ¶ 804.01 for a discussion.

[41] Code Sec. 1375.

[42] Code Sec. 1362(d)(3).

[43] Reg. § 1.1362-2(c)(1).

[44] Reg. § 1.1362-2(c)(3).

.02 Elimination of C Corporation Earnings and Profits

The problem regarding C corporation earnings and profits can be avoided if the corporation distributes its E&P to shareholders (as dividends) prior to the effective date of the election. Alternatively, the S corporation can distribute the E&P after the election, though this approach may require the S corporation to elect to make distributions from E&P before distributing its AAA.[45] Alternatively, if there are insufficient funds to make an actual distribution, the corporation can elect to make a deemed dividend of all or part of its E&P.[46] For S corporations with subsidiaries, there are special rules for elimination of the C corporation earnings and profits (see discussion at Chapter 14).

¶ 1205 Waiver of Termination

.01 Inadvertent Termination

An inadvertent termination occurs when an S corporation loses its S election pursuant to Code Sec. 1362(d)(2) and (3) (failure to satisfy requirements on excess passive income for three consecutive years) and the IRS deems the termination was inadvertent. To prevent unwarranted tax results from an inadvertent termination, Congress has provided ways for an S status to be restored. For example, if the corporation, within a reasonable time after discovering the inadvertent termination, takes steps to restore S status, and/or the corporation and all persons who were shareholders during the effective period agree to make whatever adjustments are required by the IRS, the S status will be restored pursuant to Code Sec. 1362(f).

However, Code Sec. 1362(f) does not describe the types of inadvertent terminations that are covered. The Senate Finance Committee Report to the Subchapter S Revision Act of 1982 (SSRA Senate Finance Committee Report) states that the IRS should grant waivers and restore S status when no tax avoidance will result.[47] Examples of what the SSRA Senate Finance Committee Report felt would not be tax avoidance were inadvertent breaches of the one-class-of-stock requirements of Code Sec. 1361(b)(1)(D) and inadvertent violations of the passive income rules of Code Sec. 1362(d)(3) if the shareholders agreed to treat any additional income from C corporation years, arising from an audit, as a dividend.

Further examples are found in IRS Letter Rulings. In IRS Letter Ruling 8523097,[48] an attorney advised a major shareholder of an S corporation that he would not cause the S status of the corporation to terminate if he transferred a portion of his stock to two trusts established for the benefit of the shareholder's children. The attorney who rendered this advice was also the attorney for the S corporation. In fact, the attorney's advice was wrong, and the trusts were not permitted shareholders under Code Sec. 1361. In the year subsequent to termination, a new attorney discovered that the S corporation terminated in the prior year when the trusts became shareholders. When the new attorney learned about the inadvertent termination, steps were immediately taken to transfer the stock held by

---

[45] Code Sec. 1368(e)(3). See discussion at ¶ 1004.03 for the means to make this distribution.

[46] Reg. § 1.1368-1(f)(3). See discussion at ¶ 1004.03 for the means to make this distribution.

[47] Senate Report No. 640 to the 97th Congress, Second Session, 12 (1982).

[48] IRS Letter Ruling 8523097 (March 15, 1985).

the trusts to permitted shareholders. The IRS, under Code Sec. 1362(f), restored the S status retroactive to the terminating event.

> ***Tax Pointer:*** Code Sec. 1362(f) (waiver of termination) does not apply to voluntary revocations under Code Sec. 1362(d)(1). Consequently, if an S corporation revokes its S status under Code Sec. 1362(d)(1), and it wants to have its S status restored, it will have to wait five years before reelecting.[49]

.02 Requesting Relief for Inadvertent Termination

Proof that termination was inadverent. A corporation has the burden of proof that termination was inadvertent according to Reg. § 1.1362-4(b):

> The fact that the terminating event was not reasonably within the control of the corporation and was not part of a plan to terminate the election, or the fact that the event took place without the knowledge of the corporation, notwithstanding its due diligence to safeguard itself against such an event, tends to establish that the termination was inadvertent.

Request for relief ruling. A corporation must file a ruling request to obtain relief for a termination, setting forth (among other points per Reg. § 1.1362-4(c)):

> the date of the corporation's election under section 1362(a), a detailed explanation of the event causing termination, when and how the event was discovered, and the steps taken to return the corporation to small business corporation status.

Required adjustments. Reg. § 1.1362-4(d) prescribes that the IRS can require any "adjustments that are appropriate" for the termination to be deemed "inadvertent." For instance, when stock is transferred to an ineligible shareholder causing an inadvertent termination under Code Sec. 1362(f), the Commissioner may require that the ineligible shareholder be treated as a shareholder of the S corporation during the period the ineligible shareholder actually held the corporation's stock. Moreover, the Commissioner may require protective adjustments to prevent any loss of revenue due to the stock being transferred to an ineligible shareholder (e.g., a nonresident alien).

Status determination. Reg. § 1.1362-4(f) prescribes that:

> Inadvertent termination relief may be granted retroactive for all years for which the terminating event was effective, in which case the corporation is treated as if its election had not terminated. Alternatively, relief may be granted only for the period in which the corporation again became eligible for subchapter S treatment, in which case the corporation is treated as a C corporation during the period for which the corporation was not eligible to be an S corporation.

> ***Tax Pointer:*** Neither the regulations nor the Code indicate what is a reasonable time between the termination event, discovering an inadvertent S status termination, and taking the necessary steps to restore S status. IRS Letter Rulings provide some guidance, specifically IRS Letter Ruling 9017010,[50] which sustained a four-year period between the termination event and discovery.

---

[49] Code Sec. 1362(g).

[50] IRS Letter Ruling 9017010 (January 24, 1990).

¶1205.02

.03 Invalid Elections

Code Sec. 1362(f)(1) also authorizes the IRS to provide relief in situations where an S corporation's S election was invalid. As with inadvertent terminations, the S corporation must: show that the "circumstances resulting in such ineffectiveness" were inadvertent; take immediate steps to correct the problem (e.g., having an unforeseen shareholder consent to the election); and (along with each shareholder) agree to any adjustments deemed appropriate by the IRS.

¶ 1206 Reelection After Termination

If an S corporation terminates its S status, either intentionally or inadvertently, it can elect S status again. However, under Code Sec. 1362(g), the corporation or its successor corporation must wait five years to reelect S status unless the IRS consents to a shorter waiting period.

.01 Successor Corporations

A successor corporation is not defined in Code Sec. 1362(g), but Reg. § 1.1362-5(b) states that a corporation is a successor corporation to a corporation whose election under Code Sec. 1362 has been terminated if

(1) 50 percent or more of the stock of the corporation (the new corporation) is owned, directly or indirectly, by the same persons who, on the date of the termination, owned 50 percent or more of the stock of the corporation whose election terminated (the old corporation); and

(2) Either the new corporation acquires a substantial portion of the assets of the old corporation, or a substantial portion of the assets of the new corporation were assets of the old corporation.

.02 Reelecting S Status

The following should be noted when reelecting S status:

- Code Sec. 1362(g) applies only to corporations that lost their S election. If the corporation filed an invalid election, Code Sec. 1362(g) can never apply since the corporation never was an S corporation. Thus the corporation can elect S status at any time.[51]

- The S corporation that has lost its S status has a choice: It can wait the full five-year waiting period and then reelect S status, or it can request reapplication with the IRS's permission during the five-year waiting period with the burden of convincing the IRS to allow reelection on the corporation.

.03 Grounds for Consent to Reelection

Reg. § 1.1362-5(a) lists the following grounds for being able to reelect S status before expiration of the five-year waiting period:

- If stock ownership in the corporation changed by more than 50 percent after the year of termination, this will tend to establish that consent should be granted.

---

[51] Rev. Rul. 71-549, 1971-2 CB 319. See also Reg. § 1.1362-5(c).

- If the events causing the termination were not reasonably within the control of the corporation or shareholders having a substantial interest in the corporation, and these substantial shareholders were not participating in any plan to terminate the election, consent to a new election may be granted.

A number of Revenue Rulings and IRS Letter Rulings have been issued under Code Sec. 1362(g) that apply to various S corporation terminations. Examples of when permission to reelect S status has been granted include:

- Rev. Rul. 78-275[52] —Permission was granted because a recession caused a drop in sales, and the bank required a deposit that caused disqualifying interest income.

- Rev. Rul. 78-333[53] —Permission was granted when a corporation's assets were leased to another party while the shareholder-manager was temporarily disabled and no replacement manager could be found.

- IRS Letter Ruling 8351065[54] —Permission was granted when a real estate downturn caused a lack of home sales for the corporation, resulting in its investment income exceeding 25 percent of gross receipts for three consecutive years.

IRS Letter Ruling 9047010 (August 22, 1990) details a situation where the Internal Revenue Service refused to waive the 5 year re-election period. In IRS Letter Ruling 9047010, the S corporation terminated its election at the request of its bonding company. When the bonding ended, the S corporation, which was composed of the same shareholders at the time it terminated its status, requested waiver under Code Sec. 1362(g). The Internal Revenue Service denied the waiver stating that there was no evidence that the S corporation could not have received a bond from another bonding company which would have allowed them to keep the S election.

.04 Effect of Re-Election after Revocation of S Corporate Status

A C corporation could elect S status, then revoke it, and subsequently re-elect it, selling the S corporate assets, with the question being the operation of Code Sec. 1374 in terms of the sale of the assets. The Department of the Treasury promulgated Reg. §1.1374-8T and 10T to address this point. For a discussion of the temporary regulations, see ¶ 802.01.

¶ 1207 Tax Effects of Termination

When an S corporation's S status is terminated under Code Sec. 1362(d)(1)-(3), various tax effects occur. If the termination is intentional, that is, if the revocation falls under Code Sec. 1362(d)(1)(D) or under the *T.J. Henry Associates*[55] rationale, some tax planning can occur. The discussion in ¶ 1207.01–¶ 1207.04

[52] Rev. Rul. 78-275, 1978-2 CB 221.

[53] Rev. Rul. 78-333, 1978-2 CB 224.

[54] IRS Letter Ruling 8351065 (September 20, 1983).

[55] *T.J. Henry Associates, Inc.*, 80 TC 886, Dec. 40,110. Acq., 1984-1 CB 2. where a father, a principal shareholder

in an S corporation, transferred stock to himself as custodian for his four children and as such a custodian refused to consent to continue the S status thereby terminating the S election.

describes the consequences of termination and identifies options to minimize any adverse tax consequences.

.01 S Termination Year

If an S corporation terminates at a point other than at the beginning or end of the tax year, the tax year is divided into two segments: an S short year and a C short year. The S short year ends on the day before the occurrence of the terminating event, and the C short year begins on the terminating date.[56] As a general rule, items of income, loss, deduction, or credit are allocated proportionately to the C and S short years based on the number of days in each year, using the corporation's normal accounting method as determined under Code Sec. 446.[57] Exceptions to the rule are as follows:

- The pro-rata allocation rules of Code Sec. 1362(e)(2) cannot be used if there is a sale or exchange of 50 percent or more of the S stock during an S termination year.[58]

- If all persons who held stock in the corporation at any time during the S short year and those who were shareholders on the first day of the C short year unanimously consent, the shareholders can have the items of income, loss, and so on reported in each short tax year under normal tax accounting rules using the book method.[59] (See a sample form to make this election at Appendix 13, Consent to Election to Have Items Assigned Under Normal Accounting Rules.)

- Gains recognized by the S corporation in a deemed sale of its assets under Code Sec. 338 (acquisition of stock treated as acquisition of assets) must be allocated to the S corporation tax year ending on the date of the deemed sale of assets.[60]

The tax for a C short year is determined on an annualized basis.[61] Example 12-6 shows the effect of two short years.

> **Example 12-6:** Buena Inc. is a calendar-year S corporation having one shareholder, Fred Fowler. On July 1, 2010, pursuant to Code Sec. 1362(d)(1)(D), Buena's S status terminated. Buena's tax year was thereby divided into two segments: the S short year from January 1 to June 30, 2010, and the C short year from July 1 to December 31, 2010. An analysis of the books indicated that Buena Inc. had profits of $100,000 from January 1 to June 30, 2010, and losses of $40,000 from July 1 to December 31, 2010, or net income of $60,000 for the year. Income, losses, and so on for calendar-year 2010 will be prorated between the S and C short years on a daily basis pursuant to Code Sec. 1362(e)(2), showing $30,000 net income for the S and C short years, unless shareholders elect under Code Sec. 1362(e)(3) to report the taxable income on each return on the basis of income or loss shown on its permanent records ($100,000 of income for the S short year, and $40,000 of loss for the C short year).

---

[56] Code Sec. 1362(e)(1)(A).
[57] Code Sec. 1362(e)(2) and Reg. § 1.1362-3(a).
[58] Code Sec. 1362(e)(6)(D).

[59] Code Sec. 1362(e)(3)(B).
[60] Code Sec. 1362(e)(6)(C).
[61] Code Sec. 1362(e)(5).

Carrybacks or carryovers. The S and C short years are treated as one year for determining the number of tax years to which any item may be carried back or forward by the corporation.[62]

> *Example 12-7:* Kromer Inc., a calendar-year, cash-basis S corporation, terminates its S status on July 1, 2010. At the time of the termination, Kromer Inc. was operating at a loss; however, it was projected that in the C short year (July 1 to December 31, 2010), the company would operate profitably. Based on the accounting analysis for 2010, it was projected that if the pro rata method was used, a profit would be shown in both the S and C short years. However, if the book method were used, the S short year would show a loss and the C year would show income. If the shareholders have basis in their S stock, they may consider electing the book method as a desirable alternative since they can reduce their Form 1040 taxable income from the S short year, assuming no difficulties with various other Code provisions, such as passive loss or at-risk rules, etc. (Because the C corporation's income is not passed through to them, it will not affect the shareholders' Form 1040s.)

Tax return due dates. The due date for filing tax returns for the S short year is the same date as that for the C short year, including extensions.[63]

Stock transfers. If during an S termination year, one or more shareholders sell or exchange 50 percent or more of the corporation's stock, the S corporation must close its books to allocate income between the S and C corporation short years.[64] Pro rata allocation between the short years is not allowed. A gift of stock is not a sale or exchange for this purpose.

> *Example 12-8:* Carl Davis and Dan King are shareholders in Saltry Inc., a calendar-year S corporation. Each owns 50 percent of the issued and outstanding shares of the corporation on December 31, 2009. On March 1, 2010, Davis makes a gift of his entire shareholder interest to Terry Thomas, a nonresident alien. As a result, on March 1, 2010, Saltry Inc. ceases to be a small business corporation and its S election is terminated. As a result of the gift, Thomas owns 50 percent of Saltry Inc.'s issued and outstanding stock. However, because Thomas acquired the stock by gift from Davis rather than by sale or exchange, there has not been a more than 50 percent change in ownership by sale or exchange that would cause the rules of Code Sec. 1362(e)(6)(D) to apply. Saltry Inc. can allocate its 2000 income between the short S and C years on a pro rata daily basis.

.02 Distributions During a Post-Termination Transition Period (PTTP)

S corporation income that has been taxed but not previously distributed to shareholders may be distributed to shareholders as a nontaxable reduction in basis rather than as dividends during the one-year post-termination transition period.[65]

---

[62] Reg. § 1.1362-3(c)(4).
[63] Code Sec. 1362(e)(6)(B).

[64] Code Sec. 1362(e)(6)(D).
[65] Code Sec. 1371(e). For a discussion of the post-termination transition period, see ¶ 912.

.03 No Carryover of S Corporation Attributes

Code Sec. 1371(b)(2) requires that there shall be "no carryforward, and no carryback, . . . at the corporate level for a taxable year for which a corporation is an S corporation." There have been no regulations or IRS letter rulings issued on this area of law, so guidance is limited as to what this provision means.

.04 C Corporation Taxes

When an S corporation election terminates, a C corporation begins. Important tax issues for the C corporation are given below. Note that different tax issues occur depending on whether the S corporation ever was a C corporation before.

S corporations de novo. C corporations, whether or not they were C corporatons prior to their S status, should consider the following:

Borrowing from a retirement plan. Termination of S corporation status is not a trigger event for the repayment of any shareholder-employee loans from the retirement plan; rather, the payment schedule that the shareholder-employee debtor has for the payment of the loan will continue unabated.[66]

Members of a controlled group. When an S corporation becomes a C corporation, it becomes subject to the (1) controlled group rules and the corporate rates under Code Sec. 11, (2) accumulated earnings credit under Code Sec. 535, and so on.[67]

Estimated taxes. Because there may be taxable income under Code Sec. 11 when an S election terminates, the C corporation is liable for estimated taxes.

Former S corporations that were former C corporations. A C corporation, when it elects S status, basically keeps in limbo its C corporation attributes, namely, net operating losses (NOLs), passive losses under Code Sec. 469, etc. (unless the newly elected S corporation disposes of the assets as detailed at ¶ 404.13). When the S corporation returns to being a C corporation, the former C corporation attributes come into play. For example, assume that in the year a C corporation elected S status, it had an NOL of $10,000. When the corporation terminates its S status after five years and regains its C status, it will be able to apply the NOL carryforward against its C corporation income. Note, however, that five years of the NOL carryforward period will have lapsed.

¶ 1208 Sale of Stock

There are two ways to sell an S corporation—the sale of its assets or the sale of its stock.[68] Sale of stock presents a difficult situation because a buyer of the stock is stuck with what the prior shareholders have done with the corporation. Also, the new shareholders, unless they elect a Code Sec. 338 liquidation,[69] are stuck with the basis, not the fair market value, of the corporate assets. Sellers of S corporation stock prefer sales of stock because sellers receive capital gains rather than ordinary

---

[66] See ¶ 1302.06 for a fuller discussion of retirement plan shareholder loans.

[67] Code Sec. 1561 et seq. Controlled groups are also discussed at ¶ 205.

[68] See ¶ 1112.02 and ¶ 1112.03 for more discussion.

[69] See ¶ 1210.09 for discussion.

income. The rules and consequences of stock sales are discussed from ¶ 1208.01–¶ 1208.09.

Alternatives to the sale of stock. In contrast to selling stock, sales of assets can yield ordinary income depending on the type of assets being sold (e.g., depreciation recapture). Another alternative to the sale of stock may be a redemption of a shareholder's stock.[70] A redemption is used when a corporation has the necessary funds to make the acquisition of the stock while the remaining shareholders remain and run the company. Yet another alternative is a reorganization.[71]

.01 Computing a Seller's Gain and Loss

An S shareholder's gain or loss on the sale of S corporation stock is computed under Code Sec. 1001(a) just as if stock in a C corporation was sold. Gain or loss is determined by the difference between the amount received for the stock and the seller's basis. A shareholder's basis in S corporation stock is adjusted for the amount of income and loss passed through to the shareholders plus the amount of distributions (other than distributions from E&P). If a sale occurs other than at the beginning or end of the S corporation tax year, adverse tax consequences could develop because the selling shareholder will not know his, her, or its basis until the end of the tax year, unless the books are closed pursuant to Code Sec. 1377(a)(2).

> **Tax Pointer:** A shareholders' agreement should be in place restricting the sales of stock as well as handling the effects of any sale; in particular, the agreement should address the procedure for determining whether the corporation will make the Code Sec. 1377(a)(2) election to close the S corporation books on the day of sale.[72]

> **Example 12-9:** There is no shareholders' agreement for Breadmakers Inc., a calendar-year S corporation, composed of three sisters who are equal shareholders, Connie, Brenda, and Joanne Topper. On March 1, 2010, Joanne sells her stock to Darla Peters, a qualified S corporation shareholder. Darla refuses to consent to the Code Sec. 1377(a)(2) election to close the S corporation books; however, Joanne is confident that a capital loss will result on the sale. At the time of the sale, Joanne projects that her basis at $10,000 will produce a capital loss since Darla is only paying $7,500 for the stock. At the end of the year when the income and loss of Breadmakers Inc. is determined, it is found that Joanne's basis at the time of sale was $6,500 instead of $10,000 since Breadmakers Inc. operated at a loss for 2010 and Joanne's share of the loss (up to the March 1 sale) was $3,500 based on the pro rata method of Code Sec. 1362(e)(2). Thus, Joanne realizes a $1,000 gain on the sale ($7,500 – [$10,000 – $6,500] stock basis) instead of the $2,500 projected loss.

.02 Requirements for Making a Code Sec. 1377(a)(2) Election

Code Sec. 1377(a)(2) election. To terminate the year and close the S corporation books by making a Code Sec. 1377(a)(2) election, the following requirements must be met.

---

[70] See ¶ 1209 for discussion.
[71] See ¶ 1211 for discussion.

[72] See ¶ 1106 for a discussion of shareholders' agreements and Appendix 4 for example language.

Entire interest terminated with consent. The Code Sec. 1377(a)(2) election can only be made if the selling shareholder terminates his, her, or its entire interest in the S corporation and all the "affected shareholders" consent. Reg. § 1.1377-1(b)(2) defines an "affected shareholder" as "the shareholder whose interest is terminated and all shareholders to whom such shareholder has transferred shares during the taxable year." If such a shareholder has transferred shares to the corporation, the term "affected shareholder" includes all persons who were its shareholders during that tax year.

A shareholder's entire interest in an S corporation is not terminated if the shareholder retains ownership of any stock (including an interest treated as stock under Reg. § 1.1361-1(l)) that would result in the shareholder continuing to be considered a shareholder of the corporation for purposes of Code Sec. 1362(a)(2). Thus, in determining whether a shareholder's entire interest in an S corporation has been terminated, any interest held by the shareholder as a creditor, employee, director, or in any other nonshareholder capacity is disregarded.

Termination events. Reg. § 1.1377-1(b)(4) lists the following events, any of which will satisfy the requirement that a shareholder's entire interest be terminated:

- A sale, exchange, or other disposition of all the shareholder's stock
- A gift of all the shareholder's stock
- A spousal transfer under Code Sec. 1041(a) of all the shareholder's stock
- A redemption, as defined in Code Sec. 317(b), of all the shareholder's stock, regardless of the tax treatment of the redemption under Code Sec. 302
- The death of the shareholder

Election requirements. Reg. § 1.1377-1(b)(5) provides specific requirements that must be met if the Code Sec. 1377(a)(2) election is to occur:

- A statement must be filed with the S corporation's tax returns for the year when the election is made. (See sample form at Appendix 14, Election to Close Books Upon Termination of Interest by S Corporation Shareholder.)
- The affected S shareholders must sign a consent form. (See sample form at Appendix 15, Shareholders' Consent.)

Examples 12-10 and 12-11 are adapted from Reg. § 1.1377-1(c).

Example 12-10: *Shareholder's pro rata share in a partial stock disposition.* On January 6, 2010, DimSum incorporates as a calendar-year corporation, issues 100 shares of common stock to both Kim Wall and Carl Case, and files an election to be an S corporation for its 2010 tax year. On July 24, 2010, Case sells 50 shares of his DimSum stock to Mike Lee. Thus, in 2010, Wall owned 50 percent of the outstanding shares of DimSum on each day of DimSum's 2010 tax year, Case owned 50 percent on each day from January 6, 2010, to July 24, 2010 (200 days), and 25 percent from July 25, 2010, to December 31, 2010 (160 days), and Lee owned 25 percent from July 25, 2010, to December 31, 2010 (160 days).

¶1208.02

Because Case's entire interest in DimSum is not terminated when he sells 50 shares to Lee on July 24, 2010, DimSum cannot make a terminating election under Code Sec. 1377(a)(2). Although Case's sale of 50 shares to Lee is a qualifying disposition under Reg. § 1.1368-1(g)(2)(i), DimSum does not make an election to terminate its tax year under Reg. § 1.1368-1(g)(2). During its 2000 tax year, DimSum has nonseparately computed income of $720,000.

For each day in DimSum's 2010 tax year, Wall's daily pro rata share of DimSum's nonseparately computed income is $1,000 (($720,000 ÷ 360 days) × .50 ownership). Thus, Wall's pro rata share of DimSum's nonseparately computed income for 2010 is $360,000 ($1,000 × 360 days). Case's daily pro rata share of DimSum's nonseparately computed income is $1,000 (($720,000 ÷ 360 days × .50 ownership) for the first 200 days and $500 (($720,000 ÷ 360 days × .25 ownership) for the following 160 days. Thus, Case's pro rata share of DimSum's nonseparately computed income for 2010 is $280,000 (($1,000 × 200 days) + ($500 × 160 days)). Lee's daily pro rata share of DimSum's nonseparately computed income is $500 (($720,000 ÷ 360 days × .25 ownership) for 160 days. Thus, Lee's pro rata share of DimSum's nonseparately computed income for 2010 is $80,000 ($500 × 160 days).

Example 12-11: *Shareholder's pro rata share when an S corporation makes a terminating election under Code Sec. 1377(a)(2).* On January 6, 2010, Ferret Inc. incorporates as a calendar-year corporation, issues 100 shares of common stock to both Susan Adler and Barb Brady, and files an election to be an S corporation for its 2010 tax year. On July 24, 2010, Brady sells her entire 100 shares of Ferret Inc. stock to Jake Searle. With the consent of Brady and Searle, Ferret Inc. makes an election under Code Sec. 1377(a)(2) for the termination of Brady's entire interest arising from Brady's sale of 100 shares to Searle. As a result of the election, the pro rata shares of Brady and Searle are determined as if Ferret Inc.'s tax year consisted of two separate tax years, the first of which ends on July 24, 2010, the date Brady's entire interest in Ferret Inc. terminates. Because Adler is not an affected shareholder as defined by Code Sec. 1377(a)(2)(B), the treatment as separate tax years does not apply to Adler.

Requirements for electing to terminate a tax year under Reg. § 1.1368-1(g)(2). Reg. § 1.1368-1(g)(2) prescribes that if there is a "qualifying disposition" of stock in an S corporation, the books can be closed at the transfer of that substantial stock interest. A shareholder may want this when less than an entire stock interest is transferred or sold (as could have occurred in Example 12-10), or if the stock is issued to one or more new shareholders. Specifically, Reg. § 1.1368-1(g)(1) provides that if an election is made under Reg. § 1.1368-1(g)(2) to terminate the year when there is a qualifying disposition, then the tax year is divided into separate tax years for purposes of allocating income, loss, etc. among the shareholders, the first of which ends at the close of the day on which there is a qualifying disposition of stock. (Note that the S corporation files only one return for the year.) A qualifying disposition is defined as:

¶1208.02

(A) A disposition by a shareholder of 20 percent or more of the outstanding stock of the corporation in one or more transactions during any thirty-day period during the corporation's taxable year;

(B) A redemption treated as an exchange under section 302(a) or section 303(a) of 20 percent or more of the outstanding stock of the corporation from a shareholder in one or more transactions during any thirty-day period during the corporation's taxable year; or

(C) An issuance of an amount of stock equal to or greater than 25 percent of the previously outstanding stock to one or more new shareholders during any thirty-day period during the corporation's taxable year.

Making the election under Reg. § 1.1368-1(g)(2). Reg. § 1.1368-1(g)(2)(iii) prescribes the time, manner, and means of making the election. (See a sample form at Appendix 16, Election to Close Books Under Reg. § 1.1368-1(g)(2)(i).)

Coordinating with Code Sec, 1377(a)(2)'s election to close the books. An election to close the S corporation books under Code Sec. 1377(a)(2) takes precedence over an election under Reg. § 1.1368-2(g)(2).

.03 Character of a Seller's Gain or Loss

The gain or loss from a stock sale will generally be treated as a capital gain or loss.[73] If the stock is qualified Code Sec. 1244 stock, up to $50,000 ($100,000 for married taxpayers filing jointly) of any loss realized may be deductible as ordinary loss.

.04 Tax Consequences of a Sale

A sale of S corporation stock generates the following tax consequences.

Risks in buying stock. When S corporation stock is sold, the buyer of the stock is assuming a risk that the corporation may have unforeseen liabilities (e.g., environmental liabilities) that, if they arise after the sale, will be payable by the buyer unless the buyer protects him-, her-, or itself as discussed below.

> *Example 12-12:* Bernie Houser formed ColdAir Inc. in 1999 and was its sole shareholder. In 2008, a driver driving a truck owned by ColdAir Inc. was involved in an accident in which another motorist was injured. However, the victim did not sue the corporation until 2010. Houser was never told of the accident by the driver, nor did he see any evidence of damages on the truck. In 2009, Jim West purchased all of Houser's stock, receiving an indemnification and hold harmless agreement from Houser. In 2010, West requests Houser to indemnify and hold him harmless for the truck accident victim's lawsuit; however, Houser, who is having financial difficulty, declares bankruptcy, leaving West to defend the lawsuit on his own.

It is possible to minimize the risks of buying stock by (1) having the seller of the stock indemnify and hold the buyer harmless in case of losses (securitizing the hold harmless agreement with an irrevocable letter of credit); (2) having the buyer purchase the stock with long-term notes that contain the right of set-off in the event that the representations of the seller in the sales agreement prove untrue; or (3)

---

[73] Code Sec. 1222.

having the seller personally guarantee and warrant that the representations contained in the contract are true. However, there is still the risk that claims will be made that will exceed the indemnity, set-off, guarantee, etc. Accordingly, buyers should consider the risks very carefully before purchasing stock rather than assets.

No depreciation recapture. When sale of S corporation stock occurs, there appears to be no statutory provision requiring recapture of depreciable property.[74] Thus, a seller of S corporation stock could leave an unsophisticated buyer with a large amount of unforeseen future tax liability.

> *Example 12-13:* Streeter Inc., a calendar-year S corporation formed on January 1, 1970, has one shareholder, Hana Barron. In 1970, Steeter Inc. purchased $500,000 of depreciable business assets that have since been completely depreciated. Barron sold her stock in Streeter Inc. to Geoff Lane, a qualified S corporation shareholder, for $500,000 on January 1, 2009, with the $500,000 representing the fair market value of Streeter Inc. at the time (no Code Sec. 338 election was made). At the time of the stock sale, Steeter Inc. had no assets other than the fully depreciated business assets purchased in 1970. In 2010, Streeter Inc. disposed of all of its assets for $600,000. Lane will have to report depreciation recapture of $500,000 on the sale of the Code Sec. 1231 assets.

> *Example 12-14:* Assume the same facts as in Example 12-13, but instead of buying Streeter Inc.'s stock from Barron, Lane bought the business assets from Steeter Inc. for $500,000 and then disposed of them in 2009. Now, Barron faces the depreciation recapture of $500,000, not Lane. Upon obtaining Streeter Inc.'s assets, Lane sold them immediately for $600,000. Lane only has $100,000 of income ($600,000 – $500,000).

No step up in basis of assets. As Example 12-13 indicates, when S corporation stock is acquired, the buyer does not obtain a step up in basis for the assets. Thus, in Example 12-13, Lane owns a corporation that is worth $500,000, but if the corporation sells the assets, depreciation recapture will be generated for a maximum of $500,000. Further, Lane cannot obtain a depreciation deduction from Streeter Inc.'s assets because they are completely depreciated. If Lane could step up Streeter Inc.'s assets to their fair market value, $500,000, then Lane could depreciate his investment, simultaneously minimizing the tax consequences of any sale of Streeter Inc.'s assets. However, the only statutory method to step up Streeter Inc.'s assets when a stock acquisition is made is to use Code Sec. 338, but acquisitions of stock under Code Sec. 338 are prohibitive from a tax point of view for the buyer, unless the seller compensates the buyer for the taxes incurred in the acquisition. Thus, in many cases, buyers will prefer to buy assets instead of stock to obtain a step up in basis.

Alternatively, the buyer of S corporation stock could ask the selling shareholder(s) to allocate part of the purchase price to a noncompete agreement or similar right subject to amortization under Code Sec. 197. Of course, the selling shareholder(s) would have to recognize ordinary income if a consulting agreement

---

[74] Code Secs. 1245 and 1250 et seq.

or a covenant not to compete was used, thereby making the result less attractive from their perspective. Notwithstanding, there may be a middle ground that could satisfy both the buyer and seller of the stock.[75]

Using covenants not to compete. Covenants not to compete provide attractive tax benefits to the buyer, but also offer important nontax benefits as well. Foreseeably, after the sale of stock (or assets), the selling shareholder could compete with the buyer thereby depriving the buyer of the full benefits of the newly acquired purchase. Accordingly, to protect themselves against unfair competition, buyers should ask the selling shareholder (and if the sale of assets occurs, the S corporation) to sign a covenant not to compete, assuming they are in a bargaining position to obtain one. The covenant's terms, length, etc. should be created according to local law.

Using consulting agreements. Consulting agreements paid to selling shareholders are also used in the sale of S corporation stock since the buyer can allocate part of the purchase price to the agreement and amortize the cost under Code Sec. 197, providing the agreement is reasonable in term and amount. In contrast, if a buyer purchases just assets, the buyer must depreciate or amortize them over their useful lives (vs. the 15 years in a covenant not to compete).[76] Depending on the typical business, a significant portion of the purchase price for the business can be allocated to the consulting agreement, thereby allowing the United States to finance the purchase.[77]

Losses from the sale of stock. The Code Sec. 1244 treatment of losses (losses on small business stock) also applies to the sale of S corporation stock when the selling shareholder has a larger basis than the amount received from the sale. Code Sec. 1244, if it is elected by the shareholder, allows a qualifying seller to take an ordinary loss instead of a capital loss.[78]

Reporting a stock sale on Form 8594. Form 8594, "Asset Acquisition Statement," is used to report the allocation of the purchase price among the assets acquired in a taxable acquisition under Code Sec. 1060. It is also used to report allocations permitted under Code Sec. 197, such as an allocation of a purchase price to a customer list.[79]

Shareholder-employee bonuses. If an S corporation pays a bonus to a shareholder-employee in the year his or her stock is sold to the remaining shareholders, the bonus is deductible by the remaining shareholders providing the compensation is reasonable, not a disguised dividend, etc. For example, if an S corporation has a number of shareholder-employees and one is selling his or her stock, and if there is leeway in arriving at a purchase price for the selling shareholder-employee's stock because the selling shareholder-employee is not in a strong bargaining position, a portion of the stock price could be paid to the selling

---

[75] See Michael Schlesinger, "Covenants Not to Compete Are Still Useful After RRA '93," *Taxation for Accountants,* Vol. 51, No. 4 at 204 (October 1993); Michael Schlesinger, "Consider Consulting and Non-Compete Agreements When Selling a Business," *Practical Tax Strategies*, Vol. 68, No. 5 at 260 (May 2002).

[76] *Ibid.*

[77] *Ibid.*

[78] See ¶ 1114 for a discussion of Code Sec. 1244.

[79] For an interesting case regarding an allocation of purchase price to a customer list, see ¶ 1210.09 and *Martin Ice Cream Co.,* 110 TC 189, Dec. 52,624.

shareholder-employee as compensation (i.e., a bonus) thereby allowing the remaining shareholders to purchase the stock with before-tax dollars rather than after-tax dollars. For an example of a similar situation, see IRS Letter Ruling 8609052[80] in which a payment of a bonus to a shareholder-employee in a liquidation under former Code Sec. 337 occurred. The result of the IRS Letter Ruling was that depreciation recapture, in effect, was offset by the buyer's deduction for the bonus payment to the seller, thereby allowing the selling shareholder-employee to receive earned income from the sale for purposes of a pension contribution.

Termination of S status. If there is more than a 50 percent change of stock ownership, the new shareholder(s) may revoke the S status.[81] Likewise, if a shareholder(s) sells stock to a nonpermitted S corporation shareholder (e.g., a partnership), the S status will be terminated.[82] Accordingly, care should be exercised when selling S corporation stock to ensure that it is not a terminating event.

.05 Reasons a Stock Sale Is Desired

As would be expected, there may be situations in which a stock sale may be the only way to proceed, even though there are risks in purchasing the stock of an S corporation. The following situations might make a stock sale advantageous.

Assets are subject to the installment method. On December 17, 1999, Congress severely limited the use of installment sales for most assets by prescribing that the gain from such a sale has to be reported in the year of sale notwithstanding the terms of any installment note(s) used by the buyer with respect to the sale.[83] The IRS in Rev. Proc. 2001-10[84] has attempted to limit the harsh effects of Code Sec. 453A(d)(4) by prescribing that if the S corporation has average annual gross receipts of $1 million or less for three consecutive years, the S corporation can use the installment method to report the gain on the sale.[85] Practitioners should also be aware that Congress may repeal the amendments to Code Sec. 453 that limit use of installment sales.

If the S corporation cannot qualify for Rev. Proc. 2001-10's "break," then the S corporation shareholder(s) may be forced to sell his, her, or its stock to obtain installment sale treatment—a task that may be impossible to achieve because of all the risks the buyer will assume on the purchase of the stock, unless the selling shareholder(s) significantly reduces its price. Alternatively, allocation of the purchase price can occur, such as having the selling shareholder(s) enter into a consulting agreement with the buyer.[86] While utilization of a consulting agreement to a selling shareholder produces ordinary income and self-employment tax rather than capital gain from the installment sale, the advantage to the selling shareholder, if the consulting agreement is for more than one year, is to spread out the income over the life of the agreement, rather than computing the capital gain in one year, and possibly incur alternative minimum tax.

---

[80] IRS Letter Ruling 8609052 (December 2, 1985).
[81] Code Sec. 1362(d)(1).
[82] Code Sec. 1362(d)(2).
[83] Code Sec. 453A(d)(4).
[84] Rev. Proc. 2001-10, 2001-1 CB 272.

[85] Besides assisting "small" S corporations (annual gross receipts of $1 million or less) sell their assets, Rev. Proc. 2000-22 also helps them use the cash method to report income, expense, etc. while having inventories.
[86] See discussion at ¶ 1208.04.

Example 12-15: Freedom Inc. is an S corporation with one shareholder, Philip Rose. When Freedom Inc. was incorporated, Rose acquired all its stock for $10 million. Freedom Inc. used the $10 million to acquire a piece of land that it rents out to third parties. In 2010, Freedom Inc. was approached by a buyer offering $25 million for the land under the installment method, meaning that Freedom Inc. receives a mortgage to secure the debt. The mortgage terms include no down payment, a balloon of $25 million due 10 years from the date of sale, and a two-points-above-prime interest rate.

If Freedom Inc. goes ahead with selling the land through the corporation, it has the problem of Code Sec. 453A rules and limitations. However, if Rose were to sell his stock in Freedom Inc. to the buyer, securing the installment sale of his stock with the land, by definition, Code Sec. 453A will not apply. Note that when the buyer buys stock instead of property, the buyer will not obtain a stepped-up basis; however, the buyer may be willing to buy the stock if he or she can get a balloon mortgage similar to the one described above for the land.

Assets with a short depreciation life. Congress is constantly changing depreciable lives for various reasons. Foreseeably, an S corporation could purchase an asset with a depreciable life that increases by the time it is being sold. Accordingly, a buyer, sensing the disparity, may be more inclined to purchase the stock of the S corporation rather than its assets so that the corporation can keep the advantage of the asset's shorter depreciation life.

Avoidance of Code Sec. 1374's gain on the sale. Code Sec. 1374, if it applies, can impose a double tax on the sale of corporate assets. To avoid this consequence, shareholders may want to utilize a sale of S corporate stock to a buyer with the buyer utilizing a Code Sec. 338(h)(10) election to step up the basis of the assets acquired through the stock purchase to fair market value. For a discussion of built in gain, see ¶ 802; for a discussion of a Code Sec. 338(h)(10) election, see ¶ 1210.09 and ¶ 1404.02.

.06 Removing Assets from a Sale

When a buyer purchasing S corporation stock does not wish to purchase certain assets of the corporation (or when a selling shareholder wishes to keep certain assets), the shareholders can use a *Zenz v. Quinlivan*[87] redemption to eliminate the unwanted assets from the sale. Basically, a *Zenz v. Quinlivan* redemption occurs at the time of the sale—the selling shareholder redeems stock in exchange for the unwanted assets, and the buyer buys the remaining stock.

Example 12-16: Assume the same facts as in Example 12-15, except that Freedom Inc., besides having the land on its balance sheet, also has $1 million in cash. Further, the total capital stock issued to Rose is 26 shares of common stock. The buyer has indicated to Rose that in the purchase of Rose's stock he only wants one asset, the corporation's land. Accordingly, Rose will sell his stock to the buyer as follows: he will sell 25 shares for the buyer's $25 million

[87] *Zenz v. Quinlivan*, CA-6, 54-2 USTC ¶ 9445, 213 F2d 914.

note and will redeem one share for the $1 million in cash based on the *Zenz v. Quinlivan* rationale.

.07 Effect That a Sale of Stock Has on the Accumulated Adjustments Account and Retained Earnings and Profits

An S corporation's accumulated adjustments account (AAA) is a corporate level account, just like a C corporation's retained earnings and profits (E&P) account is a corporate level account—neither belongs to the shareholders.[88] However, the shareholders are able to withdraw earnings left in the corporate AAA account tax free. Similarly, if an S corporation has retained E&P from a predecessor C corporation, or due to a reorganization under Code Sec. 368, it also is a corporate account, not a personal one.

When an S corporation shareholder sells his, her, or its stock interest, the sale has no effect on the S corporation's AAA and E&P, and nothing has to be eliminated from the corporate balance sheet. The purchasing shareholder has a proportionate claim to the AAA, just like the selling shareholder did during his, her, or its tenure. No dividend or distribution of AAA is taxed to the selling shareholder.

> **Example 12-17:** Quash Inc., a calendar-year S corporation since inception, has two equal shareholders, Sol Binder and Yuri Feldman. Binder sells his entire stock interest to Art Metz on December 31, 2009, for $2,000. At the time of the sale, Quash Inc. had AAA of $500 because the shareholders (Binder and Feldman) decided to leave the S corporation earnings in the S corporation, rather than distribute them. For the year 2010, Quash Inc. broke even; notwithstanding, the corporation distributed $500 of AAA to both shareholders ($250 each). The distribution is tax free to Metz and Feldman, even though Metz was not a shareholder when the AAA earnings were created.

¶ 1209 Redemptions

A redemption of S corporation stock occurs when an S corporation shareholder sells his, her, or its stock to the corporation.[89] The tax treatment of redemptions is discussed in the following sections.

.01 Code Sec. 302 Redemptions

If the requirements of Code Secs. 302 or 303 are met (i.e., a redemption of stock is not essentially equivalent to a dividend), then a shareholder's redemption will be treated as a capital transaction, allowing a redeeming shareholder capital gain or loss treatment.[90]

An S corporation shareholder selling his, her, or its interest in an S corporation should consider a redemption under the following circumstances:

(1) There is no buyer willing to pay the price desired for the stock, but the corporation has sufficient assets to make the acquisition.

---

[88] Code Sec. 1368(e)(1)(A). For a discussion of the AAA account, see ¶ 1004.

[89] Code Sec. 317 and Code Sec. 1371(a).

[90] Code Sec. 302 and 302(b)(1).

(2) A buyer does not want certain assets, and, under the *Zenz v. Quinlivan*[91] rationale, a selling shareholder can redeem a pro rata portion of his, her, or its stock for those unwanted assets.

(3) A buyer has funds to acquire a shareholder's interest, but, for various reasons, does not wish to use them to acquire all the stock, preferring that a portion of the stock be redeemed by the S corporation while buying the rest (i.e., a part-redemption/ part-sale). (This alternative usually arises in a family S corporation when one family member is leaving but the others are staying.)

(4) The shareholder needs a distribution of cash or other property, but other shareholders will not receive comparable distributions. When one share-holder is to receive a distribution but others are not, the parties should consider structuring the transaction as a stock redemption in order to avoid a challenge from the IRS that the S corporation has two classes of stock. If the redemption does not qualify under Code Secs. 302 or 303 (e.g., because the other shareholders are related to the one redeeming shares), the redemption will be treated as a distribution for tax purposes. Consequently, to the extent the redemption proceeds do not exceed the tax basis of all the shareholder's stock (rather than just the redeemed shares), no gain or loss will be recognized by the shareholder.

Tax Pointer: The IRS does not like part-redemption/part-sales because the remaining acquiring shareholder(s) are using corporate funds to relieve them of an obligation to purchase corporate stock.[92]

When a corporation engages in a redemption, it can pay for the stock with cash, property, or notes,[93] or in any combination of the three. Alternatively, the corporation can redeem a shareholder's interest using a private annuity.[94]

.02 Qualifying for Capital Gain Treatment

For capital gain treatment to apply to a redemption, a shareholder must completely redeem his, her, or its interest in the corporation.[95] Frequently, in an S corporation composed of family members, the redeemed shareholder (e.g., Dad) wants to retain control of the corporation or the remaining family members (e.g., the children). However, the IRS has struck down attempts at control. See, for example, Rev. Rul. 71-426[96] where a former shareholder's redemption transaction was treated as ordinary income rather than capital gains because the shareholder acted as a voting trustee of a trust that held the remaining corporate stock for the benefit of the remaining shareholder's children. Rev. Rul. 81-233[97] likewise pre-

---

[91] *Zenz v. Quinlivan,* CA-6, 54-2 USTC ¶ 9445, 213 F2d 914.

[92] See, e.g., *D. Jacobs,* 41 TCM 951, Dec. 37,709(M), TC Memo. 1981-81. Aff'd, per curiam, CA-6, 83-1 USTC ¶ 9193, 698 F2d 850.

[93] For the interest expense that the S corporation incurs, there is scant guidance to detail how the S corporation characterizes it (i.e., investment interest, business interest, etc.). Presumably, the general rules discussed at ¶ 702 and ¶ 911 will apply.

[94] See ¶ 1110 for a discussion of private annuities.

[95] Code Sec. 302(b)(3).

[96] Rev. Rul. 71-426, 1971-2 CB 173.

[97] Rev. Rul. 81-233, 1981-2 CB 83. But see *R.E. Hurst,* 124 TC No. 16, where a seller's continuing ties to the business did not bar capital gains treatment for an S corporate redemption.

scribed ordinary income treatment for a redemption when the redeemed share-holder was the custodian of stock held under the Uniform Gift to Minors Act (now the Uniform Transfers to Minors Act (UTMA)). Alternatively, the remaining share-holders (i.e., the children) want a tax advantage to result from the redemption by paying compensation to the departing shareholder (i.e., Dad) through a consulting agreement. The consulting agreement reduced the payment needed for the stock by paying the redeeming shareholder with money that was deductible by the corporation. However, cases interpreting this ploy of using compensation have been struck down (see, e.g., *Seda*[98]). Likewise, covenants not to compete cannot be used for tax planning for family members unless there is an economic reality to them.[99]

> ***Tax Pointer:*** Code Sec. 1(h)(11) prescribes that dividends received after 2002 and before 2013 are taxed to shareholders at the rate of 5 percent for individuals in the 10 percent-15 percent bracket, and then a maximum of 15 percent thereafter. Consequently, if an S corporate shareholder fails to qualify for capital gains treatment under Code Sec. 302, the redemption will then be taxed at the special dividend rate as set forth in Code Sec. 1(h)(11). See discussion at ¶ 1209.04 under "Consequences if Redemption Fails to Satisfy Code Sec. 302(b)(1)-3's Tests."

.03 Tax Effect on Remaining Shareholders

When a corporation redeems a shareholder's stock, no tax benefit is produced; in contrast, a tax benefit is produced when a shareholder sells his, her, or its stock to others.

> ***Example 12-18:*** Jerry Sand and Eric Ervin, two individuals, form Servin Ltd. on January 1, 2000, a calendar-year corporation electing S status on formation. The shareholders acquire capital stock for $1,000 each. Servin Ltd. acquires vacant land with the $2,000 on January 1, 2000. The corporation does not engage in any other transactions during its entire tenure. On January 1, 2010, when the vacant land is worth $1 million, Sand approaches Ervin to sell his interest. The shareholders examine their stock basis, determining that each has a stock basis of $1,000. If Sand redeems his stock or sells it to Ervin for $500,000 (one-half of $1 million), Ervin will realize a capital gain of $499,000. If Ervin purchases Sand's stock for $500,000, Ervin's basis for taking losses or computing gain on the sale of the stock will be $501,000 ($1,000 original basis + $500,000). If the corporation redeemed Sand's stock for $500,000, then Ervin's basis for computing gain or taking S corporation losses will be $1,000, because a redemption does not affect his stock basis.

.04 Computing a Shareholder's Gain or Loss

Since a shareholder's redemption of stock is in effect a "sale" of stock to the corporation, the same concepts that enter into a sale (i.e., closing the books, computing basis, etc.) occur with a redemption. The following points should be noted.

---

[98] *L.V. Seda,* 82 TC 484, Dec. 41,067.   [99] See ¶ 1119.06 for buyouts of family members.

Closing the books. If there is a complete termination of a shareholder's interest by redemption, then two short tax years for the redeeming shareholder will be created if the redemption occurs other than on the first or last day of the S corporation's tax year; one for the period before the redemption, and the other for the period after the redemption.[100] When there is not a complete redemption of a shareholder's interest, the S corporation can still elect to treat its tax year as two tax years[101] provided that the shareholder redeemed 20 percent or more of the outstanding corporate stock in one or more transactions during a 30-day period during the corporation's tax year.[102]

Losses—Code Secs. 1244 and 469(g). If a loss is generated on a redemption, then the shareholder (provided Code Sec. 1244 applies in the year of redemption) can, if married, write off up to $100,000 of the loss as ordinary, providing the taxpayer is married at the end of the year, or $50,000 if the taxpayer is single.

When a taxpayer completely terminates his or her interest in a passive activity, any unused passive loss carryforwards attributable to that activity can be deducted at that time. Sale or redemption of a shareholder's entire interest in S corporation stock will generally constitute a complete disposition of his or her interest in the associated activity.[103]

> **Example 12-19:** Cliff and Brad Jones, two brothers, form Bradcliff Inc., a calendar-year S corporation, to engage in the restaurant business. Cliff and Brad are equal shareholders, but Cliff lives in New York and takes no role in the business while Brad lives in California where the restaurant is located and works as the chef, officer, etc. Cliff and Brad each contribute $50,000 in cash for the stock. Each year of Bradcliff Inc.'s operation has generated losses of $20,000 ($10,000 to each shareholder), and after five years of operations, Cliff decides that he wants out. He redeems his stock for $1.00, its fair market value. While Cliff had $10,000 of losses for each of Bradcliff Inc.'s five years of operation pursuant to Code Sec. 1366(d)(1), Code Sec. 469 precluded any deduction because Cliff's interest was passive. However, as discussed at ¶ 911.01, Code Sec. 469 allows Cliff to recognize the $50,000 in the year he redeems his stock.

Consequence if redemption fails to satisfy Code Sec. 302(b)(1)-(3)'s tests. For a redemption to be eligible for capital gains treatment, it has to meet certain requirements (e.g., it cannot be essentially equivalent to a dividend per Code Sec. 302(b)(1)). When Code Sec. 302(b)(1)-(3)'s rules are satisfied, then Code Sec. 1001 provides that gain or loss (except if a Code Sec. 1244 loss is generated) will arise in the same manner as gain or loss arises if the shareholder sold his, her, or its stock (i.e., the shareholder determines gain or loss as the difference between his, her, or its basis and the amount received). If the redemption does not qualify for capital gains treatment under Code Sec. 302(b)(1)-(3) (i.e., it is deemed a dividend), Code Sec. 302(d) prescribes that the money and/or

---

[100] Code Sec. 1377(a)(2). See the discussion at ¶ 901.02 for the tax consequences which could arise regarding the closing of the corporate books.

[101] Reg. § 1.1368-1(g)(2)(B).
[102] Code Secs. 302(a) and 303.
[103] Code Sec. 469(g).

property received is treated as a distribution under Code Sec. 1368 and Code Sec. 301. Thus, the distribution rules of Code Sec. 1368(b) and (c) apply. Accordingly, the proceeds received for the nonqualifying redemption will be allocated in the following order: (1) to the corporation's accumulated adjustments account (AAA) as nontaxable; (2) taxed as an ordinary dividend to the extent the corporation has earnings and profits as a C corporation; (3) tax free to the extent of a shareholder's entire basis in his, her, or its stock (redeemed portion and nonredeemed portion); and (4) the balance as gain.

For an S corporation shareholder, if a redemption qualifies for capital treatment under Code Sec. 302(b), any realized loss recognized on the exchange will be treated as capital, but if a redemption is classified as a distribution under Code Sec. 302(d), then no loss can be recognized.

Tax Pointer: Code Sec. 1(h)(11), for the period after 2002 and before 2013, has taken some of the sting out of failing to qualify for capital gains treatment with respect to a redemption, by prescribing that dividends are taxed at the same rate as capital gains, namely 5 percent for individuals in the 10 percent-15 percent bracket, and then a maximum of 15 percent thereafter. Thus, if a redemption fails to satisfy Code Sec. 302(b)(1)-3's tests, being classified as a dividend, the tax rate will be same as for capital gains.

Unused losses. Losses that a shareholder cannot use because of insufficient basis are carried forward until basis is established to deduct the losses.[104] However, if a shareholder completely terminates his, her, or its interest under Code Sec. 302(b) or Code Sec. 303(a), or an estate or trust terminates, then any unused losses are lost forever.[105] Accordingly, since redemptions under Code Sec. 302(b) are controllable by the shareholder, the shareholder should attempt tax planning before a redemption to prevent the expiration of loss carryforwards. One approach might be to not completely redeem a shareholder's interest, retaining one share to utilize the suspended losses.[106] Likewise, a fiduciary of a trust or will should do similar tax planning to prevent the loss of losses.

Changes to the S corporation AAA and/or E&P. If a redemption qualifies for capital gain treatment under Code Secs. 302(b) and 303(a), then the corporation's AAA and earnings and profits must be reduced by an amount proportional to the percentage of shares redeemed.[107]

Example 12-20: Shermer Inc. is a calendar-year S corporation composed of a number of shareholders. At the beginning of its tax year 2010, it has an AAA account of $10,000 and its shareholders' aggregate stock basis is $500,000. On July 1, 2010, the corporation redeemed 25 percent of its stock in a qualified redemption for $30,000. In 2010, the corporation earned $12,000 income from operations. Shermer Inc. did not distribute any of its earnings during the tax year. To account for the redemption on July 1, 2010, first the AAA account is increased by $6,000 (one-half of $12,000) to $16,000; then it is

[104] Code Sec. 1366(d)(2).
[105] Code Sec. 1366(d)(2).
[106] For an illustration of this point, see discussion at ¶1124.01 under "Carryover of Unused Losses."
[107] Code Sec. 1368(e)(1)(B) and Code Sec. 1371(c)(2).

reduced by $4,000 (25%) to $12,000; and at the end of the year, it is raised by $6,000 (the remaining profit) to a balance of $18,000.

If a corporation uses appreciated property to effect the redemption in whole or in part, then the corporation must recognize gain (but not loss) under Code Sec. 311 as if the property had been sold for its fair market value. If the property is depreciable, then the corporation will report depreciation recapture under Code Sec. 1245, Code Sec. 1250, etc. If the depreciable property is distributed to the shareholders in redemption, Code Sec. 311(a) precludes the S corporation from recognizing a loss on the distribution. Alternatively, the corporation may consider selling the "loss" property to the shareholders, subject to the rules of Code Sec. 267, or sell the "loss" property on the open market free of the restrictions under Code Sec. 267, thereby creating a loss to be passed through to the shareholder(s).

If the corporation incurs debt to finance the redemption, presumably the debt allocation rules apply to characterize the interest expense.[108]

.05 Code Sec. 303 Redemptions

If the value of S corporation stock has been included in a decedent's estate for federal estate tax purposes, subject to certain conditions, the redemption of the decedent's stock will qualify as a Code Sec. 303 redemption, meaning it is treated as a sale or exchange (i.e., capital gains).[109] The amount of the redemption that will qualify is equal to the total of all the estate, inheritance, generation-skipping transfers, legacy, and successor taxes (including any interest collected as part of such taxes), plus funeral and administrative expenses allowed as deductions from the gross estate of the deceased shareholder.[110]

If a redemption does not qualify as a Code Sec. 303 redemption, then the estate will have to use other provisions, mainly Code Sec. 302(b)(1)-(3) to effect capital gains treatment for the redemption. However, because the shares of the decedent are redeemed after the decedent's death, the amount of capital gain or loss should be minimal due to the step up of the decedent's stock to fair market value at the date of death. Note that a Code Sec. 303 redemption only applies to a decedent's estate, not to a beneficiary who receives stock in satisfaction of a specific monetary bequest.[111]

Requirements to use. Generally, for the capital gains treatment prescribed by Code Sec. 303(a) to apply, the value of the corporate stock that is included in a decedent's estate must exceed 35 percent of the decedent's adjusted gross estate.[112] If the decedent owned stock of two or more corporations at his or her death, then the stocks can be aggregated for the redemption, providing that 20 percent or more in value of each corporation's total outstanding stock is included in the gross estate.[113] Since the decedent could hold stock in joint tenancy, tenancy in common, etc. prior to his or her death,[114] those stock holdings are included in determining whether the decedent's gross estate meets the 20 percent test.

---

[108] Code Sec. 163. For a discussion of the debt allocation rules, see ¶ 702.
[109] Code Sec. 303.
[110] Code Sec. 303(a).
[111] Rev. Rul. 70-297, 1970-1 CB 66.
[112] Code Sec. 303(b)(2)(A).
[113] Code Sec. 303(b)(2)(B).
[114] Code Sec. 303(b)(3).

Example 12-21: Jane Gray is the sole shareholder of Best Inc., an S corporation. Gray's adjusted gross estate is $2,000,000 ($2,200,000 gross estate − $200,000 of debt). The 35 percent rule of Code Sec. 303(b)(2)'s test is met if Gray's stock is worth $700,000 or more (.35 × $2,000,000).

Reasons to use. If an S corporation has accumulated earnings and profits from a C corporation predecessor, or due to a merger, a Code Sec. 303 redemption provides an excellent means to reduce those earnings with little or no tax cost since a decedent's stock is stepped up to fair market value at the date of death. If the corporation is illiquid, notes can be used to fund the redemption.[115] Also, if a corporation has excess cash, a Code Sec. 303 redemption allows an estate to attain liquidity at little or no tax cost. Also, the proceeds from the Code Sec. 303 redemption do not have to be used for the payment of estate taxes, funeral expenses, etc.

Time requirements. For the special treatment of Code Sec. 303 to apply, the redemption must occur within a specified time, namely no later than 90 days after the statute of limitations for the assessment of additional tax under Code Sec. 6501(a) (i.e., four years following the decedent's death).[116]

Closing the tax year and unused losses. Because a redemption under Code Sec. 303 could result in a change of more than 20 percent ownership, the rules of Reg. § 1.1368-1(g)(2) could come into operation.

.06 Redemptions Treated as Partial Liquidations

An S corporation can engage in a partial liquidation under Code Sec. 302(b)(4). One classic example of a partial liquidation is the case of *Imler*,[117] which involved a non-S corporation. In *Imler*, the distribution of unused fire insurance proceeds in redemption of stock was treated as a partial liquidation, thereby yielding capital gains treatment to the shareholders (the corporation decided not to rebuild floors destroyed by fire and discontinued operations carried out in part on these floors).

¶ 1210 Complete Liquidations

.01 Introduction

An S corporation's liquidation is similar to a liquidation of a C corporation. Initially, Code Sec. 336(a) applies to the liquidation of an S corporation.[118] Code Secs. 336(a) and 331 prescribe that the S corporation recognizes gain or loss when the property is distributed in complete liquidation of the corporation, with the calculation made as if the corporation sold its assets to the shareholders at fair market value as of the date of liquidation. The characterization of the gain realized on the assets distributed to the shareholders depends on the type of assets being

---

[115] Rev. Rul. 65-289, 1965-2 CB 86.

[116] Code Sec. 303(b)(1)(A). Note that Rev. Rul. 67-425, 1967-2 CB 134 prescribes rules for coordination of redemptions under Code Sec. 302 and Code Sec. 303.

[117] *J.W. Imler*, 11 TC 836, Dec. 16,691 (Acq.).

[118] It is important to note that liquidation is a tax concept governed by Code Secs. 331-338. Dissolution of an S corporation is a state concept, governed by state law. A corporation is dissolved under state law by the corporation's filing of a certificate of dissolution (or similar document) or by state law if the corporation does not pay its franchise taxes.

distributed, with the recapture rules of Code Sec. 1245, Code Sec. 1250, Code Sec. 1254, and Code Sec. 617 applying to recast all or a portion of the gain as ordinary.

Because shareholders generally bear the tax consequences of corporate activities (with the exception of Code Secs. 1374 and 1375), no tax is paid at the corporate level on the liquidation.[119] As to shareholders, their basis in the distributed assets is the fair market value of the assets.[120] A shareholder's stock basis is increased or decreased by gain or loss recognized when the shareholder receives the assets in liquidation.[121]

> *Example 12-22:* Dunsten Inc., a calendar-year S corporation since January 1, 1999, has one shareholder, Ann Foster. Dunsten Inc. purchased land for $100,000 on incorporation as an investment. As of December 31, 2010, Dunsten Inc. had no liability and only the land on its balance sheet, with a fair market value of $300,000 and a cost basis of $100,000. On December 31, 2010, Foster's basis in her stock is $75,000. On December 31, 2010, Dunsten Inc. adopts a plan of liquidation, filing Form 966, and distributes the land to Foster with the $200,000 gain on the liquidation ($300,000 fair market value – $100,000 basis) being passed through to Foster as long-term capital gain (the corporation held the land for more than one year), making Foster's basis $275,000 ($75,000 originally + $200,000 of gain). When Foster receives the land on liquidation that has a fair market value of $300,000, Foster will recognize an additional $25,000 of gain ($300,000 – $275,000 of basis). Since Foster held the stock for more than one year, the $25,000 gain is long-term capital gain.

> *Example 12-23:* Assume the same facts as in Example 12-22, except that instead of distributing the land to the shareholder, Dunsten Inc. sells it to Joe Forbes, a complete stranger, for $300,000. The same results as in Example 12-22 apply.

> *Example 12-24:* Assume the same facts as in Example 12-22, except that the land is a Code Sec. 1245 depreciable asset that was purchased for $300,000 on January 1, 1999, and has been depreciated on the corporate books to $100,000 as of December 31, 2010 (the depreciable asset has a fair market value of $300,000 as of December 31, 2010). Foster reports the following in the liquidation: Foster's basis is increased from $75,000 to $275,000, with Foster reporting $200,000 of Code Sec. 1245 ordinary income and $25,000 of long-term capital gain.

.02 Importance of Timing

Timing is critical in liquidations when there is a sale of assets.[122]

> *Example 12-25:* Assume the same facts as in Example 12-22, except that Foster's basis in her stock is $500,000 instead of $75,000. Foster will realize $200,000 of long-term capital gain pass-through on liquidation of the corporation, increasing Foster's basis to $700,000. When Foster receives the land, she will receive a $400,000 long-term loss (($500,000 of initial stock basis +

---

[119] Code Sec. 1363(a).
[120] Code Sec. 334(a).

[121] Code Sec. 1367.
[122] Code Sec. 331.

$200,000 long-term capital gain) – $300,000 fair market value of the land), with the result being a net loss of $200,000 long-term capital loss ($200,000 long-term capital gain pursuant to Code Sec. 336(a) when the corporation liquidated – $400,000 of long-term capital loss when Foster received the land).

> *Example 12-26:* Assume the same facts as in Example 12-25, except that instead of liquidating on December 31, 2009, Dunsten Inc. sold the land on December 31, 2009, for $300,000, liquidating on January 1, 2010. The result is that Foster reports the following transaction from Dunsten Inc.: $200,000 of capital gain for 2009 and $400,000 of capital loss for 2010—there is no ability to offset the gain against the loss since they arose in different years. If Foster does not have enough capital gain to offset the $400,000 loss in 2010, Foster will only be able to deduct $3,000 per year pursuant to Code Sec. 1211(b), but she will be required to pay tax on $200,000 of long-term capital gains in 2009. Accordingly, timing is critical on a sale with a liquidation.

.03 Installment Sales

If an S corporation sells an asset using the installment method as part of the liquidation, the installment obligation is passed through to the shareholder pursuant to Code Sec. 453B(h), generally without any recognition at the corporate level, with the S corporation reporting the gain realized on the sale pursuant to the installment note.

> *Example 12-27:* Assume the same facts as in Example 12-22, except that instead of receiving $300,000 in cash, Dunsten Inc. receives a $300,000 installment note, which bears the applicable federal rate of interest and there is no original discount with the note. The note is payable over five years in equal yearly installments of $60,000, the first installment being due December 31, 2010, with interest and every year thereafter until paid. Dunsten Inc. distributes the installment note to Foster on December 31, 2009, in complete liquidation and pursuant to Code Sec. 453B(h). The corporation recognizes no gain or loss on the distribution of the note; Dunsten reports the $225,000 of gain on the stock pursuant to the installment method in accordance with Code Sec. 453B(h)(1) and (2).

> *Tax Pointer:* The rules for installment sales of assets were substantially changed as of December 17, 1999. See ¶ 1208.05 for a discussion of these changes.

.04 Effect of Code Sec. 1374

A corporate level tax is imposed on an S corporation when an S corporation has C corporation assets with built-in gain and disposes of them within ten tax years of their acquisition.[123]

Code Sec. 1374 in installment sales. When an S corporation sells Code Sec. 1374 assets on an installment basis as part of a corporation liquidation, Code Sec. 453B(h) requires that the S corporation must recognize gain on the liquidating

---

[123] Code Sec. 1374.

¶1210.03

distribution, having the shareholders who receive a distribution recognize the amount of tax paid by the corporation.

> ***Example 12-28:*** Assume the same facts as in Example 12-22, except that the corporation was a C corporation before converting to an S, and at the time of conversion, it had $135,000 of Code Sec. 1374 built-in gain, with the tax on $135,000 being $40,000. Dunsten Inc. has to pay $40,000 of tax on December 31, 2009, when the corporation liquidates. Foster's basis in her stock increases from $75,000 to $170,000 ($75,000 + ($135,000 – $40,000 of Code Sec. 1374 tax)) with Foster reporting the remaining portion of the gain, $65,000 ($200,000 – $135,000), under the installment method.

.05 Code Sec. 336 Rules

Liabilities. If a shareholder assumes a liability of the liquidating corporation on liquidation, or the property distributed is subject to a liability, the fair market value of the property shall not be less than the amount of the liability.[124] Accordingly, if the corporation's liability(ies) is in excess of the corporation's basis in its assets, then gain will be recognized to the extent the liability(ies) exceeds the distributing corporation's basis. Chief Counsel Advice 201237017 (May 03, 2012) held when there was a distribution of property encumbered by a liability in a complete liquidation of an S corporation and a shareholder assumes the liability, this assumption of liability does not increase a shareholder's basis. Rather, the shareholder will reduce the amount realized by the amount of the liability assumed and if the liability exceeds the value of the property, the taxpayer will recognize a loss.

Limitation on recognition of losses. A liquidating corporation will not be permitted to recognize a loss on liquidation for property distributed to a related party as defined by Code Sec. 267 if the distribution is not pro rata to the parties, or if the property is disqualified property.[125]

Related parties. The liquidating corporation will only be able to recognize a loss if the property is distributed pro rata to a related person, as defined under Code Sec. 267.[126] Code Sec. 267(b)(2) prescribes that an individual is related to the liquidating corporation if the shareholder owns, directly or indirectly, more than 50 percent of the value of the corporation's outstanding stock. The Conference Committee Report[127] prescribes that the loss property itself has to be distributed pro rata to each shareholder to avoid disallowance of the loss.

> ***Example 12-29:*** Glovers, an S corporation, is owned 60% by Hank Miller, and 40% by Nancy Chung. Glovers owns two assets that it purchased: the first with a gain (basis of $800 and a fair market value of $1,000); and the second with a loss (basis of $500 and a value of $100). Glovers liquidates pursuant to Code Sec. 331, distributing 60% of each asset to Miller and 40% to Chung. The $400 loss on liquidation will be recognized by Glovers.

---

[124] Code Sec. 336(b).
[125] Code Sec. 336(d).

[126] Code Sec. 336(d)(1)(A)(i), subject to Code Sec. 336(d)(1)(A)(ii).
[127] Conference Committee Report to the Tax Reform Act of 1986 (P.L. 99-514).

Example 12-30: Assume the same facts as in Example 12-29, except that Glovers distributes the second asset (with the loss) only to Miller while distributing the first asset (with the gain) 60% to Miller and 40% to Chung. Glovers will not be able to recognize any of the $400 loss on liquidation.

Tax Pointer: To avoid having a corporation not be able to recognize its losses (as in Example 12-30), the corporation could sell its assets with losses to an unrelated party, thus passing the loss onto the shareholders.

In the event a loss is not recognized by a corporation on liquidation, Code Sec. 334(a) precludes the shareholders from recognizing the loss. In contrast, Code Sec. 267 permits a related party to recognize losses suspended because of the related-party rules.[128]

Disqualified property rules. Code Sec. 336(d)(1)(A)(ii) and (d)(2) states that if a principal purpose of the contribution of property to a corporation in advance of its liquidation is to recognize a loss upon the sale or distribution of the property and thus eliminate or otherwise limit corporate level gain, then the basis (for purposes of determining loss) of any property acquired by such corporation in a Code Sec. 351 transaction or as a contribution to capital will be reduced, but not below zero, by the excess of the basis of the property on the date of contribution over its fair market value on such date. For purposes of this rule, it is presumed, except to the extent provided in the regulations, that any Code Sec. 351 transaction or contribution to capital within the five-year period prior to the adoption of a plan to complete liquidation (or thereafter) has such a principal purpose.

While Congress, when it passed Code Sec. 336(d)(1)(A)(ii) and (d)(2), anticipated that regulations would be issued to detail tax treatment for this area, to date, regulations have not been issued. However, the Conference Committee Report[129] provides guidance for some situations. Below is an extract of the Conference Committee Reports.

> If the adoption of a plan of complete liquidation occurs in a taxable year following the date on which the tax return including the loss disallowed by this provision is filed, the conferees intend that, in appropriate cases, the liquidating corporation may recapture the disallowed loss on the tax return for the taxable year in which such plan of liquidation is adopted. In the alternative, the corporation could file an amended return for the taxable year in which the loss was reported.
>
> The conferees intend that the Treasury Department will issue regulations generally providing that the presumed prohibited purpose for contributions of property two years in advance of the adoption of a plan of liquidation will be disregarded *unless* there is no clear and substantial relationship between the contributed property and the conduct of the corporation's current or future business enterprises. For example, assume that A owns Z Corporation which operates a widget business in New Jersey. That business operates exclusively in the northeastern region of the United States and there are no plans to expand those operations. In his individual capacity, A had acquired unimproved real estate in New Mexico that has declined in value. On March 22, 1988, A contributes such real estate to Z and six months later a plan of complete

---

[128] See discussion at ¶ 712.

[129] Conference Committee Report to the Tax Reform Act of 1986 (P.L. 99-514).

liquidation is adopted. Thereafter, all of Z's assets are sold to an unrelated party and the liquidation proceeds are distributed. A contributed no other property to Z during the two-year period prior to the adoption of the plan of liquidation. Because A contributed the property to Z less than two years prior to the adoption of the plan of liquidation, it is presumed to have been contributed with a prohibited purpose. Moreover, because there is no clear and substantial relationship between the contributed property and the conduct of Z's business, the conferees do no expect that any loss arising from the disposition of the New Mexico real estate would be allowed under the Treasury regulations.

As another example, the conferees expect that such regulations would permit the allowance of any resulting loss from the disposition of any of the assets of a trade or business (or a line of business) that are contributed to a corporation. In such circumstance, application of the loss disallowance rule is inappropriate assuming there is a meaningful relationship between the contribution and the utilization of the corporate form to conduct a business enterprise, i.e., the contributed business, as distinguished from a portion of its assets, is not disposed of immediately after the contribution. The conferees also anticipate that the basis adjustment rules will generally not apply to a corporation's acquisition of property during its first two years of existence.

To illustrate the mechanical aspects of the basis adjustment rules, assume that on June 1, 1987, a shareholder who owns a 10-percent interest in X corporation ("X") contributes nondepreciable property with a basis of $1,000 and a value of $100 to X in exchange for additional stock; X is a calendar year taxpayer. Assume further that on September 30, 1987, X sells the property to an unrelated third party for $200, and includes the resulting $800 loss on its 1987 tax return. Finally, assume that X adopts a plan of liquidation on December 31, 1988. Thereafter, X could file an amended return reflecting the fact that the $800 loss was disallowed, because the property's basis would be reduced to $200. Alternatively, the conferees intend that X, under regulations, may be permitted to recapture the loss on its 1998 tax return. The amount of loss recapture in such circumstances would be limited to the lesser of the built-in loss ($900, or $1,000, the transferred basis under section 362, less $100, the value of the property on that date it was contributed to X) or the loss actually recognized on the disposition of such property ($800, or the $1,000 transferred basis less the $200 amount realized). Thus, unless X files an amended return, X must recapture $800 on its return for its taxable year ending December 31, 1988.

.06 Shareholder Treatment

In a complete liquidation of the S corporation, each shareholder's gain or loss is equal to the difference between the amount received in the liquidating distribution and the shareholder's adjusted basis in the stock.[130] If a shareholder assumes any liabilities or receives property subject to a liability, the amount that the shareholder receives is reduced by the amount of the liability.[131]

Example 12-31: Jazz Inc., a calendar-year S corporation from inception, had no assets subject to the Code Sec. 1374 tax on built-in gains. On January 1, 2010, it liquidated. Jazz Inc. had the following assets and liabilities on January 1, 2010: a garage on Beech Avenue with a fair market value of $125,000 after payment of taxes on the property without consideration of the mortgage for $30,000. Paul Peterson, an individual, is the only shareholder of Jazz Inc.

---

[130] Code Sec. 1001(a) and Reg. § 1.331-1(b).   [131] *H.W. Evans,* 5 TCM 336, Dec. 15,153(M).

Peterson's basis in his stock is $50,000. Peterson reports a net gain of $45,000 on the liquidating distribution (($125,000 – $30,000) – $50,000 stock basis).

Tax Pointer: If an individual acquires stock at various times and at various prices (e.g., different stock purchases from original shareholders), then Reg. § 1.331-1(e) requires that any gain or loss when receiving a liquidating distribution be computed on a per-share basis.

Code Sec. 1244 treatment. Code Sec. 1244 applies to a transaction, providing it was elected, if a loss arises on liquidation. For a discussion of Code Sec. 1244, see ¶ 1113.

Shareholder's basis in assets. A shareholder's basis in assets received in a liquidation is the fair market value at the time of distribution, providing gain or loss is recognized by the corporation on the distribution.[132] If the shareholder acquired stock at various times, an allocation is required pursuant to Reg. § 1.331-1(e).

Example 12-32: Marc Eng, an individual who files his income tax returns on the calendar-year basis, owns 20 shares of stock in WindFarm corporation, an S corporation, 10 shares of which were acquired in 1995 at a cost of $1,500 and another 10 shares were acquired in November 2009 at a cost of $2,900. He receives in April 2010 a distribution of $250 per share in complete liquidation, or $2,500 on the 10 shares acquired in 1995, and $2,500 on the 10 shares acquired in November 2009. The gain of $1,000 on the shares acquired in 1995 is a long-term capital gain. The loss of $400 on the shares acquired in 2009 is a short-term capital loss.

Pursuant to Code Secs. 1221 and 1222, a shareholder reports a capital gain or loss, assuming Code Sec. 1244 is not available, as long- or short-term, depending upon the holding period that the shareholder has for his, her, or its stock.

Code Sec. 444 election of fiscal year. If an S corporation made an election under Code Sec. 444 to report income, loss, etc. on a September 30, October 31, or November 30 fiscal year, the Code Sec. 444 fiscal-year election terminates on liquidation. Accordingly, Code Sec. 7519(c)(2) prescribes that an S corporation can obtain a refund of the excess of required payments during the period the Code Sec. 444 election was in effect.

LIFO recapture. If a C corporation using the LIFO method of inventory converts to S status, it has to pay tax on the LIFO recapture inherent in its inventory. The tax is paid in four equal installments. If the S corporation liquidates before the expiration of the four-year period, then the corporation has to pay any unpaid tax installments when the corporation files its final tax return.[133]

Shareholder's unused losses. If a shareholder has insufficient basis to take losses arising from operations of the S corporation, and the corporation liquidates, then the unused losses are lost forever on the liquidation. To prevent unwarranted tax results, shareholders should carefully review their basis calculations to ensure use of the losses. Alternatively, if unused losses generated by Code Sec. 1366(d)(2) cannot be used, the shareholder should consider terminating the S election and

---

[132] Code Sec. 334(a) and Reg. § 1.334-1(a).

[133] Rev. Proc. 94-61, 1994-2 CB 775 (Q-8).

becoming a C corporation, assuming this is feasible, using the post-termination rules given in Code Sec. 1371(e).[134]

.07 Corporate Reporting

Forms 966, 1096, and 1099. An S corporation is required to file a Form 966 within thirty days after the adoption of any plan of liquidation.[135] If the plan of liquidation is amended or supplemented, Reg. § 1.6043-1(a) requires that an additional Form 966 be filed upon the adoption of such amendment or supplement.

An S corporation is required to file Forms 1096 and 1099-DIV to report the liquidating distributions to the shareholders.[136]

Final tax return. The S corporation is required to file its final Form 1120S by the fifteenth day of the third month after the end of the month in which it liquidates.[137] Code Sec. 1366(a) prescribes that all items of income, loss, etc. from the S corporation for the period of its tax year prior to liquidation pass through to the shareholders on a per-day, per-share basis. Code Sec. 381 prescribes that on liquidation of the S corporation, all S corporation attributes such as accumulated adjustments account, net operating losses from a former C corporation, etc. cease to exist.

Taxation of a qualified subchapter S trust (QSST). The taxation of a termination of a QSST is explained in IRS Letter Ruling 9721020 (February 20, 1997).

.08 Recapture of Goodwill

When a corporation liquidates, the shareholder realizes the sum of any money received plus the fair market value of property received other than money.[138] The IRS has consistently taken the position that goodwill must be considered amoung the assets received by the shareholder(s) where appropriate, although measurement of the value of goodwill received is generally problematic. *MacDonald*[139] holds that in measuring goodwill, there is no specific rule, and each case must be considered in light of its own particular facts, with the earning power of the business being an important factor.[140] In determining if goodwill is present, and to be recognized, a number of factors have to be considered: Did the shareholder use the corporate name, keep the address of the business, keep the corporation's customers, etc.? In *Norwalk*,[141] shareholders of an incorporated public accounting firm did not have taxable goodwill when the corporation liquidated, mainly because the shareholder-employees were not bound by a covenant not to compete at the time of liquidation of the corporation. Accordingly, because there was no covenant not to compete, the shareholders' personal relationship was not corporate property. Likewise, *Martin Ice Cream Co.*[142] reached the same result in an S corporation,

---

[134] See discussion at ¶ 912.

[135] Code Sec. 6043(a)(1).

[136] Code Sec. 6043(a)(2).

[137] Code Sec. 6037 and Code Sec. 6012.

[138] Reg. § 1.331-1(e).

[139] *D.K. MacDonald,* 3 TC 720, 727, Dec. 13,898.

[140] *W. Krafft Est.,* 20 TCM 1571, Dec. 25,114(M), TC Memo. 1961-305.

[141] *W. Norwalk,* 76 TCM 208, Dec. 52,817(M), TC Memo. 1998-279.

[142] *Martin Ice Cream Co.,* 110 TC 189, Dec. 52,624.

holding that "personal relationships of a shareholder-employee are not corporate assets when the employee has no employment contract with the corporation."

.09 Code Sec. 338 Liquidations

A purchaser may only be able to acquire a corporation by purchasing its stock. Besides the inherent difficulties in purchasing stock, the purchaser acquires the carryover basis of the property in the corporation; not the fair market value as would be the case if the purchaser were purchasing the assets. However, Code Sec. 338 allows a purchaser to step up the corporate assets to fair market value. To do so, however, the purchaser has to pay tax on the difference between the price paid for the stock and the book value of the assets, a cost that could be prohibitive in obtaining a step up in basis for the assets. It is beyond the scope of this book to provide a discussion of Code Sec. 338, except to advise that it is permitted for S corporations, IRS Letter Ruling 8532076 (May 16, 1985) gives an example of where it was applied when a C corporation acquired stock of an S corporation.

¶ 1211 Reorganizations

.01 Introduction

One primary benefit for operating in the S corporation form is that the corporation and its shareholders can avail themselves of the tax-free reorganization sections of Code Sec. 368 to accomplish various objectives (partnerships have no comparable provisions). However, because of certain reorganization provisions under Code Sec. 368 (e.g., a B or C type reorganization), some reorganizations may not be practical for an S corporation, particularly if an S corporation is to be the surviving corporation. The field of tax-free reorganizations is a highly technical one, and the following discussions are general and not intended to be exhaustive. However, each type of reorganization is discussed as it pertains to S corporations along with some of the problems and situations encountered. Note that the six basic types of reorganizations and the two hybrid types are often referred to by their Code Sec. letter, (e.g., an A merger means a merger under Code Sec. 368(a)(1)(A), etc.).

In any reorganization involving S corporations, the key is Code Sec. 1371(a). Code Sec. 1371(a) provides that subchapter C (which contains the reorganization statutes, among others) shall apply to S corporations except to the extent it is inconsistent with S corporation taxation. Thus, an S corporation can be the acquiring corporation in an A merger and keep its S status after the merger, providing that the acquired corporation's shareholders are permitted S shareholders, there will be less than 100 shareholders after the merger, and so on. However, if the acquiring corporation in the merger is a C corporation, the S election will be terminated as of the date of the merger. To prevent unwarranted tax results, the S corporation shareholders should consider the consequences of termination of the S status on the general business credit recapture, distributions, flow-through of income and loss in the terminating year, and so on (discussed below).

Merger and consolidations involving wholly-owned pass-through entities. On November 15, 2001, Proposed Reg. § 1.368-2(b)(1) was issued to deal with mergers where disregarded entities such as QSUBs and one-member LLCs formed under Reg. § 301.7701-2(a) are utilized. For a discussion of this topic, see ¶ 1211.09.

Danger of reorganizations and their alternatives. Because in many reorganizations, stock is being exchanged with or acquired from another corporation, care should be exercised because of the inherent problems that stock ownership brings. An S corporation should consider the purchase of assets, or, if the S corporation wants subsidiaries, form QSubs[143] or one-member LLCs.[144]

Depending on how a reorganization is structured, an S corporation may lose its election, or if it survives, it may receive C corporation earnings and profits that could affect future operations (tax on excess passive income, etc.). Rather than engage in post-termination procedures for an S corporation,[145] the S corporation shareholders may want to structure the transactions prior to engaging in the reorganization to minimize the effect(s) of loss of S status, such as distributing the entire accumulated adjustments account (AAA) to the corporate shareholders prior to the reorganization, thereby not sharing the AAA with the shareholders of the other corporation engaged in the reorganization. As is the case with a stock sale, one of the parties in a reorganization may not want some assets of the other party (e.g., the president's desk, automobile, etc.). Accordingly, the reorganization has to be engineered to remove the undesired assets.[146] Note, however, that other reorganization rules, such as continuity of business interest, may come into play that would affect the removal of these unwanted assets. Code Sec. 356 prescribes the taxation of "boot" if the property is distributed to the shareholders.

.02 Code Sec. 368(a)(1)(A) Statutory Mergers and Consolidations (Type A Reorganizations)

In a statutory merger under Code Sec. 368(a)(1)(A), an acquired corporation is merged into a surviving one, and in a consolidation, two corporations are consolidated into a new one. In a merger, if an S corporation is the acquiring corporation, usually the S status is retained, unless the acquired corporation causes the S corporation to lose its S status (e.g., as a result of having a nonpermitted shareholder). To prevent the loss of the acquiring corporation's S status, the corporation to be acquired should take steps prior to the merger to eliminate any problems (e.g., reducing the number of shareholders so that there will be 100 or less after the merger, or eliminating nonpermitted shareholders by having them redeem their shares or sell their shares to permitted shareholders). However, if a C corporation is going to be the acquiring corporation, Code Sec. 1362(d)(2)(B) prescribes that the S termination will occur on the date of the merger. For reorganizations under Code Sec. 368(a)(1)(A), a number of situations can arise. For instance, two C corporations could merge and then elect S status, or the acquiring corporation could be a C corporation that previously had an S election that was lost, and so on. Again, careful tax planning before the reorganization is required so that no adverse tax consequences will develop.

---

[143] See Chapter 14 for a discussion.
[144] See ¶ 1307 for a discussion.

[145] See ¶ 912 for a discussion of the post-termination transition period.
[146] See ¶ 1208.06 for a discussion of removing assets from a sale.

Reelection of S status after a merger. If S status is lost after a reorganization under Code Sec. 368(a)(1)(A), the acquiring corporation may want to reelect S status under Code Sec. 1362. However, because a reorganization under Code Sec. 368 is a voluntary event, conceptually, the corporation that lost its S status cannot say it was inadvertent. Thus, the S corporation that lost its S status in the merger will have to wait the five-year waiting period prescribed in Code Sec. 1362(g), unless the Secretary of the Treasury is willing to waive all or part of the five-year statutory period.

S corporation attributes. If an S corporation is the surviving corporation in a merger (i.e., the acquiring corporation), Code Sec. 1377(a)(1) prescribes that its income, loss, etc. are allocated on a per-share, per-day basis. This allocation rule of Code Sec. 1377(a)(1) also includes the shareholders of the other corporation (i.e., the target corporation) involved in the merger.

> **Example 12-33:** Omni Inc., a calendar-year S corporation, acquires Trak Inc., a C corporation, on July 1, 2010, in a merger. The S corporation's status is not terminated by the merger. As a result of the merger, the shareholders of Trak Inc. will receive for the year 2010 25% of Omni's income, loss, etc. for the period July 1 through December 31, 2010.

In Example 12-33, it is important to note that, pursuant to Code Sec. 1377(a)(1)'s rules, it makes no difference what income, loss, etc. is generated; it will be allocated on a per-day, per-share basis.

Carryover of S corporation attributes. Generally the corporate tax attributes of a target corporation become the corporate tax attributes of the acquiring corporation.[147] Code Sec. 381 prescribes that if a target corporation merges into an acquiring S corporation, and the acquiring S corporation's status does not terminate due to the merger (i.e., it has less than 100 or less shareholders, etc.), the acquiring corporation's AAA is the sum of both the target's AAA and the acquiring corporation's AAA. If one corporation has negative AAA and one positive, the two AAAs are netted to arrive at a new total.[148]

If the target is a C corporation possessing unused capital losses, passive losses, etc., Code Sec. 381 prescribes that the target's corporate attributes stay as such since they are not capable of being used by the S corporation (However, see ¶ 404.13 as to how the S corporation shareholders could utilize the C corporation's Code Sec. 469 passive losses). If the target is a C corporation, then the surviving corporation is plagued with Code Sec. 1374 built-in gain assets.[149] Likewise, Code Sec. 1363(d)'s rules regarding LIFO recapture apply, as well as Code Sec. 1375 and Code Sec. 1362(d).

Unused losses. If an S corporation ceases to exist because it, among other things, merges with a C corporation that survives, then the post-termination rules of Code Sec. 1366(d)(3) apply.[150] Likewise, two tax years will be created if the S

---

[147] Code Sec. 381.
[148] Reg. § 1.1368-2(d)(2).

[149] Code Sec. 1374(a).
[150] See ¶ 912 for a discussion of the post-termination transition period.

status is lost: one for the portion of the year as an S corporation, and one for the portion as a C corporation.

Forward triangular merger. Code Sec. 368(a)(2)(D) establishes a variation of the classic Code Sec. 368(a)(1)(A) merger, namely: an A reorganization with a subsidiary involved. Specifically, a forward triangle merger is the merger of a target corporation into the subsidiary of the parent, which uses the stock of the parent to make the acquisition. The parent's stock received by the target is then distributed to its shareholders with the target ceasing to exist. It is possible to do a forward triangle merger with qualified subchapter S subsidiaries (QSubs).[151]

Reverse triangular merger. Code Sec. 368(a)(2)(E) prescribes another variation of a Code Sec. 368(a)(1)(A) merger. In a reverse triangular merger, a subsidiary of a parent is merged into a target corporation, with the target surviving, and the shareholders of the target exchanging their stock for the stock of the subsidiary's parent corporation. Because of Code Sec. 1361(b)(1), an S corporation cannot be the merged subsidiary corporation since a corporate shareholder cannot be the parent, unless the reorganization qualifies under Code Sec. 1361(b)(3).[152]

Business purpose, continuity of business enterprise, and continuity of interest. Besides qualifying a merger or consolidation under state law, Reg. § 1.368-1(b) requires that there be a business purpose for the transaction, and that it satisfy other concepts, such as a continuity of business enterprise and continuity of interest. The courts have held that the failure to comply with any one of these three requirements will preclude tax-free treatment of the merger or consolidation. While it is beyond the scope of this book to provide a detailed discussion of the area, the case of *Honbarrier*[153] is helpful to understand the doctrine of continuity of business enterprise. In *Honbarrier*, the taxpayer was the sole shareholder of P. P was engaged in the business of hauling packaged freight. P's operations were terminated in 1988. In 1990, P sold its operating assets, investing the proceeds in tax-exempt bonds and a municipal bond fund. C was a private-held trucking company that operated as a bulk carrier of chemicals. The taxpayer was the majority shareholder of C, with his family owning the rest of the shares. C was an S corporation, and at the end of 1993 had AAA with a positive balance of $10.7 million, and cash and short-term investments of $11.9 million. On December 31, 1993, P was merged into C, and on the day of the merger, P liquidated one of its tax-exempt bond funds, with C distributing $7 million to C's shareholders. Within four months after the merger, C had disposed of the remaining tax-exempt bonds that it had acquired from P in the merger. The Court refused to sustain a tax-free merger, claiming that C did not continue P's historic business or use a significant portion of P's historic business assets in a business. Therefore, the merger flunked the continuity of business enterprise requirement.

Regulatory procedures for mergers and consolidations. For a discussion of this topic see, ¶ 1211.10.

---

[151] See Chapter 14 for a discussion.
[152] *Ibid.*
[153] *A.L. Honbarrier*, 115 TC 300, Dec. 54,070.

.03 Code Sec. 368(a)(1)(B) Reorganizations

Code Sec. 368(a)(1)(B) prescribes that a B reorganization occurs when an acquiring corporation acquires the stock of a subsidiary (i.e., the target) solely for the stock of the parent, and the acquiring corporation, immediately after the exchange of stock, has control of the target. An S corporation, when it is the acquirer, likes this method for acquisition, because it does not involve the direct use of any of its assets—all it is doing is exchanging its stock for the stock of another. B reorganizations can be used in qualified subchapter S subsidiaries (QSubs) (discussed at Chapter 14).

Carryover of tax attributes, AAA, unused losses, two tax years, etc. As is the case with an A merger, there is a carryover of tax attributes of the target. Depending upon how the structure of the reorganization occurs, S status could be lost, the post-termination rules of Code Sec. 1366(d)(3) could apply, there could be two tax years, etc.

AAA is a corporate account. Accordingly, the new shareholders of the parent, assuming the S corporation parent survives, are allocated a proportional amount of AAA, where they can receive tax-free distributions from the S corporation even though the old shareholders had paid the tax on the income that caused the AAA to exist.

The target (i.e., the subsidiary) is not dissolved; rather, it survives intact with its assets, tax attributes, etc.; the only difference is that it has a new owner of its stock—the acquiring corporation (i.e., the parent). If the parent is a C corporation, then the subsidiary will lose its S election on the date it first has the C corporation as a shareholder because a C corporation cannot be a shareholder in any S corporation. The S corporation is relegated to pursuing post-termination procedures as discussed at ¶ 912.

.04 Code Sec. 368(a)(1)(C) Reorganizations

Code Sec. 368(a)(1)(C) prescribes that a C reorganization is an acquisition by the acquiring corporation of substantially all the assets of a target corporation in exchange for all or part of the acquiring corporation's stock (or that of its parent), or for exchange of voting stock and a limited amount of money. Depending on the structure, the S corporation could lose its S status; however, for wholly-owned C corporation subsidiaries (discussed at ¶ 1409), an S corporation's wholly-owned C corporation subsidiary could engage in a C reorganization. Notwithstanding, IRS Letter Ruling 8739010 allowed an S corporation to engage in a C reorganization.[154]

An S corporation is allowed to be the target or the acquiring corporation in a C reorganization.[155]

Carryover of tax attributes, AAA, unused losses, two tax years, etc. As is the case with an A merger, there is carryover of tax attributes and AAA, there can be unused losses, etc., two tax years could be created, etc.

---

[154] IRS Letter Ruling 8739010 (June 26, 1987).   [155] Code Sec. 1371(a).

¶1211.03

.05 Code Sec. 368(a)(1)(D) Reorganizations

There are basically two different types of situations that qualify as a Code Sec. 368(a)(1)(D) reorganization: a divisive and a nondivisive reorganization. A nondivisive D reorganization can take two forms: a merger or a nonmerger situation. Nondivisive D reorganizations can be done with S corporations; however, S status may be lost by the S corporation participating in the situations. As to the divisive situations, if a corporation transfers part of its assets to another corporation, immediately thereafter, the transferor corporation controls the transferee, and when the transferor corporation distributes stock or securities of the controlled corporation to one or more of its shareholders, the result will be tax free.[156]

Example 12-34 shows where an S corporation would undertake a divisive reorganization as found in the factual situation of Rev. Rul. 72-320:[157]

> **Example 12-34:** Zap Inc., an S corporation, was owned by four brothers, Ben, Jerry, Chip, and Dale Zappa, who were all equal shareholders. The corporation was engaged in the manufacture of heavy construction equipment. The corporation had a division in California, which was operated by Ben and Jerry, and another in New York, which was operated by Chip and Dale. Disputes broke out among the four brothers, with Ben and Jerry looking for expansion and Chip and Dale not. To solve the dispute, pursuant to Code Sec. 368(a)(1)(D), Zap Inc. created a subsidiary, Yap Inc., and transferred all the assets of the New York division to Yap Inc., subject to its liabilities, taking back all the stock and then immediately transferring all the stock of Yap Inc. to Chip and Dale in exchange for their stock in Zap Inc.

In a variation of Example 12-34, IRS Letter Ruling 200121061 sustained a tax-free D reorganization involving a five-shareholder corporation, where one shareholder director constantly fought with the others and was removed as a director. To eliminate the dissident shareholder, the S corporation created a subsidiary with a portion of the business assets so that it would qualify as a separate trade or business with a five-year history as required by Code Sec. 355. Then, the S corporation spun off the subsidiary's stock to the dissident shareholder in exchange for the dissident shareholder's stock.

To obtain nonrecognition treatment for a Code Sec. 355 transaction, Reg. § 1.355-2 prescribes that there must be a valid business purpose for the transaction, not just a tax-avoidance scheme. Further, Reg. § 1.355-3 prescribes that after the transaction, both the distributing corporation and controlled corporation must actively conduct the business previously owned and operated by the distributing corporation for at least five years. In interpreting the five-year active business requirement, the case of *McLaulin*[158] is helpful in understanding the parameters of this test.

McLaulin involved two corporations—Ridge Pallet, Inc. (Ridge) and Sunbelt Forest Products, Inc. (Sunbelt). Ridge was incorporated in 1959 and was an S corporation. Sunbelt was incorporated in 1981 and, until January 15, 1993, had two

---

[156] Code Sec. 368(a)(1)(D).

[157] Rev. Rul. 72-320, 1972-1 CB 270.

[158] *D.P. McLaulin, Jr.,* 115 TC 255, Dec. 54,047.

equal shareholders: Ridge and Hutto (Hutto was the president of Sunbelt and Chairman of its board of directors). Ridge, engaged in the forest and products business, was profitable; Sunbelt produced and sold pressure-treated lumber, and while it was profitable, needed Ridge to guarantee its loans with the bank. Ridge was unable to outvote Hutto in Sunbelt. Accordingly, Ridge withdrew its guarantee of Sunbelt's loans, with the result being that Hutto's stock was redeemed, with Sunbelt borrowing money from Ridge the day before the redemption distribution, with the cash borrowed representing over 96 percent of the total consideration paid to Hutto for his stock. On the same day as the redemption, Ridge distributed its 100 percent stock interest in Sunbelt to Ridge's shareholders, with the intent to have it qualify as a tax-free spin-off under Code Sec. 355. Because the spin-off occurred less than five years after Ridge acquired control of Sunbelt in a transaction where gain or loss was recognized (i.e., the redemption of Hutto's stock), the redemption failed to satisfy the active business requirement of Code Sec. 355.

.06 Code Sec. 368(a)(1)(E) Recapitalizations (Type E Reorganizations)

In a typical recapitalization under Code Sec. 368(a)(1)(E), stock and/or securities in a corporation is exchanged for new stock and/or securities in the same corporation. The exchange only involves the corporation's existing shareholders or security holders. If an S corporation is undertaking an E reorganization, it will not lose its S status unless two or more classes of stock result after the reorganization. An example of a recapitalization used with S corporations would be an exchange of old debt for new stock and old stock for new stock. A C corporation, prior to electing S status, may want to engage in an E reorganization to ensure that its capital structure when it elects S status will qualify under Code Sec. 1361. For instance, a C corporation could have common stock or preferred; by using an E reorganization, the preferred shareholders could exchange their preferred stock for common stock, thereby satisfying the one-class-of-stock requirement for S status.

.07 Code Sec. 368(a)(1)(F) Reorganizations

Code Sec. 368(a)(1)(F) prescribes that an F reorganization occurs when there is a "mere change in identity, form, or place or organization of one corporation, however effected."[159] A type F reorganization can resemble an A, C, or D reorganization. An example of a type A and F reorganization is found in Rev. Rul. 64-250.[160] An example illustrating the reasons for a reorganization under Rev. Rul. 64-250 is given below:

> **Example 12-35:** Al Braine formed Absolutely Inc. in Nebraska and elected S status on formation. Braine also qualified the corporation to do business in North Dakota. Over time, Absolutely Inc.'s operations changed, and it solely did business in North Dakota. To avoid having to pay tax to both North Dakota and Nebraska for future operations, Braine incorporated Absolutely Inc. in North Dakota and merged Absolutely Inc. of Nebraska into it tax-

---

[159] See IRS Letter Ruling 9213026 (December 30, 1991) for an example of when an S corporation was involved in an F reorganization.

[160] Rev. Rul. 64-250, 1964-2 CB 333.

free, pursuant to Code Sec. 368(a)(1)(F), keeping the same federal identification number.

Note that an F reorganization may also take the form of an A, C, or D reorganization; however, Code Sec. 381(b)'s rules of terminating the tax year of the transferor corporation do not apply; thus, there is no bunching of income.

Rev. Rul. 64-250[161] and Rev. Rul. 2004-85[162] prescribe that an F reorganization does not terminate the corporation's S election; likewise, the S election does not terminate when the S corporate subsidiaries elect QSub status (see Chapter 14 for a discussion of QSubs). IRS Letter Ruling 9309033 details that the transfer of an S corporation's assets to another corporation in connection with an F reorganization: (a) will not trigger Code Sec. 1374's rules; and (b) the S corporation's Accumulated Adjustment Account carries over to the newly-formed corporation, thereby allowing the new corporation, pursuant to Code Sec. 1368 to make tax-free distributions. With respect to the taxable year of the S corporation, IRS Letter Ruling 9001021 prescribes that the taxable year of the S corporation does not change; there is not acceleration of any items of income, loss, etc. reported by the shareholder due to the F reorganization.

.08 Utilizing a Reorganization under Code Sec. 368(a)(1)(F) to Establish an S Corporation for Federal Tax Purposes, but a Partnership for State Tax Purposes

In certain jurisdictions under present law, it is cheaper for S corporations in certain circumstances to operate as a partnership rather than as an S corporation. However, the S corporation may not want to liquidate and dissolve to be a partnership because it would be too costly. The IRS has sanctioned a situation where the S corporation can operate as a partnership for tax purposes, but as an S corporation for federal tax purposes. In IRS Letter Ruling 200450012, the following steps were utilized by an S corporation to establish itself as a partnership under state law, but an S corporation for purposes of federal tax law: The shareholders formed a general partnership (GP), which elected, pursuant to Reg. § 301.7701-3, to be treated as a corporation for federal tax purposes, filing a Form 2553. Then, the shareholders' existing S corporation (A) merged under state law into GP, with GP surviving, utilizing an F reorganization. The ruling held that the S election did not terminate as a result of the F reorganization, providing that GP met the requirements of Code Sec. 1361. Accordingly, the partnership agreement prescribed that no distribution and/or liquidation and/or equity interest would be created that would be treated as a second class of stock. Further, in sustaining the S election for GP, the IRS held that there cannot be any special allocations of income or losses; rather, the distributions have to be pursuant to ownership percentage.

.09 Code Sec. 368(a)(1)(G) Reorganizations

Code Sec. 368(a)(1)(G) prescribes the tax treatment for insolvent reorganizations in bankruptcy. Depending upon how the reorganization occurs, the S corporation could lose its status.

---

[161] 1964-2 CB 333. [162] 2004-33 IRB 1.

.10 Code Sec. 368(a)(1) Statutory Merger and Consolidations Involving, inter alia a Wholly-Owned Pass-Through Entity

States sensitive to the needs of their taxpayers have authorized the merger of corporations into LLCs. For an example of this, see Delaware General Corporation Law § 264. While the states are charging ahead, the IRS has been slow to develop a tax policy regarding these "mergers," with the result being that the IRS has flip-flopped with regulations in the area. Final regulations were promulgated for mergers and consolidations under Code Sec. 368(a)(1)(A) with January 23, 2006 being the basic effective date. Besides clarifying the rules regarding mergers and consolidations, the regulations also deal with disregarded entities, i.e., LLCs.

Basic definitions.

Mergers and consolidations. Code Sec. 368(a)(1)(A) covers two types of transactions, mergers and consolidations (these two types of transactions are called "A" reorganizations). Code Sec. 368(a)(1)(A) prescribes that in a statutory merger, the target corporation is absorbed into the acquiring corporation with the acquiring corporation receiving the assets and liabilities of the target in exchange for stock being issued to the shareholders of the acquiring corporation. In a consolidation, Code Sec. 368(a)(1)(A) prescribes that two or more corporations combine to form a new corporation.

An A reorganization can be effected under federal, state law or foreign law. However, for the reorganization to be recognized as an A reorganization, Reg. § 1.368-2(b)(ii) details that:

(A) All of the assets (other than those distributed in the transaction) and liabilities (except to the extent such liabilities are satisfied or discharged in the transaction or are nonrecourse liabilities to which assets distributed in the transaction are subject) of each member of one or more combining units (each a transferor unit) become the assets and liabilities of one or more members of one other combining unit (the transferee unit); and

(B) The combining entity of each transferor unit ceases its separate legal existence for all purposes, except it can defend itself against certain legal actions arising prior to the transaction.

Combining entity. Reg. § 1.368-2(b)(1)(i)(B) defines a combining entity as a business entity that is a corporation as defined in Reg. § 301.7701-2(b) that is not a disregarded entity.

Disregarded entity. Reg. § 1.368-2(b)(1)(i)(A) defines a disregarded entity as a business entity separate from its owner for Federal income tax purposes. Examples of disregarded entities include a domestic single member limited liability company that does not elect to be classified as a corporation for Federal income tax purposes, a corporation, REIT subsidiary within the meaning of Code Sec. 856(i)(2) and a Qualified S Corporation Subsidiary (Qsub).

Combining unit. Reg. § 1.368-2(b)(1)(i)(C) defines a combining unit as one composed solely of a combining entity and all disregarded entities, if any, the assets

¶1211.10

of which are treated as owned by such combining entity for Federal income tax purposes.

Forward and reverse triangular mergers. To allow flexibility, Congress has authorized forward and reverse triangular mergers to be classified as A reorganizations.

Forward triangular merger. Code Sec. 368(a)(2)(D) prescribes that a forward triangular merger is one where there is a merger of a target corporation into the subsidiary of another corporation where a subsidiary acquires "substantially all of the assets" of the acquired corporation in exchange for its parent's (voting or nonvoting) stock and:

(a) the acquired corporation is merged (in an A merger) into the acquiring subsidiary;

(b) the merger would have qualified as an "A" reorganization had the acquired corporation been merged into the parent instead of the subsidiary; and

(c) none of the subsidiary's stock is used in the transaction.

An S corporation can own all or a portion of the subsidiary stock. If the S corporation is the target of the merger, its existence will cease on the date of the merger. While stock of the acquiring subsidiary cannot be used in the transaction, there is no prohibition against using other property, such as cash or securities, of either the parent or the acquiring corporation, or both. However, in order to accomplish a tax free A reorganization, the amount of other property used in the exchange must not violate Code Sec. 368's continuity of interest rules. Further, the target's liabilities may also be assumed by the parent corporation without disqualifying the reorganization. In order to accomplish the forward triangular merger Reg. § 1.368-2(b)(2) prescribes that it can be effected regardless of whether the parent or the subsidiary are formed immediately before the merger, in anticipation of the merger, or after some preliminary steps have been taken to merge the target into the parent. An example will illustrate:

> **Example 12-36:** Under state law W, Alpha, Inc. merges into Beta, Inc., a wholly owned subsidiary of Omega, Inc. in exchange for Omega, Inc. stock. All the assets and liabilities of Alpha, Inc. are transferred to Beta, Inc., and Beta, Inc. ceases its separate legal existence in the merger. Alpha, Inc. shareholders exchange their Alpha, Inc. stock for the stock of Omega, Inc. The transaction qualifies as a forward triangular merger under Code Sec. 368(a)(1) and (a)(2)(D).

> **Tax Pointer 1:** If the Omega, Inc. stock received in the exchange were voting stock, the transaction would also qualify as a "C" reorganization under Code Sec. 368(a)(1)(C).

Reverse triangular merger. Code Sec. 368(a)(2)(E) defines this merger as one where a subsidiary corporation merges into a target corporation (which emerges as the surviving corporation) and the shareholders of the target corporation exchange their stock for stock of the subsidiary's parent. The surviving target corporation after the merger becomes a subsidiary of the merged subsidiary corporation's parent. To obtain a qualified reverse triangular merger:

(a) The target corporation retains substantially all of its assets and the assets of the merged subsidiary (other than the stock of its parent);

(b) the target corporation shareholders must exchange stock equaling control of the target corporation (i.e., at least 80%); and

(c) The target corporation shareholders. must receive voting stock of the parent corporation in exchange for at least 80 percent of the target corporation stock. An example will illustrate:

Example 12-37: The stock of Omega, Inc. has a value of $25,000. The stock of Beta, Inc. has a value of $75,000. On January 1, 2007, Omega, Inc., a wholly owned subsidiary of Theta, Inc., merges into Beta, Inc. In the merger, Beta, Inc.'s shareholders surrender all of their Beta, Inc. stock in exchange for Theta, Inc. voting stock. After the transaction, Beta, Inc. holds all of its own assets and all of Omega, Inc.'s assets. Based on these facts, the transaction qualifies under Code Sec. 368(a)(1)(A) by reason of the application of Code Sec. 368(a)(2)(E). In the transaction, former shareholders of Beta, Inc. surrender, in exchange for Theta, Inc. voting stock, an amount of Beta, Inc. stock (1,000/1,000 shares or 100 percent) which constitutes control of Beta, Inc. The stock of Beta, Inc. received by Theta, Inc. in exchange for Theta, Inc.'s prior interest in Omega, Inc. is not taken into account for purposes of Code Sec. 368(a)(2)(E)(ii) since the amount of Beta, Inc. stock constituting control of Beta, Inc. is measured before the transaction.

Tax Pointer 2: An S corporation can be the target corporation but its S election will terminate at the time of the merger because it will become a subsidiary and have a corporate shareholder.

Reg. § 1.368-2(j)(4) permits the parent's assumption of the liabilities of the acquired corporation; in such event this does not disqualify the reverse triangular merger because it is considered a contribution to capital. Reg. § 1.368-2(j)(3)(iii) permits the acquired corporation to transfer assets to a controlled corporation of the parent-acquiring corporation without violating the "substantially all" requirement. Also, IRS Letter Ruling 9520046 permits successive drop downs of target stock.

Examples explaining A reorganizations. To explain the regulations, the Internal Revenue Service at Reg. § 1.368-2(b)(1)(iii) set forth a number of examples with analysis to explain the operation of same. Pertinent examples are set forth below. In each of the examples, except as otherwise provided, each of R, V, Y, and Z is a C corporation. X is a domestic limited liability company. Except as otherwise provided, X is wholly owned by Y and is disregarded as an entity separate from Y for federal income tax purposes.

Example 12-38: Divisive transaction pursuant to a merger statute. Under State W law, Z transfers some of its assets and liabilities to Y, but retains the remainder of its assets and liabilities, remaining in existence for Federal income tax purposes following the transaction. The transaction qualifies as a merger under State W corporate law. The transaction does not qualify as an A

¶1211.10

reorganization because (a) all of the assets and liabilities of Z, the combining entity of the transferor unit, do not become the assets and liabilities of Y, the combining entity and sole member of the transferee unit; and (b) the separate legal existence of Z does not cease for all purposes.

Example 12-39: Merger of a target corporation into a disregarded entity in exchange for stock of the owner. Under State W law, Z, a C corporation, merges into X, an LLC. Pursuant to such law, the following events occur simultaneously at the effective time of the transaction: all of the assets and liabilities of Z become the assets and liabilities of X, and Z's separate legal existence ceases for all purposes. In the merger, the Z shareholders exchange their stock of Z for stock of Y. This transaction qualifies as an A reorganization because the transaction is effected pursuant to State W law and the following events occur simultaneously at the effective time of the transaction: all of the assets and liabilities of Z, the combining entity and sole member of the transferor unit, become the assets and liabilities of one or more members of the transferee unit that is comprised of Y, the combining entity of the transferee unit, and X, a disregarded entity the assets of which Y is treated as owning for federal income tax purposes, and Z ceases its separate legal existence for all purposes.

Example 12-40: Merger of a target S corporation that owns a QSub into a disregarded entity. Under State W law, Z, an S corporation which has a wholly owned Qsub, U, merges into X, an LLC. Pursuant to such law, the following events occur simultaneously at the effective time of the transaction: all of the assets and liabilities of Z become the assets and liabilities of X, and Z's separate legal existence ceases for all purposes. In the merger, the Z shareholders exchange their stock of Z for stock of Y. The transaction pursuant to Reg. § 1.1361-5(b)(3) Example 9 is treated as a transfer of the assets of U to X, followed by X's transfer of these assets to U in exchange for stock of U. This transaction qualifies as an A reorganization because:

(i) The transaction is effected pursuant to State W law and the following events occur simultaneously at the effective time of the transaction: (A) all of the assets and liabilities of Z and U, the sole members of the transferor unit, become the assets and liabilities of one or more members of the transferee unit that is comprised of Y, the combining entity of the transferee unit, and X, a disregarded entity the assets of which Y is treated as owning for federal income tax purposes; and (B) Z ceases its separate legal existence for all purposes; and

(ii) The deemed formation by Z of U pursuant to Reg. § 1.1361-5(b)(1) (as a consequence of the termination of U's QSub election) is disregarded for Federal income tax purposes.

Moreover, the deemed transfer of the assets of U in exchange for U stock does not cause the transaction to fail to qualify as a statutory merger or consolidation.

¶1211.10

Example 12-41: Triangular merger of a target corporation into a disregarded entity. Under State W law, Z, a C corporation, merges into X, an LLC. V owns 100 percent of the outstanding stock of Y and in the merger of Z into X, the Z shareholders exchange their stock of Z for stock of V with Z transfering substantially all of its properties to X. Pursuant to such law, the following events occur simultaneously at the effective time of the transaction: all of the assets and liabilities of Z become the assets and liabilities of X, and Z's separate legal existence ceases for all purposes. In the merger, the Z shareholders exchange their stock of Z for stock of Y. This transaction qualifies as an A reorganization because the transaction is effected pursuant to State W law and the following events occur simultaneously at the effective time of the transaction: all of the assets and liabilities of Z, the combining entity and sole member of the transferor unit, become the assets and liabilities of one or more members of the transferee unit that is comprised of Y, the combining entity of the transferee unit, and X, a disregarded entity the assets of which Y is treated as owning for federal income tax purposes, and Z ceases its separate legal existence for all purposes.

Example 12-42: Merger of a target corporation into a disregarded entity owned by a partnership. Under State W law, Z, a C corporation, merges into X, an LLC. Pursuant to such law, the following events occur simultaneously at the effective time of the transaction: all of the assets and liabilities of Z become the assets and liabilities of X, and Z's separate legal existence ceases for all purposes. In the merger, the Z shareholders exchange their stock of Z for a partnership interest in Y, an entity which is classified as a partnership for Federal income tax purposes. The transaction does not qualify as a tax free A reorganization because all of the assets and liabilities of Z, the combining entity and sole member of the transferor unit, do not become the assets and liabilities of one or more members of a transferee unit because neither X nor Y qualifies as a combining entity.

Example 12-43: Merger of a disregarded entity into a corporation. Under State W law, X merges into Z. Pursuant to such law, the following events occur simultaneously at the effective time of the transaction: all of the assets and liabilities of X (but not the assets and liabilities of Y other than those of X) become the assets and liabilities of Z, and X's separate legal existence ceases for all purposes. This transaction does not qualify as a tax free A reorganization because all of the assets and liabilities of a transferor unit do not become the assets and liabilities of one or more members of the transferee unit. Also, X does not qualify as a combining entity.

Example 12-44: Merger of a corporation into a disregarded entity in exchange for interests in the disregarded entity. Under State W law, Z merges into X. Pursuant to such law, the following events occur simultaneously at the effective time of the transaction: all of the assets and liabilities of Z become the assets and liabilities of X, and Z's separate legal existence ceases for all purposes. In the merger of Z into X, the Z shareholders exchange their stock of Z for interests in X so that, immediately after the merger, X is not disregarded as an entity separate from Y for federal income tax purposes. Following the merger, pursuant to Reg. §301.7701-3(b)(1)(i), X is classified as a partnership for federal income tax purposes. The transaction does not qualify as a tax free A reorganization because immediately after the merger X is not disregarded as an entity separate from Y and, consequently, all of the assets and liabilities of Z, the combining entity of the transferor unit, do not become the assets and liabilities of one or more members of a transferee unit.

Example 12-45: *Merger transaction preceded by distribution.* Z operates two unrelated businesses, Business P and Business Q, each of which represents 50 percent of the value of the assets of Z. Y desires to acquire and continue operating Business P, but does not want to acquire Business Q. Pursuant to a single plan, Z sells Business Q for cash to parties unrelated to Z and Y in a taxable transaction, and then distributes the proceeds of the sale pro rata to its shareholders. Then, pursuant to State W law, Z merges into Y. Pursuant to such law, the following events occur simultaneously at the effective time of the transaction: all of the assets and liabilities of Z related to Business P become the assets and liabilities of Y, and Z's separate legal existence ceases for all purposes. In the merger, the Z shareholders exchange their Z stock for Y stock. The transaction qualifies as a tax free A reorganization because the transaction is effected pursuant to State W law and the following events occur simultaneously at the effective time of the transaction: all of the assets and liabilities of Z, the combining entity and sole member of the transferor unit, become the assets and liabilities of Y, the combining entity and sole member of the transferee unit, and Z ceases its separate legal existence for all purposes.

Example 12-46: *State law conversion of target corporation into a limited liability company.* Y acquires the stock of V from the V shareholders in exchange for consideration that consists of 50 percent voting stock of Y and 50 percent cash. Immediately after the stock acquisition, V files the necessary documents to convert from a corporation to a limited liability company under State W law. Y's acquisition of the stock of V and the conversion of V to a limited liability company are steps in a single integrated acquisition by Y of the assets of V. The transaction does not qualify as a tax free A reorganization because V, the combining entity of the transferor unit, does not cease its separate legal existence. Although V is an entity disregarded from its owner for Federal income tax purposes, it continues to exist as a juridical entity after the conversion.

Example 12-47: *Dissolution of target corporation.* Y acquires the stock of Z from the Z shareholders in exchange for consideration that consists of 50 percent voting stock of Y and 50 percent cash. Immediately after the stock acquisition, Z files a certificate of dissolution pursuant to State W law and commences winding up its activities. Under State W dissolution law, ownership and title to Z's assets does not automatically vest in Y upon dissolution. Instead, Z transfers assets to its creditors in satisfaction of its liabilities and transfers its remaining assets to Y in the liquidation stage of the dissolution.

¶1211.10

Y's acquisition of the stock of Z and the dissolution of Z are steps in a single integrated acquisition by Y of the assets of Z. The transaction does not qualify as a tax free A reorganization because Y does not acquire all of the assets of Z as a result of Z filing the certificate of dissolution or simultaneously with Z ceasing its separate legal existence. Instead, Y acquires the assets of Z by reason of Z's transfer of its assets to Y.

Example 12-48: Merger of corporate partner into a partnership. Y owns an interest in X, an entity classified as a partnership for federal income tax purposes, that represents a 60 percent capital and profits interest in X. Z owns an interest in X that represents a 40 percent capital and profits interest. Under State W law, Z merges into X. Pursuant to such law, the following events occur simultaneously at the effective time of the transaction: all of the assets and liabilities of Z become the assets and liabilities of X, and Z ceases its separate legal existence for all purposes. In the merger, the Z shareholders exchange their stock of Z for stock of Y. As a result of the merger, X becomes an entity that is disregarded as an entity separate from Y for federal income tax purposes. The transaction qualifies as a tax free A reorganization because the transaction is effected pursuant to State W law and the following events occur simultaneously at the effective time of the transaction: all of the assets and liabilities of Z, the combining entity and sole member of the transferor unit, become the assets and liabilities of one or more members of the transferee unit that is comprised of Y, the combining entity of the transferee unit, and X, a disregarded entity the assets of which Y is treated as owning for federal income tax purposes immediately after the transaction, and Z ceases its separate legal existence for all purposes.

Example 12-49: State law consolidation. Under State W law, Z and V consolidate. Pursuant to such law, the following events occur simultaneously at the effective time of the transaction: all of the assets and liabilities of Z and V become the assets and liabilities of Y, an entity that is created in the transaction, and the existence of Z and V continues in Y. In the consolidation, the Z shareholders and the V shareholders exchange their stock of Z and V, respectively, for stock of Y. The transaction qualifies as a tax free A reorganization because the transaction is effected pursuant to State W law and the following events occur simultaneously at the effective time of the transaction: all of the assets and liabilities of Z and V, respectively, each of which is the combining entity of a transferor unit, become the assets and liabilities of Y, the combining entity and sole member of the transferee unit, and Z and V each ceases its separate legal existence for all purposes.

Example 12-50: Transaction effected pursuant to foreign statutes. Z and Y are entities organized under the laws of Country Q and classified as corporations for federal income tax purposes. Z and Y combine. Pursuant to statutes of Country Q the following events occur simultaneously: all of the assets and liabilities of Z become the assets and liabilities of Y, and Z's separate legal existence ceases for all purposes. The transaction qualifies as a tax free A reorganization because the transaction is effected pursuant to statutes of

Country Q and the following events occur simultaneously at the effective time of the transaction: all of the assets and liabilities of Z, the combining entity of the transferor unit, become the assets and liabilities of Y, the combining entity and sole member of the transferee unit, and Z ceases its separate legal existence for all purposes.

Example 12-51: *Foreign law amalgamation using parent stock.* Z and V are entities organized under the laws of Country Q and classified as corporations for Federal income tax purposes. Z and V amalgamate. Pursuant to statutes of Country Q, the following events occur simultaneously: all the assets and liabilities of Z and V become the assets and liabilities of R, an entity that is created in the transaction and that is wholly owned by Y immediately after the transaction, and Z's and V's separate legal existences cease for all purposes. In the transaction, the Z and V shareholders exchange their Z and V stock, respectively, for stock of Y. The transaction qualifies as a tax free A reorganization because the transaction is effected pursuant to Country Q law and the following events occur simultaneously at the effective time of the transaction: all of the assets and liabilities of Z and V, respectively, each of which is the combining entity of a transferor unit, become the assets and liabilities of R, the combining entity and sole member of the transferee unit, with regard to each of the above transfers, and Z and V each ceases its separate legal existence for all purposes. Because Y is in control of R immediately after the transaction, the Z shareholders and the V shareholders will be treated as receiving stock of a corporation that is in control of R, the combining entity of the transferee unit that is deemed the acquiring corporation.

.11 Short Form Merger

Under state law, corporations have the statutory ability to eliminate minority shareholders by engaging in a short form merger paying the minority shareholders the appraisal value for their shares. The process is very simple. In the usual situation, a corporation forms a subsidiary and then merges itself into the subsidiary with the required shareholder super majority vote. In Delaware, the vote requires 90% of the shareholders to agree to the merger; in Pennsylvania, per the recent case involving *Colorcon, Inc. v. USA*,[163] the majority only had to be 80% of the shareholders. The only rights the minority shareholders have when a short form merger occurs is, as illustrated in *Colorcon*, to contest the value of the appraisal rights.

---

[163] 2013-1 USTC ¶ 50,310 (Ct. Claims 2013).

Chapter 13

Comparisons to Other Business Entities

A person today faces a complex choice of entities to use in business, income, and estate tax planning. Should a corporation be used, and if so, should subchapter S status be chosen? If not a corporation, then should one operate as a sole proprietorship, a partnership, or limited liability company (LLC)? If a partnership is used, should it be a general partnership or limited partnership? The paragraphs in this chapter compare the various business entities to S corporations, pointing out the advantages and disadvantages of each type.

¶ 1301 C Corporations

.01 Definition of a C Corporation

A C corporation files a federal income tax Form 1120 and a state franchise tax form in the states where it is doing business and/or in which it is incorporated. Examples of C corporations are AT&T, IBM, and any other corporation that does not elect S status. A C corporation is established by filing its articles of incorporation in the state where it plans to operate. The organization can be formed by as few as one individual. Also, depending on its general makeup, a C corporation may have to satisfy various security laws to operate.

.02 Numbers and Types of Shareholders

A C corporation can have unlimited shares, common stock, voting and nonvoting rights, preferred stock, convertible preferred stock, etc., and anyone can be a shareholder (i.e., an individual, a trust, an estate, a nonresident alien, another C corporation, an LLC, and an S corporation).

¶1301.02

.03 Estate and Income Tax Planning

A C corporation, compared to other business entities (e.g., an S corporation and/or a personal service corporation), has numerous income and estate tax planning possibilities because it can have many classes of stock: voting and nonvoting, common, and preferred. The advantages of having more than one class of stock are illustrated in Example 13-1.

> **Example 13-1:** A mother, Muriel, and daughter, Dellie, desire to establish AMD Inc., a C corporation. Muriel is wealthy. Dellie just graduated from college and has never held a job. Muriel proposes that she put in the necessary capital to start AMD Inc. Dellie will manage the business. They decide to capitalize the business at $1,000,001 with $1,000,000 in preferred stock and $1 in common stock. Dellie will contribute $1 and take back all the common stock. Muriel will contribute $1,000,000 and take the preferred. To provide a return on Muriel's investment, the preferred stock will pay a cumulative 9 percent dividend, even though this is substantially higher than the prime rate of interest at the time the stock is issued. At the time of Muriel's death, the business is worth $10,000,000. Besides Dellie, Muriel has a son, Sam, who is emotionally disturbed. In Muriel's will, she bequeaths the preferred stock to Sam in trust, with directions to the trustee to use the income from the stock for the care of Sam. By using this approach, the following has been achieved: (1) Muriel obtains a high rate of return on her funds during her life; (2) at her death, Muriel has used the investment to provide a source of funds for Sam; (3) Dellie is able to start a business venture with the necessary funds, providing she is willing to pay Muriel a high rate of return; and (4) Muriel has avoided including the corporation's increase in value in her estate.

.04 Medical Reimbursement Plan

Shareholders of a C corporation can be participants in a medical reimbursement plan, whereby the government subsidizes all medical bills without regard to the 7.5 percent of AGI floor imposed on medical expenses claimed as itemized deductions. Example 13-2 illustrates the benefits of a medical reimbursement plan.

> **Example 13-2:** Assume the same facts as in Example 13-1. Muriel and Dellie are the sole shareholder-employees of AMD Inc. They establish a medical reimbursement plan for the corporation that pays all medical expenses, medical insurance premiums, dental bills, etc. Muriel, in the first tax year of the corporation, receives reimbursement from the corporation for $5,000 of medical expenses that were not reimbursed by insurance paid for by the corporation for all the employees. Muriel had adjusted gross income of $100,000. If AMD Inc. did not have a medical reimbursement plan, then Muriel would not be able to deduct any medical expenses on her Form 1040, Schedule A, because her medical expenses do not exceed her threshold deductibility amount of $7,500 (7½% × $100,000). The corporation can deduct $5,000 from its taxable income if there is a medical reimbursement plan in effect. So, if the corporation had net income of $5,000 before reimbursing Muriel for her

medical expenses and insurance, then AMD Inc. would not have to pay any income tax because its expenses would equal its income.

.05 Income Tax Brackets

Corporations, other than personal service corporations, are subject to federal income taxes at the following tax rates.

2010 Corporate Income Tax Rate Schedule

Taxable Income				
Over	Not Over	Pay	Tax Rate	On Excess Over
$ 0	$ 50,000	$ 0	+ 15%	$ 0
50,000	75,000	7,500	+ 25%	50,000
75,000	100,000	13,750	+ 34%	75,000
100,000	335,000	22,250	+ 39%	100,000
335,000	10,000,000	113,900	+ 34%	335,000
10,000,000	15,000,000	3,400,000	+ 35%	10,000,000
15,000,000	18,333,333	5,150,000	+ 38%	15,000,000
18,333,333			+ 35%	

In comparison, individuals are subject to federal income tax rates of up to 35 percent. There are four basic filing statuses for individuals: single, married filing jointly, married filing separately, or head of household. The single tax rate schedule for 2011 is shown below.

Single Taxpayer
For Tax Years Beginning in 2011 (Projected)

Taxable Income				
Over	But not over	Pay	% on excess	Of the amount over
$ 0	$ 8,375	$ 0	10	$ 0
8,375	34,000	837.50	15	8,375
34,000	82,400	4,681.25	25	34,000
82,400	171,850	16,781.25	28	82,400
171,850	373,650	41,827.25	33	171,850
373,650		108,421.25	35	373,650

Example 13-3 shows a simplified version of tax savings available using a C corporation, excluding the payment of payroll taxes, unemployment insurance, health and welfare benefits, state and local taxes, etc.

Example 13-3: Assume that Alicia, a single individual, earns $373,650 in 2010, but only needs $100,000 to live, and invests the rest after payment of income tax in stocks for retirement. Alicia's maximum tax bracket is 35 percent, and her income tax on $373,650 based on the table above is $108,421.25 leaving her a net of $265,228.75. Assume that Alicia forms X, Inc. as a C corporation and Alicia uses this to operate her business. X, Inc. pays Alicia a salary of $201,800, leaving her net income of $150,089.25 after payment of income taxes ($201,800 – $51,710.75 = $150,089.25 [tax per tax table above; Alicia is in the 33 percent bracket]). The corporation has $121,578.50 ($373,650 – $201,800 – $50,271.50 [corporate income taxes of $50,271.50 ($22,250 + $28,021.50) on $171,850 of income ($373,650 – $201,800 = $171,850)]) of funds before payment of FICA and FUTA to invest. By using a C corporation, Alicia saves $6,439 on a gross basis ($108,421.25 [income tax on $373,650 of income if Alicia did not utilize X, Inc. in her tax planning] less $101,982.25 [the combined tax of $51,710.75 on $201,800 of salary plus $50,271.50, the corporate tax on $171,850]= $6,439 each year. Note: this tax savings is in addition to a medical reimbursement plan discussed above and other benefits discussed herein. [It also should be noted that under Code Sec. 531 *et seq.*, a corporation is prevented from accumulating too many funds under this procedure. If a corporation is found to have accumulated too much, then a penalty tax is imposed.]

Tax Pointer: By accumulating funds in a C corporation, other than paying salary, a shareholder-employee is potentially depriving him- or herself of a tax benefit, especially in retirement plans. If a corporation is using a defined benefit plan, the amount of contribution is geared to compensation. By only declaring a limited amount of salary, a shareholder-employee is precluded from accumulating a large amount of funds in the retirement plan.

.06 Health, Welfare, and Retirement Plans

Retirement plans today are basically standardized for all business entities. Thus, a participant in a pension plan can borrow up to 50 percent of the vested balance up to $50,000. However, there are certain benefits available to C corporations. For instance, a C corporation can also establish group life insurance for its shareholder-employees, deducting the premiums and thereby reducing the cost of life insurance. Note, however, that all employees, and not just those who are shareholders, must generally be covered under such plans.

.07 Dividends-Received Deduction

C corporations generally are allowed a dividends-received deduction under Code Sec. 243 for dividends they receive from their stock investments. Generally, Code Sec. 243's dividends-received deduction produces benefits for corporations in comparison to individuals, but due to Code Sec. 1(h)'s special tax break given to individuals, the maximum tax on dividends is now 15 percent. Example 13-4 illustrates the effect Code Sec. 1(h) has on corporate planning. Example 13-4 illustrates the advantage of this tax break.

Example 13-4: Assume that Alicia Lowe in Example 13-3 owns shares of IBM stock which pays a dividend of $1,000 per year. Lowe is in the 35 percent tax bracket; notwithstanding, Alicia pays only $150 of tax on the dividend (15 percent times $1,000). If Alicia contributed her IBM stock to her wholly-owned

¶1301.06

C corporation, Bandy, Inc., which is in the 35 percent bracket, the tax on the dividend would be $105 ($1,000 minus $700 [70% times $1,000] times 35%), reflecting Code Sec. 243's dividends-received deduction. Note: while this example illustrates the tax benefits produced by a dividends-received deduction, the problem of double taxation remains when removing the dividends from the corporation.

.08 Ease of Formation

The formation of a C corporation is easy: all one has to do is file a certificate of incorporation with the secretary of state in the state where the C corporation will be conducting its business and then obtain a federal identification number. There are no elections that have to be made. If the C corporation will be operating in another jurisdiction, then it must qualify itself in this other jurisdiction as well.

.09 Creditor Protection

All shareholders are immune from the creditors of a C corporation providing they observe corporate formalities such as holding an annual shareholders' and directors' meeting and having officers sign all documents with their titles (for instance, in Examples 13-3 and 13-4, Alicia Lowe should sign all Bandy Inc. documents as "Alicia Lowe, President").

.10 Principal Advantages and Disadvantages

As discussed, a C corporation offers a number of tax advantages: a medical reimbursement plan, progressive tax brackets, and various forms of equity ownership (see Examples 13-3 and 13-4 for illustrations of these principles). A basic tax problem with a C corporation is removing funds from the corporation after they are taxed at the corporate level. Example 13-5 illustrates this point.

Example 13-5: Assume the same facts as in Example 13-3. Alicia Lowe is the sole shareholder-employee and she needs funds to buy a house. If the corporation declares a dividend, Alicia would be taxed, pursuant to Code Sec. 1(h), at the rate of 15 percent. Thus, if the dividend was $100,000, Alicia would pay a tax of $15,000. However, the corporation is in the 35 percent bracket. This means that the corporation must pay $35,000 of tax on each $100,000 earned. Thus, the combined corporate and personal tax on this dividend is 50 percent (35 percent on the corporation; 15 percent on Alicia). If the corporation paid Alicia a salary of $100,000, then Alicia (who is in the 35 percent bracket) would pay tax of $35,000 on $100,000 worth of salary. In addition, besides payroll taxes as discussed below, the corporation would have to pay unemployment insurance, Workers Compensation insurance, and disability insurance geared to Alicia's salary. In addition to the above, the IRS could attack the salary as unreasonable, with the consequence being that there would be a combined corporate and personal income tax rate of 50 percent (35 percent to the corporation, 15 percent personal) if a portion of the salary was deemed a dividend and not compensation.

Lowe could, of course, liquidate the corporation, but this would terminate the corporate activities. On liquidation, Lowe would generally recognize capital gains equal to the difference between her basis in her capital stock and the amount realized from the net sales of the corporate assets (because the gain would be taxed at capital gains rates, there would be a savings over ordinary income taxation). But liquidation is an extraordinary step and means that the corporation will go out of existence forever.

Lowe could also sell a portion of her stock, but with small, closely held businesses, there are very few taxpayers willing to buy the stock due to control issues; Lowe will hold the controlling block of stock effectively rendering the buyer without a meaningful vote on issues of corporate management. Thus, even if Lowe could find a willing buyer for a portion of her stock, she will likely have to sell at a steep discount (lack of control discount).

Even if Lowe does find a buyer for a minority portion of her stock, she is still inviting difficulty, assuming she maintains a role in the company either as a director or an officer. This is because the buyer could sue Lowe in state court in a derivative action for corporate waste if he or she is dissatisfied with Lowe's management (in a derivative action, others can be brought into the lawsuit, namely the corporation's accountant and/or lawyer if their involvement can be proven).[1]

For small, closely-held businesses operating as a C corporation, the benefits of Code Sec. 199's 9 percent deduction for domestic producers offers no direct benefit personally to the shareholders. In contrast, operating as an S corporation allows the shareholders to benefit from Code Sec. 199's 9 percent deduction, because the deduction is passed through directly to the shareholders. For a discussion of Code Sec. 199, see ¶ 722.

¶ 1302 S Corporations

.01 Definition of an S Corporation

An S corporation is a C corporation where the shareholders file an election to be taxed personally on the corporation's income. To make the S election, the S corporation files a Form 2553[2] within the required statutory period.[3] If it files the S election on formation, all income, losses, capital gains and losses, charitable deductions, etc. of the corporation pass through to the shareholders to be taxed on a shareholder's Form 1040, or the Form 1041 if the shareholder is an estate or trust. In contrast, shareholders of a C corporation pay a double tax on their earnings (as discussed at ¶ 1301.10). An S corporation can be formed by just one individual.

.02 Numbers and Types of Shareholders

Unlike a C corporation, an S corporation is restricted to two types of stock: voting and nonvoting. Nonvoting stock is stock that is entitled to the same distributions from the corporation, except that it cannot vote in shareholders' meetings. However, ownership of nonvoting stock does not preclude the shareholders from

---

[1] The buyer could also sue Lowe for securities law violations. See *Landreth Timber Co. v. Landreth*, SCt, 1985, 471 US 681, 685.

[2] See a sample of Form 2553 at Appendix 1.
[3] See ¶ 401.03.

participating in a derivative action in state court against the corporation's officers, directors, and controlling shareholders. Also, only certain taxpayers can be shareholders: individuals (other than nonresident aliens), estates, certain S corporations,[4] and certain trusts. Consequently, a C corporation cannot be a shareholder in an S corporation, a partnership cannot be a shareholder in an S corporation, etc. Interestingly, the converse is not prohibited: an S corporation can be a shareholder in a C corporation, a partner in a partnership, or a member in an LLC. Further, an S corporation can only have 100 shareholders. Thus, because of these restrictions, estate and individual tax planning becomes limited. (Refer to Example 13-1 where the benefits of preferred stock are illustrated in family estate planning.) Also, because all earnings are reported by the shareholder yearly, an S corporation cannot be used to accumulate income as shown in Example 13-3.

The trusts that can be established to hold S corporation stock are restricted in their operation by their need to meet certain standards (e.g., a qualified subchapter S trust (QSST) must distribute all its income each year). Contrast this with other business entities such as limited liability companies (LLCs) where trusts accumulate income for children without the punitive provisions of electing small business trusts (ESBTs) (see Example 13-13 for an illustration of the use of trusts with LLCs).

.03 Estate and Income Tax Planning

Because of the restrictions on the numbers and types of shareholders, estate tax planning with an S corporation is limited.[5] However, there are income tax planning possibilities because all the income, losses, expenses, etc. pass through to the shareholders directly. Example 13-6 illustrates family tax-planning possibilities:

Example 13-6: David Gates forms DG Inc., which elects S status. David has two children, Bruce and Charles, both of whom are going to medical school. David owns 50 percent of the stock, and his two children, Bruce and Charles, own 25 percent each. The corporation earns $100,000. David would receive $50,000, and Bruce and Charles would each receive $25,000, allowing them to use the funds for medical school. (Note that David must be fairly compensated for services or capital provided to the S corporation before allocating a share of remaining S corporation income to his sons.)

Tax Pointer: Code Sec. 2036 impacts family planning to a considerable degree. See ¶ 1109.03 for a discussion of Code Sec. 2036 as it applies to closely-held family S corporations.

.04 Medical Reimbursement Plan

Medical reimbursement plans are precluded for more-than-2-percent shareholder-employees. However, Code Sec. 162(l) provides some amelioratory relief to the shareholders as illustrated in Example 13-7.

Example 13-7: Alpha Inc., a calendar-year S corporation, has one shareholder-employee, Ronald Levy. In 2010, Alpha Inc. pays $10,000 for Levy's health insurance. Ronald has $18,000 of dental bills which are not covered by

---

[4] See discussion at Chapter 14.   [5] See discussion at ¶ 1109.02.

his health insurance. Because Levy is not an employee for purposes of Code Sec. 106, Levy must recognize $10,000 of income. However, Code Sec. 162(l) does provide some relief in that Levy can deduct the whole premium of $10,000. As to deducting his $18,000 of dental bills, he is subject to Code Sec. 213(a)'s 7.5 percent limit geared to adjusted gross income.

.05 Income Tax Brackets

As a general rule, an S corporation does not pay any income tax. Thus, the tax brackets are those of the individual shareholders. Accordingly, if children are shareholders, the income could bear no tax depending upon the amount allocated to the child and the child's bracket. Of course, in the case of a high-bracket shareholder, the S corporation's income could be taxed at rates as high as 35 percent. The only time an S corporation pays income tax is when it violates (1) the 10-year rule for built-in gains of Code Sec. 1374; (2) the 25-percent-of-gross-income limit for passive investment income of Code Sec. 1375; and/or tax on LIFO recognition under Code Sec. 1363(d). For state tax purposes, the S corporation may wish to operate as a partnership. See ¶ 206, which provides a discussion on this point.

.06 Health, Welfare, and Retirement Plans

For tax years beginning after December 31, 2001, Code Sec. 4975 was amended by adding Code Sec. 4975(f)(6)(B)(iii) to provide that S corporation shareholder-employees can borrow from their retirement plans, just like shareholder-employees of C corporations can, subject to the limitations of Code Sec. 72(b)(2). Their loan has to equal the lesser of: (1) $50,000 (reduced as explained below) or (2) half the present value (but not less than $10,000) of the participant's vested benefits under the plan. The $50,000 amount must be reduced per Code Sec. 72(p)(2) by the excess (if any) of (1) the highest outstanding balance of loans from the plan during the one-year period ending on the day preceding the date of the loan over (2) the outstanding balance of those loans on the date of the loan. Loans to participants are permitted if loans are available to all participants on a reasonably equivalent basis, are not made available to highly compensated employees in an amount greater than made available to other employees, are made in accordance with specific provisions in the plan, bear a reasonable rate of interest, and are adequately secured.

Several points should be noted: (1) Congress hopes that by permitting owner-employees to borrow from their plans, employers (S corporations, partnerships, LLCs and Schedule C filers) will adopt and maintain qualified plans as opposed to SEPs and SIMPLE plans; and (2) the changes to Code Sec. 4975 with respect to borrowing by owner-employees does not apply to IRAs.

Care should be practiced in borrowing from a retirement plan. Code Sec. 4975 requires that the loan be repaid in five years, using "substantially level amounts over the term of the loan." Plotkin[6] held that Code Sec. 4975's level payment procedure does not include a balloon payment at the end.

---

[6] *C.W. Plotkin*, 81 TCM 1395, Dec. 54,285(M), TC Memo. 2001-71.

¶1302.05

Premiums for group life insurance are not deductible for a more-than-2-percent shareholder-employee.

.07 Dividends-Received Deduction

Code Sec. 243 prescribes that there is no dividends-received deduction for an S corporation since dividends are reported directly by individuals. Because individuals do not receive a dividends-received deduction, as opposed to C corporations that do, this tax benefit is not available to S corporations.

.08 Ease of Formation

Formation of an S corporation is relatively simple: the same steps are followed as with a C corporation, except that it must file a Form 2553 to elect S status. Also, the state where the corporation is formed may allow it to elect S status as well, allowing all the income from the corporation to pass state-tax-free to the shareholder. State law should be checked to determine taxability of corporations that elect S status in the state. If an S corporation will be operating in another jurisdiction, then it must qualify itself in that other jurisdiction. Upon qualifying in that jurisdiction, the S corporation should check the jurisdiction's law to see if it recognizes S status.

.09 Creditor Protection

Like a C corporation, shareholders of an S corporation are immune from attack from creditors, providing they observe certain corporate formalities such as annual shareholders' and directors' meetings, etc.

.10 Principal Advantages and Disadvantages

There are a number of advantages to operating in an S corporation format. For instance, an individual shareholder can receive creditor protection for business activities, yet report the income on the individual's Form 1040. Also, because there is one level of taxation, sale of the corporate business becomes easier than with a C corporation. As discussed at ¶ 102.17 and ¶ 722, S corporations provide an easy vehicle to obtain a Code Sec. 199's 9 percent domestic producer deduction for the sole shareholder for his or her activities, because salary can be generated easily—a requirement for the Code Sec. 199. In contrast, sole proprietorships, one-person limited liability companies, and a two-person limited liability company operating as a partnership, cannot generate salaries for its owners, by definition, since all income from these activities are treated as self-employment income.

The primary disadvantages of an S corporation are that there can be no medical reimbursement plan, no group life insurance, no home office deduction (but see ¶ 1307.06 for a limited exception to this rule), and limited estate and income tax planning.

Another disadvantage is that there is no ability to control reporting of income to shareholders, as is the case with a C corporation or PSC, where generally income distribution can be regulated by salary. For individuals in the 35 percent tax bracket, this can be an important consideration, especially when the highest tax rate for a C corporation and PSC is 35 percent.

¶1302.10

¶ 1303 Personal Service Corporations (PSCs)

.01 Definition of a Personal Service Corporation (PSC)

A personal service corporation (PSC) is a C corporation whose principal activity is the performance of personal services by employee-owners (employees owning more than 10 percent of the corporation's stock). Various Code provisions define PSCs, but the primary definitions are found in Code Sec. 269A and the regulations under Code Sec. 448. The organization can be formed by as few as one individual.

A PSC is a nebulous concept. Included in the definition are the normal businesses one would think would be included, such as medical, nursing, veterinary, legal, and accounting practices. However, the regulations under Code Sec. 448 add consulting, but exclude athletes and insurance brokers.

The consequence of being a PSC is that there are no graduated tax rates—all income is taxed at 35 percent, in contrast to a C corporation which has graduated rates. Also, the Code restricts certain tax attributes of a PSC, such as the amount of money that can be accumulated in the corporation and during the tax year.

Furthermore, there may be restrictions under state law as to ownership. For instance, if a doctor incorporates, state law may require that only doctors can be shareholders in the corporation. Thus, if a mother is a physician and a son is a lawyer, the son could not be a shareholder in the mother's corporation and vice versa.[7]

> **Tax Pointer:** Because the graduated rates of income tax on corporate income are not available, and the tax rate on corporate income is so high, the businessperson should consider adopting S corporation status for his or her PSC, thereby benefitting from graduated income tax rates on the income. The drawback is that the businessperson will generally lose certain tax benefits such as a full medical reimbursement plan, life insurance, and the dividends-received deduction.

.02 Numbers and Types of Shareholders

Anyone can be a shareholder in a PSC. However, if a professional such as a doctor, lawyer, etc. wishes to incorporate as a PSC, state law may restrict exactly who can become a shareholder.[8] Accordingly, the professional, prior to incorporation, should verify who can be a shareholder in the PSC under state law.

.03 Estate and Income Tax Planning

For PSCs where there are no limitations under state law (i.e., for professionals, etc.), the same estate and income tax planning opportunities exist as for regular C corporations. With PSCs that involve professionals, the estate and income tax planning possibilities become limited because of state restrictions on who can be a shareholder.

---

[7] This type of professional restriction is changing in a number of states. For instance, in New Jersey, lay people can own up to 49 percent of an accountant's practice (N.J.S.A. 45:2B-54.1).

[8] *Ibid.*

.04 Medical Reimbursement Plan

Medical reimbursement plans are available because a PSC is a C corporation.

.05 Income Tax Brackets

Unlike a regular C corporation, as discussed above, the graduated income tax brackets are not available to the PSC; all income is taxed at the rate of 35 percent.

.06 Health, Welfare, and Retirement Plans

Because a PSC is a C corporation, it has the same health, welfare, and retirement benefits as C corporations.

.07 Dividends-Received Deduction

Because a PSC is a C corporation, it is entitled to the dividends-received deduction.

.08 Ease of Formation

A PSC, like a C corporation, is easy to form; however, if professionals are to be shareholders, there may be additional requirements under state law that have to be met. If the PSC will be operating in another jurisdiction, then it must qualify itself in that other jurisdiction.

.09 Creditor Protection

Like a C corporation, all shareholders of a PSC are protected from general creditors, providing certain corporate formalities are observed, such as holding annual shareholders' and directors' meetings, having officers sign all documents with their title, etc. However, state law may prescribe that professionals (such as doctors, nurses, lawyers, accountants, etc.) cannot be exempted from liability for malpractice.

.10 Principal Advantages and Disadvantages

The primary advantage is that a PSC has the same benefits as a C corporation, such as liability protection from creditors in most instances, borrowing from the retirement plan, medical reimbursement plan, etc. The primary disadvantage of a PSC for businesses other than licensed professionals is that the Code is nebulous. Thus, if a business is formed as a C corporation, there is always the possibility that, unless it is engaged in some definite activity where corporate resources have to be used (such as manufacturing, real estate, etc.), the IRS could classify the corporation as a PSC imposing the onerous corporate income tax rate of 35 percent on each dollar of income, and restricting the ability of the corporation to accumulate income under the regular C corporation tax rates. This is why many businesses elect S status or LLC status for operation instead of PSCs.

It also should be noted that while shareholders of a PSC may be exempt from claims of creditors, state law may prescribe that professionals will not be exempt from malpractice claims.

¶1303.10

¶ 1304 Limited Liability Companies (LLCs) with Two or More Members

.01 Definition of a Limited Liability Company (LLC)

A limited liability company (LLC) is a creation of state statute, taxable as a partnership under federal tax law. An LLC can be composed of two or more members or just one member (see discussion at ¶ 1307). An LLC is a new concept, with a new body of law being created for it each day. Like an S corporation, C corporation, or PSC, the members (unless they are professionals and malpractice is committed) are not personally liable for the debts of an LLC, providing certain formalities are followed.

In many ways, an LLC is like an S corporation; however, the LLC is not limited to 100 members, and anyone can be a member, such as a nonresident alien, a trust that allows a trustee's discretion on income distribution, S corporations, etc. Like an S corporation or PSC, the LLC can engage in any business operation.

.02 Numbers and Types of Members

Anyone can be a member. Thus, nonresident aliens, S corporations, partnerships, other LLCs, PSCs, etc. can be members. There is no restriction on the number or types of members that an LLC can have, unless it is engaged in a professional practice. (In that event, state law will probably prescribe the professional requirements for membership.) Also, depending upon its makeup, the LLC may have to satisfy various security laws to operate.

.03 Estate and Income Tax Planning

An LLC offers tremendous possibilities in estate and income tax planning, while at the same time offering the members liability protection from creditors like an S corporation, C corporation, or PSC. In a nutshell, an LLC offers three distinct advantages that an S corporation, C corporation, or PSC cannot offer: (1) Code Sec. 754 step up in basis at death or transfer of an interest, (2) flexible allocation of income, and (3) use of debt basis. Further, because LLCs are subject to partnership taxation, there can be many classes of ownership interest. Three examples illustrating the three principal tax advantages of LLCs for both estate and income tax planning are given below:

Code Sec. 754 step up in basis.

Example 13-8: ABC, composed of three brothers who are equal members, Alvin, Bruce, and Charles Gray, is a cash-basis service LLC engaged in accounting, and ABC has the following balance sheet:

	Adjusted Basis	Fair Market Value
Assets		
Cash	3	3
Accounts Receivable	0	30
	3	33
Capital		
Alvin	1	11
Bruce	1	11
Charles	1	11
	3	33

On December 31, 2009, Charles sells his LLC interest for $11 to David Harris. On January 2, 2010, the LLC collects its accounts receivable of $30.

If a Code Sec. 754 election is not in effect, the result would be that Alvin, Bruce, and David would each report $10 of ordinary income from the accounts receivable. This result is not unfair to Alvin and Bruce, but to David it is an unfair result, since David just paid Charles $11 (one-third of the fair market value of the LLC) to become a member. If a Code Sec. 754 election was in effect, however, then the basis of the accounts receivable would have been increased to $10 on David's acquisition of Charles' interest, and the LLC would recognize only $20 income on collection of its accounts receivable. This $20 would have been allocated entirely to Alvin and Bruce. Example 13-9 illustrates what would have occurred if a Code Sec. 754 election had been made by the LLC when Charles transferred the interest to David.

Example 13-9: ABC, composed of three equal members, Alvin, Bruce, and Charles Gray, is a cash-basis service LLC engaged in accounting that made a Code Sec. 754 election. On December 31, 2009, Charles sells his LLC interest for $11 to David Harris. On January 2, 2010, the LLC collects its accounts receivable of $30. The LLCs balance sheet would be adjusted under Code Sec. 754 as follows upon David's admission:

	Adjusted Basis	Fair Market Value
Assets		
Cash	3	3
Accounts Receivable	10	30
	13	33

Capital

Alvin	1	11
Bruce	1	11
David	11	11
	13	33

Note that the $10 increase in the basis of the accounts receivable was credited to David's capital account; thus, he recognizes no income on the collection of his one-third share of the receivables. The $10 income attributable to this one-third share of the receivables was recognized by Charles upon the sale of his interest in the LLC to David.

Allocation of income, loss, etc.

Example 13-10: Edward and Frank Jones enter into an LLC agreement to develop and market experimental electronic devices. Edward contributes $2,500 cash and agrees to devote his full-time services to the LLC. Frank contributes $100,000 cash and agrees to obtain a loan for the LLC for any additional capital needs. The LLC agreement provides that all deductions for research and experimental expenditures and interest on LLC loans are to be allocated to Frank. In addition, Frank will be allocated 90 percent, and Edward 10 percent, of LLC taxable income or loss, computed net of the deductions for such research and experimental expenditures and interest, until Frank has received allocations of such taxable income equal to the sum of such research and experimental expenditures, such interest expense, and his share of such taxable loss. Thereafter, Edward and Frank will share all taxable income and loss equally. Operating cash flow will be distributed equally between Edward and Frank. These allocations have substantial economic effect because this is what normal business people would do.

By definition this type of "special" allocation is not allowed in an S corporation since the only method to distribute income, loss, expense, etc. to shareholders, other than by salary, is equally on a per-share basis.

Debt basis. Under Code Sec. 752, liabilities of the LLC are deemed "contributions" of the members. As such, the debt increases basis. In contrast, debts of an S corporation do not increase a shareholder's basis unless a shareholder lends money or property to the corporation. Examples 13-11 and 13-12 illustrate the effect that liabilities have on LLCs.

Example 13-11: Assume on December 31, 2010, two individuals, Alan and Bruce Hernandez, decide to form an LLC, contributing $5,000 each as their only investment in the business enterprise. They intend to share profits, losses, etc. equally, and they entitled the LLC "AB Business." AB Business, on January 2, 2011, decides to buy a building for $390,000 that will be depreciated over 39 years, using straight-line depreciation without any salvage value. To finance the cost of the building, AB Business will borrow $380,000 from a bank, using a balloon note due in 39 years, interest only, payable yearly, and use the $10,000 cash from the capital contributions to make up the balance of

¶1304.03

the purchase price. AB Business estimates that the building will break even each year, but the building will generate a loss of $10,000 each year equal to the depreciation on the building ($390,000 ÷ 39 years). For purposes of discussion, and to simplify matters, assume that no part of the $390,000 purchase price for the building is allocated to land, and that the passive loss rules of Code Sec. 469 are not applicable. The result will be that, for the first tax year, assuming that Alan's and Bruce's projections hold true, Alan and Bruce will be able to deduct $5,000 each and will continue to receive a $5,000 annual deduction every year thereafter, until the LLC debt basis is used up.

Example 13-12: Assume the same facts as in Example 13-11, except AB Business is an S corporation, not an LLC. Alan and Bruce will each be able to write off $5 of loss in the first year because of their capital contribution, but for the second year and thereafter, no additional losses will be deductible. The $380,000 bank loan does not give them basis in S corporation stock.

The shareholders in Example 13-12 could produce the same results as those in Example 13-11; however, to do this, the shareholders would have to borrow the money personally from the bank and then lend the money to the business. If the shareholders follow this two-step personal borrowing scenario, they are liable to the bank if the loan is not repaid. In contrast, if the shareholders follow the scenario in Example 13-11, they have no personal liability, assuming a bank is willing to lend money in this fashion without asking them to personally guarantee the debt.[9]

Examples 13-11 and 13-12 illustrate one reason why an LLC is superior to an S corporation—members get liability protection from creditors and can use the bank's money to generate losses. Nonrecourse loans (i.e., when LLC members are not personally liable) do not increase the at-risk amount, unless attributable to real estate, but the facts in Examples 13-11 and 13-12 do not indicate that either loan was nonrecourse. Recourse loans (i.e., when LLC members are personally liable) (except seller-financing) do increase the at-risk amount.

In addition to the above, if a discretionary trust for family members (i.e., one where the trustee has discretion for distribution of principal and/ or income) becomes a member of an LLC, the trust is not bound by the punitive tax treatment that the electing small business trusts (ESBTs) face.[10]

Example 13-13: Harold and Wendy Willard, husband and wife, decide to form an LLC where they will each have a 40 percent interest in the company. They have two teenage boys, Philip and Charles, both over the age of fourteen, whom they desire to make 10 percent owners each. Because they do not think the boys will have the maturity to handle this investment when they reach majority, they establish two trusts to hold the ownership of the LLC interest for their children. Harold's brother, Sam, is named as trustee. The trust documents provide that: (1) the trustees will have discretion to distribute or accumulate any income from the LLC interest; (2) the boys will not receive

---

[9] There are potential problems in deducting the interest expense; if the interest constitutes investment interest expense, as will likely be the case, Code Sec. 163 limits their deductions each year to their investment income.

[10] See discussion at ¶ 306.

their 10 percent interest until they turn 30; and (3) principal and/or income can be used to pay for the beneficiary's (i.e., the child's) health, education, welfare, and maintenance. Another reason why the parents have chosen such a long vesting period is that their children, by the time they receive their interest, will be out of school, hopefully married, and interested in buying a house. The trustees distribute all the income to the beneficiaries after the trusts are established; however, Charles, when he turns 21, develops a drug problem. Sam, the trustee, because of the discretionary powers given him under the trust, does not distribute the income to Charles that is earned from the LLC investment; rather, he uses the income to pay for a drug treatment program for Charles. Charles, at the age of 25, straightens out his life. Sam is satisfied that Charles is off drugs, and starts distribution of income again to Charles. The trust pays no income tax when it distributes all the income to the beneficiaries, and when the trustee withholds income to Charles, it pays no income tax on the income distributed to Philip. In contrast, if this same type of trust was established in an S corporation, it would be classified as an ESBT, and the trustees would pay tax at 35 percent, the highest individual tax bracket, from the first dollar earned, regardless of how much is distributed to the beneficiaries. Thus, ESBTs should only be used for beneficiaries in the 35 percent tax bracket.

Tax Pointer: The same type of discretionary trust for an LLC is available in every other business entity except S corporations, with the same tax treatment given an LLC.

Because LLCs are subject to partnership taxation, they are likewise subject to the family partnership rules of Code Sec. 704(e).

Transfer of economic benefit of entity's assets to family members but retaining voting control. In *Byrum*,[11] the Supreme Court allowed a donor to transfer the economic benefit of stock ownership while maintaining control of the corporation, without the inclusion of the stock in the donor's taxable estate. Congress reversed *Byrum* by enacting Code Sec. 2036(b), which states that retention of voting stock is tantamount to retaining economic value, with the donor, following a *Byrum* transfer, having the stock's value included in the donor's estate.

The specific facts of *Byrum* are that Mr. Byrum, while he was alive, created an irrevocable trust for the benefit of his children. He funded the trust with shares of three closely held corporations but retained the right to vote the shares and to veto any sale or transfer of the stock. As a result, Mr. Byrum at his death continued to have the right to vote not less than 71 percent of the common stock in each of the three corporations. The three corporations were involved in lithography-related businesses and had a substantial number of minority shareholders unrelated to Mr. Byrum. (The Supreme Court noted that 11 of 12, 5 of 8, and 11 of 14 stockholders, respectively, in the three corporations appeared to be unrelated to Mr. Byrum). The trust instrument specified that there be, and Mr. Byrum named, an indepen-

---

[11] *M.A. Byrum*, SCt, 72-2 USTC ¶ 12,859, 92 SCt 2382, 408 US 125.

¶1304.03

dent corporate trustee. The trustee was authorized in its "absolute and sole discretion" to pay income and principal to or for the benefit of the beneficiaries.

The Supreme Court noted that while Mr. Byrum could select the corporate directors and thereby control the corporate dividend policy with respect to payments to the trusts established for his children, Mr. Byrum could not direct the flow of income to the trust beneficiaries. Furthermore, the Supreme Court stressed that "A majority shareholder has a fiduciary duty not to misuse his power by promoting his personal interests at the expense of corporate interests" and the directors of a corporation "have a fiduciary duty to promote the interests of the corporation." Such duties were legally enforceable by means of, for example, a derivative suit.

However, Code Sec. 2036(b), by definition, only applies to corporations, not to partnerships and LLCs classified as a partnership; thus, parents who want to transfer the economic value of a two or more member LLC to children but retain voting control can utilize the *Byrum* principle to accomplish their objectives.

> *Tax Pointer:* Notwithstanding the *Byrum* decision, the reader should consult Code Sec. 2036 to ensure compliance with this provision. For a discussion of Code Sec. 2036, see ¶ 1109.03.

.04 Medical Reimbursement Plan

Because it is treated as a partnership for federal income tax purposes, an LLC is ineligible to have a medical reimbursement plan for its members. However, Code Sec. 162(l) provides some ameliorative relief to the members by allowing them to deduct 100 percent of health insurance premiums in computing their AGIs.

.05 Income Tax Brackets

By definition, an LLC never pays any income tax; rather, like an S corporation, the tax brackets are determined by the individual members from their respective tax returns. So, if the LLC is composed of family members, and there are family members in the 15 percent bracket as well as the 35 percent bracket, the income distributed to the 15 percent bracketed taxpayers will be reported at 15 percent, with the 35 percent tax bracketed individuals paying tax at 35 percent on the same income.

.06 Health, Welfare, and Retirement Plans

As with an S corporation, members of an LLC can borrow from their retirement plans. Also, no deduction is allowed for group life insurance premiums paid on behalf of the members.

.07 Dividends-Received Deduction

Because an LLC is not a C or PSC corporation, it is ineligible for the dividends-received deduction.

.08 Ease of Formation

The formation of an LLC is relatively easy: all you have to do is file a certificate with the secretary of state in the state where the LLC will be conducting its

¶ 1304.08

business; then obtain a federal identification number. In some states, advertising is required similar to what occurs with limited partnerships. There are no elections to be made. However, an LLC is a complex entity, and before one is established, the members should have a thorough grasp of federal partnership taxation, as well as use a written operating agreement among the members to prevent difficulties on death of a member, bankruptcy of a member, etc.

.09 Creditor Protection

All members of an LLC are immune from creditors, providing certain formalities are observed, such as holding annual meetings, having managers sign as such, etc. However, state law may prescribe that professionals (such as doctors, nurses, lawyers, accountants, etc.) cannot exempt themselves from liability for their own malpractice.

.10 Principal Advantages and Disadvantages

The principal advantage of an LLC is, as expressed throughout, the benefits of partnership taxation and liability protection from general creditors (again, professionals will be liable for their own malpractice but not for general liabilities such as rent to a landlord).

The principal disadvantage of an LLC is the complexity due to the vagueness of partnership taxation. Another disadvantage is that there is no ability to control reporting of income to members, as is the case with a C corporation or PSC, where generally income distribution can be regulated by salary to shareholder-employees.

¶ 1305 General Partnerships

.01 Definition of a General Partnership

A general partnership is one where everyone can vote and all are equally liable to partnership creditors. A general partnership can be formed either in writing or by oral agreement. If a written partnership agreement is not used, state law controls operations.

.02 Numbers and Types of Partners

Like an LLC, anyone can be a partner, but you need at least two taxpayers to have a partnership. Thus, nonresident aliens, S corporations, partnerships, LLCs, PSCs, etc. can be partners. There is no restriction on the number of partners that a general partnership can have. Also, depending on its makeup, a general partnership may have to satisfy various security laws to operate.

.03 Estate and Income Tax Planning

A general partnership offers the same income and estate tax planning benefits that an LLC provides.

.04 Medical Reimbursement Plan

As with an LLC, a general partnership is ineligible to have a medical reimbursement plan for partners. However, Code Sec. 162(l) provides some ameliorative relief for the partners.

¶1304.09

.05 Income Tax Brackets

A partnership never pays any income tax; rather, like an S corporation, the tax brackets are determined by the individual partners. So, if the partnership is composed of 15 percent bracketed taxpayers as well 35 percent bracketed taxpayers, the income distributed to the 15 percent bracketed taxpayers will be reported at 15 percent, with the 35 percent tax bracketed individuals paying tax at 35 percent on the same income.

.06 Health, Welfare, and Retirement Plans

As with an S corporation, partners in a general partnership can borrow from their retirement plans. There is also no group life insurance available for partners.

.07 Dividends-Received Deduction

Because a general partnership is not a corporation, it is ineligible for the dividends-received deduction.

.08 Ease of Formation

The formation of a general partnership is an easy matter since the partnership can be either in writing or by oral agreement. However, to prevent difficulties at the death of a partner, sale of a partnership interest, etc., a written partnership agreement is recommended. In fact, a written partnership agreement helps to establish a general partnership for tax purposes.

.09 Creditor Protection

A general partnership provides no protection to its partners against the creditors of the partnership.[12] They are all individually liable to the extent of their assets. This is why a general partnership is not favored as an operating vehicle for businesses. LLCs, limited partnerships, and S corporations are favored because of their liability protection while at the same time passing income, loss, expense, etc. through to their owners.

.10 Code Sec. 761(f)—Spouses Can Elect Out of Partnership Reporting

Code Sec. 761 was amended by adding Code Sec. 761(f) effective for taxable years beginning after December 31, 2006 to provide that if a "qualified joint venture" is conducted by a husband and wife who file a joint return, they can elect to have this venture not treated as a partnership for federal tax purposes. All items of income, gain, loss, deduction and credit are divided between the spouses in accordance with their respective interests in the venture. Each spouse takes into account his or her respective share of these items as a sole proprietor. Thus, it is anticipated that each spouse would account for his or her respective share on the appropriate form, such as separate Schedule Cs. The provision is not intended to change the determination under present law of whether an entity is a partnership for federal tax purposes (without regard to the election provided by the provision).

---

[12] Rev. Rul. 2004-41, 2004-18 IRB 845. For an example of where partners are held personally liable, see *W. Remington,* DC Tex., 98-2 USTC ¶ 50,739 (Code Sec. 6672's "responsible person" provision does not preempt state partnership law; partners in a law firm are personally liable for unpaid payroll taxes pursuant to state partnership law provisions).

¶1305.10

For purposes of determining net earnings from self-employment, each spouse's share of income or loss from a qualified joint venture is taken into account just as it is for federal income tax purposes under the provision (i.e., in accordance with their respective interests in the venture). Congress provided a corresponding change to the definition of net earnings from self-employment under the Social Security Act. The Small Business and Work Opportunity Tax Act of 2007 Committee Reports detail that the change to Code Sec. 761 is not intended to prevent allocations or reallocations, to the extent permitted under present law, by courts or by the Social Security Administration of net earnings from self-employment for purposes of determining Social Security benefits of an individual.

Qualified joint venture. Code Sec. 761(f)(2) states that a qualified joint venture is one where (1) the only members of the joint venture are a husband and wife, (2) both spouses materially participate in the trade or business, and (3) both spouses elect to have the provision apply.

Tax Pointer 1: Married couples may not want to make this election if they want partnership provisions such as having all the income allocated to one spouse.

Tax Pointer 2: Code Sec. 761(f) does not detail how to make the election. Presumably, it will be done on a timely filed Form 1040 for the couple showing two Schedule Cs for the husband and wife.

Tax Pointer 3: While a partnership could obtain the same thing, the married couple may want to pursue Code Sec. 761(f)'s procedure avoiding the strictures of filing partnership tax returns to pass money to a non-working spouse so that he or she can build up assets for estate planning purposes or a social security base for disability benefits and to provide survivorship benefits. In that regard, see *Collier v. Barnhart*,[13] discussed at ¶ 1104 (Female who contracted ALS (Lou Gehrig's disease) denied Social Security Disability Insurance (SSDI) and medicare benefits because she does not have the required recent work history under the 20/40 rule, no violation found under the 14th Amendment for discrimination).

Tax Pointer 4: There are pros and cons for a Code Sec. 761(f) election for married couples:

(A) A tax deductible medical reimbursement plan for partnerships of a married couple is not allowed: however, if one spouse utilizing a Schedule C format hires another spouse and the hired spouse requires a medical reimbursement plan to become an employee, a tax deductible medical reimbursement plan can be established covering the hired spouse, his or her dependents plus the hiring spouse.

(B) Many married couples who work together report all the income on one spouse's Schedule C saving self-employment tax, among other things, for the spouse not reporting income. Result: on a divorce or legal separation, all the assets are in Schedule C filer's name and the

---

[13] 473 F. 3d 444 (2nd Cir. 2007).

"non-reporter" has to establish that 50% of the business, income, etc. belongs to this spouse, a difficult task. Conversely, the "non-reporter" will have an easier time with obtaining innocent spouse status with respect to this Schedule C income.

.11 Principal Advantages and Disadvantages

The principal advantage of a general partnership is ease of formation since it can be either in writing or by oral agreement.

The main disadvantage of a general partnership is the lack of creditor protection. Also, the IRS frequently reclassifies joint tenancy situations into partnerships and imposes penalties on the joint tenants for failure to file partnership returns (see, e.g., *Cusick,*[14] where co-owners of property were treated as a partnership pursuant to Reg. § 1.761-1(a)). The IRS can make this reclassification because partnerships can be oral. Thus, to be safe, when there are joint tenancy situations, the parties should form a partnership (and/or an LLC), draft a partnership agreement and file Form 1065 (the partnership tax return).

Another disadvantage is that there is no ability to control reporting of income to partners, as is the case with a C corporation or PSC, where generally income distribution can be regulated by salary to the shareholder-employee. For partners in the 35 percent tax bracket, this can be an important consideration, especially when the highest tax rate for a C corporation and PSC is 35 percent. S corporations, in contrast, can regulate to some degree the amount of Social Security and Medicare tax paid by shareholder-employees.[15]

¶ 1306 Limited Partnerships

.01 Definition of a Limited Partnership

A limited partnership is a creation of state statute. It is composed of at least one or more general partners and one or more limited partners. It is used because, as the name suggests, liability protection is offered to some degree to limited partners. A limited partner is one who basically cannot vote but whose liability to partnership creditors is limited to his or her equity contribution, plus whatever capital calls are placed on the limited partnership interest (i.e., the limited partner may be required to make additional capital contributions each year for a period of time). Because of the liability protection that a limited partner receives, a limited partnership has been among the most common vehicles used to raise capital for business investment. However, with the advent of two-or-more-member LLCs, which offer liability protection plus voting rights, the use of limited partnerships is waning.

.02 Numbers and Types of Partners

A limited partnership can have an unlimited number of limited partners; however, depending on the limited partnership makeup and the number of partners, the limited partnership may have to satisfy various security laws to operate. While a limited partnership can have an unlimited number of limited partners, it

---

[14] *T.H. Cusick,* 76 TCM 241, Dec. 52,824(M), TC Memo. 1998-286.

[15] For a discussion of these taxes, see ¶ 1307.06.

has to have at least one general partner to satisfy state law. Any one can be a partner in a limited partnership. Note, however, that if the general partner is in a form other than an individual (such as an S corporation), then the IRS limits the amount of ownership that the limited partners can have in the general partner.

.03 Estate and Income Tax Planning

The same estate and income tax benefits that exist with a general partnership and LLC apply to a limited partnership.

.04 Medical Reimbursement Plan

As with an LLC and a general partnership, a limited partnership is ineligible to have a medical reimbursement plan for partners.

.05 Income Tax Brackets

A limited partnership never pays any income tax; rather, like an S corporation, the tax brackets are determined by the individual members. So, if the limited partnership is composed of 15 percent bracketed taxpayers as well 35 percent bracketed taxpayers, the income distributed to the 15 percent bracketed taxpayers will be reported at 15 percent, with the 35 percent tax bracketed individuals paying tax at 35 percent on the same income.

.06 Health, Welfare, and Retirement Plans

As with an S corporation, LLC, and general partnership, general partners in a limited partnership can borrow from their retirement plans. There is also no deduction for group life insurance premiums paid on behalf of partners.

.07 Dividends-Received Deduction

Because a limited partnership is not a corporation, it is ineligible for the dividends-received deduction.

.08 Ease of Formation

A limited partnership is not easily formed because of the various state filing requirements, including publication, which must be made.

.09 Creditor Protection

By definition, only the limited partners have limited liability protection against partnership creditors. Thus, the general partner has unlimitedly liability to partnership creditors.

.10 Principal Advantages and Disadvantages

The principal advantage of a limited partnership is, as the case with general partnership and limited liability companies, the benefit of partnership taxation, with some degree of liability protection for the limited partners. As in other cases, professionals have no liability protection for malpractice acts, assuming that they can practice in a limited partnership capacity.

The principal disadvantages of a limited partnership are that the limited partners "must pay their money and take their chances"—they have no vote. In an LLC, all members of the LLC may have the right to vote.

¶1306.03

Another disadvantage is that there is no ability to control reporting of income to partners, as is the case with a C corporation or PSC, where generally income distribution can be regulated by salary to the shareholder-employee. For partners in the 35 percent tax bracket, this can be an important consideration, especially when the highest tax rate for a C corporation and PSC is 35 percent.

¶ 1307 One-Member Limited Liability Companies (LLCs)

.01 Introduction

Because of the recent creation of one-member LLCs, the discussion about this business entity will provide guidance on how to operate one-member LLCs with S corporations, as well as the advantages that one-member LLCs offer individuals in comparison to S corporation or two-member LLCs. Because of the expansive nature of the discussion, it does not follow this chapter's outline for the other business entities. The comparison chart at ¶ 1308 should be consulted for a complete perspective.

.02 Definition

A one-member LLC is a creature of state statute. Using New York state's law as a guide, anyone in the state of New York can form an LLC—a natural person, a corporation, another LLC, etc. An LLC is formed by filing articles of organization with the secretary of state.[16] Reg. § 301.7701-2(a) states that for tax purposes, a one-member LLC is deemed to have the same status as its owner, unless the LLC makes an election on Form 8832 to elect corporate status. Thus, if an individual forms a one-member LLC, the LLC is treated for tax purposes (for purposes of reporting income, loss, etc.) as a Form 1040 filer, filing Schedule C for business operations and Schedule E for rental activities. If an S corporation forms a one-member LLC, the one-member LLC, for federal tax purposes, will report its income, loss, etc. on the same Form 1120S that the S corporation files (e.g., the S corporation just combines the LLC operations with its own).[17]

.03 Situations Where One-Member LLCs Could Arise

While one may think that one-member LLC status is elective (i.e., a taxpayer decides to form a one-member LLC), in actuality, one-member LLC status could arise by operation of law. To illustrate: assume that two individuals, Amy and Beth Orr, form an LLC (AB LLC) to operate a business in a state that, besides allowing two or more persons to operate as an LLC, recognizes one-member LLCs as well. Amy dies, and pursuant to the operating agreement for the two-member LLC, Beth purchases Amy's interest, thereby leaving Beth as the sole owner of the LLC. While for tax purposes, AB LLC has lost its partnership tax status due to the fact that there is only one member left, for state purposes, AB LLC still exists as a one-member LLC unless Amy and Beth, in their operating agreement for AB LLC, prescribed that the LLC would dissolve when it is owned by only one member.[18]

---

[16] New York State Limited Company Law, Code Sec. 701.

[17] However, for S corporation operations, the less complicated one-member LLCs are preferred for their simplic-

ity over qualified S corporation subsidiaries (QSubs) (see discussion of QSubs at Chapter 14).

[18] As to the tax consequences of the termination of partnership status, see Rev. Rul. 99-5, 1999-1 CB 434.

¶1307.03

Individuals prefer a one-member LLC when they want an LLC's liability protection and the simplicity of filing their tax return by filing Schedule C and/or E to report the activities of the operation. Additionally, there are tax benefits provided to Schedule C filers not available to one-person S corporations and one-person C corporations. For professionals, while a one-member LLC does protect the individual from his or her creditors, the one-member LLC does not protect the professional from professional liability.

It is also important to note that while one-member LLCs protect individuals from general creditors, they do not provide protection to the individual owners from all liabilities. Thus, one-member LLC owners can be held liable for violation of environmental laws, Code Sec. 6672 penalties, etc.[19]

.04 When Not to Operate as a One-Member LLC

LLCs are creations of state statute, and each state establishes its own laws for the operation of a one-member LLC.[20] There is no uniform state law regarding LLC operations, nor is there a uniform state income tax system. Thus, state law has to be researched to determine which state provides flexible operations and tax benefits. This is particularly important for LLCs engaged in interstate commerce.

Steps can be taken, however, by a one-member LLC to minimize liability. One obvious solution (although it could prove to be expensive) is insurance. Thus, let us assume that a one-member LLC is established in New York and as part of its activities, its trucks make deliveries to another state where one-member LLC status is not recognized. One of the delivery trucks is involved in an accident in that state; however, because there is adequate insurance on the truck, the owner of the LLC is not held personally responsible because the insurance policy covered the damages.

The second means of protection is by use of contract, in that the one-member LLC in contracts could prescribe that the venue for all contractual disputes is in the state and city where the LLC was formed, and/or for purposes of resolving disputes, the law of the state where the one-member LLC was formed would be applicable. While these "forum" clauses in contracts are not 100 percent enforced by states, they do have a large percentage of acceptance in contractual disputes.

Also, notwithstanding the above steps, there is the corporate concept of "piercing the veil," which could hold an individual owner of a one-member LLC liable. The corporate concept of "piercing the veil" is used against shareholders to hold them personally responsible if they do not observe corporate formalities. To avoid liability, a one-member LLC should take certain obvious steps, such as holding annual meetings and/or having the owner, when signing LLC documents, sign in an LLC capacity rather than as an individual.

If a husband and wife operate a business together, but report the income, loss, etc. on one spouse's Form 1040, Schedule C, then the non-reporting spouse has no income for purposes of (i) obtaining social security benefits; (ii) establishing an IRA

---

[19] See, e.g., IRS Legal Memorandum (ILM) 1999-22053 (a sole owner of a one-member LLC was personally liable for employment taxes); Notice 99-6, 1999-1 CB 321 (details reporting procedures for one-member LLCs when employees exist at two levels: the owner of the LLC and the one-member LLC).

[20] See discussion at ¶ 1304.01.

or other type of retirement benefit; and (iii) no income record in the event that the spouse desires to return to the workforce, etc. Consequently, to prevent this disparity, the spouses may consider utilizing a partnership, S corporation, etc. or a Code Sec. 761(f) joint venture as discussed at ¶ 1305.10.

.05 Taxation of One-Member LLCs

Federal taxation. At present, while one-member LLCs are subject to the vagaries of state law for their operation, federal tax law is uniform due to the check-the-box regulations. However, the check-the-box regulations are the Treasury Department's regulations. Congress has not ruled on this matter, and, as a result, it is possible that Congress may one day decide that they want to tax one-member LLCs in a similar manner to S corporations and C corporations. While congressional legislation for one-member LLCs does not appear imminent, it is something to consider for the future. Also, a one-member LLC can change status and become a one-person S corporation or C corporation. Thus, if Congress does pass federal legislation, a one-member LLC can minimize any adverse tax effect by adopting S corporation or C corporation status.

State and local taxation. Unfortunately, there is no standard state taxation of one-member LLCs. State and local tax laws where the LLC operates and is qualified to do business should be consulted to determine taxation.

.06 Operation of One-Member LLCs for Individuals

Unincorporated businesses file Form 1040, Schedule C and individuals engaged in real estate file Form 1040, Schedule E.

Taxation of sole proprietorships (Schedule C). A sole proprietorship is not an entity separate and apart from the individual who owns it; thus, it has no separate existence.[21] Income flows directly to the owner who pays income tax (state, federal, and local) on any profits on his or her personal return, deducting the payments for state and local taxation as an itemized deduction on Schedule A. The individual deducts ordinary and necessary expenses on Schedule C. Examples of such expenses would be interest payments, advertising, tax return preparation, etc. However, the Form 1040, Schedule C is not all-inclusive; thus, an individual has to file a number of forms to report transactions. For instance, if an individual engages in the disposition of Code Sec. 1231 business property, the individual, depending on how long the property was held, has to file Form 4797 and Schedule D. Additionally, some of the business operations will be reported on the Form 1040 itself (e.g., retirement plan contributions, the deduction for self-employment tax).

As detailed in ¶ 722, it is easier to obtain Code Sec. 199's 9 percent domestic production deduction in an S corporate format, because wages can be paid to S corporate shareholder employees easily. In contrast, all income earned by Schedule C filers is self-employment income, and not eligible for Code Sec. 199's deduction by definition. Consequently, a sole proprietor, if Code Sec. 199's 9 percent deduc-

[21] *Williams v. McGowan*, CA-2, 46-1 USTC ¶ 9120, 152 F2d 570.

tion significantly affects the proprietor's taxes, may consider converting the business operations to an S corporation.

Depending on the jurisdiction, a state and/or local government could impose taxation on the one-member LLC. Accordingly, before forming a one-member LLC, the owner should review state and local taxation of the entity to ensure that the owner will not be adversely taxed in comparison to other business entities (e.g., a one-person S corporation).

Additionally, other business entities may offer unique tax advantages that a one-member LLC cannot furnish. For instance, a shareholder, pursuant to *Radtke*,[22] only has to receive a reasonable salary from the business, taking the rest of the earnings as a distribution from the S corporation free of Social Security and Medicare tax. In contrast, an owner of a one-member LLC filing Schedule C has to pay Medicare tax on the entire earnings and self-employment tax on all the income to the threshold amount prescribed.

Health insurance. Health insurance deductions for the individual require a bifurcated approach—if the LLC has employees, the employees' premiums are deducted on Schedule C; however, the owner's premiums are deducted as an itemized deduction on Schedule A, or as a deduction for AGI under Code Sec. 162(l).

Home office expenses. Code Sec. 280A(c)(1) permits individuals to deduct costs attributable to those portions of a dwelling unit used exclusively and regularly

    (a) as the principal place of business for any trade or business of the taxpayer;

    (b) as a place of business which is used by patients, clients, or customers in meeting or dealing with the taxpayer in the normal course of his trade or business;

    (c) in the case of a separate structure which is not attached to the dwelling unit, in connection with the taxpayer's trade or business; or

    (d) by the taxpayer for administration or management activities of any trade or business of the taxpayer.[23]

In contrast, Code Sec. 280A(a) denies a deduction of losses to S corporations if the S corporation operates out of the shareholder's home. While rental by the sole shareholder of an S corporation of a home office in his personal residence to the S corporation does not allow the shareholder to deduct, on his Form 1040, Schedule E depreciation or maintenance expenses in connection with the rental, the shareholder can allocate a portion of his mortgage interest and property taxes to the home office, but the owner must reduce the owner's itemized deductions. High income taxpayers who have their itemized deductions phased out and/or who have mortgages greater than $1,000,000 may want to utilize this allocation to obtain deductions where not available previously.

Tax year and tax elections. No restrictions are imposed on the method of accounting that an individual must use to report income, expenses, etc. arising from

---

[22] *J. Radtke*, CA-7, 90-1 USTC ¶ 50,113, 895 F2d 1196.

[23] The home office deduction cannot be taken if the taxpayer reports a loss from the activity in which the home office is used (see Code Sec. 280A(c)(5)).

¶1307.06

the one-member LLC.[24] Accordingly, an individual can use the accrual method for a one-member LLC while keeping personal records on the cash method.[25] Like any other business, the one-member LLC will be permitted to use the four methods of accounting prescribed by Code Sec. 446(c)—cash, accrual, other, and hybrid. However, unlike certain business entities, a one-member LLC has no statutory restrictions on the use of accounting method.[26] As to its tax year, unless the one-member LLC can justify to the contrary, the one-member LLC will most likely use a calendar year to report income, loss, etc. In tax elections, there is only one taxpayer, and thus elections are made on the Form 1040.

Formation issues. As previously discussed, the one-member LLC has no separate tax significance. Consequently, from a tax perspective, the transfer of assets, depreciated or appreciated, for use in the one-member LLC, and the retransfer of the assets (depreciated or appreciated) from the one-member LLC to the owner, will have no tax effect. However, if an asset that has been held for personal use is transferred to a one-member LLC for business use, the one-member LLC must use the lower of the fair market value of the property at the time the property is converted to business use, or the adjusted basis determined at the time of conversion for purposes of computing depreciation, gain, loss, etc.[27]

Leveraging. By design, the one-member LLC does not have a capital structure independent of itself like a corporation, two-member LLC, etc. However, the LLC can borrow funds. If so, the debt by definition becomes nonrecourse debt, and unless a lender protects him-, her- or itself, the lender may not be able to proceed against the owner personally.[28] State laws may also affect the interest rate charged. For instance, New York prescribes in Limited Liability Company Law Code Sec. 1104 that an LLC formed for any purpose other than the ownership of a one- or two-family dwelling may not interpose the defense of usury in any civil action. However, the LLC can interpose a defense of commercial usury under Code Sec. 190.40 of the Penal Law of the State of New York. As to tax deductibility of the interest, Code Sec. 163 has to be consulted; particularly Reg. § 1.163-8T to determine the amount and manner in which the interest can be deducted.

Deflection of income. Because a one-member LLC is owned by one person, income from the business cannot be allocated to another as can occur in other closely held family business situations such as partnerships and S corporations. The only means to have income allocated to other family members is to have them become employees, lease property to the one-member LLC, buy goods from them, etc..

---

[24] Reg. § 1.446-1(c)(1)(iv) *(b)*.

[25] See e.g., *Old Merchant National Bank & Trust Co. of Battle Creek,* CA-6, 41-1 USTC ¶ 9150, 117 F2d 737.

[26] Code Sec. 448(a)(1) states that generally, C corporations with gross receipts over $5 million dollars are not allowed to use the cash method of accounting.

[27] *L.Y.S. Au,* 40 TC 264, Dec. 26,110. Aff'd, per curium, CA-9, 1964, 30 F2d 1008. Cf. Reg. § 1.167(g)-1.

[28] Care should be practiced with respect to non-recourse debt when the debt significantly exceeds the fair market value of the property securing the debt. In *K.A. Bergstrom,* FedCl, 97-1 USTC ¶ 50,143, 37 FedCl 164, the Court of Claims disregarded in its entirety, for depreciation and interest calculation purposes, the non-recourse debt when it found that the debt significantly exceeded the fair market value of the property. Contra, *Pleasant Summit Land Corp.,* CA-3, 88-2 USTC ¶ 9601, 863 F2d 263 (when non-recourse financing exceeds the value of the property, the debt will be recognized for tax purposes to the extent of the property's value).

¶ 1307.06

Sale of a one-member LLC. The sale of a one-member LLC is the sale of the individual assets of the business.[29] Accordingly, the seller will recognize and be taxed on the gain (or reflect as a loss) equal to the difference between the amount received for each individual asset from the business and the owner's tax basis in each asset. In characterizing the gain or loss as capital or ordinary, short or long term, this will depend likewise on how long each asset was held by the owner.

The purchaser treats the transaction as the purchase of individual assets of a business, with the purchase price allocated to the individual assets pursuant to Code Sec. 1012 and Code Sec. 1060. Because there is fragmented tax reporting of a sale, an owner may desire a lump-sum reporting. Accordingly, prior to the sale, the owner may consider incorporating the one-member LLC and having the buyer purchase the stock of the business. Also, buyers frequently do not like to purchase stock of a corporation due to the hidden liability problems which arise with stock ownership transfers.

In the sale of an asset, the owner of an LLC may be asked to restrict him- or herself by means of a covenant not to compete. Likewise, the buyer may ask the seller to sign a consulting agreement to assist the buyer in operating the newly acquired business. If the buyer is astute, the buyer will place a dollar value on these agreements, thereby leading to tax write-offs for the buyer—a 15-year write-off pursuant to Code Sec. 197 for the covenant not to compete, and a faster write-off for the consulting agreement, provided it is reasonable "compensation for the services actually rendered by the former owner."[30] While the seller may have reservations about the covenant not to compete and consulting agreement because the seller will have to report the income received as ordinary, and self-employment tax on the consulting portion, the seller may have no choice about this approach because it may be the only means to sell the business. Also, while a seller will have to report ordinary income from the covenant not to compete and consulting agreement, the seller will probably try for a higher allocation for the covenant not to compete because it is not subject to self-employment tax. The buyer will prefer allocating the price to the consulting agreement because of the Committee Report's permissibility in allowing a faster write-off for the consulting agreement rather than the 15-year period required for covenants not to compete required by Code Sec. 197.[31]

> **Tax Pointer:** For more detailed discussion on buying and selling a business, see the discussion under the subheading "Using Covenants Not to Compete" and "Using Consulting Agreements" discussed at ¶ 1208.04.

Borrowing from retirement plans. As with an S corporation, a member engaged in an employment situation can borrow from his or her retirement plan.

.07 Like-Kind Exchanges

Code Sec. 1031 treatment for swapping certain assets of an LLC is available. Assets eligible for Code Sec. 1031 treatment are land and building, machinery,

---

[29] *Williams v. McGowan*, CA-2, 46-1 USTC ¶ 9120, 152 F2d 570.

[30] Committee Report to the Omnibus Budget Reconciliation Act of 1993 (P.L. 103-66).

[31] Landlords generally would be precluded from a covenant not to compete on general principles because landlords do not have a unique business where a covenant not to compete would be applicable.

patents, technology, and other property held for the productive use in a trade or business or for investment. Code Sec. 1031(a)(2) details what assets cannot be swapped, such as interests in a partnership, choses in actions, stock, bonds, notes, etc. If a one-member LLC wishes to engage in a tax-free swap under Code Sec. 1031, Code Sec. 1031 imposes restrictions, such as the time limits imposed by Code Sec. 1031(a)(3) and the limitations on exchanges between related persons (Code Sec. 1031(f)).

.08 Estate and Income Tax Planning

Because a one-member LLC is basically a sole proprietorship for tax purposes, the estate-planning options available with other closely held business forms is not available to it. Thus, a parent cannot make a child an owner with him or her, because if a parent makes the child a part owner, then this action will probably effectively create a partnership. For estate tax purposes, by definition, a person can bequeath an LLC to another; however, all that would be accomplished would be a bequest of individual assets that make up the one-member LLC, with the assets being stepped up or down to reflect the fair market value at death (or the alternate valuation date). Likewise, a person can give the LLC to another, but for tax purposes, it is really a gift of the individual assets to another.

Notwithstanding the above, it is possible for an individual owning a one-member LLC engaged in real estate to do some family planning and include family members in the operation by conveying a portion of the real estate to these family members as tenants in common, or, if so desired, joint tenants with right of survivorship. An individual might consider this creation of tenancy for purposes of (1) taking advantage of the minority and lack of marketability discounts available under *Mandelbaum*[32] and *LeFrak*,[33] and/or (2) to pass property to family members when the property might appreciate. However, if there is no business purpose for the joint tenancy, the IRS could attack it, utilizing the concept set forth in Field Service Advice 200143004, discussed at ¶ 1126.01.

Burden of proof—Code Sec. 7491. In 1998, Congress provided, pursuant to Code Sec. 7491(a), that if a taxpayer produces credible evidence in a civil proceeding, the burden of proof on the factual issues will be shifted to the IRS. Recently, in *Dailey*,[34] a taxpayer was able to shift the burden of proof to the IRS on the question of valuation in connection with gifts by a parent of interest in a family business to children.

Minority discounts allowed for gift transfer of interest in a family business even if the family business assets are marketable securities or non-income-producing assets. In the field of partnership taxation, minority discounts for gift tax purposes in connection with transfers of interest in a family business to children of the partners were sustained. For example, in *Knight*,[35] a husband and wife created a family partnership with their two unmarried children, with assets

---

[32] *B. Mandelbaum,* 69 TCM 2852, Dec. 50,687(M), TC Memo. 1995-255. Aff'd, CA-3, 96-2 USTC ¶ 60,240, 91 F3d 124.

[33] *S. LeFrak,* 66 TCM 1297, Dec. 49,396(M), TC Memo. 1993-526.

[34] *E.M. Dailey Est.,* 82 TCM 710, Dec. 54,506(M), TC Memo. 2001-263.

[35] *I.F. Knight,* 115 TC 506, Dec. 54,136.

valued at approximately $2,000,000. The parents' ranch with mineral rights, and the children's residence where they were living rent-free, were transferred to the partnership (the residences represented approximately 24 percent of the partnership assets). Trusts were established for the children, with each trust owing 44.6 percent of the partnership units; however, neither the children nor their trust participated in the management of the partnership. The partnership kept no records, prepared no annual reports, and had no employees. The Court sustained the partnership for gift tax purposes, permitting a 15 percent discount with respect to transfers of partnership interest, claiming that if the partnership was validly formed under state law, it was valid for gift tax purposes. The Court also rejected the IRS's attempt to strike down the partnership under Code Sec. 2704(b) because the restrictions imposed by the partnership (i.e., a lack of withdrawal rights by the limited partners and the fifty-year term of the partnership) was no more restrictive than state law. By definition, the principles of these cases apply to S corporations.

In *Strangi*,[36] a partnership was established two months before the decedent's death by his attorney in fact (his son-in-law). The partnership assets had a value of approximately $9.8 million, of which roughly 75 percent of the assets was either cash or securities. Further, the partnership basically followed the Fortress Plan established by the Fortress Financial Group, Inc. One part of the Fortress Plan included the utilization of establishing a charity as a partner. The Court refused to apply Code Sec. 2703(a)(2) to prevent minority discounts on transfers of the partnership interest to family members. Further, the Court sustained a 31 percent discount for minority interest and lack of marketability, exactly what the IRS's expert witness stated was a proper discount. However, as the textual discussion at ¶ 1109.03 details, the *Strangi* Court, utilizing Code Sec. 2036, looks with great disdain at family businesses where passive assets are the bulk of the assets; rather, the Court prefers active businesses to be utilized where there will be such problems as cash flow with respect to operations of the business. Further, the Court wants business plans to be developed with the assets, not just continuing the status quo.

.09 Medical Reimbursement Plans and Medical Savings Accounts

In an Industry Specialization Program (ISP) Coordinated Issue Paper,[37] the IRS concedes that self-employed individuals—whether in partnerships, LLCs, S corporations, or sole proprietorships—can hire their spouses as employees and legitimately transform otherwise nondeductible personal expenses into deductible business expenses. The IRS concludes that one spouse can hire the other spouse as an employee, and pay and deduct that employee's medical benefits—including coverage for the employer-spouse and any dependents—as long as the employment arrangement is deemed legitimate. However, the spouse of a more-than-2-percent shareholder of an S corporation cannot be treated as an employee.[38] Thus, the ISP offers a distinct advantage over S corporations when coupled with the other benefits that one-member LLCs offer, such as the home office deduction discussed

---

[36] *A. Strangi Est.*, 115 TC 478, Dec. 54,135. *Aff'd* 2005-2 USTC ¶ 60,506 (5th Cir. 2005).

[37] Industry Specialization Program (ISP) Coordinated Issue Paper, Uniform Issue List (UIL) No. 162.35-02.

[38] *Ibid.*

¶1307.09

at ¶ 1307.06. Accordingly, these tax benefits may tip the scales for individuals to opt for one-member LLCs as a means to do business. Note also that Code Sec. 162(l) provides a special deduction for health insurance premiums paid by the self-employed.

In addition, Code Sec. 220 of the Internal Revenue Code allows self-employed individuals to establish medical savings accounts. So, individuals have a choice of how to cover their health costs from a tax perspective.

.10 Liquidation and Dissolution

An owner can dissolve a one-member LLC, causing the LLC to go out of business; however, for tax purposes, it should not be a taxable event. If a one-member LLC dissolves under state law and liquidates under tax law, the individual will just continue to treat the assets in the same manner as held before—there is no step up or down in value caused by the dissolution and/or liquidation of the LLC.

.11 Estimated Tax Payments

A one-member LLC owned by an individual has to make estimated tax payments if, after subtracting tax withholdings and credits, the amount of income tax that will be owed at the time of filing the tax return for the pertinent year will be at least $1,000, and the withholding tax and the tax credits are less than the smaller of: (1) 90 percent of the tax shown on the current year's return; (2) 100 percent of the tax shown on the prior year's tax return (assuming that a return was filed and it covered twelve months); or (3) 110 percent (for 2002 and thereafter) of the tax shown on the prior year's tax return if the individual's adjusted gross income shown on the preceding year's return exceeds $150,000 ($75,000 for married filing separately).[39]

.12 Conversion of a One-Member LLC to a C or S Corporation or Partnership

C or S corporation. Because a one-member LLC is not a separate entity from its owner, conversion of a one-member LLC to a corporation under Code Sec. 351 is not a taxable event unless other provisions of the Internal Revenue Code cause a taxable event to occur (e.g., Code Sec. 357). At the time of conversion of the LLC to a corporation, the corporation can make its election to become an S corporation as detailed at Chapter 4. In the conversion, *Pittsfield Coal & Oil Co.*[40] prescribes that there will not be a change in accounting method, thus allowing the corporation to continue the accounting method used for the one-member LLC.[41]

Partnership. If the owner of a one-member LLC wishes to take another member (e.g., a child, spouse, other business entity, etc.) into the business operation, then a partnership can be created under the provisions of Code Sec. 701 et seq. As is the case with the one-member LLC converting into a corporation, this will not be a taxable event to the owner of the one-member LLC except as prescribed in the Internal Revenue Code (see, e.g., Reg. § 1.731-1(c)(3)).

---

[39] Code Sec. 6654.

[40] *Pittsfield Coal & Oil Co., Inc.,* 25 TCM 11, Dec. 27,806(M), TC Memo. 1966-4.

[41] For guidance on conversion of an LLC to a partnership for tax purposes, see Rev. Rul. 99-5, 1999-1 CB 434.

.13 A One-Member LLC Can Be a Joint Venturer

A one-member LLC could enter into a joint venture with others while still maintaining its business operations. For instance, assume that a physician, Dr. Miles, decides to form a one-member LLC (Dr. Miles LLC) to conduct a medical practice. At the same time, Dr. Miles LLC decides to enter into a joint venture with the local hospital, contributing some assets from the one-member LLC (e.g., know-how) to the hospital joint venture. Dr. Miles would report operations from the one-member LLC and the hospital joint venture by filing Form 1040, Schedule C (for Dr. Miles' operations) and Schedule E (for the joint venture operations).

.14 Tax Planning with One-Member LLCs

As the above discussion indicates, the area of one-member LLCs is a complex one, notwithstanding the fact that one-member LLCs are easy to establish. Knowledge of state law is required so that the owners of the venture will know how to operate. Thus, annual meetings will be a requirement, and other formalities associated with corporations will have to be followed. If the one-member LLC becomes a debtor, then knowledge of the various lending laws (including usury) will be applicable. From a tax perspective, besides knowing the concept of Form 1040, Schedules C and E taxation, Forms 1120S, etc., the owner will have to understand the concept of nonrecourse debt. Notwithstanding the complexities detailed above, it is probable that, because of the ease of formation and single taxation of operations, one-member LLCs will likely become a significant vehicle in the business community.

.15 S Corporation Can Have One-Member LLCs Instead of Subsidiaries or QSubs

An S corporation may decide to limit its liability exposure by operating its business through a series of one-member LLCs. Reg. § 301.7701-3(a) prescribes that an S corporation can be the owner of a one-person LLC. An example will illustrate the operation of an S corporation with a single-member LLC.

> **Example 13-14:** Taylor Lincoln owns Alpha, Inc., a calendar-year S corporation. Alpha, Inc. operates three jewelry concessions in major department stores, and it is concerned about liability in the event the insurance policies the corporation has on its operations are insufficient to cover claims made. Alpha, Inc. also contemplates that, at various concessions, it has to free up its capital, be able to easily bring in partners, etc. The states where Alpha, Inc. has it concessions recognize one-taxpayer LLCs. Alpha, Inc. forms a one-member LLC for each of the concessions. By utilizing a one-member LLC, Alpha, Inc. accomplishes all its objectives—liability protection from creditors (providing they observe LLC formalities, such as holding annual meetings, to prevent creditors from piercing the veil), and tremendous flexibility if Alpha, Inc. wants to include individuals such as managers with a profit interest, or investors with an equity interest, utilizing partnership tax principles discussed at ¶ 1304.03 and ¶ 1307.01 et seq. Code Sec. 721 would generally allow the inclusion of a partner easily, without adverse tax consequences to the S corporation, who would now be a partner. In contrast, if the concession was

operated as a QSUB,[42] the inclusion of other shareholders in the QSUB would cause the QSUB's status to terminate.

.16 One-Member LLCs Can Be Useful for Exchanges

IRS Letter Ruling 200118023 illustrates the use of a one-member LLC with respect to a Code Sec. 1031 exchange by allowing the corporation to avoid state transfer fees with respect to real estate. The facts in Letter Ruling 200118023 are as follows.

The taxpayer arranged for an intermediary, QI, a single-member LLC not classified as an association, to facilitate the exchange of its real property, RQ, for like-kind property, RP. QI, which owns RP, is owned by XX, and per the taxpayer's specifications, XX constructed improvements on RP. The conveyance of RP to the taxpayer was subject to real estate transfer fees under state law; however, the transfer of an ownership interest in an LLC to the taxpayer is not subject to real estate transfer fees. The ruling states that the taxpayer's receipt of the sole ownership interest in QI will be treated as the receipt of RP directly by the taxpayer for purposes of qualifying the receipt of such RP for nonrecognition of gain under Code Sec. 1031.

.17 One-Member LLCs Can Facilitate a Merger of S Corporations, Allowing Avoidance of Franchise Taxes

In IRS Letter Ruling 200107018, the following facts were presented.

The taxpayer was the 100 percent shareholder of two brother-sister S corporations, X and Y. X was incorporated in State 1, and Y was incorporated in State 2. Y had a wholly-owned subsidiary, Z, also located in State 2. The taxpayer, in addition, was 100 percent owner of LLC-1, a disregarded entity, which was formed in State 3. Z and LLC-1 owned 100 percent of a foreign LLC, F-1. F-1 and LLC-1 owned 100 percent of another foreign LLC, F-2. The taxpayer wanted to relocate assets of X from State 1 to State 4; X planned to either sell certain assets to a related entity, or distribute those assets to the taxpayer. The taxpayer would then contribute the assets to a newly formed S corporation.

To avoid franchise taxes imposed by State 1 and gain more operating structure flexibility, the parties planned to take a number of steps, including:

- they would organize another LLC (LLC-2) in State 2, contributing a portion of Z to LLC-2, converting Z to a limited partnership, LP-1, with Y as a limited partner and LLC-2 as the general partner;
- Y and LLC-1 would organize another limited partnership, LP-2 in State 2, with Y as a limited partner and LLC-2 as a general partner;
- LP-1 will transfer its interest in F-1 to LLP-2;
- F-1 will distribute its interest in F-2 to LP-2;
- X will merge into Y under an A statutory merger with Y surviving, and Y will contribute the assets received from X to LP-1.

---

[42] See Chapter 14.

No one will elect to have LP-1, LP-2 or LLC-2 treated as an organization. The IRS sustained the transaction.

¶ 1308 Comparison Chart of Seven Business Entities

For determining the best form of business entity for a particular business and owner, use the comparison chart on the following four pages. It illustrates how the seven business entities discussed in this chapter differ on nine factors.

Comparison Chart of Seven Business Entities

Factor	I. C Corporations	II. S Corporations	III. Personal Service Corporations
1. Numbers and Types of Owners	Unlimited amount and types of shareholders.	Maximum of 100 shareholders, and only certain types of shareholders. However, depending on state law, if professionals incorporate, only professionals can be shareholders. Family members can elect to join as a family, thereby creating only one shareholder.	Unlimited, but as a rule, depending on state law, only professionals can be shareholders in the corporation engaged in that professional activity; unlimited shareholders for other personal service corporations (e.g., a consulting business).
2. Estate and Income Tax Planning	As a general rule, good.	Limited.	Limited because frequently, in the case of a professional corporation, depending on state law, only the professionals licensed to practice in that particular profession can be shareholders of the corporation.
3. Medical Reimbursement Plan	Yes.	None available to more-than-2-percent shareholder-employees.	Yes.
4. Income Tax Brackets	Progressive.	Income tax brackets of the shareholders.	One bracket: 35% percent on all income.
5. Health, Welfare, and Retirement Plans	Yes, with borrowing from the retirement plans possible up to the statutory amount.	Yes, and borrowing from the retirement plans for participants.	Yes, and borrowing permitted from the retirement plans up to certain statutory limits.

¶1308

Factor	I. C Corporations	II. S Corporations	III. Personal Service Corporations
6. Dividends-Received Deduction	Yes.	No.	Yes.
7. Ease of Formation	Easy.	Relatively easy.	Relatively easy; however, in the case of professionals, depending on state law, only professionals licensed in that state can be shareholders of that professional corporation.
8. Creditor Protection	Yes.	Yes, except for professional malpractice.	Yes, except for professional malpractice.

¶1308

Factor	*I.* *C Corporations*	*II.* *S Corporations*	*III.* *Personal Service Corporations*
9. Principal Advantages and Disadvantages	**Advantages:** tax planning is easy because there are two taxpayers in a closely-held business: the shareholder-employee and the corporation; also, the various classes of stock that can be issued and the taxable entities that can hold the stock allows flexible tax planning. **Disadvantages:** removing funds from the corporation; problems with unreasonable accumulation of funds and unreasonable salary; potential double taxation on audit disallowance for items involving shareholder-employees; difficult to obtain benefits from Code Sec. 199's 9 percent domestic production deduction.	**Advantages:** generally one level of taxation; provides the shareholders with liability protection except for professional malpractice; obtain benefit of Code Sec. 199's 9 percent domestic production deduction. **Disadvantages:** limited estate and income tax planning possibilities because there can only be one class of stock; the type of taxpayers that can be shareholders.	**Advantages:** same benefits as a C corporation. **Disadvantages:** the primary disadvantage is that the tax rate is 35 percent and there is a danger that a C corporation can be classified as a personal service corporation, depending upon the type of activities in which it engages. Also, same problems as a C corporation removing funds, etc; difficult to obtain benefits from Code Sec. 199's 9 percent domestic production deduction.
10. Self-Employment Taxes	No. Shareholder subject to employment taxes on compensation paid for services rendered	No. Shareholder subject to employment taxes on compensation paid for services rendered (Note: IRS can recharacterize distributions as compensation if reasonable salary not paid)	No. Shareholder subject to employment taxes on compensation paid for services rendered

¶ 1308

Factor	I. C Corporations	II. S Corporations	III. Personal Service Corporations
11. Subsidiaries	Yes. Wholly owned LLC treated as disregarded entity; ownership of foreign corporation permitted, but Section 1504(b)(3) precludes it from being a member of a consolidated group	Yes. Wholly owned subsidiary can elect Qsub status, foreign corporation ownership permitted, but no Qsub because Section 1361(b)(3) permits only domestic corporations to be Qsubs (unless foreign corporation treated as a disregarded entity); wholly owned LLC treated as disregarded entity	Yes. Wholly owned LLC treated as disregarded entity; ownership of foreign corporation permitted
12. Ownership Participation in Management	Permitted	Permitted	Permitted, but Section 280H restricts amounts paid to owners if it has elected non-calendar tax year
13. Tax Year	Generally, accounting year	Generally, calendar year subject to Section 444	Generally, calendar year subject to Section 444
14. Method of Accounting	Accrual, unless average gross receipts under $5 million	Accrual or cash; but if tax shelter, accrual	Accrual or cash
15. Tax Matters Partner	No	No	No
16. Conversion of Entities	Conversion of S Corp or LLC/partnership has tax implications; conversion to S Corp may create entity level tax	Conversion to C Corp permitted but tax implications to shareholders if have unrecognized losses; conversion to LLC/partnership has tax implications	Conversion to S Corp or LLC/partnership has tax implications; conversions to S Corp may create entity level tax

Factor	I. C Corporations	II. S Corporations	III. Personal Service Corporations
17. Reorganizations	Tax-free reorganizations, applicable	Tax-free reorganization applicable (but certain reorganizations may not be practical for an S corporation such as B or C if S to be surviving corporation)	Tax-free reorganizations applicable
18. Code Sec. 1411	Not subject to taxation	Operations will directly affect shareholders	Not subject to taxation

Comparison Chart of Seven Business Entities (cont'd)

Factor	IV. Limited Liability Companies (Two or More Members)	V. General Partnerships	VI. Limited Partnerships	VII. One-Member Limited Liability Companies
1. Numbers and Types of Owners	Unlimited as to type of members and individuals who can be members.	Unlimited as to number of partners and types of partners.	Requires at least one general partner and one limited partner.	One member.
2. Estate and Income Tax Planning	Good, since partnership taxation principles are used.	Good, since partnership taxation principles can be used for tax purposes.	Good, since partnership taxation principles apply.	None, except for medical reimbursement plans for self-employed individuals.
3. Medical Reimbursement Plan	No.	No.	No.	Yes, for self-employed individuals.
4. Income Tax Brackets	Income tax brackets of the members.	Tax brackets of individual partners.	Tax brackets of individual partners.	Income tax brackets of the member.
5. Health, Welfare, and Retirement Plans	Yes, and borrowing from the retirement plans.	Yes, and borrowing from the retirement plans.	Yes, and borrowing from the retirement plans.	Yes, and borrowing from the retirement plans.
6. Dividends-Received Deduction	No.	No.	No.	No.
7. Ease of Formation	Complicated, because LLC agreement should be used.	Easy.	Complicated, because state limited partnership act must be followed.	Easy.

Factor	IV. Limited Liability Companies (Two or More Members)	V. General Partnerships	VI. Limited Partnerships	VII. One-Member Limited Liability Companies
8. Creditor Protection	Yes, except for professional malpractice.	No creditor protection for individual partners.	Yes, but only for the limited partners to the extent of their capital contribution, and no protection for professional malpractice.	Yes, except for professional malpractice.
9. Principle Advantages and Disadvantages	**Advantages:** benefits of liability protection while at the same time having partnership taxation and members can vote. **Disadvantages:** complexity, and as a general rule, two or more members are needed to form an LLC; difficult to obtain benefits from Code Sec. 199's 9 percent domestic production deduction.	**Advantages:** ease of formation and partnership tax principles apply. **Disadvantages:** no protection from creditors for individual partners; possible reclassification by IRS of joint tenancy situations into partnership tax situations; difficult to obtain benefits from Code Sec. 199's 9 percent domestic production deduction.	**Advantages:** benefits of partnership taxation with some degree of liability protection for the limited partners, with the exception of professionals who cannot exempt their malpractice acts. **Disadvantages:** no vote for limited partners; difficult to obtain benefits from Code Sec. 199's 9 percent domestic production deduction.	**Advantages:** ease of formation and easier to operate than a subsidiary for a corporation or tiered LLC or partnership. **Disadvantages:** difficult to obtain benefits from Code Sec. 199's 9 percent domestic production deduction.

¶1308

Factor	IV. Limited Liability Companies (Two or More Members)	V. General Partnerships	VI. Limited Partnerships	VII. One-Member Limited Liability Companies
10. Self-Employment Taxes	Yes, if members involved in service partnership where they cannot be classified as limited partners under state law (law, health, accounting, architecture, etc.).	Yes.	General partner, yes; limited partner in service partnership where they cannot be classified as limited partners under state law (law, health, accounting, architecture, etc.)	Yes.
11. Subsidiaries	Yes. Wholly owned LLC treated as disregarded entity; ownership of foreign corporation permitted, but Section 1504(b) (3) precludes it from being a member of consolidated group.	Yes. Wholly owned LLC treated as disregarded entity; ownership of foreign entity permitted.	Yes. Wholly owned LLC treated as disregarded entity; ownership of foreign entity permitted.	Yes.
12. Ownership Participation in Management	Permitted, but may cause member to become liable for self-employment tax.	Permitted.	Permitted, subject to state law limitations.	Yes.
13. Tax Year	Generally, tax year of principal member, subject to Section 444.	Generally, tax year of principal partner, subject to Section 444.	Generally, tax year of principal partner subject to Section 444.	Tax year of owner.

¶1308

Factor	IV. Limited Liability Companies (Two or More Members)	V. General Partnerships	VI. Limited Partnerships	VII. One-Member Limited Liability Companies
14. Method of Accounting	Accrual, if classified as partnership and C corporation other than a PSC a partner; per Section 446 if has gross receipts greater than $5 million; a tax shelter; engaged in farming or tree raising business.	Accrual, if have a C corporation other than a PSC a partner; per Section 446 if have gross receipts greater than $5 million; a tax shelter; engaged in farming or tree raising business.	Accrual, if have a C corporation other than a PSC a partner; per Section 446 if have gross receipts greater than $5 million; a tax shelter; engaged in farming or tree raising business.	Owner's method.
15. Tax Matters Partner	Member-Manager; if no manager, then any member so designated.	Any partner so designated.	General partner.	N/A
16. Conversion of Entities	If classified as partnership, conversion to another business entity has tax consequences.	Conversion to another business entity has tax consequences.	Conversion to another business entity has tax consequences.	Can be taxable depending on transaction.
17. Reorganizations	Generally no tax consequence to members unless members' shares are altered.	Generally no tax consequence to partners unless partners' shares altered.	Generally no tax consequence to partners unless partners' shares altered.	N/A
18. Code Sec. 1411	Operations will directly affect members.	Operations will directly affect partners.	Operations will directly affect partners.	Operations will directly affect individual members, trusts and estates.

¶1308

Chapter 14

Subsidiaries

¶ 1401 Introduction

Prior to the Small Business Job Protection Act of 1996 (SBJPA), an S corporation could not own 80 percent or more of the stock of another corporation. The SBJPA changed all that by implementing Code Sec. 1361(b)(3) and amending Code Sec. 1361(b)(2). It made the S corporation a more viable business entity by, among other things, allowing it to own all of the stock of a subsidiary, and, except for very limited circumstances, to elect to have the subsidiary not be taxed on its operations separately but as part of the parent S corporation's operations. The elective subsidiary is called a qualified subchapter S subsidiary (QSub), and has also been referred to as a QSSS.

Subsidiaries are important from a state law perspective in that they allow a parent (providing it observes corporate formalities, such as holding annual meetings, recording major events in the corporate minutes, etc.) to limit its liability by conducting its business through separate subsidiaries.

While the idea of allowing an S corporation to operate subsidiaries sounds simple from a state law perspective, from a tax perspective, it is complex partly because Congress enacted Code Sec. 1361(b) in a cursory manner, allowing the law to be defined by regulations to be issued by the Secretary. On January 20, 2000, the Secretary, in an attempt to provide some guidance in the area, published final regulations (Reg. §§ 1.1361-2, 1.1361-6, and 1.1362-8).

This chapter discusses two subsidiaries—QSubs in ¶ 1402–¶ 1408 and C corporation subsidiaries in ¶ 1409.

.01 One-Member Limited Liability Companies—A More Flexible Alternative for Business Operations

Under present law, as discussed at ¶ 1304, one-member LLCs offer liability protection with tremendous flexibility from a tax perspective to conduct operations, thereby making them a preferable alternative to a QSub because of their unique tax advantages. Thus, an S corporation seeking liability protection in its operations should carefully consider utilization of a one-member LLC, because they are easier to operate from a tax perspective.

¶ 1402 Qualified Subchapter S Subsidiaries (QSubs)

A "qualified subchapter S subsidiary" (QSub) is defined as any domestic corporation that is not an ineligible corporation if (1) an S corporation holds 100 percent of the stock of the subsidiary and (2) the S corporation parent elects to treat the subsidiary as a QSub.[1] Except for certain situations (e.g., with a bank), a corporation for which a QSub election is made[2] is not treated as a separate corporation; rather, all assets, liabilities, and items of income, deduction, and credit of the QSub are treated as being part of its parent S corporation.[3]

.01 Definition of a QSub

To satisfy Code Sec. 1361(b)(3)(B)(i)'s 100-percent-stock-ownership test, stock of a corporation is treated as held by an S corporation if the S corporation is the owner of the stock for income tax purposes.[4]

> **Example 14-1:** Hands Inc. is an S corporation that owns 100% of Digits Inc., a corporation that has a valid QSub election in effect for the tax year. Digits Inc. owns 100% of Nails Etc. Inc., a corporation otherwise eligible for QSub status. Hands Inc. may elect to treat Nails Etc. Inc. as a QSub and have its operations included as part of its activities.
>
> If Digits Inc. owns 50% of Nails Etc. Inc. and Hands Inc. owns the other 50%, Hands Inc. may elect to treat Nails Etc. as a QSub. However, if Digits Inc. is a C corporation that is otherwise eligible to be a QSub but no QSub election has been made for Digits Inc., Hands Inc. is deemed not to hold the stock of Nails Etc. Inc. under Reg. § 1.1361-2, and thus Hands Inc. cannot elect to treat Nails Etc. Inc. as a QSub.

For a QSub election, the General Explanation[5] prescribes that the election does not have to be made for all subsidiaries eligible to be a QSub. Thus, if Corporation A, an S corporation, owns 100 percent of the stock of Corporation B, which in turn owns 100 percent the stock of Corporation C, and Corporations B and C could each qualify as a QSub, Code Sec. 1361(b)(3) allows Corporation A to make an election only for Corporation B.

---

[1] Code Sec. 1361(b)(3)(B).
[2] Code Sec. 1361(b)(3)(B)(ii).
[3] Reg. § 1.1361-4(a)(1).

[4] Reg. § 1.1361-2(a) and (b).
[5] The term "General Explanation" refers to the Staff of Joint Committee on Taxation General Explanation of Tax Legislation enacted in the 104th Congress, p. 119-22.

.02 Reasons for Establishing a QSub

Under current law, distributions from a C corporation subsidiary to its S corporation parent are treated generally as if an individual were receiving distributions from a C corporation.[6] If the S corporation has earnings and profits from its operations as a predecessor C corporation, or acquired the earnings or profits in a merger, the S corporation could be subject to tax under the passive investment income tax rules of Code Sec. 1375 and lose its election under Code Sec. 1362(d)(3). For a loss of election to happen, the dividends from the S corporation's stock investment in the C corporation, together with the S corporation's other passive investment income, have to total more than 25 percent of its gross receipts.[7] However, if the dividends are attributable to C corporation earnings and profits derived from the active conduct of a trade or business, and the S corporation owns at least 80 percent of the total value and voting power of the C corporation's stock, then the dividends are not deemed passive investment income for Code Secs. 1362(d)(3) and 1375.[8]

If an S corporation owns more than 50 percent of a C corporation subsidiary's stock, the related-party rules of Code Secs. 267, 453, and 1239 affect transactions between the S corporation parent and C corporation subsidiary. The effect of Code Sec. 1239 is to recharacterize as ordinary income the gain on the sale of depreciable assets between the C corporation subsidiary and the S corporation parent. Code Sec. 453(e) et seq. affects installment sales between the S corporation parent and C corporation subsidiary, triggering the recognition of gain at the time of sale if certain conditions are met rather than permit reporting of the gain under the installment method. Code Sec. 267 denies the recognition of loss between the S corporation parent and C corporation subsidiary based on the mere ownership of more than 50 percent of stock of the C corporation subsidiary by the S corporation parent.

A QSub appears to be the answer to an S corporation parent's dilemma in that all of the QSub's assets, liabilities, and items of income, deduction, and credit are treated as being of the parent S corporation. However, in operation, the QSub rules, even with the issuance of the Regulations, present as many unanswered questions as answered.

Code Sec. 1361(b)(2)(A) basically treats the QSub as a non-entity, similar to the way S corporations would treat a wholly-owned one-member LLC. Thus, there is no basic tax effect for transactions between the subsidiary and the parent. Accordingly, if the parent S corporation transfers LIFO recapture inventory, taxable under Code Sec. 1363(d) to a QSub, this transfer would not qualify as a disposition to trigger tax under Code Sec. 1363(d).[9] Likewise, if a shareholder of the parent S

---

[6] Code Sec. 1363(b).

[7] Code Sec. 1362(d)(3) specifies that the S corporation will lose its election if the S corporation has gross receipts from passive investment income that total more than 25 percent for three consecutive years, and at the end of each tax year, the corporation had subchapter C earnings and profits.

[8] Code Sec. 1362(d)(3)(E). For a discussion of the exception to the rule of Code Secs. 1362(d)(3) and 1375, see ¶ 1409.02 on dividends received from C corporation subsidiaries.

[9] IRS Letter Ruling 9807023.

corporation makes a loan to a QSub, the loan would be considered a loan to the parent for purposes of establishing basis for the shareholder to take losses.[10]

¶ 1403 Four Requirements for the Establishment of a QSub

A simple reading of Code Sec. 1361(b)(3) yields four statutory requirements that must be satisfied to have a QSub. The QSub must

   (1) be a domestic corporation,

   (2) not be an ineligible corporation (defined in Code Sec. 1361(b)(2)),

   (3) have 100 percent of its stock held by its S corporation parent, and

   (4) have its parent elect for it to be treated as a QSub.

.01 Domestic Corporation

A "domestic corporation" is defined by referring to Reg. § 301.7701-5.[11] The regulation states that a "domestic corporation is one organized and created in the United States, . . . and the District of Columbia, or under the laws of the United States or of any State or Territory." A foreign corporation is not a domestic one.[12]

.02 Ineligible Corporation

An "ineligible corporation" is defined in Code Sec. 1361(b)(2) as "(A) a financial institution which uses the reserve method of accounting for bad debts described in section 585," and "(B) an insurance company subject to tax under subchapter L." If the S corporation is a bank, or if an S corporation makes a valid QSub election for a subsidiary that is a bank, any special rules for banks under the Internal Revenue Code continue to apply separately to the bank parent or bank subsidiary.[13]

.03 100 Percent of Stock Owned by Its S Corporation Parent

As illustrated in Example 14-1, there can be various ownership patterns of parent and subsidiary stock that will qualify for QSub treatment. There can be a direct chain of subsidiaries or triangle ownership. A subsidiary could also be a business entity that is disregarded as an entity separate from its owner under Reg. § 301.7701-2(c)(2).

.04 Parent Must Elect QSub Treatment for Its Subsidiary

An S corporation parent must elect to treat its subsidiary as a QSub.[14] The means, manner, and time to make such an election are detailed in Reg. § 1.1361-3.

---

[10] General Explanation (as described in Footnote 5), p. 121. For a discussion of basis, see Chapter 9.

[11] Reg. § 1.1361-1(c).

[12] Reg. § 301.7701-5. However, IRS Letter Ruling 9512001 (September 30, 1994) prescribes that if a corporation formed in a foreign country domesticates itself by filing a certificate of domestication and certificate of incorporation in a state of the United States that permits such a procedure, then the corporation can elect S status. For the foreign corporation in this ruling to qualify as a domestic one, it stated in its ruling request that it did not have any nonresident aliens as shareholders, that all shares of stock issued by the corporation would confer identical rights to distributions and liquidation proceeds, and that shares of stock issued in the foreign country could be transferred without transferring the corresponding shares issued by the corporation where it domesticates itself. Another alternative to IRS Letter Ruling 9512001 (assuming the S corporation has foreign activities) is to form a foreign one-member LLC (assuming that such an entity exists in the jurisdiction(s) where the foreign operation(s) occur) and use the check-the-box regulations to ensure flow-through status from the entity to the "parent" S corporation.

[13] Reg. § 1.1361-4(a)(3).

[14] Code Sec. 1361(b)(3)(B)(ii).

Generally, except as provided in Code Sec. 1361(b)(3)(D) (the five-year prohibition on reelection), an S corporation may elect to treat an eligible subsidiary as a QSub by filing a completed form to be prescribed by the IRS.[15] The election form must be signed by a person authorized to sign the S corporation's return that is required to be filed under Code Sec. 6037 and must be submitted to the service center where the subsidiary filed its most recent tax return (if applicable). If an S corporation forms a subsidiary and makes a valid QSub election for the subsidiary (effective upon the date of the subsidiary's formation), the election should be submitted to the service center where the S corporation filed its most recent return.

Time of making the election. A QSub election may be made by the S corporation parent at any time during the tax year.[16] In contrast, the election for S status for the parent has to be made pursuant to Code Sec. 1362(b) no later than the 15th day of the third month of the tax year.

Effective date of election. Reg. § 1.1361-3(a)(4) states the following:

> A QSub election will be effective on the date specified on the election form or on the date the election form is filed if no date is specified. The effective date specified on the form cannot be more than two months[17] and 15 days prior to the date of filing and cannot be more than 12 months after the date of filing . . . . If an election form specifies an effective date more than 12 months after the date on which the election is filed, it will be effective 12 months after the date it is filed.

Extra time is available to make the QSub election providing the procedures in Reg. §§ 301.9100-1 and 301.9100-3 are followed.[18]

Code Sec. 1362(f) allows the IRS to grant relief where a QSub inadvertently makes an invalid election or termination. Code Sec. 1361(b)(1)(A) prescribes that the IRS, for taxable years beginning after December 31, 2004, can provide, by regulations, when information returns will be required to be filed with respect to QSubs.

¶ 1404 Effect of a QSub Election—A Deemed Liquidation

When an S corporation parent makes a valid QSub election for an existing subsidiary, the subsidiary is considered to have liquidated into the parent per Code Secs. 332 and 337.[19] The tax treatment of the liquidation, alone or in the context of a larger transaction (e.g., a transaction that includes the acquisition of the subsidiary's stock), will (except for the transitional rules discussed at ¶ 1406) be determined under all relevant provisions of the Internal Revenue Code and general principles of tax law, including the step transaction doctrine.[20] Accordingly, if an S corporation forms a subsidiary and makes a valid QSub election for the subsidiary (effective upon the date of the subsidiary's formation), there will be no deemed

---

[15] Reg. § 1.1361-3(a)(2).

[16] Reg. § 1.1361-3(a)(3).

[17] The definition of the term "month" is found in Reg. § 1.1362-6(a)(2)(ii)(C).

[18] Reg. § 1.1361-3(a)(6); Rev. Proc. 2004-49, 2004-33 IRB, which details procedures for late elections.

[19] Reg. § 1.1361-4(a)(2).

[20] In corporations, the "step transaction doctrine" deals with how long "control" is in the formation or other aspects of corporate operation where a percentage requirement of ownership is mandated—does it mean "momentarily" or a longer period of time? For a discussion of the step transaction doctrine, see B. Bittker and J. Eustice, *Federal Income Taxation of Corporations and Shareholders,* 6th ed., ¶ 3.09(2) (1994).

liquidation of the new subsidiary. Instead, the corporation will be considered a QSub from its inception.

Generally, once an election is made for a QSub, the stock of the QSub shall be disregarded for federal tax purposes.[21] Further, Reg. § 1.1361-4(a)(1) states that a corporation that is a QSub shall not be treated as a separate corporation, with all assets, liabilities, and items of income, deduction, and credit of the QSub to be treated as being part of the S corporation. Likewise, debt between the QSub and the parent is disregarded. Example 14-2, adapted from Example 4 in Reg. § 1.1361-4(d), illustrates this point.

> *Example 14-2:* Kleen Inc., an S corporation, owns 100% of Windows Inc., a corporation for which a QSub election is in effect. On May 12, 2010, a date on which the QSub election is in effect, Kleen Inc. issues a $10,000 note to Windows Inc. under state law that matures in 10 years with a market rate of interest. Windows Inc. is not treated as a separate corporation, and Kleen's issuance of the note to Windows Inc. on May 12, 2010, is disregarded for federal tax purposes.

In a loan by a shareholder of a parent S corporation to a QSub, the General Explanation prescribes that the loan be treated as being from the shareholder to the parent for determining its basis for pass-through losses. Specifically, the General Explanation states that

> [b]ecause the parent and each subsidiary corporation that is a qualified sub-chapter S subsidiary are treated for federal income tax purposes as a single corporation, debt issued by a subsidiary to a shareholder of the parent corporation will be treated as debt of the parent for purposes of determining the amount of losses that may flow through to shareholders of the parent corporation under section 1366(d)(1)(B).[22]

.01 Timing of a Liquidation

Generally, except for acquisitions and Code Sec. 338 situations, the deemed liquidation procedure given in Reg. § 1.1361-4(a)(2) shall occur at the close of the day before the QSub election is effective.[23] Thus, if a C corporation elects to be treated as an S corporation and makes a QSub election for a subsidiary (effective the same date as the S election), the QSub's liquidation occurs immediately before the S election becomes effective, while the S electing parent is still a C corporation. However, if an S corporation forms a subsidiary and makes a valid QSub election for the subsidiary (effective upon the date of the subsidiary's formation), there will be no deemed liquidation of the new subsidiary. Instead, the corporation will be considered a QSub from its inception.

Acquisition. If an S corporation does not own 100 percent of the stock of a subsidiary on the day before the QSub election is effective, the QSub's liquidation occurs immediately after the S corporation first owns 100 percent of the stock.[24]

---

[21] Reg. § 1.1361-4(a)(4).
[22] General Explanation (as described at footnote 5), p. 121.
[23] Reg. § 1.1361-4(b)(1).
[24] Reg. § 1.1361-4(b)(3).

¶1404.01

.02 Coordination with a Code Sec. 338 Election

If an S corporation elects under Code Sec. 338 to treat the acquisition of stock in a subsidiary as an acquisition of assets, a QSub election made for that subsidiary is not effective before the day after the deemed acquisition date (within the meaning of Code Sec. 338(h)(2)). If the QSub election is effective on the day after the acquisition date, the liquidation occurs immediately after the deemed asset purchase by the new target corporation under Code Sec. 338. If an S corporation makes an election under Code Sec. 338 for a target (without a Code Sec. 338(h)(10) election), the target must file a final or deemed sale return as a C corporation reflecting the deemed sale under Reg. § 1.338-10T(a).[25]

Examples 14-3 through 14-5 illustrate the timing of liquidations.

Example 14-3: Sigma Inc., an S corporation, owns 100% of the stock of Delta Inc., a C corporation. On June 2, 2010, Sigma Inc. makes a valid QSub election for Delta Inc., effective June 2, 2010. Assume that, under general principles of tax law, including the step transaction doctrine, Sigma Inc.'s acquisition of the Delta Inc. stock and the subsequent QSub election would not be treated as related. The Reg. § 1.1361-4(a)(2) liquidation occurs at the close of the day on June 1, 2010, the day before the QSub election is effective, and the plan of liquidation is considered adopted on that date. Delta's tax year and separate existence for federal tax purposes end at the close of June 1, 2010.

Example 14-4: Monet Inc., a C corporation, owns 100% of the stock of Cherry Inc., another C corporation. On December 31, 2009, Monet Inc. makes an election under Code Sec. 1362 to be treated as an S corporation and a valid QSub election for Cherry Inc., both effective January 1, 2010. Assume that, under general principles of tax law, including the step transaction doctrine, Monet Inc.'s acquisition of the Cherry Inc. stock and the subsequent QSub election would not be treated as related. The Reg. § 1.1361-4(a)(2) liquidation occurs at the close of December 31, 2009, the day before the QSub election is effective. The QSub election for Cherry Inc. is effective on the same day that Monet Inc.'s S election is effective, when Monet Inc. is still a C corporation. Cherry Inc.'s tax year ends at the close of December 31, 2009.

Example 14-5: On June 1, 2010, Buffet Inc., an S corporation, acquires 100% of the stock of Lancer Inc., an existing S corporation, for cash in a transaction meeting the requirements of a qualified stock purchase (QSP) under Code Sec. 338. Buffet Inc. immediately makes a QSub election for Lancer Inc. effective June 2, 2010, and also makes a joint election under Code Sec. 338(h)(10) with the shareholder of Lancer Inc. Under Code Sec. 338(a) and Reg. § 1.338(h)(10)-1T(d)(3), Lancer Inc. is treated as having sold all of its assets at the close of the acquisition date, June 1, 2010. Lancer Inc. is treated as a new corporation that purchased all of those assets as of the beginning of June 2, 2010, the day after the acquisition date. The QSub election is effective on June 2, 2010, and the liquidation occurs immediately after the deemed asset purchase by the new corporation.

---

[25] Reg. § 1.1361-4(b)(3).

¶ 1405 Quirks of Liquidations Under Code Secs. 332 and 337

.01 Insolvent Subsidiaries

A basic understanding of Code Secs. 332 and 337 is needed to understand Example 14-6 (adapted from Reg. § 1.1361-4(d)'s Example 5).

> **Example 14-6:** Alexa Inc., an S corporation, owns 100% of the stock of Wyatt Inc., a C corporation. At a time when Wyatt Inc. is indebted to Alexa Inc. in an amount that exceeds the fair market value of Wyatt Inc.'s assets, Alexa Inc. makes a QSub election (effective on the date it is filed) for Wyatt Inc. The Reg. § 1.1361-4(a)(2) liquidation does not qualify under Code Secs. 332 and 337 and, thus, Wyatt Inc. recognizes gain or loss on the assets distributed, subject to the limitations of Code Sec. 267.

The reason why the QSub election in Example 14-6 cannot occur is because Reg. § 1.332-2(b) prescribes that Code Sec. 332 "applies only to those cases in which the recipient corporation receives at least partial payment for the stock which it owns in the liquidating corporation. If section 332 is not applicable, see section 165(g) relative to allowance of losses on worthless securities."

If Code Sec. 332 cannot apply to the "subsidiary" corporation liquidation of the insolvent subsidiary, then Code Sec. 337 is inapplicable as well. As shown in Example 14-6, the S corporation parent will generally be required to recognize a loss equal to its basis in its insolvent subsidiary stock.

.02 Built-In Gains and How They Affect a QSub

When a C corporation converts to S status, the S corporation may be liable for corporate income tax on the gain at the time of the disposition if the corporation disposes of its assets within 10 tax years from the conversion, and the assets' fair market value at the time of conversion is greater than the C corporation's cost basis (i.e., built-in gain).[26] The General Explanation prescribes that with the acquisition of a C corporation subsidiary by an S corporation parent under the QSub election procedure, the subsidiary will be subject to Code Sec. 1374.[27]

> **Example 14-7:** Alpha Inc., an S corporation from inception, acquired the stock of Beta Inc. for $1,000 from an unrelated third party. Beta Inc. has one asset: a piece of land costing $10 and having a fair market value of $1,000. At the time of the acquisition, Alpha Inc. immediately filed a QSub election for Beta Inc. Beta Inc.'s built-in gain is $990 ($1,000 – $10). If within 10 tax years from the QSub election (assuming that the QSub election stays in effect), Beta Inc. sells the land for $1,000, a corporate-level tax will have to be paid pursuant to Code Sec. 1374 on the $990 of built-in gain.

---

[26] Code Sec. 1374.

[27] General Explanation (as described at footnote 5), p. 121. The chances of a Code Sec. 1374 transaction arising in a QSub election are slight, mainly because it is dangerous to acquire stock of a subsidiary by a purchase or merger. Rather, the S corporation could buy the assets of the subsidiary corporation, obtain a stepped-up value for the assets, and then drop the assets into a QSub that it forms.

.03 LIFO Inventory Recapture

A corporation that uses LIFO for inventory accounting and converts to S status must include the LIFO recapture amount in the four-year period following the S election.[28] Because the General Explanation requires that a parent that owns a subsidiary in a QSub relationship is bound by Code Sec. 1363(d)(3), the S corporation parent may decide not to make the QSub election if the "LIFO" tax is too large.

.04 Inability to Use C Corporation Attributes

When an S corporation acquires a C corporation subsidiary and makes a QSub election, the C corporation attributes, such as net operating losses (NOLs) and unused passive losses, stay with the C corporation and cannot be used by the S corporation.[29] With NOLs, the carryforward period is currently 20 years, and if the losses are not used within the 20-year period, the NOLs are lost forever. Accordingly, an S corporation parent may decide not to elect QSub status for the C corporation subsidiary, to allow the subsidiary to use up its NOL, or to terminate the QSub election after it is made but before the 20-year NOL period expires.[30]

.05 Consolidated Return Issues

For deferred intercompany transactions occurring after July 12, 1995, any deferred gains must be recognized upon the liquidation of a subsidiary into a parent.[31] Thus, if a C holding company owning subsidiaries decides to elect S status for itself and elect QSubs for its subsidiaries after July 12, 1995, and there is a deferred gain not recognized arising from the sale of an asset from one subsidiary to another, the QSub election will trigger the recognition of the deferred gain. Accordingly, a parent, when there is deferred gain on the consolidated returns filed for C corporation subsidiaries, may choose not to adopt a QSub for the subsidiaries affected if the amount of tax on the gain recognition is too high.

.06 Reg. § 1.1374-3(b)'s Relief for Duplicative Recognition of Built-In Gain in Transactions with QSubs

To cover a duplication of S corporation built-in gain or loss under Code Sec. 1374, Reg. § 1.1374-3 and 10 provide for an adjustment to the amount subject to the built-in gains tax under Code Sec. 1374 if an S corporation acquires a C corporation's assets in a carry-over basis transaction to which Code Sec. 1374(d)(8) applies. To illustrate, Alpha, Inc., a C corporation, acquires all the stock of Beta, Inc., creating a parent-subsidiary relationship. Alpha, Inc. decides to become an S corporation on January 1, 2XX1, electing QSUB status for Beta, Inc. at the time of electing S status. At the time of the S corporation election, Alpha, Inc. had net unrealized built-in gain (NUBIG) of $30,000 due to the corporate assets of Beta, Inc. If later, Beta, Inc. transfers its assets to Alpha, Inc. in a Code Sec. 332 liquidation, the NUBIG would be reflected twice; once on the date of the election to S status,

---

[28] Code Sec. 1363(d). See discussion at ¶ 806.

[29] IRS Letter Ruling 9628002 (October 10, 1995) refused to allow C corporation passive losses to be used against S corporation income. For a discussion of C corporation attributes, see ¶ 404 and ¶ 1301.

[30] For the tax consequences of terminating a QSub election for a subsidiary, see discussion at ¶ 1408.

[31] Reg. § 1.1502-13(d)(1).

and the second time on the liquidation. To remedy this, Reg. § 1.1374-3(b)(1) prescribes that:

> If Code Sec. 1374(d)(8) applies to an S corporation's acquisition of assets, some or all of the stock of the corporation from which such assets were acquired was taken into account in the computation of the net unrealized built-in gain for a pool of assets of the S corporation, and some or all of such stock is redeemed or canceled in such transaction, then, subject to the limitations of Reg. § 1.1374-3(b)(2), such net unrealized built-gain is adjusted to eliminate any effect any built-in gain or built-in loss in the redeemed or canceled stock (other than stock with respect to which a loss under Code Sec. 165 is claimed) had on the initial computation of net unrealized built-in gain for that pool of assets. For purposes of this paragraph, stock described in Code Sec. 1374(d)(6) shall be treated as taken into account in the computation of the net unrealized built-in gain for a pool of assets of the S corporation.

Examples 14-8 through 14-10 adapted from Reg. § 1.1374-3(c) set forth the situations illustrating the application of the adjustments to be made with a duplicative situation.

Example 14-8: Adjustment to net unrealized built-in gain for built-in gain in eliminated C corporation stock. (i) X, a calendar year C corporation, elects to become an S corporation effective January 1, 2005. On that date, X's assets (the first pool of assets) have a net unrealized built-in gain of $15,000. Among the assets in the first pool of assets is all of the outstanding stock of Y, a C corporation, with a fair market value of $33,000 and an adjusted basis of $18,000. On March 1, 2010, X sells an asset that it owned on January 1, 2005, and as a result has $10,000 of recognized built-in gain. X has had no other recognized built-in gain or built-in loss. X's taxable income limitation for 2010 is $50,000. Effective June 1, 2010, X elects under Code Sec. 1362 to treat Y as a qualified subchapter S subsidiary (QSub). The election is treated as a transfer of Y's assets to X in a liquidation to which Code Sec. 332 and Code Sec. 337(a) apply.

(ii) Under Reg. § 1.1374-3, the net unrealized built in-gain of the first pool of assets is adjusted to account for the elimination of the Y stock in the liquidation. The net unrealized built-in gain of the first pool of assets, therefore, is decreased by $15,000, the amount by which the fair market value of the Y stock exceeded its adjusted basis as of January 1, 2005. Accordingly, for taxable years ending after June 1, 2010, the net unrealized built-in gain of the first pool of assets is $0.

(iii) Under Reg. § 1.1374-2(a), X's net recognized built-in gain for any taxable year equals the least of X's pre-limitation amount, taxable income limitation, and net unrealized built-in gain limitation. In 2010, X's pre-limitation amount is $10,000, X's taxable income limitation is $50,000, and X's net unrealized built-in gain limitation is $0. Because the net unrealized built-in gain of the first pool of assets has been adjusted to $0, despite the $10,000 of recognized built-in gain in 2010, X has $0 net recognized built-in gain for the taxable year ending on December 31, 2010.

¶1405.06

*Example 14-9: Adjustment to net unrealized built-in gain for built-in loss
in eliminated C corporation stock.* (i) X, a calendar year C corporation, elects to
become an S corporation effective January 1, 2005. On that date, X's assets (the
first pool of assets) have a net unrealized built-in gain of negative $5,000.
Among the assets in the first pool of assets is 10 percent of the outstanding
stock of Y, a C corporation, with a fair market value of $18,000 and an adjusted
basis of $33,000. On March 1, 2010, X sells an asset that it owned on January 1,
2005, resulting in $8,000 of recognized built-in gain. X has had no other
recognized built-in gains or built-in losses. X's taxable income limitation for
2010 is $50,000. On June 1, 2010, Y transfers its assets to X in a reorganization
under Code Sec. 368(a)(1)(C).

(ii) Under Reg. § 1.1374-3(b), the net unrealized built-in gain of the first
pool of assets is adjusted to account for the elimination of the Y stock in the
reorganization. The net unrealized built-in gain of the first pool of assets,
therefore, is increased by $15,000, the amount by which the adjusted basis of
the Y stock exceeded its fair market value as of January 1, 2005. Accordingly,
for taxable years ending after June 1, 2010, the net unrealized built-in gain of
the first pool of assets is $10,000.

(iii) Under Reg. § 1.1374-2(a), X's net recognized built-in gain for any
taxable year equals the least of X's pre-limitation amount, taxable income
limitation, and net unrealized built-in gain limitation. In 2010, X's pre-limitation
amount is $8,000 and X's taxable income limitation is $50,000. The net unrealized built-in gain of the first pool of assets has been adjusted to $10,000, so X's
net unrealized built-in gain limitation is $10,000. X, therefore, has $8,000 net
recognized built-in gain for the taxable year ending on December 31, 2010. X's
net unrealized built-in gain limitation for 2011 is $2,000.

*Example 14-10: Adjustment to net unrealized built-in gain in case of prior
gain recognition.* (i) X, a calendar year C corporation, elects to become an S
corporation effective January 1, 2005. On that date, X's assets (the first pool of
assets) have a net unrealized built-in gain of $30,000. Among the assets in the
first pool of assets is all of the outstanding stock of Y, a C corporation, with a
fair market value of $45,000 and an adjusted basis of $10,000. Y has no current
or accumulated earnings and profits. On April 1, 2007, Y distributes $18,000 to
X, $8,000 of which is treated as gain to X from the sale or exchange of property
under Code Sec. 301(c)(3). That $8,000 is recognized built-in gain to X under
Code Sec. 1374(d)(3), and results in $8,000 of net recognized built-in gain to X
for 2007. X's net unrealized built-in gain limitation for 2008 is $22,000. On June
1, 2010, Y transfers its assets to X in a liquidation to which Code Sec. 332 and
Code Sec. 337(a) apply.

(ii) Under Reg. § 1.1374-3(b), the net unrealized built in-gain of the first
pool of assets is adjusted to account for the elimination of the Y stock in the
liquidation. The net unrealized built-in gain of that pool of assets, however, can
only be adjusted to reflect the amount of built-in gain that was inherent in the Y
stock on January 1, 2005 that has not resulted in recognized built-in gain
during the recognition period. In this case, therefore, the net unrealized built-

¶1405.06

in gain of the first pool of assets cannot be reduced by more than $27,000 ($35,000, the amount by which the fair market value of the Y stock exceeded its adjusted basis as of January 1, 2005, minus $8,000, the recognized built-in gain with respect to the stock during the recognition period). Accordingly, for taxable years ending after June 1, 2010, the net unrealized built-in gain of the first pool of assets is $3,000. The net unrealized built-in gain limitation for 2010 is $0.

¶ 1406 Transitional Relief for All QSub Elections Effective Before January 1, 2001

The step transaction doctrine will not apply to determine the tax consequences of a corporate acquisition if an S corporation and another corporation are "related persons" as defined in Code Sec. 267(b) prior to an acquisition by the S corporation of some or all of the stock of the related corporation followed by a QSub election for the acquired corporation.[32] Examples 14-11 and 14-12, adapted from the regulations,[33] show how the transitional relief rules apply.

Example 14-11: Tom Mora owns 100% of the stock of Granite Inc., an S corporation. Granite Inc. owns 79% of the stock of Stone Inc., a solvent corporation, and Mora owns the remaining 21%. On May 4, 1998, Mora contributes his Stone Inc. stock to Granite Inc. in exchange for Granite Inc. stock. Granite Inc. makes a QSub election for Stone Inc. effective immediately following the transfer. The Reg. § 1.1361-4(a)(2) liquidation is respected as an independent step separate from the stock acquisition, and the tax consequences of the liquidation are determined under Code Secs. 332 and 337. The contribution by Mora of the Stone Inc. stock qualifies under Code Sec. 351, and no gain or loss is recognized by Mora, Granite Inc., or Stone Inc.

Example 14-12: Mary Dixon owns 100% of the stock of two solvent S corporations, Peabody Inc. and Beach Inc. On May 4, 2004, Dixon contributes the stock of Beach Inc. to Peabody Inc. Peabody Inc. makes a QSub election for Beach Inc. immediately following the transfer. The Reg. § 1.1361-4(a)(2) liquidation is respected as an independent step separate from the stock acquisition, and the tax consequences of the liquidation are determined under Code Secs. 332 and 337. The contribution by Dixon of the Beach Inc. stock to Peabody Inc. qualifies under Code Sec. 351, and no gain or loss is recognized by Dixon, Peabody Inc., or Beach Inc. Beach Inc. is not treated as a C corporation for any period solely because of the transfer of its stock to Peabody Inc., an ineligible shareholder.

¶ 1407 State Income Tax Issues

Before making a QSub election, a parent company should undertake an analysis of the state tax law to determine how the deemed liquidation will be treated. For instance, in *Universal Leaf Tobacco Co., Inc.,*[34] a Code Sec. 332 liquidation occurred which, for federal tax purposes, was tax free; however, the

---

[32] Reg. § 1.1361-4(a)(5).
[33] Reg. § 1.1361-4(a)(5)(ii).

[34] *Universal Leaf Tobacco Co., Inc.,* CA-4, 63-2 USTC ¶ 9520, 318 F2d 658.

state of Virginia required income tax to be paid on the receipt of the subsidiary's assets. Notwithstanding, the parent company was able to deduct Virginia's tax under Code Sec. 164. There also could be sales tax issues. For a discussion of sales tax as it affects S corporations, see ¶ 103.

¶ 1408 Termination of a QSub Election

Once elected, the QSub status of a corporation continues until it terminates.

.01 Forming a New Corporation After Terminating a QSub Election

Reg. § 1.1361-5(b)(1) states the following:

> If a QSub election terminates, . . . the former QSub is treated as a new corporation acquiring all of its assets (and assuming all of its liabilities) immediately before the termination from the S corporation parent in exchange for stock of the new corporation. The tax treatment of this transaction or of a larger transaction that includes this transaction will be determined under the Internal Revenue Code and general principles of tax law, including the step transaction doctrine.

Note, however, that if stock is transferred between a QSub and its parent, this transfer will not constitute a termination of QSub status. Example 14-13 below, adapted from the regulations, illustrates the point.[35]

> **Example 14-13:** Iron Inc., an S corporation, owns 100% of the stock of Steel Corp., and Steel Corp. owns 100% of the stock of Metalics Inc. QSub elections are in effect for both Steel Corp. and Metalics Inc. Steel Corp. transfers all of its Metalics Inc. stock to Iron Inc. Because Iron Inc. is treated as owning the stock of Metalics Inc. both before and after the transfer of stock solely for purposes of determining whether the requirements of Code Sec. 1361(b)(3)(B)(i) and Reg. § 1.1361-2(a)(1) have been satisfied, the transfer of Metalics Inc. stock does not terminate Metalics Inc.'s QSub election. Because the stock of Metalics Inc. is disregarded for all other federal tax purposes, no gain is recognized under Code Sec. 311.

.02 Revoking a QSub Election

A QSub election could terminate in three ways: (1) voluntary revocation, (2) the S corporation terminating its S election, or (3) occurrence of an event that renders the subsidiary ineligible for QSub status.[36]

A voluntary revocation. An S corporation may revoke a QSub election under Code Sec. 1361 by filing a statement with the service center where the S corporation's most recent tax return was properly filed.[37] The revocation statement must include the names, addresses, and taxpayer identification numbers of both the parent S corporation and the QSub. The statement must be signed by a person authorized to sign the S corporation's return that is required to be filed under Code Sec. 6037. Revocation of the QSub election is effective on the date specified on the revocation statement or on the date the revocation statement is filed if no date is specified.[38] The effective date specified on the revocation statement cannot be more

---

[35] Reg. § 1.1361-5(a)(4), Example 3.
[36] Reg. §§ 1.1361-3(b) and 1.1361-5(a)(1).
[37] Reg. § 1.1361-3(b)(1).
[38] Reg. § 1.1361-3(b)(2).

than two months and 15 days prior to the date on which the revocation statement is filed and cannot be more than 12 months after the date on which the revocation statement is filed. If a revocation statement specifies an effective date more than two months and 15 days prior to the date on which the revocation statement is filed, it will be effective two months and 15 days prior to the date on which it is filed. If a revocation statement specifies an effective date more than 12 months after the date on which the revocation statement is filed, it will be effective 12 months after the date on which the revocation statement is filed.

The termination of a parent's S election. A QSub election terminates if the S corporation parent terminates its S election under Reg. § 1.1362-2.[39]

A subsidiary that becomes ineligible for QSub status. A QSub could lose its S status by a number of acts (other than its parent filing a revocation), such as the QSub's parent conveying one or more shares of the QSub's stock so that the parent fails Code Sec. 1361(b)(3)(B)(i)'s 100-percent-stock-ownership requirement or the subsidiary becoming an ineligible corporation or losing its domestic status.

If a subsidiary becomes ineligible to be a QSub (e.g., its parent transfers one share of QSub stock to a shareholder of the parent), a revocation may not be made after the occurrence of an event that renders the subsidiary ineligible for QSub status.[40]

.03 Effective Date of Termination

The following are the effective dates for the revocation events detailed in ¶ 1408.02.[41]

- **A voluntary revocation** uses the effective date contained in the revocation statement.

- **The termination of a parent's S election** causes the revocation date to occur at the close of the last day of the parent's last tax year as an S corporation.

- **A subsidiary that becomes ineligible for QSub status** uses the close of the day on which the event occurs that renders the subsidiary ineligible to be a QSub.

If a QSub election terminates because a subsidiary is ineligible to be a QSub, the S corporation must attach to its return for the tax year in which the termination occurs a notification that the QSub election has terminated, the date of the termination, and the names, addresses, and employer identification numbers of both the parent corporation and the QSub.[42]

Examples 14-14 and 14-15 illustrate the effective dates for termination.

Example 14-14: Termination because parent's S election terminates. Downs Inc., an S corporation, owns 100% of Catera Inc. A QSub election is in effect for Catera Inc. for 2009. Effective on January 1, 2010, Downs Inc. revokes

---

[39] Reg. § 1.1361-5(a)(1).
[40] Reg. § 1.1361-3(b)(3).

[41] Reg. § 1.1361-5(a).
[42] Reg. § 1.1361-5(a)(2).

its S election. Because Downs Inc. is no longer an S corporation, Catera Inc. no longer qualifies as a QSub at the close of December 31, 2009.

Example 14-15: Termination due to transfer of QSub stock. Milburn Corp., an S corporation, owns 100% of Daisy Inc. A QSub election is in effect for Daisy Inc. for 2010. On December 10, 2010, Milburn Corp. sells one share of Daisy Inc. stock to Mike Jobs, an individual. Because Milburn Corp. no longer owns 100% of the stock of Daisy Inc., Daisy Inc. no longer qualifies as a QSub. Accordingly, the QSub election made for Daisy Inc. terminates as of December 10, 2010.

.04 Effect of Terminating a QSub Election

A number of tax consequences flow from the termination of a QSub election. A new corporation is formed, with the new corporation being subject to Code Sec. 351's 80-percent-control requirement, and it acquires all of the assets and liabilities held by it immediately before the QSub status terminates.[43] Code Sec. 351 generally prescribes that for a parent company to have a tax-free exchange, it must own 80 percent of its subsidiary's stock (both vote and value) immediately after the exchange.

Treatment of the sale of interest in a qualified Subchapter S subsidiary. If the subsidiary corporation ceases to be a QSub (e.g., fails to meet the wholly-owned requirement) the subsidiary is treated as a new corporation acquiring all its assets (and assuming all of its liabilities) immediately before such cessation from the parent S corporation in exchange for its stock. Under prior law, if more than 20% of the stock of the Qsub was disposed of, the parent S corporation would be required to report as gain any unrealized gain in the Qsub's assets. Example 14-16, adapted from Reg. § 1.1361-5(b)(3), Example 1, illustrates the taxable transaction.

Example 14-16: Green Corp., an S corporation, owns 100% of the stock of WiteWay Inc., a corporation for which a QSub election is in effect. Green Corp. sells 21% of the WiteWay Inc. stock to Golda Inc., an unrelated corporation, for cash, thereby terminating WiteWay's QSub election. WiteWay Inc. is treated as a new corporation acquiring all of its assets (and assuming all of its liabilities) in exchange for WiteWay Inc. stock immediately before the termination from the S corporation. The deemed exchange by Green Corp. of assets for WiteWay Inc. stock does not qualify under Code Sec. 351 because Green Corp. is not in control of WiteWay Inc. within the meaning of Code Sec. 368(c) immediately after the transfer as a result of the sale of stock to Golda Inc. Therefore, Green Corp. must recognize gain, if any, on the assets transferred to WiteWay Inc. in exchange for its stock. Green Corp.'s losses, if any, on the assets transferred are subject to the limitations of Code Sec. 267.

If WiteWay's balance sheet at the time of the QSub-terminating event had land with a cost basis of $10,000 and a fair market value of $500,000 along with a mortgage on the land of $100,000, then Green Corp. would recognize $490,000 of gain.

---

[43] Reg. § 1.1361-5(b)(1).

In the above example, the deemed transfer of all the assets to the QSub is treated as a taxable sale because the S corporation was not in 80% control of the QSub immediately after the transfer by reason of the sale, and thus the transfer did not qualify for nonrecognition treatment under Code Sec. 351.

Effective for taxable years after December 31, 2006, Code Sec. 1361(b)(3)(C) provides that where the sale of stock of a QSub results in the termination of the QSub election, the sale is treated as a sale of an undivided interest in the assets of the QSub (based on the percentage of the stock sold) followed by a deemed transfer to the QSub in a transaction to which Code Sec. 351 applies.

Thus, in the above example, the S corporation will be treated as selling a 21 percent-interest in all the assets of the QSub to the unrelated party, followed by a transfer of all the assets to a new corporation in a transaction to which Code Sec. 351 applies. Accordingly, the S corporation will recognize 21 percent of the gain or loss in the assets of the QSub rather than causing 100% of the gain to be recognized on the sale.

The amendment to Code Sec. 1361 is not intended to change the present-law treatment of the disposition of stock of a QSub by an S corporation in connection with an otherwise non-taxable transaction. For example, the transfer of stock of a QSub by an S corporation pro rata to its shareholders can qualify as a distribution to which Code Secs. 368(a)(1)(D) and 355 apply if the transaction otherwise satisfies the requirements of those sections. Thus, Reg. § 1.1361-5(b) (3) Example 4 discussed below as Example 14-18 remains in full force and effect.

.05 Alternatives to Creating a Taxable Termination

In Example 14-16, if Green Corp. did some of the following tax planning before its taxable transaction, it could have avoided the adverse tax consequences.

Following the mandates of Code Sec. 351. Code Sec. 351 mandates that taxpayers transferring assets to a corporation own an 80 percent controlling interest by value and vote in the stock of the corporation immediately after the exchange. So, in Example 14-16, assume that instead of Green Corp. selling 21 percent of the stock to Golda Inc., Golda Inc. contributes to WiteWay Inc. an operating asset in exchange for 21 percent of the stock. Reg. § 1.1361-5(b)(3), Example 3, prescribes that no taxable exchange will occur. (Note, however, that $90,000 of taxable gain would still be recognized under Code Sec. 357(c) as a result of the excess liabilities transferred to WiteWay.)

Example 14-17, adapted from the regulations, describes other means to avoid immediate taxation on a QSub termination.[44]

Example 14-17: Ring Inc., an S corporation, owns 100% of the stock of Sterling Inc., a corporation for which a QSub election is in effect. Ring Inc. subsequently revokes the QSub election. Sterling Inc. is treated as a new corporation acquiring all of its assets (and assuming all of its liabilities) immediately before the revocation from its S corporation parent in a deemed exchange for Sterling Inc. stock. On a subsequent date, Ring Inc. sells 21% of

---

[44] Reg. § 1.1361-5(b)(3), Example 5.

the stock of Sterling Inc. to Goshen Inc., an unrelated corporation, for cash. Assume that under general principles of tax law including the step transaction doctrine, the sale is not taken into account in determining whether Ring Inc. is in control of Sterling Inc. immediately after the deemed exchange of assets for stock. The deemed exchange by Ring Inc. of assets for Sterling Inc. stock and the deemed assumption by Sterling Inc. of its liabilities qualify under Code Sec. 351 because, for purposes of that section, Ring Inc. is in control of Sterling Inc. within the meaning of Code Sec. 368(c) immediately after the transfer.

A Code Sec. 355 breakup. Another alternative to a taxable QSub termination is a Code Sec. 355 breakup. Reg. § 1.1361-5(b)(2) provides that if a QSub terminates because the S corporation distributes the QSub stock to some or all of the S corporation's shareholders in a transaction to which Code Sec. 368(a)(1)(D) applies by reason of Code Sec. 355 (or so much of Code Sec. 356 as relates to Code Sec. 355), any loss or deduction disallowed under Code Sec. 1366(d) with respect to a shareholder of the S corporation immediately before the distribution is allocated between the S corporation and the former QSub with respect to the shareholder. Example 14-18, adapted from Example 4 of Reg. § 1.1361-5(b)(3), illustrates Reg. § 1.1361-5(b)(2)'s pronouncement.

> ***Example 14-18:*** Denimo Corp., an S corporation, owns 100% of the stock of Runna Inc., a corporation for which a QSub election is in effect. Denimo Corp. distributes all of the Runna Inc. stock pro rata to its shareholders, and the distribution terminates the QSub election. The transaction can qualify as a distribution to which Code Secs. 368(a)(1) and 355 apply if the transaction otherwise satisfies the requirements of those sections.

Code Sec. 357(c)(1)(B) prescribes that for transactions after October 22, 2004, Code Sec. 357(c) will not apply to a "D" reorganization that also qualifies under Code Sec. 355. Thus, the rules for gain recognition on liabilities assumed in excess of basis will not apply where the transferor does not survive the reorganization.

.06 Inadvertent Terminations

In the event of an "inadvertent termination" (as that term is defined in Reg. § 1.1362-4), relief is available in the same manner as if an S corporation inadvertently lost its S election.[45] Thus, if the parent takes immediate steps to correct the problem, and convinces the IRS that the termination was inadvertent, the IRS may overlook the terminating event or allow the election to be reinstated.

.07 Election After QSub Termination

For a corporation where a QSub election has terminated, the corporation or a successor corporation cannot make an S election or have a QSub election made for it for five tax years following the termination without the consent of the IRS.[46] Notwithstanding, the regulations say that in the case of S and QSub elections effective after December 31, 1996, without requesting the IRS's consent, a corporation can make an election to be treated as an S corporation, or may have a QSub election made for it before the expiration of the five-year period under certain

---

[45] Reg. § 1.1361-5(c).

[46] Code Sec. 1361(b)(3)(D).

["

as discussed at ¶ 1402.02, receiving distributions from the C corporation as an individual would apply.[50]

.01 Consolidated Returns

In the operation of an S corporation and its subsidiary(ies), Code Sec. 1504(b)(8) prevents an S corporation from joining in the filing of a consolidated return with any of its affiliated C corporation subsidiaries. Notwithstanding, a C corporation subsidiary of an S corporation may file consolidated returns with other affiliated C corporations that meet the definitions of Code Secs. 1361(b)(3) and 1504.[51]

Consolidated returns offer a number of advantages to the parent S corporation; namely that within the C corporation consolidated return, Code Sec. 1504 permits operating losses of one group to offset operating profits of other members. There is also a 100 percent deduction for intercompany dividends. Consolidated returns are a complex area and fraught with difficulties. However, with careful planning, desired tax results can be obtained.

.02 Dividends from C Corporation Subsidiaries

Distributions from a C corporation subsidiary (e.g., dividends) are taxed to the S corporation parent as if the S corporation parent was an individual.[52] Thus, the S corporation cannot claim the dividends-received deduction for dividends received from C corporation subsidiaries. While this statutory denial of Code Sec. 243's dividends-received deduction may have an impact on the S corporation parent's operations, a greater impact occurs if the S corporation has earnings and profits from its operations as a C corporation before electing S status or due to a merger with a C corporation that had earnings and profits.

If an S corporation parent has at least $1 of earnings and profits at the end of its tax year for three consecutive tax years and had passive investment income (as that term is defined in the statute) greater than 25 percent of gross receipts, then the S corporation parent will lose its election as an S corporation effective the end of its third tax year.[53] Furthermore, Code Sec. 1375 imposes a tax on the S corporation for each tax year it meets the above conditions for earnings and profits, passive investment income, and gross receipts.

However, the SBJPA, when it amended Code Sec. 1361(b)(2) to allow C corporation subsidiaries, removed some of the harshness of Code Secs. 1362(d)(3) and 1375 by prescribing that if an S corporation holds 80-percent-or-greater owner-ship interest in a C corporation (80 pecent C subsidiary), any dividends received from the C corporation are not treated as passive investment income for purposes of Code Secs. 1362 and 1375, provided the dividends are "attributable to earnings and profits of said C corporation derived from the active conduct of a trade or business."[54]

---

[50] As discussed in the reasons for establishing a QSub at ¶ 1402.02, transactions between an S parent and its C corporation subsidiary(ies), depending upon the amount of ownership, are subject to Code Secs. 267, 1239, etc.

[51] General Explanation (as described at footnote 5), p. 119-20.

[52] Code Sec. 1363(b).

[53] Code Sec. 1362(d)(3).

[54] Code Sec. 1362(d)(3)(E).

.03 Determination of Active or Passive Earnings and Profits

Earnings and profits of a C corporation subsidiary are active earnings and profits (active E&P) to the extent that the earnings and profits are derived from activities that would not produce passive investment income (as defined in Code Sec. 1362(d)(3)) if the C corporation were an S corporation.[55]

In determining dividends that derive from active E&P, the S corporation can use "any reasonable method" to make a determination.[56] To assist, the Preamble to Proposed Reg. § 1.1361-0 et seq. (April 22, 1998) provided a safe harbor as follows:

> The corporation may determine the amount of the active earnings and profits by comparing the corporation's gross receipts derived from non-passive investment income-producing activities with the corporation's total gross receipts in the year the earnings and profits are produced (and then multiplying this ratio times the C corporation earnings and profits for the year to arrive at the amount of active earnings and profits). Further, if less than 10% of the C corporation's earnings and profits for a taxable year are derived from activities that would produce passive investment income, all earnings and profits produced by the corporation during the taxable year are considered active earnings and profits.

Additionally, Reg. § 1.1362-8(b)(4) provides that an 80 percent C subsidiary

> may treat all earnings and profits accumulated by the corporation in all taxable years ending before the S corporation held stock meeting the requirements of section 1504(a)(2) as active earnings and profits in the same proportion as the C corporation's active earnings and profits for the three taxable years ending prior to the time when the S corporation acquired 80 percent of the C corporation bears to the C corporation's total earnings and profits for those three taxable years.

.04 Consolidated Groups

To deal with an S corporation acquiring a string of C subsidiaries, if an 80 percent C subsidiary holds stock in another 80 percent C subsidiary meeting the requirements of Code Sec. 1504(a)(2), the upper-tier corporation's gross receipts attributable to a dividend from the lower-tier subsidiary are considered to be derived from the active conduct of a trade or business to the extent the lower-tier subsidiary's earnings and profits are attributable to the active conduct of a trade or business by the subsidiary.[57]

.05 Allocating Distributions to Active and Passive Earnings and Profits

Once the active earnings and profits (active E&P) of an 80 percent C subsidiary are determined, Reg. § 1.1362-8(c)(1) and (2) prescribes the following allocation rules.

> *Distributions from current earnings and profits.* Dividends distributed by a C corporation from current earnings and profits are attributable to active earnings and profits in the same proportion as current active earnings and profits bear to total current earnings and profits of the C corporation.

> *Distributions from accumulated earnings and profits.* Dividends distributed by a C corporation out of accumulated earnings and profits for a taxable year are attributable to active earnings and profits in the same proportion as accumulated

---

[55] Reg. § 1.1362-8(a).
[56] Reg. § 1.1362-8(b)(1).
[57] Reg. § 1.1362-8(b)(2).

active earnings and profits for that taxable year bear to total accumulated earnings and profits for that taxable year immediately prior to the distribution.

In the adjustment of the active E&P after the above distributions have been made, the active E&P of a corporation are reduced by the amount of any prior distribution properly treated as attributable to active E&P from the same tax year.[58]

Consolidated groups. Reg. § 1.1362-8(c)(4) outlines the following rules for determining dividends received by an S corporation from the common parent of a consolidated group (as defined in Reg. § 1.1502-1(h)).

(i) The current earnings and profits, accumulated earnings and profits, and active earnings and profits of the common parent shall be determined under the principles of § 1.1502-33 (relating to earnings and profits of any member of a consolidated group owning stock of another member); and

(ii) The gross receipts of the common parent shall be the sum of the gross receipts of each member of the consolidated group (including the common parent), adjusted to eliminate gross receipts from intercompany transactions (as defined in § 1.1502-13(b)(1)(i)).

Examples 14-21 and 14-22, adapted from Reg. § 1.1362-8(d), illustrate the application of the dividend procedure for 80 percent C corporation subsidiaries.

Example 14-21: Gobi Inc., an S corporation, owns 85% of the one class of stock of Minuta Inc. On December 31, 2010, Minuta Inc. declares a dividend of $100 ($85 to Gobi Inc.), which is equal to Minuta Inc.'s current earnings and profits. In 2010, Minuta Inc. has total gross receipts of $1,000, $200 of which would be passive investment income if Minuta Inc. were an S corporation.

One-fifth ($200 ÷ $1,000) of Minuta Inc.'s gross receipts for 2010 is attributable to activities that would produce passive investment income. Accordingly, one-fifth of the $100 of earnings and profits is passive, and $17 (1/5 of $85) of the dividend from Minuta Inc. to Gobi Inc. is passive investment income.

Example 14-22: Assume the same facts as in Example 14-21, except that Minuta Inc. owns 90% of the stock of Ocean Inc. Minuta Inc. and Ocean Inc. do not join in the filing of a consolidated return. In 2010, Ocean Inc. has gross receipts of $15,000, $12,000 of which are derived from activities that would produce passive investment income. On December 31, 2010, Ocean Inc. declares a dividend of $1,000 ($900 to Minuta Inc.) from current earnings and profits.

Four-fifths ($12,000 ÷ $15,000) of the dividend from Ocean Inc. to Minuta Inc. is attributable to passive earnings and profits. Accordingly, $720 (4/5 of $900) of the dividend from Ocean Inc. to Minuta Inc. is considered gross receipts from an activity that would produce passive investment income. The $900 dividend to Minuta Inc. gives Minuta Inc. a total of $1,900 ($1,000 + $900) in gross receipts, $920 ($200 + $720) of which is attributable to passive investment income-producing activities. Under these facts, $41 ($920/1900 of $85) of Minuta Inc.'s distribution to Gobi Inc. is passive investment income to Gobi Inc.

---

[58] Reg. § 1.1362-8(c)(3).

¶ 1410 Tax Planning with Q Subsidiaries

QSubs are inherently, by statutory design, a complex undertaking requiring constant attention. Technical requirements must be followed, such as making the election (as detailed in ¶ 1403.04); the subsidiary must be a domestic corporation (as outlined in ¶ 1403.01); etc. ¶ 1408.02 details that QSub status could be lost if the S corporation parent, to spread the risk of operation, brings in another shareholder to be a partial owner of the QSub. Since adverse tax consequences could result, the S corporation may want to pursue some tax planning to ease operations. ¶ 1408.05 details some tax planning procedures, such as a Code Sec. 355 break-up. Other approaches are listed below.

.01 Formation of a Partnership or LLC with Another Taxpayer to Spread the Risk of QSub Operations

¶ 1108 details that a QSub could form an LLC with another taxpayer which, for tax purposes, would be taxed as a partnership. As discussed in ¶ 1304, partnership taxation currently offers more flexibility and planning opportunities than S corporation taxation, depending on the objectives desired.

.02 Merger of a QSub into a One-Member LLC Owned by QSub's Parent

Because of state law considerations, it might be less expensive to operate the QSub as a single-person LLC than as a corporation. To accomplish this goal, the parent of the QSub could cause the QSub to merge into a wholly-owned single-taxpayer LLC, with the LLC being wholly-owned by the QSub's parent. IRS Letter Ruling 9822037 views this merger as liquidation of the QSub. Under Code Sec. 332, the parent does not recognize any gain or loss on a liquidation of a QSub. Code Sec. 337(a) prescribes that the parent will not recognize any gain or loss because of the liquidating distribution to it. Code Sec. 334(b)(1) prescribes that the parent takes a transferred basis and a tacked holding period for the assets received in the Code Sec. 332 liquidation.

In terms of how the wholly-owned single-taxpayer LLC will operate for the S corporation parent, see the discussion at ¶ 1107 and ¶ 1307.

Tax Pointer: One-taxpayer LLC status may be desirable for QSubs if a Code Sec. 1031 exchange is being utilized or if a merger of the entities is being considered. For a discussion of these points, see ¶ 1307.01 et seq.

¶ 1411 Merger of QSubs Under Code Sec. 368(a)(1)(A) with Other Entities

On November 15, 2001, the IRS issued Proposed Reg. § 1.368-2(d), allowing the merger of a corporation into a wholly-owned passthrough entity such as a QSub under Code Sec. 368(a)(1)(A). The IRS withdrew the prior proposed regulations it had issued in 2000. For a discussion of Proposed Reg. § 1.368-2(d), see ¶ 1211.09.

Emplo... ...*lans*

Employer stock ownership plans (ESOPs) have been in existence for a number of years, and while they are complex and intricate, they do offer unique planning opportunities to C corporations, whether the C corporation is a publicly traded entity or a small, closely held business. In the Small Business Job Protection Act of 1996 (SBJPA), Congress extended the concept of ESOPs to S corporations in a limited format, effective January 1, 1998.

¶ 1501 Features of Employee Stock Ownership Plans (ESOPs)

When a taxpayer sells stock owned in a C corporation to an ESOP established by the C corporation, then, assuming certain terms are met, the taxpayer will not recognize any gain on the sale.[1]

> *Example 15-1:* Patricia Moore starts a C corporation (XIT Inc.) as a one-person corporation, making a stock investment of only $1,000. XIT Inc. grows through the years, acquires employees, etc., and eventually it is worth $10,000,000. Moore can sell her XIT Inc. stock to XIT Inc.'s ESOP for $10,000,000, realizing a gain of $9,999,000 tax free. Payment for the stock will be provided by the employees of XIT with tax-deductible contributions to the ESOP,[2] and the employees of the C corporation will acquire ownership in a C corporation at the same time.

Unfortunately, when Congress extended ESOPs to S corporations, it deliberately excluded the ability of the owners (i.e., taxpayers[3]) of the S corporation stock

---

[1] Code Sec. 1042(a)(1).

[2] Code Secs. 1042, 4975, 404, and 409.

[3] Code Sec. 1042 does not define "taxpayer." However, Code Sec. 1042(c)(7) excludes C corporations from mak-

ing a Code Sec. 1042 election to exclude gain. Thus, by definition, grantor trusts, estates, partnerships, LLCs, and S corporations can be the taxpayer making the election.

to roll over their gain tax free when they sell the S corporation stock to an ESOP.[4] In addition, Congress also removed certain C corporation ESOP taxable benefits for S corporation ESOPs, thereby making them less attractive than C corporation ESOPs. However, there is some benefit for S corporation ESOPs that make them a viable tax-planning device. Because of the unique advantages that C corporation ESOPs offer over S corporation ESOPs, the shareholders of an S corporation may consider terminating the S corporation status and sell its stock to a C corporation ESOP.

¶ 1502 Two Types of ESOPs

An ESOP is basically either leveraged or nonleveraged. A "leveraged ESOP" arises when a third-party lender finances the entire purchase transaction or when the ESOP issues an installment note to the selling shareholder(s). A "nonleveraged ESOP" arises when the ESOP has the funds to purchase the selling shareholder(s)' stock and converts it from an existing employee benefit plan (e.g., a profit-sharing plan) to an ESOP. There is also a hybrid ESOP: an ESOP that uses existing cash as well as a note for the balance of the purchase price (or that finances the balance of the purchase price).

¶ 1503 General Requirements

.01 Code Sec. 401(a) Requirements

An ESOP must satisfy the general requirements of Code Sec. 401(a). An ESOP is a stock bonus plan created pursuant to Code Sec. 401(a). Code Sec. 4975(e)(7) exempts ESOPs from tax on prohibited transactions if the ESOP is a (1) defined contribution plan and (2) is either a qualified stock bonus plan or a qualified Code Sec. 401(a) stock bonus plan with a qualified Code Sec. 401(a) money purchase plan that invests primarily in employer securities.[5]

.02 Definition of Employer Securities

Code Sec. 4975(e)(8), which exempts ESOPs from prohibited transactions, defines "employer securities" by using the definition found in Code Sec. 409(l). Code Sec. 409(l) provides a number of definitions for "employer securities," namely: "common stock issued by the employer (or by a member of the corporation which is a member of the same controlled group) which is readily tradable on an established securities market";[6] preferred stock;[7] and nontradable common stock.[8]

By definition, S corporations do not have preferred stock due to their one-class-of-stock limitation, and are not traded on any established securities market. Thus, the only viable stock that an S corporation can use for an ESOP is nontraded common stock. Nontraded common stock has to meet a number of requirements given in Code Sec. 409: the corporate voting rights have to pass through to the

---

[4] Code Sec. 1042(c)(1)(A).

[5] Code Sec. 401 et seq. does not define the phrase "invests primarily in employer securities"; however, common sense dictates that the plan have more than 51 percent of its assets in the securities of the employer that established the plan.

[6] Code Sec. 409(l)(1).

[7] Code Sec. 409(l)(3).

[8] Code Sec. 409(l)(2).

participants or the beneficiaries of the ESOP, but these individuals can only vote on certain transactions that involve mergers, consolidations, recapitalizations, reclassifications, liquidations, dissolutions, sale of substantially all assets of a trade or business, or such similar transactions as the Treasury may prescribe by regulation[9] (all other voting rights are done by the trustee[10]). For an ESOP to be a qualified plan under Code Sec. 401, a participant who is entitled to receive a distribution from the plan generally has the right to demand that his or her benefits be distributed in the form of employer securities.[11]

Stock bonus plan. A "stock bonus plan" is defined as a plan established to provide employees or their beneficiaries benefits similar to those of a profit-sharing plan, except that such benefits are distributable in stock of the employer.[12] A stock bonus plan is subject to the same general qualification requirements as a profit-sharing plan, with either type of plan providing for discretionary employer contributions.[13] However, there are differences between a stock bonus plan and a profit-sharing plan.

For instance, a stock bonus plan is exempt from any "fair return requirements" on its investment in employer stock,[14] and Code Sec. 409(l)'s voting requirements apply to stock bonus plans of employers when stock is not publicly traded, while profit-sharing plans are not subject to such requirements.[15]

Money purchase plans. A money purchase plan is permitted to be part of an ESOP;[16] however, by itself, a money purchase plan cannot be an ESOP. Generally speaking, the use of money purchase plans with C corporation ESOPs is limited unless they are used in a nonleveraged ESOP.[17]

Contributions. Code Sec. 404 prescribes that an employer contributing to an ESOP receive a tax deduction for the contribution. Thus, with careful planning, the shareholders' sale of shares to the ESOP is tax free to them while generating a corporate-level deduction (for funds contributed to the ESOP to be used to purchase stock). The contributions to a stock bonus plan are deductible to a maximum of 15 percent of the plan participant's compensation.[18] In a leveraged

---

[9] Code Sec. 409(e)(3).

[10] Depending on how an ESOP is established, the trustee could be the selling shareholder(s). However, trustees are subject, among other things, to the "prudent man rule" (House Report No. 533, 93rd Cong. 1st Sess. 12, 13 (1973)); thus, the selling shareholder/trustee cannot play "games" for votes. For participant's votes, Code Sec. 409(e)(5) adopts a one-person, one-vote approach by prescribing that each participant is permitted one vote on an issue, and the trustee voting the shares held by the plan casts votes in proportion to the votes cast by the plan participants.

[11] Code Sec. 409(h). For employer securities, if the participant does not make a demand for distribution of the stock, the benefits may be distributed in cash by the plan. Further, for stock to be recognized as employer securities in establishing an ESOP, Temp. Reg. §1.1042-1T, Q&A-1(b) prescribes other requirements be met: (1) the employer securities were issued by a domestic corporation; (2) for at least one year before and immediately after the sale, the domestic corporation that

issued the employer securities (and each corporation that is a member of a "controlled group of corporations" with such corporation for purposes of Code Sec. 409(l)) has no stock outstanding that is readily tradable on an established market; (3) as of the time of the sale, the employer securities have been held by the taxpayer for more than 1 year; and (4) the employer securities were not received by the taxpayer in a distribution from a plan described in Code Sec. 401(a) or in a transfer pursuant to an option or other right to acquire stock to which Code Secs. 83, 422, 423, or 424 applies.

[12] Reg. §1.401-1(a)(2)(iii) and (b)(1)(iii). Code Sec. 4975(e)(7) prescribes that a stock bonus plan may be designated as an ESOP.

[13] Code Sec. 401(a)(22), (23), and (27).

[14] Rev. Rul. 69-65, 1969-1 CB 114.

[15] Code Sec. 401(a)(22).

[16] Code Sec. 4975(e)(7).

[17] Code Sec. 404(a)(9).

[18] Code Sec. 404(a)(3).

ESOP, the deduction for payment of an ESOP loan is raised to 25 percent of the participant's compensation.[19] For S corporations, the 25 percent maximum deduction will not be available if an ESOP is structured as a stock bonus plan or a profit-sharing plan.[20] However, the 25 percent deduction will be available to an S corporation if its ESOP is structured as a money purchase plan or a combination money purchase plan and stock bonus plan.[21] For a leveraged ESOP plan, the 25 percent contribution of Code Sec. 409 does not apply to the payments of interest on its ESOP loan. Also, depending on how an ESOP is created (i.e., using preferred stock with dividends), an employer (other than an S corporation) can deduct dividend payments.

Code Sec. 415(c)(1) prescribes limits on the contributions which can be made to an ESOP, namely a participant's annual addition cannot exceed the lesser of $40,000 or 100 percent of the participant's compensation. IRS Letter Ruling 200243055 prescribes that distributions from an S corporation's Accumulated Adjustment Account are not deemed to constitute an annual addition; consequently, the distributions do not cause the ESOP to violate the annual additions limitation.

IRS Letter Ruling 201124030 (March 22, 2011) allowed an S corporation which operated through a single member limited liability company ("LLC") to have an ESOP. Because the limited liability company was a disregarded entity, the LLC was treated as a division of the S corporation; thus, the stock issued to the employees of the LLC was deemed "employer securities."

¶ 1504 ESOP Benefits

Generally speaking, a small, closely held business is difficult to sell. Besides the difficulty in finding a financially sound buyer who can afford to pay the seller's price for the business, there is also the "tax bite" on the gain. In a C corporation framework, shareholders, when they sell stock to an ESOP, can roll over the gain tax free (i.e., engage in a tax-free bailout).[22] The difficulty with a tax-free bailout of this type, since all the employees own the company, is in assembling a management team who would run the company without having any equity control.[23] Assuming that this hurdle can be overcome, then the elements of Code Sec. 1042 have to be met to ensure the tax-free rollover of the gain (this tax-free rollover provision is specifically denied to S corporations by Code Sec. 1042(c)(1)(A)).

.01 Code Sec. 1042

To qualify for tax-free treatment on the sale to the ESOP, Code Sec. 1042(a) and (b) have a number of provisions that must be satisfied:

---

[19] Code Sec. 404(a)(9)(A) and (B).

[20] Code Sec. 404(a)(9)(C).

[21] Note, however, that Code Sec. 415(c)(6) prescribes restrictions for highly compensated employees by limiting the amount of contributions to them (this limitation depends on how the employer contributions are allocated).

[22] Code Sec. 1042(a).

[23] If the ESOP engages in a leveraged buyout with a third-party lender, the selling shareholder(s) may be required to personally guarantee the loan. However, as discussed at ¶ 1504.03, an ESOP can be established with as little as 30 percent of the corporation's outstanding stock, with the establishment to be done all at once or gradually.

(1) The taxpayer has to sell (a) the ESOP employer securities and (b) make a written election to defer the gain by reinvesting the proceeds in qualified replacement securities.[24]

(2) The sale otherwise qualifies for long-term capital gain.

(3) Immediately after the sale (with Code Sec. 318(a)(4)'s rules applying), the ESOP has to own at least 30 percent of either (a) each class of outstanding stock of the corporation or (b) the total value of all the corporation's outstanding stock (in both cases, nonvoting and nonconvertible preferred stock are excluded).

(4) The taxpayer must have held the stock for at least three years prior to the date of the sale to the ESOP.[25]

(5) The employer sponsoring the ESOP must sign a verified written statement consenting to the application of the excise tax provisions of Code Secs. 4978 and 4979A (generally, Code Sec. 4978 subjects the employer to a 10 percent excise tax on the proceeds from the dispositions of any qualified securities by the ESOP within three years after acquisition of qualified securities in a Code Sec. 1042 transaction, and Code Sec. 4979A subjects the employer to a 50 percent excise tax on certain prohibited allocations made in the ESOP).[26]

(6) The taxpayer purchases "qualified replacement property" within the replacement period (the period that begins three months before the date on which the sale of the qualified security occurs, and which ends twelve months after the date of such sale).[27]

.02 Estates Can Make the Sale to an ESOP

An executor or executrix can elect to sell the stock of a corporation to an ESOP.[28] Thus, ESOPs become an important estate-planning tool in that a decedent's estate can create a market for its closely held stock. In a typical situation, a closely held corporation is owned by a family where a decedent is the driving force behind the business. The decedent, while alive, did not plan for successive ownership, even though the stock of the closely held company is the major asset in the decedent's estate. The decedent's heirs, however, are incapable of running the business but the closely held business employees are. Consequently, an ESOP offers a viable means to dispose of the closely held stock for fair value to a buyer who would be

---

[24] Temp. Reg. § 1.1042-1T Q&A-3(b) prescribes that a Code Sec. 1042(a)(1) election contain the following information: (1) a description of the qualified securities sold, including the type and number of shares; (2) the date of the sale of the qualified securities; (3) the adjusted basis of the qualified securities; (4) the amount realized upon the sale of the qualified securities; (5) the identity of the employee stock ownership plan or eligible worker-owned cooperative to which the qualified securities were sold; and (6) if the sale was part of a single, interrelated transaction under a prearranged agreement between taxpayers involving other sales of qualified securities, the names and taxpayer identification numbers of the other taxpayers under the agreement and the number of shares sold by the other taxpayers.

[25] IRS Letter Ruling 200003014 (October 20, 1999) prescribed that for purposes of Code Sec. 1042(b)(4)'s three-year holding period, it can include the time during which a corporation's subchapter S election was in effect. Thus, a corporation can operate as an S corporation until just before establishment of the ESOP (assuming the three-year period can be met), acquiring the benefits of a C corporation ESOP on conversion. For a discussion of the features of ESOPs, see ¶ 1501.

[26] See discussion at ¶ 1504.08 and ¶ 1505.08 about Code Sec. 4979A and Code Sec. 4978.

[27] Code Sec. 1042(c)(3).

[28] Code Sec. 1042(a)(1).

responsible, as opposed to attempting to go into the marketplace to find such a buyer (as discussed generally at ¶ 1504.09 and ¶ 1505.07). An ESOP must pay fair market value for stock.[29]

.03 30 Percent Ownership Rule

An ESOP is required to hold at least 30 percent of its corporation's stock after the sale.[30] Thus, if a taxpayer wanted to keep majority ownership in the corporation while disposing of a portion of the stock, it is possible. However, from a practical point of view, the partial sale may not be viable in that the majority owner may be subject to attack from the ESOP for corporate waste in a state derivative action (e.g., the ESOP could allege that the corporation paid the shareholder-employee too much salary) or that the corporation paid excessively for the shareholder-employee's transportation, travel, entertainment expenses, etc. (e.g., the share-holder should have stayed at a budget hotel rather than a five-star hotel). Also, as discussed at ¶ 1504.08, Code Sec. 409(n) imposes restrictions on the selling shareholder if he or she remains as a shareholder-employee. In the event there are two or more shareholders who want to sell stock to an ESOP, the sales must be part of a single, integrated transaction under a prearranged agreement between the taxpayers.[31]

For stock transferred to an ESOP, the taxpayer must not have received the stock in (1) a distribution from a qualified retirement plan or (2) a transfer under an option or other right to acquire stock to which Code Secs. 83 (transfer of property for services), 422 (incentive stock options), or 423 (employee stock purchase plans) applied.

.04 Qualified Replacement Property

A shareholder selling stock to an ESOP will have nonrecognition treatment applied to the gain to the extent that the selling shareholder purchases qualified replacement property during a 15-month period, beginning three months before and ending 12 months after the date the shares are sold to the ESOP.[32] "Qualified replacement property" is defined as any security that has the meaning given the term by Code Sec. 165(g)(2), except that the term shall not include any security issued by a governmental unit or political subdivision thereof.[33] Thus, qualified replacement property, by definition, does not include tax-free municipal bonds, partnership interests, and other business investments of such ilk. However, qualified replacement property does include corporate stock, corporate bonds, debentures, notes, certificates, or other evidences of indebtedness, and corporate rights to subscribe to or receive stock.

Other limitations are provided regarding what constitutes replacement property.[34] Specifically, the proceeds must be invested as follows:

---

[29] IRS Letter Ruling 9644024 (July 24, 1996) held that an estate's basis in qualifying replacement stock that it acquired after the decedent's death to replace the corporation's stock that the decedent sold to the corporation's ESOP is determined under Code Sec. 1042(d); thus, the basis is reduced by gain not recognized due to Code Sec. 1042(a), not the fair market value as determined by Code Sec. 2031.

[30] Code Sec. 1042(b)(2).

[31] Temp. Reg. § 1.1042-1T Q&A-2(b).

[32] Code Sec. 1042(c)(4).

[33] Code Sec. 1042(c)(4)(A). By definition, qualified replacement property can include stock in an S corporation.

[34] Code Sec. 1042(c)(4) and Temp. Reg. § 1.1042-1T, Q&A-1(d).

- A corporation issuing qualified securities does not have passive investment income (as that term is defined for S corporations in Code Sec. 1362(d)(3)(D)) that exceeds 25 percent of its gross receipts for the tax year preceding the tax year in which the security was purchased.

- An ESOP cannot purchase shares issued by the employer that established the ESOP or by another corporation that is a member of the same control group.[35]

- A corporation issuing qualified replacement securities must be an operating corporation using more than 50 percent of its assets in the active conduct of a trade or business, either on the taxpayer's acquisition of qualified replacement property, or by the end of the replacement property period (i.e., the 15-month replacement period in Code Sec. 1042(c)(3)).[36]

.05 Selling Shareholder's Basis in Qualified Replacement Property

A selling shareholder's basis in each item of qualified replacement property is the cost of the property reduced by the amount of realized gain not recognized under Code Sec. 1042.[37]

.06 Deferral Tax on Capital Gain

Code Sec. 1042 does not require that a selling shareholder make a complete replacement of securities; the replacement can be partial with tax due on the proceeds not reinvested pursuant to Code Sec. 1042. For any replacement property, if a taxpayer disposes of replacement property for which an election has been made under Code Sec. 1042(a) after the initial 12-month period to acquire replacement property under Code Sec. 1042(c)(3), then tax will be due on the capital gain.[38] Thus, care must be taken as to what investments are made during the replacement period. As discussed at ¶ 1504.04, the selling shareholder must make an election after the replacement property is purchased, describing the qualified replacement property, date of purchase, etc.

For ESOP capital gains, the IRS advised that it will issue advance rulings for the sale of employer securities to an ESOP if all of the following conditions are satisfied:[39]

(1) There is no plan, intention, or understanding for the employer to redeem stock from the ESOP.

(2) The combined beneficial interest in the plan of each selling shareholder and related parties does not exceed 20 percent.

(3) The restrictions on disposing of the selling shareholder's stock will be no more onerous than the restrictions applied to at least a majority of the stock generally.

---

[35] The attribution rules of Code Sec. 318 apply to define "control."

[36] Code Sec. 1042(c)(4). Code Sec. 1042(c)(4)(B)(ii) prescribes that financial institutions and insurance companies are specifically included as "operating corporations."

[37] Code Sec. 1042(d). Also see IRS Letter Ruling 9644024 (July 24, 1996) as to the consequences of Code Sec. 1042(d) basis (footnote 29 also discusses this letter ruling).

[38] Code Sec. 1042(a)(1).

[39] Rev. Proc. 87-22, 1987-1 CB 718.

In the case of a complete bailout by a selling shareholder and his or her family, the above provisions can be easily met; however, if the goal is to maintain a family in their closely held business while allowing an active family member to bail out through an ESOP, then the provisions become onerous.[40] The IRS has ruled in the area, however, thereby providing some limited guidance. Capital gains were found in the following transaction: a shareholder owned 45 percent of the outstanding stock of a corporation; his wife and family in addition owned 17 percent directly and indirectly. The 45 percent shareholder was a participant in the ESOP where he received approximately 5 percent of the total covered compensation. The shareholder sold unspecified securities to the ESOP. He represented to the IRS that he had no plan or intention to redeem stock from the ESOP, and that the ESOP would have the first option on the remaining shares owned by the 45 percent shareholder.[41]

.07 Nonrecognition Events

No gain will be recognized if the disposition of replacement properties is caused by the death of a selling shareholder after making a Code Sec. 1042 election, a gift, another Code Sec. 1042 transaction, by a re-organization under Code Sec. 368, such as a merger occurring with replacement securities, consolidation, etc., or by a divorce-related transfer.[42] Replacement properties held at death will step up income tax free to fair market value at the date of death, or the alternate valuation date if an alternative valuation is used.[43] From a tax-planning perspective, Code Sec. 1042(e) offers a number of income and estate tax-planning possibilities. One logical scenario, given below, involves an elderly married taxpayer with children, who is a sole shareholder in a C corporation. This taxpayer sells his or her stock to an ESOP, electing tax deferral with replacement property pursuant to Code Sec. 1042, thereby realizing no capital gain tax on the sale, holding the replacement property until his or her death (however, making gifts during life to reduce his or her estate). Any replacement property remaining at death will pass to the surviving spouse estate-tax free with stepped-up value. For support during life, the selling shareholder lives off the income produced from the replacement securities, and if this is inadequate, the selling shareholder can sell off some replacement property, realizing capital gains as described in Code Sec. 1042.

.08 Restrictions When a Selling Shareholder or Member Remains a Plan Participant

When a selling shareholder, or a member of the shareholder's family as defined by Code Secs. 267 and 318, remains as a participant in a plan after a sale, no portion of the assets of the plan attributable to employer securities sold to the plan during the nonallocation period (defined below) may be allocated to the individual accounts of (1) the taxpayer who made the election under Code Sec. 1042(a) (i.e., the seller); (2) any individual who is related to the taxpayer pursuant to Code Sec.

---

[40] Rev. Proc. 87-22, 1987-1 CB 718.
[41] IRS Letter Ruling 7802015 (October 12, 1977).

[42] Code Sec. 1042(e)(3); IRS Letter Ruling 201024005 (June 18, 2010).
[43] Code Secs. 1014 and 2031 et seq.

267(b); and (3) any other person who owns more than 25 percent in value of any class of outstanding qualified securities (after application of Code Sec. 318(a)).[44]

A 25 percent shareholder. A "25 percent shareholder" is defined as one who has that percentage of interest at any time during the one-year period ending on the date of the sale of the employer's securities to an ESOP or on the date the employer's securities are allocated to the participant in the plan.[45]

The nonallocation period. The period when a selling shareholder and members of his or her family, as defined above, cannot receive an allocation of ESOP assets as participants; namely, the later of (1) 10 years after the date of the sale of the employer's securities to the plan or (2) if indebtedness is involved in the sale, the date of the plan allocation attributable to the final payment of acquisition debt incurred in the sale.[46]

Excise tax. If Code Sec. 1042 stock should be allocated to any of the persons described in Code Sec. 409(n) (see discussion at ¶ 1504.03), an excise tax equal to 50 percent of the prohibited allocation will be imposed against the corporation.[47]

Practical consequences of the restrictions imposed by Code Secs. 409(n) and 4979A. Code Secs. 409(n) and 4979A impose severe restrictions (see discussion at ¶ 1504.03) on a selling shareholder if he or she seeks to use an ESOP to pass the family business from one generation to the next. One means to solve this problem is to have the selling shareholder(s) not elect to defer the gain under Code Sec. 1042 for a portion of the employer's securities allocated to family members and/or the 25 percent shareholder. While the selling shareholder(s) would have to pay tax on the capital gains realized on the appreciated securities, the result would be that the selling shareholder structures the transactions to provide family members and the 25 percent shareholder with continued growth of the corporation for the stock where no Code Sec. 1042 gain deferral is taken, and tax-free treatment for the rest. If the family members and 25 percent shareholders are capable of running the business, then this option is a very viable one, since the selling shareholder has increased his or her chances of having the corporation continue and meet its obligations under the ESOP.

.09 Security Laws and ESOPs

In *Landreth Timber Co. v. Landreth,*[48] the Court held that when selling shareholders in a closely held business made misrepresentations to a buyer, they were actionable under Rule 10b-5 and Code Sec. 10(b) of the Securities Exchange Act of 1934 (1934 Act), notwithstanding that the securities were not traded over a national exchange. It remains to be seen if the selling shareholder of employer securities that are not publicly traded will be held liable with respect to an ESOP using the *Landreth* concept. If liability is found, then ESOPs will have a number of arrows in their quiver to attack fraudulent sales by a selling shareholder, with the injured

---

[44] Code Sec. 409(n). Code Sec. 409(n)(3)(A) exempts an allocation from disqualifying the ESOP if no more than 5 percent of the employer securities purchased from the selling ancestor shareholder will be allocated to lineal descendants in the aggregate.

[45] Code Sec. 409(n)(3)(B).
[46] Code Sec. 409(n)(3)(C).
[47] Code Sec. 4979A.
[48] *Landreth Timber Co. v. Landreth,* SCt, 1985, 471 US 681, 685.

permitted to use federal courts that, as a rule, are more sophisticated than state courts.

.10 Professional Corporations

The ESOP provisions do apply to professional corporations. However, state laws may prevent ESOPs from being established because of the restriction that nonprofessional employees of a professional corporation cannot be shareholders, unless they own a minority interest.[49]

¶ 1505 Elements of an ESOP

For an ESOP to produce tax and successive benefits, the ESOP has to meet certain requirements such as those outlined at ¶ 1503 and ¶ 1504.03.

.01 General Requirements

An ESOP plan must invest in qualified employer securities and be a qualified plan under Code Sec. 401(a). An ESOP is subject to (1) the nondiscrimination rules of qualified plans (Code Sec. 401(a)(4) and (5) and Code Sec. 410); (2) the top-heavy rules of Code Sec. 416 (provisions regarding defined contribution plans such as minimum vesting standards as provided in Code Secs. 203 and 411); and (3) the various rules for plan distributions as provided in Code Sec. 402(d). A discussion of some of the unique rules, as well as the general rules, that apply to ESOPs are given at ¶ 1505.02–¶ 1505.08.

.02 Allocation of Employer Contributions and Forfeitures

Code Sec. 404 governs the size of a contribution that can be made to an ESOP. For employer contributions and forfeitures, like all qualified defined contribution plans, an ESOP is required to establish a definite form for all the allocations of employer contributions and forfeitures, with any allocation formula permitted to be used, provided the formula does not discriminate in favor of the officers, shareholders, or highly paid individuals.[50] Subject to this restriction, a formula geared to the relative compensation of each plan participant will pass muster.

.03 Coverage and Participation Requirements

An ESOP must cover at least 70 percent of all nonhighly compensated employees.[51] ESOPs can prescribe a minimum age and service requirement;[52] however, they cannot have a maximum age limitation.[53] ESOPs can mandate that employee-participants make mandatory contributions to the plan pursuant to Code Sec. 411(a)(4)(B); otherwise, the employee will not receive employer contributions.[54]

---

[49] For a discussion of shareholder ownership by non-professionals in a professional corporation, see Chapter 13.

[50] Reg. § 1.401-1(b)(l)(ii) and (iii).

[51] Code Sec. 410(b)(1)(A) and (B).

[52] Code Sec. 410(a)(1) and (2).

[53] Code Sec. 410(a)(2).

[54] Whether or not a selling shareholder establishing an ESOP for a small, closely held business wants this mandatory contribution requirement is a business call (i.e., the advantage is that the mandatory contributions will ensure that only dedicated employees will be participants, and they will provide the additional funds needed to make the ESOP viable; however, the negative consequence is that the participants may feel that the mandatory contributions are extremely onerous since employee-participants are required not only to make sufficient profits to pay for the stock, but contribute their own personal funds as well.

.04 Vesting

The ESOP must allow participants to become vested in their account balances.[55] Code Sec. 411(a)(2) prescribes two basic ESOP vesting schedules: (1) full vesting at the end of the fifth year or (2) gradual vesting over three to seven years, with 100 percent vesting after seven years. A plan can also be more generous than the minimum vesting schedule.

.05 Distribution of ESOP Benefits

A distinction is made between a leveraged and nonleveraged plan. If a plan is leveraged, the distribution of employer securities acquired with the proceeds of an ESOP loan generally can be postponed until the plan year when the loan is repaid.[56] Unless a participant elects otherwise, the ESOP must commence distribution to the participant or his or her beneficiary no later than one year after the close of the plan year in which the participant separates from service by reason of the attainment of normal retirement age under the plan, disability, or death.[57] The distribution of stock must be made over a period of no more than five years in substantially equal periodic payments, at least annually.[58] If a participant's account exceeds $500,000, then the distribution is extended for one additional year for each $100,000 or fraction thereof.[59]

While an IRA cannot be an S corporation shareholder, it is possible, in connection with an ESOP, that the ESOP could provide that every participant who receives a distribution of stock can direct that the distribution be rolled over to an IRA. IRS Letter Ruling 200122034 prescribes that the S corporation's status will not be terminated if the S corporation redeems the stock immediately on the rollover designation before the IRS custodian receives the stock.

.06 Mandatory Put Option and Required Diversification of Investments

Participants have mandatory "put options",[60] and there must be diversification of investments for the plan.[61] Mandatory put options and the diversification of investments, as illustrated below, put a strain on an ESOP's cash position. Thus, careful planning has to occur at the onset of the establishment of the ESOP to ensure that there will be enough cash to acquire the employer securities from the selling shareholder and meet the requirements as provided in Code Secs. 409(h) and 401(a)(28)(B).

Mandatory put options. If a participant receives stock from an ESOP, the participant has the right to require that the employer repurchase the stock for a price determined pursuant to a "fair valuation formula."[62] The terms of the payment, the period that the participant must exercise the put option, etc. are detailed in Code Sec. 409(h).

Required diversification of investments. An ESOP has to provide participants, when they are at least 55 and have completed 10 years of participation in the

---

[55] Code Sec. 411.
[56] Code Sec. 409(o)(1)(B).
[57] Code Sec. 409(o)(1)(A).
[58] Code Sec. 409(o)(1)(C)(ii).

[59] Code Sec. 409(o)(1)(C)(ii).
[60] Code Sec. 409(h).
[61] Code Sec. 401(a)(28)(B).
[62] Code Sec. 409(h).

plan, with the right to diversify their accounts.[63] A participant is eligible to diversify his or her investments for six years following the plan year when the participant becomes eligible for diversification,[64] with Code Sec. 401(a)(28)(B)(i) defining the method of diversification, the elections which must be made by the participant, etc.

.07 Valuation

All ESOP assets are required to be valued at least once a year.[65] For an ESOP holding stock that is not publicly traded, there is little guidance prescribed by the Code as to how an appraisal must be conducted. However, if the purchase price paid for the put options discussed above is too low, then the participant will have a cause of action against the plan, subjecting the trustee to legal liability. Accordingly, the trustee should consider using outside counsel to determine the price paid for the stock, with the admonition to outside counsel that if they err, they will held liable for the consequences.

.08 Excise Tax

If the ESOP disposes of the securities within three years after acquiring qualified securities in a Code Sec. 1042 transaction, the employer is liable for a 10 percent excise tax on the amount realized if either of the following occurs:[66]

- The total shares held by the ESOP after the disposition is less than the total shares held immediately after the Code Sec. 1042 acquisition.

- The value of the qualified securities held by the ESOP after the disposition is less than 30 percent of the value of all employer securities as of the disposition. However, Code Sec. 4978(d) prescribes that if the distribution of qualified securities or the sale of securities to provide cash for distributions occurs because of the participant's death, disability, retirement after age 59½, or separation from service, there will be no excise tax imposed. Likewise, reorganization under Code Sec. 368 will not cause the imposition of excise tax.

¶ 1506 Leveraged ESOP

An ESOP is permitted to leverage its purchase of employer securities, thereby allowing a selling shareholder to "cash out."[67] IRS Letter Ruling 9102017 (October 12, 1990) permitted a taxpayer to sell stock to an ESOP in exchange for cash and an installment note.[68]

An ESOP is also permitted to leverage the entire transaction by borrowing funds to purchase the employer's stock from a third-party lender.[69] For this type of leveraged ESOP purchase to occur, the following steps have to be met:

(1) The employer establishes an ESOP and contracts to have the ESOP acquire the selling shareholder's stock.

---

[63] Code Sec. 401(a)(28)(B).
[64] Code Sec. 401(a)(28)(B)(ii).
[65] Code Sec. 401(a)(28)(C).
[66] Code Sec. 4978(a)(1) and (2).
[67] Code Sec. 4975.

[68] The IRS ruled that the Code Sec. 1042 deferral of gain was available to the extent that the taxpayer purchased qualified replacement securities equal to the amount realized on the sale.
[69] Code Sec. 4975(d)(3).

(2) The ESOP borrows the shares with the employer guaranteeing the purchase, or the employer can borrow the funds, lending the money to the ESOP.

(3) The ESOP uses the borrowed funds to buy the selling shareholder's securities, with the employer in future years using tax deductible contributions to the plan to pay off the loan (pursuant to Code Sec. 404(a)(9)) equal to 25 percent of the compensation paid or accrued during the tax year to the employees under the stock ownership plan. This contribution deduction provision under Code Sec. 404(a)(9) is not available to S corporations pursuant to Code Sec. 409(a)(9)(C).

.01 Leveraged ESOPs Can Be Used for Merger Transactions

Technical Advice Memorandum 9705004 (December 15, 1995) is illustrative in that it involved an acquisition by an acquiring corporation ("B") of a target closely held company ("A"). B established an ESOP. In B's acquisition of A, the parties discussed the tax advantage to A's shareholders of an ESOP, the Code Sec. 1042 election, etc. The plan approved by the IRS was as follows: A formed an ESOP, which purchased A's nontraded common shares by means of financing provided by B; then A's ESOP merged into B's ESOP; after the merger of the ESOPs, A and B merged; then A stock was converted to B stock, with A becoming a wholly-owned subsidiary of B.

¶ 1507 Practicalities of ESOPs for S Corporations

.01 ESOPs Count as One Shareholder

An ESOP is permitted to be a shareholder in an S corporation.[70] The Committee Reports to the Small Business Job Protection Act of 1996 (SBJPA) state that "for the purposes of determining the number of shareholders in an S corporation, a qualified tax-exempt shareholder [i.e., an ESOP] will count as one shareholder."

.02 Restrictions in ESOP Formations and Operations

Congress passed a number of restrictions on ESOPs for S corporations; the denial of tax-free capital gain treatment under Code Sec. 1042 for the sale to ESOPs by shareholders, and a limitation on contributions to ESOPs pursuant to Code Sec. 404(a)(9)(C). An ESOP's holding of shares in an S corporation will not be treated as an interest in an unrelated trade or business.[71]

.03 Planning Opportunities

As ¶ 1501–¶ 1506 indicate, C corporation ESOPs offer more planning opportunities than S corporation ESOPs. However, it is probable that some utility exists for S corporation ESOPs. One example may be with an estate where S corporation stock, pursuant to Code Sec. 2031, etc., is stepped up to fair market value at death. If the step up will be accomplished tax free due to the use of the marital deduction, unified credit, etc., then, by definition, there is no need for the Code Sec. 1042 tax-free rollover since there will be no taxable gain. Another use may be the merger

---

[70] Code Sec. 1361.

[71] Code Sec. 512(e)(3).

takeover route outlined in Technical Advice Memorandum 9705004 (December 15, 1995) (discussed at ¶ 1506.01).

IRS Letter Ruling 200003014 provides an interesting planning possibility by allowing the shareholders to utilize the S corporation with its passthrough abilities for growth, taking losses, etc., and then terminating the S election, forming a C corporation ESOP to take advantage of tax planning opportunities offered by S corporation ESOPs. Code Sec. 1042, which provides favorable tax treatment to C corporation shareholders, prescribes in Code Sec. 1042(b)(4) that the shareholder must hold stock for three years. The ruling prescribes that the taxpayer's holding period, for purposes of Code Sec. 1042(b)(4), will include the time during which the company's subchapter S election was in effect.

Love[72] provides another example of tax planning; however, the case is fact intensive and may not apply to all situations. In a nutshell, Taxpayers operated McDonald franchises, and to motivate employees of a management company owned by the taxpayers as the sole shareholders, decided to institute an ESOP and a non-qualified deferred compensation plan ("NQDCP"). However, because of personal financial situations and the need for current funds, no employees of the management company other than petitioners chose to participate in the NQDCP. In 2002, 2003, and early 2004 a total $3,066,000 of petitioners' management company salaries were deferred under the NQDCP in exchange for the management company's commitment to pay petitioners the deferred compensation in future years. Because of the large amounts of petitioners' compensation that were deferred under the NQDCP, significant portions of the management company's income (consisting of the fees it received from the operating company) reflected the deferred compensation and were not made available for distribution to the ESOP and to the rank-and-file employee-beneficiaries of the ESOP. The management company on July 12, 2004 decided to scuttle the ESOP selling the shares to the Taxpayers for $103,000. This low valuation reflected the management company's total $3,066,000 deferred compensation payment obligation to petitioners. One of the major reasons for terminating the ESOP was the high cost of operating same due to the high turnover of employees. Right after the Taxpayers acquired the company stock from the ESOP, they established a profit sharing plan, terminating the ESOP and merging it into the profit sharing plan. Then, the company paid out to petitioners the $3,066,000 it owed to them as deferred compensation under the NQDCP. Petitioners did recognize the receipt of the $3,066,000 as ordinary income on their joint Federal income tax return. This created a loss for the management company of $2,969,000 and to be able to recognize the loss, the Taxpayers transferred $2,965,000 to the management company as a capital contribution. Thus, the Taxpayers were able to receive almost $3,000,000 of ordinary income untaxed.

.04 Terminating S Status and Forming a C Corporation ESOP

Code Sec. 1362(d)(1) allows an S corporation to terminate its S status. If the termination occurs during the tax year, the consequences are that the S corporation has two tax returns—one as an S for the period prior to termination of the S

---

[72] TC Memo 2012-166.

election and the other as a C for the balance of the tax year. If a S corporation forms an ESOP and terminates its S status, then unless the tax doctrines of "substance over form," "sham," etc. apply, it appears that the ESOP and selling shareholder(s) will be able to avail themselves of the C corporation ESOP rules (Code Sec. 1042's tax-free rollover of gain).

.05 Charitable Organizations Selling Stock to an ESOP

A charitable organization organized under Code Sec. 501(c)(3) is now permitted to be a shareholder in an S corporation.[73] If, after an ESOP is formed, an S corporation shareholder makes a charitable contribution of S corporation stock to a charity, and the charity then sells the stock to an ESOP, converting its stock to cash, then the following will occur: (1) the selling shareholder may reap considerable tax benefits through the charitable contribution and (2) the S status can be maintained. However, for this approach to be beneficial, a computation must be made to determine if the charitable contribution route will produce more tax benefits overall than using a C corporation format with a Code Sec. 1042 tax-free gain rollover, and ensuring that the various tax doctrines such as "form over substance," "step transaction," "sham," etc. do not apply to this type of transaction.

¶ 1508 Prohibited Allocations of Stock in an S Corporation ESOP

Under prior law, the Small Business Job Protection Act of 1996 (SBJPA) allowed qualified retirement plan trusts described in Code Sec. 401(a) to own stock in an S corporation. The SBJPA treated the plan's share of the S corporation's income (and gain on the disposition of the stock) as includible in full in the trust's unrelated business taxable income (UBTI).

The Tax Relief Act of 1997 repealed the provision treating items of income or loss of an S corporation as UBTI in the case of an employee stock ownership plan (ESOP). Thus, the income of an S corporation allocable to an ESOP was not subject to current taxation.

Code Sec. 1042 provides a deferral of income on the sales of certain employer securities to an ESOP. A 50 percent excise tax is imposed on certain prohibited allocations of securities acquired by an ESOP in a transaction to which Code Sec. 1042 applies. In addition, such allocations are currently includible in the gross income of the individual receiving the prohibited allocation.

However, under prior law, in small, closely held S corporation ESOPs, the S shares of stock could be allocated to a small group of shareholder-employees who control the S corporation, thus sheltering the S corporation income with no tax disadvantage, while allowing the shareholder-employee to control the corporation. Accordingly, Congress amended Code Sec. 409(p) and Code Sec. 4975 for plan years beginning after December 31, 2004,[74] to provide that if there is a nonallocation year (as defined below) with respect to an ESOP maintained by an S corpora-

---

[73] Code Sec. 1361(c)(6)(A).

[74] In the case of an ESOP established after March 14, 2001, or an ESOP established on or before such date if the employer maintaining the plan was not an S corporation on such date, the provision is effective with respect to plan years ending after March 14, 2001.

tion: (1) the amount allocated in a prohibited allocation to an individual who is a disqualified person is treated as distributed to such individual (i.e., the value of the prohibited allocation is includible in the gross income of the individual receiving the prohibited allocation); (2) an excise tax is imposed on the S corporation equal to 50 percent of the amount involved in a prohibited allocation; and (3) an excise tax is imposed on the S corporation with respect to any synthetic equity owned by a disqualified person.[75] Accordingly, it is intended that the amendments to Code Sec. 409(p) and Code Sec. 4975 will limit the establishment of ESOPs by S corporations to those that provide broad-based employee coverage and that benefit rank-and-file employees as well as highly compensated employees and historical owners. An example will illustrate.

> *Example 15-2:* The taxpayer is a 60% shareholder of XYZ, Inc., an S corporation which established an ESOP. Because the taxpayer owns more than 20% of the company, income from the S corporation stock cannot be allocated to the taxpayer's account.

In terms of specific guidance, Reg. § 1.409(p)-1T was promulgated to detail the operation of Code Sec. 409(p). A plan is not treated as an ESOP under the Internal Revenue Code (Code) unless it meets the following requirements, to the extent applicable: Code Sec. 409(e) (relating to participants' voting rights if the employer has a registration-type class of securities); Code Sec. 409(h) (relating to participants' right to receive employer securities; put options); Code Sec. 409(o) (relating to participants' distribution rights and payment requirements); Code Sec. 409(n) (relating to securities received in transactions to which Code Sec. 1042 applies); Code Sec. 409(p) (relating to prohibited allocations of securities in an S corporation); and Code Sec. 664(g) (relating to qualified gratuitous transfers of qualified employer securities).

Code Sec. 511 imposes an income tax on unrelated business taxable income (UBTI), as defined in Code Sec. 512. Code Sec. 512(e)(1) generally provides that an interest in an S corporation held by an organization described in Code Sec. 1361(c)(6), including a qualified plan, is treated as an interest in an unrelated trade or business. However, Code Sec. 512(e)(3) has an exception for employer securities held by an ESOP, so that an ESOP of an S corporation generally does not have UBTI under Code Sec. 512 with respect to the S corporation stock held by the ESOP.

Code Sec. 409(p)(1) requires an ESOP holding employer securities[76] consisting of stock in an S corporation to provide that no portion of the assets of the plan attributable to (or allocable in lieu of) such employer securities may, during a "non-allocation year," accrue (or be allocated directly or indirectly under any plan of the employer meeting the requirements of Code Sec. 401(a)) for the benefit of any "disqualified person," as defined in Code Sec. 409(p). Code Sec. 409(p)(3)(A) provides that a "non-allocation year" includes any plan year during which the ownership of the S corporation is so concentrated among disqualified persons that

---

[75] The plan is not disqualified merely because an excise tax is imposed under the provision.

[76] For a definition of "employer securities," see Code Sec. 409(l).

they own or are deemed to own at least 50 percent of its shares. Code Sec. 409(p)(4) provides, in general, that whether someone is a "disqualified person" depends on a person's deemed-owned shares of S corporation stock held by an ESOP (deemed-owned ESOP shares). Code Sec. 409(p)(4) provides, in general, that a "disqualified person" means any person whose deemed-owned ESOP shares are at least 10 percent of the number of deemed-owned ESOP shares or for whom the aggregate number of deemed-owned ESOP shares of such person and the members of such person's family is at least 20 percent of the number of deemed-owned ESOP shares.

The determination of whether someone is a disqualified person and whether a plan year is a non-allocation year is also made separately taking into account "synthetic equity." Reg. § 1.409(p)-1T(f)(2)(i) defines "synthetic equity" as any stock option, warrant, restricted stock, deferred issuance stock right, stock appreciation right payable in stock, or similar interest or right that gives the holder the right to acquire or receive stock of the S corporation in the future. Rights to acquire stock in an S corporation with respect to stock that is, at all times during the period when such rights are effective, both issued and outstanding and held by persons (who are subject to federal income taxes) other than the ESOP, the S corporation, or a related entity are not synthetic equity.

"Synthetic equity" is a general classification unique to Code Sec. 409(p). Under the rules for the treatment of synthetic equity at Code Sec. 409(p)(5), if a person owns synthetic equity in an S corporation, then the shares of stock in such corporation on which such synthetic equity is based are treated as outstanding stock in such corporation, and as deemed-owned shares of such person, "if such treatment of synthetic equity of 1 or more such persons results in... the treatment of any person as a disqualified person or... the treatment of any year as a non-allocation year."

Reg. § 1.409(p)-1T(f)(2)(ii)-(iv) prescribes special rules for certain stock rights, deferred compensation.[77] Code Sec. 4979A imposes a 50 percent excise tax on certain prohibited allocations in an ESOP, including any allocation of employer securities that violates Code Sec. 409(p), and on any synthetic equity owned by a disqualified person during a non-allocation year under Code Sec. 409(p). In addition, Code Sec. 4979A includes special rules for the first non-allocation year of an ESOP under which the excise tax applies with respect to all deemed-owned ESOP shares and all synthetic equity of disqualified persons, even if there is no prohibited allocation in that year.[78] Thus, for example, any unallocated shares in an ESOP loan suspense account that are treated as deemed-owned shares of a disqualified person pursuant to Code Sec. 409(p)(4)(C) are taken into account in determining the amount involved under Code Sec. 4979A(e)(2)(C). In addition, under Code Sec. 4979A(e)(3)(D), a special statute of limitations applies to the first year of an ESOP that is a non-allocation year.

---

[77] See ¶ 723 for a discussion of Code Sec. 409A's rules regarding deferred compensation.

[78] See Code Sec. 4979A(a)(3), (a)(4), and (e)(2)(C).

.01 Definition of Prohibited Allocation

Code Sec. 409(p) prescribes that in order to prevent imposition of penalties under Code Sec. 4979A, an ESOP holding employer securities consisting of stock in an S corporation must provide that no portion of the assets of the plan attributable to (or allocable in lieu of) such employer securities may, during a non-allocation year, accrue under the ESOP, or be allocated directly or indirectly under any plan of the employer (including the ESOP) meeting the requirements of Code Sec. 401(a), for the benefit of any disqualified person. This requirement has two elements; it prohibits accruals and allocations. Reg. § 1.409(p)-1T(b)(2)(ii) and (iii) provides two new terms, impermissible accrual and impermissible allocation, to reflect these two elements. Under the regulations, if there is an impermissible accrual or an impermissible allocation, then there is a prohibited allocation in violation of this requirement.

Under the definition of impermissible accrual, Reg. § 1.409(p)-1T(b)(2)(ii) prescribes that there is a prohibited allocation to the extent (and only to the extent) that employer securities consisting of stock in an S corporation owned by the ESOP and any assets attributable thereto are held under the ESOP for the benefit of a disqualified person during a non-allocation year. For this purpose, assets attributable to S corporation securities include not only S corporation stock held in a disqualified person's account in the ESOP, but also any distributions, within the meaning of Code Sec. 1368, made on S corporation stock held in a disqualified person's account in the ESOP (including earnings thereon), plus any proceeds from the sale of S corporation securities held for a disqualified person's account in the ESOP (including any earnings thereon).

Under the definition of impermissible allocation, Reg. § 1.409(p)-1T(b)(2)(iii) prescribes that prohibited allocations include any allocation for a disqualified person directly or indirectly under any plan of the employer qualified under Code Sec. 401(a) that occurs during a non-allocation year to the extent that a contribution or other annual addition is made, or the disqualified person otherwise accrues additional benefits, under the ESOP or any other plan of the employer qualified under Code Sec. 401(a) (including a release and allocation of assets from a suspense account, as described at Reg. § 54.4975-11(c) and (d)) that, for the non-allocation year, would otherwise have been added to the account of the disqualified person under the ESOP and invested in employer securities consisting of stock in an S corporation owned by the ESOP but for a provision in the ESOP to comply with Code Sec. 409(p).

.02 Effect of a Prohibited Allocation

Under Code Sec. 409(p)(2) and Reg. § 1.409(p)-1T(b)(2)(iv), if there is a prohibited allocation, then the amount of the prohibited allocation is treated as distributed to the disqualified person at the time of the prohibited allocation. Accordingly, the fair market value of the disqualified person's account under the ESOP would generally be included in his or her gross income (to the extent in excess of his or her allocable investment in the contract, if any, under Code Sec.

¶ 1508.01

72). The additional income tax imposed by Code Sec. 72(t) would also apply if the disqualified person is less than age 59 1/2 (and no other exception applies).

Like a deemed distribution under Code Sec. 72(p),[79] a deemed distribution under Code Sec. 409(p) is not an actual distribution from the ESOP. Thus, the amount of the prohibited allocation is not an eligible rollover distribution and, for purposes of applying Code Sec. 72 and Code Sec. 402 with respect to any subsequent distribution from the ESOP, the amount previously taken into account by the disqualified person as income as a result of the deemed distribution is treated as an investment in the contract.

Under Reg. § 1.409(p)-1T(b)(2)(iv)(B), if there is a non-allocation year and there are prohibited allocations in that year, the plan would fail to satisfy the requirements of Code Sec. 4975(e)(7) and would cease to be an ESOP. As a result, not only would the plan lose the prohibited transaction exemption for loans to an ESOP under Code Sec. 4975(d)(3) of the Code and Code Sec. 408(b)(3) of Title I of the Employee Retirement Income Security Act of 1974, as amended (ERISA), but also the exception in Code Sec. 512(e)(3) would cease to apply to the plan, so that the plan would owe income tax as a result of unrelated business taxable income under Code Sec. 512 with respect to S corporation stock held by the plan from and after the date of the prohibited allocation.[80]

Other consequences include imposition of an excise tax under Code Sec. 4979A and, assuming that the plan's provisions do not permit a prohibited allocation under Code Sec. 409(p), loss of tax qualification for failure to operate the plan in accordance with its terms.

.03 Prevention of a Non-Allocation Year

Compliance with the requirements of Code Sec. 409(p) is required on a current operational basis, as well as a plan document basis. Thus, for example, if S corporation shares are held in a disqualified person's account during a non-allocation year, then there is a failure to satisfy Code Sec. 409(p), without regard to whether the terms of the ESOP prohibit such actions or require preventative action to be taken. Factors that might be considered in determining whether there has been a failure to comply with the requirements of Code Sec. 409(p) on a current operational basis include, for example, the exercise of voting rights of shares in the disqualified person's account, distributions from the S corporation to the disqualified person's account, and plan account statements showing allocations to the disqualified person's account.

A plan might choose to take a number of steps before the beginning of a year in order to ensure that the year is not a non-allocation year, such as steps to prevent an individual from becoming a disqualified person. These include:

---

[79] See Reg. § 1.72(p)-1, Q&A-11 and 12.

[80] It should be noted that transactions that give rise to loss of the prohibited transaction exemptions under Code Sec. 4975(d)(3) of the Code and Code Sec. 408(b)(3) of Title I of ERISA for loans to an ESOP could also give rise to other prohibited transactions under Code Sec. 4975 of the Code, as well as violations of Title I of ERISA, including prohibited transactions under Code Sec. 406 of Title I of ERISA, resulting in, among other things, the assessment of additional excise taxes under Code Sec. 4975(a) and (b) of the Code, as well as civil penalties under Code Sec. 502(i) of ERISA.

- Reduction of synthetic equity, e.g., by cancellation or distribution of the synthetic equity.

- A sale of the S corporation securities held in the participant's ESOP account so that the account is not invested in S corporation stock.

- A distribution of the S corporation securities held in the participant's account from the ESOP to the participant. Such a distribution is only permissible to the extent the amount is otherwise permitted to be distributed (e.g., for amounts that are subject to Code Sec. 401(k), the distribution does not violate the distribution restrictions of Code Sec. 401(k)(2)(B)(i)).

- A transfer of the S corporation securities held for the participant under the ESOP into a separate portion of the plan that is not an ESOP (as permitted under Code Sec. 54.4975-11(a)(5) of the Excise Tax Regulations) or to another qualified plan of the employer that is not an ESOP.

Any of these steps must satisfy applicable legal and qualification requirements, including the nondiscrimination requirements of Code Sec. 401(a)(4).[81] Reg. § 1.409(p)-1T(b)(v) provides that, if a transfer is made from an ESOP to a separate portion of the plan or to another qualified plan of the employer that is not an ESOP in order to prevent a non-allocation year, then both the ESOP and the plan that is not an ESOP will not fail to satisfy the requirements of Reg. § 1.401(a)(4)-4 merely because of the transfer. Further, subsequent to the transfer, the plan that is not an ESOP will not fail to satisfy the requirements of Reg. § 1.401(a)(4)-4 merely because of the benefits, rights, or features with respect to the transferred benefits if those benefits, rights, or features would satisfy the requirements of Reg. § 1.401(a)(4)-4 if the mandatory disaggregation rule for ESOPs at Reg. § 1.410(b)-7(c)(2) did not apply.

In the event of such a transfer, the transferee plan would be subject to tax on unrelated business taxable income with respect to its pro rata share of income from the S corporation securities, with that expense to be charged to the account holding the transferred amount. However, the ESOP would be able to continue to satisfy the requirements of Code Sec. 4975(e)(7) and the allocations could be made for the participant for the year.

.04 Determination of Non-Allocation Year

Code Sec. 409(p) prescribes that a "non-allocation year" generally means a plan year during which on any date disqualified persons own 50 percent or more of the stock in the S corporation, separately applied by taking into account all outstanding shares of stock in the S corporation (including shares held by the ESOP) and by taking into account all outstanding shares of stock in the S corporation and synthetic equity.

Reg. § 1.409(p)-1T(c)(1) prescribes that a non-allocation year means a plan year of an ESOP during which, at any time, the ESOP holds any employer securities that are shares of an S corporation and either:

---

[81] Additionally, any sale or transfer of plan assets must comply with the requirements of Part 4 of Subtitle B of Title I of ERISA.

¶1508.04

(i) Disqualified persons own at least 50 percent of the number of outstanding shares of stock in the S corporation (including deemed-owned ESOP shares); or

(ii) Disqualified persons own at least 50 percent of the sum of:

(A) The outstanding shares of stock in the S corporation (including deemed-owned ESOP shares), plus

(B) The shares of synthetic equity in the S corporation owned by disqualified persons.

Reg. § 1.409(p)-1T(c)(2) prescribes attribution rules, to wit: the rules of Code Sec. 318(a) apply to determine ownership of shares in the S corporation (including deemed-owned ESOP shares) and synthetic equity. However, for this purpose, Code Sec. 318(a)(4) (relating to options to acquire stock) is disregarded and, in applying Code Sec. 318(a)(1), the members of an individual's family include members of the individual's family under Reg. § 1.409(p)-1T(d)(2). In addition, an individual is treated as owning deemed-owned ESOP shares of that individual notwithstanding the employee trust exception in Code Sec. 318(a)(2)(B)(i). If the attribution rules in Reg. § 1.409(p)-1T(f)(1) apply, then the rules of Reg. § 1.409(p)-1T(f)(1) are applied before the rules of Reg. § 1.409(p)-1T(c)(2). Further, Reg. § 1.409(p)-1T(c)(3)-(6) detail special rules to prevent avoidance or evasion as well as deal with stock rights where shares are treated as owned by more than one person.

.05 Disqualified Persons

Reg. § 1.409(p)-1T(d)(1) prescribes that a "disqualified person" means any person for whom:

(i) The number of such person's deemed-owned ESOP shares of the S corporation is at least 10 percent of the number of the deemed-owned ESOP shares of the S corporation;

(ii) The aggregate number of such person's deemed-owned ESOP shares and synthetic equity shares of the S corporation is at least 10 percent of the sum of: (A) The total number of deemed-owned ESOP shares, and (B) The person's synthetic equity shares of the S corporation;

(iii) The aggregate number of the S corporation's deemed-owned ESOP shares of such person and of the members of such person's family is at least 20 percent of the number of deemed-owned ESOP shares of the S corporation; or

(iv) The aggregate number of the S corporation's deemed-owned ESOP shares and synthetic equity shares of such person and of the members of such person's family is at least 20 percent of the sum of: (A) The total number of deemed-owned ESOP shares, and (B) The synthetic equity shares of the S corporation owned by such person and the members of such person's family.

Reg. § 1.409(p)-1T(d)(2)(ii) defines "member of the family" with respect to an individual as follows:

¶1508.05

(A) The spouse of the individual;

(B) An ancestor or lineal descendant of the individual or the individual's spouse;

(C) A brother or sister of the individual or of the individual's spouse and any lineal descendant of the brother or sister; and

(D) The spouse of any individual described in (B) or (C).

Reg. § 1.409(p)-1T(d)(2)(i), (iii) and (iv) prescribe special attribution rules such as Reg. § 1.409(p)-1T(d)(2)(iii), which details that "A spouse of an individual who is legally separated from such individual under a decree of divorce or separate maintenance is not treated as such individual's spouse under Reg. § 1.409(p)-1T(d)(2)(ii)(A)."

An example illustrating the determination of a non-qualifying person is set forth below:

> **Example 15-3:** An S corporation has 800 outstanding shares of which 100 are owned by individual O and 700 are held in an employee stock ownership plan (ESOP) during 2010, including 200 shares held in the ESOP account of O, 65 shares held in the ESOP account of participant P, and 40 shares held in the ESOP account of participant Q who is P's spouse. The S corporation has no synthetic equity. O is a disqualified person during 2010 because O's account in the ESOP holds at least 10 percent of the shares owned by the ESOP (200 is 28.6 percent of 700). In addition, P is a disqualified person during 2010 because P is treated as owning the shares held by Q, and P's total deemed-owned shares are thus at least 10 percent of the shares owned by the plan (65 plus 40 is more than 10 percent of 700). In addition, Q is a disqualified person because of being a spouse. As a result, disqualified persons own at least 50 percent of the outstanding shares of the S corporation during 2010 (O's 100 directly owned shares, O's 200 deemed-owned shares, P's 65 deemed owned shares, plus Q's 40 deemed owned shares are 50.6 percent of 800).

.06 Determination of Disqualified Persons on Person-by-Person Basis

For purposes of determining "synthetic equity," Reg. § 1.409(p)-1T(f) looks only at the synthetic equity of the person being tested to determine if he or she is a disqualified person. In addition, Reg. § 1.409(p)-1T(c)(1)(ii) prescribes a non-allocation year occurs as a result of synthetic equity if the total share ownership of disqualified persons (actual ownership, deemed-owned ESOP shares, plus synthetic equity) is at least 50 percent of the total shares outstanding plus the synthetic equity of disqualified persons. This "person-by-person approach" is more consistent with the statutory rule that synthetic equity is counted for one person if it results in any person being treated as a disqualified person.

Reg. § 1.409(p)-1T(f)(i)-(v) prescribes that the person-by-person approach applies to synthetic equity in the form of non-qualified deferred compensation, as well as in the form of options or other rights related to stock. This approach prevents dilution of the disqualified person's ownership and also addresses an abuse situation involving stock options or stock appreciation rights that are unlikely to be

¶1508.06

exercised. In this abuse, the S corporation issues a large number of stock options or stock appreciation rights to lower paid employees which are only exercisable at a strike price far exceeding even the likely future value of the shares or the strike price is periodically reset to exceed the expected value during the term of the option or right. These options or rights would never be exercised by the employees, but are designed to count as synthetic equity shares in order to prevent shareholders who actually have the right to own 10 percent or more of the S corporation from being treated as disqualified persons. Under the person-by person approach adopted in Reg. § 1.409(p)-1T, these options or rights would be ignored in determining whether other shareholders were disqualified persons and would not prevent persons who have actual rights to become 10 percent shareholders from being treated as disqualified persons.

.07 Synthetic Equity

Reg. § 1.409(p)-1T(f)(4)(i) prescribes that in the case of synthetic equity that is determined by reference to shares of stock of the S corporation, the person who is entitled to the synthetic equity is treated as owning the number of shares of stock deliverable pursuant to such synthetic equity. In the case of synthetic equity that is determined by reference to shares of stock of the S corporation, but for which payment is made in cash or other property (besides stock of the S corporation), the number of shares of synthetic equity treated as owned is equal to the number of shares of stock having a fair market value equal to the cash or other property (disregarding lapse restrictions as described in Reg. § 1.83-3(i)). Where such synthetic equity is a right to purchase or receive S corporation shares, the corresponding number of shares of synthetic equity is determined without regard to lapse restrictions as described in Reg. § 1.83-3(i) or to any amount required to be paid in exchange for the shares. Thus, for example, if a corporation grants an employee of an S corporation an option to purchase 100 shares of the corporation's stock, exercisable in the future only after the satisfaction of certain performance conditions, the employee is the deemed owner of 100 synthetic equity shares of the corporation as of the date the option is granted. If the same employee were granted 100 shares of restricted S corporation stock (or restricted stock units), subject to forfeiture until the satisfaction of performance or service conditions, the employee would likewise be the deemed owner of 100 synthetic equity shares from the grant date. However, if the same employee were granted a stock appreciation right with regard to 100 shares of S corporation stock (whether payable in stock or in cash), the number of synthetic equity shares the employee is deemed to own equals the number of shares having a value equal to the appreciation at the time of measurement (determined without regard to lapse restrictions).

Reg. § 1.409(p)-1T(f)(4)(ii) prescribes that in the case of synthetic equity that is determined by reference to shares of stock (or similar interests) in a related entity, the person who is entitled to the synthetic equity is treated as owning shares of stock of the S corporation with the same aggregate value as the number of shares of stock (or similar interests) of the related entity (with such value determined without regard to any lapse restriction as defined at Reg. § 1.83-3(i)).

¶ 1508.07

Reg. § 1.409(p)-1T develops a three-part test to determine the number of shares of synthetic equity. First, Reg. § 1.409(p)-1T includes a special rule with respect to voting rights. While Code Sec. 409(l) and Code Sec. 4975(e)(7) generally require that the employer securities of an ESOP have voting rights at least equal to the voting rights of that class of common stock having the greatest voting rights (assuming the employer has no stock readily traded on an established securities market), there might be rights to acquire a class of shares that are not currently outstanding and that have greater voting rights. Under Reg. § 1.409(p)-1T(f)(4)(v), if a synthetic equity right includes (directly or indirectly) a right to purchase or receive shares of S corporation stock that have per-share voting rights greater than the per-share voting rights of one or more shares of S corporation stock held by the ESOP, then the number of shares of deemed owned synthetic equity attributable to such right is at least equal to the number of shares that would have the same voting rights if such shares had the same per-share voting rights as shares held by the ESOP.

Second, Reg. § 1.409(p)-1T permits the number of synthetic equity shares for non-qualified deferred compensation (that is not determined by reference to shares of stock of the S corporation or shares of stock or similar interests in a related entity) to be determined as of the first day of the ESOP's plan year, or any other reasonable determination date or dates during a plan year that is consistently used by the ESOP for this purpose for all persons. Reg. § 1.409(p)-1T require that the date used be reasonably representative of the share value of the S corporation's stock. The number of shares of synthetic equity treated as owned for any period from a determination date through the date immediately preceding the next following determination date is the number of shares treated as owned on the first day of that period. In addition, Reg. § 1.409(p)-1T(f)(4)(iii)(B) includes a rule intended to address the administrative and planning difficulties that arise from a daily, or even annual, determination of synthetic equity shares where the number is affected both by the potential volatility of the S corporation stock value and separately by the potential volatility of the non-qualified deferred compensation. Under Reg. § 1.409(p)-1T, the ESOP may provide, on a reasonable and consistent basis used by the ESOP for this purpose for all persons, that the number of shares of synthetic equity treated as owned on an identified determination date remain constant for the period from that determination date until the date that is immediately preceding the third anniversary of the identified determination date. As new grants are made during this three-year period, the appropriate number of shares of synthetic equity resulting from the new grant would be determined at the next determination date, which would likewise remain constant during the remainder of the same three-year period. However, the ESOP must recalculate the number of shares of this type of synthetic equity at least every three years, based on the S corporation share value on the applicable determination date and the aggregate present value of non-qualified deferred compensation on that determination date.

Third, Reg. § 1.409(p)-1T(f)(4)(iv) includes a rule for cases in which the ESOP does not own all of the stock of the S corporation. This rule reflects the view that the dilutive effect of synthetic equity only affects an ESOP to the extent of the ESOP's ownership interest in the S corporation. Under this rule, the number of

¶1508.07

synthetic shares otherwise determined is reduced ratably to the extent that shares of the S corporation are owned by a person who is not an ESOP (and who is subject to federal income taxes). For example, if an S corporation has 200 outstanding shares, of which individual A owns 50 shares and the ESOP owns the other 150 shares, and individual B would be treated as owning 200 synthetic equity shares of the S corporation but for the special rule for cases in which the ESOP does not own all of the stock of the S corporation, then the number of synthetic shares treated as owned by B is decreased from 200 to 150 (because the ESOP only owns 75 percent of the outstanding stock of the S corporation, rather than 100 percent).

.08 Avoidance or Evasion of Code Sec. 409(p)

Reg. § 1.409(p)-1T(g)(2) includes a standard for determining whether the principal purpose of the ownership structure of an S corporation involving synthetic equity constitutes an avoidance or evasion of Code Sec. 409(p). Under this standard, whether the principal purpose of the ownership structure of an S corporation involving synthetic equity constitutes an avoidance or evasion of Code Sec. 409(p) is determined by taking into account all the surrounding facts and circumstances. An avoidance or evasion of Code Sec. 409(p) does not occur where the ESOP receives the economic benefits of ownership in the S corporation, taking into account all features of the ownership of the S corporation's outstanding stock and related obligations (including synthetic equity), any shareholders who are taxable entities, and the rights of the ESOP, to determine whether, to the extent of the ESOP's stock ownership, the ESOP receives the economic benefits of ownership in the S corporation that occur during the period that stock of the S corporation is owned by the ESOP. Among the factors indicating that the ESOP receives these economic benefits include shareholder voting rights, the right to receive distributions made to shareholders, and the right to benefit from the profits earned by the S corporation, including the extent to which actual distributions of profits are made from the S corporation to the ESOP and the extent to which the ESOP's ownership interest in undistributed profits and future profits is subject to dilution as a result of synthetic equity. For example, the ESOP's ownership interest is not subject to dilution if the total amount of synthetic equity is a relatively small portion of the total number of shares and deemed-owned shares of the S corporation.

As an example of evasion, Rev. Rul. 2004-4[82] was promulgated to illustrate a situation involving avoidance or evasion of Code Sec. 409(p) and provide that there is a non-allocation year not only in the situations described in the revenue ruling but also in situations in which profits are segregated using a method other than QSUBs. Under Reg. § 1.409(p)-1T(g)(3)'s rules, the principal purpose of the ownership structure of an S corporation constitutes an avoidance or evasion of Code Sec. 409(p), and a non-allocation year results, in any case in which (i) the profits of the S corporation generated by the business activities of a specific individual or individuals are substantially accumulated and held for the benefit of that individual or individuals on a tax-deferred basis within an entity related to the S corporation, such as a partnership, trust, or corporation (such as in a subsidiary that is a

[82] IRB 2004-6.

disregarded entity), or through any other method that has the same effect of segregating profits for the benefit of such individual or individuals (such as non-qualified deferred compensation); (ii) the individual or individuals for whom profits are segregated have rights to acquire 50 percent or more of those profits directly or indirectly (for example, by purchase of the subsidiary); and (iii) a non-allocation year would occur if this Code Sec. were separately applied with respect to either the separate entity or whatever method has the effect of segregating profits of the individual or individuals, treating such entity as a separate S corporation owned by an ESOP (or in the case of any other method of segregation of profits by treating those profits as the only assets of a separate S corporation owned by an ESOP).

Examples illustrating the application of Reg. § 1.409(p)-1T's rules are set forth below:

> ***Example 15-4:*** **Determination of disqualified persons and non-allocation year if there is no synthetic equity.** Corporation X is a calendar year S corporation that maintains an ESOP. X has a single class of common stock, of which there are a total of 1,200 shares outstanding. X has no synthetic equity. In 2010, individual A, who is not an employee of X (and is not related to any employee of X), owns 100 shares directly, individual B owns 100 shares directly, and the remaining 1,000 shares are owned by an ESOP maintained by X for its employees. The ESOP's 1,000 shares are allocated to the accounts of individuals who are employees of X (none of whom are related), as set forth in columns 1 and 2 in the following table:

1	2	3	4
Shareholders	Deemed-Owned ESOP Shares (total of 1,000)	Percentage Deemed-Owned ESOP Shares	Disqualified Person
B	330	33%	Yes
C	145	14.5%	Yes
D	75	7.5%	No
E	30	3%	No
F	20	2%	No
Other participants	400 (none exceed 10 shares)	1% or less	No

Disqualified Persons. Per column 4 in the table above, individuals B and C are disqualified persons for 2010 because each owns at least 10 percent of X's deemed-owned ESOP shares.

Non-Allocation Year. 2010 is not a non-allocation year under Code Sec. 409(p) because disqualified persons do not own at least 50 percent of X's outstanding shares (the 100 shares owned directly by B, B's 330 deemed-owned ESOP shares, plus C's 145 deemed-owned ESOP shares equal only 47.9 percent of the 1,200 outstanding shares of X).

Example 15-5: **Determination of disqualified persons and non-allocation year if there is synthetic equity.** The facts are the same as in Example 15-4, except that, as shown in column 4 of the table in this Example 15-5, individuals E and F have options to acquire 110 and 130 shares, respectively, of the common stock of X from X.

1 Share-holders	2 Deemed-Owned ESOP Shares (total of 1,000)	3 Percentage Deemed-Owned ESOP Shares	4 Options (240)	5 Shareholder Percentage of Deemed-Owned ESOP plus Synthetic Equity Shares	6 Disqualified Person
B	330	33%			Yes (col. 3)
C	145	14.5%			Yes (col. 3)
D	75	7.5%			No
E	30	3%	110	11.1% ([30 + 91.7] divided by 1,091.7)	Yes (col. 5)
F	20	2%	130	11.6% ([20 + 108.3] divided by 1,108.3)	Yes (col. 5)
Other participants	400 (none exceeds 10 shares)	1% or less			No

Disqualified Persons. E's option to acquire 110 shares of the S corporation converts into 91.7 shares of synthetic equity (110 times the ratio of the 1,000 deemed-owned ESOP shares to the sum of the 1,000 deemed-owned ESOP shares plus the 200 shares held outside the ESOP by A and B). Similarly, F's option to acquire 130 shares of the S corporation converts into 108.3 shares of synthetic equity (130 times the ratio of the 1,000 deemed-owned ESOP shares to the sum of the 1,000 deemed-owned ESOP shares plus the 200 shares held outside the ESOP by A and B). Accordingly, as shown in column 6 in the table above, individual E's synthetic equity shares are counted in determining whether E is a disqualified person for 2006, and individual F's synthetic equity shares are counted in determining whether F is a disqualified person for 2006, but the synthetic equity shares owned by any person do not affect the calculation for any other person's ownership of shares. Accordingly, individuals B, C, E, and F are disqualified persons for 2006.

Non-Allocation Year. The 100 shares owned directly by B, B's 330 deemed-owned ESOP shares, C's 145 deemed-owned ESOP shares, E's 30 deemed-owned ESOP shares, E's 91.7 synthetic equity shares, F's 20 deemed-owned ESOP shares, plus F's 108.3 synthetic equity shares total 825, which equals 58.9 percent of 1,400, which is the sum of the 1,200 outstanding shares of X and the 200 shares of synthetic equity shares of X held by disqualified persons. Thus, 2006 is a non-allocation year for X's ESOP under Code Sec. 409(p) because disqualified persons own at least 50 percent of the total shares of outstanding stock of X and the total synthetic equity shares of X held by disqualified persons. In addition, independent of the preceding conclusion, 2006 would be a non-allocation year because disqualified persons own at least 50 percent of X's outstanding shares because the 100 shares owned directly by B, B's 330 deemed-owned ESOP shares, C's 145 deemed-owned ESOP shares, E's 30 deemed-owned ESOP shares, plus F's 20 deemed-owned ESOP shares equal 52.1 percent of the 1,200 outstanding shares of X.

Example 15-6: **Relating to Determination of Number of Shares of Synthetic Equity.** (i) Corporation Y is a calendar year S corporation that maintains an ESOP. Y has a single class of common stock, of which there are a total of 1,000 shares outstanding, all of which are owned by the ESOP. Y has no synthetic equity, except for four grants of non-qualified deferred compensation that are made to an individual during the period from 2005 through 2011, as set forth in column 2 in the following table, and the ESOP uses the special rules regarding synthetic equity to determine the number of shares of synthetic equity owned by that individual, as shown in columns 4 and 5:

1 Determination Date	2 Present Value of Non-qualified Deferred Compensation Date on Determination Date	3 Share Value on Determination Date	4 New Shares of Synthetic Equity on Determination Date	5 Aggregate Number of Synthetic Equity Shares on Determination Date
January 1, 2005	A grant is made on January 1, 2005 with a present value of $1,000. An additional grant of non-qualified deferred compensation with a present value of $775 is made on March 1, 2005.	$10 per share	100	100
January 1, 2006	An additional grant is made on December 31, 2005 which has a present value of $800 on January 1, 2006. The March 1, 2005 grant has a present value on January 1, 2006 of $800.	$8 per share	200	300
January 1, 2007	No new grants made.	$12 per share	300	

January 1, 2008	An additional grant is made on December 31, 2007 which has a present value of $3,000 on January 1, 2008. The grants made during 2005 through 2007 have an aggregate present value on January 1, 2008 of $3,750.	$15 per share	200	450
January 1, 2009	No new grants made.	$11 per share	450	
January 1, 2010	No new grants are made.	$22 per share	450	
January 1, 2011	No new grants are made. The grants made during 2005 through 2008 have an aggregate present value on January 1, 2011 of $7,600.	$20 per share	380	

The grant made on January 1, 2005, is treated as 100 shares until the determination date in 2008. The grant made on March 1, 2005, is not taken into account until the 2006 determination date and its present value on that date, along with the then present value of the grant made on the preceding day, is treated as a number of shares that are based on the $8 per share value on the 2006 determination date, with the resulting number of shares continuing to apply until the determination date in 2008. On the January 1, 2008 determination date, the grant made on the preceding day is taken into account at its present value of $3,000 on January 1, 2008 and the $15 per share value on that date with the resulting number of shares (200) continuing to apply until the next determination date. In addition, on the January 1, 2008 determination date, the number of shares determined under other grants made between January 1, 2005 and December 31, 2007 must be revalued. Accordingly, the aggregate value of all non-qualified deferred compensation granted during that period is determined to be $3750 on January 1, 2008, and the corresponding number of shares of synthetic equity based on the $15 per share value is determined to be 250 shares on the 2008 determination date, with the resulting aggregate number of shares (450) continuing to apply until the determination

¶1508.08

date in 2011. On the January 1, 2011, determination date, the aggregate value of all non-qualified deferred compensation is determined to be $7,600 and the corresponding number of shares of synthetic equity based on the $20 per share value on the 2011 determination date is determined to be 380 shares (with the resulting number of shares continuing to apply until the determination date in 2014, assuming no further grants are made).

.09 Application of Excise Tax

Code Sec. 4979A imposes a 50 percent excise tax on certain prohibited allocations in an ESOP, including any allocation of employer securities that violates Code Sec. 409(p), and on any synthetic equity owned by a disqualified person during a non-allocation year under Code Sec. 409(p). In addition, Code Sec. 4979A includes special rules as set forth in Code Sec. 4979A(a)(3), (a)(4), and (e)(2)(C) for the first non-allocation year of an ESOP under which the excise tax applies with respect to all deemed-owned ESOP shares and all synthetic equity of disqualified persons, even if there is no prohibited allocation in that year. Thus, for example, any unallocated shares in an ESOP loan suspense account that are treated as deemed-owned shares of a disqualified person pursuant to Code Sec. 409(p)(4)(C) are taken into account in determining the amount involved under Code Sec. 4979A(e)(2)(C). In addition, under Code Sec. 4979A(e)(3)(D), a special statute of limitations applies to the first year of an ESOP that is a non-allocation year.

.10 Effective Dates

Reg. § 1.409(p)-1T(i) prescribes that generally, the rules of Reg. § 1.409(p)-1T are applicable for plan years beginning on or after January 1, 2005. However, Reg. § 1.409(p)-1T(i) prescribes a number of special effective date and transition rules; thus, this regulation must be consulted to ensure compliance.

.11 ESOP Dividends May Be Reinvested Without Loss of Dividend Deduction

Under prior law, a corporation is entitled to deduct certain dividends paid in cash during the employer's taxable year with respect to stock of the employer that is held by an employee stock ownership plan (ESOP). The deduction is allowed with respect to dividends that, in accordance with plan provisions, are (1) paid in cash directly to the plan participants or their beneficiaries, (2) paid to the plan and subsequently distributed to the participants or beneficiaries in cash no later than 90 days after the close of the plan year in which the dividends are paid to the plan, or (3) used to make payments on loans (including payments of interest as well as principal) that were used to acquire the employer securities (whether or not allocated to participants) with respect to which the dividend is paid.

Congress has determined that the present law rules concerning the deduction of dividends on employer stock held by an ESOP discourage employers from permitting such dividends to be reinvested in employer stock and accumulated for retirement purposes.

Accordingly, for taxable years beginning after December 31, 2001, Code Sec. 404(k)(2)(A)(iii) and Code Sec. 404(k)(5)(A) are amended to provide that in

¶1508.09

addition to the deductions permitted under present law for dividends paid with respect to employer securities that are held by an ESOP (to use the dividends to make payments on the loan, the ESOP used to acquire the employer's stock [Code Sec. 404(k)(2)(A)(iv)]), an employer is entitled to deduct dividends that, at the election of plan participants or their beneficiaries, are (1) payable in cash directly to plan participants or beneficiaries, (2) paid to the plan and subsequently distributed to the participants or beneficiaries in cash no later than 90 days after the close of the plan year in which the dividends are paid to the plan, or (3) paid to the plan and reinvested in qualifying employer securities.

In terms of the dividends, the Committee Reports[83] state that for purposes of the Code Sec. 404(k)(2)(A)(iii) reinvested dividends, a dividend paid on common stock that is primarily and regularly traded on an established securities market would be reasonable. In addition, for this purpose in the case of employers with no common stock (determined on a controlled group basis) that is primarily and regularly traded on an established securities market, the reasonableness of a dividend is determined by comparing the dividend rate on stock held by the ESOP with the dividend rate for common stock of comparable corporations whose stock is primarily and regularly traded on an established securities market. Whether a corporation is comparable is determined by comparing relevant corporate characteristics such as industry, corporate size, earnings, debt-equity structure and dividend history.

To enforce this change, the Conference Committee Report[84] states that the Secretary is authorized to disallow the deduction for any ESOP dividend if the Secretary determines that the dividend constitutes, in substance, the avoidance or evasion of taxation.

¶ 1509 Abusive Transactions

Rev. Rul. 2004-4[85] details situations allowing the IRS to attack transactions involving S corporations participating in tax shelters. As an example, see Rev. Rul. 2003-6,[86] which struck down a scheme whereby promoters were offering shell S corporations which had ESOPs established to take advantage of the rules pre-Temp. Reg. § 1.469(p)-1T, utilizing a merger.

---

[83] *Ibid.*
[84] H.R. 1836, 107-84.

[85] 2004-6 IRB 414.
[86] 2003-3 IRB 286.

Chapter 16

The Effect That Code Sec. 1411 Has on S Corporate Shareholders

¶ 1601 Introduction

Congress enacted several provisions to implement and finance Obamacare, namely Code Secs. 1411 and 3101(b)(2)(A).[1] On December 5, 2012, the Department of the Treasury issued proposed regulations to interpret Code Secs. 1411 and 3101(b)(2)(A). Set forth below is a brief analysis of the pertinent part of these regulations. Section 1411's tax applies to individuals; however, since an individual could be a shareholder in an S corporation either directly or indirectly, as a beneficiary of a trust and/or estate, the proposed regulations detail how to compute the income which is passed through to the shareholders. Likewise, an S corporation could be part of a tiered structure with partnerships and Qsubs (See Chapter 14 for a discussion of Qsubs); thus, the proposed regulations set forth rules for reflecting their transactions for the shareholders.

For individuals, Code Sec. 1411(a)(1) imposes a tax (in addition to any other tax imposed by subtitle A of the Internal Revenue Code of 1986, as amended) for

---

[1] ¶ 615 sets forth a discussion of the tax imposed by Code Sec. 3101(b)(2)(A).

each taxable year equal to 3.8 percent of the lesser of (A) the individual's net investment income for such taxable year, or (B) the excess (if any) of (i) the individual's modified adjusted gross income ("MAGI") for such taxable year, over (ii) the threshold amount. Code Sec. 1411(b) provides that the "threshold amount" is: (1) In the case of a taxpayer making a joint return under Code Sec. 6013 or a surviving spouse (as defined in Code Sec. 2(a)), $250,000; (2) in the case of a married taxpayer (as defined in Code Sec. 7703) filing a separate return, $125,000; and (3) in any other case, $200,000. Code Sec. 1411(d) defines MAGI as adjusted gross income increased by the excess of (1) the amount excluded from gross income under Code Sec. 911(a)(1), over (2) the amount of any deductions (taken into account in computing adjusted gross income) or exclusions disallowed under Code Sec. 911(d)(6) with respect to the amount excluded from gross income under Code Sec. 911(a)(1). Code Sec. 1411(e) prescribes that the tax does not apply to a nonresident alien or to a trust where all of the unexpired interests are devoted to one or more of the purposes described in Code Sec. 170(c)(2)(B).

With respect to an estate or trust, Code Sec. 1411(a)(2) imposes a tax for each taxable year equal to 3.8 percent of the lesser of (A) the estate's or trust's undistributed net investment income, or (B) the excess (if any) of (I) the estate's or trust's adjusted gross income (as defined in Code Sec. 67(e)) for such taxable year, over (II) the dollar amount at which the highest tax bracket in Code Sec. 1(e) begins for such taxable year indexed for inflation (the projected estate and non-grantor trust highest bracket for 2013 is $11,950). See ¶ 1603 for a discussion of Section 1411's rules as they apply to trusts and estates.

Code Sec. 1411(c)(1) provides that net investment income means the excess (if any) of (A) the sum of (I) gross income from interest, dividends, annuities, royalties, and rents, other than such income derived in the ordinary course of a trade or business to which the tax does not apply, (II) other gross income derived from a trade or business to which the tax applies, and (III) net gain (to the extent taken into account in computing taxable income) attributable to the disposition of property other than property held in a trade or business to which the tax does not apply; over (B) the deductions allowed by subtitle A which are properly allocable to such gross income or net gain. Code Sec. 1411(c)(1)(A) defines net investment income, in part, by reference to trades or businesses described in Code Sec. 1411(c)(2). A trade or business is described in Code Sec. 1411(c)(2) as one if it is (A) a passive activity (within the meaning of Code Sec. 469) with respect to the taxpayer, or (B) a trade or business engaged in trading in financial instruments or commodities (as defined in Code Sec. 475(e)(2)). Code Sec. 1411(c)(5) prescribes that net investment income does not include distributions from a plan or arrangement described in Code Secs. 401(a), 403(a), 403(b), 408, 408A, or 457(b). Code Sec. 1411(c)(6) details that net investment income does not include any item taken into account in determining self-employment income for a taxable year on which a tax is imposed by Code Sec. 1401(b). See ¶ 1604 for a definition of net investment income.

Code Sec. 1411(c)(3) states that while income from the investment of working capital is not treated as derived from a trade or business for purposes of Code Sec.

¶1601

1411(c)(1); it is subject to tax under Code Sec. 1411. See ¶ 1606 for a discussion of Section 1411's rules as they apply to working capital. Section 1411 exempts earned income from the definition of net investment income; however, earned income is a component of MAGI, another component of Section 1411's tax. (See ¶ 1604.02 for a discussion of the rules as they are employed with earned income from the S corporation.)

In the case of the disposition of an interest in a partnership or an S corporation, Code Sec. 1411(c)(4) provides that gain or loss from such disposition is taken into account for purposes of Code Sec. 1411(c)(1)(A)(iii) only to the extent of the net gain or net loss which would be so taken into account by the transferor if all property of the partnership or S corporation were sold at fair market value immediately before the disposition of such interest. See ¶ 1607 for a discussion of Section 1411's rules as they apply to disposition of partnership and S corporate interests.

¶ 1602 Application to Individuals

.01 Non-Resident Aliens Married to an S Corporation Shareholder

Code Sec. 1411(e)(1) prescribes that Code Sec. 1411's tax does not apply to a nonresident alien. Prop. Reg. § 1.1411-2(a)(2)(i)(A) details that in the event a joint return is filed by a nonresident alien married to a U.S. citizen or resident, the spouses will be treated as married filing separately for purposes of Code Sec. 1411. For purposes of calculating the tax imposed under Code Sec. 1411(a)(1), the U.S. citizen or resident spouse will be subject to the threshold amount for a married taxpayer filing a separate return (i.e., $125,000), and the nonresident alien spouse will not be subject to tax under Code Sec. 1411. In accordance with the rules for married individuals filing separate returns, the spouse that is a U.S. citizen or resident must determine his or her own net investment income and modified adjusted gross income. Prop. Reg. § 1.1411-2(a)(2)(i)(B) states that married individuals who file separately must abide by the same rules as for nonresident aliens filing a joint return with a U.S. citizen.

.02 Calculation of Code Sec. 1411's Tax

Prop. Reg. § 1.1411-2(b) reiterates Code Sec. 1411(a)(2)'s provision set forth above and sets forth an example of how to calculate the tax as follows: In 2013, A, an unmarried U.S. citizen, has modified adjusted gross income ("MAGI") of $190,000, which includes $50,000 of net investment income. A owes no tax under Code Sec. 1411 because the threshold amount for a single individual is $200,000. If for 2013, A had net investment income of $100,000 and MAGI of $220,000, A would pay a Code Sec. 1411 tax only on the $20,000 ($220,000 less his MAGI threshold of $200,000 = $20,000) with the surtax being $760.00 (3.8% × $20,000 = $760). While his net investment income is $100,000, Code Sec. 1411's tax is only imposed on the lesser of the net investment income or the amount which exceeds the threshold amount. If during 2014, A has modified adjusted gross income of $220,000, which includes $5,000 of net investment income, then the individual has a Code Sec. 1411 tax of $190 (Code Sec. 1411's MAGI/threshold computation is $20,000; A's net investment income is $5,000. Since $5,000 is less than $20,000; A's Code Sec. 1411's tax is computed on the lower amount of $5,000 or $190 [$5,000 × 3.8% = $190].).

Tax Pointer 1: Code Sec. 1411's tax is in addition to Code Sec. 1401's 0.9% tax on wages and on self-employment income in excess of Code Sec. 1401's 0.9% threshold amounts of $200,000 if single, $250,000 if married, etc. To illustrate: In 2013, a single taxpayer has net investment income of $100,000, wages of $300,000, and MAGI of $375,000. The taxpayer will pay a Code Sec. 1411 tax of $3,800 (3.8% × $100,000) and an additional Code Sec. 1401 tax of $900 ($100,000 × 0.9%) on his wages in excess of $200,000. (See ¶ 616 for a discussion of the application of Code Sec. 1401's 0.9% tax on wages.)

Tax Pointer 2: Code Sec. 1411(b)'s and 1401's threshold amounts are not indexed for inflation. Accordingly, in years to come more taxpayers will become subject to Code Sec. 1411 and 1401.

.03 Taxable Year of Less Than Twelve Months

Prop. Reg. § 1.1411-2(d)(1) states that in the case of an individual who has a taxable year consisting of less than twelve months (e.g., in the case of death) the threshold amount is not reduced or prorated. For example, in the case of an unmarried decedent who dies on June 1, the threshold amount is $200,000 for the decedent's short taxable year that begins on January 1 and ends on June 1.

¶ 1603 Application to Estates and Trusts

Code Sec. 1411(a)(2) prescribes that certain estates and trusts will for each taxable year pay a tax equal to 3.8% of the lesser of (A) The estate's or trust's undistributed net investment income for such taxable year; or (B) The excess (if any) of: (1) the estate's or trust's adjusted gross income (as defined in Code Sec. 67(e) and adjusted by Reg. § 1.1411-10(e)(2) [controlled foreign corporations and passive foreign investment companies, if applicable] for such taxable year; over (2) the dollar amount at which the highest tax bracket in Code Sec. 1(e) begins for such taxable year indexed for inflation (the projected estate and non-grantor trust highest bracket for 2013 is $11,950).

.01 Taxable Year of Less Than Twelve Months

Prop. Reg. § 1.1411-3(a)(2) prescribes that if an estate has a short year, a taxable year consisting of less than twelve months, the projected estate and non-grantor trust highest bracket for 2013 dollar amount of $11,950 is not reduced or prorated.

.02 Exception for Certain Trusts

Prop. Reg. § 1.1411-3(b) states that Code Sec. 1411 will not apply to certain trusts, such as a charitable remainder trust subject to certain exceptions, a foreign trust (with some exceptions), a trust exempt from tax under Code Sec. 501, et seq.

In the case of the grantor trust, Code Sec. 671 et seq income and deductions attributable to the grantor trust are treated as the owner's taxable income and subject to taxation under Code Sec. 1411. An example will illustrate.

Example 16-1: Ruth Carol established a grantor trust in 2013 called the Ruth Carol Grantor Trust ("RCGT"). In 2013, the RCGT had $50,000 of trust net investment income. Ruth who is single earned $170,000 of salary. Ruth would owe $760 of Code Sec. 1411 tax ($50,000 + $170,000 = $220,000; $220,000 - $200,000 threshold amount = $20,000. $20,000 x 3.8% tax = $760. The reason Ruth pays tax on $20,000 instead of $50,000 is that her MAGI threshold computation is lesser than her net investment income.

.03 Application to Electing Small Business Trusts, Charitable Remainder Trusts, and Bankruptcy and Foreign Estates

Prop. Reg. § 1.1411-3(c) sets forth rules for application of Code Sec. 1411's rules to certain trusts and estates, namely Subchapter S corporations electing small business trusts ("ESBTs"), charitable remainder trusts, and bankruptcy and foreign estates.

ESBTs. As discussed at ¶ 306, an ESBT can have two types of income - S corporate income and non-S corporate income with these two types of income divided into separate trusts for tax reporting. For purposes of Code Sec. 1411, Prop. Reg. § 1.1411-3(c)(1) combines the income from the two trusts to determine Code Sec. 1411's threshold amount as follows: First, the ESBT will separately calculate the undistributed net investment income of the S portion and non-S portion in accordance with the general rules for trusts under Chapter 1 of the Internal Revenue Code of 1986, as amended, and combine the undistributed net investment income of the S portion and the non-S portion. Second, the ESBT will determine its adjusted gross income, solely for purposes of Code Sec. 1411, by adding the net income or net loss from the S portion to that of the non-S portion as a single item of income or loss. Finally, to determine whether the ESBT is subject to Code Sec. 1411, and if so, the Code Sec. 1411 tax base, the ESBT will compare the combined undistributed net investment income with the excess of its adjusted gross income over the Code Sec. 1411 threshold amount. Example 16-4 below illustrates the application of Prop. Reg. § 1.1411-3(c)(1)'s rules for computing Code Sec. 1411's tax. The ESBT will pay tax on the lesser of (1) The ESBT's total undistributed net investment income; or (2) The excess of the ESBT's adjusted gross income over the dollar amount at which the highest tax bracket in Code Sec. 1(e) begins for the taxable year (estimated to be $11,950).

Charitable remainder trusts. While charitable remainder trusts are not subject to Code Sec. 1411, annuity and unitrust distributions from the trusts can be net investment income to the non-charitable recipient beneficiary. Prop. Reg. § 1.1411-3(c)(2)(i) provides that distributions from a charitable remainder trust to a beneficiary for a taxable year consist of net investment income in an amount equal to the lesser of the total amount of the distributions for that year, or the current and accumulated net investment income of the charitable remainder trust. Accumulated net investment income of a charitable remainder trust is defined to mean the total amount of net investment income received by the charitable remainder trust for all tax years that begin after 12/31/12, decreased by the sum of all distributed net investment income attributable to all prior tax years of the trust that began after 12/31/12. In the case of multiple beneficiaries Prop. Reg. § 1.1411-3 states that net investment income will be attributed to beneficiaries based on their respective shares of the total annuity or unitrust distribution. So, if one beneficiary receives 60% of the total unitrust distributions and the other, 40%. The beneficiary receiving

60% of the total unitrust distributions would increase his or her investment income by 60% of the total distributions; the 40% beneficiary would do likewise, except for 40% of the total distributions.

.04 Calculation of Undistributed Net Investment Income for Estates and Trusts

Prop. Reg. § 1.1411-3(e) details that generally, an estate's or trust's net investment income is calculated in the same manner as that of an individual. However, since an estate or trust could have undistributed net investment income, the net investment income computation to determine taxability is reduced by distributions of net investment income to beneficiaries and trust deductions. The deduction allowed is limited to the lesser of the amount deductible to the estate or trust under Code Sec. 651 or Code Sec. 661, as applicable, or the net investment income of the estate or trust. In the case of a deduction under Code Sec. 651 or Code Sec. 661 that consists of both net investment income and excluded income, the distribution must be allocated between net investment income and excluded income in a manner similar to Reg. § 1.661(b)-1 as if net investment income constituted gross income and excluded income constituted amounts not includible in gross income. For trusts where amounts are paid or permanently set aside for charitable purposes, Prop. Reg. § 1.1411-3(e)(4) prescribes special rules. Lastly, Prop. Reg. § 1.1411-3(e)(5) prescribes that items of excluded income like tax exempt interest is excluded in the Code Sec. 1411's computation.

Prop. Reg. § 1.1411-3(f) sets forth examples to explain the provisions set forth above. In each example, unless otherwise indicated, the taxpayer uses a calendar taxable year, the taxpayer is not a foreign trust, and Year 1 is a taxable year in which Code Sec. 1411 is in effect:

Example 16-2: Calculation of undistributed net investment income (with no deduction under Code Sec. 642(c) [deductions for amounts paid or permanently set aside for a charitable purpose]).

(i) In Year 1, Trust, reporting its income using a calendar year, has dividend income of $15,000, interest income of $10,000, capital gain of $5,000, and $60,000 of taxable income relating to a distribution from an individual retirement account (as defined under Code Sec. 408). Trust has no expenses. Trust distributes $10,000 of its current year trust accounting income to A, a beneficiary of Trust. For trust accounting purposes, $25,000 of the distribution from the individual retirement account is attributable to income. Trust allocates the remaining $35,000 of taxable income from the individual retirement account and the $5,000 of capital gain to principal, and therefore these amounts do not enter into the calculation of Trust's distributable net income for Year 1.

(ii) Trust's distributable net income is $50,000 ($15,000 in dividends plus $10,000 in interest plus $25,000 of taxable income from an individual retirement account), from which the $10,000 distribution to A is paid. Trust's deduction under Code Sec. 661 is $10,000.

Under Reg. § 1.662(b)-1, the deduction reduces each class of income comprising distributable net income on a proportional basis. The $10,000 distribution equals 20 percent of distributable net income ($10,000 divided by $50,000). Therefore, the distribution consists of dividend income of $3,000, interest income of $2,000, and ordinary income attributable to the individual retirement account of $5,000. Because the $5,000 of capital gain allocated to principal for trust accounting purposes did not enter into distributable net income, no portion of that amount is included in the $10,000 distribution, nor does it qualify for the deduction under Code Sec. 661.

(iii)   Trust's net investment income is $30,000 ($15,000 in dividends plus $10,000 in interest plus $5,000 in capital gain). Trust's $60,000 of taxable income attributable to the individual retirement account is excluded income (within the meaning of Prop. Reg. § 1.1411-3(e)(5)) because it is excluded from net investment income under Prop. Reg.§ 1.1411-8. Trust's undistributed net investment income under Proposed Reg.§ 1.1411-3(e)(2) is $25,000, which is Trust's net investment income ($30,000) less the amount of dividend income ($3,000) and interest income ($2,000) distributed to A. The $25,000 of undistributed net investment income is comprised of the capital gain allocated to principal ($5,000), the remaining undistributed dividend income ($12,000), and the remaining undistributed interest income ($8,000).

(iv)   A's net investment income includes dividend income of $3,000 and interest income of $2,000, but does not include the $5,000 of ordinary income attributable to the individual retirement account because it is excluded from net investment income under Prop. Reg. § 1.1411-8.

Example 16-3: **Calculation of undistributed net investment income (with deduction under Code Sec. 642(c)).**

(i)   Same facts as Example 16-2, except Trust is required to distribute $30,000 to A. In addition, Trust has a $10,000 deduction under Code Sec. 642(c) (deduction for amounts paid for a charitable purpose). Trust also makes an additional discretionary distribution of $10,000 to B, a beneficiary of Trust. As in Example 16-2, Trust's net investment income is $30,000 ($15,000 in dividends plus $10,000 in interest plus $5,000 in capital gain). In accordance with Reg. § § 1.661(b)-2 and 1.662(b)-2, the items of income must be allocated between the mandatory distribution to A, the discretionary distribution to B, and the $10,000 distribution to a charity.

(ii)   For purposes of the mandatory distribution to A, Trust's distributable net income is $50,000. See Reg. § 1.662(b)-2, Example 1(b). Trust's deduction under Code Sec. 661 for the distribution to A is $30,000. Under Reg. § 1.662(b)-1, the deduction reduces each class of income comprising distributable net income on a proportional basis. The $30,000 distribution equals 60 percent of distributable net income ($30,000 divided by $50,000). Therefore, the distribution consists of dividend income of $9,000, interest income of $6,000, and ordinary income attributable to the individual retirement account of $15,000. A's mandatory distribution thus consists of $15,000 of net investment income and $15,000 of excluded income.

(iii) Trust's remaining distributable net income is $20,000. Trust's remaining undistributed net investment income is $15,000. The $10,000 deduction under Code Sec. 642(c) is allocated in the same manner as the distribution to A, where the $10,000 distribution equals 20 percent of distributable net income ($10,000 divided by $50,000). For purposes of determining undistributed net investment income, Trust's net investment income is reduced by $5,000 under Prop. Reg. § 1.1411-3(e)(4) (dividend income of $3,000, interest income of $2,000, but with no reduction for amounts attributable to the individual retirement account of $5,000).

(iv) With respect to the discretionary distribution to B, Trust's remaining distributable net income is $10,000. Trust's remaining undistributed net investment income is $10,000. Trust's deduction under Code Sec. 661 for the distribution to B is $10,000. The $10,000 distribution equals 20 percent of distributable net income ($10,000 divided by $50,000). Therefore, the distribution consists of dividend income of $3,000, interest income of $2,000, and ordinary income attributable to the individual retirement account of $5,000. B's distribution consists of $5,000 of net investment income and $5,000 of excluded income.

(v) Trust's undistributed net investment income is $5,000 after taking into account distribution deductions and Code Sec. 642(c) in accordance with Prop. Reg. § 1.1411-3(e)(3) and (e)(4), respectively. To arrive at Trust's undistributed net investment income of $5,000, Trust's net investment income of $30,000 is reduced by $15,000 of the mandatory distribution to A, $5,000 of the Code Sec. 642(c) deduction, and $5,000 of the discretionary distribution to B.

Example 16-4: **Calculation of an ESBT's tax for purposes of Code Sec. 1411.**

(i) In Year 1, the non-ESBT portion of Trust has dividend income of $15,000, interest income of $10,000, and capital gain of $5,000. Trust's ESBT portion has net rental income of $21,000 and a capital loss of $7,000. The Trustee's annual fee of $1,000 is allocated 60 percent to the non-ESBT portion and 40 percent to the ESBT portion. Trust makes a distribution from income to a single beneficiary of $9,000.

(ii) Step one.

    (A) The undistributed net investment income ("UNII") for the ESBT portion is $20,600 determined as follows: Net Rental Income $21,000 less Trustee Annual Fee $400 [40% × $1,000] = $20,600.[2]

    (B) The undistributed net investment income for the non-ESBT portion is $20,400 determined as follows: $15,000 (dividend income) + $10,000 (interest income) + $5,000 (capital gain) = $30,000 less [$600 (portion of trustee annual fee) + $9,000 (distributable net income distribution "DNI")] = $20,400.

    (C) The Trust's combined undistributed net investment income of the ESBT portion and the non-ESBT portion is $41,000 ($20,400 + $20,600).

(iii) Step two.

    (A) The ESBT will calculate its adjusted gross income. The ESBT's adjusted gross income is the non-ESBT portion's adjusted gross income increased or decreased by the net income or net loss of the ESBT portion.

    (B) The adjusted gross income for the ESBT is $38,000 and is determined as follows:

First: Calculate the S Portion of income: $21,000 of rental income less ($3,000 of the $7,000 of capital loss allowed under Code Sec. 1211(b)(1) + $400 trustee commission) = $17,600.

Second: add the non-ESBT portion of income, $20,400 $15,000 (dividend income) + $10,000 (Interest Income) + $5,000 (Capital Gain) = $30,000 less [$600 (portion of trustee annual fee) + $9,000 (Distributable net income distribution "DNI")]. Total: $38,000 ($17,600 + $20,400).

(iv) Step three. Trust will pay tax on the lesser of—

    (A) The combined undistributed net investment income ($41,000); or

    (B) The excess of adjusted gross income ($38,000 over the dollar amount at which the highest tax bracket in Code Sec. 1(e) applicable to a trust begins for the taxable year ($11,950 [the projected amount]), or $26,050. Since $26,050 is the lesser amount, the tax the ESBT will pay is $989.90 (3.8% × 26,050 = 989.90).

---

[2] No portion of the capital loss is allowed because, pursuant to Reg. §1.1411-4(d)(2), net gain cannot be less than zero and excess capital losses are not properly allocable deductions under Prop. Reg. §1.1411-4(f). See Example 16-10 set forth below. In addition, pursuant to Reg. §1.641(c)-1(l), no portion of the $9,000 distribution is allocable to the S portion.

¶ 1604 Definition of Net Investment Income

Code Sec. 1411 prescribes that net investment income ("NII") is the excess (if any) of (A) the sum of (i) gross income from interest, dividends, royalties, rents, annuities, substitute interest payments, and substitute dividend payments except if such income is derived in the ordinary course of a trade or business to which Code Sec. 1411 would not apply; (ii) other gross income from trades or businesses to which Code Sec. 1411 would apply and (iii) net gain to the extent taken into account to calculate taxable income attributable to the disposition of property other than property held in a trade or business to which the tax does not apply over (B) deductions which are properly allocable to such gross income or net gain.

When items of net investment income (including the properly allocable deductions) pass through to an individual, estate, or trust from a partnership or S corporation, the allocation of such items must be separately stated under Code Sec. 702 or Code Sec. 1366 and the regulations thereunder.

.01 Gross Income Items Described in Code Sec. 1411(c)(1)(A)(i)

The Preamble to Prop. Reg. § 1.1411-1 et seq ("Preamble") provides definitions for these terms. Set forth below is guidance from the Preamble with respect to certain items of gross income.

Annuities. Gross income from annuities includes the amount received as an annuity under an annuity, endowment, or life insurance contract that is includible in gross income as a result of the application of Code Sec. 72(a) and Code Sec. 72(b), and an amount not received as an annuity under an annuity contract that is includible in gross income under Code Sec. 72(e).

Gain or loss from the sale of an annuity would be treated as net investment income for purposes of Code Sec. 1411. To the extent the sales price of the annuity does not exceed its surrender value, the gain recognized would be treated as gross income described in Code Sec. 1411(c)(1)(A)(I). If the sales price of the annuity exceeds its surrender value, the seller would treat the gain equal to the difference between the basis in the annuity and the surrender value as gross income described in Code Sec. 1411(c)(1)(A)(I), and would treat the excess of the sales price over the surrender value as gain from the disposition of property under Code Sec. 1411(c)(1)(A)(iii).

Royalties. Gross income from royalties includes amounts received from mineral, oil, and gas royalties, and amounts received for the privilege of using patents, copyrights, secret processes and formulas, goodwill, trademarks, tradebrands, franchises, and other like property.

Rents. Gross income from rents includes amounts paid or to be paid principally for the use of (or the right to use) tangible property. However, if the gross income is derived in the ordinary course of a trade or business (except (A) a passive activity (within the meaning of Code Sec. 469) with respect to the taxpayer, or (B) trading in financial instruments (as defined in proposed Reg. § 1.1411-5(c)(1)) or commodities (as defined in Code Sec. 475(e)(2)), it is not classified as net investment income. There is a special rule regarding Code Sec. 1411's taxation of working capital at ¶ 1606.

.02 Ordinary Course of a Trade or Business—Code Sec. 1411(c)(1)(A)(ii)

Prop. Reg. § 1.1411-4(b) states that to determine whether gross income is derived in the ordinary course of a trade or business, the following rules apply:

(1) In the case of an individual, estate, or trust that owns or engages in a trade or business directly (or indirectly through ownership of an interest in an entity that is disregarded as an entity separate from its owner under Reg. § 301.7701-3), the determination of whether gross income is derived in a trade or business is made at the individual level.

(2) In the case of an individual, estate, or trust that owns an interest in a trade or business through one or more passthrough entities for Federal tax purposes (for example, through a partnership or S corporation), the determination of whether gross income is derived from

    (i) a passive activity is made at the owner level; and

    (ii) the trade or business of a trader trading in financial instruments or commodities is made at the entity level.

Prop. Reg. § 1.1411-4(b) sets forth the following examples to explain the provisions for the ordinary course of a trade or business rules to apply:

Example 16-5: *Multiple passthrough entities.* A, an individual, owns an interest in UTP, a partnership, which is engaged in a trade or business. UTP owns an interest in LTP, also a partnership, which is not engaged in a trade or business. LTP receives $10,000 in dividends, $5,000 of which is allocated to A through UTP. The $5,000 of dividends is not derived in a trade or business because LTP is not engaged in a trade or business. This is true even though UTP is engaged in a trade or business. Accordingly, the ordinary course of a trade or business exception does not apply, and A's $5,000 of dividends is net investment income.

Example 16-6: *Entity engaged in trading in financial instruments.* B, an individual, owns an interest in PRS, a partnership, which is engaged in a trade or business of trading in financial instruments. PRS' trade or business is not a passive activity (within the meaning of Code Sec. 469) with respect to B. In addition, B is not directly engaged in a trade or business of trading in financial instruments or commodities. PRS earns interest of $50,000, and B's distributive share of the interest is $25,000. Because PRS is engaged in trading in financial instruments or commodities, the ordinary course of a trade or business exception does not apply, and B's $25,000 distributive share of the interest is net investment income.

Example 16-7: *Application of ordinary course of a trade or business exception.* C, an individual, owns stock in S corporation, S. S is engaged in a banking trade or business (that is not a trade or business of trading in financial instruments or commodities), and S's trade or business is not a passive activity (within the meaning of Code Sec. 469) with respect to C. S earns $100,000 of interest in the ordinary course of its trade or business, of which $5,000 is C's pro rata share. Because S is not engaged in a trade or business of trading in financial instruments or commodities and because S's trade or business is not a passive activity with respect to C, the ordinary course of a trade or business exception applies, and C's $5,000 of interest is not included as net investment income. (However, If C is passive with respect to S's banking business as defined per Code Sec. 469, then even though the interest was not "tainted" trader income, C's pro rata share of S's interest is net investment income.)

Income from employment, trades or businesses conducted by a sole proprietor, partnership or S corporation. For purposes of Code Sec. 1411, an employee is treated as engaged in the trade or business of being an employee. Accordingly, amounts paid by an employer to an employee that are treated as wages for purposes of Code Sec. 3401 are not net investment income because such amounts are derived in the ordinary course of a trade or business to which Code Sec. 1411 does not apply. For example, amounts paid to an employee under a nonqualified deferred compensation plan for such employee (or that otherwise become includible in income under Code Secs. 409A, 457(f), 457A, or other Code Code Secs. or tax doctrine) that include gross income from interest or other earnings are not treated as net investment income, regardless of whether such amounts are not subject to Federal Insurance Contributions Act tax due to the earlier application of Code Sec. 3121(v)(2).

The Joint Committee on Taxation Report states that Code Sec. 1411 generally does not apply to trades or businesses conducted by a sole proprietor, partnership or S corporation, providing the business or trade is not a passive activity or involved in the trading of financial instruments or commodities.

Coordination with portfolio income rules in Code Sec. 469. Because Code Sec. 469 treats portfolio income (which includes, for example, gross income from interest and dividends) as not derived in the ordinary course of a trade or business, portfolio income is classified as net investment income per Prop. Reg. § 1.1411-4(a)(1)(i).

Veteran's benefits, tax-exempt income, Code Sec. 121's excluded gain from the sale of a primary residence are not subject to taxation under Code Sec. 1411 per the Joint Committee on Taxation Report.

Code Sec. 1411(c)(1)(A)(ii)'s other trade or business gross income. Prop. Reg. § 1.1411-4(c) states that any gain from marking to market under Code Sec. 475(f) or Code Sec. 1256 and any realized gain from the disposition of property held in the trade or business is classified as arising from a passive activity or trading in financial instruments or commodities.

.03 Net Gain Described in Code Sec. 1411(c)(1)(A)(iii)

Code Sec. 1411(c)(1)(A)(iii) states that net investment income includes net gain (to the extent taken into account in computing taxable income) attributable to the disposition of property other than property arising from a passive activity or trading in financial instruments or commodities.

¶1604.03

Disposition. Generally, Prop. Reg. § 1.1411-4(d) provides that net investment income includes net gain (to the extent taken into account in computing taxable income) attributable to the sale, exchange, transfer, conversion, cash settlement, cancellation, termination, lapse, expiration, or other disposition (collectively, referred to as the disposition) of property other than property held in a trade or business.

Distributions from an S corporation or partnership: If a partner receives a distribution of money from a partnership in excess of the adjusted basis of the partner's interest in the partnership and recognizes gain under Code Sec. 731(a), or if an S corporation shareholder receives a distribution of money from the S corporation in excess of the adjusted basis of the shareholder's stock in the corporation and recognizes gain under Code Sec. 1368(b)(2), the gain is treated as gain from the sale or exchange of such partnership interest or S corporation stock for purposes of Code Sec. 1411(c)(1)(A)(iii) and taxable under Code Sec. 1411.

Sale of S corporate stock utilizing Code Sec. 338(h)(10): If stock of an S corporation is sold and a Code Sec. 338(h)(10) election is made, each shareholder's pro rata share of the deemed asset sale gain or loss may be taken into account in determining net investment income under Code Sec. 1411(c)(1)(A)(iii). Furthermore, each shareholder may have additional gain or loss upon the deemed liquidation of the S corporation resulting from the Code Sec. 338(h)(10) election, which gain or loss will also generally be taken into account under Code Sec. 1411(c)(1)(A)(iii) in determining net investment income.

Capital gain dividends from regulated investment companies and real estate investment trusts: Capital gain dividends from regulated investment companies and real estate investment trusts described in Code Secs. 852(b)(3)(c) and 857(b)(3)(c), respectively, and undistributed capital gains described in Code Secs. 852(b)(3)(D) and 857(b)(3)(D), are included in net investment income as net gain under Code Sec. 1411(c)(1)(A)(iii), and not as dividend income under Code Sec. 1411(c)(1)(A)(i).

Calculation of Code Sec. 1411 net gain can never be less than zero: Prop. Reg. § 1.1411-4(d)(1) states that the calculation of net gain shall not be less than zero. Losses allowable under Code Sec. 1211(b) are permitted to offset gain from the disposition of assets other than capital assets that are subject to Code Sec. 1411. Further, net gain shall include gain or loss attributable to the disposition of property from the investment of working capital.

> **Tax Pointer:** Because the proposed regulations include for taxation under Code Sec. 1411 income from working capital, a special breakout of this income will be required. See ¶ 1606 for a discussion of this point.

Mark-to-market rules for non-traders. The proposed regulations treat amounts of gain or loss recognized as a result of marking to market as net investment income.

¶1604.03

.04 Determination of Net Gain From Disposition

Generally, the rules under Chapter 1 of the Internal Revenue Code of 1986, as amended apply for purposes of determining net gain under Code Sec. 1411. Thus, for example, to the extent gain from a like-kind exchange is not recognized for income tax purposes under Code Sec. 1031, it is not recognized for purposes of determining net investment income under Code Sec. 1411. Losses properly taken into account in determining net gain include all losses deductible under Code Sec. 165, including losses attributable to casualty, theft, and abandonment or other worthlessness to the extent they are attributable to property.

The amount of net gain on the disposition of an interest in a partnership or an S corporation taken into account for purposes of Code Sec. 1411(c)(1)(A)(iii) may be adjusted in accordance with a special rule discussed at ¶ 1607.

With respect to the term net gain (which contemplates a positive number), the proposed regulations provide that the amount of net gain included in net investment income may not be less than zero. Thus, generally, capital losses in excess of capital gains are not recognized for purposes of Code Sec. 1411.

Property held in a trade or business. Prop. Reg. § 1.1411-4(d)(3)(ii) sets forth special rules for determining whether property is held in a trade or business:

(1) A partnership interest or S corporation stock generally is not property held in a trade or business. Therefore, gain from the sale of a partnership interest or S corporation stock is generally gain subject to taxation under Code Sec. 1411 subject to some special rules discussed at ¶ 1607.

(2) In the case of an individual, estate, or trust that owns or engages in a trade or business directly (or indirectly through ownership of an interest in an entity that is disregarded as an entity separate from its owner under Reg. § 301.7701-3), the determination of whether net gain subject to taxation under Code Sec. 1411 is attributable to property held in a trade or business is made at the individual level.

(3) In the case of an individual, estate, or trust that owns an interest in a trade or business through one or more passthrough entities for Federal tax purposes (for example, through a partnership or S corporation), the determination of whether net gain from (I) a passive activity is made at the owner level; and (II) from a business engaged in trading in financial instruments or commodities is made at the entity level.

Prop. Reg. § 1.1411-4(d)(3)(c) sets forth an example to illustrate the application of the above rules:

Example 16-8: *Gain from rental activity.* A, an unmarried individual, rents a boat to B for $100,000 in Year 1. A's rental activity does not involve the conduct of a Code Sec. 162 trade or business, but under Code Sec. 469(c)(2), A's rental activity is a passive activity. In Year 2, A sells the boat to B, and A realizes and recognizes taxable gain attributable to the disposition of the boat of $500,000. Because A is not in a trade or business, A's $500,000 gain will be subject to taxation under Code Sec. 1411.

Code Sec. 1411(c)(1)(A)(iii) generally applies if the property disposed of is either not held in a trade or business, or arises from a passive activity or trading in financial instruments or commodities.

The determination of whether property is "held" in a trade or business is determined in the same manner as whether gross income is "derived in" a trade or business for purposes of Code Sec. 1411(c)(1)(A)(i). Thus, for individuals directly engaged in a trade or business, the determination is made at the individual level. If an individual, estate, or trust holds an interest in a passthrough entity and such entity disposes of its property, the determination of whether property is held in a trade or business that is a passive activity is made at the taxpayer level (that is, the individual, estate, or trust level), and the determination of whether property is held in a trade or business of trading in financial instruments or commodities is made at the entity level. For example, SAM, an S corporation, is engaged in a trade or business, and Alex, an individual, owns stock in SAM. If SAM sells its Property 1 for a gain, the determination of whether Alex's gain from the disposition of SAM's Property 1 is subject to Code Sec. 1411(c)(1)(A)(iii) depends on (1) whether SAM held Property 1 in its trade or business, and (2) if SAM held Property 1 in its trade or business, whether SAM's trade or business arises from a passive activity or trading in financial instruments or commodities. If SAM held Property 1 in its trade or business and SAM's trade or business is neither a passive activity with respect to A nor trading in financial instruments or commodities with respect to SAM, net gain from the disposition of Property 1 will not be subject to Code Sec. 1411's tax under Code Sec. 1411(c)(1)(A)(iii).

.05 Distributions From Trusts

As discussed at ¶ 1603, the character of income distributions from trusts will determine if it is net investment income subject to tax by the beneficiary under Code Sec. 1411.

.06 Properly Allocable Deductions

Prop. Reg. § 1.1411-4(f) prescribes extensive rules for deductions allowed against net investment income. Set forth below are pertinent descriptions of the deductions allowed.

Limitations and carryovers. Deductions allowed shall not exceed the total amount of gross income and net gain of investment income. Any deductions in excess of such gross income and net gain shall not be taken into account in determining net investment income in any other taxable year, except as allowed under Chapter 1 of the Internal Revenue Code of 1986, as amended. Examples of carryforwards of expenses would be carryforward of investment interest under Code Sec. 163(d), a suspended passive activity loss that is allowed in a later year under Code Sec. 469(b), or a capital loss carryforward under Code Sec. 1212 However, in no event will a net operating loss deduction allowed under Code Sec. 172 be taken into account in determining net investment income for any taxable year.

Properly allocable deductions described in Code Sec. 62.

Rents and Royalties: Deductions described in Code Sec. 62(a)(4) allocable to rents and royalties shall be taken into account in determining net investment income.

Deductions allocable to gross income from trades or businesses for passive activities and business of trading in financial instruments or commodities: Deductions described in Code Sec. 62(a)(1) shall be taken into account in determining net investment income to the extent the deductions have not been taken into account in determining self-employment income. An example will illustrate:

> **Example 16-9:** A, an individual, is engaged in the trade or business of trading in commodities, and made an election under Code Sec. 475(f)(2). A earns $500,000 of gross income and A also incurs $100,000 of expenses relating to the trading business. Under Code Sec. 1402, none of the $500,000 of gross income would be taken into account in determining A's self-employment income (as provided in Code Secs. 475(f)(1)(D) and 1402(a)(3)(A)), but all of the $100,000 of expenses would be taken into account, even though there are no net earnings from self-employment and thus no self-employment income to reduce.

Penalty on early withdrawal of savings: Net investment income shall take into account deductions described in Code Sec. 62(a)(9).

Properly allocable itemized deductions described in Code Sec. 63(d): The following are set forth as items to be included:

(A) Investment interest expense as defined in Code Sec. 163(d)(3)) to the extent allowed under Code Sec. 163(d)(1). Any investment interest not allowed under Code Sec. 163(d)(1) shall be treated as investment interest paid or accrued by the taxpayer in the succeeding taxable year.

(B) Investment expenses as defined in Code Sec. 163(d)(4)(C).

(C) Taxes deductible under Code Sec. 164(a)(3) and imposed on gross income.

(D) Any deductions that are subject to Code Sec. 67 (the 2-percent floor on miscellaneous itemized deductions) or Code Sec. 68 (the overall limitation on itemized deductions) are allowed in determining net investment income only to the extent the items are deductible for Chapter 1 of the Internal Revenue Code of 1986, as amended, after the application of Code Secs. 67 and 68. For this purpose, Code Sec. 67 is applied before Code Sec. 68 (note there are extensive rules for application of deductions under Code Secs. 67 and 68).

Loss deductions: Losses deductible under Code Sec. 165 are deductible only in determining net gain to the extent of gains.

Prop. Reg. § 1.1411-4(h) sets forth the following examples to determine net investment income:

¶1604.06

Example 16-10: Calculation of net gain.

(i) In Year 1, A, an unmarried individual, realizes a capital loss of $40,000 on the sale of P stock and realizes a capital gain of $10,000 on the sale of Q stock, resulting in a net capital loss of $30,000. Both P and Q are C corporations. A has no other capital gain or capital loss in Year 1. In addition, A receives wages of $300,000 and earns $5,000 of gross income from interest. For income tax purposes, under Code Sec. 1211(b), A may use $3,000 of the net capital loss against other income. Under Code Sec. 1212(b)(1), the remaining $27,000 is a capital loss carryover. A's Year 1 net gain for taxation under Code Sec. 1411 is A's gain of $10,000 on the sale of the Q stock reduced by A's loss of $40,000 on the sale of the P stock. However, because net gain may not be less than zero, A may not reduce net investment income by the $3,000 of the excess of capital losses over capital gains allowed for income tax purposes under Code Sec. 1211(b).

(ii) In Year 2, A has a capital gain of $30,000 on the sale of Y stock. Y is a C corporation. A has no other capital gain or capital loss in Year 2. For income tax purposes, A may reduce the $30,000 gain by the Year 1 Code Sec. 1212(b) $27,000 capital loss carryover. For purposes of determining A's Year 2 net gain for Code Sec. 1411 purposes, A's $30,000 gain may also be reduced by the $27,000 capital loss carryover from Year 1. Therefore, in Year 2, A has $3,000 of net gain for purposes of taxation under Code Sec. 1411.

Example 16-11: Calculation of net gain. The facts are the same as in Example 16-10, except that in Year 1, A also realizes a gain of $20,000 on the sale of Rental Property D, all of which is treated as ordinary income under Code Sec. 1250. For income tax purposes, under Code Sec. 1211(b), A may use $3,000 of the net capital loss against other income. Under Code Sec. 1212(b)(1) the remaining $27,000 is a capital loss carryover. For purposes of determining A's net gain for taxation under Code Sec. 1411, A's gain of $10,000 on the sale of the Q stock is reduced by A's loss of $40,000 on the sale of the P stock. A's $20,000 gain on the sale of Rental Property D is reduced to the extent of the $3,000 loss allowed under Code Sec. 1211(b). Therefore, A's net gain for Year 1 is $17,000 ($20,000 gain treated as ordinary income on the sale of Rental Property D reduced by $3,000 loss allowed under Code Sec. 1211).

Example 16-12: Code Sec. 172 net operating loss deduction.

(i) In Year 1, A, an unmarried individual, has the following items of income and deduction: $60,000 in wages, $20,000 in gross income from a trade or business of trading in financial instruments or commodities, $70,000 in loss from his sole proprietorship (which is not a passive activity or a business engaged in trading in financial instruments or commodities), and $30,000 in trading activity expense deductions. As a result, for income tax purposes A sustains a Code Sec. 172(c) net operating loss of $20,000. A makes an election

¶1604.06

under Code Sec. 172(b)(3) to waive the carryback period for this net operating loss.

(ii) For purposes of Code Sec. 1411, A's net investment income for Year 1 is the excess (if any) of the $20,000 in gross income from the trading activity over the $30,000 deduction for the trading activity expenses. Net investment income cannot be less than zero for a taxable year. Therefore, A's net investment income for Year 1 is $0.

(iii) For Year 2, A has $200,000 of wages, $100,000 of gross income from the trading activity, $80,000 of income from his sole proprietorship, and $10,000 in trading activity expense deductions. For income tax purposes, A's $20,000 net operating loss carryover from Year 1 will be allowed as a deduction. In addition, A's Year 1 $20,000 net operating loss will be allowed as a deduction in computing A's Year 2 modified adjusted gross income.

(iv) For purposes of Code Sec. 1411, A's $20,000 net operating loss carryover from Year 1 is not allowed in computing A's Year 2 net investment income. As a result, A's Year 2 net investment income is $90,000 ($100,000 gross income from the trading activity minus the $10,000 of trading activity expenses).

Example 16-13: *Code Sec. 121(a) exclusion.*

(i) In Year 1, A, an unmarried individual, sells a house that he has owned and used as his principal residence for five years and realizes $200,000 in gain. In addition to the gain realized from the sale of his principal residence, A also realizes $7,000 in long-term capital gain. A has a $5,000 short-term capital loss carryover from a year preceding the effective date of Code Sec. 1411.

(ii) For income tax purposes, under Code Sec. 121(a), A excludes the $200,000 gain realized from the sale of his principal residence from his Year 1 gross income. In determining A's Year 1 adjusted gross income, A also reduces the $7,000 capital gain by the $5,000 capital loss carryover allowed under Code Sec. 1211(b).

(iii) For Code Sec. 1411 purposes, under Code Sec. 121(a), A excludes the $200,000 gain realized from the sale of his principal residence from his Year 1 gross income and, consequently, net investment income. In determining A's Year 1 net investment income under Code Sec. 1411, A reduces the $7,000 capital gain by the $5,000 capital loss carryover allowed under Code Sec. 1211(b).

Example 16-14: *Code Sec. 163(d) limitation.*

(i) In Year 1, A, an unmarried individual, pays interest of $4,000 on debt incurred to purchase stock.

Under Reg. §1.163-8T, this interest is allocable to the stock and is investment interest within the meaning of Code Sec. 163(d)(3). A has no investment income as defined by Code Sec. 163(d)(4). A has $10,000 of income from a trade or business that is a passive activity with respect to A. For income tax purposes, under Code Sec. 163(d)(1) A may not deduct the $4,000 investment interest in Year 1. Under Code Sec. 163(d)(2), the $4,000 investment interest is a carryforward of disallowed interest that is treated as investment interest paid by A in the succeeding taxable year. Similarly, for purposes of determining A's Year 1 net investment income, A may not deduct the $4,000 investment interest.

(ii) In Year 2, A has $5,000 of Code Sec. 163(d)(4) net investment income. For both income tax purposes and for determining Code Sec. 1411 net investment income, A's $4,000 carryforward of interest expense disallowed in Year 1 may be deducted in Year 2.

Example 16-15: *Code Secs. 67 and 68 limitations on itemized deductions.*

(i) A, an unmarried individual, has adjusted gross income in Year 1 as follows: Wages, $1,600,000; Interest income, 400,000; and adjusted gross income, $2,000,000. In addition, A has the following items of expense qualifying as itemized deductions: investment expenses, $70,000; job-related expenses, $30,000; investment interest expense, $80,000; and state income taxes, $120,000. A's investment expenses and job-related expenses are miscellaneous itemized deductions. In addition, A's investment interest expense and investment expenses are properly allocable to net investment income. A's job-related expenses are not properly allocable to net investment income. Of the state income tax expense, $20,000 is properly allocable to net investment income and $100,000 is not properly allocable to net investment income.

(ii) A's 2-percent floor under Code Sec. 67 is $40,000 (2 percent of $2,000,000). Assume that the Code Sec. 68 limitation for this taxable year starts at adjusted gross income of $200,000. The Code Sec. 68 overall limitation disallows $54,000 of A's itemized deductions that are subject to Code Sec. 68 (3 percent of the excess of $2,000,000 adjusted gross income over the $200,000 limitation threshold).

(iii)

    (A) A's total miscellaneous itemized deductions allowable before the application of Code Sec. 67 is $100,000 ($70,000 in investment expenses plus $30,000 in job-related expenses), and the total miscellaneous deductions allowed after the application of Code Sec. 67 is $60,000 ($100,000 minus $40,000).

    (B) The amount of the deduction allowed for investment expenses after the application of Code Sec. 67 is computed as follows: $70,000 x $60,000/$100,000 = $42,000.

    (C) The amount of the deduction allowed for job-related expenses after the application of Code Sec. 67 is computed as follows: $30,000 x $60,000/$100,000 =$18,000.

¶1604.06

(iv)

(A) Under Code Sec. 68, the $80,000 deduction for the investment interest expense is not subject to the Code Sec. 68 limitation on itemized deductions.

(B) A's itemized deductions subject to the limitation under Code Sec. 68 and allowed after application of Code Sec. 67, but before the application of Code Sec. 68, are the following: investment expenses, $42,000; job-related expenses, $18,000; and state income tax, $120,000 totaling $180,000.

(C) Of A's itemized deductions that are subject to the limitation under Code Sec. 68, the amount allowed after the application of Code Sec. 68 is $126,000 ($180,000 minus the $54,000 disallowed in paragraph (ii) of this Example 16-15).

(D) The amount of the investment expense deduction allowed after the application of Code Sec. 68 is determined as follows: $42,000 x $126,000/$180.000 = $29,400.

(E) The amount of the state income tax deduction allowed after the application of Code Sec. 68 and properly allocable to net investment income is determined as follows: $20,000 × $126,000/$180,000 = $14,000.

(F) The itemized deductions allowed after applying Code Secs. 67 and 68 and properly allocable to A's net investment income are the following: Investment interest expense, $80,000; Investment expenses, $29,400; State income taxes, $14,000 totaling $123,400.

(G) The amount of the state income tax deduction allowed after the application of Code Sec. 68 and not properly allocable to net investment income is determined as follows: $100,000 × $126,000/$180,000 = $70,000.

(H) The job-related expenses deduction and $70,000 of the state income tax deduction are not properly allocable deductions for purposes of Code Sec. 1411.

Example 16-16: Code Sec. 1031 like-kind exchange. (I) In Year 1, A, an unmarried individual who is not a dealer in real estate, purchases Greenacre, a piece of undeveloped land, for $10,000. A intends to hold Greenacre for investment.

(ii) In Year 3, A enters into an exchange in which he transfers Greenacre, now valued at $20,000, and $5,000 cash for Blackacre, another piece of undeveloped land, which has a fair market value of $25,000. The exchange is a transaction for which no gain or loss is recognized under Code Sec. 1031.

(iii) In Year 3, for income tax purposes A does not recognize any gain from the exchange of Greenacre for Blackacre. A's basis in Blackacre is

$15,000 ($10,000 substituted basis in Greenacre plus $5,000 additional cost of acquisition). For purposes of Code Sec. 1411, A's net investment income for Year 3 does not include any realized gain from the exchange of Greenacre for Blackacre.

(iv) In Year 5, A sells Blackacre to an unrelated party for $35,000 in cash.

(v) In Year 5, for income tax purposes B recognizes capital gain of $20,000 ($35,000 sale price minus $15,000 basis). For purposes of Code Sec. 1411, A's net investment income includes the $20,000 gain recognized from the sale of Blackacre.

¶ 1605 Passive Activity Situations and Trade or Business of a Trader Trading in Financial Instruments or Commodities

.01 Passive Activity

Prop. Reg. § 1.1411-5(b)(1) defines a passive activity as a trade or business (within the meaning of Code Sec. 162) and such trade or business is a passive activity within the meaning of Code Sec. 469 and the regulations thereunder.

Prop. Reg. § 1.1411-5(b)(2) sets forth the following examples to illustrate the application of this definition to Code Sec. 1411 to passive activities:

Example 16-17: Rental activity. A, an unmarried individual, rents a commercial building to B for $50,000 in Year 1. A's rental activity does not involve the conduct of a Code Sec. 162 trade or business, but under Code Sec. 469(c)(2), A's rental activity is a passive activity; thus A's rental income of $50,000 is not derived from a trade or business. Therefore, A's rental income of $50,000 constitutes gross income from rents subject to taxation under Code Sec. 1411.

Example 16-18: Application of grouping rules under Code Sec. 469. In Year 1, A, an unmarried individual, owns an interest in PRS, a partnership for Federal income tax purposes. PRS is engaged in two activities, X and Y, which constitute trades or businesses (within the meaning of Code Sec. 162), and neither of which constitute trading in financial instruments or commodities. Pursuant to Reg. § 1.469-4, A has properly grouped X and Y (the grouped activity). A participates in X for more than 500 hours during Year 1 and would be treated as materially participating in the activity within the meaning of Reg. § 1.469-5T(a)(1). A only participates in Y for 50 hours during Year 1, and, but for the grouping of the two activities together, A would not be treated as materially participating in Y within the meaning of Reg. 1.469-5T(a). However, pursuant to Reg. § § 1.469-4 and 1.469-5T(a)(1), A materially participates in the grouped activity, and therefore, for purposes of Code Sec. 1411, neither X nor Y is a passive activity with respect to A; thus, the income or loss generated is not subject to Code Sec. 1411's tax.

Example 16-19: Application of the rental activity exceptions. B, an unmarried individual, is a partner in PRS, which is engaged in an equipment leasing activity. The average period of customer use of the equipment is seven days or less (and therefore meets the exception in Reg. § 1.469-1T(e)(3)(ii)(A)). B materially participates in the equipment leasing activity (within the meaning of Reg.§ 1.469-5T(a)). The equipment meaning of Code Sec. 162. In Year 1, B has modified adjusted gross income (as defined in Reg. § 1.1411-2(c) of $300,000, all of which is derived from PRS. All of the income from PRS is derived in the ordinary course of the equipment leasing activity, and all of PRS's property is held in the equipment leasing activity. Of B's allocable share of income from PRS, $275,000 constitutes gross income from rents (within the meaning of Reg. § 1.1411-4(a)(1)(I)). While $275,000 of the gross income from the equipment leasing activity meets the definition of rents in Reg. § 1.1411-4(a)(1)(I), the activity meets one of the exceptions to rental activity in Reg. § 1.469-1T(e)(3)(ii) and B materially participates in the activity. Therefore, the trade or business is not a passive activity with respect to B for purposes of Code Sec. 1411; thus, the ordinary course of a trade or business exception in Reg. § 1.1411-4(b) applies, which means that the rents are not subject to taxation under Code Sec. 1411. Furthermore, because the equipment leasing trade or business is a trade or business, the $25,000 of other gross income is not subject to Code Sec. 1411's tax.

Example 16-20: Application of Code Sec. 469's passive activity rules. Assume the same facts as Example 16-19, except B does not materially participate in the equipment leasing trade or business and therefore the trade or business is a passive activity with respect to B and is subject to taxation under Code Sec. 1411. Accordingly, the $275,000 of gross income from rents is subject to Code Sec. 1411's tax because the rents are derived from a passive activity. Furthermore, the $25,000 of other gross income from the equipment leasing trade or business is subject to Code Sec. 1411's tax because of the nature of the business being a passive activity. Finally, gain or loss from the sale of the property used in the equipment leasing trade or business is subject to Code Sec. 1411(c)(1)(A)(iii) because the trade or business is a passive activity with respect to B.

Example 16-21: Application of the portfolio income rule and Code Sec. 469. C, an unmarried individual, is a partner in PRS, a partnership engaged in a trade or business (within the meaning of Code Sec. 162) that does not involve a rental activity. C does not materially participate in PRS within the meaning of Reg. § 1.469-5T(a), and therefore the trade or business of PRS is a passive activity with respect to C for purposes of Code Sec. 1411. C's $500,000 allocable share of PRS's income consists of $450,000 of gross income from a trade or business and $50,000 of gross income from dividends and interest that is not derived in the ordinary course of the trade or business of PRS. Thus, under Code Sec. 469(e)(1)(A)(i)(I) and the regulations thereunder, C's allocable share of gross income from dividends and interest consists of portfolio income. Therefore, C's $500,000 allocable share of PRS's income is subject to Code Sec. 1411. C's $50,000 allocable share of PRS's income from dividends and interest is subject to taxation under Code Sec. 1411(c)(1)(A)(i) because the share is gross income from dividends and interest that is not derived in the ordinary course of a trade or business. C's $450,000 allocable share of PRS's income is subject to taxation under Code Sec. 1411(c)(1)(A)(ii) because it is gross income from a trade or business that is a passive activity.

.02 Trading in Financial Instruments or Commodities

Prop. Reg. § 1.1411-5(c)(1) prescribes that financial instruments includes stocks and other equity interests, evidences of indebtedness, options, forward or futures contracts, notional principal contracts, any other derivatives, or any evidence of an interest in any of the items fitting this definition. An evidence of an interest in any of the items described herein includes, but is not limited to, short positions or partial units in any of the items. Prop. Reg. § 1.1411-5(c)(2) defines commodities by reference to Code Sec. 475(e)(2).

¶ 1606 Income on Investment of Working Capital Subject to Tax

Code Sec. 1411(c)(3) states that any item of gross income from the investment of working capital will be treated as not derived in the ordinary course of a trade or business, and any net gain that is attributable to the investment of working capital will be treated as not derived in the ordinary course of a trade or business. In determining whether any item is gross income from or net gain attributable to an investment of working capital, principles similar to those described in Reg. § 1.469-2T(c)(3)(iii) apply. There are special rules involving working capital related to the adjustment to net gain on the disposition of interests in a partnership or S corporation; this is discussed at ¶ 1607. Code Sec. 1411(c)(3) provides that a rule similar to the rule of Code Sec. 469(e)(1)(B) applies for purposes of Code Sec. 1411 (the working capital rule). Code Sec. 469(e)(1)(B) provides that, for purposes of determining whether income is treated as from a passive activity, any income or gain attributable to an investment of working capital shall be treated as not derived in the ordinary course of a trade or business.

The term working capital is not defined in either Code Sec. 469 or Code Sec. 1411, but it generally refers to capital set aside for use in and the future needs of a trade or business. Because the capital may not be necessary for the immediate conduct of the trade or business, the amounts are often invested by businesses in income-producing liquid assets such as savings accounts, certificates of deposit, money market accounts, short-term government and commercial bonds, and other similar investments. These investment assets will usually produce portfolio-type income, such as interest. Under Code Sec. 469(e)(1)(B), portfolio-type income generated by working capital is not derived in the ordinary course of a trade or business, and therefore, it is not treated as passive income. Under Code Sec. 1411(c)(3), gross income from and net gain attributable to the investment of working capital is not derived in the ordinary course of a trade or business, and therefore such gross income and net gain is subject to Code Sec. 1411.

Prop. Reg. § 1.1411-6(b) sets forth an example to illustrate the rules regarding working capital:

> **Example 16-22:** A, an unmarried individual, operates a restaurant through his wholly owned S corporation, "ABC". The restaurant is a Code Sec.

162 trade or business. ABC is able to pay all of the restaurant's current obligations with cash flow generated by the restaurant. ABC utilizes an interest-bearing checking account at a local bank to make daily deposits of cash receipts generated by the restaurant, and also to pay the recurring ordinary and necessary business expenses of the restaurant. The average daily balance of the checking account is approximately $2,500, but at any given time the balance may be significantly more or less than this amount depending on the short-term cash flow needs of the business. In addition, ABC has set aside $20,000 for the potential future needs of the business in case the daily cash flow into and from the checking account becomes insufficient to pay the restaurant's recurring business expenses. ABC does not currently need to spend or use the $20,000 capital to conduct the restaurant business, and ABC deposits and maintains the $20,000 in an interest-bearing savings account at a local bank. Both the $2,500 average daily balance of the checking account and the $20,000 savings account balance constitute working capital; thus, the interest generated by this working capital will not be treated as derived in the ordinary course of ABC's restaurant business. Accordingly, the interest income derived by ABC from its checking and savings accounts and allocated to A under Code Sec. 1366 will be subject to tax under Code Sec. 1411(c)(1)(A)(i).

¶ 1607 Exception for Dispositions of Interests in Partnerships and S Corporations

.01 Introduction

Section 8 of the Preamble to the proposed Code Sec. 1411 regulations states that in most cases, an interest in a partnership or S corporation is not property held in a trade or business. Therefore, gain or loss from the sale of a partnership interest or S corporation stock will be subject to taxation under Code Sec. 1411(c)(1)(A)(iii). See also Code Sec. 731(a) and Code Sec. 1368(b)(2) (providing that the gain recognized when cash is distributed in excess of the adjusted basis of, as applicable, a partner's interest in a partnership or a shareholder's stock in an S corporation is treated as gain from the sale or exchange of such partnership interest or S corporation stock).

Code Sec. 1411(c)(4)(A) provides that, in the case of a disposition of an interest in a partnership or S corporation, gain from such disposition shall be taken into account under Code Sec. 1411(c)(1)(A)(iii) only to the extent of the net gain which would be so taken into account by the transferor under Code Sec. 1411(c)(1)(A)(iii) if all property of the partnership or S corporation were sold for fair market value immediately before the disposition of such interest. Code Sec. 1411(c)(4)(B) applies a similar rule to a loss from a disposition. The purpose of this provision is to put a transferor of an interest in a partnership or S corporation in a similar position as if the partnership or S corporation had disposed of all of its properties and the accompanying gain or loss from the disposition of such properties passed through to its owners (including the transferor). However, the gain or loss upon the sale of an interest in the entity and a sale of the entity's underlying properties will not always match. First, there may be disparities between the transferor's adjusted basis in the partnership interest or S corporation stock and the transferor's share of the entity's adjusted basis in the underlying properties. Example 16-24 set forth below illustrates this point. Second, the sales price of the interest may not reflect the proportionate share of the underlying properties' fair market value with respect to the interest sold.

So, in an effort to achieve parity between an interest sale and an asset sale, Code Sec. 1411(c)(4) must be applied on a property-by-property basis, which requires a determination of how the property was held in order to determine whether the gain or loss to the transferor from the hypothetical disposition of such property would have been gain or loss subject to taxation under Code Sec. 1411(c)(1)(A)(iii). Further, to maintain the separateness of taxation for situations involving passive activities and situations involving financial instruments and commodities, Code Sec. 1411(c)(4) is only applicable to active businesses not engaged in financial instruments and commodities. This means that the exception in Code Sec. 1411(c)(4) does not apply where (1) there is no trade or business, (2) the trade or business is a passive activity under Code Sec. 469 with respect to the transferor, or (3) where the partnership or the S corporation is in the trade or business of trading in financial instruments or commodities. Example 16-29 illustrates a situation involving the transferor of an interest in an S corporation with two trades or businesses, one of which is a passive business situation.

.02 Mechanics of Code Sec. 1411(c)(4)

To achieve the parity between sale by a partnership or an S corporation of assets and sale of partnership or S corporate stock interest, the proposed regulations provide that, for purposes of Code Sec. 1411(c)(4), a transferor computes the gain or loss from the sale of the underlying properties of the partnership or S corporation using a deemed asset sale method ("Deemed Sale"), and then determines if, based on the Deemed Sale, there is an adjustment (either positive or negative) to the transferor's gain or loss on the disposition of the partnership or S corporation interest for purposes of taxation under Code Sec. 1411(c)(1)(A)(iii). An adjustment only occurs if the underlying property is used in an active trade or business (not one that is passive or engaged in financial instruments or commodities) with the result being that a positive adjustment reduces a loss on the disposition of the interest, and a negative adjustment reduces the gain on the disposition of the interest. Because the proposed regulations apply a Deemed Sale by the passthrough entity of all its assets for cash equal to the fair market value of the entity's properties, any gain or loss on the interest sale that is not reflected in the underlying properties of the passthrough entity (as the result of an inside-outside basis disparity) would not create an adjustment. This is illustrated in Example 16-24 below.

The proposed regulations provide that the Deemed Sale under Code Sec. 1411(c)(4) applies, in part, rules similar to Reg. § 1.743-1(d)(2). However, because the Deemed Sale approach may impose an administrative burden on owners of partnerships and S corporations in certain circumstances, the rules are still subject to review.

.03 Deemed Sale

Prop. Reg. § 1.1411-7(c)(2) prescribed that the first step of the Deemed Sale computation is a hypothetical disposition of all the entity's properties (including goodwill) in a fully taxable transaction for cash equal to the fair market value of the entity's properties immediately before the disposition of the interest.

Step two of the Deemed Sale computation as set forth in Prop. Reg. § 1.1411-7(c)(3) is to compute the gain or loss on each of the entity's properties (including goodwill). The calculation of gain or loss is determined by comparing the fair market value of each property with such property's adjusted basis. The gain or loss from each property must be computed separately.

Prop. Reg. § 1.1411-7's third step of the Deemed Sale computation as set forth in Prop. Reg. § 1.1411-7(c)(4) is to allocate the gain or loss from each property determined in the second step to the transferor. In the case of a partnership, the amount of gain or loss allocated to the transferor must take into account the allocations provided in the partnership agreement and any allocations required by Code Secs. 704(b) and 704(c) (and the regulations thereunder), as well as basis adjustments under Code Sec. 743 with respect to the transferor. In the case of an S corporation, the amount of gain or loss allocated to the transferor is determined under Code Sec. 1366(a), and the allocation should not take into account any reduction in the transferor's distributive share in Code Sec. 1366(f)(2) resulting from the hypothetical imposition of tax under Code Sec. 1374 as a result of the Deemed Sale.

Prop. Reg. § 1.1411-7(c)(5) prescribes that the fourth step of the Deemed Sale computation is to determine whether the amount of gain or loss allocated to the transferor with respect to each property under the Deemed Sale would have been taken into account in determining the transferor's net gain under Code Sec. 1411(c)(1)(A)(iii) if it were an actual disposition. If the entity's property is either held in a trade or business described in Code Sec. 1411(c)(2) (i.e., a passive situation or trading in financial instruments or commodities) with respect to the partnership, the S corporation, or the transferor, or is not held in a trade or business, there will be no adjustment under Code Sec. 1411(c)(4) with respect to that property. However, if the property is held in a trade or business not described in Code Sec. 1411(c)(2), there is an adjustment under Code Sec. 1411(c)(4) calculated in the following manner as set forth in Prop. Reg. § 1.1411-7(c)(5). First, the transferor's gains or losses from such property (or properties) are aggregated to create a net gain (which will be treated as a negative adjustment) or a net loss (which will be treated as a positive adjustment). Second, based on the adjustment calculated and subject to certain limitations, the transferor then must adjust the gain or loss from the disposition of the partnership or S corporation interest determined in Code Sec. 1411(c)(1)(A)(iii) (without regard to Code Sec. 1411(c)(4)) by the positive or negative adjustment.

For example, if in the Deemed Sale the transferor would have been allocated a net gain from property held in a trade or business not described in Code Sec. 1411(c)(2) (thus, a negative adjustment) and the transferor had a gain on the disposition of the interest, then the gain on the disposition of the interest will be reduced for purposes of determining net investment income. However, in a situation in which a transferor has a gain (determined without regard to Code Sec. 1411(c)(4)) from the disposition of the partnership or S corporation interest, Prop. Reg. § 1.1411-7(c)(5)(iii)(B) prescribes that a negative adjustment cannot result in the transferor having a loss on the disposition of the partnership or S corporation interest for purposes of Code Sec. 1411(c)(1)(A)(iii), and a positive adjustment is not taken into account. For example, if a transferor has a $100,000 gain on the disposition of S corporation stock, the Code Sec. 1411(c)(4) adjustment cannot result in a gain for Code Sec. 1411 purposes greater than $100,000, and cannot result in a loss for Code Sec. 1411 purposes. Example 16-25 set forth below illustrates this point. Similarly, in a situation where a transferor has a loss (determined without regard to Code Sec. 1411(c)(4)) from the disposition of the partnership or S corporation interest, a positive adjustment cannot result in the transferor having a gain on the disposition of the partnership or S corporation interest for purposes of Code Sec. 1411(c)(1)(A)(iii), and a negative adjustment is not taken into account. For example, if a transferor has a $50,000 loss on the disposition of S corporation stock, the Code Sec. 1411(c)(4) adjustment cannot result in a loss for Code Sec. 1411 purposes greater than $50,000, and cannot result in a gain for Code Sec. 1411 purposes.

The proposed regulations provide a special rule for property held in more than one trade or business during the twelve-month period ending on the date of the disposition. In such case, the fair market value and the adjusted basis of such property must be allocated among the trades or businesses on a basis that reasonably reflects the use of the property. This allocation rule is illustrated in Example 16-29 set forth below.

The proposed regulations provide rules to determine the treatment of gain or loss from goodwill for purposes of Code Sec. 1411(c)(4). If the entity is engaged in one trade or business, the entire gain or loss on the goodwill will be treated as gain or loss from the disposition of property held for use in that trade or business, and no portion of such gain or loss will be treated as attributable property not held for use in the trade or business. If the entity is engaged in more than one trade or business, the gain or loss on the goodwill is allocated between the trades or businesses based on the relative fair market value of the property (excluding cash) held for use in each trade or business. For example, if the entity has total assets with a fair market value of $110,000 (consisting of assets of $10,000 not held in any trade or business, $15,000 of assets held for use in Business 1, $45,000 of assets held for use in Business 2, $10,000 of cash, and goodwill of $30,000), and if the gain on the goodwill is $20,000, $5,000 of such gain is allocated to Business 1 and the remaining $15,000 gain is allocated to Business 2. Example 16-30 set forth below illustrates this point.

.04 Special Situations—Code Sec. 338(h)(10) Sales; Installment Sales; and Sales by QSSTs

Interaction of Code Sec. 1411(c)(4) and Code Sec. 338(h)(10) election. In the case of a disposition of stock in an S corporation with respect to which a Code Sec. 338(h)(10) election is made, Code Sec. 1411(c)(4) is inapplicable to the deemed asset sale and liquidation transactions that result from the Code Sec. 338(h)(10) election. Under Code Sec. 338(h)(10), the sale of the S corporation stock is treated as an actual asset sale by the S corporation. Code Sec. 1411(c)(4) is inapplicable to such an asset sale. In the deemed liquidation of the former S corporation, Code Sec. 1411(c)(4) is also inapplicable to the shareholders because the underlying character of the gain or loss in the assets at the former S corporation level is already fully taken into account in the deemed asset sale.

Installment sales. In the case of a disposition of a partnership or S corporation interest in an installment sale transaction to which Code Sec. 453 applies, the adjustment to net gain will be calculated in the year of the disposition. However, the gain and any applicable adjustment are deferred and recognized proportionally pursuant to Code Sec. 453.

Installment sales—election to have taxation under Code Sec. 1411 apply. In the event that the year of the disposition of the interest occurs before the effective date of Code Sec. 1411, the adjustment under Code Sec. 1411(c)(4) will not be applicable. However, the proposed regulations allow taxpayers to elect into the rules of Code Sec. 1411(c)(4) if they receive installment sale payments attributable to a disposition of an interest in a partnership or S corporation that occurred before the effective date of Code Sec. 1411. This election allows taxpayers that sell their interests in installment sales before the effective date of Code Sec. 1411 to be treated similarly with taxpayers that sell their interests after the effective date. In submitting the required statement of adjustment, this election will require the taxpayer to have the information (such as basis and fair market value of each property) as of the date of disposition.

> *Planning Point:* While having Code Sec. 1411's surtax apply to an existing installment sale may seem to be an oxymoron, Code Sec. 1411's tax does not differentiate between past and current transactions; it lumps all capital gains in its computation. Thus, to minimize Net Investment Income, assuming that Code Sec. 1411(c)(4) will apply to reduce the gain, S corporation shareholder(s), assuming that the Deemed Sale computation will eliminate all or most of the capital gain should make the election to have this retroactive procedure apply.

Sale by a qualified subchapter S trust (QSST). Under Reg. § 1.1361-1(j)(8) the income beneficiary of the QSST is treated as the owner, for purposes of Code Sec. 678(a), of that portion of the trust that consists of the stock of the S corporation for which the QSST election was made. However, solely for purposes of this rule, an income beneficiary who is a deemed Code Sec. 678 owner only by reason of Code Sec. 1361(d)(1) will not be treated as the owner of the S corporation stock in determining and attributing the Federal income tax consequences of a disposition of the stock by the QSST. Therefore, if the QSST sells some (or all) of its S corporation stock, any gain or loss recognized on the sale will be that of the trust, not the income beneficiary. (On the other hand, the disposition is treated as a disposition by the income beneficiary for purposes of applying Code Secs. 465 and 469 to the income beneficiary of a QSST.)

¶1607.04

Tax Pointer: The Treasury Department has requested comment about taxation of the QSST on sale of the stock. Because trust taxation may prove to be onerous compared to sale by the beneficiary, taxpayers may want to carefully review utilization of QSSTs for estate and income tax planning. For a discussion of QSSTS see ¶ 307.

The proposed regulations do not address whether special rules are needed to coordinate the QSST rules regarding dispositions of stock in an S corporation in Reg. § 1.1361-1(j)(8) and Code Sec. 1411(c)(4). Hopefully, the IRS will furnish some direction in the near future regarding this issue.

.05 Required Statements

Prop. Reg. § 1.1411-7(c)(5) prescribes that any transferor selling or disposing of S corporate stock or a partnership interest making an adjustment under must attach a statement to the transferor's return for the year of disposition. The statement must include: (1) a description of the disposed-of interest; (2) the name and taxpayer identification number of the entity disposed of; (3) the fair market value of each property of the entity; (4) the entity's adjusted basis in each property; (5) the transferor's allocable share of gain or loss with respect to each property of the entity; (6) information regarding whether the property is a passive activity or involved with financial instruments or trading of commodities; (7) the amount of gain arising from the sale of the stock or partnership interest; and (8) the computation to arrive at the gain.

In cases involving partnerships without a Code Sec. 754 election in effect (or where there is no mandatory Code Sec. 743 adjustment) and S corporations, the transferor may not have access to the information that is necessary to make the adjustment and to file the required statements. Hopefully, the IRS will provide a means to resolve this issue.

.06 Examples to Illustrate the Application of the Deemed Sales Rules

Examples 16-23 to 16-30 are set forth below to illustrate the application of the "Deemed Sales Rules" for S corporations and partnerships. In each case, unless otherwise indicated, the taxpayer uses a calendar taxable year, the taxpayer is a U.S. citizen, and the partnership (PRS) or S corporation (S) is not engaged in a trade or business of trading in financial instruments or commodities.

Example 16-23: Basic application.

(i) *Facts.* Individuals A and B are shareholders of S Corporation (S). A owns 75 percent of the stock in S, and B owns 25 percent of the stock in S. During Year 1, S is engaged in a single trade or business. With respect to S's trade or business, A is not engaged in a passive activity; but B is so engaged. S has three properties (1, 2, and 3) held exclusively in S's trade or business that have an aggregate fair market value of $120,000. On September 1 of Year 1, A and B sell their S stock to C for the fair market value of S's properties (that is, A sells for $90,000 and B sells for $30,000). At the time of the disposition, A's adjusted basis in his S stock is $75,000, and B's

¶1607.06

adjusted basis in his S stock is $25,000. S's properties have the following adjusted bases and fair market values immediately before the disposition:

Property	Adjusted Basis	Fair Market Value
1	$10,000	$50,000
2	$70,000	$30,000
3	$20,000	$40,000

(ii) *Calculation of net gain.* On the stock sale to C, both recognize gain under Code Sec. 1411(c)(1)(A)(iii): A recognizes a gain of $15,000 ($90,000 minus $75,000), and B recognizes a gain of $5,000 ($30,000 minus $25,000).

(iii) *Application of Code Sec. 1411(c)(4).*

    (A) **In general.** Code Sec. 1411(c)(4) is applicable to A because with respect to S's trade or business, A is not in a passive activity. On the other hand, with respect to B, S's trade or business is passive to B; thus, Code Sec. 1411(c)(4) is inapplicable to B, and B may not make any adjustment to his $5,000 gain upon the stock disposition since it arises from a passive activity.

    (B) **Deemed sale—**

        (1) **Step one:** *deemed sale of properties.* Upon a hypothetical disposition of S's properties for cash equal to fair market value, S would receive $50,000 for Property 1, $30,000 for Property 2, and $40,000 for Property 3.

        (2) **Step two:** *determination of gain or loss.* The determination of gain or loss on the deemed sale of S's properties is as follows:

Property	Adjusted Basis	Fair Market Value	Gain or Loss
1	$10,000	$50,000	$40,000
2	$70,000	$30,000	($40,000)
3	$20,000	$40,000	$20,000

        (3) **Step three:** *allocation of gain or loss.* Under Code Sec. 1366, A is allocated $30,000 gain from Property 1, $30,000 loss from Property 2, and $15,000 gain from Property 3.

        (4) **Step four:** *adjustment to net gain.* Because all three properties are held in S's trade or business, A must make an adjustment to determine if any of the gain is subject to Code Sec. 1411's

tax. The gain or loss on each of the three properties are added together ($30,000 minus $30,000 plus $15,000), resulting in a negative adjustment of $15,000 ($90,000 amount realized less basis of $75,000 = $15,000 of gain); however, since this gain arose from sale of stock in an active trade or business, Prop. Reg. § 1.1411-7(c)(5) applies to eliminate gain realized from taxation under Code Sec. 1411 using the deemed sale rules. So, A's gain of $15,000 on the disposition of the interest under Code Sec. 1411(c)(1)(A)(iii) is reduced by $15,000, A has zero gain from the sale of S stock for Code Sec. 1411(c)(1)(A)(iii) purposes. However, A must still report the $15,000 gain from the sale of his S corporate stock on Form 1040, Schedule D and use that gain to determine his MAGI under Code Sec. 1411(a)(1)(B)(i) to see if A owes Code Sec. 1411 tax under Code Sec. 1411(a)(1).

Example 16-24: *Inside-outside basis disparity.*

(i) *Facts.* Same facts as Example 16-23, except that A's adjusted basis in his S stock is $70,000.

(ii) *Analysis.* On the stock sale to C, A recognizes a gain of $20,000 ($90,000 minus $70,000). The deemed sale would result in a negative adjustment of $15,000 ($30,000 minus $30,000 plus $15,000). Under, Prop. Reg. § 1.1411-7(c)(5) A's net gain of $20,000 on the disposition of his stock interest is reduced by $15,000, and A has $5,000 net gain with respect to the stock disposition for purposes of Code Sec. 1411(c)(1)(A)(iii). Thus, he will have $5,000 of net investment income subject to taxation under Code Sec. 1411.

Example 16-25: *Limitation of adjustment.*

(i) *Facts.* Same facts as Example 16-23, except that A's adjusted basis in his S stock is $80,000.

(ii) *Analysis.* On the stock sale to C, A recognizes a gain of $10,000 ($90,000 minus $80,000). The deemed sale utilizing Prop. Reg. § 1.1411-7(c)(5) would result in a negative adjustment of $15,000 ($30,000 minus $30,000 plus $15,000). However, under Prop. Reg. § 1.1411-7(c)(5)(iii)(B), A's net gain of $10,000 on the disposition is reduced by the negative adjustment, but the negative adjustment under is limited to $10,000 so as not to create negative net investment income from this sale of stock. As a result, A has zero net gain with respect to the stock disposition for purposes of Code Sec. 1411(c)(1)(A)(iii)'s computation for net investment income.

Example 16-26: *Loss on disposition.*

(i) *Facts.* Same facts as Example 16-23 except that A's adjusted basis in his stock is $105,000, Property 3 has an adjusted basis of $60,000 and fair market value of $10,000, and A sells his interest for $67,500.

(ii) *Analysis.* On the stock sale to C, A recognizes a loss of $37,500 ($67,500 minus $105,000). Under the deemed sale rules of Code Sec. 1411(c)(4), A would be allocated $30,000 gain from Property 1, $30,000 loss from Property 2, and $37,500 loss from Property 3. The deemed sale would result in a positive adjustment of $37,500 ($30,000 minus $30,000 minus $37,500). Under Prop. Reg. § 1.1411-7(c)(5), A's loss of $37,500 on the disposition of his stock is increased by the positive adjustment of $37,500, and A has zero loss with respect to the stock disposition for purposes of Code Sec. 1411(c)(1)(A)(iii)'s computation for net investment income.

Example 16-27: *Property not held in trade or business.*

(i) *Facts.* Same facts as Example 16-23, except that S owns a fourth property (adjusted basis of $20,000 and fair market value of $100,000) that is not held in S's trade or business and only A sells his S stock to C for A's proportionate share of the fair market value of S's properties. At the time of the disposition, A's adjusted basis in his S stock is $90,000.

(ii) *Calculation of net gain under Code Sec. 1411(c)(1)(A)(iii).* On the stock sale to C, A recognizes a gain of $75,000 ($165,000 minus $90,000).

(iii) *Application of Code Sec. 1411(c)(4):*

    (A) **In general.** Code Sec. 1411(c)(4) is applicable to A because S's trade or business is not a trade or business described in Reg. § 1.1411-5(a)(1) with respect to A.

    (B) **Deemed sale—**

        (1) **Step one:** *deemed sale of properties.* Upon a hypothetical disposition of S's properties for cash equal to fair market value, S would receive $50,000 for Property 1, $30,000 for Property 2, $40,000 for Property 3, and $100,000 for Property 4.

        (2) **Step two:** *determination of gain or loss.* The determination of gain or loss on the deemed sale of S's properties is as follows:

Property	Adjusted Basis	Fair Market Value	Gain or Loss
1	$10,000	$50,000	$40,000
2	$70,000	$30,000	($40,000)

Property	Adjusted Basis	Fair Market Value	Gain or Loss
3	$20,000	$40,000	$20,000
4	$20,000	$100,000	$80,000

(3) **Step three:** *allocation of gain or loss.* Under Code Sec. 1366, A who owns 75% of S is allocated $30,000 gain from Property 1 (75% × $40,000 = $30,000); $30,000 loss from Property 2 (75% × ($40,000) = ($30,000); $15,000 gain from Property 3 (75% × $20,000 = $15,000); and $60,000 gain from Property 4 (75% x $80,000 = $60,000). A's total gain is $75,000 (30,000 + (30,000) + 15.000 + 60,000).

(4) **Step four:** *adjustment to net gain.* Because Property 4 is passive to S, A's $60,000 gain from Property 4 is not taken into account Prop. Reg. § 1.1411-7(c)(5) to eliminate the gain. The gain or loss on Property 1, Property 2, and Property 3 are added together ($30,000 minus $30,000 plus $15,000), resulting in a negative adjustment of $15,000. Under Prop. Reg. § 1.1411-7(c)(5), A's net gain of $75,000 on the disposition of his stock interest is reduced by $15,000, and A has $60,000 net gain for purposes of Code Sec. 1411(c)(1)(A)(iii). For purposes of A's Form 1040, Schedule D he reports a net of $75,000 which likewise would be used to determine his MAGI for purposes of Code Sec. 1411(a)(1)(B)(i) to see if A owes Code Sec. 1411 tax under Code Sec. 1411(a)(1).

Example 16-28: Calculation of gain in general where a partnership is involved.

(i) *Facts.* D and E are equal partners in PRS, a partnership, and PRS's partnership agreement provides that allocations are 50 percent to D and 50 percent to E. PRS is engaged in a single trade or business. D contributed Property 1 with an adjusted basis of $100,000 and a fair market value of $200,000 at the time of the contribution. E contributed Property 2 with an adjusted basis of $120,000 and a fair market value of $200,000 at the time of the contribution. PRS is engaged in a single trade or business in which both Property 1 and Property 2 are used. PRS's trade or business is "active," not "passive" or engaged in trading financial instruments or commodities with respect to D. On November 1 of Year 1, D sells his interest in PRS to F for $320,000, which is based on the fair market value of PRS's properties. At the

¶1607.06

time of the sale, D has an adjusted basis in his partnership interest of $100,000 and the properties of PRS have the following adjusted bases and fair market values:

Property	Adjusted Basis	Fair Market Value
1	$100,000	$240,000
2	$120,000	$400,000

(ii) *Calculation of net gain under Code Sec. 1411(c)(1)(A)(iii).* D recognizes $220,000 ($320,000 minus $100,000) of gain on the sale of his partnership interest to F and such gain is subject to Code Sec. 1411(c)(4) to determine the amount of gain to be reported.

(iii) *Application of Code Sec. 1411(c)(4).*

(A) **In general.** Code Sec. 1411(c)(4) is applicable to D because PRS's trade or business is "active" with respect to A.

(B) *Deemed sale.*

(1) **Step one:** *deemed sale of properties.* Upon a hypothetical disposition of PRS's properties for cash equal to fair market value, PRS would receive $240,000 for Property 1 and $400,000 for Property 2 as set forth above.

(2) **Step two:** *determination of PRS's gain or loss.* The determination of gain or loss on the deemed sale of PRS's properties is as follows:

Property	Adjusted Basis	Fair Market Value	Gain or Loss
1	$100,000	$240,000	$140,000
2	$120,000	$400,000	$280,000

(3) **Step three:** *allocation of gain or loss.* Pursuant to Code Sec. 704(c), D is allocated $120,000 gain from the deemed sale of Property 1 and $100,000 gain from the deemed sale of Property 2 computed as follows: Property 1 has a gain of $140,000: D's untaxed gain on contribution of Property 1 was $100,000; thus, from the gain of $140,000 subtract D's gain of $100,000 leaving $40,000 to be shared equally with E; or, $20,000 to each. So, from property 1, D's gain is $120,00 (100,000 + 20,000). Property 2 has a gain of $280,000: E's untaxed gain of $80,000 on contribution of Property 1 is $80,000; subtracting $80,000 from $280,000 leaves $200,000 of gain to be shared equally by D and E, or D's gain from Property 2 is $100,000.

(4) **Step four:** *adjustment to net gain.* Because both properties are used in PRS's trade or business, D must make an adjustment under Prop. Reg. § 1.1411-7(c)(5) to the amount of net gain determined under Code Sec. 1411(c)(1)(A)(iii). The total gain allocated to D in the deemed sale is $220,000 ($120,000 plus $100,000), resulting in a negative adjustment of $220,000. Under Prop. Reg. § 1.1411-7(c)(5) and Code Sec. 1411(c)(4), D's net gain of $220,000 is reduced by $220,000, and D has zero net gain with respect to his partnership interest disposition under Code Sec. 1411(c)(1)(A)(iii). However, D must report his gain from the sale of his partnership interest on Form 1040, Schedule D and utilize this gain for purposes of calculating his MAGI under Code Sec. 1411(a)(1)(B)(i).

Example 16-29: Multiple trades or businesses.

(i) *Facts.* Individuals A and B are shareholders of an S corporation (S). A owns 50 percent of the stock in S. During Year 2, S is engaged in two trades or businesses (Business X and Business Y).

With respect to Business X, this is an "active" business for A, but with respect to Business Y, this business is "passive" for A. S has five properties. Property 1 and Property 2 are held exclusively in Business X, and Property 3 and Property 4 are held exclusively in Business Y. Property 5 is used half of the time in Business X and the rest of the time in Business Y. On December 1 of Year 2, A sells his S stock to C for A's proportionate share of the fair market value of S's properties. At the time of the disposition, A's adjusted basis in his S stock is $110,000. S's properties have the following adjusted bases and fair market values immediately before the disposition:

Property	Adjusted Basis	Fair Market Value
1	$10,000	$30,000
2	$70,000	$30,000
3	$20,000	$40,000
4	$20,000	$100,000
5	$100,000	$120,000
Total	$220,000	$320,000

Total net gain, Property 1, $20,000; Property 2, ($40,000); Property 3, $20,000; Property 4, $80,000; and Property 5, $20,000.

(ii) *Calculation of gain under Code Sec. 1411(c)(1)(A)(iii).* On the stock sale to C, A recognizes a gain of $50,000 ($320,000 fair market value of the property divided by 2 =$160,000; less A's stock basis of $110,000 = $50,000 of gain).

(iii) *Application of Code Sec. 1411(c)(4).*

  (A) **In general.** Code Sec. 1411(c)(4) is applicable to A. However, any adjustment will only relate to property held in Business X and not to property held in Business Y (because Business Y is a "passive" business with respect to A).

  (B) **Deemed sale—**

   (1) **Step one:** *deemed sale of properties.* Upon a hypothetical disposition of S's properties for cash equal to fair market value, S would receive $30,000 for Property 1, $30,000 for Property 2, $40,000 for Property 3, $100,000 for Property 4, and $120,000 for Property 5.

   (2) **Step two:** *determination of gain or loss.* The determination of gain or loss on the deemed sale of S's properties is as follows:

Property	Adjusted Basis	Fair Market Value	Gain or Loss
1	$10,000	$30,000	$20,000
2	$70,000	$30,000	($40,000)
3	$20,000	$40,000	$20,000
4	$20,000	$100,000	$80,000
5	$100,000	$120,000	$20,000

   (3) **Step three:** *allocation of gain or loss.* Under Code Sec. 1366, A is allocated $10,000 gain from Property 1, $20,000 loss from Property 2, $10,000 gain from Property 3, $40,000 gain from Property 4, and $10,000 gain from Property 5.

   (4) **Step four:** *adjustment to net gain.* A must make an adjustment under an adjustment under Prop. Reg. § 1.1411-7(c)(5) to the amount of net gain determined under Code Sec. 1411(c)(1)(A)(iii), but only with respect to the gain or loss on the properties used in Business X (that is, Property 1, Property 2, and a portion of Property 5 which is used 50% for "active" business purposes). Because Property 5 is used 50 percent of the time in Business X, 50 percent of the gain $20,000 × 50% = $10,000) would be attributable to Business X (and A's share would be $5,000 since he is selling his 50% stock interest in the S corpora-

tion). The gain or loss on Property 1, Property 2, and Property 5 are added together ($10,000 minus $20,000 plus $5,000 = ($5,000)), and results in a positive adjustment of $5,000. Under Code Sec. 1411(c)(4), A makes no adjustment for his $5,000 of loss realized on the sale of his stock; thus, he reports $50,000 of gain under Code Sec. 1411(c)(1)(A)(iii).

Example 16-30: *Goodwill and multiple trades or businesses.*

(i) *Facts.* Individuals A and B are shareholders of an S corporation (S). A owns 50 percent of the stock in S. During Year 2, S is engaged in two trades or businesses (Business X and Business Y). With respect to Business X, this business is "active" for A; but with respect to Business Y, this business is "passive" for A. In addition to cash and goodwill, S has five properties. Property 1 and Property 2 are used exclusively in Business X. Property 3 is not held for use in either Business X or Business Y. Property 4 and Property 5 are used exclusively in Business Y. On June 1 of Year 2, A sells his S stock to C for A's proportionate share of the fair market value of S's properties. At the time of the disposition, A's adjusted basis in his S stock is $30,000. S's properties have the following adjusted bases and fair market value immediately before the disposition:

Property	Adjusted Basis	Fair Market Value
1	$5,000	$10,000
2	$5,000	$5,000
3	$0	$10,000
4	$20,000	$30,000
5	$10,000	$15,000
Cash	$10,000	$10,000
Goodwill	$10,000	$30,000

(ii) *Calculation of gain under Code Sec. 1411(c)(1)(A)(iii).* On the stock sale to C, A recognizes a gain of $25,000 ($55,000 minus $30,000).

(iii) *Application of Code Sec. 1411(c)(4).*

(A) **In general.** Code Sec. 1411(c)(4) is applicable to A. However, any adjustment will only relate to property used in Business X and not to property used in Business Y (because Business Y is "passive" with respect to A).

(B) **Deemed sale—**

(1) **Step one:** *deemed sale of properties.* Upon a hypothetical disposition of S's properties for cash equal to fair market value, S would receive $10,000 for Property 1, $5,000 for Property 2, $10,000 for Property 3, $30,000 for Property 4,

$15,000 for Property 5, $10,000 for the cash, and $30,000 for goodwill.

(2) **Step two:** *determination of gain or loss.* The determination of gain or loss on the deemed sale of S's properties is as follows:

Property	Adjusted Basis	Fair Market Value	Gain or Loss
1	$5,000	$10,000	$5,000
2	$5,000	$5,000	$0
3	$0	$10,000	$10,000
4	$20,000	$30,000	$10,000
5	$10,000	$15,000	$5,000
Cash	$10,000	$10,000	$0
Goodwill	$10,000	$30,000	$20,000

(3) **Step three:** *allocation of gain or loss.* Under Code Sec. 1366, A is allocated a $25,000 gain ($2,500 gain from Property 1, $0 gain from Property 2, $5,000 gain from Property 3, $5,000 gain from Property 4, $2,500 gain from Property 5, $0 from cash, and $10,000 from goodwill).

(4) **Step four:** *adjustment to net gain.* A must make an adjustment under Prop. Reg. § 1.1411-7(c)(5) to the amount of net gain determined under Code Sec. 1411(c)(1)(A)(iii), but only with respect to the gain or loss on the properties used in Business X (that is, Property 1, Property 2, and a portion of the goodwill). Under Prop. Reg. § 1.1411-7(c)(5)(ii)(B), the goodwill is allocated to Business X and Business Y based on the relative fair market value of the property (other than cash) held for use in each trade or business. For this purpose, the fair market value of the property held for use in Business X is $15,000 ($10,000 + $5,000), and the fair market value of the property held for use in Business Y is $45,000 ($30,000 + $15,000); the total fair market value of these properties is $60,000 ($15,000 + $45,000 = $60,000). Therefore, 25 percent of A's gain on the goodwill is attributable to Business X (25% × $10,000 = $2,500). A's share of the gain on Property 1, Property 2, and goodwill are added together ($2,500 plus zero plus $2,500), which results in a negative adjustment of $5,000. Under Code Sec. 1411(c)(4), A takes into account the negative adjustment of $5,000, and A has a $20,000 gain ($25,000 [$55,000 fair market value of the stock less $30,000 basis] minus $5,000 adjustment) for purposes Code Sec. 1411(c)(1)(A)(iii).

¶ 1608 Code Sec. 1411 Does Not Apply to Distributions from Qualified Plans

Code Sec. 1411(c)(5) provides that net investment income does not include any distribution from the following plans or arrangements:

(1) A qualified pension, stock bonus, or profit-sharing plan under Code Sec. 401(a);

(2) A qualified annuity plan under Code Sec. 403(a);

(3) A tax-sheltered annuity under Code Sec. 403(b);

(4) An individual retirement account (IRA) under Code Sec. 408;

(5) A Roth IRA under Code Sec. 408A; or

(6) A deferred compensation plan of a State and local government or a tax-exempt organization under Code Sec. 457(b).

Prop. Reg. § 1.1411-8 sets forth the general rule that for purposes of Code Sec. 1411, any amount actually distributed from a qualified plan or arrangement is a distribution within the meaning of Code Sec. 1411(c)(5), and thus is not included in net investment income. Examples of distributions which would be exempt would be actual distributions, including a rollover to an eligible retirement plan within the meaning of Code Sec. 402(c)(8)(B), a distribution of a plan offset amount within the meaning of Q&A-13(b) of Reg. § 1.72(p)-1, and corrective distributions from a qualified plan or arrangement to maintain its tax-favored status. The term "corrective distribution" includes any of the following distributions: (1) A distribution of excess deferrals as described in Reg. § 1.402(g)-1(e)(3); (2) for purposes of Code Sec. 408 IRAs, a distribution of excess contributions as described in Reg. § 1.408-4(c); (3) for purposes of Code Sec. 408A Roth IRAs, a distribution of excess contributions as described in Q&A-1(d) of Reg. § 1.408A-6; and (4) for purposes of eligible Code Sec. 457(b) plans, a distribution of excess deferrals as described in Reg. § 1.457-4(e)(2) through (4).

Prop. Reg. § 1.1411-8(b)(2) states that, for purposes of Code Sec. 1411, amounts that are deemed distributions under the Code for purposes of income tax are distributions for purposes of Code Sec. 1411(c)(5), even if these distributions are not treated as actual distributions for purposes of the qualification requirements under Code Sec. 401(a). Examples of deemed distributions include conversions to a Roth IRA described in Code Sec. 408A and deemed distributions under Code Sec. 72(p).

Prop. Reg. § 1.1411-8(b)(3) details that any amount that is not treated as a distribution, but is otherwise includible in gross income pursuant to a rule relating to amounts held in a qualified plan or arrangement, is a distribution within the meaning of Code Sec. 1411(c)(5), and thus is not included in net investment income. For example, any income of the trust of a qualified plan or arrangement that is applied to purchase a participant's life insurance coverage (the P.S. 58 costs) is a distribution within the meaning of Code Sec. 1411(c)(5), and thus is not included in net investment income.

While distributions from qualified plans or arrangements are not includible in net investment income, as defined in Code Sec. 1411(c)(1), distributions from a qualified plan or arrangement that are includible in gross income under Chapter 1 of the Internal Revenue Code of 1986, as amended are taken into account in determining the taxpayer's modified adjusted gross income or adjusted gross income for purposes of calculating the amount subject to tax under Code Sec. 1411(a)(1)(B) or (a)(2)(B).

¶ 1609 Controlled Foreign Corporations and Passive Foreign Investment Companies

The proposed regulations provide rules that apply to an individual, estate, or trust that owns stock of a controlled foreign corporation ("CFC") or qualified electing fund ("QEF") through a domestic partnership or S corporation. Because of the different timing rules under Chapter 1 of the Internal Revenue Code of 1986, as amended and Chapter 2A of the Internal Revenue Code of 1986, as amended and the fact that partnerships and S corporations are passthrough entities, the proposed regulations provide rules on the determination for Code Sec. 1411 purposes of (1) the partner's or shareholder's outside basis in his interest, and (2) the partnership's or S corporation's adjusted basis in its CFC or QEF stock. The Treasury Department and the IRS believe that the partnership or S corporation will need to separately state, in addition to a partner's distributive share of the amounts included in the partnership's income under Code Sec. 951(a) or Code Sec. 1293(a), a partner's distributive share of any distributions of previously taxed earnings and profits of a CFC or QEF received by the partnership or S corporation that are dividends for purposes of Chapter 2A of the Internal Revenue Code of 1986, as amended. However, no rules have been promulgated to deal with this situation. So, it remains to be seen what will occur in this area.

The proposed regulations also provide conforming rules for estates, trusts, and their beneficiaries. Prop. Reg. § 1.1411-10(c)(5), (e)(2), and (f) coordinate the rules relating to the computation of net investment income and any associated increase or decrease to adjusted gross income with the distributable net income regime and other general operating rules governing the income taxation of estates and trusts contained in Subchapter J and Code Sec. 1411. There is no clear direction from the Treasury as to how to report these items.

¶ 1610 Regrouping for Taxpayers Subject to Code Sec. 1411

Reg. § 1.469-4 provides rules for defining an activity for purposes of applying the passive activity loss rules of Code Sec. 469 (grouping rules). The grouping rules will apply in determining the scope of a taxpayer's trade or business in order to determine whether such trade or business is a passive activity for purposes of Code Sec. 1411(c)(2)(A).

Reg. § 1.469-4(e)(1) provides that, except as provided in Reg. §§ 1.469-4(e)(2) and 1.469-11, once a taxpayer has grouped activities, the taxpayer may not regroup those activities in subsequent taxable years. The Treasury Department and the IRS have determined on prior occasions that taxpayers should be given a "fresh start" to redetermine their groupings. The enactment of Code Sec. 1411 may cause taxpayers to reconsider their previous grouping determinations, and therefore the Treasury Department and the IRS have determined that taxpayers should be given the opportunity to regroup. Thus, the proposed regulations provide that taxpayers may regroup their activities in the first taxable year beginning after December 31, 2013, in which the taxpayer meets the applicable income threshold as set forth at Code Sec. 1411(b) and has net investment income as defined in Code Sec. 1411(a)(1). The determination in the preceding sentence is made without regard to the effect of the regrouping. Taxpayers may regroup their activities in reliance on this proposed regulation for any taxable year that begins during 2013 if Code Sec. 1411 would apply to such taxpayer in such taxable year. A taxpayer may only regroup activities once pursuant to Reg. §1.469-11(b)(3)(iv)(A), and any such regrouping will apply to the taxable year for which the regrouping is done and all subsequent years.

The regrouping must comply with the existing requirements under Reg. §1.469-4. For example, Reg. §1.469-4(e) provides that taxpayers must comply with disclosure requirements that the Commissioner may prescribe with respect to both their original groupings and the addition and disposition of specific activities within those chosen groupings in subsequent taxable years. On January 25, 2010, the Treasury Department and the IRS published Revenue Procedure 2010-13 (2010-4 IRB 329), which requires taxpayers to report to the IRS their groupings and regroupings of activities and the addition of specific activities within their existing groupings of activities for purposes of Code Sec. 469 and Reg. §1.469-4. Thus, the disclosure requirements of Reg. §1.469-4(e) and Revenue Procedure 2010-13 require taxpayers who regroup their activities pursuant to Prop. Reg. §1.469-11(b)(3)(iv) to report their regroupings to the IRS. See Reg. §601.601(d)(2). If a taxpayer chooses not to regroup activities under the proposed regulations, Part 12 of the Preamble to the Proposed Code Sec. 1411 regulations states that the taxpayer will not be precluded from regrouping once the regulations are finalized.

¶ 1611 Tax Planning under Code Sec. 1411

As the above discussion details, Code Secs. 1411, 1401(b)(2) and 3101(b)(2)(A)[3] are complex and interrelated to some degree. A simple reading of these Code sections reveals that there are several major steps which individual taxpayers must undertake to minimize the effect of the tax surcharges being generated by Code Secs. 1411, 3101(b)(2)(A) and 1401(b)(2).

.01 Minimize MAGI and Employment Income Below the Threshold Amounts

A key step in a taxable year, attempt to keep one's MAGI below the threshold amounts for imposition of tax set forth in Code Sec. 1411(b), namely $200,000 for a single person, $250,000 in the case of a joint return and $125,000 in the case of a married taxpayer filing separately. The reason is simple: if MAGI is below the threshold amount, Code Sec. 1411 cannot be imposed because Code Sec. 1411's tax can only be imposed on the lesser of net investment income or MAGI over the

---

[3] ¶ 616 sets forth a discussion of Code Secs. 3101(b)(2)(A) and 1402(b)(2)(A),

threshold amounts. Example 16-31 set forth below clearly illustrates MAGI's effect on Code Sec. 1411 taxation:

> **Example 16-31:** A owes no tax under Code Sec. 1411 because the threshold amount for a single individual is $200,000. If for 2013, A had net investment income of $100,000 and MAGI of $220,000, A would pay a Code Sec. 1411 tax only on the $20,000 ($220,000 less his MAGI threshold of $200,000 = $20,000) with the surtax being $760.00 (3.8% × $20,000 = $760). While his net investment income is $100,000, Code Sec. 1411's tax is only imposed on the lesser of the net investment income or the amount which exceeds the threshold amount. If during 2014, A has modified adjusted gross income of $220,000, which includes $5,000 of net investment income, then the individual has a Code Sec. 1411 tax of $190 (Code Sec. 1411's MAGI/threshold computation is $20,000; A's net investment income is $5,000. Since $5,000 is less than $20,000; A's Code Sec. 1411's tax is computed on the lower amount of $5,000 or $190 [$5,000 × 3.8% = $190]).

For wage earners and self-employed individuals, while the threshold amounts are the same for imposition of the additional medicare tax, the criteria for imposing the additional medicare tax is not MAGI, but employment income.

Above the line deductions from adjusted gross income. MAGI is created from Adjusted Gross Income ("AGI") on a taxpayer's income tax return. So, if AGI can be reduced, then *a fortiori*, MAGI is reduced. The most common way to reduce MAGI would be contributions to an IRA, SEP, Simple and Qualified plans; however, there are deductions for educator expenses, student loans interest and self-employed health insurance deduction.

.02 Eliminate Code Sec. 469's Passive Income from Net Investment Income

Code Sec. 1411(c)(1)(A)(ii) prescribes that Code Sec. 469's passive income constitutes net investment income. So, if this passive income can be converted to "active," then, an individual taxpayer only has to deal with the other two aspects of net investment income: capital gains and interest, dividends, etc. The key to eliminate the tag of "passive" on income is to have a familiarity with Code Sec. 469 and its various tests to impose restrictive taxability on individuals, namely to have the taxpayer materially participate in the activity. For instance, Reg. § 1.469-5T(a) details various standards for finding material participation:

- the taxpayer participates for more than 500 hours in the activity for the year;

- the taxpayer's participation in the activity for the taxable year constitutes substantially all of the participation of all individuals in the activity for the year;

- the taxpayer participates for more than 100 hours, and this is more than the participation of all other individuals;

- the taxpayer's participation is "significant," and his "significant" participation in all activities exceeds a total of 500 hours for the year—significant participation in the activity requires more than 100 hours of participation during the year;

- the taxpayer materially participated in the activity for any five taxable years during the last 10 taxable years;

- in the case of a personal service activity (such as health, law, engineering, accounting, and the performing arts), the taxpayer materially participated in the activity during only three prior years; or

- the taxpayer, based on all the facts and circumstances, participates in the activity on a regular, continuous, and substantial basis.

.03 Group Passive Activities to Accomplish Material Participation

If the S corporation is involved in more than one passive activity, proving material participation for each activity pursuant to the standards set forth above by Reg. § 1.469-5T(a) may be difficult. However, Prop. Reg. § 1.469-11(b)(3)(iv) will allow taxpayers to group their passive activities to obtain material participation thereby eliminating the "activity" from being classified as net investment income. The Prop. Reg. § 1.469-11(b)(3)(iv) discussion in the text above sets forth the requirements for regrouping.

.04 Installment Sale

An installment sale allows income to be deferred over a period of time thereby allowing a taxpayer to minimize MAGI. However, installment sales present one major problem, receiving payment for the property sold. Taxpayers are also deprived of all the funds arising from the sale at the time of sale, so investment opportunities are reduced.

.05 Tax Exempt Income

Code Sec. 1411 excludes tax exempt income from MAGI. However, gains and losses from the sale of the tax exempt securities are included in the computation of MAGI. While an S corporation can invest in tax exempt securities, it may not be a wise investment strategy. See the discussion at ¶ 1118.

.06 Eliminate Passive Activities at the S Corporate Level

Due to Code Sec. 1411 taxing the S corporation's passive activities, the S corporation may want to eliminate ownership or severely minimize its ownership in passive activities which generate the passive income like real estate, royalties, dividends and interest. In the situation where an S corporation has earnings and profits from a C corporation predecessor, this may provide the incentive to dispose of the assets generating the passive income to eliminate taxation under Code Sec. 1375 and avoid losing its S status after 3 years under Code Sec. 1362 (for a discussion of these points see ¶ ¶ 804-805).

.07 Code Sec. 1031 Exchange

As illustrated at Example 16-16, Code Sec. 1411 does not impose taxation on a Code Sec. 1031 exchange. Thus, taxpayers may want to explore a Code Sec. 1031 exchange if they will be exposed to Code Sec. 1411's 3.8% surcharge and/or income taxation.

.08 Trusts and Estates

To minimize Code Sec. 1411's tax on estates and trusts, these taxpayers should, in the event they have net investment income, distribute the net investment income to the beneficiaries to just below Code Sec. 1411(a)(2)(B)(ii)'s threshold amount. However, the distribution from the these taxpayers could cause the beneficiaries to be subject to Code Sec. 1411's taxation. Thus, if possible, trust and estate fiduciaries should consult with the beneficiaries to discuss the implications of the distributions. Given the fact that tax exempt income is not subject to Code Sec. 1411's taxation, fiduciaries should consider investing in these types of securities keeping in mind that they are interest rate sensitive.

.09 Shareholder Loans to S Corporation

If a shareholder lends money to his or her S corporation, interest, imputed or paid results. "Interest" per Code Sec. 1411 is net investment income; so, contributions to capital should be made instead to avoid the creation of net investment income.

Appendices

Caution: Before using any of these appendices,
consult the laws in the jurisdiction
where the material will be used.

Appendix 1

Form 2553
(Rev. December 2007)
Department of the Treasury
Internal Revenue Service

Election by a Small Business Corporation
(Under section 1362 of the Internal Revenue Code)
▶ See Parts II and III on page 3 and the separate instructions.
▶ The corporation can fax this form to the IRS (see separate instructions).

OMB No. 1545-0146

Note. This election to be an S corporation can be accepted only if all the tests are met under **Who May Elect** on page 1 of the instructions; all shareholders have signed the consent statement; an officer has signed below; and the exact name and address of the corporation and other required form information are provided.

Part I   Election Information

Type or Print

Name (see instructions)

Number, street, and room or suite no. (If a P.O. box, see instructions.)

City or town, state, and ZIP code

A Employer identification number

B Date incorporated

C State of incorporation

D Check the applicable box(es) if the corporation, after applying for the EIN shown in **A** above, changed its ☐ name or ☐ address

E Election is to be effective for tax year beginning (month, day, year) (see instructions) . . . . . ▶ / /

Caution. A corporation (entity) making the election for its first tax year in existence will usually enter the beginning date of a short tax year that begins on a date other than January 1.

F Selected tax year:

(1) ☐ Calendar year

(2) ☐ Fiscal year ending (month and day) ▶ _____

(3) ☐ 52-53-week year ending with reference to the month of December

(4) ☐ 52-53-week year ending with reference to the month of ▶ _____

If box (2) or (4) is checked, complete Part II

G If more than 100 shareholders are listed for item J (see page 2), check this box if treating members of a family as one shareholder results in no more than 100 shareholders (see test 2 under **Who May Elect** in the instructions) ▶ ☐

H Name and title of officer or legal representative who the IRS may call for more information

I Telephone number of officer or legal representative ( )

If this S corporation election is being filed with Form 1120S, I declare that I had reasonable cause for not filing Form 2553 timely, and if this election is made by an entity eligible to elect to be treated as a corporation, I declare that I also had reasonable cause for not filing an entity classification election timely. See below for my explanation of the reasons the election or elections were not made on time (see instructions).

Sign Here

Under penalties of perjury, I declare that I have examined this election, including accompanying schedules and statements, and to the best of my knowledge and belief, it is true, correct, and complete.

▶ Signature of officer   Title   Date

For Paperwork Reduction Act Notice, see separate instructions.   Cat. No. 18629R   Form **2553** (Rev. 12-2007)

Appendix 1

Form 2553 (Rev. 12-2007) Page **2**

Part I **Election Information** (continued)

J Name and address of each shareholder or former shareholder required to consent to the election. (See the instructions for column K.)	K Shareholders' Consent Statement. Under penalties of perjury, we declare that we consent to the election of the above-named corporation to be an S corporation under section 1362(a) and that we have examined this consent statement, including accompanying schedules and statements, and to the best of our knowledge and belief, it is true, correct, and complete. We understand our consent is binding and may not be withdrawn after the corporation has made a valid election. (Sign and date below.)		L Stock owned or percentage of ownership (see instructions)		M Social security number or employer identification number (see instructions)	N Shareholder's tax year ends (month and day)
	Signature	Date	Number of shares or percentage of ownership	Date(s) acquired		

Form **2553** (Rev. 12-2007)

Appendix 1

Form 2553 (Rev. 12-2007)   Page **3**

Part II   Selection of Fiscal Tax Year (see instructions)

Note. All corporations using this part must complete item O and item P, Q, or R.

O   Check the applicable box to indicate whether the corporation is:

    1. ☐ A new corporation **adopting** the tax year entered in item F, Part I.

    2. ☐ An existing corporation **retaining** the tax year entered in item F, Part I.

    3. ☐ An existing corporation **changing** to the tax year entered in item F, Part I.

P   Complete item P if the corporation is using the automatic approval provisions of Rev. Proc. 2006-46, 2006-45 I.R.B. 859, to request **(1)** a natural business year (as defined in section 5.07 of Rev. Proc. 2006-46) or **(2)** a year that satisfies the ownership tax year test (as defined in section 5.08 of Rev. Proc. 2006-46). Check the applicable box below to indicate the representation statement the corporation is making.

    1. Natural Business Year ▶ ☐ I represent that the corporation is adopting, retaining, or changing to a tax year that qualifies as its natural business year (as defined in section 5.07 of Rev. Proc. 2006-46) and has attached a statement showing separately for each month the gross receipts for the most recent 47 months (see instructions). I also represent that the corporation is not precluded by section 4.02 of Rev. Proc. 2006-46 from obtaining automatic approval of such adoption, retention, or change in tax year.

    2. Ownership Tax Year ▶ ☐ I represent that shareholders (as described in section 5.08 of Rev. Proc. 2006-46) holding more than half of the shares of the stock (as of the first day of the tax year to which the request relates) of the corporation have the same tax year or are concurrently changing to the tax year that the corporation adopts, retains, or changes to per item F, Part I, and that such tax year satisfies the requirement of section 4.01(3) of Rev. Proc. 2006-46. I also represent that the corporation is not precluded by section 4.02 of Rev. Proc. 2006-46 from obtaining automatic approval of such adoption, retention, or change in tax year.

Note. If you do not use item P and the corporation wants a fiscal tax year, complete either item Q or R below. Item Q is used to request a fiscal tax year based on a business purpose and to make a back-up section 444 election. Item R is used to make a regular section 444 election.

Q   Business Purpose—To request a fiscal tax year based on a business purpose, check box Q1. See instructions for details including payment of a user fee. You may also check box Q2 and/or box Q3.

    1. Check here ▶ ☐ if the fiscal year entered in item F, Part I, is requested under the prior approval provisions of Rev. Proc. 2002-39, 2002-22 I.R.B. 1046. Attach to Form 2553 a statement describing the relevant facts and circumstances and, if applicable, the gross receipts from sales and services necessary to establish a business purpose. See the instructions for details regarding the gross receipts from sales and services. If the IRS proposes to disapprove the requested fiscal year, do you want a conference with the IRS National Office?

    ☐ Yes   ☐ No

    2. Check here ▶ ☐ to show that the corporation intends to make a back-up section 444 election in the event the corporation's business purpose request is not approved by the IRS. (See instructions for more information.)

    3. Check here ▶ ☐ to show that the corporation agrees to adopt or change to a tax year ending December 31 if necessary for the IRS to accept this election for S corporation status in the event (1) the corporation's business purpose request is not approved and the corporation makes a back-up section 444 election, but is ultimately not qualified to make a section 444 election, or (2) the corporation's business purpose request is not approved and the corporation did not make a back-up section 444 election.

R   Section 444 Election—To make a section 444 election, check box R1. You may also check box R2.

    1. Check here ▶ ☐ to show that the corporation will make, if qualified, a section 444 election to have the fiscal tax year shown in item F, Part I. To make the election, you must complete **Form 8716,** Election To Have a Tax Year Other Than a Required Tax Year, and either attach it to Form 2553 or file it separately.

    2. Check here ▶ ☐ to show that the corporation agrees to adopt or change to a tax year ending December 31 if necessary for the IRS to accept this election for S corporation status in the event the corporation is ultimately not qualified to make a section 444 election.

Part III   Qualified Subchapter S Trust (QSST) Election Under Section 1361(d)(2)*

Income beneficiary's name and address	Social security number
Trust's name and address	Employer identification number

Date on which stock of the corporation was transferred to the trust (month, day, year) . . . . ▶   / /

In order for the trust named above to be a QSST and thus a qualifying shareholder of the S corporation for which this Form 2553 is filed, I hereby make the election under section 1361(d)(2). Under penalties of perjury, I certify that the trust meets the definitional requirements of section 1361(d)(3) and that all other information provided in Part III is true, correct, and complete.

_____   _____
Signature of income beneficiary or signature and title of legal representative or other qualified person making the election   Date

*Use Part III to make the QSST election only if stock of the corporation has been transferred to the trust on or before the date on which the corporation makes its election to be an S corporation. The QSST election must be made and filed separately if stock of the corporation is transferred to the trust **after** the date on which the corporation makes the S election.

Form **2553** (Rev. 12-2007)

Appendix 1

Appendix 2

Consent to Election to Be Treated
as an S Corporation

The undersigned shareholder hereby consents to the election of [name of corporation, address, and employer identification number] to be treated as an S corporation under §1362(a) of the Internal Revenue Code of 1986.

Name and address of consenting shareholder:

Number of shares owed:

Date(s) shares were acquired:

Social Security number of consenting shareholder or employer identification number:

Month and day on which shareholder's taxable year ends:

Date: (Signature)

Consent of Spouse*

The shares listed above are community property. I hereby consent to the election of [name of corporation] to be treated as an S corporation under §1362(a) of the Internal Revenue Code of 1986.

Date: (Signature)

Spouse's name:

Address:

Social Security number:

Taxable year:

---

* *Commentary:* Consent of spouse to be used only in community property states. For a discussion of this form, see ¶402.02.

Appendix 2

Appendix 3

§1368(e)(3) Election to Distribute Accumulated Earnings and Profits Before Accumulated Adjustments Account

CERTIFIED MAIL
RETURN RECEIPT REQUESTED
Internal Revenue Service
[Address]

[Name of corporation, address, and employer identification number] hereby elects under §1368(e)(3) to treat those distributions not exceeding accumulated adjustments accounts during the taxable year as distributions out of accumulated earnings and profits rather than distributions from the accumulated adjustments accounts. This election applies only to distributions made during the taxable year ending [date].

Dated: [Name of corporation]

                      By: _____
                           [Name and title]

Consent of Shareholders

The undersigned being all the shareholders of [name of corporation] receiving a distribution during the taxable year ending [date] hereby consent to the above election under §1368(e)(3) being made by the corporation with respect to distributions made during the taxable year.

Shareholder Signature	Shareholder Identification Number	
_____	_____	_____
[Name of shareholder]		Date
_____	_____	_____
[Name of shareholder]		Date

Commentary: For a discussion of this form, see ¶804.17 and ¶1004.03.

Appendix 3

Appendix 4

Shareholders' Agreement

This Agreement entered into this _____ day of _____, 2000, by and between _____, a [state] corporation with its principal place of business at _____ (hereinafter referred to as the "Corporation") and the individuals detailed on Schedule Shareholders.

(Each of the aforementioned individuals hereinafter sometimes referred to as a "Shareholder" or collectively referred to as the "Shareholders").

WHEREAS, the shareholders are the sole shareholders of the corporation which has made an S corporate election pursuant to the Internal Revenue Code of 1986; and

WHEREAS, if the corporation lost its S status without the written consent of more than 50% of the outstanding stock prior thereto it would tend to disrupt the affairs of the corporation; and

WHEREAS, the corporation and the shareholders realize that in the event of the death of any one of them, or the sale of his, her or its stock during his or her lifetime, should in any such event the stock of the corporation owned by such shareholder pass into the ownership or control of a person other than the remaining shareholders it would tend to disrupt the harmonious and successful management and control of the corporation; and

WHEREAS, it is the earnest desire of the corporation and the shareholders to avoid the happening of any such unfortunate contingency by assuring to the remaining shareholders an orderly succession to the ownership and control of the corporation through the acquisition of the shares of a shareholder at the time of his or her death or upon prior sale;

NOW, THEREFORE, in consideration of the mutual promises of the parties hereto and of the mutual benefits to be gained by the performance thereof, the parties hereto hereby AGREE:

Appendix 4

1. The outstanding capital stock of the corporation consists of _____ (__) shares of common stock, which are owned by the shareholders as detailed in Schedule Shareholders.

The shareholders agree to endorse the certificate or certificates of stock held by them, or hereafter acquired, as follows: "This certificate of stock is subject to a stock purchase agreement dated _____ ___, 2002, between _____ and its shareholders to, *inter alia*, preserve S corporate status and is transferable only in accordance with such agreement."

A. Except as herein provided each shareholder, as a party hereto, shall not sell, give, assign, transfer, encumber, pledge, hypothecate or otherwise dispose of his or her shares of the corporation now or hereafter owned by him or her, except under and pursuant and in compliance with the terms and conditions of this agreement and the corporation agrees that it will not transfer or recognize any transfer of such shares except in compliance herewith, and any such transfer or attempted transfer not in accordance with the terms and conditions contained in this agreement shall be of no effect, null and void. Further, each shareholder agrees that no person may acquire the ownership of any shares (beneficial or otherwise) of the corporation's stock, if such transfer or acquisition would cause this corporation to lose its S status, unless the shareholder(s) owning more than 50% of the outstanding stock in writing consent otherwise prior to the transfer. A copy of this agreement shall be filed in the offices of the corporation.

B. Except as herein provided, each of the shareholders covenants and agrees with each other and the corporation to keep registered in his, her or its respective name upon the books of the corporation the certificates representing the ownership of his, her or its capital stock in the corporation.

C. The Corporation shall: (i) take no action which would cause it to become an "ineligible corporation" pursuant to §1361(b)(2) of the Internal Revenue Code of 1986, as amended or modified; or (ii) not issue any debt which would cause it to be classified other than "straight debt" under §1361(c)(5)(B).

Appendix 4

2. Upon the death of any natural shareholder (i.e., a human being), the surviving shareholders shall purchase, and the executor or administrator (hereinafter called the "legal representative") of the deceased shareholder will sell to the surviving shareholders, all of the stock of the corporation owned by the deceased at the time of his or her death, for the price and upon the terms and conditions hereinafter stipulated.

* * *

6. A. If a shareholder wishes to dispose of his, her or its stock in the corporation during life, the terms of paragraph 3 through 5 (detailing the procedure for sale and the price determination) shall govern except that:

(1) The selling shareholder shall give written notice to the other shareholders and the corporation of the desire to sell and they shall have 30 days to respond as to whether or not they wish to purchase the stock with closing to occur no later than 150 days after notice is given of the desire to sell.

* * *

B. A shareholder shall be required to sell his or her stock pursuant to Paragraph 6A, hereof if an event of transfer detailed in Paragraph 7 [see Appendix 8] occurs, except that the shareholder who commits an event of transfer shall not be required to give written notice to the corporation and shareholder of the sale of stock.

C. In the event that anyone purchases the stock pursuant to Paragraph 6, the terms and conditions of this shareholders' agreement shall be binding upon the stock so purchased in regard to sales, transfers, gifts, etc.

D. The shareholder selling the stock shall abstain with respect to any corporate action involving the sale of the shareholder's stock.

Commentary: For a discussion of this form, see ¶1106.02 and ¶1203.01.

Appendix 4

Appendix 5

Disposition of Stock
Upon Shareholder's Death—
Valuation Language

3. Upon the death of a natural shareholder (hereinafter the "decedent"), the purchase price of the decedent's stock of the corporation shall be determined as of the date of death of the shareholder and this price shall be composed of three categories of corporate assets: Assets capable of being appraised; assets determined by market value; and all others, as follows:

I. As to assets capable of being appraised, the price shall be determined as follows: Within 30 days after the legal representative is qualified and appointed, the decedent's estate shall select an appraiser with the corporation to select an appraiser 30 days after the death of the decedent. Both appraisers shall then select an appraiser at random. The three appraisers shall each then appraise the assets capable of being appraised of the corporation within 60 days after their appointment, submitting their appraisals in writing to the corporation and the decedent's estate to value the corporation's assets capable of being appraised at the date of death of the decedent. The accountant for the corporation shall add the appraisals together and then divide them by the number of appraisals submitted to arrive at the average fair market value of the corporation's assets capable of being appraised at the date of death of the decedent. After the fair market value of the assets capable of being appraised is arrived at by the accountant for the corporation, the decedent's percentage of stock ownership at death in the corporation shall be multiplied by the corporation against the fair market value of the assets capable of being appraised to arrive at the appraised asset portion of the purchase price for the stock.

II. As to corporate assets capable of being determined by market value, such as stock listed on a national securities exchange, cash, Treasury Bills, etc., the market value of these assets shall be determined as of the date of death of the decedent shareholder by the accountant for the Corporation; after the market value segment of the assets of the Corporation

Appendix 5

Appendices

is determined, the decedent's percentage of stock in the corporation at date of death is to be multiplied against the market value of the corporate assets to determine the market value portion of the purchase price for the stock.

III. As to the remaining assets of the corporation not reflected in the appraisals and market value set forth above, the book value of these assets shall be determined as of the date of death the decedent, and the decedent's percentage of stock at death in the corporation shall be multiplied against the book value of the assets to arrive at the book value portion of the purchase price for the stock.

IV. At the date of death of the decedent shareholder, the accountant for the corporation shall determine the liabilities of the corporation, actual and/or contingent (including tax liabilities accrued to the date of death), and the accountant shall multiply decedent's percentage of stock ownership at death in the corporation against the total amount of corporate liabilities determined by the accountant as of the date of death of the decedent shareholder, to determine the portion of liabilities to be subtracted from the valuation of gross assets as outlined in Paragraphs 3(I)-(III) hereof.

V. The purchase price of the stock at decedent's death shall be the sum of the book value portion, the market value portion and the appraised asset portion less the liability portion computed above and the corporation shall serve written notice on each of the shareholders of this price. An example will clarify:

Example

Assume that shareholder A dies owning 5% of the corporation. At the time of death of shareholder A, the corporation has a $100,000 mortgage on the real estate plus liability to suppliers of $500,000. Three appraisers are selected, one by the estate, one by the corporation and the last at random. All the appraisals deduct the mortgage and the estate's appraisal was for $1 million; the corporation's, $1,100,000 and the

Appendix 5

random appraisal, $900,000. These three appraisals are added together and divided by three to arrive at $1 million for the fair market value at date of death for the real estate. Multiplying $1 million by 5% yields $50,000, the fair market value of the real estate at death for shareholder A. The only other asset the corporation has at the date of death of shareholder A is a bank account which has $100,000 in it. 5% times $100,000 yields $5,000; A's stock is worth $30,000 at death ($5,000 plus $50,000 less $25,000 [5% of $500,000 of supplier liabilities]).

VI. In terms of the appraisals and valuation of the stock, the following shall govern:

1. If the legal representative of the decedent's estate is not appointed within 30 days of decedent's death, an appraiser in _____ County shall be selected by the Corporation at random for the deceased shareholder. If the corporation does not have an accountant as of the date of death of the decedent shareholder, one shall be selected at random from the list of accountants detailed in the [state] Telephone Book/Yellow Pages.

2. The corporation and the decedent's estate shall each bear the costs of their respective appraisals and shall share equally the cost of the appraiser chosen at random.

3. In the event that a party to this agreement fails to chose an appraiser within the time limits prescribed, this shall be deemed a default and the appraisal process shall be conducted without this appraisal.

4. All parties to this agreement should use their best efforts to ensure that the appraisals required herein should be completed within 90 days of decedent's death. For purposes of this agreement, if a legal representative is not appointed for a decedent within 45 days after a decedent's death, the Corporation and/or a shareholder who is a party to this agreement will have the right to file a petition in a court of law to have temporary letters of administration granted so as to allow the appraisal process set forth herein to operate.

Appendix 5

5. In the event that it cannot be verified that a shareholder died (e.g., he or she is missing in action in a war), the shareholder's interest shall not be conveyed until there is an official proceeding determining the shareholder's death.

6. Any appraiser to be selected at random shall be selected from the list of appraisers in the County of _____ capable of performing these functions, with the accountant for the corporation assisting.

7. If any appraisal is 15% more or less than the appraisal submitted by the appraiser selected at random by the corporation and the decedent's estate, then this appraisal shall not be used to determine the fair market value of the real estate.

8. The book value at the date of death of the shareholder of all assets that are not subject to valuation by market value and/or appraisal shall be determined by the accountant for the corporation using generally accepted accounting principles consistently applied with the accrual basis method of accounting to be used to report income and expenses of the corporation. The accountant shall only value the assets on the balance sheet and no consideration shall be given to the assets not reflected therein such as goodwill. The book value and market value computation by the accountant shall be completed at the same time the appraisals detailed in Paragraph 3(I) are completed.

9. The corporation shall furnish upon receipt copies of all appraisals and notices to the shareholders.

10. The accountant, in performing the valuation process as set forth in Paragraph 3(I)-(IV) shall use generally accepted accounting principles consistently applied. If the accountant has any question about including or excluding an asset, liability or portion thereof, the accountant shall use his or her best judgment for valuing same, with the accountant to rely on counsel of his or her own choosing to assist in the case a question arises, informing the parties to this agreement of such a difficulty, with the corporation and decedent's estate to

Appendix 5

pay equally for the counsel. If, subsequently, the accountant makes his or her determination for the purchase price of the stock, and the valuation of the asset and/or liability changes, no adjustment shall be made to the price determination set forth in Paragraph 3(V) hereof. An example will illustrate:

Example

On the date the shareholder dies, the corporation: (1) receives notice from the Internal Revenue Service that it will audit three tax years prior to death of the decedent; and (2) is embroiled in two litigations: (i) whether an individual is a shareholder of the corporation; and (ii) whether the corporation owes a creditor $75,000 or $125,000 plus attorneys' fees. The accountant obtains a legal opinion from an attorney paid for equally by the corporation and the decedent's estate as to the effect that the three items above will have on the purchase price, with that determination to be final. The accountant believes that the tax audit will not produce any tax liability, and thus puts down "zero" for any contingent liability regarding the audit; deems that the individual is not a shareholder of the corporation; and believes that the liability with the creditor will settle for $75,000. Subsequently, after the accountant determines the purchase price, the Internal Revenue Service and the corporation settle for a tax liability of $1,000,000; the individual is deemed a shareholder of the corporation, and the liability is settled for $125,000 plus attorneys' fees. The IRS tax liability of $1,000,000, the determination that the individual is a shareholder, and the liability being settled for $125,000 plus attorneys' fees, has no effect on the purchase price.

11. If one party disputes the accountant's determination as to the purchase price, the disputing party shall serve notice on the other party(ies) within ten (10) days after receipt by the party of the price determination set forth in Paragraph 3(V), with arbitration to commence twenty (20) days after the party disputing the valuation serves notice on the

Appendix 5

other party(ies). Each party to the disagreement shall select one arbitrator, and the arbitrators so selected shall appoint either one or two arbitrators, so as to create an odd number of arbitrators. In the event the arbitrators selected by the parties cannot agree on the appointment of the additional arbitrator or arbitrators, then the missing arbitrator shall be selected at random from the list of arbitrators of the American Arbitration Association. The award of the arbitrators so selected need only be by majority and not unanimous. Any award rendered by said arbitrators shall be conclusive and binding upon all persons interested hereunder and judgment may be entered in any court having jurisdiction thereof. The loser shall bear all costs of the arbitration, and in the case of two or more losers, jointly and severally. All arbitrations shall be conducted in the City where the Corporation has its principal offices. The losing party(ies) shall bear the entire costs of the arbitration, including the winning party(ies)' legal fees and costs with the arbitrators to make a finding as to winning and losing parties.

Commentary: For a discussion of this form, see ¶1106.03.

Appendix 5

Appendix 6

*Resolution of Disputes**

If one party disputes the accountant's determination as to the purchase price, the disputing party shall serve notice on the other party(ies) within ten (10) days after receipt by the party of the price determination set forth in Paragraph 3(V), with arbitration to commence twenty (20) days after the party disputing the valuation serves notice on the other party(ies). Each party to the disagreement shall select one arbitrator, and the arbitrators so selected shall appoint either one or two arbitrators, so as to create an odd number of arbitrators. In the event the arbitrators selected by the parties cannot agree on the appointment of the additional arbitrator or arbitrators, then the missing arbitrator shall be selected at random from the list of arbitrators of the American Arbitration Association. The award of the arbitrators so selected need only be by majority and not unanimous. Any award rendered by said arbitrators shall be conclusive and binding upon all persons interested hereunder and judgment may be entered in any court having jurisdiction thereof. The loser shall bear all costs of the arbitration, and in the case of two or more losers, jointly and severally. All arbitrations shall be conducted in the City where the Corporation has its principal offices. The losing party(ies) shall bear the entire costs of the arbitration, including the winning party(ies)' legal fees and costs with the arbitrators to make a finding as to winning and losing parties.

---

* Commentary: This language is the same as included in Appendix 5, Par. 3(VI)(11), Disposition of Stock Upon Shareholder's Death—Valuation Language. For a discussion of this form, see ¶1106.05.

Appendix 6

Appendix 7

Minimum Distribution

4.4. Minimum Distribution

(a) Each Shareholder recognizes that the Shareholder will be taxed individually for Federal, State and local tax purposes on their pro rata share of the S corporation's taxable income for each taxable year. The S corporation shall deliver to each Shareholder as promptly as practicable following the end of each taxable year a Schedule K-1 and such other materials relating to the Shareholder's holdings in the S corporation as reasonably necessary to permit the Shareholder to complete and file the Shareholder's Federal and State income tax returns with respect to that taxable year. To the extent it shall be consistent with the provisions of the laws of the State of _____ and existing credit and other obligations of the S corporation, the S corporation shall (subject to not being rendered insolvent) distribute to each Shareholder with respect to each taxable year, if practicable in installments consistent with the Shareholder's obligations to make estimated tax payments, an amount not less than the amount of tax the Shareholder would be required to pay if (a) the Shareholder was a _____ resident and (b) all the income attributable to the Shareholder was taxable at the highest marginal tax rate for individuals by the federal government, _____ State and [city] (taking into account the deductibility of _____ State and [city] taxes in computing federal taxes).

(b) For purposes of this minimum distribution provision of income detailed in §4.4 hereof: (i) No provision shall be made for alternative minimum tax or similar provision; and (ii) the distributions of cash shall be made on or before March 15 of the year following the taxable year when the income was earned, and the S corporation can make the distribution of cash based on estimated income, with the distribution to be reduced by the amount of cash previously distributed to the Shareholders during the taxable year when the income was earned. An example will illustrate how the minimum distribution provision works for federal tax purposes (state tax considerations are not reflected:

Appendix 7

Example

Assume that an S corporation is composed of two individual Shareholders, Lauren and Roz, each owning a 50% interest. At the end of the S corporation's first year of operations, the S corporation had the following income reported on its federal tax return (Form 1120S): capital gains of $100,000; ordinary income of $200,000. The minimum distribution for each Shareholder for federal tax purposes shall be (assuming that the taxable year is 2000) $49,600 ((20% x $100,000 = $20,000) + (39.6% x $200,000 = $79,200) ÷ 2)).

(c) For purposes of determining the amount of distribution required by §4.4(a) and (b), the accountant for the S corporation shall make this determination each taxable year using generally accepted accounting principles consistently applied.

Commentary: For a discussion of this form, see ¶1106.06.

Appendix 7

Appendix 8

Events Requiring Transfer of Stock

7. A. For purposes of this agreement each of the following events shall be deemed an "Event of Transfer" which shall give rise to the transfer of shares referred to above per Paragraph 6 (see Appendix 4*]:

(1) bankruptcy, not discharged within 30 days after the filing of a petition, or the pursuit of the shareholder of any state creditor remedy;

(2) the attempt to transfer any of the shareholder's shares in the corporation to another person without the prior written consent of all parties hereto in the manner herein provided;

(3) conviction of a crime involving moral turpitude.

---

* *Commentary:* Appendix 4, Paragraph 6, should be read in conjunction with this appendix. For a discussion of this form, see ¶1106.07.

Appendix 8

Appendix 9

Best Efforts Language

The Shareholder shall not, directly or indirectly, at any time during the term of this Agreement, be engaged in any other professional or business activity (such as teaching at a university), other than serving as an Employee of the S Corporation pursuant to the employment agreement the shareholder entered into as a condition for signing this Agreement, whether or not such activity is pursued for gain, profit or pecuniary advantage. However, the Shareholder may invest his or her assets in such form or manner as will not require his or her services to the operation of the affairs of the Company in which such investments are made, and ownership of 5% or less of a company traded on any securities exchange will not be deemed a default hereunder. If the Shareholder is elected or appointed a Director or Officer of the S Corporation, at any time during the term hereof, the Shareholder will serve in such capacity or capacities without further compensation; but nothing herein shall be constructed as requiring the election or employment of the Shareholder as such Director or Officer.

Commentary: For a discussion of this form, see ¶1106.08.

Appendix 9

Appendix 10

Covenant Not to Compete Language

23. A. While an individual is a shareholder and/or consultant, he or she will not, directly or indirectly, during the term of this Agreement and for a period of two (2) years thereafter:

I. engage in, be involved in or participate in any manner either as an owner, member, partner, proprietor, shareholder, agent, consultant, salesperson, broker, employer, employee, principal, director, manager, participant, officer, joint venturer, etc., in a business or company engaged in or involved in a business like the Company in countries [state(s) for purposes of the United States] where the Company is doing more than 5% of its business, however, ownership of less than 5% interest in a company traded on any public stock exchange shall not be deemed a default hereunder;

II. canvass, solicit or accept any business from any other business competing with the Company or from any present or past customers of the Company;

III. give any other person, company, employer, firm, business, entity or corporation the right to canvass, solicit, or accept any business from any other business competing with the Company or from any present or past customers of it;

IV. request or advise any present or future users of the Company's services to withdraw, curtail, or cancel their business with the Company;

V. disclose to any other business, entity, company, employer, firm or corporation the names of past or present customers of the Company;

VI. directly or indirectly induce, or attempt to influence, any shareholder, agent, manager, director, officer, consultant, broker, salesperson of the Company to terminate his, her or its employment;

VII. disclose to anyone other than the Company's present shareholders the names of the Company's customers, their specifications, requirements, needs, products sold to them, etc.; and/or

VIII. disclose to anyone the Company's products and pricing cost information; customer prospects, customer lists, and various sales techniques; and methods and tools of how to run the Company's operations.

B. Notwithstanding anything to the contrary herein, a Shareholder recognizes and acknowledges that the Company's trade secrets and confidential or proprietary information, including such trade secrets or information as may exist from time to time, and information as to the identity of customers of the Company, and other similar items, are valuable, special and unique assets of the Company's business, access to and knowledge of which are essential to the performance of the duties of Shareholder hereunder. Shareholder will not, in whole or in part, disclose, during the term of this Agreement and for a period ending two (2) years from and after the termination of this Agreement, such secrets or confidential or proprietary information to any person, firm, corporation, association or other entity for any reason or purpose whatsoever, except as required by Shareholder's duties to the Company, nor shall Shareholder make use of any such property for his own purposes or for the benefit of any person, firm, corporation or other entity (except the Company) under any circumstances. As used in this Agreement, "Affiliate" shall mean any person, firm or corporation that, directly or indirectly, through one or more intermediaries, controls, is controlled by, or is under common control with, the Company, whether such control is through stock ownership, contract or otherwise; or

C. Because of the fact that the Company values its customers, prospects, sales techniques, methods and tools, its price lists, etc., the Shareholder is willing to enter into these covenants to protect the Company against unfair competition. Shareholder further realizes that by entering into these covenants he or she will seriously be affecting his or her income for the future. Notwithstanding this limitation, he or she is agreeable to these covenants for the reasons aforesaid.

Appendix 10

D. It is the desire and intent of the parties that the provisions of all Paragraph 23 shall be enforced to the fullest extent permissible under the laws and public policies applied in each jurisdiction in which enforcement is sought, including the right to an injunction.

Commentary: For a discussion of this form, see ¶1106.08.

Appendix 10

Appendix 11

Closing S Corporation Books
on Sale of S Corporation Stock

In the event of a sale of stock, other than at the beginning or end of the S corporation's taxable year, then all the shareholders of the S corporation shall take all necessary steps to ensure that the books of the corporation are closed for the selling shareholder so that the selling shareholder will report income, expense, loss, gain, etc. as if the corporation ended its taxable year on the date of sale; there shall be no proration of income, expense, loss, gain, etc. for the selling shareholder for the portion of the corporation's taxable year that the selling shareholder was a stockholder of the S corporation. An example will illustrate:

Example

A, B and C are equal shareholders in XYZ, Inc., a calendar year S corporation. A sells her shares to B and C on 6/30. As of 6/30, XYZ, Inc. had a profit of $300 ($100 to each shareholder); as of 12/31, XYZ, Inc. broke even. Under the closing of books method which A, B and C elected on 6/30, A will report her $100 of income. If the proration method had been used, A would have no income to report.

Commentary: For a discussion of this form, see ¶1106.09.

Appendix 11

Appendix 12

Notice of Revocation of
Subchapter S Election Under §1362(a)

CERTIFIED MAIL
RETURN RECEIPT REQUESTED
Internal Revenue Service Center
[Address]

Name:

Address:

Employer Identification Number:

Service Center:

Voting shares issued and outstanding:

Nonvoting shares issued and outstanding:

　　The above corporation, [name of corporation], hereby revokes its election made under §1362(a) to be taxed as an S corporation, made by it on Form 2553 filed with the District Director, on _____. It is intended that this revocation shall be effective on _____. Attached are the consents to the revocation by shareholders owning more than one-half of the issued and outstanding shares.

Dated:

　　　　　　　　　　　　　　　　　[Name of corporation]

　　　　　　　By:　　_____
　　　　　　　　　　　　[Name and title]

Commentary: For a discussion of this form, see ¶1202 and ¶1203.02.

Appendix 12

Appendix 13

Consent to Election to
Have Items Assigned Under
Normal Accounting Rules—§1362(e)(3)(B)

The undersigned, being all of the shareholders of [name of corporation], at any time during the S short year beginning _____, and all shareholders on the first day of the C short year, beginning _____, hereby consent to the aforementioned corporation's election under §1362(e)(3)(B) to have the rules in §1362(e)(2) not apply.

Dated:

                               [Name of corporation]

                 By: _____

                                 [Name and title]

Shareholder Signature	Shareholder Identification Number	
_____ [Name of shareholder]	_____	_____ Date
_____ [Name of shareholder]	_____	_____ Date

Commentary: For a discussion of this form, see ¶1207.01.

Appendix 14

Election to Close Books Upon Termination of Interest by S Corporation Shareholder—§1377(a)(2)

CERTIFIED MAIL
RETURN RECEIPT REQUESTED
Internal Revenue Service Center
[Address]

Name:

Address:

Employer Identification Number:

Service Center:

Voting shares issued and outstanding:

Nonvoting shares issued and outstanding:

The above corporation, [name of corporation], hereby elects under §1377(a)(2) to have the rules provided in §1377(a)(1) applied as if the taxable year consisted of two taxable years.

Date corporate year ends:

Name of shareholder who terminated
entire interest in corporation:

Cause of termination:

Date of termination:

Dated: [Name of corporation]

By: _____
[Name and title]

Commentary: For a discussion of this form, see ¶1208.02.

Appendix 14

Appendix 15

*Shareholders' Consent—§1377(a)(2)**

We, the undersigned shareholders of [name of corporation, address, identification number] hereby consent to the election to close the books of the corporation pursuant to §1377(a)(2).

Shareholder   Shareholder
Signature   Identification Number

_____   _____
[Name of shareholder]   Date

_____   _____   _____
[Name of shareholder]   Date

---

* *Commentary:* This consent form should be appended to Appendix 14, Election to Close Books. For a discussion of this form, see ¶1208.02.

Appendix 15

Appendix 16

Election to Close Books Under Reg. §1.1368-1(g)(2)(i)

[Name of corporation, address, identification number] hereby elects, pursuant to Reg. §1.1368-1(g)(2)(i) to close its book as of [date of disposition of stock] and to treat its taxable year consisting of two taxable years, the first of which ends on [date of disposition of stock]. This election is made because [detail facts and circumstances concerning disposition of stock as well as specify the number of shares effected].

The shareholders detailed below consent to this election for the corporation's taxable year ended [current taxable year]. This election is being made under penalties of perjury.

Consent of Shareholders

The undersigned being all the shareholders of [name of corporation hereby consent to the above election under Reg. §1.1368-1(g)(2)(i) being made by the corporation.

Shareholder   Shareholder
Signature   Identification No.

_____   _____   _____
[Name of shareholder]   Date

_____   _____   _____
[Name of shareholder]   Date

Commentary: For a discussion of this form, see ¶1208.02.

Appendix 16

Case Table

Cases found in this book's text and footnotes are listed below.

References are to paragraph (¶) numbers.

A

Al Assaf 911.11
Allen, V. 908
Allison, W.M., Est. 208.05
Anclote Psychiatric Center, Inc. .714.04
Arrowsmith, F.D. 605.01
Au, L.Y.S. 1307.06
Auld, F.G. 403.13
Austin, L.E. 501.03

B

Bank of Winnfield & Trust Co. . 205.04,
    603.01
Barden Development, Inc.: The
    Majestic Star Casino, LLC v. . 203.03,
    1202.04, 1408.08
Barnes. 910
Barnhart: Collier v. . . . 1104.01, 1305.10
Barron, W.L. 716.02
Barr, B. 904.08, 904.14
Beard .902.02
Bell, III, W.H. 205.04
Bergstrom, K.A. 1307.06
Bianchi, A.J. 707.02
Bingo, W. 711
Black, Estate of 1109.03
Bolding, D.E. 904.10
Braun, Jr., F.C. 1119.04
Bresler, D. 605.01
Brooks 904.14
Brown Group 806.01
Brutsche, R.E. 402.02, 603.01
Buono, G. 606
Burnstein, S.P. 904.10
Byrum, M.A. 1109.03, 1304.03

C

Cain, R.L. 1110

Carlos, T.R. 911.05, 911.11
Carter, Mattie K., Trust v. U.S. . 301.02,
    911.10
Chesterton, Inc. v. Chesterton 210
Chevy Chase Motor Co., Inc. . . .802.18
Chiapetti, D.L. 1119.06
Chilton, R.G., In re 1103.16
Chin 712
Cibotti 1115.02
Coggin Automotive Corporation .806.01
Collier v. Barnhart 1104.01, 1305.10
Colorado Gas Compression, Inc. .802.01
Colorcon, Inc. v. USA 1211.11
Corn Products Ref. Co. 605.01
Craft 715
Crummey, D.C. 303.02
Culnen, D.J. 205.05, 904.01, 904.10
Cusick, T.H. 1305.11

D

Dailey, Est. of E.M. . . 1109.08, 1116.04,
    1307.08
D'Angelo 715
David Dung Le, M.D., Inc. 209
Davis, C. 102.09
Davis, E.D. 1119.05
Davis, T.C. 716.04
Dean, W.K. 606
DeLorean 716.06
Dessauer, R. 603.01
DiLeonardo, S.P. 903.04
Ding, P.B. . 707.04, 716.03, 722.10, 1105
Dynamic Energy, Inc. 1121

E

Eisenberg, I. 1106.10, 1109.07
Elkins, Jr., Est. 703.05
Evans, H.W. 1210.06

EVA

References are to paragraph (¶) numbers.

Merritt, Sr., J.H. 712.01
Mitchell Offset Plate Serv., Inc. . . .401.04

N

Nessa 1103.16
Nielsen Co., A.F. 208.05
Norwalk, W. 1210.08
Novell, S. 208.05

O

Oden .904.01
Ofria, C. 606
Old Colony Trust Co. 1109.03
Old Merchant National Bank & Trust
  Co. of Battle Creek 1307.06
Old Virginia Brick Co., Inc. 1109.06
Oren, D.G. 904.10
Osteen, H.E. 711
Osteopathic Medical Oncology and
  Hematology, P.C. 501.03
Oswald, V.E. 102.13, 208.07

P

Pacific Coast Music Jobbers,
  Inc. 403.14
Pahl, S.D. 202.07
Papermaster, M. 908
Parker, R. v. Saunders, C.R. 1202.04
Patterson v. Shumate 1103.15
Payne, A.H. 711
Peracchi, D.J. 904.01, 1117.01
Petroleum Corp. of Texas 806.01
Pfaff .1127.01
Pierre 1126.01
Pike, S.J. 904.11
Pittsfield Coal & Oil Co., Inc. . . . 1307.12
Pleasant Summit Land Corp. 1307.06
Plotkin, C.W. 1302.06
Poulter, F.E. 1202.02
Prashker, R.M. 904.10
Prewitt 1007
Proctor: Watson v. 707.03

Q

Quinlivan: Zenz v. 1208.06, 1209.01

R

Rabinowitz, L. 711
RACMP Enterprises 501.03, 722.06
Radtke, J. 102.09, 716.02, 716.03,
  722.10, 1105, 1126.01, 1307.06
Reichardt, Est. of 1109.03
Remington, W. 1305.09
Reser, R.J. 1121
Ringgold Telephone Company . .802.22
Rogers 718
Rosenberg, A. 404.08
Rountree Cotton Co., Inc. 904.13
Rousey v. Jacoway 1103.15
Russon, S.C. 404.10

S

S & B Realty Co. 802.18
Sather, L.L. 1109.10
Saunders, C.R.: Parker, R. v. . . .1202.04
Sauvigne, D.J. 907.02
Sawaf, A.H. 1103
Schauerhomer, Est. of 1109.03
Schumacher, E.J. 911.11
Schutt, Estate of 1109.03
Seda, L.V. 1209.02
Selfe, E.M. 904.05
Selig, A.H. 1108
Settimo, Frank 1103.10
Shapiro, Bernard 103.03
Shea, Est. of J.F. 605.01
Shumate: Patterson v. 1103.15
Smith, E.G. 722.06
St. Charles Investment Co. 404.08,
  404.13, 710.01, 804.02, 911.08, 911.11
St. Louis County Bank, Exr. . . .1120.03
Stamoulis 703.01
Stinnett, Jr., J.L. 208.05
Stone III, Estate 1109.03
Strangi, Est. of 1109.03, 1109.09,
  1120.03, 1307.08
Sunny Vending Co. 103.01

SUN

Finding Lists

Citations found in this book's text are listed below under the following categories:

Internal Revenue Code Sections, Regulations, Temporary Regulations, Proposed Regulations, Revenue Rulings, Revenue Procedures, IRS Letter Rulings, Technical Advice Memoranda, and Notices.

References are to paragraph (¶) numbers.

Internal Revenue Code Sections

1(e) 1601; 1603; 1603.03; 1603.04	45F(c)(3)(a) 1129
1(g) 1102	45F(c)(3)(b) 1129
1(h) 611; 1301.07; 1301.10	45F(d) 1129
	45F(d)(2) 1129
1(h)(11) 609.04; 804.16; 804.17; 1209.02; 1209.04	45F(f) 1129
	47 .... 1004.02
	50 .... 903.02
1(h)(11)(D)(i) 702	50(a)(1) 903.02
2(a) 1601	50(c)(1) 903.02
10(b) 1504.09	52 .... 722.07
11 .... 205.04; 1207.04	52(a) 205.03; 722.07
11(b) 609.02; 802.01; 802.18; 804.01; 804.12	52(b)(1) 614
	54 .... 1508.03
	55 .... 404.11
16(a) 723.02	56 .... 102.12
21 .... 905.01	56(b)(2) 301.02
34 .... 804.13; 905.01; 905.05	56(g)(6) 909
	57 .... 602; 905.01
38 .... 404.03; 709; 1129	61 .... 610.08; 1125.04
38(b) 903.02	61(a) 703.04
38(b)(14) 1103.04	61(a)(12) 610.01
38(c) 802.15	62 .... 1604.06
39(d)(10) 1103.04	62(a)(1) 1604.06
41(f) 205.03	62(a)(4) 1604.06
44(d)(7) 722.06	62(a)(9) 1604.06
45E 1103.04	62(a)(19) 721.07
45E(a) 1103.04	63(a) 804.11; 804.17
45E(b) 1103.04	67 .... 715; 1604.06
45E(d)(1)(B) 1103.04	67(e) 1601; 1603
45E(e)(1) 1103.04	68 .... 1604.06
45F 1129	72 .... 1508.02
45F(a) 1129	72(a) 1604.01
45F(b) 1129	72(b) 1604.01
45F(c)(1) 1129	72(b)(2) 1302.06
45F(c)(2) 1129	72(e) 1604.01
	72(p) 1508.02; 1608

References are to paragraph (¶) numbers.

1221(a)(8) 722.06

1221(b)(2)(A) 722.06

1222 .... 1208.03

1223(2) 1126.02

1231 .... 602; 605.02; 606;
608.01; 901; 903.02;
905.01; 1002.01;
1106.10; 1208.04;
1307.06

1239 .... 102.11; 205.02; 607;
716.04; 1402.02

1239(c) 607

1244 .... 11; 910; 911.07;
1113; 1208.03;
1208.04; 1209.04;
1210.06

1244(b) 1113

1244(d)(4) 1113

1245 .... 710; 1209.04;
1210.01

1245(a)(3) 710

1250 .... 1209.04; 1210.01;
1604.06

1254 .... 102.11; 1210.01

1256 .... 1604.02

1256(a)(1) 603.02

1271(a)(1) 904.08; 904.14; 1117

1272(a)(2)(C) 603.02

1275(a)(1) 904.08

1281(b)(2)(A) 603.02

1293(a) 1609

1313(a) 912.02

1361 .... 202.01; 204.01;
204.02; 206.01;
208.02; 208.07;
208.08; 306.03;
704.01; 716.03;
1109.06; 1111; 1203;
1205.01; 1211.06;
1211.08; 1408.02;
1408.04; 1507.01

1361(b) 202.01; 202.03;
204.06; 401.05;
401.08; 1203.02;
1401

1361(b)(1) 201; 203; 206;
206.01; 208.05;
1211.02

1361(b)(1)(A) 202.01; 306.03;
1403.04

1361(b)(1)(B) 203.04; 204.02;
204.03; 204.04;
304.02

1361(b)(1)(C) 203.01; 204.01;
1109.05; 1127

1361(b)(1)(D) 208; 208.01; 208.02;
1205.01

1361(b)(2) 205.01; 207; 1401;
1403; 1403.02; 1409;
1409.02

1361(b)(2)(A) 206; 1402.02

1361(b)(2)(B) 403.11

1361(b)(3) 1211.02; 1401;
1402.01; 1403

1361(b)(3)(B) 1402

1361(b)(3)(B)(i) 1402.01; 1408.01;
1408.02

1361(b)(3)(B)(ii) 1402; 1403.04

1361(b)(3)(C) 1408.04

1361(b)(3)(D) 403.18; 1403.04;
1408.07

1361(c) 208.05

1361(c)(1) 202.02; 202.08;
203.03; 403.04

1361(c)(1)(B)(i) 202.08

1361(c)(1)(B)(ii) 202.08

1361(c)(1)(D) 403.20

1361(c)(2) 203.02; 301; 1109.05

1361(c)(2)(A) 203.07; 204.02;
303.03; 1109.06

1361(c)(2)(A)(i) 302.01; 303.01;
307.03

1361(c)(2)(A)(i)-(iv) 204.02

1361(c)(2)(A)(ii) 302.02; 303.02

1361(c)(2)(A)(iv) 305.01

1361(c)(2)(B) 202.08

1361(c)(2)(B)(i) 403.08

1361(c)(2)(B)(iii) 403.09

1361(c)(2)(B)(iv) 305.02; 403.07

1361(c)(2)(B)(v) 306.02; 306.03

References are to paragraph (¶) numbers.

666 Finding Lists

1368(c)(2) 911.06; 1004.02

1368(d)(1) 1002.01; 1002.03

1368(e) 1003.03

1368(e)(1) 1003.04; 1006

1368(e)(1)(A) 1003.03; 1208.07

1368(e)(1)(B) 1209.04

1368(e)(2) 912.02

1368(e)(3) 404.05; 609.03;
804.16; 804.17;
1004.03; 1204.02

1371 . . . . 208.07; 306.02

1371(a) 903.01; 1209;
1211.01; 1211.04

1371(b)(1) 404.08; 404.13;
804.02; 911.08

1371(b)(2) 1207.03

1371(b)(3) 404.08

1371(c)(1) 609.01; 1004.01

1371(c)(2) 609.04; 1209.04

1371(c)(3) 1004.02

1371(d)(1) 404.03

1371(d)(2) 803

1371(d)(3) 1004.02

1371(e) 912; 1207.02;
1210.06

1371(e)(1) 912.01

1372 . . . . 404.06; 706.01;
721.07; 1103

1372(a)(1) 706.01

1372(b) 706.02; 1103.19

1372(d)(2) 404.03

1374 . . . . 102.03; 102.08;
404.08; 404.11;
502.04; 608.01;
802.01; 802.03;
802.06; 802.07;
802.10; 802.15;
802.16; 802.18;
802.19; 802.20;
802.22; 804.13;
806.03; 905.05;
1109.05; 1112.02;
1202.05; 1206.04;
1208.05; 1210.04;
1210.06; 1211.02;
1211.07; 1302.05;
1405.02; 1405.06;
1607.03

1374(a) 404.07; 802.03;
1211.02

1374(a)-(b) 802.01

1374(b)(1) 802.03

1374(b)(2) 802.03; 802.15;
802.20

1374(b)(3) 802.03; 802.15;
802.20

1374(c) 908

1374(d) 802.11; 804.13

1374(d)(2) 802.01; 802.03

1374(d)(2)(A)(ii) 802.18

1374(d)(3) 802.01; 802.05;
802.11; 802.13;
1405.06

1374(d)(4) 802.01; 802.11

1374(d)(5) 802.01

1374(d)(6) 802.11; 802.18;
1405.06

1374(d)(7)(E) 802.10

1374(d)(8) 802.16; 1405.06

References are to paragraph (¶) numbers.

1375 . . . . 205.01; 609.02;
609.04; 802.19;
804.01; 804.02;
804.09; 804.13;
804.14; 804.16;
804.17; 905.05;
1004.03; 1109.05;
1204; 1204.01;
1211.02; 1302.05;
1402.02; 1409.02;
1611.06

1375(a) 804.12; 804.13;
804.14

1375(a)(1) 804.02

1375(a)(2) 804.02

1375(b)(1)(B) 802.01; 802.04;
804.02; 804.11

1375(b)(2) 804.02; 804.09;
804.13

1375(b)(4) 802.19; 804.13

1375(c) 804.13

1375(d) 804.14

1377 612

1377(a) 903.05; 905.05

1377(a)(1) 901; 901.01; 1106.09;
1211.02

1377(a)(2) 901.02; 903.03;
904.07; 1106.09;
1208.01; 1208.02;
1209.04

1377(a)(2)(B) 1208.02

1377(b)(1) 912.02

1377(b)(1)(B) 912.02

1377(b)(2)(B) 912.02

1378 . . . . 404.04; 502.02;
802.01

1381(a) 911.06

1401 . . . . 1602.02

1401(b) 1601

1401(b)(2) 615.02

1402 . . . . 203.06; 716.03;
716.05; 1604.06

1402(a)(13) 716.03

1411 . . . . 16; 102.09; 301.01;
306.07; 615.02;
1118.01; 1308; 1601;
1602.01; 1602.02;
1603.02; 1603.03;
1603.04; 1604;
1604.01; 1604.02;
1604.03; 1604.04;
1604.05; 1604.06;
1605.01; 1606;
1607.01; 1607.03;
1607.04; 1607.06;
1608; 1609; 1610;
1611; 1611.01;
1611.05; 1611.06;
1611.07; 1611.08;
1611.09

1411(a)(1) 1601; 1602.01;
1607.06; 1610

1411(a)(1)(B) 1608

1411(a)(1)(B)(i) 1607.06

1411(a)(2) 1601; 1602.02; 1603

1411(a)(2)(B)(ii) 1611.08

1411(b) 1601; 1602.02; 1610;
1611.01

1411(c)(1) 1601; 1608

1411(c)(1)(A) 1601

1411(c)(1)(A)(I) 1604.01

1411(c)(1)(A)(i) 1604.01; 1604.03;
1604.04; 1605.01;
1606

1411(c)(1)(A)(ii) 1604.02; 1605.01;
1611.02

1411(c)(1)(A)(iii) 1601; 1604.01;
1604.03; 1604.04;
1605.01; 1607.01;
1607.02; 1607.03;
1607.06

1411(c)(2) 1601; 1607.03

1411(c)(2)(A) 1610

1411(c)(3) 1601; 1606

1411(c)(4) 1601; 1607.01;
1607.02; 1607.03;
1607.04; 1607.06

1411(c)(4)(A) 1607.01

1411(c)(4)(B) 1607.01

1411(c)(5) 1601; 1608

References are to paragraph (¶) numbers.

Regulations

References are to paragraph (¶) numbers.

References are to paragraph (¶) numbers.

1.1375-1 (b) (1)	804.10
1.1375-1 (b) (3) (i)	804.09
1.1375-1 (b) (3) (ii)	804.09
1.1375-1 (d)	606
1.1375-1 (d) (2)	804.14
1.1375-l (d) (2)	804.14
1.1377-1 (a) (2) (i)	202.07
1.1377-1 (a) (2) (ii)	901.02
1.1377-1 (b) (1)	901.02
1.1377-1 (b) (2)	1208.02
1.1377-1 (b) (4)	901.02; 1208.02
1.1377-1 (b) (5)	1208.02
1.1377-1 (c)	1208.02
1.1377-2 (b)	912.01
1.1402 (a)-2 (h)	716.03
1.1411-2 (c)	1605.01
1.1411-4 (a) (1) (I)	1605.01
1.1411-4 (b)	1605.01
1.1411-4 (d) (2)	1603.04
1.1411-5 (a) (1)	1607.06
1.1411-5 (c) (1)	1604.01
1.1411-10 (e) (2)	1603
1.1502-1 (h)	1409.05
1.1502-13 (d) (1)	1405.05
1.6015-5 (b) (1)	1121
1.6037-1 (c)	405.04
1.6037-2	405.03
1.6043-1 (a)	1210.07
1.6161-1 (b)	1109.01
1.7872-4 (d) (1)	904.13
31.3121 (v) (2)-1 (e) (4)	723.11
53.6011-4 (a)	405.04
54.4975-11 (c)	1508.01
54.4980B-8	615.01
199-3 (n) (1)	722.06
199-3 (n) (2)	722.06
199-3 (n) (4)	722.06
199-3 (n) (5)	722.06
199-3 (n) (6)	722.06
301.7701-1	401.08
301.7701-2 (a)	1211.01; 1307.02
301.7701-2 (b)	1211.10
301.7701-2 (c) (2)	1403.03
301.7701-3	904.01; 1211.08; 1604.02; 1604.04
301.7701-3 (a)	1307.15
301.7701-3 (a);	401.04
301.7701-3 (b)	203.06
301.7701-3 (b) (1) (i)	1211.10
301.7701-3 (b) (2) (ii)	102.09; 716.03
301.7701-3 (c) (1) (i)	401.04
301.7701-3 (c) (1) (v) (C);	401.04
301.7701-5	206; 1403.01
301.9100-1	401.04; 1403.04
301.9100-3	401.04; 1403.04
601.601 (d) (2)	1610

Temporary Regulations

1.67-2T (b) (1)	715
1.163-8T (a) (3)	714.01; 911.06
1.163-8T (a) (4)	702
1.163-8T (a) (4) (i)	702
1.163-8T (a) (4) (i) (B)	911.06
1.163-8T (c) (4) (i)	714.01
1.163-8T (j)	714.01
1.163-8T (n) (3)	702
1.444-1T (a) (5) (i) (A)-(E)	502.04
1.444-1T (a) (5) (i) (C)	502.04
1.444-1T (b) (2) (iii)	502.04
1.444-1T (b) (5) (iii) (B)	502.04
1.444-3T (b) (1)	502.04
1.444-3T (b) (4) (i)	502.03
1.469 (p)-1T	1509
1.469-1T (e) (3) (vii)	911.05
1.469-2T	911.09
1.469-2T (c) (3)	911.07
1.469-2T (e) (1)	911.03; 911.04
1.469-5T (b) (2) (ii)	911.04
1.469-5T (c) (2)	911.04

References are to paragraph (¶) numbers.

Proposed Regulations

8113107 .... 723.01	9115020 .... 307.04
8203017 .... 401.06	9119070 .... 307.04
8211103 .... 804.03	9125010 .... 610.03
8336014 1202	9131006 .... 1109.03
8336069 .... 307.02	9213026 .... 1211.07
8351065 .... 1206.03	9309033 .... 1211.07
8411057 .... 1106.01	9310039 .... 1109.03
8417042 .... 603.01; 603.02	9311021 .... 303.02
8435153 .... 307.02	9314022 .... 403.11; 403.15
8506114 .... 208.02	9316015 .... 403.11
8515056 .... 804.05	9332006 .... 1109.03
8523097 .... 1205.01	9415007 .... 1109.03
8530100 .... 401.03	9424022 .... 401.04
8532076 .... 1210.09	9506011 .... 303.02; 307.04
8609052 .... 802.18; 1208.04	9512001 ...... 206; 401.08; 1403.01
8646036 .... 102.14	9520046 .... 1211.10
8711020 .... 1108.01	9526021 .... 403.08
8717024 .... 307.02	9546006 .... 1109.03
8721045 .... 307.04	9625031 .... 303.02
8739010 .... 1211.04	9626035 .... 403.11
8804015 .... 1108.01	9628002 .... 1405.04
8819041 .... 208.01	9644024 .... 1504.02; 1504.05
8823027 .... 1108.01	9703028 703
8828029 .... 208.01	9719009 .... 401.04
8835011 .... 401.04; 402.02	9721020 .... 1210.07
8904012 .... 804.03	9732023 703
8906035 .... 804.03	9735006 .... 1125.04
8915067 .... 204.05	9735008 .... 401.04
8921039 .... 804.03	9735019 .... 401.04
8938079 .... 404.12	9739014 .... 203.06
9003029 .... 1202.03	9745017 .... 203.06
9009010 .... 303.02	9750036 .... 1202; 1203.02
9011055 .... 208.02	9803008 .... 403.03; 403.10
9017010 .... 1205.02	9807023 .... 1402.02
9022045 .... 1109.05; 1109.07	9846005 .... 707.05
9026021 .... 1109.03	20008015 .... 203.06
9037011 .... 302.02	20010718 .... 103.01
9043013 .... 208.01	199935035 .... 1106.01
9046036 .... 1003.02	199936031 .... 204.02
9047010 .... 1206.03	199949019 .... 203.06
9049049 .... 208.01	200003014 .... 102.16; 1504.01;
9050021 .... 1108.01	1507.03
9101019 .... 208.01	200029050 .... 208.01
9102017 1506	200107018 .... 1307.17
9112017 .... 208.02	200118023 .... 103.01; 1307.16

Technical Advice Memoranda

Notices

Index

References are to paragraph (¶) numbers.

A

References are to paragraph (¶) numbers.

Built-in gains—continued
. rules for determining recognized . . . 903.01

Built-in gains tax, S corporation . . . 404.07, 802.01-802.22
. on accounts receivable during C corporation conversion to S corporation . . . 802.06
. anti-stuffing rules . . . 802.17
. for C corporation assets sold . . . 1112.02
. compared to passive investment income tax . . . 802.02
. computing . . . 802.03
. credits against . . . 802.15
. deductions against . . . 802.15
. estimated tax payments of . . . 802.21
. excess net passive income tax coordinated with . . . 804.13
. minimizing . . . 802.18
. passive investment income tax and . . . 802.19
. premium payment for an asset, use of minority discount for tax computation, . . . 802.22
. for QSubs . . . 802.16, 1405.06
. reduction in pass-through of . . . 804.15, 905.05
. reporting . . . 802.20

Built-in losses
. from bad debts . . . 802.08
. from completion of contract . . . 802.09
. in eliminated C corporation stock, adjustment to net unrealized built-in gain for . . . 1405.06
. limitations on partnership recognized . . . 802.12

Bundled rights . . . 1120.02

Burden of proof
. Code Sec. . . . 7491 1116.04, 1307.08
. cross-purchase agreements . . . 1125.03
. split dollar . . . 1125.04
. valuation of gifts . . . 1109.08

Business expenses, cash method required for deducting . . . 501.01

Business meals and trips . . . 102.13

Buy-sell agreements
. for family transfers, restrictions on . . . 1120.03
. for stock . . . 208.02

C

C corporation shareholders
. deceased, election of S corporation status for . . . 203.01
. health, welfare, and retirement plans for . . . 1301.06
. medical reimbursement plans for . . . 1301.04
. numbers and types of . . . 1301.02

C corporation subsidiaries . . . 1409-1409.05
. acquired by S corporation under QSub election as subject to built-in gains . . . 1405.02
. consolidated groups of . . . 1409.04, 1409.05
. consolidated returns for . . . 1409.01
. dividends from . . . 1409.02
. dividends-received deduction not available for S corporation parent of . . . 1409.02
. earnings and profits . . . 1409.03, 1409.05
. 80 percent . . . 1409.02-1409.05
. reasons not to elect QSub status for acquired . . . 1405.04
. recharacterized transactions for S corporations owning . . . 205.02, 1402.02
. wholly owned by S corporation . . . 1409

C corporations . . . 1301.01-1301.10
. advantages and disadvantages of . . . 1301.10
. carry back provision, . . . 404.14
. charitable contributions of inventory and scientific equipment allowed to . . . 102.04
. classified as tax shelters . . . 404.02
. closely held . . . 102.13, 911.08
. comparison of other business entities and . . . 1308
. conversion of one-member LLCs to . . . 1307.12
. conversion of S corporations to, considerations for . . . 711, 1115
. converted to S corporations, considerations for . . . 102.03, 404-404.14, 605.01, 802.05, 804.01, 804.06, 805.03, 806, 911.08, 911.11
. creditor protection by . . . 1301.09
. debt of . . . 404.09
. defined . . . 1301.01
. dividends-received deduction for . . . 1301.07
. double taxation of earnings of . . . 102.03
. ease of forming . . . 1301.08

C C

COD

References are to paragraph (¶) numbers.

COD

Controlled foreign corporation, Code
Sec. 1411 regulations . . . 1609

Controlled group
. related-persons designation for
corporations in same . . . 712.01
. tax consequences of membership in . . .
205.03, 1207.04

Cooperative patron income as portfolio
income . . . 911.06

Copyright royalties . . . 804.04

Corporate debt, "piercing corporate veil"
to place shareholder liability for . . .
102.02

Corporate income, zeroing out . . . 802.18

Corporate income tax for S
corporations . . . 801-806.03

Corporate officers, signatures of
. on Form 1120S . . . 405.02
. on Form 2553 for S corporation
election . . . 403.19

Corporate separations, effects on
carryover of losses on . . . 906.03

Corporate tax return
. penalties for failing to file an S corporate
return . . . 405.05
. shareholder notice to IRS of nonfiling
of . . . 1116.03
. shareholder's return conforming to . . .
1116.02

Corporate veil, formalities of corporation
necessary to avoid piercing . . . 102.02

Cost of goods sold (CGS) allocable to
DPGR . . . 722.04

Covenant not to compete
. by parent in family S corporation . . .
1119.06, 1209.02
. in sale of S corporation stock . . . 1208.04
. in shareholders' agreement . . . 1106.08

Coverdell education savings accounts,
prohibited transactions under . . .
1103.17

Creditor protection for shareholders,
members, and partners
. by C corporation . . . 1301.09
. by general partnership, lack of . . .
1305.09
. by limited liability companies . . . 1304.09
. by limited partnership . . . 1306.09
. by personal service corporation . . .
1303.09
. by S corporation . . . 102.02, 1302.09

Credits and credit carryforwards . . .
802.15

Cross-purchase buyout of stock . . . 102.12

Crummey power, ownership of Code,
Sec. 678 trust determined by holder
of . . . 303.02

Current income beneficiary of QSST,
distribution of trust corpus to . . . 307.03

Custodian, S corporation stock held
by . . . 202.05, 403.02

Customer list
. allocation of purchase price to . . . 1208.04
. sold to family S corporation . . . 1119.06

D

Dealer transactions of S corporations . . .
606
. taint on property in . . . 905.05

Debt
. of C corporation converting to S
corporation . . . 404.09
. consequences of using . . . 904.04
. defining . . . 904.05
. discharge of, built-in gains from . . .
802.08
. discharge of, income reporting of . . .
610.01
. disregarded between parent corporation
and QSub . . . 1404
. distribution rules and . . . 1002.04
. guarantee of . . . 904.05
. nonrecourse one-member LLC . . .
1307.06
. open account . . . 904.03, 904.05-.08,
904.14, 906.02
. repayment of, by shareholder . . . 904.08
. safe harbor for straight . . . 208.05, 904.04
. second class of stock created by . . .
904.04
. straight debt . . . 904.04
. tax planning with repayment of . . . 904.08
. written note . . . 904.03

Debt basis . . . 902, 904.01-904.14
. as cost . . . 904.05
. creating . . . 904.05
. to deduct S corporation losses . . . 904.01
. distributions and . . . 904.02
. economic reality of loans . . . 904.11
. effective date of adjustments to . . . 904.07
. forms of loans to S corporation for . . .
904.03
. increasing . . . 904.05, 904.06, 1117.01,
1304.03

DEB

Debt basis—continued
. loan from related entities . . . 904.10
. restoration of . . . 904.06, 904.08
. S corporation income taxation . . . 601
. total loss and deduction claim limited to adjusted stock basis and adjusted . . . 906

Decedent's final tax return, decision about closing S corporation books for . . . 901.02

Deductions
. Code Sec. 1411 effect on shareholders . . . 1604.06
. compensation-related . . . 716.04
. limits to shareholders' . . . 906-906.04
. against net investment income . . . 1604.06
. passed on to shareholders as separately stated items . . . 601, 602, 701
. of S corporation expenses. *See* Expenses, deductible S corporation *and* individual expense items
. of shareholders aggregated with pro rata shares of S corporation separately stated deductions . . . 905.04

Deemed liquidation of existing subsidiary
. application of Code Secs. 332 and 337 to . . . 1405.01-1405.06
. coordinated with Code Sec. 338 election for purchase of stock as assets . . . 1404.02
. as effect of QSub election . . . 1404-1404.02
. for insolvent subsidiaries . . . 1405.01
. state income tax issues for . . . 1407
. timing of . . . 1404.01, 1404.02

Deemed sale
. Code Sec. 1411 and . . . 1607.02, 1607.03, 1607.06
. examples to illustrate rules . . . 1607.06

Deferred compensation plans
. aggregation rules for . . . 723.10
. Code Sec. 409A's provision to curtail abuses in . . . 716.01, 723.02
. Code Sec. 1411 not applicable to . . . 1608
. defined . . . 723.01
. distribution rules for . . . 723.06
. effective date for . . . 723.12
. election rules for . . . 723.07
. funding . . . 723.08
. interest in, treatment of . . . 723.09
. partnership transactions . . . 723.05
. planning opportunities . . . 723.13

Deferred compensation plans—continued
. plans considered to be . . . 723.03
. reporting requirements for . . . 723.11
. stock appreciation rights . . . 723.04
. transactions of . . . 723.05

Deferred prepayment income . . . 802.06

Defined benefit plans, benefit limitations for . . . 1103.21

Defined contribution plans
. diversification requirements for . . . 707.07
. eligible investment advice arrangement for . . . 1103.17

Depreciated property that appreciates subsequently, gifts of . . . 903.01

Depreciation recapture
. not required in sale of S corporation stock . . . 1208.04
. offset by buyer's deduction for bonus payment to seller of S corporation stock . . . 1208.04
. in sale of assets . . . 1208

Discharge of indebtedness . . . 610.01-610.09

Dispositions
. Code Sec. 1411 effect on shareholders . . . 1601
. of interests in partnerships and S corporations . . . 1607-1607.06
. net gain described in Code Sec. 1411 . . . 1604.03

Dispute resolution . . . 1006.05, 1106.05

Disqualified individuals, compensation to . . . 720.01

Disqualified person for ERISA qualified retirement plans and welfare benefit plans . . . 1103.17

Disqualified persons for ESOPs . . . 1508.05, 1508.06

Distribution rights, taxation of . . . 1120.02

Distributions
. AAA decreased by . . . 1003.05
. applied against stock basis but not debt basis . . . 904.02
. of appreciated property . . . 102.11, 603.02, 608.01
. Code Sec. 1411 not applicable to . . . 1608
. from C corporation subsidiary . . . 1402.02
. constructive vs. actual . . . 208.02
. debt-financed, interest expense allocated to . . . 714.07
. decreasing stock basis . . . 903.02
. of depreciated property . . . 608.02

References are to paragraph (¶) numbers.

References are to paragraph (¶) numbers.

References are to paragraph (¶) numbers.

S C

References are to paragraph (¶) numbers.

SUB

References are to paragraph (¶) numbers.

References are to paragraph (¶) numbers.

Tax-exempt bonds
. reporting gain from holding . . . 1118.01
. S corporations as generally not to hold . . . 602

Tax-exempt income
. items included in . . . 605.03, 905.01
. not reflected in AAA but in shareholder basis . . . 1004
. as separately stated item . . . 905.01

Tax-exempt obligations, corporate interest on . . . 714.04

Tax-free bailout . . . 1504-1504.01, 1504.06

Taxable income, S corporation
. excess net passive income tax on . . . 804.13, 805.04, 905.05
. reducing . . . 804.17

Taxes paid by S corporation
. foreign, itemized deduction or foreign tax credit taken by shareholders for . . . 704.01
. state income, deduction passed through to shareholders for . . . 704.02

Taxpayer attributes, reductions to . . . 610.02

Taxpayer Relief Act of 1997 stipulations about limited partners' self-employment tax . . . 716.03

Technical and Miscellaneous Act of 1988 (TAMRA) . . . 802.01

Tenants in common
. S corporation stock held by married . . . 202.02, 403.03
. S corporation stock held by unmarried . . . 202.06, 403.03

Term interest in property, rules for consideration as gift of . . . 1120.05

Terminating event for S corporation status
. deliberate . . . 401.07, 1203
. effective date of loss of S status on date of . . . 1203
. inadvertent, admission of ineligible trust as shareholder triggering . . . 203.02
. inadvertent, admission of nonresident alien as shareholder triggering . . . 204.01
. inadvertent, transfer of S corporation stock to IRA triggering . . . 204.05
. inadvertent, earnings and profits triggering . . . 205.01
. inadvertent, restoring S status following . . . 1205.01-1205.02

Terminating event for S corporation status—continued
. inadvertent, sale of stock to nonpermitted shareholder triggering . . . 1208.04
. inadvertent, testamentary trust as shareholder for more than two years triggering . . . 304.02
. preventing . . . 1203.01
. proof of inadvertent . . . 1205.02
. request for relief ruling for inadvertent . . . 1205.02
. rules for . . . 1203.01

Testamentary trusts . . . 304-304.03
. advantages of . . . 304.03, 307.04
. characteristics of . . . 304.02
. as eligible S corporation shareholders . . . 203.02
. executor of estate as consenting to S corporation election for . . . 403.09
. reasons for . . . 304.01

Texas Limited Partnership Act . . . 1109.03

Trade or business activities
. expenses . . . 705
. restraints on grouping, . . . 911.03, 911.05

Transfers of interest to family members . . . 1120.02

Travel and entertainment expenses . . . 706.03, 1103.14, 1130
. single level of taxation on disallowed . . . 102.13

Trusts. *See also* individual types
. Code Sec. 1411 effect on shareholders . . . 1601, 1603-1603.04
. continuation as S corporation shareholder after death of trust owner . . . 302.02, 303.02
. distributions from . . . 1604.05
. fiduciary and beneficiary of, considered related persons . . . 712.01
. fiduciary and grantor of, considered related persons . . . 712.01
. material participation of trustee . . . 911.10
. members of family for . . . 202.08
. ineligible to be S corporation shareholders . . . 203.02, 204.02
. primary use for control in estate and income tax planning . . . 307.04
. qualifying to be S corporation shareholders . . . 203.02, 301-307.04, 1109.04
. tax minimization on . . . 1611.08
. taxable year of less than twelve months . . . 1603.01

TRU